BSF | CRPF | CISF | ITBP | SSB

CAPF AC

Assistant Commandant

Paper II : Descriptive

(Essays, Comprehension, Precis Writing & Language Skills)

BSF | CRPF | CISF | ITBP | SSB

CAPF AC

Assistant Commandant

Paper II : Descriptive

(Essays, Comprehension, Precis Writing & Language Skills)

Sristi Agarwal & Prerna
(MA English)
(UGC Net)

arihant
SUCCESS AND NOTHING LESS

arihant
SUCCESS AND NOTHING LESS

ARIHANT PUBLICATIONS (INDIA) LIMITED

卐 **Administrative & Production Offices**

Regd. Office
'Ramchhaya' 4577/15, Agarwal Road, Darya Ganj, New Delhi -110002
Tele: 011- 47630600, 43518550

卐 **Head Office**
Kalindi, TP Nagar, Meerut (UP) - 250002
Tel: 0121-7156203, 7156204

卐 **Sales & Support Offices**
Agra, Ahmedabad, Bengaluru, Bareilly, Chennai, Delhi, Guwahati, Hyderabad, Jaipur, Jhansi, Kolkata, Lucknow, Nagpur & Pune.

卐 **PRICE** ₹245.00

卐 **PO No :** TXT-XX-XXXXXXX-X-XX

Published by Arihant Publications (India) Ltd.

For further information about the books published by Arihant, log on to www.arihantbooks.com or e-mail at info@arihantbooks.com

Follow us on

CONTENTS

Get to Know CAPF AC

The Union Public Service Commission (UPSC) conducts CAPF AC exam once a year for various security forces such as BSF, CRPF, CISF, ITBP, and SSB. The UPSC CAPF AC Selection Process consists of three main stages: the Written examination, the Medical test, and the PET.

CAPF Written Exam comprises two papers and candidates' performance in each round will be considered for the final selection.

A distinct category of young individuals nationwide are attracted to the Paramilitary Forces and are ambitious to serve as Assistant Commandants (Group A). It offers job security and attractive incentives and perks, making the CAPF Exam highly desirable and a dream career opportunity in the Armed Forces.

UPSC CAPF Syllabus for Paper-II

The CAPF AC Syllabus for Paper II has descriptive-type questions that must be answered according to the Commission's guidelines. This section carries a weightage of 200 marks and assesses a candidate's language proficiency, comprehension, and essay-writing skills. It is important to note that only candidates who meet the CAPF Cut Off in Paper I will be evaluated for Paper II.

To perform well in this section and manage time effectively, students should revise their English grammar and regularly practice writing essays on relevant topics.

- Paper-II is descriptive type, hence no negative marking is applicable.

Paper	Topic	CAPF Syllabus
Paper II	Essay	Syllabus includes key topics such as modern Indian history, with a specific focus on the freedom struggle, as well as geography, politics, economy, knowledge of security and human rights issues, and analytical ability.
	Comprehension, précis writing language skills	Syllabus includes subjects such as reading comprehension, précis writing, developing counterarguments, basic grammar, and other aspects of language testing.

01 Essay Writing

SPECIAL FOCUS

In essay writing pay special attention to
Word count (300 words) • Reference to data from legitimate sources • Correct use of grammar

An essay is a piece of writing outlining the writer's opinion on a particular topic. Essays can be **augmentative** (explore a topic and establish point of view), **expository** (explain something), narrative (tell a story) and **descriptive** (paint a mental picture).

In the UPSC CAPF AC exam, Essay writing is of **80 (20 × 4) marks.** A student has to attempt any four essays out of the six topics in **300 words** each. As it is a scoring section, it is crucial to select and present an essay as per your command over the content and ideas.

Scoring Points

You can score good marks in your essay easily by

- writing a **well-structured** essay
- presenting a balanced approach
- **giving data** that supports your arguments
- prioritising which argument will come first
- writing a **comprehensive** essays
- Following ABC
  - Accuracy – Brevity/conciseness – Correctness
- Making your essay interesting by including **flowcharts**, **diagrams**, etc.
- Wherever possible including data from
  - Government authorities
  - UN and other important international organisations
  - Speeches made by leaders
  - High Courts or Supreme Court verdicts

TOPICS FOR CAPF ESSAYS

CAPF can ask an essay from variety of issues. These include History, Political, Social and Developmental Literature, Economic, Internal Security, Environmental, Science and Technology, Disaster Management, International Relations, Quote based topics, Human Rights, Armed Forces, etc.

Format of an Essay

An essay does not follow any specific format except the differentiation between the introduction, body and the conclusion.

Introduction

An introduction should reflect that you have understood the topic completely.

Try to write it in a single paragraph i.e., **30 to 40 words** maximum in a crisp and clear manner. You can write an introduction in different ways like,

- Definition
- Quotes that are related to the topic
- Current events/Context related to the topic
- Fact and figure (data)
- Meaning of terms of the Essay topic

Body Paragraph

The second and other paragraphs form the body of the essay. This part comprises the **writer's opinion** and thoughts which are proved with evidence (data/examples/case study). It must contain **arguments**, their **reasons** and **explanations**, and current examples.

It also includes Government schemes and programmes and current news related to the topic. An important component of the body of an essay is that it presents both the sides related to the topics.

Conclusion

Conclusion of the essay is supposed to satisfy the readers such that they should be convinced with what they have read in the essay.

Hence, it contains the writer's opinions, suggestions and solutions and is **futuristic** and **positive** in tone.

Useful Quotes for Essay Writing

- The only good is knowledge and the only evil is ignorance. *– Socrates*
- The artist is nothing without the gift, but the gift is nothing without work. *– Emile Zola*
- Life contains but two tragedies. One is not to get your heart's desire, the other is to get it *– Socrates*
- If women didn't exist, all the money in the world would have no meaning *– Aristotle Onasis*
- Righteousness is the foundation stone of peace and good governance. *– Confucius*
- Peace and Justice are two sides of the same coin. *– Eisenhower*
- The price good men pay for indifference to public affairs is to be ruled by evil men. *– Plato*
- Our scientific power has outrun our spiritual power. We have guided missiles and misguided men. *– Martin Luther King*
- Doubt everything. Find your own light. *– Gautam Buddha*
- Science without religion is lame, and Religion without Science is blind. *– Einstein*
- Education is the most powerful weapon you can use to change the world. *– Nelson Mandela*
- It is the mark of an educated mind to be able to entertain a thought without accepting it. *– Aristotle*
- I measure the progress of a community by the degree of progress which women have achieved. *– BR Ambedkar*
- Blind belief in authority is the greatest enemy of truth. *– Einstein*
- Peace begins with a smile. *– Mother Teresa*
- Poverty is the worst form of violence. *– MK Gandhi*
- A right delayed is a right denied. *– Martin Luther King*
- The three key societal members who can make a difference are father, mother and teacher. *– APJ Abdul Kalam*
- We need to create pedestrian crossings on the highway of globalisation. *– KR Narayanan*

■ Sample Question

Write an essay on 'The Crying Need For Embracing Minimalism' in about 300 words. **20 Marks**

SAMPLE FOR ESSAY

Introduction

A dictum by Ludwig Mies van der Rohe, 'Less is More', brings out a new phenomenon of minimalism. Minimalism, essentially, is a lifestyle which means living a life wherein one possess things one needs and nothing more. It means being satisfied with the little we have and sustaining and enjoying life with what is needed. Being a minimalist means valuing oneself more than material things. The decisions are based on the needs instead of desires. Also, it does not mean buying only cheap things to cut costs.

Body

While the word and the concept may seem a little complex and negative, it is not so. People often believe that being a minimalist, one has to sacrifice materialistic possessions and renounce the world to live like a recluse. They feel that the minimalists do not take advantages of the modern technologies available in today's world. However, in the modern world, wherein our desires, needs and demands are increasing exponentially in the face of technological advancement, minimalism presents a way out of consumerism. Rather than working toward a financial gain to buy more stuff we can't afford and don't really need, it helps in saving money by spending less on futile materialistic possessions. Therefore, more money and disposable income will be available to channelise towards experiences that will remain in one's memory forever. Minimalism is a living that helps getting rid of impulses. Hence, it encourages a reassessment of priorities so that the excess stuff — the possessions, ideas, relationships and activities that don't bring value to one's life and put us in stress can be stripped away. When there is nothing to stress about as our needs are fulfilled, we feel internally satisfied. Fewer commitments help in taking out time to do what we actually love thus, making us satisfied. A minimalist does not over-consume but rather lives more in line with nature and its beauty. As a result, a minimalist lives a peaceful, satisfied and a content life.

Conclusion

A wave of minimalism as a lifestyle choice has been sweeping the developed world, where more and more people are walking away from the tiresome update-and-upgrade consumerist lifestyle. They are now embracing minimalism with a focus on needs, quality, experiences and decluttering.

Practice EXERCISE

Directions (Essay 1-68) *Write an Essay on each of the given topic in about 300 words.*

1. Artificial Intelligence—A Look into the Future

Artificial intelligence (AI) is rapidly transforming the world we live in. From the way we work and communicate to the products and services we use every day, AI is playing an increasingly important role in our lives. Artificial intelligence (AI) essentially is the ability of a machine to display human-like capabilities such as reasoning, learning, planning and creativity. It enables technical systems to perceive their environment, deal with what they perceive, solve problems and act to achieve a specific goal.

With its ability to perceive its environment, deal with what they perceive, quickly solve problems and act to help with tasks to make everyday life easier, AI has been integrated in many fields. Some of the important applications of AI are as follows

- **Voice Assistants** Digital assistants like Siri, Google Home and Alexa use AI-backed Voice User Interfaces (VUI) to process and decipher voice commands.
- **Healthcare and Hospitals** The emergence of Artificial Intelligence (AI) in healthcare has been groundbreaking, reshaping the way we diagnose, treat and monitor patients. This technology is drastically improving healthcare research and outcomes by producing more accurate diagnoses and enabling more personalised treatments. With AI, healthcare's ability to analyse vast amounts of clinical documentation quickly helps medical professionals identify disease markers and trends that would otherwise be overlooked. By using artificial intelligence in hospital settings and clinics, healthcare systems can become smarter, faster and more efficient in providing care to millions of people worldwide.
- **Entertainment Streaming Apps** Streaming giants like Netflix, Spotify and Disney Hotstar are continually feeding data into machine learning algorithms to make the user experience seamless and customised. Using AI to review through the user data, these Apps create catalogs of music, movies and TV series suited to each individual user's liking.
- **Facial Recognition Technologies** The most popular application of AI is the Face ID unlock feature which is present in most of the flagship smartphone models today. Various industries are also developing AI software that picks up facial expressions to identify mood and intention. Emotion AI or Affective Computing is an emerging area of interest to measure customer experience.
- **Internet of Things** The confluence of AI and the Internet of Things (IoT) opens up an abundance of opportunities to develop smarter home appliances that require minimal human interference to operate. While IoT deals with devices interacting with the internet, the AI part helps these devices to learn from data. AI unlocks the potential of the data aggregated by IoT devices via sensors. Learnings from this data over multiple iterations enable IoT devices to respond to human stimuli and requirements better.

As the world is witnessing unprecedented growth in Artificial Intelligence (AI) technologies, it is also facing some potential risks. These are as follows

- **Privacy Concerns** The AI technologies often collect and analyse large amounts of personal data, raising issues related to data privacy and security.
- **Misinformation and Manipulation** AI generated content, such as Deep-Fakes, contributes to the spread of false information and the manipulation of public opinion.
- **Job Displacement** The AI driven automation can lead to job losses across various industries, particularly for low skilled workers. As AI technologies continue to develop and become more efficient, the workforce must adapt and acquire new skills to remain relevant in the changing landscape.

Conclusion

In the 21st Century, innovations are becoming faster, more efficient and more widely accessible than before. Technology is also becoming increasingly connected. New technologies are enabling societal shifts by having an effect on economics, values, identities and possibilities for future generations. In this light, Artificial Intelligence holds tremendous potential in different sectors of India. However we need more discussions to make AI systems responsible, fair and just to our society.

2. Youth Unrest- Causes and Remedies

Youth is the most important part of the population of a country and are its asset and future. Going through a 'youth bulge' with maximum portion of its population being children and young adults, the future of India should be great. Thus, we can say that the grand image of the future of India is dependent on its youth. But what if the youth is in a state of unrest, anxious and alienated?

Causes of Youth Unrest

This is the reality seen in the present day world wherein the youth is afflicted with stress, anxieties, depression and fear due to many reasons. Some of these reasons are given below

- **Disoriented Upbringing** The complexities of the modern world have adversely affects the social family setup in India. As a result, children face a lack of care and love due to which the youth becomes more stubborn and disoriented.
- **Lack of a Better Future** When the youth foresees a bleak future due to lack of growth opportunities, they become

frustrated and disillusioned with the existing system and sometimes become cynical (negative).

- **Unemployment** The current education system in India, which charges huge amounts to provide good education, does not fulfil the criteria of getting a well-paid job. This makes the youth feel cheated, confused, frustrated and express their feelings with the acts of violence and unruly behaviour.
- **Generation Gap** The youth are rationalistic in their nature and pragmatic in their approach. They oppose the old values and cultures and try to establish the new. As a result, there is either a confrontation between the old and the new value or dilemma.. This leads a conflict in the minds of youth making them restless.
- **Identity Crisis** Youth in contemporary period try to define their own identity in order to obtain the resources for survival and try to get a place in the existing social order. The struggle or the inability to do so frustrates them.

Conclusion

With this growing unrest, we need to take urgent step to create a climate of hope, confidence and trust for the youth to grow and flourish. These are some initiatives that has to be taken for mobilising the young generation. The very first step to solving the unrest faced by the youth needs the awareness of the root cause of the issue. Despite the differences existing between characteristics of the youth in different regions, certain common problems can be identified.

Once we know the reason behind the feelings of frustration, one can easily strategise and effectively implement ways to tackle it. Further, open conversation and discussion can also help the youth in doing away with their feelings of unrest.

3. Dual board exams for 10th and 12th from 2025: boon or bane

The Indian education system, recognised globally for its rigorous curriculum and emphasis on academics, has been at the crossroads of reform for several years. One of the transformative proposals discussed extensively is the introduction of Dual Board Exams for students of 10th and 12th grades starting from 2025.

Traditionally, students in India face a single board examination at the end of their 10th and 12th grades, which plays a critical role in determining their academic and professional futures. The proposal for dual exams emerges against the backdrop of increasing concerns over student stress levels, the diverse learning pace of students and the need for a more holistic assessment framework.

Need of Dual Board Exams

The need to reform the way of evaluation of Indian students has been in talks for years due to various challenges that students face in terms of competition, pressure to perform well and expectations. In this light, dual board exams offer various benefits to both students and teachers. These benefits are-

- **Reduces Pressure** Dual exams offer the opportunity for students to be assessed at different intervals, potentially reducing the pressure of a single, high-stakes test. It allows educators to identify learning gaps and provide targeted interventions midway, fostering a more adaptive and responsive teaching approach.
- **Reduces Stress** By splitting the final assessment into two parts, it is believed that the psychological burden on students could be significantly alleviated. Further, students who may not perform well due to illness or other unforeseen circumstances will have another opportunity to prove their capabilities.
- **Higher Educational Standards** Dual board exam will encourage students to maintain consistent study habits rather than relying on last-minute preparations. It would subsequently pave the way for more skill-based assessments, aligning with the National Education Policy's (NEP) focus on holistic development.

Challenges Ahead

While the idea of dual board exams seems to bring much relief to students, there are various challenges that it faced. They are as follows

Resource Allocation As of now many schools, especially in rural and underpriviledged regions, lack even the basic of facilities to support proper learning and evaluation. In this light, ensuring that all schools, especially in rural and underprivileged areas, have the infrastructure and resources to conduct two sets of exams annually is daunting

Standardisation With dual Board exams, maintaining a consistent standard of examination across two sessions to ensure fairness could be challenging.

Academic Pressure There is a concern that instead of reducing stress, the model might lead to continuous pressure on students to perform throughout the year. This is so because, dual exams can inadvertently increase parental expectations, adding to the students' stress levels.

Curriculum Coverage and Depth Dual Board exams might push teachers to rush through curriculums to prepare students for the first exam, potentially compromising the depth of understanding. As a result, curriculum may become more test-oriented, rather than knowledge and application-based.

While the dual examination system promises several benefits, including reduced student stress, improved educational outcomes and early identification of learning gaps, its success hinges on careful implementation. The Central Board of Secondary Education (CBSE) and relevant educational authorities must undertake pilot studies and phased rollouts to address potential challenges. Moreover, comprehensive training programs for educators, substantial infrastructure investments and a clear communication strategy with stakeholders are imperative to navigate the transition smoothly.

Conclusion

In conclusion, the proposal for Dual Board Exams from 2025 represents a bold step towards educational reform in India. As noted by the Ministry of Education, the objective is not merely to change the examination pattern but to transform the educational landscape by fostering a more adaptive, student-centric learning environment. While the road ahead is fraught with challenges, the potential to create a more equitable, less stressful and more engaging educational system is an opportunity that merits serious consideration and effort from all sectors of society.

4. Towards Making the 21st Century the Century of Peace

The 21st century has dawned with a myriad of challenges, ranging from climate change to technological disruption. The Century has seen huge devastation caused by the various natural disasters, Health Crises, Wars among others. Amidst the chaos, one overarching aspiration persists, the quest for peace.

As humanity navigates through the complexities of this era, there exists an unprecedented opportunity to steer the course towards a century marked by harmony and cooperation. There are possibilities, strategies and imperative actions required to make the 21st century the century of peace.

Peace transcends the mere absence of conflict. It embodies a state of societal calm built upon foundations of justice, equality, and mutual respect. Achieving peace demands a holistic approach, encompassing political, economic, social, and environmental dimensions. Moreover, peace isn't static; it requires continual nurturing, adaptation and innovation.

Strategies for Peace-Building

To realize the vision of a peaceful 21st century, concerted efforts are imperative

- **Diplomacy and Conflict Resolution** Prioritising early warning mechanisms, preventive diplomacy and addressing root causes of conflicts preemptively averts the escalation of violence and human suffering. Thus, making space for dialogue, mediation, and negotiation over coercion and militarism is essential.

  Political leaders must prioritise peace- building over short-term gains, demonstrating the courage and commitment to resolve conflicts through dialogue and diplomacy. Investing in diplomatic institutions like the United Nations and strengthening multilateral frameworks enhances conflict resolution capabilities. As of 2020, the UN Peacekeeping Operations involve 100,000 personnel deployed in 13 missions across four continents, illustrating the global commitment to conflict resolution through diplomacy.

- **Sustainable Development** Addressing socio-economic disparities and promoting inclusive growth mitigates grievances and fosters stability. Sustainable development goals (SDGs), focusing on poverty alleviation, education, healthcare and gender equality, are indispensable in this regard. According to the World Bank, achieving the SDGs could lift 68 million people out of extreme poverty by 2030, contributing to peace and stability.

- **Environmental Stewardship** Recognising the intrinsic link between peace and environmental sustainability is crucial. Adopting eco-friendly policies, investing in renewable energy and combating climate change is imperative for preventing resource-driven conflicts. The Intergovernmental Panel on Climate Change (IPCC) warns that unchecked climate change could exacerbate conflicts over resources, displacing millions and destabilising regions.

- **Education and Cultural Exchange** Promoting cross-cultural understanding, empathy and tolerance through education and cultural exchange programs nurtures a culture of peace. Emphasising critical thinking, conflict resolution skills and global citizenship fosters a generation committed to peace-building. UNESCO reports that every additional year of education can reduce the risk of conflict by 20%, highlighting the transformative potential of education in fostering peace.

- **Disarmament and Non-Proliferation** Reducing the proliferation of conventional and nuclear weapons diminishes the likelihood of conflicts escalating into full-scale wars. Embracing arms control treaties, disarmament agreements and confidence-building measures are paramount. The Stockholm International Peace Research Institute (SIPRI) reports that global military expenditure reached $1.9 trillion in 2020, underscoring the urgent need for reallocating resources towards peace-building initiatives.

- **Technology for Peace** Harnessing technology for humanitarian purposes and conflict prevention is pivotal. From early warning systems to digital platforms for peace-building initiatives, leveraging technological innovations facilitates proactive responses to emerging threats. For instance, the United Nations utilises satellite imagery and geospatial data for early warning of potential conflicts and natural disasters, enabling timely interventions.

- **Empowering Civil Society** Empowering grassroots movements, NGOs, and civil society organizations amplify voices for peace and foster bottom-up initiatives. Civil society engagement holds governments and institutions accountable while catalysing social change. The Global Peace Index highlights the role of civil society in peace-building, citing community-driven initiatives as key contributors to peaceful societies.

- **Promoting Good Governance** Upholding principles of transparency, accountability and the rule of law strengthens democratic institutions and fosters societal trust. Combating corruption and ensuring equitable distribution of resources enhance social cohesion and resilience against conflicts. According to Transparency International, corruption costs the global economy $2.6 trillion annually, underscoring the significance of good governance in promoting peace and prosperity.

- **Gender Equality** Empowering women and promoting their meaningful participation in peace processes is not only a matter of rights but also a pragmatic approach to conflict prevention and resolution.
- **Global Solidarity** Recognising the interconnectedness of global challenges, and fostering solidarity and cooperation among nations is imperative. Collective responses to crises, such as pandemics or climate disasters, underscore the urgency of global collaboration.
- **Youth Engagement** Engaging youth as agents of change and investing in their education, empowerment and participation in decision-making processes cultivates a culture of peace and sustainability.

Conclusion

As humanity navigates through the complexities of the 21st century, the aspiration for peace remains paramount. Making the 21st century the century of peace requires unwavering commitment, collaboration, and innovative approaches. By prioritising diplomacy, sustainable development, environmental stewardship, and empowerment of communities, nations can collectively pave the path towards a future characterised by harmony, justice, and prosperity for all. As individuals, communities, and nations, let us seize this historic opportunity to realise the vision of a peaceful 21st century, leaving behind a legacy of hope and resilience for future generations.

5. G-20 Summit 2023: A Roadmap for Global Growth

The G-20, a collection of twenty of the world's largest economies formed in 1999, was conceived as a bloc that would bring together the most important industrialised and developing economies to discuss international economic and financial stability. It is essentially a key forum for the most important industrial and emerging countries to discuss major issues of international currency and financial policy.

The G-20 comprises nineteen countries including are Argentina, Australia, Brazil, Canada, China, France, Germany, India, Indonesia, Italy, Japan, Republic of Korea, Mexico, Russia, Saudi Arabia, South Africa (Now The African Union), Turkey, United Kingdom and United States of America and the European Union (EU). It functions by hosting a Summit which is held annually, under the leadership of a rotating Presidency. The country holding the presidency for the year organises the Summit and directs the agenda for the Summit.

While G-20 may seem like any other international meet, it is not so. G-20 is critical in creating an atmosphere favourable to equitable global growth and development. Its efforts to create prosperity, guarantee financial stability and avoid and manage crises are crucial. It provides policy coherence, analysis and practical tools which helps its members to better target their cooperation with developing countries. Further, it promotes inclusive societies and opportunities for all which fosters a global economy.

G-20 2023 Important For India

G-20 2023 is crucial for India as the nation took over its presidency from Indonesia and organised its Summit in November 2023. India's theme for its G-20 Presidency, '*Vasudhaiva Kutumbakam*' (One Earth - One Family - One Future) was aimed to build unanimity to address global challenges collectively and effectively. Under its presidency, India undertook discussions and initiatives among the world's major economies to address complex challenges. During its presidency, India focused on various issues like inclusive growth, digital innovation, climate resilience and equitable global health access. It took about 200 hours of non-stop negotiations to reach a consensus in the 'Delhi Declaration' that the G20 leaders adopted on 9th September, 2023.

The major Agendas for 18th G-20 Summit 2023 are as follows

- **First Agenda** The first agenda relates to financing tomorrow's cities and establishing them as the foremost engines of economic growth. It is estimated that by 2050, nearly twice as many people will live in cities. To sustain their economic potential, cities need to become more livable through upgraded infrastructure and services. The G-20 platform could be used to mobilise international support to bridge this financing need.
- **Second Agenda** The second agenda where the G-20 summit led the way is in energy transition. Enabling an orderly and equal transition from carbon-intensive energy to renewable energy would not only help combat climate change, but also help bolster energy security.
- **Third Agenda** The third agenda was related to health care. The COVID-19 pandemic highlighted the compelling need for a united global approach to strengthen health systems to effectively address emerging health crises. India's G-20 Presidency became mode of change towards more resilient, responsive and sustainable health systems and to advance previously established G-20 pandemic preparedness efforts.

Key Outcomes of G-20 Summit 2023

Leaders of the world's 20 big economies ended the G-20 Summit in New Delhi with adoption of 'New Delhi Declaration' with ending deep divisions over the war in Ukraine to produce a consensus document and move forward. The major outcomes of the G-20 Summit are as follows

- The G-20 nations agreed that states cannot grab territory by force and highlighted the suffering of the people of Ukraine, but avoided direct criticism of Russia for the war. However, everyone including Russia committed themselves to not seizing territory by force.
- The 55 member African Union was formally made permanent member of the G-20, on par with the European Union, in order to make the grouping more

representatives. Until now, only South Africa was a member of the G20.

- During the G-20 Summit, US President Joe Biden, Indian Prime Minister Narendra Modi and European Commission President Ursula von der Leyen announced the project and named this as the 'Partnership for Global Infrastructure Investment'. The corridor would help to boost trade, transport energy resources and improve digital connectivity. It would include India, Saudi Arabia, the United Arab Emirates, Jordan, Israel and the European Union.
- G-20 leaders in 'New Delhi Declaration' committed for WTO reforms through a fully functional dispute settlement system by 2024. It will be achieved through an inclusive member driven process and a fully and well-functioning dispute settlement system accessible to all members.
- The G-20 leaders agreed to pursue tripling renewable energy capacity globally by 2030 and accepted the need to phase down unabated coal power, but stopped short of setting major climate goals.

Conclusion

India's significant role in global economic governance has given advantage it to participate in the G-20 process more actively. Giving priority to enhancing health emergency prevention and preparedness and linkages between climate change and health, India has stressed for strengthen cooperation in the pharmaceutical sector. India also pushed for leveraging digital health innovations and solutions to aid universal health coverage. India can lend its experience to not only G-20 nations but across the globe in framing a successful national digital health architecture through supportive regulatory environment, private public partnerships and digital health interventions such as National Digital Health Mission.

6. Promoting Artisans and Handicrafts

India has a long and unique history of art, with several indigenous crafts and practices passed down across generations of artisan communities. It has nearly 3,000 unique arts and crafts, many of which are as old as the Indian civilisation itself and are an embodiment of India's intellectual and aesthetic properties. It comes as no surprise that India has earned appreciation from all across the world for its richness in culture, heritage and art.

Historically, artisans were given tremendous respect, admiration and appreciation.

Role of Artisans

Artisans were the backbone of India's non-farm rural economy, engaged in craft production to earn a livelihood. However, propelled by loss of markets, declining skills and difficulty catering to new markets, the number of Indian artisans has been rapidly decreasing. As India industrialised and the demand for traditional handicrafts decreased, the local craftsmen started to struggle to earn even a basic livelihood. As a result, over the past 30 years, the number of Indian artisans has decreased by 30 percent and the vast majority of artisans operate in informal work settings where their excellence, creativity and hard work is generally overshadowed.

In the situation, the need of the hour is to create and craft a livelihood for reinvestment in India's artisans to safeguard history, culture and an important source of livelihood. This can be done if we all come together to promote Indian artisans and handicrafts.

Ways to Promote Artisans and Handicrafts

- We can reinvest capital in rural artisans and craftsmen to preserve the traditional art culture and talent of India. This investment will also help the rural artisans to kickstart their lost careers and India's exquisite artistry will gain the long due recognition and popularity it deserves.
- Businesses can use their online presence to spread awareness about the lost traditional artistry and craftsmanship.
- Apart from financial and technical help, we can provide information, knowledge and guidance that can truly help artisans create a career and income source for themselves. Through e-commerce platforms, the artisans and craftsmen can sell their fine work products to a large number of customers while operating comfortably from their hometowns. The craftsmanship of India can gain global reach and demand, increasing the revenue of the country and improving their lives.
- The government has also taken various initiatives like the 'Atmanirbhar Bharat Abhiyan' which aims at empowering local Indian brands to manufacture locally rather than importing from other countries. It also encourages citizens to become 'vocal for local' and enables the resurgence of the Indian economy. Under Atmanirbhar Bharat with its focus on vocal for local and products to be made in India and their promotion, the Ministry of Textiles has launched an initiative to set up an e-commerce platform for artisans.

Conclusion

Concluding, to preserve the ancient culture, artistry and heritage of our country, we should scale up the local art and handmade products created by skilled artisans. Through online presence and business marketing, let us join hands in bringing light to the wonderful culture of our country. Only by ensuring and providing opportunities in the local and rural communities can we grow the industry and retain the traditional art and hidden talents of Indian craftsmen.

7. The New Trend of Organic Farming

The introduction of chemicals such as fertilisers, pesticides and insecticides in farming got many delirious at the sight of what they could accomplish. It was not surprising that soon chemicals revolutionised the field of agriculture. Almost every farmer in the world started to use chemicals during the cultivation process. As a result, yields exploded without any significant impact on soil. However, it did not take long before the negative impact of chemical was seen not only in soil and the environment but also on the health of all living organisms on the planet.

In a world battered by new diseases and degradation of the environment and the demand for healthy and safe food, organic farming and organic foods came into being. Organic farming or organic agriculture is a technique which involves the cultivation of plants and rearing of animals without the use of toxic and persistent pesticides, fertilisers, antibiotics, synthetic hormones, genetic engineering or other excluded practices. It essentially involves the use of biological materials, to maintain soil fertility and ecological balance, thereby minimising pollution and wastage. The food products, thus, produced are fresh and chemical free gaining them the name organic foods.

The concept of organic farming is not new in India. Indian farmers, especially in the North-Eastern states, the tribal and island territories, have been tilling their lands without the use of chemicals largely relying on organic residues, cow dung, composts, etc., since time immemorial. As a result, it does not come as a surprise that India ranks first in number of organic farmers and ninth in terms of area under organic farming.

To further show the rising popularity of organic foods, it has been found that Sikkim became the first State in the world to become fully organic in 2016 and other states including Tripura and Uttarakhand have set similar targets.

There are many reasons why people today are inclining more and more towards organic food, thus, turning farmers towards organic farming.

- **To Accrue the Benefits of Nutrients** Organic food is loaded with nutrients such as vitamins, enzymes, minerals and other macro nutrients compared to those from conventional farms. Further, products from organic farms have a natural and better taste which stems from the well balanced and nourished soil.
- **Helps us Stay Healthy** Studies reveal that a large section of the population fed on toxic substances used in conventional agriculture has fallen prey to diseases like cancer. As organic farming avoids these toxins and uses natural farming techniques that don't harm humans, it keeps dangerous diseases like cancer and diabetes at bay.
- **To Conserve Environment and Agricultural Diversity** In commercial farms, the chemicals are applied to infiltrate into the soil which severely affects all life. In contrast, the chemical free organic farming methods guarantee a sustainable future in the face of environmental concerns and the loss of 75% of the agricultural diversity of crops.
- **Builds Soil Fertility** As opposed to modern and conventional agricultural methods, organic farming does not depend on synthetic chemicals. It utilises natural, biological methods to build up soil fertility such as microbial activity boosting plant nutrition. Further, the multiple cropping practiced in organic farming boosts soil quality which enhances productivity and resilience and contributes to a healthy farming system.

To promote organic farming, the Government of India has introduced two central schemes namely– Mission Organic Value Chain Development for North East Region (MOVCD) and Paramparagat Krishi Vikas Yojana (PKVY) to promote organic farming.

In the face of food and health crisis, the world needs an integrated system that gives equal importance to all sustainability dimensions across the value chain and thus helps establish a healthy and well fed society. Organic agriculture is the best insurance policy that the world can have with better performance on productivity, environmental impact, economic viability and social well-being.

8. The Role of NGOs in Social Change

Non-Governmental Organisations, popularly known as NGOs are not for profit, voluntary citizen's groups, which are organised on local, national and/ or international levels to address issues in support of the public good. Also known as non-profit organisations, they work toward a social cause and social justice. In the present society, NGOs have assumed a significant space in civil society. NGOs with the support given by the government has been accelerating its development activities by taking up specific issues like poverty alleviation, casteism and discrimination, women rights, child labour, rural development, environmental issues etc. They play a key role in the following sectors

- **Health** NGOs like Armman, Mother and Child Health And Nutrition (MACHAN), Mamta-Health Institute for Mother and Child, etc., work to improve maternal and child health and nutrition. Other than this, Akshay Patra is a Bengaluru based NPO which strives to eliminate classroom hunger by organising mid-day meal schemes in government schools.
- **Education** Numerous NGOs in India work to provide quality education to children, youth and even adults, particularly belonging to the weaker sections of the society. Bharti Foundation, Bhumi, Pratham Education Foundation, Room to Read India trust are such NGOs.
- **Social Development** Social development means equal development of all individuals irrespective of their age, gender, caste, etc. NGOs help in creating awareness among people to fight for their own rights and bring about social development.
- **Poverty Alleviation** Prerna, Navjyoti India Foundation, Scope for Social Change are such NGOs working to alleviate the poverty and improve the lives of the poor in India.
- **Women Empowerment** Sewa, Sathin, Eklavya, Disha, etc., are some of the thousands of NGOs known for their role in development by creating awareness among people and interventions regarding women, their rights and their freedoms.

- **Child Protection** Children are the most vulnerable groups. The cases of child abuse, trafficking, harassment, child labour etc., have been on rise in the country. Therefore, various NGOs work to protect children from any kind of exploitation. Smile Foundation, CRY, Save the Children, Childline, etc., are some of the many NGOs working for the cause.
- **Environmental Awareness** Today, thousands of voluntary organisations work to awaken people and governments against environmental degradation and depletion of resources. Some of these organisations are Vanashakti NGO, Gram Chetna Kendra, Janmitram Kalyan Samiti, etc.

Conclusion

These are only some of the hundreds of cause that NGOs work for and these numbers are increasing rapidly. Citizens today are more aware of their civil society and are coming forward to promote social justice, gender equity, inclusion, etc. Hence, in such a active society, NGOs are bound to grow and flourish to work towards a better living.

9. The Indian Judicial System needs overhauling

The Indian judiciary is regarded as one of the most important foundations of the three Constitutional pillars simply because it is an independent entity. It is not hidden that the powerful independent judiciary is of great importance for India's development. Yet by its definition Indian judiciary has been very weak and inefficient.

According to the World Bank's Ease of Doing Business survey, India ranks 168 out of 190 countries on 'contract compliance.' India has one of the highest numbers of under-trial prisoners in the country. A little more than two-thirds of the nearly 4.2 lakh inmates in India are awaiting trial. The problem, despite the overwhelming power, is that the Indian judiciary faces certain integral issues. The Indian judicial system, for example, is erratic, underemployed and above all, appallingly slow.

Some issues faced by the Indian judiciary are as follows

- **Delay in Justice** 'The delay in the trials is one of the greatest drawbacks of a court system. Justice delay creates disillusionment among the litigants and also undermines the capacity of the judicial system. The huge backlog of cases is proving to be the primary judicial problem. There are over three crores pending cases in India. This figure is increasingly growing and in fact, reflects the inadequacy of the judicial system.
- **Transparency** The lack of transparency is another issue faced by the Indian judiciary. Substantial issues like the quality of justice and accountability are not properly known in the functioning of the judiciary as the judiciary does not fall within the scope of the Right to the Information Act.
- **Judicial Capacity** One of the main reasons for the delay of justice is that the institution of court cases exceeds its disposition. The judge population ratio in the country is not very appreciable. India is a country with a population of more than 135 million and total strength of judges with only around 25000.While for the other countries, the ratio is about 50-70 judges per million people, in India it is 20 judges per million heads. The posts in the judiciary are not filled up as expeditiously as required. Almost 400 posts are vacant (40%) in the high courts. Around 35% of the posts are lying vacant in the lower judiciary.

Judiciary is essential for the state and a priority must be given to it. There has to be an improvement in the funding for the justice system and an improvement in efficiency. The first thing the government can do is to increase the number of magistrates. The number of judges needs to be increased including the Supreme Court, the High Court and the Lower Courts. Then, the Indian judiciary needs a dedicated branch of the registrar, administration and management. This along with reforms in civil and criminal practices, as well as reporting and regulatory processes, will go a long way towards streamlining trials and reducing court delays.

Conclusion

For a long time in India, there have been disputes regarding the system of judiciary. Judiciary is considered as one of the most important pillars in the Constitutional framework. During the 75 years of independence, the judiciary system has overhauled itself in many ways. Irrespective of these reforms and amendments, there is still a lot of development that must be made. Probably the important thing to humanity is an efficient and effective judiciary system.

10. Journalism has been rendered into Sensationalism

In the modern society, Journalism and Media has gained a prominent role in its function as a medium through which each and every person becomes aware of what is happening in the world. Journalism, then essentially, is an industry which collects, organises and presents meaningful content on a variety of platforms to make the public aware.

With such a huge task, comes a huge social responsibility. Everyone working in the journalism industry is required to follow certain ethics that include objective and unbiased reporting of useful information while maintaining factual accuracy.

However, with the need to increase viewership and profit in the middle of great competition, the ethical values associated with journalism are being replaced by exaggerated versions of controversial and non-important issues. Such an aspect of journalism is called sensationalism. Sensationalism, often termed as Yellow Journalism, simply refers to presenting an exaggerated, distorted and perverted version of the most insignificant events. It is an editorial tactic using which truth is often manipulated, or not verified to grab attention and create extreme emotional responses. Thus, journalism becomes yet another means of developing propaganda instead of becoming a trustworthy source of information.

Sensationalism as a part of journalism comes with a plethora of problems. These are

- **Validity of Truth** Since, a news story or an event is often repeated to be seen from different perspectives; the truth value of the story is lost. The public is left to wonder what actually is the real factual truth regarding the event. This not only reduces the credibility associated with media houses but also hinders the growth and development of society.
- **Lack of Focus on Important Issues** With the unimportant and insignificant issues blown out of proportion, the areas that need proper discussions and understanding are often ignored and neglected.
- **Communal Conflicts** Sensationalism can very easily create biasness in a country of diversity like India. It can promote the differences of opinions, beliefs and practices between people leading to communal conflicts which can lead to violent situations like riots. Such situations break the integrity of a nation and leads it towards destruction.
- **Political Propaganda** With media houses supporting certain organisations, it is not surprising to find journalists flattering some with exaggerated praises and heavily criticising others.
  This creates a bias in people creating blind supporters and critiques. In order to gain popularity, media houses forget their need to remain unbiased so that it can effectively perform its role in checking the government decisions and holding it responsible for its actions.

Conclusion

With these problems, there is a greater need for all to identify and avoid sensationalism. This responsibility of dealing with sensationalism is a two-way street. There is a need to work towards less sensationalism by discouraging the irresponsible breaking news cycle, from both the media and the common man's perspective.

For journalists and media people, it is important to understand that when people want information, they look at the various media platforms.

Thus, the truth and reality of an event without any biasness should be the first and foremost priority of any journalist. There is a need to recognise the importance of demanding journalistic ethics as part of media in addressing other societal problems. Further, people should always be cautious of all information that they get. They must verify all data before taking any action in regards to the event.

11. E-Commerce- Market Trend of the 21st Century

In the year 1994, the first sale of the first online product took place as a man named Phil Brandenberger, purchased 'Ten Summoner's Tale', a studio album from Sting. Now, more than 20 years later, online commerce has become an integral part of our lives and a significantly more profitable business model than brick-and-mortar stores. It has taken over the market as e-commerce sales worldwide has grown up to 4.8 trillion dollars serving more than 2.14 billion people.

Electronic commerce or e-commerce, essentially, is an online market where people can transact on a digital platform. It includes all activities that involve buying or selling of goods and services online from any part of the world sitting within the comfort of homes. Before comfort and convince, e-commerce offers many benefits that make it popular. Some of these benefits are

- **Choose from Wide Range of Goods** E-commerce allows customers to choose a product or service they want from any supplier present anywhere in the world without any stress or hurry.
- **Enjoy Simplicity and Comfort** Customers can buy any product from any e-commerce without having to leave their workplace or home. There is no hassle of coming out of the house, driving car, braving the traffic and so on.
- **Cost Effective and Flexible Payments** Products offered over the e-commerce platforms are generally found to be cheaper than those found in shops. These platforms offer many discount offers and coupons which further facilitates saving of money. In addition, there is also no need for cash. An individual is simply make and digital payment or even pay in cash.
- **Save Time** E-commerce offers consumers 24*7*365 services. This means that customers can order anything they need online at any time. The period required to choose, buy and pay for an online product is 15 minutes or less. Products are often delivered within a maximum of one week, depending on the sort of service.
- **Get Detailed Information** E-commerce allows customers to search for product information, compare prices and benefits and ultimately evaluate whether it is really worth the money. Everything needed for making an informed decision is on the tip of one's fingertips–reviews, product descriptions, usage videos, warranty information etc. All customers, therefore, are fully aware of the conditions before purchasing the product. An individual can also modify their orders and track the delivery status. If there is any doubt about product handling, they may contact the company for clarifications.

Although it may seem like the ideal way of buying and selling goods and services, e-commerce comes with its own set of disadvantages such as

- The customer does not communicate with the seller face to face, which may cause doubts or distrust. Some customers are therefore more cautious when buying over the Internet and prefer personal contact.
- Another disadvantage of online shopping is that customers often pay for customer shipping or packaging which increases the overall money spent on the product.
- As mentioned, shopping online includes the waiting period for the required produce to get shipped and then delivered which can take days or weeks. Customers cannot 'walk into' the online store and take the product immediately, as it is in the case of brick-and-mortar shops.

- Many customers are concerned that e-commerce is not safe. As the E-commerce websites are highly dependent on the internet, they are prone to cyber-attacks.

Propelled by the many benefits offered by e-commerce, the Government of India in 2019 released a Draft National E-commerce Policy which encourages FDI (Foreign Direct Investment) in the e-commerce marketplace model. Further, the Department of Commerce initiated an exercise and established a Think Tank on 'Framework for National Policy on e-commerce' and a Task Force under it to deliberate on the challenges confronting India in the arena of the digital economy and electronic commerce (e-commerce).

Conclusion

Thus, it can be said that e-commerce has revolutionised the marketplace offering many benefits to all. As a growing sector with huge interest from both domestic and international players, it becomes pertinent to regulate it keeping in mind the interest of both entrepreneurs and consumers.

12. Deep Sea Mining- Potential Resource or Ecological Destruction

In the race to cut greenhouse gas emissions and increasing climate change, demand for critical minerals is booming worldwide. Materials such as lithium, cobalt and graphite are essential components of EV batteries, wind turbines, solar panels and other low carbon technologies increasingly powering the world's energy systems. Mining for these materials on land is already underway, but with demand surging, some are now looking to tap the seafloor for its millions of square kilometres of metal ores. Hence, deep sea mining or the process of extracting and often excavating mineral deposits from the deep seabed, has become a emergent industry in the current economy.

The reasons for such a rising focus on deep sea mining is only one it can help meet the world's pressing need for critical minerals, which will likely only continue to grow as countries scale their decarbonisation efforts. There is common understanding that deep sea mining is an alternative pathway that can minimise certain risks associated with mining activities on land.

However, the potential opening of the international seabed for mining raises concerns about its impact on fragile marine ecosystems and deep sea habitats. Some of the environmental and biodiversity risks related to deep sea mining are as follows

- **Direct Harm to Marine Life** The heavy equipment used can mining poses huge risks for marine life. Mining equipment and mining wastewater could kill marine life through overheating and poisoning. Further, it could impair the feeding and reproduction of deep sea species through the creation of intense noise and light pollution, posing further risk to populations already strained by climate change and other human activities.
  As many deep sea species are rare, long-lived and slow to reproduce and because polymetallic nodules (potential deep mining site) are an important habitat for deep sea species, scientists are fairly certain that some species would face extinction from habitat removal due to deep sea mining. Further, the loss of deep sea biodiversity following mining activity may impact the ocean's carbon cycle and reduce its ability to help in reducing global temperature rise.
- **Economic and Social Risks** While extraction would occur offshore, the deep-sea mining industry would still need shoreline facilities, whether for processing or trans-shipment of material. This would require land acquisition and development, which has historically driven habitat loss affecting coastal communities' dependent on marine resources the most.

As the deep sea remains understudied and poorly understood, there are many gaps in our understanding of its biodiversity and ecosystems. This makes it difficult to assess the potential impacts of deep-sea mining or to put in place adequate safeguards to protect the marine environment and the three billion people whose livelihoods depend on marine and coastal biodiversity.

With this knowledge and the prediction that the global supply of critical minerals and rare Earth elements will grow in the coming years, the world must address how to responsibly scale up mining and processing operations in a way that minimises environmental and social risks.

Some of the alternatives that can help us meet the demand without harming the environment are

- **Mineral Recycling** The World Bank estimates that if recycling rates for end of life batteries increase significantly by 2050, it could decrease the need for newly mined minerals by around one-quarter for copper, nickel and lithium and by about 15% for cobalt.
  Better recycling practices in established waste streams, such as from electronics and electrical equipment, can help reduce some short-term supply pressure and can also handle a large volume of end of life zero-carbon energy products in the future.

Conclusion

The ocean and its resources are the common heritage of humankind. It must be managed on behalf of and in the interests of all humanity by sharing of economic benefits, support for marine scientific research and the effective protection of the marine environment.

There is an urgent and dire need of establishing comprehensive regulations and environmental safeguards to mitigate the potential risks associated with deep sea mining and other activities.

13. One Nation, One Election -Is it Practical?

The Union government on 1st September, 2023 has constituted a committee headed by former President Ram Nath Kovind to explore the feasibility of 'one nation, one election' to the Lok Sabha and State Assemblies, either on a single day or within a specific time frame. The government cited mainly the financial burden that caused by the continuous election cycle and an obstacle to development work during polls.

The concept 'One Nation, One Election' refers to holding simultaneous polls across the country. In other words, it proposes to conduct elections for Lok Sabha and all State Assemblies at the same time. The idea of 'One Nation, One Election' is not new and dates back to the very independence wherein simultaneous elections were held until 1967.

However, due to premature dissolutions, the system was dropped until 1983 when the Election Commission proposed to again adopt it.

Keeping the past in mind, the current committee suggests the adopted of 'One Nation, One Election' for various reasons cited below

- **Massive Expenditure** With so many states, there's always an election in some or the other part of the country, leading to excessive expenditure in the process both by the Election Commission of India (ECI). Holding simultaneous elections would reduce the massive expenditure incurred to conduct of separate elections every year.
- **Disruption in Public Life** Frequent elections lead to disruption of normal public life and impact the functioning of essential services. The holding of political rallies disrupts road traffic and also leads to noise pollution. Such kind of disruptions would be limited only to a certain pre-determined period of time if elections are held simultaneously.
- **Focus on Governance** Simultaneous elections also help ruling parties focus on governance instead of being constantly in election mode.

While the idea seems to have great many positive impacts, there are some challenges that need to be tackled before the system of simultaneous elections is adopted. Some of these are

- **Lack of Manpower** The deployment of security forces and officials for prolonged periods in more than 700,000 polling stations located in widely varying geographic and climatic conditions, all at the same time is going to be extremely difficult.
- **Against Spirit of Democracy** Critics suggests that forcing simultaneous elections is against democracy because India is a multi-party democracy where elections are held for State Assemblies and the Lok Sabha separately. The voters are better placed to express their voting choices keeping in mind the two different governments which they would be electing by exercising their franchise.
- **Election Issues/Agendas** State and national elections are often fought on different sets of issues and agendas, whereas in simultaneous elections, voters may end up giving advantage to one set over the other in ways they might not have done otherwise.

Conclusion

Holding of simultaneous elections is theoretically very attractive, but practically there are a lot of challenges to be met. It's desirable but is not going to be easy as the Constitution and other laws would need to be amended for implementing simultaneous elections. However, it should be done in such a way that it doesn't hurt the basic structure of democracy and federalism. Moreover if India indeed opts for 'one nation, one election', the world's biggest democracy will set another unique example.

14. Understanding the Global Failure in Mitigating Climate Change

Climate change stands as one of the most pressing challenges of our time, threatening the very existence of life on Earth. Despite widespread acknowledgement of its severity and the urgent need for action, countries around the world have consistently fallen short in effectively mitigating its impact. With complex factors underlying this global failure, it is important for us to examine the political, economic, and social barriers hindering progress.

Political Inertia and Lack of Leadership

At the heart of the global failure in climate change mitigation lies political inertia and a lack of leadership. Despite numerous international agreements such as the Paris Agreement, countries have often prioritized short-term economic interests over long-term sustainability. The withdrawal of the United States from the Paris Agreement in 2017 exemplifies this trend, undermining global efforts to combat climate change.

Moreover, many governments are hesitant to implement stringent climate policies due to concerns about potential economic repercussions. Developing countries, in particular, often argue that stringent climate regulations could hinder their economic growth and development. This friction between economic development and environmental sustainability has impeded the adoption of effective mitigation strategies.

Inadequate Funding and Resource Allocation

Another significant obstacle to mitigating climate change is the inadequate funding and resource allocation dedicated to this cause. Despite the enormity of the challenge, global investments in renewable energy and climate adaptation are insufficient. According to the International Energy Agency (IEA), only a fraction of global energy investments are directed towards renewable sources, with fossil fuels continuing to dominate the energy landscape.

Developing countries encounter barriers to accessing climate finance to support their adaptation and mitigation efforts. The Green Climate Fund was established to assist developing countries in addressing climate change. It is struggling to mobilize the necessary funding. As a result, vulnerable nations remain ill-equipped to cope with the adverse effects of climate change, exacerbating global inequalities.

Corporate Influence and Lobbying

The influence of powerful corporate interests and industry lobbying presents another formidable barrier to effective climate action. Fossil fuel companies, in particular, have consistently opposed regulations aimed at curbing greenhouse gas emissions, fearing the potential impact on their profits. The fossil fuel industry's extensive lobbying efforts have often succeeded in weakening or delaying climate legislation, perpetuating reliance on carbon-intensive energy sources. Corporate interests frequently intersect with political agendas, further entrenching the status quo. The revolving door between government and industry allows corporate executives to occupy key positions of power, shaping policies that prioritize corporate interests over environmental sustainability. This collusion between government and industry undermines public trust and hampers efforts to implement meaningful climate policies.

Public Apathy and Misinformation

Despite growing awareness of the urgency of climate change, public apathy and misinformation continue to impede progress. Climate change denialism, fueled by vested interests and ideological biases, has sowed doubt and confusion among the public, hindering consensus on the need for decisive action. Moreover, the complex and abstract nature of climate science often makes it difficult for the general public to grasp the severity of the problem and the urgency of the required response. The psychological phenomenon of "psychological distance" often leads individuals to perceive climate change as a distant threat, diminishing their sense of personal responsibility and urgency. This disconnect between individual actions and global consequences further undermines efforts to mobilize public support for climate action.

Conclusion

In conclusion, the failure to effectively mitigate climate change stems from a complex interplay of political, economic, and social factors. Political inertia, inadequate funding, corporate influence, and public apathy all contribute to the inertia and lack of progress in addressing this existential threat.

To overcome these barriers, concerted international cooperation, bold political leadership, and a paradigm shift in societal attitudes are imperative. Only through collective action and a genuine commitment to sustainability can we hope to avert the worst impacts of climate change and safeguard the planet for future generations.

15. Increasing competition and expectations: impact on youth

In an era marked by rapid technological advancement and globalisation, the youth face an unprecedented level of competition and escalating expectations. This intensification is evident across various spheres, including education, employment, and social interaction, predominantly fueled by societal benchmarks and digital platforms that amplify peer comparison. The consequences of these pressures encompass a broad spectrum, affecting psychological health, social relationships, and economic prospects. As mental health issues, social isolation, and economic disparities become increasingly pronounced among young individuals, it is essential to examine the root causes and implications of these challenges.

The landscape of opportunity and achievement has dramatically evolved over the past few decades, influenced by technological advancements, globalisation, and demographic shifts. According to the World Bank, the global youth population—defined as individuals aged 15 to 24—stood at approximately 1.3 billion in 2020, representing a significant portion of the world's populace engaging with an increasingly competitive environment.

Issues Associated with Increasing Competition and Expectations

When we talk of competition and expectations, we need to understand that both of them are beneficial to a certain extent. They act as motivators and encourage students to give their best everywhere. However, in the present day scenario, the exponentially high competition and unreal expectation has negatively impacted the youth.

The various issues that crop up due to them are

Educational Pressures The pursuit of academic excellence has intensified, with institutions like the OECD highlighting the surging demand for higher education. This trend is compounded by the growing significance of rankings and standardised testing, setting a global benchmark and intensifying competition.

Job Market Challenges The International Labour Organization (ILO) has consistently documented the hurdles facing youths in securing employment. Advanced economies demand a higher skillset, while automation and outsourcing reshape labour needs, complicating the employment landscape for the newer generations.

Social Media and Peer Comparison Platforms such as Facebook, Instagram, and LinkedIn have introduced a new arena for competition, perpetuating a cycle of comparison and expectation setting, as noted by numerous studies including those published in the Journal of Social and Clinical Psychology.

Family and Societal Pressures The generational shift has seen parents and guardians placing higher academic and professional expectations on the youth, partly influenced by societal benchmarks of success.

Personal Aspirations With exposure to global standards and success stories, young individuals often set elevated personal goals, further feeding into the cycle of competition and expectations.

The Multidimensional Impact

The convergence of increasing competition and expectations crafts a complex tapestry of impacts on the youth, spanning psychological, social, and economic realms. These impacts are as follows

Stress and Mental Health Issues The American Psychological Association (APA) reports a notable increase in stress-related disorders among the youth, directly correlated to academic and career pressures. Anxiety, depression, and even burnout have become more prevalent, necessitating a paradigm shift in how society addresses mental health.

Identity and Self-Esteem The relentless chase for achievement can erode self-worth, tying identity and self-esteem closely to external validations of success, as highlighted by mental health advocacy groups.

Altered Interpersonal Relationships Competition and high expectations can distort social interactions, promoting rivalry over camaraderie. The erosion of community bonds in pursuit of individual success has broader implications for societal cohesion.

Diverging Socioeconomic Trajectories Those unable to meet societal benchmarks often face marginalisation, deepening socioeconomic divides and fostering an environment of inequity, as examined in studies by the United Nations Development Programme (UNDP).

Innovative Drive vs. Risk Aversion On one hand, the push for excellence has fostered innovation, with young entrepreneurs and leaders emerging. However, the fear of failure has also instigated a risk-averse mindset among significant sections of the youth, potentially stymieing economic dynamism.

The Skill Gap Dilemma Despite higher educational attainment, the mismatch between academic qualifications and market needs continues, as noted by the World Economic Forum. This gap underscores the importance of aligning education systems with the evolving demands of the global economy.

A Call for Balanced Approaches

Addressing the multifaceted impact of increasing competition and expectations on youth necessitates a holistic and nuanced approach, involving stakeholders across the spectrum.

Educational Reforms Tailoring education to foster critical thinking, creativity, and emotional intelligence over rote learning and standardisation can mitigate undue stress and better prepare students for real-world challenges.

Mental Health Advocacy Normalising mental health discussions and ensuring accessible support services are crucial. Initiatives like the Mental Health in Schools Act in the U.S. serve as commendable efforts in integrating mental health education and services in schools.

Policy Interventions for Inclusive Growth Governments and international bodies must implement policies that ensure equitable opportunities for all youths, thereby reducing disparities and creating a more inclusive economic landscape.

Community and Family Support Systems Encouraging a culture of understanding and support within families and communities can alleviate the pressures faced by young individuals, fostering environments where failure is seen as a stepping stone rather than a setback.

Conclusion

The journey toward mitigating the impact of increasing competition and expectations on youth is complex, yet imperative. Cultivating a society that values individual uniqueness over uniform benchmarks of achievement and that sees failure as an integral part of learning and growth, is fundamental. As policymakers, educators, parents and the youth navigate this challenging landscape, the collective aim should be to champion a future where success is diversely defined, and where the youth can thrive unencumbered by undue pressures. Only then can the true potential of the next generation be unlocked, steering the world towards a more compassionate, innovative, and inclusive era.

16. Women in Indian Politics

Politics can be understood as the activities that deal with the governance of a geographical region. It ensures proper working of a society, a better life for every individual and overall growth and development. As a democracy, India is a nation that has established equal rights and opportunities for all, notwithstanding the differences of society. Yet, India stands at 149th position in terms of women representation in executive government and Parliament as per the UN Women in Politics 2019 report.

Like most other fields, the Indian politics has also been dominated by male members primarily. Even though many women have entered politics since the Indian Independence, the number is infinitesimal in comparison to that of men. The reasons behind this include

- gender stereotypes
- lack of political education
- uneven distribution of responsibilities
- scarcity of resources
- social conditioning

Women's representation in parliament was only 3% at the eve of independence, and more than 70 years later, this figure has risen to just 12%. At present, women make up 14.39% (77 MPs) of Lok Sabha's 542 members and 11 % (27 MPs) of Rajya Sabha's 245 members.

Some of the key female politicians in Indian history include

Droupadi Murmu	First Tribal Woman President of India
Nirmala Sitharaman	Current Finance Minister of India
Indira Gandhi	First and Only Female Prime Minister of India
Sucheta Kripalani	First Female Chief Minister in India (UP)
Pratibha Patil	First Female President of India
Jayalalitha	Former Chief Minister of Tamil Nadu
Sheila Dikshit	Former Chief Minister of Delhi
Sushma Swaraj	Second Woman to serve as the Minister of External Affairs of India
Sonia Gandhi	Former President of the Indian National Congress
Mamata Banerjee	Current Chief Minister of West Bengal

In improving the status of women in the Indian society, the Government of India has played an integral role. It has taken many steps to ensure that women are provided with equal opportunities and are treated equally. From ensuring education of every girl child to providing them with ample career opportunities and choices, the government has made many efforts, two of which are

- **Women's Reservation Bill** The 108th Amendment in the Indian Constitution sought to amend the Constitution of India to reserve 1/3rd of all seats in the Lok Sabha and in all State Legislative Assemblies for women.
- **The 73rd and 74th Amendments** The Indian political system, which is a three-step political system – the grass root level (panchayats), the state level and the national level – guarantees one-third reservation to women in the local bodies. As a result of this law, currently, India has about 13,00,000 women in politics at the grassroots, giving way to increased participation of younger women.

It is imperative that a democratic nation like India does more to provide equal opportunities to all the sections of society in political sphere. This can be achieved by ensuring proper education to every citizen, putting a minimum percentage of women in state and central assemblies, promoting the notion of democracy, breaking down gender stereotypes and recognising the experience of the women members of local bodies and providing them with a better opportunity and larger roles. Women have proved themselves equal to men in every sector of life, time and again. It is time that we realise that they deserve an equal chance at governance and can do much good in the field of politics too.

17. Can Hindi become out National Language?

Language is a medium and a means of conveying one's thoughts and opinions to others. In a land of several cultures and ethnicities, like India, language forms the core of an individual's identity. India has around 1,635 languages (as per the 2011 census) of which 22 languages, including Hindi and English, have been recognised as official languages and another 41 are queued to find a place in the eighth schedule of the Indian Constitution.

A national language is a representation of the history and heritage of a country. It shows that the majority of the citizens in the country knows and speaks that language. But in a country with many languages, to declare one language to be the national language is the issue of debate. India's affair with this debate dates back to when it got its independence.

Call for Hindi as National Language

Time and again, people have called for Hindi to be declared as the national language of the county. The call was supported with the claims that the complete usage of Hindi language whilst respecting the various native languages would ensure better co-ordination and cooperation among all the states and act as a strong unifying factor to eliminate all regional differences. Further, if India uses Hindi in the international forum the prestige of Hindi and India would be significantly raised.

However, these claims had a many clapbacks. India is a land of many wonderful languages. The languages of locals differ in different states and within regions of these states. The dialects of Hindi also change after every 100km. Research shows locals either speak in dialects associated with their communities or converse in a form of Hindi that is drastically different from the mainstream version. For instance, in Bihar, the Bhojpuri dialect or the mother tongue Maithili are more common, in Chhattisgarh, people use a dialect known as Chhattisgarhi.

Moreover, promoting one language as the national language, it promotes the growth of one and the death of other languages. The best example for this is the death of Pali language. It was a language of commons but recognising Sanskrit as the court language brought death of Pali language. Further, as per the 2011 census, which is the last reliable information on India's diverse population, only about 44% of Indians speak Hindi. Many in states like Tamil Nadu, Parts of Karnataka, Kerala, Telangana, Andhra Pradesh, Odisha and North-Eastern states don't know how to read, write or speak Hindi. Therefore, it would be grossly inappropriate to enforce Hindi upon them.

Conclusion

India is the birth place of many language and dialects. Declaring one language as a national language will create a linguistic barrier among people and will collapse the national integration. The duty of the government is to build bridges not the walls. Thus, a certain framework should be established between the centre and all the state governments where Hindi can be used up to a certain level while giving due respect to the various regional languages and thus mutually benefiting everyone.

18. The Future of Space Exploration: India's Role

In only six decades, India has rapidly ascended as a global frontrunner in space technology and exploration, with much credit attributed to the ISRO. The overarching objective of India's space endeavour to harness space technology for national progress, simultaneously pursuing scientific research in space and venturing into planetary exploration came up to many successes with the latest one being the triumphant soft landing of Chandrayaan-3 on the lunar south pole.

Achievements in Space Exploration

- ISRO's remarkable track record is a living testament to its accomplishments. The cadre of engineers and scientists at ISRO has crafted an array of launch vehicles, homegrown satellites and associated technologies that cater to diverse domains such as Earth observation, communication, navigation, meteorology and space science.
- Pivotal milestones encompass the creation and launch of the Indian National Satellite System (INSAT) to satisfy the telecommunications, broadcasting, meteorology and search and rescue needs of India, the series of Indian

Remote Sensing Satellites (IRS) catering to the needs of the country in managing its natural resources and the development and deployment of the Polar Satellite Launch Vehicle (PSLV) and the Geosynchronous Satellite Launch Vehicle (GSLV), enabling the launch of both domestic and international satellites.

- Through its historical timeline, ISRO scripted numerous technological breakthroughs and initiated the launch of indigenous spacefaring entities. Hallmarks include the maiden flight of Aryabhata in 1975, the deployment of Rohini Satellite (RS-1) in 1980 and the resounding triumph of the Chandrayaan lunar venture in 2008.
- The Mangalyaan in 2013 further consolidated ISRO's stature as the fourth space agency to reach Mars. Further, ISRO initiated AstroSat in 2015, marking the country's first dedicated astronomical pursuit. With India, now standing alongside the United States, Russia and China as one of the selected few nations to achieve a successful lunar soft landing, it is evident that India is charting a bold trajectory in space exploration.

Future Prospects

India's prospects in space exploration shine brightly, with an array of upcoming missions and collaborations poised to elevate the nation's standing on the global stage including the Aditya L-1 Mission and the Gaganyaan Mission. In addition to these missions, there is a lineup of forthcoming endeavours. The Lunar Polar Exploration (LUPEX) mission, a collaborative effort between ISRO and JAXA (Japan), is set to explore the lunar polar regions focusing on permanently shaded areas. X-ray Polarimeter Satellite (XPoSat) and NASA-ISRO SAR (NISAR) will contribute to Earth observation and human spaceflight endeavours. Additionally, Shukrayaan-1, the mission to Venus, promises to unveil the secrets of our neighbouring planet.

Conclusion

As we gaze into the future, the prospects are rife with promise. Upcoming missions such as Aditya L1 and Gaganyaan hold the potential to reshape our understanding of the cosmos, enhance technological capabilities and solidify India's position as a prominent player in the realm of space exploration.

19. Even A Layman can Change Society

Our society is bound by the ever present concept of transformation wherein the basic structures, beliefs, norms, values and hierarchies undergo a change. This change is often believed to be initiated by the leaders of the time who spread a revolutionary idea and motivated people to such an extent that the social setup transformed. However, the belief is not correct. It is not necessary that to transform a society for the good requires only professionals. Even a layman, who is not involved in governmental or public services, holds the power to change the society. Even a layman can make a difference to the society in small ways. Some of these ways are listed below

- **Doing the 'Right'** Making laws is not an achievement. A society cannot be run by laws if the participating people don't follow these laws. Therefore, by doing the 'right' thing, one can set examples for others motivating them to do the same. Starting with very basic things like following proper etiquettes, following rules and laws, etc., one can change the society.
- **Exercising Fundamental Rights Fairly** The Constitution provides certain fundamental rights to its citizens like right to freedom, right to freedom of religion, etc. It is the responsibility of the citizens not to abuse the given rights. One should be aware of one's rights and practice them as and when required.
- **Raising Voice** It is said that tolerating injustice is a bigger crime than committing one. Therefore, it is important to raise voice when injustice happens. With the advent of internet and technology, one can raise voice and stand against injustice with the help of internet. One post against any malpractice can help in starting discussions resulting in strong actions against the unjust.
- **Educating Self, Family and Friends** We all know the importance of education in our lives. Education helps in learning the difference between good and bad, just and unjust, fair and cheating, etc. It also helps in realising and practicing rights and protects us from fraudulent practices prevailing. An educated individual is capable of doing the right thing and motivating others to do the same.
- **Breaking Social Barriers** Orthodox and conservative societal norms which compel one section of the society to lag behind the other are not meant to be followed. Social evils like dowry, women illiteracy, discrimination in any form, etc., have to be stopped. Equal respect should be given to every individual.

Thus, it is not necessary to be a professional to transform a society. It is equal responsibility of every layman and professionals to make the society a healthy and conducive place to live in.

20. Role of Films in Promotion of Freedom Struggle

It was as early as in the 1890s, long before the Partition (1947), that cinema was introduced in India. Today, the Indian cinema is one of the most popular and vibrant cultural practices that reflects a plethora of social, economic and cultural phenomena that we can find in modern societies. It is an ensemble of all aspects be it the social norms, ambitions, language and everything that constitutes the everyday life in a society.

Cinema, as the art form of the 20th century, essentially is a fluid phenomenon. It is sometimes the cultural reconstruction of our daily lives and sometimes an entry to a different time or place or idea that otherwise is difficult or even impossible to access. Cinema remixes the real, the unreal, the present, the past, the future, memory and dream on the same shared mental level. All of this makes cinema a very powerful and successful medium with a global reach and a language of universality.

Cinema Influencing People's Mindset

In the Indian context, cinema plays a great role in the formation of the mindset of people. It has entertained and influenced people across the spectrum in a place as diverse as India.

This great impact of cinema and films was seen at its very onset wherein the freedom struggle was at height. The film industry was particularly charged with patriotism during the struggle days.

The filmmakers thought of new vistas and brought in a new vision that altogether changed the outlook, text and tenor of the Hindi cinema. Hence, a large number of films in the patriotic mode were made which made the audience/people realise that no price is too high to defend the honour of the country and safeguard it. The films inspired the youth of those days to join the armed forces or atleast to serve the country in their own way.

During the shooting of Bombay Talkies 'Kismet' (1943) starring Ashok Kumar and Mumtaz Shanti, the Quit India Movement was at its peak. Kavi Pradeep wrote the lyrics of this film, the music of which was composed by Anil Biswas. Pradeep had strong nationalistic feelings. He came up with lyrics '*Aaj Himalaya ki choti se hum ne yeh lalkara hai/Door hato ae duniya walo Hindustan Hamara hai...*'.

The song was passed by the Censor Board and it was only when they noticed the tremendous enthusiasm of the audience did the Censor Board realise they had blundered. But they did not recall 'Kismet' for recensoring. The underlying content of Kismet was nationalist and anti-British, not only did that escape the censors, it seems to have ensured that the public would greet the film with acclaim for that very dimension.

Patriotic Genre of Filmmaking

This patriotic genre of filmmaking became very popular in the years between the 1940s and 1960s. These are really period films but they bring alive the atmosphere of the times. Directed by Ramesh Saigal for Filmistan's production, 'Shaheed' (1948) starring Dilip Kumar, Kamini Kaushal, Chander Mohan etc. was a nationalist melodrama set in the context of Quit India Movement and the ensuing wave of terrorist actions, during the mid-40s. The film had contemporary subject and was relevant to the troubled times.

The song '*Wattan ki rah men wattan ke naujawan shaheed ho......*' sung soulfully by Mohd. Rafi and Khan Mastana became almost a national anthem.

Conclusion

It is true that through the freedom movement threw up hundreds of stalwarts; there are few stories that can match Bhagat Singh's for sheer heroism, idealism and dare-devilry. People should realise that the freedom they take for granted did not just come to them on a platter. It was bitterly fought and hard on.

21. Inspiration for Creativity Springs from the Effort to Look for the Magical in the Mundane

Creativity as a Driving Force

Creativity is the driving force behind artistic expression. It engenders innovation, which often enables the advancement of human civilisation. It encourages an endeavour to peer beyond the commonplace and unearth the extraordinary concealed within the everyday facets of existence.

However, we sometimes forget that the mundane can hold just as much enchantment if we take the time to appreciate it. We miss out on the beauty of our neighbourhoods, the simple joys of everyday life, and the opportunity to find magic in the ordinary. It's time to shift our perspective and recognize that adventure and creativity are not limited to far-off places; they can be discovered right at home if we open our eyes to the possibilities around us.

The given adage reminds us just this. It means that creativity is born from the endeavour to uncover enchantment within everyday simplicity, where the ordinary becomes a wellspring of inspiration and innovation. To understand the idea of finding magic in the mundane, it's important to first recognise what we mean by the word, 'mundane'. The mundane refers to the ordinary, the everyday things we often don't pay much attention to in our daily lives. It includes our daily routines, common objects, and regular experiences. These seemingly unremarkable aspects of life provide a limitless canvas for creativity and self-expression when viewed through an imaginative perspective.

Inspiration of Artists

Artists often find inspiration in the ordinary. For example, Dutch painter Johannes Vermeer created masterful paintings like 'Girl with a Pearl Earring' and 'The Milkmaid' that celebrated everyday life. Similarly, poets like William Wordsworth found profound beauty in the natural world and ordinary experiences.

His poems often celebrated the tranquility of rural life and the emotional richness found in ordinary encounters. Scientific discovery also begins with the observation of ordinary phenomena. For example, Sir Isaac Newton's exploration of gravity began with the simple observation of an apple falling from a tree. Albert Einstein's theory of relativity was rooted in the mundane experience of riding a train and wondering about the consequences of its motion. Charles Darwin's fascination with the diverse forms of plant life during his travels on the HMS Beagle led to his revolutionary theory of evolution by natural selection.

Creativity extends beyond the realms of arts and sciences, proving to be a catalyst for innovative solutions to practical challenges. When faced with a problem, individuals and organizations that embrace creative thinking often discover ingenious ways to overcome obstacles.

Example of Space X

Consider the example of the SpaceX's innovative approach to rocket recovery showcases creativity in problem-solving. They turned the mundane idea of reusing rocket components into a groundbreaking practice, drastically reducing the cost of space travel. Many companies are creatively addressing environmental concerns through mundane objects like sustainable packaging, using biodegradable materials and minimalistic designs, are aimed at reducing waste and environmental impact.

Further, the education sector has witnessed a surge in creativity, especially with the rise of e-learning platforms. Creative approaches to digital education, such as interactive content, have transformed the mundane process of learning into engaging and effective experiences. Innovation in the business world also relies on the ability to find the magic in the mundane.

Companies that thrive often do so by identifying unmet needs or overlooked opportunities in everyday life. Uber, for example, transformed the mundane act of hailing a taxi into a convenient and efficient experience by leveraging smartphone technology.

However, in today's fast-paced world filled with constant distractions and obligations, finding the time and mental space to meditate on the magic in the mundane can be a significant challenge.

The prevalence of smartphones, social media, and the constant influx of notifications can make it hard for people to take a break and pay attention to what's happening right now. Always being connected can distract us from the ordinary parts of life. This means people have very little time to stop and think about the simple beauty of everyday life.

Society's focus on getting immediate gratification and always chasing after new things might make people look for thrills in new experiences instead of appreciating the wonder in what they already know. Advertisements and consumer culture often promote the idea that happiness and magic can be purchased through products or experiences, encouraging people to constantly seek the next big thing.

Conclusion

On the surface, it might seem that observing the mundane or insignificant things around us diverts our attention from the more important tasks in life. However, when we decide to relax and find meaning in simpler things, we pay more attention to the small but significant details of our existence. Joy and beauty in such simpler things help us appreciate and fill us with a sense of gratitude and satisfaction. When we make an effort to look for the magical in the mundane, we are opening ourselves up to new possibilities and perspectives. We begin to see the world in a different light, noticing details and nuances that we may have overlooked before. This shift in perception can be incredibly powerful, leading to new ideas and insights that can fuel our creativity.

22. Religious Fundamentalism : a Challenge to National Security

'A house divided against itself cannot stand together' is an old saying and it holds true in the present context of increasing communal disharmony in the society. These dividing forces weaken and mutilate the society.

Cultural Richness of India

The culture, civilisation and tradition of India is approximately 12,000 years old. The spirit of tolerance and assimilation has made it possible for our civilisation to survive the test of time. But with the passage of time, the growing attachment to one's own ethnic, religious, racial or cultural group rather than being a part of a wider circle of the entire social milieu, has posed one of the gravest problems of modern times. Somehow with the increase in science and technology, people should have opened up to assimilation and integration. But they have instead receded into their own cocoons and have become more conservative and protective of their own culture and community. Fear, suspicion and a sense of insecurity towards the other communities has given rise to hatred, which acts as a fuel, feeding the flame of religious fundamentalism or communalism.

Role of Divide and Rule Policy

India has had a long and proud history of mutual cooperation and trust. People belonging to various ethnic groups, races, religions, creeds, cultures have come and settled on this land and since centuries have made it their home. But the 'Divide and Rule policy', that took root deeper than what the colonial masters could have imagined, shows its predatory signs time and again. The seeds of communal divide, sown by colonial leaders to meet short-term selfish political ends, now threaten to uproot the century old harmony and unity of the country.

This hatred was at its worst during the ill-fated partition of the country. The articulation of two-nation theory and creation of the state of Pakistan implied that the enmity between the two communities/ religions was so great that it was virtually impossible for them to live together in peace as one nation.

Conclusion

Even today, India's fragile peace is shattered by communal riots every now and then. The recent communal violence of Gujarat, the anti-Sikh campaigns during the mid-80s, the Mumbai Riots, the Ayodhya episode, the evacuation of Kashmiri Pandits, the attacks on the pilgrims on their way to pilgrimage are all blots on the secular fabric of the country. Not just these, today religious ostracising, crimes against women, love jihad, honour killing and many other unlawful activities are done under the guise of religious fundamentalism. Such activities not only threaten the internal security and peace of the nation but also allow external forces to take advantage of the situation and create chaos over boundaries.

Thus, it is important to tackle religious fundamentalism as they are a challenge to national security.

23. Nexus between Health Practitioners and Pharmaceutical Companies, a concern

Since vedic era, human beings suffer from various ailments and diseases. To treat the patients, ayurvedic vaidyas were there. With passage of time, this pious, holy alliance of doctor and patient is expanded and entered the third party of retail chemist. Slowly, the fourth and fifth party of manufacturer and distributor entered this triangle. In modern era, the Indian pharmaceutical industry of allopathic medicines started with a Calcutta based company named Bengal Chemical and Pharmaceutical Company, in the year 1901. This tiny step of manufacturing medicine in our country has now grown into a vast industry with more than 24000 pharmaceutical companies.

Change in Imperative Pharmacy Knowledge

Initially, the pharmaceutical company's representative met medical health professionals (Doctors) and imparted knowledge about new drugs/ medicines, launched by their pharmaceutical company.

With passage of time, this practice of imparting only knowledge of medicines was modified and supplemented with additional points like giving physician's trial samples of new drugs/ medicines. These trial packs are supposed to be given to poor patients, free of charge, by the physician. By this, doctor will also check the quality of product by seeing the improvement in the condition of patient. This tradition of free sample is further augmented by occasional gifts on New Year, diwali, holi or other festival or on the occasion of new product launch. The small gifts include pen, writing pads, stethoscope, calendar, table top, paper weight or other utility items, which are helpful in the examination of patients.

Profits Making Ideology of Pharmacy Companies

The greed and hunger for more sales in various pharmaceuticals companies leads to various ponzy, lucrative schemes of offering big gifts, from latest and sophisticated electronic gazettes like mobile phones, laptop, tablet, AC, refrigerator, LED TV etc., to hard cash.

However, this nexus has come to question as petitions have been filed in the supreme court regarding the nexus between doctors and pharmaceutical companies. In the petition regarding the nexus of companies and doctors for the sale of medicines, it has been alleged that several doctors have been prescribing particular medicine excessively after receiving gifts without any care for the sick and the ailing. This is a serious allegation and casts a shadow on the noble profession wherein a simple salt which costs the bare minimum are sold at high prices to provide luxury to the health professionals as well as the pharmaceutical companies.

It is imperative to know here that the Medical Council of India has a code of conduct for doctors that prohibits them from accepting any gifts, cash, travel facilities or hospitality from pharma companies. Although there is a voluntary code for pharmaceutical companies known as the Uniform Code of Pharmaceutical Marketing Practice or UCMP, experts say that it is not a very effective mechanism for checking prevalent misconduct.

Conclusion

Hence, there is a dire need to bring in a new law under which pharmaceutical companies will be required to disclose the amount paid to doctors for research, lectures, travel and entertainment. There should also be a code of ethics, under which pharma companies cannot give any kind of gift, money, or other benefits to doctors for promoting their medicines, nor should they organise meetings or conferences in such places which are associated with entertainment, sporting events or providing fun and leisure.

There should also be an emphasis on the need to punish anyone for adopting unethical methods. Only legal intervention can work to break this immoral nexus of doctors and pharma companies besides awareness campaigns that could help patients to understand the system better.

24. Gandhi's idea in the 21st century

In the annals of history, few have left as indelible a mark on the tapestry of human thought and action as Mohandas Karamchand Gandhi.

Known to the world as Mahatma Gandhi, his philosophy of non-violent resistance and profound spirituality has transcended the confines of time, finding profound relevance and resonance in the contemporary 21st century. At a juncture where the global community grapples with unprecedented challenges—ranging from climate crises to deep-seated social injustices, rampant consumerism to the scourge of war—Gandhi's teachings emerge not merely as historical footnotes but as navigational beacons.

Gandhi's Principles in the Contemporary World

Non violence and Peacekeeping The principle of 'Ahimsa' or non-violence stands at the core of Gandhi's philosophy, advocating for resolution of conflict through peaceful means. This principle finds its echo in modern peacekeeping efforts around the globe. The United Nations, recognizing the universality of Gandhi's message, commemorates his birthday, October 2nd, as the International Day of Non-Violence, underscoring the global aspiration towards peace. Noteworthy leaders such as Martin Luther King Jr. in the United States, Nelson Mandela in South Africa and the Dalai Lama have drawn inspiration from Gandhi, illustrating the transcultural appeal of his teachings. Their successes lend credence to the potent force of non-violent action in achieving societal and political milestones.

Sustainability and Environmentalism At a time when environmental degradation threatens the very survival of the planet, Gandhi's ethos of living in harmony with nature and advocating for minimalistic lifestyles resonate more than ever. His principle of 'Swadeshi', promoting local self-sufficiency, mirrors modern movements against overconsumption and for carbon footprint reduction. The Intergovernmental Panel on Climate Change (IPCC) emphasises transformative changes in human activities, paralleling Gandhi's caution against unrestrained industrialization. Environmental activists worldwide adopt Gandhian methods in their fight for ecological conservation, demonstrating the adaptability of his ideas to contemporary environmental challenges.

Social Justice and Inclusion Gandhi's life was a testament to the fight against social discrimination and for inclusivity. The resurgence of global movements advocating for social justice—be it Black Lives Matter, Indigenous rights, or LGBTQ+ equality—reflects the ongoing relevance of his vision for a society predicated on empathy, respect and community dialogues. Organisations like the United Nations through its various programs reiterate the importance of inclusive policies for achieving sustainable development, embodying Gandhi's vision of 'Sarvodaya' or welfare for all.

Economic Equity In an era marked by egregious economic disparities, Gandhi's advocacy for an equitable economic system and his vision of a self-reliant, village-centric economy offer profound insights. The concept of 'Khadi' and empowerment of rural industries envisioned by Gandhi can be seen paralleled in several of the United Nations' Sustainable Development Goals (SDGs), notably those aiming at reducing poverty, ensuring economic inclusivity, and promoting sustainable communities. Gandhi's economic ideas challenge the contemporary world to rethink development paradigms, emphasising human and ecological well-being over mere economic growth.

Education and Empowerment Gandhi's revolutionary approach to education, known as 'Nai Talim', advocated for a learning process that integrates moral development with academic and vocational training. In an age where educational systems are often critiqued for their narrow focus and failure to address broader societal needs, Gandhi's holistic vision for education presents a compelling alternative. His emphasis on education as a tool for personal and societal empowerment echoes in current discussions on educational reforms and the need for more inclusive, holistic learning frameworks.

Challenges in Adopting Gandhi's Philosophy

Implementing Gandhi's teachings in the modern context is fraught with challenges, necessitating adaptation and careful interpretation:

- **Misinterpretation and Misuse** Gandhi's advocacy for non-violence and tolerance is sometimes construed as advocating passivity, potentially undermining the effectiveness of his philosophy in socio-political activism. This necessitates a nuanced understanding and application of non-violent resistance as a dynamic and potent force rather than mere passivity.
- **Economic Globalisation and Consumerism** The dominant economic narrative is marked by aggressive consumerism and globalisation, often at odds with Gandhi's vision of sustainability, moderation, and local self-sufficiency. Bridging this ideological divide demands significant policy shifts and a transformation in collective consciousness towards more sustainable lifestyles.
- **Technological Disruption** With the advent of digital technology, the world is encountering ethical dilemmas and social challenges unforeseen in Gandhi's era. Navigating these complexities while adhering to Gandhian ethics requires innovative thinking to reconcile technological advancements with principles of non-violence, compassion, and sustainability.

At the heart of Gandhi's philosophy lies the profound belief in the power of change within each individual and the potential for collective action to reshape the world. As humanity stands at the crossroads, confronting multifarious global challenges, the universality and timelessness of Gandhi's teachings offer not just hope but a pragmatic framework for action. Whether it is through fostering global peace, advocating for environmental sustainability, championing social justice, striving for economic equity, or reimagining education, Gandhi's principles provide a holistic lens through which to view and address contemporary issues.

However, translating these ideals into reality is contingent upon our collective will, resilience, and creativity. It demands a conscientious effort to not only reinterpret Gandhi's philosophy to suit the complexities of the 21st century but also to live by the adage that epitomises his belief: "Be the change that you wish to see in the world." In embracing this ethos, we affirm the enduring relevance of Gandhi's ideas, forging a path towards a future that is inclusive, sustainable and just—a testament to the enduring legacy of Mahatma Gandhi in the 21st century.

25. Emergence of Regional Parties and Its Effect on the Federal Structure of India

In a democracy, political parties provide an agency to the society to gather different views on various issues and to present these to the government. They bring various representatives together so that a responsible government could be formed. They provide a mechanism to support or restrain the government, make policies, justify or oppose them. As a democracy, India has a multi-party system with 2100 registered political parties.

Other than the 8 national parties- Indian National Congress, Bharatiya Janata Party, Nationalist Congress Party, Communist Parties, Bahujan Samaj Party, Rashtriya Janata Dal, All India Trinamool Congress and National People's Party; most of the major parties of the country are classified by the Election Commission as 'state parties'. These are commonly referred to as regional parties that have held power in specific regions or states.

For a country which has been dominated by one party since its independence, the emergence of regional parties holds as important significance. It changes the federal structure and boosts good governance.

Impacts of Political Structure

Some of its impacts on the political structure of the nation are

- They provide better governance and a stable government at the regional level
- They pose a challenge to the one-party dominant system in the country and led to a decline in the dominance of the one party.
- They make a strong impact on the nature and course of centre-state relations. The tension areas in centre-state relations and the demand for grant of greater autonomy make the central leadership more responsive to the needs of the regional actors.
- They make politics more competitive and popular participation in the political process more extensive at the grass roots.
- They widen the choice for voters in both the parliamentary and assembly elections. The voters can vote for that party which aims to promote the interest of the state/region.
- They increase the political consciousness of the people and also their interest in politics. They bring into focus the local or regional issues which immediately attract the attention of the masses.
- They provide a chance against the dictatorial tendencies of the central government. They oppose the ruling party at the centre on certain issues and force the dominant party to the more reasonable in its approach to the process of conflict resolution.
- They have succeeded in exposing the partisan role of the Governors in the appointment and dismissal of the Chief Minister, in issuing of ordinances and reservation of bills for the consideration of the President.

Conclusion

After the dawn of the era of coalition politics, the regional parties have assumed an important role in national politics. They again joined the coalition governments formed at the centre and shared power with the national parties. With the reemergence of coalition governments, the regional parties have changed the way federalism worked in India.

26. Population Stabilisation—India's Critical Need

India, the largest democracy in the world has added one more stud as the world's most populous country amongst the comity of nations. United Nations data shows India is world number one in population which grew by 1.56% to reach 142.86 crore, overtaking China which is at 142.57 crore. It has been predicted that India would reach this figure only in 2027, however, reached four years earlier (2023).

Problem of Population Explosion

The changes in the population growth have sparked dystopian future for India.

This rapid rise of population has led to various socio-economic problems in the country. Socially, population explosion leads to migration of people from rural to the urban areas leading to the growth of slum areas. People in slums live in the most unhygienic and insanitary conditions which gives birth to number of diseases. Migration also leads to several associated problems such as overcrowding, traffic congestions, frequent accidents and pollution. Further, increase in population increases the pressure on land and crop production which is compensated by using synthetic fertilisers, insecticides and pesticides which in turn pollute land, water and air. Population explosion also acts as a hurdle in addressing the problems of poverty, hunger and malnutrition effectively. This leads to an intensification of the existing problems of a nation. In addition, it puts a pressure on the several resources leading to the overall shortage in land, jobs, capital, housing transportation, employment and health services.

Need of Population Stabalisation

To cater to the demands of an ever increasing population, building the subsequent infrastructure for providing basic necessities like health, education and water becomes a challenge for various government authorities. For feeding a large population, we need more production of food. Even though new techniques of agriculture have increased our productions, there is still malnutrituon reported in parts of our country. Population explosion ultimately leads to the decrease in the per-capita income and standard of living of the people.

Conclusion

Hence, population can be our strength only when we have resources and power to feed, provide the basic facilities, healthcare and jobs. This will mould them into an asset. But in reality, we don't have the necessary resources to do this. Therefore, we should make a conscious effort as individuals to put a curb on further population increase. It is the only way through which we can secure better future for upcoming generations.

Highlighting the importance of population control, Prime Minister in his Independence Day Speech of 2019, equated 'family planning as another form of patriotism.' Hence, family planning needs to taken as another 'Jan andolan' by the citizens of the country in order to visualise the dream of making India a global superpower.

27. Do the Modern means of Telecommunication and Internet Pose a Threat to Our Culture and Society?

The present age in which we live is the age of technology and communication. With the present advancements everything is just a click away. It has made this huge world a global village and has given every infinite access to information and products and services. This is especially true for social media which has been used more effectively for communication, interactions, forming communities, entertainment, commerce and others.

In a democratic society like India, social media plays a major role by giving information to the citizens and by reflecting their opinions at a large scale impacting different communities. It affects us so much that it has a role in forming opinions in the community. Hence, it poses a various threats to the nation-

- **Nation Integrity and Harmony** Hateful contents against communities and religions harm communal harmony and raise a wall of mistrust and disgust among people. For instance, the recent Love Jihad, Muzaffarpur riots sparked because of social media video post.
- **Terrorism** Terrorism, using the social media has become one of the most concerning issues across the world. Terrorist organisations are using social media platforms for recruiting, training and communicating with their followers, supporters, donors, as it is cheaper, easier, faster and more effective method of communication. The members of the terrorist organisations are spreading their ideologies, propaganda and their activities to the world, using social media platforms.
- **Spreading Conflicts Among People** Social media is a place where people share their opinions and sometimes try to impose them on others. Sharing of religious conflicts, proving one religion/ community/ gender/ race better than the other, spreading hate, etc., give rise to conflicts among masses. These conflicts sometimes become so intense that people tend to become violent and start verbal or physical abuse.
- **Sensationalism and Commercialisation** Social media is known to be promoting sensationalism and commercialisation where it tends to exaggerate facts related to events, which definitely result in serious communal tensions and conflicts. Instead of bringing communal unrest to normalcy, social media often plays an ignorant role in inciting agitations as a consequence of which large scale rioting, arson and pillage takes place. This is being done because the current youth can be strongly influenced by anything and everything they see. They are so gullible and innocent that the media can control and manipulate their minds.
- **Communalism** Objective facts have little or no influence in shaping public opinion when compared to personal emotions and beliefs which are naturally very subjective. Thus, competition is born between reality and hoaxes, where when previously the mainstream media where people trusted the content and studies reported by them but now that trust is decreasing and people trusting more information that comes from or even favours on his own group.

Conclusion

However, this does not mean that means of telecommunication and internet pose a threat to our culture and society and have not positives.

Social media is one of the most potent and effective mediums given its wide reach, effective delivery mechanism. It is changing the way we perceive the world. It has the ability to mobilise public opinion by giving people a voice as a principle to lead our community. It plays an active role in enhancing social, religious and communal harmony for the betterment of the community, the society, the nation and the entire humanity as a whole.

Therefore, we need a movement to develop digital literacy, a movement that should grow on the basis of shared awareness of the urgency of mastery and understanding of online media.

It should be used wisely for acts of kindness or benefit to humans.. It should be used to establish friendship, spread goodness and compassion, as well as a means to strengthen national integration, not to be used as a tool for acts of sin, transgression and conflict or disintegration among people.

28. Can Laws Alone Fight Corruption?

As the world observes International Anti-Corruption Day on 9th December, it is a good time to do a stocktaking of India's efforts in tackling the most entrenched and widely visible phenomenon that devalues governance and erodes the average citizen's trusts in the state. According to Transparency International (TI), India ranks very high in the Asian region. Although the situation is lot better than 2013 when the country was ranked 94, India has a long way to go to tackle this perverse phenomenon.

The roots of corruption in India date back to British colonial rule. The British administration, which systematically excluded much of the Indian population from key political and administrative processes, helped to institutionalise graft culture by enacting the crucial Official Secret Act, 1923. This colonial act made it an offence for any public official to disclose state information or secrets. Once the malaise was borne, it was allowed to grow freely without any checks. However, even when the malaise was detected and various laws were made to curb corruption, the problem never disappeared. There are many reasons for the same.

- **Over Centralisation** The more remotely power is exercised from the people, the greater is the distance between authority and accountability. The large number of functionaries between the citizen and final decision makers makes accountability diffused and the temptation to abuse authority strong.
- **Weak Enforcement of Law** Various laws have been made to curb the evil of corruption but their weak enforcement has acted as a hindrance in curbing corruption.
- **Greed for Illegitimate Money** Various scams like the telgi stamp scam took place due to the inexhaustible appetite for illegal illegitimate funds.
- **Colonial Legacy of Unchallenged Authority** In a society which worships power, it is easy for public officials to deviate from ethical conduct.

Hence, the presence laws only cannot solve the problem of corruption. There are various other ways to curb the issue.

These are

- **Regulation of Work Procedures** Work procedures and processes need to be regularly reviewed and it needs to be ensured that such procedures are strictly followed in a systematic manner to make corruption difficult and thus act as preventive measures.
- **Regular Investigations** The audit system can be an effective tool to suggest systemic improvements and changes in the working procedures of government so that chances of corruption diminish.
- **Free and Fair Media** A free media has a crucial role in prevention, monitoring and control of corruption. Such media can inform and educate the public on corruption, expose corruption in government, private sector and civil society organisations and help monitor codes of conduct while policing itself against corruption.

Conclusion

In India, some recent anti-corruption initiatives have been taken. Measures are indeed steps in the right direction, but bringing behavioural change in society will act as the most potent weapon against corruption.

29. The Role and Impact of the International Solar Alliance in Advancing Solar Energy Cooperation

The world is at a pivotal juncture, grappling with the imperative to transition towards sustainable energy sources amid escalating environmental concerns. Emphasising the significance of solar energy collaboration, Indian Prime Minister Narendra Modi aptly stated, "The sun is the source of all energy. The world must turn to solar, the power of our future." This sentiment encapsulates the essence of the ISA's mission and the transformative potential of solar energy on a global scale. In this context, the International Solar Alliance (ISA) stands as a beacon, fostering global collaboration in advancing solar energy.

Historical Context and Formation

Established in 2015, the ISA has emerged as a transformative force, uniting nations in the quest for cleaner, more sustainable energy solutions. The International Solar Alliance was conceived on the sidelines of the 2015 United Nations Climate Change Conference (COP21) in Paris, reflecting a shared commitment among solar rich countries to harness the power of the Sun. The alliance was officially launched on 30th November, 2015, by Indian Prime Minister Narendra Modi and French President François Hollande. With India playing a pivotal role in its formation, the ISA exemplifies South-South cooperation, epitomising the spirit of global solidarity. The ISA's primary mission is to facilitate the deployment of solar energy on a massive scale, addressing energy poverty, fostering sustainable development and mitigating climate change. Its objectives include mobilising more than a trillion dollars of investment by 2030, deploying over 1,000 GW of solar capacity and facilitating the adoption of solar technologies in member countries.

Global Collaboration and Diplomacy

The ISA operates on the principle of collective action, bringing together solar-rich nations lying between the Tropics of Cancer and Capricorn. This unique geographical focus positions the alliance as a potent force in driving solar energy cooperation. Through diplomatic channels, the ISA has garnered support from over 121 countries, showcasing the global resonance of solar energy as a key driver of sustainable development.

Achievements and Impact

Since its inception, the ISA has made significant strides in advancing solar energy cooperation. One of its notable achievements is the initiation of the Common Risk Mitigation Mechanism (CRMM), a financial instrument aimed at reducing risks associated with solar projects, thereby attracting investments. The ISA has also launched various programs, including the Scaling Solar Applications for Agricultural Use and Affordable Finance at Scale, to address specific challenges and promote solar applications in diverse sectors.

Key Initiatives and Collaborative Projects

The ISA has spearheaded initiatives such as the One Sun, One World, One Grid (OSOWOG), envisioning a global interconnected solar grid to optimise solar energy utilisation.

Collaborative projects like the Rewa Ultra Mega Solar Park in India, a joint effort between the ISA and the World Bank, exemplify the alliance's capacity to mobilise international support for large-scale solar ventures.

Conclusion

In conclusion, as the International Solar Alliance continues to evolve, its impact on global solar energy cooperation is undeniable.

Beyond the tangible achievements and collaborative projects, the ISA represents a paradigm shift in international relations, where nations unite not only for economic or political reasons but also to address the shared challenges of sustainable energy and climate change. In the journey towards a cleaner, greener future, the ISA stands as a testament to the power of collective action, proving that together, nations can harness the boundless energy of the Sun to illuminate a brighter and more sustainable world.

30. Tapping the Gender Dividend for India @100

As India approaches its centennial milestone, a powerful narrative emerges the concerted effort to tap into the gender dividend, recognising the indispensable role of women in shaping the nation's trajectory. The recent data from the Election Commission of India underscores the substantial influence of women, with 470 million eligible female voters out of a total of 960 million. Let us delve into the latest developments and initiatives aimed at women's empowerment, reflecting India's commitment to harness the untapped potential of its female population.

Economic and Political Influence

The staggering number of eligible female voters, as highlighted by the Election Commission of India, signifies the significant political clout women hold in shaping the nation's political landscape. President Draupadi Murmu's address ahead of the Budget session further emphasises the commitment to women's empowerment, citing the 2024 Republic Day's Parade dedicated to showcasing the capabilities of India's daughters. The government's focus on expanding women's roles across various domains, from land to space, demonstrates a holistic approach towards recognising and leveraging women's potential.

Education as the Catalyst

Education plays a pivotal role in unleashing the gender dividend. By ensuring equal access to quality education for both genders, India can empower its youth with the skills and knowledge necessary for the challenges of the 21st century. Investing in STEM (Science, Technology, Engineering and Mathematics) education for girls, for instance, not only narrows gender gaps in these fields but also fuels innovation and technological advancements.

Changing Social Norms

Tapping the gender dividend also necessitates a cultural shift in societal norms and attitudes towards gender roles. Eradicating deeply ingrained stereotypes and prejudices is essential for creating an environment where women can thrive professionally and men can engage more actively in caregiving and domestic responsibilities. The breaking down of gender-based barriers fosters a more harmonious society and unleashes the full potential of the Indian populace.

Global Recognition and Competitiveness

Internationally, countries recognising and leveraging the gender dividend have gained a competitive edge. By harnessing the talents of the entire population, nations can innovate, compete and adapt more effectively in the global arena. As India aims to be a global powerhouse by the time it turns 100, harnessing the gender dividend is not just a matter of morality but a strategic imperative for staying competitive and relevant on the world stage.

Legislative and Policy Initiatives

Several legislative and policy initiatives underscore India's commitment to women's empowerment. The Ministry of Road Transport and Highways' emphasis on pay parity and basic amenities for women working in highway construction reflects a tangible effort to create an inclusive and supportive work environment. Amendments to the EPFO rules, allowing women government employees to nominate their children as beneficiaries, exemplify a progressive approach acknowledging diverse family structures.

Key Empowerment Initiatives

President Murmu's address highlighted key initiatives including engaging around 100 million women in self-help groups, receiving substantial financial support. The campaign to create 20 million 'Lakhpati Didis' and the NAMO Drone Didi scheme, providing 15 thousand drones to groups, represent ambitious yet transformative steps towards technological and economic empowerment. Extending maternity leave from 12 to 26 weeks, granting permanent commissions to women in the Armed Forces and admitting women cadets to prestigious military institutions demonstrate significant strides towards gender inclusivity.

Impactful Schemes

The success of the Mudra Yojana stands out as a testament to the government's commitment to economic inclusivity. Out of more than 460 million loans extended, over 310 million were granted to women, empowering countless women to become self-employed and contributing to their economic independence. As the nation progresses, the focus on women's empowerment remains at the forefront, reflecting a commitment to further bolster initiatives aimed at economic inclusivity and gender parity.

Conclusion

We can conclude that, India @100 is not merely a chronological milestone but a canvas upon which the narrative of women's empowerment unfolds. The data, legislative measures, and key initiatives outlined in President Murmu's address showcase a nation earnestly working towards unleashing the potential of its female population. It is poised to be pivotal, solidifying India's commitment to tapping into the gender dividend, ensuring that women become not just the beneficiaries but the architects of a more inclusive, prosperous and empowered nation.

31. India's Climate Action towards Building Resilience

India, standing at the forefront of climate challenges, has embarked on a transformative journey towards climate resilience, recognising the urgency and global significance of sustainable development. India has shown great leadership on this issue and worked hard to play a crucial role in adopting the Paris Agreement during its Presidency of COP21. Antonio Guterres, UN Secretary General. India's leadership in climate action has been acknowledged globally, reflecting the nation's commitment to collaborative efforts in addressing the shared challenge of climate change.

India's Climate Imperatives

With a rapidly growing population and diverse ecosystems, India faces multifaceted challenges exacerbated by climate change. Rising temperatures, extreme weather events and escalating natural disasters demand proactive measures to fortify the nation's resilience. India's climate action not only aligns with international commitments but also underscores the imperative of safeguarding its citizens and ecosystems.

Renewable Energy Revolution

India's ambitious targets for renewable energy adoption exemplify its commitment to mitigating climate change.

The country has set a goal of achieving an audacious target of 500 GW by 2030. India is one of the five largest producers of wind energy globally and has made significant strides in solar energy production. This transition towards clean energy not only reduces greenhouse gas emissions but also ensures a sustainable and resilient energy future.

Forest and Biodiversity Conservation

India's diverse ecosystems, rich in biodiversity, are integral to its climate resilience strategy. The nation has committed to restoring 26 million hectares of degraded land by 2030, an ambitious goal aimed at enhancing carbon sequestration and preserving ecosystems. Initiatives like the Green India Mission and Project Tiger emphasise the importance of biodiversity conservation, recognising the role of healthy ecosystems in building resilience against climate induced challenges.

Water Resource Management

Addressing the impacts of climate change on water resources is a priority for India. The Jal Shakti Abhiyan, a flagship programme aims to rejuvenate water bodies, enhance water conservation and improve water use efficiency. The Pradhan Mantri Krishi Sinchayee Yojana focuses on sustainable irrigation practices, ensuring farmers have access to water resources in the face of changing climate patterns.

Climate Resilient Agriculture

Recognising the vulnerability of agriculture to climate change, India is actively promoting climate-resilient agricultural practices. The National Mission for Sustainable Agriculture focuses on enhancing resilience, promoting water use efficiency and implementing climate smart technologies. By integrating traditional knowledge with modern practices, India seeks to ensure food security and farmer livelihoods in the face of changing climatic conditions.

Community Engagement and Adaptation

India's climate action extends beyond policy measures to grassroots level community engagement. The National Action Plan on Climate Change includes eight national missions, emphasising adaptation and resilience at the local level. Initiatives like the National Adaptation Fund for Climate Change (NAFCC) provide financial resources to vulnerable communities for implementing adaptation projects, fostering resilience at the community level.

Conclusion

India's journey towards climate resilience is a testament to its commitment to sustainable development and global environmental stewardship. The nation's holistic approach, encompassing renewable energy, biodiversity conservation, water resource management and community engagement, reflects a comprehensive strategy in the face of climate challenges. As India continues to lead by example, the global community looks to its transformative climate action as a beacon of hope for a more resilient and sustainable future.

32. Social Media: Turning to Antisocial Media

In the age of digitisation, social media emerged as a transformative force, promising connectivity, information dissemination and virtual communities. However, the journey from 'social' to 'antisocial' dynamics on these platforms has presented a paradoxical shift. This essay examines the multifaceted impacts of social media, analysing its evolution from a tool for societal engagement to a platform that sometimes perpetuates antisocial behaviours.

Initially hailed as a revolutionary tool for connecting people across the globe, social media platforms like Facebook, Twitter and Instagram promised to break down geographical barriers, fostering global communities and shared narratives.

The democratisation of information became a hallmark, with individuals empowered to share their perspectives and engage in meaningful conversations.

The Rise of Antisocial Dynamics

While social media held the promise of connecting diverse voices, it also witnessed the rise of antisocial dynamics. Cyberbullying, online harassment and the spread of misinformation have become prevalent issues, casting a shadow on the platforms' original intent.

Data-driven Polarisation

The algorithmic nature of social media platforms, designed to keep users engaged, has unintentionally led to echo chambers and polarisation. The platforms prioritise content based on users' preferences, creating filter bubbles that reinforce existing beliefs and limit exposure to diverse perspectives. This unintentional consequence has contributed to social divisions and a decline in constructive dialogue.

Psychological Impact

The addictive nature of social media, driven by features like endless scrolling and instant gratification through likes and shares, has led to concerns about its impact on mental health. Studies have shown a correlation between excessive social media use and issues like anxiety, depression and feelings of inadequacy. The constant comparison facilitated by curated online persons can contribute to a distorted sense of reality.

Misinformation and Fake News

The rapid dissemination of information on social media, while empowering has also given rise to the swift spread of misinformation and fake news.

The viral nature of sensational content can lead to the amplification of false narratives, impacting public opinion and even influencing real world events. The World Health Organisation termed the spread of misinformation during the COVID-19 pandemic as an 'infodemic' emphasising the urgency to address this challenge.

Regulatory Responses

Governments worldwide are grappling with the need for regulatory measures to mitigate the negative impacts of social media. India, for instance, introduced intermediary guidelines in 2021, seeking to hold social media platforms accountable for content moderation and user safety. Striking a balance between freedom of expression and preventing online harm remains a complex challenge for policymakers.

Conclusion

To summarise, social media's evolution from a conduit of connectivity to a platform fostering antisocial dynamics underscores the complex relationship between technology and society.

As we navigate this digital landscape, it is crucial to recognise the dual nature of social media, acknowledging its potential for positive social change while actively addressing the challenges it poses. The onus lies not only on regulatory bodies but also on users to cultivate a responsible and ethical online culture, ensuring that the promise of 'social' media prevails over its antisocial dimensions.

33. Quad : Future of Strategic Partnership for India

The Quadrilateral Security Dialogue (QSD), commonly known as the Quad, is a strategic security dialogue between Australia, India, Japan and the United States that is maintained by talks between member countries. The dialogue, initiated in 2007, was disbanded in 2008. However, in 2021, leaders in all four countries have become more aligned in their shared concerns about China's increasingly assertive behavior in the region and are more willing to define a constructive agenda of cooperation. All four navies participated in their first joint exercise in over a decade in November 2020. And in March 2021, US President Joe Biden convened a virtual Quad meeting attended by Australian Prime Minister Scott Morrison, Indian Prime Minister Narendra Modi and Japanese Prime Minister Yoshihide Suga.

The Quad, as such, presents India with a complex geopolitical puzzle, offering both opportunities and challenges in its pursuit of strategic interests. As India contemplates its role in this strategic alliance, it must carefully weigh the advantages of countering China's influence and expanding its global reach against the potential pitfalls of regional tensions, diplomatic balancing acts and delivery deficits.

Advantages of Quad for India

- **Countering China's Influence** The Quad provides India with a crucial platform to counterbalance China's expanding presence in the Indo-Pacific region. With China's Belt and Road Initiative causing concerns about encirclement, the Quad serves as a strategic alliance to safeguard India's interests and maintain regional stability.
- **Global Influence Beyond Indo-Pacific** Participation in the Quad allows India to transcend its middle power status and project influence beyond the Indo-Pacific. The alliance aligns with India's Act East Policy and Extended Neighbour policy, bolstering its engagement in the region and amplifying its voice on the global stage.
- **Strengthening Bilateral Relations** The Quad facilitates the strengthening of India's bilateral relations with like minded nations. Information sharing agreements, arms exchange agreements and defence ties contribute to enhanced security cooperation, aligning the strategic objectives of member countries.
- **Economic Opportunities** Economically, the Quad positions India as a preferred destination for investment, particularly in the post COVID-19 era. India's role in the Quad, coupled with initiatives like 'Vaccine Maitri,' enhances its global standing, making it an attractive partner for economic collaboration and investment.

Challenges and Considerations

- **Avoiding Anti-China Perception** The Quad must avoid devolving into an anti-China grouping to prevent reactivating tensions with China on various fronts. India, being part of international organisations like BRICS and SCO with China, needs to ensure that its involvement in the Quad complements rather than undermines its broader diplomatic engagements.
- **Balancing Allies** India's participation in the Quad may risk alienating important allies like Iran and Myanmar. While Iran is crucial for India's energy security and trade with Central Asia, China's economic deals with Iran could pose challenges. Similarly, China's presence in Myanmar, part of its Belt and Road Initiative, necessitates a delicate diplomatic balance.
- **Border Security Concerns** India, being the only Quad member sharing borders with China, faces the risk of increased tensions and potential military engagements. The Quad's initiatives should not compromise India's security interests at its borders, necessitating careful management of military dynamics.
- **Delivery Deficit and Regional Dominance** India's delivery deficit, especially in infrastructure projects, poses a challenge to the Quad's objectives. Challenges in regional connectivity projects, like the Kaladan Multi-Model Transport project, could undermine India's dominance in the region, allowing China to exert influence through its Belt and Road Initiative.

Conclusion

In general, it can be said that, the Quad's significance for India lies in its potential to shape a resilient and secure Indo-Pacific region, while also providing economic and diplomatic advantages. Navigating the complex landscape requires India to leverage the Quad's strengths in countering China strategically, enhancing global influence and fostering economic collaboration. Simultaneously, India must address challenges by diplomatically balancing allies, safeguarding border security and overcoming delivery deficits. As India charts its course in the Quad, it stands at the crossroads of seizing opportunities and managing complexities, crucial for its strategic imperatives in the evolving global order.

34. Need for energy sector reforms in India

India, with its burgeoning population and rapid economic growth, stands at the crossroads of a dynamic energy landscape. According to the International Energy Agency (IEA), India's energy demand is expected to grow by nearly 50% by 2040. The Integrated Energy Policy (IEP) estimated that India's primary energy consumption could increase from 375 million tonnes of oil equivalent (Mtoe) in 2012 to about 1,123 Mtoe by 2031–32. In this light, the need for comprehensive reforms in the energy sector has become paramount to address the challenges of sustainability, affordability and energy security. Let us deeply explore the compelling reasons behind the urgent call for transformative reforms in India's energy sector.

Energy Demand and Economic Growth

India's economic trajectory is intricately linked to its energy demands. As the country aspires to achieve double-digit economic growth, the energy sector serves as the linchpin for powering industries, fuelling transportation and lighting up homes.

The growing energy appetite necessitates a revaluation of the existing infrastructure and policies to ensure a sustainable and resilient energy future.

Renewable Energy Potential

India boasts of abundant renewable energy resources, including solar, wind and hydropower. Harnessing these resources not only addresses environmental concerns but also reduces dependence on fossil fuels. According to data from the International Renewable Energy Agency (IRENA), India is the fourth-largest renewable energy market globally, with a total renewable energy capacity of over 160 GW as of 2022. The peak power demand is expected to soar above 256 GW in 2024.

Affordability and Inclusivity

Energy reforms are imperative for ensuring affordability and inclusivity in energy access. A large population still lacks access to reliable and affordable energy sources. Reforms aimed at promoting decentralised and off grid solutions can bridge this gap, empowering rural communities and fostering inclusive growth. The Pradhan Mantri Saubhagya Yojana, aiming to provide electricity to every household, is a step in this direction. In fact, as of January 2022, India's installed renewable energy capacity stands at approximately 160 GW, with significant contributions from solar and wind power. Further, the Ministry of Power reported that over 99% of Indian villages had been electrified under the Saubhagya Yojana by the end of 2021.

Reducing Carbon Footprint

India's commitment to environmental sustainability is underscored by its pledge to reduce carbon emissions and combat climate change. Energy sector reforms need to prioritise a transition towards cleaner and greener technologies. The National Clean Air Programme (NCAP) and the ambitious target of achieving 175 GW of renewable energy capacity by 2022 are pivotal initiatives in this regard.

Enhancing Energy Efficiency

Improving energy efficiency is a key facet of the necessary reforms. The Bureau of Energy Efficiency (BEE) has been at the forefront, implementing measures to enhance energy efficiency across industries and households. The Perform, Achieve and Trade (PAT) scheme, under the National Mission for Enhanced Energy Efficiency (NMEEE) has demonstrated significant strides in this direction.

Foreign Direct Investment (FDI) and Technological Collaboration

Energy sector reforms present an attractive opportunity for foreign direct investment (FDI) and technological collaboration. As India aims to modernise its energy infrastructure, international partnerships can bring in capital, expertise and cutting-edge technologies. The easing of FDI norms and initiatives like the International Solar Alliance (ISA) showcase India's commitment to fostering global collaboration in the energy sector.

Conclusion

On the whole, the imperative for energy sector reforms in India is not merely a policy choice but a strategic necessity to fuel sustainable growth, ensure energy security and combat climate change.

As the nation navigates its trajectory towards becoming a global economic powerhouse, transformative reforms will serve as the catalyst for a resilient, inclusive and environmentally conscious energy future. Embracing these reforms is not just a national agenda (;) it is a commitment towards fostering a brighter and sustainable tomorrow for generations to come.

35. Making India a Superpower

India, with its rich history, diverse culture and robust economy, stands at the cusp of a transformative journey towards becoming a global superpower. There are multifaceted aspects that contribute to the endeavour of making India not just a regional powerhouse but a prominent player on the world stage. These aspects are as follows

Economic Growth and Development

India's economic trajectory has been nothing short of remarkable, propelling the nation to the forefront of the world's fastest growing major economies. As substantiated by the World Bank, India achieved a significant milestone in 2021 when its Gross Domestic Product (GDP) surged beyond the $3 trillion mark. This achievement not only underscores the resilience ingrained in India's economic engine but also highlights the vast potential that the nation possesses. To solidify its position on the global stage and pave the way for superpower status, India must persist in sustaining this momentum. This entails the formulation and implementation of strategic policies that not only foster continued economic growth but also prioritise inclusive development, ensuring that the benefits permeate across all segments of society.

Demographic Dividend

India's demographic advantage, often referred to as the 'youth bulge,' presents a unique opportunity. With a median age of around 28 years, India has a significant labour force that, when skilfully harnessed, can propel economic productivity, innovation and global competitiveness. Investing in education, skill development and job creation is essential to unlock the full potential of this demographic dividend.

Strategic Geopolitical Positioning

India's geopolitical positioning in South Asia, coupled with its non-aligned foreign policy, provides a strategic advantage. Strengthening diplomatic ties, fostering regional stability and actively participating in global forums amplify India's influence. Collaborative initiatives like the Quad and BRICS underscore India's commitment to shaping a multipolar world order.

Military Capabilities and Defense Preparedness

A superpower status necessitates a robust defense apparatus. India's armed forces, one of the largest in the world, are undergoing modernisation to meet evolving security challenges. Strategic investments in defense research, technology and infrastructure are imperative for maintaining a credible deterrence and contributing to global peacekeeping efforts.

Technological Advancement and Innovation

Technological prowess is a cornerstone of superpower status. India's achievements in space exploration, information technology and pharmaceuticals showcase its capabilities.

Continued investments in research and development, fostering innovation ecosystems and leveraging digital technologies will position India at the forefront of the global knowledge economy.

Global Economic Integration

India's active participation in global economic forums, trade agreements and organisations fosters economic integration. Strengthening ties with major economies, diversifying export markets and enhancing competitiveness are pivotal steps. Initiatives like 'Make in India' and 'Ease of Doing Business' reforms contribute to creating a conducive environment for foreign investments.

Environmental Sustainability

A responsible global player must prioritise environmental sustainability. India's commitment to renewable energy, as exemplified by the ambitious target of 170 GW of renewable capacity by March 2025, aligns with global efforts to combat climate change. Balancing economic growth with sustainable practices reinforces India's credentials as a responsible superpower.

Conclusion

The journey towards making India a global superpower is a dynamic process that encompasses economic, geopolitical, technological and environmental dimensions. Strategic policymaking, continued investments in human capital, innovation, and sustainable practices are the cornerstones of this endeavour.

As India navigates the complexities of the 21st century, the realisation of its superpower aspirations will not only transform the nation but contribute to shaping a more equitable and harmonious world order. The future beckons and India stands poised to embrace its destiny as a global force to be reckoned with.

36. Transgender should be allowed to join Armed Forces in India

In the ongoing pursuit of a more inclusive and egalitarian society, one domain that demands our attention is the armed forces. Traditionally perceived as bastions of discipline and order, the armed forces in India have an opportunity to lead by example by embracing transgender individuals into their ranks. There are various compelling reasons and societal benefits of allowing transgender individuals to serve in the Indian Armed Forces. These can be summarised as

Dismantling Stereotypes

The armed forces have long been associated with notions of strength, discipline and courage. By allowing transgender individuals to join, India has the chance to dismantle age old stereotypes surrounding gender and pave the way for a more progressive and accepting society. This move acknowledges that valour and commitment are not exclusive to any gender identity.

Promoting Equality and Human Rights

The Constitution of India guarantees equality and prohibits discrimination based on gender, among other factors. Embracing transgender individuals into the armed forces aligns with these constitutional values, emphasising that every citizen, regardless of gender identity has the right to contribute to the nation's defence. Inclusion in the armed forces would be a stride towards recognising transgender rights as an integral part of human rights.

Utilising Untapped Talent

Transgender individuals, like any other section of society, possess diverse skills, talents and capabilities. Allowing them to serve in the armed forces taps into a reservoir of untapped potential.

It broadens the talent pool available for defense, ensuring that the armed forces benefit from a diverse range of skills and perspectives.

Enhancing Organisational Effectiveness

Diversity is a strength in any organisation. The armed forces, with a diverse set of individuals, can enhance organisational effectiveness. Different backgrounds and experiences contribute to a more innovative and adaptable force. Transgender inclusion would foster a sense of unity, camaraderie, and shared purpose within the armed forces, strengthening the overall defense mechanism.

Global Precedents

Several countries around the world, including the United States, Canada, and Israel, have already paved the way for transgender inclusion in their armed forces. Learning from these global precedents, India can adapt policies and practices to ensure a smooth integration process. It also allows India to align its defense practices with evolving international standards of inclusivity.

Challenges and Solutions

Undoubtedly, challenges may arise during the implementation of transgender inclusion policies in the armed forces.

Sensitisation programmes, education and awareness campaigns within the armed forces can help address biases and misconceptions. Clear guidelines on accommodation and support mechanisms for transgender personnel would ensure a smooth transition.

Conclusion

In conclusion, allowing transgender individuals to join the armed forces in India is a transformative step towards building a more inclusive and progressive society. It aligns with constitutional principles, promotes equality and harnesses untapped talent for the defense of the nation. By dismantling stereotypes, embracing diversity and learning from global best practices, India can forge a path that not only strengthens its armed forces but also sets a powerful example for the entire nation. The inclusion of transgender individuals in the armed forces is not just a policy change; it is a commitment to building a more compassionate and equitable India.

37. Only Electric Vehicles should be Allowed in Cities

The rapid urbanisation and increasing vehicular emissions have exacerbated environmental concerns, making it imperative for cities to reassess their transportation policies. The transition towards a sustainable future calls for bold measures, and one such pragmatic step is the exclusive allowance of electric vehicles (EVs) within city limits.

Environmental Impact

Transportation is a significant contributor to air pollution and greenhouse gas emissions, with conventional internal combustion engine vehicles being major culprits. Electric vehicles, on the other hand, produce zero tailpipe emissions. By allowing only electric vehicles in cities, we can substantially reduce air pollution levels, mitigate the effects of climate change, and work towards achieving sustainable urban development goals.

Data from the International Energy Agency (IEA) indicates that the transport sector accounted for nearly one-quarter of global CO_2 emissions in 2019. The transition to electric vehicles is a key strategy to curtail this environmental impact. Furthermore, studies have shown that EVs have a significantly lower carbon footprint over their lifecycle compared to traditional vehicles, even when factoring in manufacturing and electricity generation.

Public Health Benefits

The health consequences of air pollution are well-documented, leading to respiratory issues, cardiovascular diseases and other adverse health effects. Electric vehicles, being emission-free at the point of use, contribute to cleaner air in urban areas. By restricting non-electric vehicles, cities can create environments conducive to better public health outcomes, reducing the burden on healthcare systems.

A report by the World Health Organisation (WHO) estimates that around 4.2 million premature deaths annually can be attributed to ambient air pollution. Transitioning to electric vehicles in cities would play a pivotal role in addressing this global health crisis and improving the overall quality of life for urban residents.

Economic Opportunities and Technological Advancements

Encouraging the use of electric vehicles fosters economic growth and technological innovation. Governments worldwide are investing heavily in EV infrastructure, creating job opportunities in manufacturing, research and development and maintenance. According to the International Renewable Energy Agency (IRENA), the global shift to electric vehicles could create over 11 million jobs by 2050.

Technological advancements in battery technology and charging infrastructure are pivotal for the widespread adoption of electric vehicles. By establishing EV-only zones, cities can accelerate these advancements and position themselves as hubs for clean and sustainable transportation solutions.

Challenges and Solutions

While the idea of exclusive electric vehicle zones is promising, it comes with challenges such as the need for robust charging infrastructure, cost considerations and potential resistance from traditional automotive industries. Governments and local authorities can address these challenges through strategic investments in charging networks, incentivising EV adoption through subsidies and collaborating with stakeholders to facilitate a smooth transition.

Conclusion

In conclusion, the exclusive allowance of electric vehicles in cities is a forward-thinking approach that aligns with global efforts towards sustainable urbanisation. The environmental, health, economic and technological benefits make a compelling case for embracing EV-only zones. As cities grapple with the complexities of urban planning, the shift towards electric vehicles emerges as a practical and impactful solution to pave the way for cleaner, healthier and more resilient urban environments. The time for decisive action is now and by embracing electric mobility, cities can lead the charge towards a greener and more sustainable future.

38. Climate Change and its Implications for National Security

Climate change, propelled by human activities, presents an immediate and profound threat to global national security. The escalating temperatures, amplified extreme weather events, and environmental degradation have shifted from distant concerns to tangible challenges, jeopardising the resilience and stability of nations worldwide. Rising heat levels and intensifying natural disasters impose health risks and economic burdens, while ecosystem degradation threatens food security and biodiversity. The intersection of climate change with existing vulnerabilities amplifies socio-economic disparities, fostering conflict and instability, particularly in fragile regions.

The global community must recognise climate change as a central security concern, demanding collaborative efforts to mitigate its impacts, adapt to inevitable changes and build a sustainable future resilient to the evolving climate challenges.

Environmental Displacement and Migration

One of the immediate consequences of climate change is the displacement of populations due to rising sea levels, droughts, and extreme weather events. This environmental migration can strain social and economic systems, leading to heightened competition for resources, increased potential for conflict, and the potential emergence of climate refugees. Nations must prepare for the challenges associated with mass migrations, both internally and across borders, to mitigate potential security threats.

Resource Scarcity and Conflict

Climate change exacerbates resource scarcity, creating conditions conducive to conflict over essential resources such as water, arable land and food. As these resources become scarcer, competition intensifies, heightening the risk of regional and international tensions. The 2007-2008 food crisis and the 'Day Zero' water crisis in Cape Town serve as stark reminders of the security implications tied to resource scarcity, underscoring the need for strategic planning to avert potential conflicts.

Melting Ice Caps and Geopolitical Shifts

The melting of polar ice caps due to rising temperatures opens up new maritime routes and access to untapped natural resources. This geopolitical shift raises the potential for increased competition among nations for control over these strategic areas, leading to heightened geopolitical tensions. The Arctic, in particular, is witnessing renewed interest and military posturing, emphasising the need for diplomatic efforts to prevent the escalation of conflicts in these sensitive regions.

Extreme Weather Events and Infrastructure Vulnerability

The increasing frequency and intensity of extreme weather events, such as hurricanes, floods and wildfires, pose a direct threat to critical infrastructure. Infrastructure vulnerabilities can disrupt essential services, strain emergency response capabilities and impact national security. Governments must prioritise climate-resilient infrastructure development to withstand and recover from the impacts of extreme weather events.

Security Risks in Fragile Regions

Climate change worsens existing vulnerabilities in regions already grappling with fragility and conflict. For instance, in regions like the Sahel and the Middle East, water scarcity and changing weather patterns contribute to resource-driven conflicts, fostering conditions conducive to terrorism and insurgency. Addressing the security risks in these fragile regions requires a comprehensive approach that integrates climate adaptation and conflict prevention strategies.

Global Cooperation and Diplomacy

Given the transboundary nature of climate change, effective solutions necessitate global cooperation and diplomatic efforts. Nations must work collaboratively to reduce greenhouse gas emissions, build climate resilience and address the root causes of climate-induced security threats. Multilateral platforms, such as the Paris Agreement, provide frameworks for collective action, emphasising the importance of international collaboration to mitigate the security risks posed by climate change.

Conclusion

In conclusion, climate change emerges as a pervasive and interconnected threat to national security, encompassing environmental displacement, resource conflicts, geopolitical shifts, infrastructure vulnerabilities and security risks in fragile regions. Recognising the intricate linkages between climate change and security is crucial for developing comprehensive strategies that safeguard nations against the impacts of a changing climate. Urgent and coordinated action is imperative to mitigate the security risks posed by climate change, ensuring a more stable and resilient future for nations worldwide.

39. Human Rights in Armed Conflicts: Balancing Security and Values

Balancing the needs of security and protecting people's rights during wars is a tough challenge. Countries must figure out how to follow security rules while also making sure to keep the dignity and rights of individuals safe in the middle of all the chaos of war. It's like walking a tightrope, finding the right balance between keeping the country safe and treating people fairly. This isn't just about following the rules already in place; it also means coming up with new ways to lessen the impact of wars on regular folks.

As the world deals with new challenges, finding a fair and thoughtful approach to handle this complicated situation is crucial. It's about making sure that both the need for security and the basic values of human rights can coexist in a balanced way.

Historical Perspective

Throughout history, armed conflicts have posed severe threats to human rights, with egregious violations documented across various theatres of war. The post-World War II era witnessed the establishment of international frameworks, such as the Geneva Conventions and the Universal Declaration of Human Rights, aiming to mitigate the impact of armed conflicts on civilian populations and delineate permissible conduct during war.

Security Imperatives vs. Human Rights

The tension between security imperatives and human rights is palpable in the discourse surrounding counterterrorism measures, where states contend with the need to protect citizens from extremist threats while ensuring that counterterrorism efforts adhere to international human rights standards. Striking this balance requires nuanced policies that prevent the erosion of civil liberties in the pursuit of security objectives.

Impact on Civilian Populations

Armed conflicts disproportionately affect civilian populations, leading to widespread displacement, loss of life, and destruction of infrastructure. The protection of civilians in conflict zones is a critical facet of human rights considerations, necessitating adherence to principles of proportionality and distinction between combatants and non-combatants.

Sexual and Gender-Based Violence

Human rights violations, particularly sexual and gender-based violence, often escalate during armed conflicts. Women and children are particularly vulnerable, and the international community must prioritise efforts to prevent and address such atrocities. The use of rape as a weapon of war, for instance, requires robust international condemnation and accountability mechanisms.

Role of International Law and Institutions

International law, through conventions and treaties, plays a pivotal role in establishing norms for the protection of human rights in armed conflicts. Institutions like the International Criminal Court (ICC) serve as a mechanism for holding individuals accountable for war crimes, crimes against humanity and genocide, reinforcing the importance of accountability in preserving human rights.

Challenges and Controversies

The implementation of human rights principles in armed conflicts is not without challenges. Controversies arise in situations where states prioritise national security interests over human rights obligations. The use of drone strikes, extrajudicial killings and mass surveillance are contentious practices that necessitate a revaluation of strategies to ensure alignment with human rights standards.

Conclusion

Overall, balancing security imperatives with the preservation of human rights in armed conflicts is an ongoing and dynamic challenge for the international community. Nations must reinforce their commitment to upholding the dignity of individuals even in the face of security threats. The evolution of international legal frameworks, coupled with diplomatic initiatives and accountability mechanisms, can pave the way for a future where the devastating impact of armed conflicts on human rights is mitigated, ensuring a more just and secure world.

40. Indian Presence in International Awards

In the global landscape of the 21st century, excellence knows no boundaries and achievements transcending geographical limits. India, with its rich heritage, diverse culture and intellectual prowess, has consistently made its mark on the international stage, earning accolades and recognition across fields ranging from arts and literature to science, peace and humanitarian efforts. The various fields and areas where India has emerged as a leader are as follows

Nobel Prize in Literature : A Legacy Initiated by Tagore The Nobel Prize in Literature awarded to Rabindranath Tagore in 1913, for his anthology 'Gitanjali,' marked the beginning of India's journey on the global literary stage. This accolade was not merely a recognition of Tagore's literary genius but also a testament to the depth and richness of Indian culture and philosophy. Following Tagore, Indian-origin authors such as Sir VS Naipaul and Kazuo Ishiguro have also been honoured, reflecting the global resonance of Indian storytelling and its themes of identity, post-colonialism, and diaspora experiences.

The Man Booker Prize: Chronicles of Indian Narratives The Man Booker Prize, an esteemed recognition in the world of literature, has been awarded to Indian authors who have captured the complexities of life in India through their ingenious narratives. From Salman Rushdie's 'Midnight's Children' to Aravind Adiga's 'The White Tiger,' these works have not only won acclaim but have significantly contributed to shaping global perceptions of India's societal transformations and challenges.

Nobel Laureates in Physics and Chemistry Illuminating the Path of Scientific Inquiry- The Nobel Prizes in Physics and Chemistry have seen Indian scientists such as Sir CV Raman and Venkatraman Ramakrishnan etch their names in history. Raman's discovery of the Raman Effect and Ramakrishnan's work on the structure of the ribosome have opened new frontiers in their respective fields, highlighting the Indian talent pool's substantial contribution to global scientific advancement.

Fields Medal: The Mathematical Marvels Celebrated as the Nobel Prize of Mathematics, the Fields Medal has recognized the contributions of Indian mathematicians like Akshay Venkatesh, whose work spans multiple mathematical disciplines. Such achievements not only showcase the analytical and intellectual rigour of Indian scholars but also inspire future generations to engage in mathematical research.

Nobel Peace Prize: Echoes of Nonviolence and Compassion India's philosophical ethos, marked by doctrines of nonviolence and compassion, found global recognition through Nobel Peace laureates like Mother Teresa and Kailash Satyarthi. Their work, oriented towards service, upliftment and protection of the marginalised, embodies the spirit of altruism and humanitarianism deeply rooted in Indian culture.

The Magsaysay Award : Leaders of Change and Reform The Ramon Magsaysay Award, often dubbed as Asia's Nobel Prize, has been conferred upon numerous Indians, including but not limited to Vinoba Bhave, Kiran Bedi and Arvind Kejriwal. Recognised for their leadership, commitment to public service and impactful social initiatives, these awardees underscore India's active engagement in addressing socio-political issues and striving for equity and justice.

Academy Awards (Oscars) **and Cannes Film Festival: Showcasing Indian Creativity and Artistry** The global film fraternity has recognised the exceptional talent of Indian artists and storytellers through prestigious awards such as the Oscars and accolades at the Cannes Film Festival. From Bhanu Athaiya's pioneering Oscar win for costume design in 'Gandhi', awards to 'Slumdog Millionaire' to the appreciation of films like "Pather Panchali' and 'Salaam Bombay!" at Cannes, these recognitions celebrate India's cinematic heritage, diversity and the compelling power of its narratives.

United Nations and Global Leadership India's Role on the World Stage- India's contribution to international diplomacy and cooperation is exemplified by personalities such as Vijaya Lakshmi Pandit, who broke gender barriers to become the first woman President of the United Nations General Assembly. Moreover, Indians like Shashi Tharoor have held significant positions within the United Nations, playing pivotal roles in fostering global dialogue and understanding, reflecting India's commitment to multilateralism and peacebuilding.

India's achievements in securing international awards and recognition are a reflection of its enduring legacy of cultural richness, intellectual curiosity, and a collective ethos of peace and service. These accolades serve not just as milestones of individual or national pride but as beacons of inspiration, showcasing the potential for human endeavour and cooperation across borders.

The international recognition of Indian talents and contributions plays a crucial role in enhancing India's soft power, opening channels for cross-cultural exchange, dialogue, and mutual respect. As a country with one of the world's oldest civilizations, India's global awards narrative underscores its vibrant contemporary presence and influential role in shaping a more inclusive, equitable and sustainable world order.

Conclusion

In charting the course of excellence, Indian awardees across domains have laid down a path for future generations to aspire, innovate and contribute to global society. Their stories are a testament to the power of perseverance, the depth of creativity and the spirit of humanitarianism that transcends geographical and cultural barriers.

Thus, the saga of Indian presence in international awards is not just a chronicle of honours received but a narrative of contribution and engagement with the world, reflecting a harmonious blend of tradition and modernity. As India continues to make its mark on the global stage, the legacy of its international awards will remain a source of national pride, motivating aspirations for continued excellence and cooperation in the quest for a better future for all.

41. Privatisation of the Space Sector

The privatisation of the space sector marks a transformative shift in the dynamics of space exploration, with private companies playing an increasingly prominent role alongside traditional government agencies. This paradigm shift is reshaping the landscape of space activities, bringing about new opportunities, challenges, and collaborative models.

Historical Context

Traditionally, space exploration has been the domain of government agencies like NASA, ESA and ISRO. However, in recent decades, private companies such as SpaceX, Blue Origin, and Virgin Galactic have emerged as key players, fostering innovation and injecting competition into the industry.

Commercial Space Launches

One of the most notable aspects of space sector privatisation is the surge in commercial space launches. SpaceX, led by Elon Musk, has achieved remarkable success in reducing launch costs and increasing launch frequency, making space more accessible to a variety of payloads, including satellites, cargo and even human spaceflight.

Technological Advancements

Private companies are driving technological advancements in space exploration. SpaceX's reusable rocket technology has demonstrated cost-effectiveness, while Blue Origin focuses on reusable suborbital space tourism. These innovations contribute to sustainable space activities and lay the groundwork for future exploration missions.

Global Collaborations

Privatisation encourages international collaborations in space exploration. Commercial partnerships between companies and countries foster shared technological advancements and cost-sharing, enabling smaller nations to participate in space endeavours. The Artemis Accords, initiated by NASA, exemplify global collaboration principles for lunar exploration.

Economic Opportunities

The space sector's privatisation unlocks economic opportunities, creating jobs and stimulating innovation. According to the Space Data Association, the global space economy was valued at $385 billion in 2020, with significant contributions from private entities. As the industry grows, it has the potential to become a key driver of economic development.

Challenges and Regulatory Framework

While privatisation brings innovation and economic benefits, it also presents challenges. Regulatory frameworks must evolve to address issues such as space debris management, spectrum allocation and ensuring responsible space practices. Governments need to strike a balance between fostering innovation and safeguarding public interests.

Emergence of Space Tourism

Privatisation has fuelled the emergence of space tourism, with companies like Virgin Galactic and Blue Origin offering suborbital flights for civilians. While this signifies a new era in space accessibility, it also raises ethical and safety concerns that necessitate careful regulation and oversight.

National Security Implications

As private entities engage in space activities, national security considerations come to the forefront. Governments must ensure that critical space assets and technologies remain secure and that private actors adhere to international norms. Collaborations between governments and private entities are crucial for addressing national security challenges.

Conclusion

It can, thus, be concluded that the privatisation of the space sector represents a significant evolution in humanity's journey beyond Earth. Private companies are driving innovation, reducing costs, and expanding access to space, fostering a more inclusive and dynamic space exploration ecosystem. While challenges persist, the collaboration between governments and private entities holds the key to unlocking the full potential of the privatised space sector. As we embark on this new era, it is imperative to navigate the complexities with foresight, ensuring that space remains a shared frontier for the benefit of all.

42. Rise of Indigenous Politics

The global resurgence of indigenous politics marks a transformative moment in the socio-political landscape, as historically marginalised communities assert their identities and advocate for rightful representation. This phenomenon reflects a profound quest for justice, cultural recognition, and the protection of indigenous rights, reshaping the narrative of contemporary politics. The rise of indigenous politics is intrinsically tied to historical injustices, cultural marginalisation and the enduring struggle for self-determination.

Historical Context

Indigenous communities across the world have endured centuries of colonisation, displacement and cultural erasure. The emergence of indigenous politics is deeply rooted in a historical context marked by systemic injustices. The United Nations Declaration on the Rights of Indigenous Peoples (UNDRIP), adopted in 2007, stands as a landmark international instrument affirming the collective and individual rights of indigenous people. This declaration serves as a foundational document that acknowledges the historical wrongs and paves the way for addressing contemporary challenges.

Identity Assertion

At the heart of the rise of indigenous politics is a fervent commitment to identity assertion. Indigenous people, possessing distinctive languages, cultures and traditions, are reclaiming their agency in the face of assimilationist policies and cultural homogenisation. The movement seeks not only to preserve indigenous identities but also to revitalise and celebrate them, fostering a renewed sense of pride and belonging within these communities.

Land Rights and Environmental Advocacy

A critical aspect of indigenous politics revolves around the demand for land rights and environmental protection. Many indigenous communities inhabit ecologically significant areas and play a pivotal role in sustainable resource management. Activism against resource extraction projects, deforestation and environmental degradation underscores their commitment to preserving ancestral lands, which are not only central to their cultural identity but also crucial for global biodiversity.

Political Representation

The pursuit of political representation stands as a cornerstone of indigenous politics. Historically underrepresented in legislative bodies and decision-making processes, indigenous communities are striving for meaningful participation. The implementation of quotas, reserved seats and affirmative action policies aims to redress historical imbalances and promote inclusive governance. The goal is to ensure that indigenous voices influence policies that directly impact their lives and territories.

Economic Empowerment

Indigenous politics extends beyond the realm of rights advocacy to encompass economic empowerment. Many indigenous communities are leveraging their unique cultural assets for sustainable tourism, artisanal enterprises and traditional knowledge-based industries. These initiatives aim to break cycles of poverty, foster self-sufficiency and ensure that economic development aligns with cultural preservation.

Digital Activism and Cultural Revitalisation

The advent of the digital age has amplified the voices of indigenous communities through social media and online platforms. Activists utilise these tools to raise awareness, mobilise support and counter misrepresentations. Digital platforms also play a crucial role in cultural revitalisation efforts, allowing indigenous communities to share traditional knowledge, language, and practices with a global audience.

Challenges and Contemporary Struggles

Despite the progress made, indigenous communities continue to face persistent challenges. Land dispossession, cultural appropriation, and systemic discrimination remain entrenched issues. The impacts of climate change disproportionately affect indigenous populations, exacerbating existing vulnerabilities. Additionally, economic disparities and limited access to education and healthcare contribute to the ongoing struggles faced by many indigenous communities.

Policy Implications

Governments and international organisations must respond to the rise of indigenous politics with inclusive policies that respect cultural diversity and safeguard indigenous rights. Collaborative efforts should prioritise meaningful dialogue, recognising the agency of indigenous communities in shaping their destinies. This involves the integration of indigenous perspectives in policymaking, addressing historical injustice and fostering partnerships based on mutual respect.

Conclusion

The rise of indigenous politics signifies a pivotal moment in the global discourse on human rights, cultural preservation, and inclusive governance.

As indigenous communities assert their identities and demand political representation, the world is called to confront historical injustices and build a future that respects and celebrates diversity. The success of this movement hinges on collaborative efforts, acknowledging the intrinsic value of indigenous perspectives in shaping a more equitable and inclusive world. In embracing the rise of indigenous politics, nations have an opportunity to rectify past wrongs, forge genuine partnerships, and contribute to a global landscape that values the richness of cultural diversity.

43. India's Necklace of Diamonds strategy v/s China's String of Pearls

In the complex geopolitics of the Indo-Pacific, India has strategically crafted its 'Necklace of Diamonds' approach to counterbalance China's expansive 'String of Pearls' initiative. This nuanced strategy reflects India's diplomatic and economic prowess, emphasising connectivity, partnerships and regional stability.

Historical Context

China's 'String of Pearls' strategy involves establishing a network of military and economic footholds in the Indian Ocean, encircling India, and securing maritime routes critical for its economic interests. In response, India has adopted the 'Necklace of Diamonds' strategy, focusing on building alliances, enhancing maritime capabilities and fostering economic partnerships to fortify its position in the region.

Connectivity Initiatives

A cornerstone of India's strategy is the proactive promotion of connectivity initiatives that strengthen ties with neighbouring nations.

The International North-South Transport Corridor (INSTC) and the Chabahar Port in Iran exemplify India's efforts to create alternative routes, reducing dependence on Chinese-dominated maritime pathways. These initiatives not only enhance India's regional influence but also contribute to the economic development of partner nations.

Economic Cooperation

Economic partnerships play a vital role in India's 'Necklace of Diamonds' strategy. Engaging with countries in the Indo-Pacific through trade agreements, infrastructure projects, and investments fosters mutual growth and stability. The Asia-Africa Growth Corridor (AAGC), a collaborative effort with Japan, aims to promote sustainable development, connectivity and economic integration, countering China's Belt and Road Initiative (BRI).

Military Preparedness

Recognising the importance of a robust military presence, India has bolstered its maritime capabilities. Strategic collaborations with like-minded nations, such as the United States, Australia and Japan, underpin a collective commitment to regional security. The Indian Navy's increased patrols and joint exercises showcase its resolve to safeguard vital sea lanes and maintain stability in the Indo-Pacific region.

Diplomatic Alliances

India's diplomatic outreach is a key aspect of its strategy, emphasising partnerships based on shared values and interests. Engaging with nations in South-East Asia, the Indian Ocean Rim and beyond, India aims to build a network of allies that collectively contribute to regional security. Participation in forums like the Quad (Quadrilateral Security Dialogue) underscores India's commitment to a free and open Indo-Pacific.

Challenges and Responses

The 'Necklace of Diamonds' strategy faces challenges, including China's economic influence and assertive territorial claims. India's response involves diplomatically addressing disputes, enhancing defense preparedness and promoting transparent and inclusive development projects.

Emphasising the principles of sovereignty and non-interference, India aims to differentiate its approach from China's and build trust within the region.

Soft Power Initiatives

Cultural diplomacy and people-to-people ties constitute an integral part of India's strategy. Educational exchanges, cultural events and initiatives like the Indian Technical and Economic Cooperation (ITEC) programme contribute to a positive image of India in the region. Leveraging its soft power, India seeks to establish enduring relationships that transcend geopolitical rivalries.

Environmental Stewardship

In a departure from traditional geopolitical strategies, India incorporates environmental stewardship into its approach. Promoting sustainability and addressing climate change concerns align with global priorities. India's efforts to balance economic development with ecological responsibility contribute to the perception of a responsible regional actor.

Conclusion

It can be sum up as, India's 'Necklace of Diamonds' strategy reflects a multifaceted approach to navigate the complex geopolitical dynamics of the Indo-Pacific. By emphasising connectivity, economic cooperation, military preparedness, diplomatic alliances and soft power initiatives, India aims to counterbalance China's influence and promote regional stability.

As both nations vie for dominance, the success of India's strategy lies in its ability to build collaborative partnerships, showcase responsible leadership and contribute to a harmonious Indo-Pacific region that values inclusivity and shared prosperity.

44. Women Reservation Bill

The Women's Reservation Bill, a transformative legislative proposal, seeks to address the historical gender imbalance in India's political landscape.

While significant progress has been made, women's representation in decision-making bodies remains disproportionately low.

The Women's Reservation Bill aims to rectify this disparity by ensuring a more equitable distribution of political power.

Historical Context

India, despite being a vibrant democracy, has struggled with gender parity in its political institutions. The patriarchal societal structure has perpetuated the underrepresentation of women in legislative bodies.

The Women's Reservation Bill, first introduced in 1996, aims to reserve one-third of seats in the Lok Sabha and state legislative assemblies for women, providing them with a meaningful platform to influence policy and governance.

Empowering Women Through Political Representation

The enactment of the Women's Reservation Bill holds immense potential for transforming the socio-political landscape of India. Increased representation for women in legislatures can serve as a catalyst for addressing pressing gender-related issues, advocating for policies that enhance women's rights and fostering a more inclusive and diverse decision-making process.

Impact on Policy and Governance

Increased women's representation in legislatures can result in more gender-sensitive policy formulations. Issues like healthcare, education and economic empowerment, which disproportionately affect women, are likely to receive greater attention and comprehensive solutions. The bill, therefore, becomes a catalyst for broader societal change.

Women's Role in Local Governance

Reserving seats for women in local governance institutions, as witnessed in Panchayati Raj institutions, has demonstrated positive outcomes. The Women's Reservation Bill extends this principle to the national level, allowing women to participate in shaping the destiny of the nation on a larger scale. The grassroots successes can be replicated at the macro-political level.

Economic Empowerment and Social Change

Enhancing women's participation in politics goes beyond symbolic representation; it translates into economic empowerment and social change. Access to political power equips women with the tools to challenge traditional norms, advocate for their rights and influence public discourse on issues ranging from education to employment.

Closing the Gender Pay Gap

The Women's Reservation Bill aligns with broader efforts to address gender disparities beyond politics. Closing the gender pay gap, promoting workplace equality and dismantling institutional barriers are complementary objectives that contribute to a more equitable and progressive society.

Challenges and Opposition

Despite its noble intent, the Women's Reservation Bill has faced resistance from certain quarters. Concerns related to tokenism, potential misuse of reserved seats and questions about the effectiveness of legislative quotas have been raised. Addressing these apprehensions through robust debate and informed discourse is crucial for the bill's eventual success.

Conclusion

The Women's Reservation Bill is not merely a legislative initiative; it symbolises a commitment to rectifying historical injustices and fostering an inclusive democracy. As India aspires to become a global leader, it is imperative to harness the untapped potential of women in shaping the nation's destiny. The passage of the Women's Reservation Bill will not only bring about a paradigm shift in India's political landscape but also signify a resounding endorsement of gender equality and women's empowerment.

The time has come to transform aspirations into action, as the empowerment of half the population is central to the nation's progress and prosperity.

45. The Himachal Ecological Crisis

Himachal Pradesh, known for its pristine landscapes and breathtaking mountains, is currently grappling with an ecological crisis that threatens its unique biodiversity and environmental balance. This essay delves into the root causes, current state and potential solutions to address the Himachal ecological crisis.

Himachal Pradesh's ecological crisis is characterised by deforestation, rampant construction, unregulated tourism and climate change impacts.

The once-lush green hills are now witnessing soil erosion, loss of bio-diversity and increased vulnerability to natural disasters.

- **Deforestation and Loss of Biodiversity** The extensive felling of trees for developmental projects, illegal logging, and agricultural expansion have led to severe deforestation. This not only disrupts the delicate ecological balance but also contributes to the loss of biodiversity, endangering numerous plant and animal species endemic to the region.
- **Rampant Construction and Urbanisation** The surge in construction activities, especially in tourist destinations like Shimla and Manali, has led to the degradation of natural habitats. Unplanned urbanisation, improper waste management, and inadequate infrastructure strain the ecosystem, posing a threat to the well-being of both residents and the environment.
- **Tourism Pressure** Himachal Pradesh's popularity as a tourist destination has soared, resulting in an influx of visitors that exceeds the region's carrying capacity. Unregulated tourism leads to littering, pollution and habitat destruction. The delicate alpine ecosystems are particularly vulnerable to the ecological footprint left by mass tourism.
- **Climate Change Impacts** The Himalayan region, including Himachal Pradesh, is witnessing the adverse impacts of climate change. Glacial melt, erratic weather patterns and the increased frequency of extreme events like flash floods and landslides pose significant challenges to the state's ecological stability.
- **Water Scarcity** The depletion of natural water sources due to deforestation, excessive use for tourism and changing precipitation patterns contribute to water scarcity issues in various regions of Himachal Pradesh. This not only affects local communities but also exacerbates the vulnerability of the ecosystem.

Community Perspectives

Local communities, especially indigenous populations, are at the forefront of the ecological crisis. Their traditional livelihoods, reliant on sustainable practices, are threatened by the degradation of natural resources. Involving these communities in conservation efforts is crucial for sustainable solutions.

Potential Solutions

- **Afforestation and Reforestation** Implementing large-scale afforestation and reforestation programmes to counteract the impact of deforestation and restore biodiversity.
- **Regulated Tourism** Implementing strict regulations on tourism activities, including the issuance of permits, waste management policies and promoting responsible tourism practices.
- **Climate-Resilient Infrastructure** Developing infrastructure that is resilient to climate change impacts, including measures to prevent landslides, flash floods and other natural disasters.
- **Community Participation** Engaging local communities in conservation efforts, respecting indigenous knowledge and promoting sustainable livelihoods that align with ecological preservation.
- **Policy Reforms** Enacting and enforcing stringent environmental laws, land-use policies and development regulations to curb unsustainable practices and promote eco-friendly alternatives.
- **Water Conservation Measures** Implementing water conservation strategies, including rainwater harvesting, watershed management and promoting responsible water usage.

Conclusion

The Himachal ecological crisis demands urgent attention and comprehensive action. Balancing development with environmental conservation is essential to ensure the state's long-term sustainability. The integration of local communities, stringent regulatory measures and a commitment to sustainable practices can pave the way for a harmonious coexistence between human activities and the delicate Himalayan ecosystem. The time to act is now, as the fate of Himachal Pradesh's ecological richness hangs in the balance.

46. Today India Needs 'Harmony in Diversity, Not Unity in Diversity'

India, with its rich tapestry of cultures, languages, and traditions, has long prided itself on the concept of 'Unity in Diversity.' However, in the contemporary socio-political landscape, the need for a shift towards 'Harmony in Diversity' becomes increasingly evident. Embracing harmony over mere unity becomes imperative considering the challenges and opportunities that India faces in its journey towards inclusive development.

Historical Perspective

The phrase 'Unity in Diversity' has been a cornerstone of India's identity, emphasising the coexistence of myriad communities, religions and languages within a singular national framework. This concept, while commendable, has sometimes masked underlying tensions and disparities, hindering the realisation of true social cohesion.

Challenges to Unity

- **Communal Strife** Instances of communal disharmony and religious tension have, at times, disrupted the nation's unity. Incidents of religious intolerance and discrimination highlight the need for a deeper understanding and acceptance of diverse faiths.
- **Linguistic Divides** Linguistic diversity, while celebrated, has also resulted in linguistic chauvinism and occasional tensions. Language-based identity politics can impede national integration if not approached with sensitivity.
- **Socio-Economic Disparities** Economic inequality and social disparities persist, with marginalised communities facing challenges in accessing education, employment and other opportunities. Bridging these gaps is crucial for building an inclusive and harmonious society.

The Shift Towards Harmony

- **Cultural Integration** Instead of a more coexistence of diverse cultures, fostering cultural integration can create a harmonious blend where each cultural element enriches the larger societal fabric. Cultural exchange programs, festivals and educational initiatives can contribute to this integration.
- **Interfaith Dialogue** Encouraging open dialogue among various religious communities promotes understanding, tolerance and coexistence. Interfaith initiatives can play a pivotal role in dispelling misconceptions and building bridges across religious divides.
- **Linguistic Pluralism** Celebrating linguistic diversity should go hand in hand with promoting multilingualism and linguistic inclusivity. Encouraging the learning of multiple languages can strengthen communication and foster a sense of shared linguistic heritage.
- **Social Justice Reforms** Prioritising social justice and inclusive policies can address economic disparities and uplift marginalised communities. Education and employment opportunities need to be accessible to all, irrespective of socio-economic backgrounds.
- **Promoting Diversity in Governance** Ensuring representation of diverse communities in political and administrative bodies enhances the inclusivity of governance. This representation helps in addressing the unique needs and concerns of various segments of the population.

Opportunities for Progress

- **Innovation and Creativity** Embracing diversity fosters innovation and creativity. Diverse perspectives bring a wealth of ideas and solutions, contributing to advancements in various fields.
- **Tourism and Cultural Heritage** India's diverse cultural heritage is a potential magnet for tourism. Promoting cultural tourism not only boosts the economy but also enhances cross-cultural understanding.
- **Global Recognition** Embracing diversity enhances India's global image as a tolerant and pluralistic society. This can attract foreign investments, collaborations and partnerships, contributing to the nation's progress.

Conclusion

While 'Unity in Diversity' remains a cherished ideal, India's contemporary challenges call for a nuanced approach. The shift towards 'Harmony in Diversity' involves fostering deeper understanding, empathy and active collaboration among diverse communities.

Embracing this paradigm shift can propel India towards a more inclusive, just and progressive future, where every citizen actively contributes to the nation's development. The choice between mere unity and harmonious diversity is pivotal in shaping the trajectory of India's societal evolution.

47. Does India need more missiles or more industries?

The question of whether India should prioritise the development of more missiles or the expansion of industries encapsulates the complex interplay between defense capabilities and economic prosperity. This interplay points out the dual necessity of enhancing defence preparedness and fostering economic growth, emphasising the imperative of striking a delicate balance.

Defense Preparedness : A Strategic Imperative

- **Security Challenges** India faces a myriad of security challenges, ranging from traditional threats along its borders to emerging asymmetric threats. A robust defense infrastructure, including missile systems, is crucial for safeguarding national sovereignty and integrity.
- **Deterrence Capability** A credible missile arsenal acts as a deterrent, dissuading potential adversaries and bolstering India's strategic position on the global stage. Investments in missile technology enhance the nation's ability to respond effectively to evolving security threats.

Economic Growth : The Engine of National Prosperity

- **Job Creation** Industrial expansion contributes significantly to job creation, addressing the pressing issue of unemployment. A thriving industrial sector can absorb the burgeoning workforce, especially among the youth.
- **Foreign Direct Investment** (FDI) Industries attract FDI, injecting capital into the economy. This influx of foreign funds enhances India's economic resilience and facilitates technology transfer, fostering innovation and competitiveness.
- **Technological Advancements** Industrial growth is synonymous with technological advancements. A technologically advanced industrial base ensures that

India remains at the forefront of innovation, making significant strides in various sectors.

The Balancing Act

- **Integrated Defence-Industrial Complex** The synergy between defence and industry is essential. Developing a robust defence-industrial complex ensures self-reliance in defence production, reducing dependence on imports and bolstering indigenous capabilities.
- **Dual-Use Technologies** Investments in industries with dual-use technologies, applicable in both defense and civilian sectors, offer a pragmatic solution. This approach aligns with India's broader goals of achieving economic growth while fortifying its defense capabilities.

Challenges and Opportunities

- **Budgetary Constraints** Allocating resources to both missile development and industrial expansion poses budgetary challenges. Efficient resource management and prioritisation become imperative to address both needs adequately.
- **Skill Development** Developing a skilled workforce is crucial for both defense and industrial sectors. Investment in education and skill development programs can bridge the existing gaps, ensuring a proficient workforce for diverse sectors.

Strategic Considerations

- **Strategic Autonomy** A well-balanced approach ensures strategic autonomy. Overemphasis on one aspect at the expense of the other could compromise India's ability to respond effectively to multifaceted challenges.
- **Geopolitical Significance** India's economic and defense capabilities contribute to its geopolitical influence. A judicious blend of missile development and industrial growth enhances the nation's standing in the global arena.

Conclusion

The conundrum of missiles versus industries is not a binary choice but a nuanced balancing act that demands careful consideration. India's path forward lies in harmonising defense preparedness with economic prosperity. A comprehensive strategy that integrates both facets ensures not only security and deterrence but also sustainable growth, job creation, and technological advancement. In navigating this complex terrain, India can forge a trajectory that fortifies its resilience and cements its role as a key player in the global landscape. The challenge is not in choosing one over the other but in orchestrating a symphony where defense and industry complement each other for the holistic advancement of the nation.

48. Transgenders : From the Margins to the Mainstream

The journey of the transgender community in India from the peripheries of society to the mainstream is an unfolding narrative of resilience, advocacy and the collective pursuit of inclusivity.

The journey covers the various challenges faced by the transgender community, the progress made in empowering them, and the imperative for continued efforts to ensure their full integration into the mainstream.

Challenges Faced by the Transgender Community

- **Social Stigma and Discrimination** Transgender individuals often encounter deep-seated social stigma and discrimination, leading to their marginalisation. This discrimination manifests in various forms, including limited access to education, employment and healthcare.
- **Legal Ambiguities** Historically, legal frameworks in India lacked clarity on transgender rights. Ambiguous laws contributed to the vulnerability of the community, with a lack of legal recognition affecting their access to entitlements and services.

Empowering the Transgender Community

- **Legal Reforms** Recognising the need for legal reforms, landmark judgments such as the NALSA verdict (2014) paved the way for the recognition of the third gender. The Transgender Persons (Protection of Rights) Act, 2019, aimed at safeguarding transgender rights, signifies a step towards legal empowerment.
- **Inclusive Policies** Initiatives like gender-neutral restrooms and inclusive workplace policies have emerged, promoting a more accepting environment. Educational institutions and corporates are gradually adopting measures to ensure equal opportunities for transgender individuals.
- **Healthcare Access** Efforts to enhance healthcare access for the transgender community have been witnessed, with some institutions providing specialised services. Addressing transgender-specific health needs is crucial for their holistic well-being.

Economic Empowerment

- **Employment Opportunities** Advocacy for equal employment opportunities has gained momentum. Inclusion in various sectors, including the government, private enterprises and the entertainment industry, reflects a positive shift towards economic empowerment.
- **Entrepreneurship** Encouraging transgender entrepreneurship fosters economic independence. Initiatives supporting transgender individuals in establishing and sustaining businesses contribute to their empowerment.

Education and Awareness

- **Inclusive Education** Creating transgender-inclusive educational environments is fundamental to dismantling stereotypes and prejudices. Inclusive curricula and awareness campaigns help foster understanding and acceptance.
- **Media Representation** Positive and accurate portrayal of transgender individuals in media plays a pivotal role in challenging stereotypes. Increased visibility contributes to changing societal perceptions.

Ongoing Challenges and the Way Forward

- **Socio-Economic Disparities** Despite progress, socio-economic disparities persist within the transgender community. Targeted interventions addressing these disparities, including poverty and homelessness, are essential for comprehensive empowerment.
- **Mental Health Support** The transgender community faces higher rates of mental health challenges. Accessible mental health support services and awareness campaigns are crucial for addressing these issues.

Conclusion

The transformation of the transgender community from the margins to the mainstream is an ongoing process marked by significant strides and persistent challenges. Legal recognition, inclusive policies, economic empowerment, and educational initiatives represent crucial pillars in this journey. To truly empower the transgender community, continued efforts are required to address existing disparities, challenge societal norms and foster an environment where every individual, irrespective of gender identity, can thrive. As India moves forward, it is imperative to recognise the agency and resilience of the transgender community and work collectively towards a society that embraces diversity and ensures equal opportunities for all.

49. The Greatest Result of Education is Tolerance

The profound impact of education extends far beyond academic knowledge and skills, transcending into the realm of fostering tolerance and inclusivity. The transformative power of education can be seen in its power to shape open-minded individuals who foster harmonious societies. The power held by education takes various shapes and forms which are discussed below

Education as a Catalyst for Tolerance

- **Promoting Understanding** Education exposes individuals to diverse perspectives, cultures and histories, fostering a deep understanding of the richness of human experience. This understanding lays the foundation for tolerance by dispelling ignorance and stereotypes.
- **Cultivating Critical Thinking** Educational systems that emphasise critical thinking instill in individuals the capacity to question biases and preconceived notions. This intellectual agility encourages open-mindedness and a willingness to consider alternative viewpoints.
- **Facilitating Empathy** Exposure to literature, arts and social sciences in education nurtures empathy by allowing individuals to vicariously experience the lives of others. This emotional connection is pivotal in developing a tolerant mindset.

Tolerance in the Educational Environment

- **Inclusive Curricula** Educational curricula that reflect the diversity of society contribute to building tolerance. Inclusive lessons that celebrate differences and highlight commonalities foster an environment where students embrace diversity.
- **Anti-Bullying Initiatives** Tolerance starts within the classroom. Schools and colleges must actively promote anti-bullying initiatives, creating safe spaces where students feel accepted, regardless of their background or identity.

Beyond Academics–Life Lessons in Tolerance

- **Teamwork and Collaboration** Co-curricular activities and group projects in educational settings provide opportunities for students to collaborate with peers from different backgrounds, promoting teamwork and tolerance.
- **Conflict Resolution Skills** Education equips individuals with the skills to navigate conflicts peacefully. Learning to resolve differences constructively contributes to a more tolerant and understanding society.

Challenges in Fostering Tolerance Through Education

- **Biases in Educational Materials** Addressing biases in textbooks and learning materials is crucial. Efforts should be made to present a balanced and inclusive narrative that reflects the true tapestry of human experiences.
- **Teacher Training** Ensuring that educators are equipped with the knowledge and skills to foster tolerance are essential. Ongoing teacher training programs should include components focused on diversity, equity and inclusion.

Global Citizenship and Tolerance

- **Preparation for a Globalised World** In an interconnected world, education plays a vital role in preparing individuals to be global citizens. Tolerance becomes imperative for effective cross-cultural communication and collaboration.
- **Resisting Extremism** Education serves as a bulwark against extremism and radicalisation. By instilling tolerance, societies can resist the allure of divisive ideologies and work towards peaceful coexistence.

Conclusion

The greatest result of education is undeniably tolerance. Through a holistic approach that encompasses curricula, educational environments and life skills, education shapes individuals into tolerant and empathetic citizens. As societies navigate the complexities of the modern world, prioritising education that fosters tolerance is not just an academic endeavour but a fundamental step towards building harmonious and inclusive communities. Education stands as the cornerstone of a tolerant society, where diversity is not merely accepted but embraced as a source of strength and enrichment.

50. GDP and GDH Would be Right Indices to Judge the Well-being of the Country

The conventional yardstick for assessing a nation's progress, Gross Domestic Product (GDP), has long been the go-to metric.

However, the limitations of GDP in capturing the multifaceted aspects of citizens' well-being have spurred a paradigm shift. Today, while GDP remains a crucial economic indicator, Gross Domestic Happiness (GDH) offers a more comprehensive lens, encompassing the holistic dimensions of national prosperity.

GDP's Limitations

- **Economic Myopia** GDP primarily gauges economic output, emphasising quantitative aspects and neglecting the qualitative facets that contribute to citizens' welfare.
- **Inequality Oversight** GDP fails to account for wealth distribution, often masking social disparities. A high GDP doesn't guarantee equitable access to opportunities and resources.

The Essence of Gross Domestic Happiness (GDH)

- **Incorporating Social and Environmental Factors** GDH expands the evaluative criteria beyond economic output. It considers social indicators like education, healthcare, and environmental sustainability, offering a more holistic view of national well-being.
- **Quality of Life Metrics** GDH integrates factors such as life satisfaction, mental health and work-life balance, providing insights into citizens' overall contentment and happiness.
- **Cultural and Community Values** GDH recognises the importance of cultural identity, social cohesion and community engagement, acknowledging that these elements contribute significantly to citizens' well-being.

Measuring Well-being Through GDH

- **Bhutan's GNH Model** Bhutan's pioneering Gross National Happiness (GNH) model, a precursor to GDH, emphasises spiritual, physical and mental well-being. It serves as an exemplary approach that values happiness alongside economic development.
- **International Recognition** GDH has gained recognition globally, prompting governments and organisations to consider a more balanced approach to development. The World Happiness Report, which incorporates GDH elements, reflects this shift in global consciousness.

GDP and GDH as Complementary Metrics

- **Economic Foundations** GDP remains indispensable for gauging a nation's economic health, tracking growth and informing fiscal policies.
- **Informed Decision-Making** Integrating GDH with GDP allows policymakers to make more informed decisions. By considering citizens' happiness and well-being, policies can be tailored to foster sustainable development.

Challenges in Adopting GDH

- **Subjectivity** GDH's reliance on subjective indicators poses challenges in standardising measurements. Efforts are needed to establish universally accepted parameters for holistic well-being.
- **Policy Implementation** Shifting from GDP-centric policies to GDH-oriented strategies requires a nuanced approach, involving careful consideration of cultural, social, and economic contexts.

Conclusion

In conclusion, the transition from a GDP-centric approach to embracing GDH as a complementary metric marks a paradigmatic evolution in assessing a nation's prosperity. While GDP provides vital economic insights, GDH illuminates the intangible dimensions that define citizens' well-being. The integration of both metrics enables a more comprehensive evaluation, fostering a holistic approach to national development. As countries strive for progress in the 21st century, the synergy between GDP and GDH emerges as a potent framework for shaping policies that prioritise not just economic growth but the overall welfare and happiness of the populace.

51. Inclusivity and Plurality are the Hallmarks of a Peaceful Society

In a world marked by diversity, the ideals of inclusivity and plurality emerge as crucial pillars for fostering a peaceful and harmonious society. In the modern world, embracing diversity and promoting inclusivity contribute to the fabric of a peaceful coexistence.

Value of Inclusivity

Inclusivity begins with acknowledging and celebrating the rich tapestry of diversity that characterises human societies. Beyond mere tolerance, a society that actively embraces differences in culture, ethnicity, religion, gender and socioeconomic background lays the foundation for inclusivity. Recognising that each individual brings a unique perspective to the collective narrative fosters a sense of belonging for all.

A society that values inclusivity becomes a cultural mosaic, where varied traditions, customs and beliefs coexist. This cultural diversity becomes a source of strength, contributing to the richness of human experience. Rather than viewing differences as divisive, an inclusive society understands that a tapestry of cultures enhances social harmony, promoting a deeper understanding and appreciation for one another.

Inclusivity extends beyond superficial acceptance, requiring active efforts to empower marginalised voices. Elevating those who have historically been sidelined ensures that a broader range of perspectives is considered in decision-making processes. Whether in governance, workplaces, or social institutions, an inclusive approach dismantles barriers, fostering a society where all individuals have the opportunity to thrive.

Education as an Agent of Inclusivity

Education plays a pivotal role in shaping inclusive societies. Curricula that reflect diverse histories and perspectives, coupled with an environment that encourages critical thinking, contribute to breaking down stereotypes and prejudices. Inclusive education equips individuals with the tools to challenge biases, fostering a generation capable of appreciating differences.

Economic Inclusivity and Social Equity

Inclusivity extends to economic spheres, ensuring equitable opportunities for all members of society. A commitment to economic inclusivity addresses disparities in wealth and access to resources. Policies that prioritise social equity contribute to reducing socio-economic inequalities, promoting a more just and stable society.

Plurality as a Catalyst for Innovation

Plurality, the coexistence of various ideas and beliefs, acts as a catalyst for innovation. A society that encourages diverse perspectives fosters creativity and problem-solving. Different viewpoints challenge the status quo, leading to solutions that consider a broad range of needs and realities. Plurality propels societies forward by embracing change and adapting to evolving circumstances.

Social Cohesion and Conflict Resolution

Inclusive societies experience higher levels of social cohesion, where individuals feel interconnected despite their differences. This interconnectedness becomes a powerful tool in conflict resolution. When conflicts arise, an inclusive approach seeks dialogue and understanding, recognising that diverse perspectives contribute to comprehensive and lasting resolutions.

Challenges and the Path Forward

Despite the inherent benefits of inclusivity and plurality, challenges persist. Prejudices, stereotypes and systemic biases can impede progress. Overcoming these challenges requires a collective commitment to dismantling discriminatory structures and promoting policies that actively prioritise inclusivity. Education, awareness campaigns and legislative measures play crucial roles in this ongoing endeavour.

Conclusion

In conclusion, inclusivity and plurality stand as not only ideals but imperative principles for constructing a peaceful society. As we navigate an increasingly interconnected world, fostering understanding, appreciation and respect for diverse perspectives becomes paramount. A commitment to inclusivity ensures that no voice is left unheard and no individual feels marginalised. Plurality becomes the driving force that propels societies toward innovation, resilience and a harmonious coexistence. In the quest for lasting peace, embracing the hallmarks of inclusivity and plurality emerges as an unequivocal imperative, shaping societies that celebrate the strength found in their inherent diversity.

52. The VIP Culture is a Bane of Indian Democracy.

The VIP culture in India, characterised by preferential treatment and excessive privileges accorded to individuals holding prominent positions, stands as a significant challenge to the principles of democracy.

The roots of the VIP culture in India can be traced back to the colonial era when hierarchies were ingrained in the administrative system.

Post-independence, the perpetuation of this culture finds expression in the extravagant privileges bestowed upon politicians, bureaucrats and other influential figures, often at the cost of democratic principles.

Erosion of Equality

One of the primary concerns associated with the VIP cult is the erosion of the principle of equality. In a democratic setup, every citizen is deemed equal before the law. However, the VIP culture fosters a sense of elitism, where certain individuals enjoy privileges that elevate them above the common citizen. This hierarchical mindset contradicts the democratic ethos of equal representation and treatment.

Impact on Governance

The VIP culture adversely affects the efficiency and accountability of governance. The undue focus on providing special treatment diverts resources and attention away from addressing the needs of the broader population. VIP privileges often result in traffic disruptions, security concerns and administrative burdens, diverting crucial resources from more pressing issues.

Symbol of Entitlement

The VIP culture becomes a symbol of entitlement, wherein individuals in positions of power perceive themselves as exempt from the rules that govern ordinary citizens. This attitude not only undermines the rule of law but also fosters a culture of impunity, where those in privileged positions believe they are beyond accountability.

Strain on Public Resources

The allocation of disproportionate resources for the comfort and security of VIPs imposes an additional burden on public finances.

Lavish accommodations, extensive security details, and VIP travel arrangements divert funds that could be utilised for essential public services. This misallocation contributes to economic inefficiency and inequality.

Erosion of Democratic Values

The VIP culture erodes the democratic values of transparency and accessibility. The preference given to VIPs in various aspects, from public events to official protocols, creates an atmosphere of exclusivity that contradicts the principles of an open and inclusive democracy. The perception of a privileged class enjoying unchecked privileges undermines public trust in democratic institutions.

Social Implications

Beyond the realm of governance, the VIP culture has social implications. It perpetuates a societal mindset that values hierarchy and reinforces traditional power structures. The emulation of VIP behaviour by the broader population further entrenches social inequalities, hindering the evolution toward a more egalitarian society.

Addressing the Issue

Effectively addressing the VIP culture requires a multifaceted approach. Stricter regulations on the allocation of resources for VIP privileges, enhanced transparency in decision-making processes and a shift in societal attitudes toward entitlement are essential. Leaders need to set an example by embracing a humbler and service-oriented approach, aligning their actions with democratic principles.

Conclusion

In conclusion, the VIP culture poses a substantial threat to the foundational principles of Indian democracy. As the nation strives for inclusive and accountable governance, it is imperative to challenge and dismantle the culture of entitlement that surrounds VIPs.

A truly democratic society is one where every citizen is treated with equality and respect, irrespective of their social or political standing. Addressing the VIP cult is not just a matter of administrative reform, it is a critical step toward fostering a democracy that is truly of the people, by the people and for the people.

53. Science and Mysticism: Are they compatible?

The relationship between science and mysticism has been a subject of contemplation and debate throughout history. While science relies on empirical evidence and rational inquiry, mysticism often delves into the realms of spiritual experience, intuition and transcendental knowledge.

Science

Science is a systematic and evidence-based approach to understanding the natural world. It relies on empirical observations, experimentation and the formulation of testable hypothesis to explain phenomena. The scientific method, with its emphasis on objectivity and reproducibility, has led to remarkable advancements in our understanding of the physical universe, from the microscopic to the cosmic.

Mysticism

Mysticism, on the other hand, is often associated with the direct experience of the divine, transcending the boundaries of reason and sensory perception.

Mystics explore altered states of consciousness, meditation and spiritual practices to attain insights into the nature of existence. Mystical traditions across cultures emphasise the interconnectedness of all things and the quest for a deeper, experiential understanding of reality.

Points of Convergence

While science and mysticism may seem divergent, there are points of convergence. Quantum physics, for example, has introduced concepts that challenge classical notions of casuality and material reality, inviting parallels with mystical ideas about interconnectedness and non-duality. Some scientists and mystics alike advocate for a holistic worldview that integrates scientific inquiry with a deeper appreciation for the mysteries that transcend purely empirical understanding.

Complementarity

The compatibility between science and mysticism lies in their potential complementarity. Science excels in explaining the 'how' of phenomena, unravelling the mechanics of the universe. Mysticism, on the other hand, often delves into the 'why' and the subjective, providing insights into the human experience, consciousness and the underlying unity of all existence. Together, they offer a more comprehensive understanding of reality.

Challenges to Compatibility

Despite points of convergence, challenges to compatibility exist. The demand for empirical evidence in science contrasts with the subjective and personal nature of mystical experiences. Scepticism within the scientific community often dismisses mysticism as unverifiable and incompatible with the rigorous standards of scientific inquiry. The tension arises when attempts are made to reconcile the inherently different methodologies and epistemologies of science and mysticism.

Navigating the Interplay

To navigate the interplay between science and mysticism, it is essential to recognise and respect the distinct domains each occupies.

Science thrives in the realm of the observable and measurable, contributing to technological progress and our understanding of the physical world. Mysticism, on the other hand, explores the subjective dimensions of consciousness and spirituality, offering insights that transcend the limitations of empirical knowledge.

Harmony through Dialogue

Harmony between science and mysticism can be fostered through open dialogue and mutual respect. Recognising the value of both perspectives enriches our collective understanding of reality. Scientists and mystics alike can engage in interdisciplinary conversations, acknowledging the limitations and strengths of each approach. This collaborative spirit encourages a more holistic worldview that accommodates diverse ways of knowing.

Conclusion

In conclusion, the compatibility between science and mysticism remains a complex and nuanced interplay. While their methodologies and objectives may differ, there is room for dialogue and mutual enrichment. Embracing the diversity of human inquiry, from empirical investigation to mystical contemplation, can contribute to a more comprehensive understanding of the profound mysteries that shape our existence. Whether through the lens of a microscope or the depths of contemplative experience, the quest for knowledge continues to unfold, inviting us to explore the unity within the diversity of our intellectual and spiritual pursuits.

54. As Civilisation Progresses, Culture Declines.

The relationship between civilisation and culture is a complex interplay that has been a subject of contemplation and debate throughout history. Some argue that as civilisation advances, cultural values may decline, while others maintain that progress can enrich and diversify cultural expressions. Thus, it becomes important for us to understand the nuanced dynamics of this relationship, exploring the impact of civilisation on culture and the intricate ways in which these forces interact.

Evolution of Civilisation

Civilisation, characterised by technological, social and economic advancements, marks the collective progress of human societies. It encompasses urbanisation, scientific achievements, governance structures and the overall development of a society's intellectual and material resources. The march of civilisation is often associated with the pursuit of knowledge, innovation, and the improvement of human conditions.

Cultural Foundations

Culture, on the other hand, represents the shared values, beliefs, traditions and artistic expressions that define a community. It is the tapestry of identity woven by generations, reflecting the collective consciousness of a society. Culture encompasses art, language, customs and rituals, providing a sense of belonging and continuity. The cultural richness of a society contributes to its unique character and legacy.

Points of Tension

The contention that as civilisation progresses, culture declines, suggests potential points of tension between these two forces. One argument is that rapid technological advancements and globalisation can lead to cultural homogenisation, eroding distinct local traditions. The commodification of culture in the face of consumerism and the dilution of traditional values in the wake of modernisation are cited as examples of this decline.

- **Consumerism and Cultural Commodification** In the pursuit of economic prosperity, civilisations often embrace consumerism. The commodification of cultural artifacts and practices for mass consumption can lead to their distortion or oversimplification. Traditional art forms may be reduced to marketable stereotypes and cultural practices may become performative spectacles, losing their authentic essence. This commercialisation is seen by some as a form of cultural decline.
- **Erosion of Traditional Values** The rapid pace of social change accompanying progress can challenge traditional values. As societies adopt new technologies, alter social structures and redefine norms, certain cultural values may be sidelined or marginalised. This erosion of traditional values is perceived by critics as a loss of cultural depth and authenticity, with the younger generations potentially dissociating from their cultural roots.
- **Cultural Homogenisation** Globalisation, while fostering interconnectedness, can also contribute to cultural homogenisation. As Western cultural influences spread worldwide through media, technology and consumer products, there is a concern that diverse local cultures may be subsumed into a more uniform, globalised culture. This potential loss of cultural diversity is viewed as a consequence of civilisation's relentless march.
- **Enrichment through Diversity** Contrary to the notion of cultural decline, others argue that civilisation's progress can enrich culture through diversity. The exchange of ideas, artistic expressions and traditions on a global scale can lead to a dynamic fusion of cultures. Technological advancements provide platforms for preserving and disseminating cultural heritage, fostering a global appreciation for diverse artistic forms and traditions.
- **Cultural Renaissance** Some civilisations experience cultural renaissances as they advance. The flourishing of arts, literature and intellectual pursuits during periods of enlightenment is an example of how progress can stimulate cultural vitality. The interplay of civilisations with diverse cultural backgrounds can give rise to syncretic forms, where the fusion of ideas results in novel and vibrant cultural expressions.

Balancing Progress and Preservation

The key lies in striking a balance between progress and the preservation of cultural heritage. Forward-looking societies can embrace innovation and modernisation while actively safeguarding and promoting their unique cultural identities. Initiatives that prioritise cultural education, support local artists and celebrate traditional practices can ensure that progress complements rather than diminishes cultural richness.

Conclusion

In conclusion, the relationship between civilisation and culture is a nuanced and multifaceted interplay. While concerns about cultural decline in the face of progress exist, it is essential to recognise the potential for enrichment and diversification.

Striking a balance between progress and the preservation of cultural heritage is crucial for societies to navigate the complexities of modernity without losing the essence of their unique identities. Civilisation's march need not entail the erosion of culture; rather, it can be an opportunity for cultural resilience, adaptation and the flourishing of diverse expressions in the tapestry of human civilisation.

55. Are the Multinational Corporations Saviours Or Saboteurs?

The role of multinational corporations (MNCs) in the global landscape has been a subject of intense debate. Some view them as saviours, bringing economic growth, technological advancement and job opportunities, while others label them as saboteurs, accusing them of exploiting resources, evading taxes and exacerbating social inequalities. With the increasing role of MNC's in the global landscape, it becomes crucial to examine both perspectives, exploring the nuanced impact of MNCs on economies, societies and the environment.

MNCs as Saviours

- **Engines of Economic Growth** One of the primary arguments in favour of MNCs is their role as catalysts for economic growth. These corporations often bring substantial investments, technological expertise and managerial know-how to host countries. Through the establishment of factories, research and development centres, and innovation hubs, MNCs contribute to the expansion of local economies.
- **Job Creation and Skill Development** MNCs, by setting up operations in different regions, create job opportunities for local populations. The transfer of skills and knowledge from these corporations to the local workforce can enhance human capital, fostering skill development and increasing employability. This, in turn, contributes to poverty reduction and overall economic improvement.
- **Access to Global Markets** For many developing countries, partnering with MNCs provides a gateway to global markets. These corporations, with their extensive networks, can facilitate the export of locally produced goods and services, enabling countries to participate in the global economy and diversify their revenue streams.

MNCs as Saboteurs

- **Resource Exploitation and Environmental Degradation** Critics argue that MNCs often engage in resource exploitation, depleting natural assets without adequate environmental safeguards. Extractive industries, in particular, face accusations of ecological damage, deforestation and pollution, leading to long-term environmental degradation and loss of biodiversity.
- **Tax Avoidance and Erosion of Public Finances** MNCs are frequently accused of engaging in aggressive tax avoidance strategies, shifting profits to low-tax jurisdictions and depriving host countries of much-needed revenues. This erosion of public finances can hinder governments' ability to invest in essential services such as education, healthcare and infrastructure.
- **Social Inequalities and Exploitative Practices** In pursuit of maximising profits, some MNCs are criticised for exploiting cheap labour, disregarding workers' rights and perpetuating social inequalities. Sweatshops, poor working conditions and inadequate wages are often associated with certain multinational operations, leading to ethical concerns regarding corporate responsibility.
- **Taking A Balanced Approach** The saviour or saboteur dichotomy oversimplifies the complex reality of MNCs' impact. The role of these corporations varies across industries, regions and regulatory environments. It is essential to recognise the nuances and adopt a more balanced perspective that considers both positive and negative aspects.

Governments play a crucial role in shaping the impact of MNCs through robust regulatory frameworks. Effective laws and enforcement mechanisms can ensure that corporations adhere to ethical standards, contribute to local development and minimise negative externalities.

Many MNCs recognise the importance of corporate social responsibility and sustainable business practices. Initiatives focusing on environmental sustainability, ethical labour practices and community development showcase a growing awareness among corporations regarding their broader impact on society.

Conclusion

In conclusion, the debate over whether multinational corporations are saviours or saboteurs reflects the dual nature of their impact on societies and economies. While acknowledging the positive contributions in terms of economic growth, job creation and global market access, it is crucial to address the challenges related to resource exploitation, environmental degradation and social inequalities. Striking a balance requires concerted efforts from governments, corporations and civil society to promote responsible business practices that prioritise both profit and the well-being of communities and the planet. Recognising MNCs as complex actors with the potential for positive transformation can pave the way for constructive engagement and the pursuit of sustainable and inclusive development.

56. Will developing rural infrastructure catalyse the faster growth of the national economy?

The question of whether developing rural infrastructure can expedite the growth of the national economy is central to the discourse on inclusive and sustainable development. The Rural-Urban divide has been a persistent challenge and investing in Rural infrastructure holds the potential to not only address this gap but also act as a catalyst for overall economic advancement.

Economic Impacts of Rural Infrastructure Development

- **Boost to Agricultural Productivity** Developing rural infrastructure, such as irrigation systems, cold storage facilities and better transport networks, directly impacts agriculture. Improved irrigation ensures consistent water supply, leading to increased crop yields. Efficient transportation reduces post-harvest losses and connects farmers to markets, enhancing overall agricultural productivity.

- **Rural Industrialisation** Robust rural infrastructure can serve as a foundation for rural industrialisation. Access to reliable power supply, better roads and telecommunications can attract industries to rural areas. This decentralisation of industries not only reduces urban congestion but also creates employment opportunities in rural regions.
- **Employment Generation** Rural infrastructure projects, from road construction to water resource management, generate employment locally. This not only addresses rural unemployment but also boosts income levels, stimulating demand for goods and services, which, in turn, contributes to economic growth.
- **Market Access and Trade** Improved connectivity through well-maintained roads and transportation networks enables farmers and local businesses to access wider markets. This enhances competitiveness and promotes a more inclusive economic growth model by integrating rural economies into the national and global supply chains.

Social Implications of Rural Infrastructure Development

- **Quality of Life Improvement** Access to basic amenities such as clean water, sanitation and healthcare services significantly improves with enhanced rural infrastructure. This leads to an improvement in the overall quality of life for rural populations, contributing to human development indices.
- **Education and Skill Development** Developing rural infrastructure includes investing in educational institutions and skill development programs. This empowers the rural workforce with the necessary skills for better employability, fostering a more knowledgeable and skilled population.
- **Women Empowerment** Improved rural infrastructure often has a pronounced impact on women's lives. Access to better healthcare, education and employment opportunities empowers women, contributing to gender equality and social development.

Challenges and Considerations

- **Funding and Resource Allocation** Implementing comprehensive rural infrastructure projects requires substantial financial resources. Governments must prioritise and allocate funds effectively, often navigating competing demands for resources in both rural and urban areas.
- **Maintenance and Sustainability** Building infrastructure is one aspect; ensuring its long-term sustainability is another. Effective maintenance mechanisms must be in place to ensure that investments continue to yield returns over the years.
- **Community Engagement** Successful rural development projects necessitate active participation and engagement with local communities. Understanding their needs, involving them in decision-making and considering local contexts are critical for project success.

Conclusion

In conclusion, developing rural infrastructure is undeniably a potent catalyst for faster national economic growth. It not only addresses the disparities between rural and urban areas but also generates a ripple effect, positively impacting various sectors of the economy. However, a nuanced and context-specific approach, taking into account local needs, community involvement and sustainable practices, is essential for reaping the full benefits of rural infrastructure development. As nations embark on this transformative journey, strategic planning, effective governance and a commitment to inclusivity will be key to ensuring that the dividends of development are shared equitably across the entire socio-economic landscape.

57. The role of literature in character building.

Literature, the eternal repository of human experiences and emotions, stands as an indomitable force in shaping character. Beyond its role as mere entertainment, literature becomes a guiding beacon for individuals, offering profound insights, diverse perspectives and moral lessons that contribute significantly to their moral and intellectual development. The various ways in which literature transforms and builds character are as follows

Literature as a Moral Compass

The pages of literary works unfold moral dilemmas, ethical considerations and choices that characters face. In traversing these narratives, readers encounter a spectrum of human behaviour, providing them with a moral compass to navigate the complexities of their own lives. The moral landscape depicted in literature becomes a reflective surface for readers to ponder upon, fostering a deep understanding of right and wrong.

Empathy and Emotional Intelligence

One of literature's most profound impacts lies in its ability to cultivate empathy and emotional intelligence. Through the lens of characters, readers vicariously experience a myriad of emotions and diverse perspectives. This emotional journey not only makes readers more compassionate but also equips them with the emotional intelligence necessary for nuanced social interactions and a deeper understanding of human nature.

Cultivation of Virtues

Classic literary characters often embody virtues that stand as pillars of strength. Whether it's the courage of Atticus Finch in 'To Kill a Mockingbird' or the resilience of Jane Eyre, these characters inspire readers to emulate virtues that contribute to the building of a robust character. The struggles and triumphs become an inspirational guide for readers on their own moral journey.

Intellectual Stimulation

The vast realm of literature is a treasure trove of intellectual stimulation. Engaging with intricate narratives, complex characters and diverse themes challenges readers to think critically.

This intellectual stimulation not only enhances their analytical abilities but also fosters a lifelong love for learning, contributing to the development of a well-rounded and intellectually curious character.

Formation of Values and Beliefs

Literature has the power to shape values and beliefs. The ideologies and philosophies portrayed in literary works resonate deeply with readers, often influencing their own worldviews. Whether it's the pursuit of justice in a legal drama or the exploration of existential questions in philosophical novels, literature becomes a crucible where individuals forge their own values, essential to the construction of character.

Literature and Ethical Decision-Making

The ethical quandaries characters face in literature provide readers with a testing ground for their moral compass. Navigating through the moral landscapes presented in literary narratives prepares readers for real-life ethical decision-making. The ability to critically analyse and reflect on ethical dilemmas in fiction becomes a skill set that individuals carry into their personal and professional lives.

Cultural and Global Awareness

In an increasingly interconnected world, literature serves as a bridge to diverse cultures and global perspectives. Exposure to narratives from different societies fosters cultural understanding and broadens one's worldview. This cultural awareness contributes significantly to the development of an inclusive and open-minded character capable of navigating the complexities of a globalised society.

Literature's Role in Nurturing Imagination

Beyond its impact on moral and intellectual aspects, literature plays a pivotal role in nurturing imagination. The imaginative realms crafted by authors encourage readers to explore possibilities beyond their immediate reality. This cultivation of imagination is crucial for creative thinking and problem-solving, enriching the cognitive aspects of character development.

Challenges and Criticisms

While extolling the virtues of literature in character building, it's essential to acknowledge the challenges. The subjective interpretation of texts and the influence of external factors on readers' perceptions can lead to varied outcomes. Moreover, ensuring the accessibility and diversity of literature is crucial to maximising its impact on character development and making it an inclusive force for all.

Conclusion

In conclusion, literature stands as a timeless and transformative force in character building. Its ability to instil moral values, foster empathy, stimulate intellectual growth and offer diverse perspectives makes it an invaluable resource for shaping individuals into ethically grounded, emotionally intelligent and culturally aware beings. As societies evolve, literature remains an enduring guide, capable of moulding generations with virtues that transcend the pages and endure in the fabric of human character. In harnessing the power of literature, societies pave the way for individuals to not only comprehend the human experience but to actively engage with it, creating a tapestry of character that reflects the richness of the literary world.

58. Indian secularism a blend of constitutional and cultural heritage

India, a cradle of diverse cultures and religions, stands as a testament to the delicate balance between constitutional ideals and cultural richness in the realm of secularism. The Indian concept of secularism transcends the mere separation of religion and state, weaving a narrative that cherishes both constitutional principles and cultural heritage.

Constitutional Foundations

The roots of Indian secularism lie deep within its Constitution. Framers of the Constitution envisioned a nation where every citizen, regardless of religious affiliation, would enjoy equal rights and opportunities. The Preamble, declaring India a 'sovereign, socialist, secular and democratic republic,' reflects this commitment to secular ideals. Constitutional provisions such as Article 15, prohibiting discrimination on grounds of religion, and Article 25, guaranteeing freedom of religion, underscore the foundational principles of Indian secularism.

Equal Treatment of All Religions

Indian secularism goes beyond mere tolerance; it advocates for equal treatment of all religions. The state neither interferes with religious practices nor promotes any particular faith. This equidistant stance fosters an environment where citizens can freely practice and profess their religions without fear of discrimination or favouritism. The judiciary, as a guardian of constitutional values, plays a crucial role in upholding this principle.

Cultural Pluralism

Secularism in India is not synonymous with irreligiosity; rather, it embraces the cultural pluralism that defines the nation. Festivals, traditions and rituals from various religions coexist harmoniously, creating a vibrant tapestry of diversity. Cultural celebrations like Diwali, Eid, Christmas, and others are not only observed but also embraced by people of different faiths, exemplifying the inclusive nature of Indian secularism.

Protection of Minority Rights

A hallmark of Indian secularism is its commitment to safeguarding the rights of religious minorities. Recognising the potential vulnerability of minority communities, the Constitution provides for the establishment of minority educational institutions under Article 30. This ensures that diverse cultural and religious groups have the autonomy to preserve and propagate their unique identities.

Legal Safeguards Against Religious Discrimination

The Indian legal system actively combats religious discrimination. The Prevention of Atrocities Act, 1989, criminalises acts that harm members of Scheduled Castes and Scheduled Tribes, often linked with religious identity. The judiciary, through landmark judgments, reinforces the constitutional commitment to secularism by ensuring justice without prejudice.

Challenges to Indian Secularism

While India's secular fabric is robust, it faces challenges. Communal tensions, identity politics and occasional outbreaks of religious violence test the resilience of Indian secularism. The rise of fundamentalism and attempts to manipulate religious sentiments for political gains pose threats to the inclusive vision of the nation's founders.

Role of Media and Education

Media and education play pivotal roles in shaping the narrative of Indian secularism. Responsible journalism that promotes understanding and tolerance can counter divisive forces. Additionally, an inclusive and secular education system that imparts values of pluralism and mutual respect is crucial for nurturing future generations committed to the ideals of Indian secularism.

Conclusion

In conclusion, Indian secularism is a delicate but resilient equilibrium between constitutional principles and cultural heritage. It is an ongoing journey towards fostering a society where diverse religions and cultures coexist, thrive, and contribute to the nation's collective identity. The Constitutional commitment to equality, protection of minority rights and legal safeguards against discrimination forms the bedrock of Indian secularism. As the nation progresses, preserving this unique blend becomes imperative to sustain the ethos that defines India as a secular, pluralistic and inclusive democracy. It is in embracing this blend that India continues to demonstrate that unity in diversity is not merely a slogan but a living, evolving reality.

59. Status of Higher Education and Research in India: Ways of Future

India, with its rich intellectual heritage, stands at a critical juncture in shaping the future of higher education and research. While significant strides have been made, challenges persist and a visionary approach is imperative for India to emerge as a global hub for education and research.

Current Landscape

India boasts a vast higher education system, evident in its Gross Enrollment Ratio (GER). However, the quality of education remains a concern. A fragmented approach, outdated curriculum, and inadequate infrastructure hinder the realisation of India's true potential in higher education.

Challenges

- **Quality Disparities** Discrepancies in educational standards across institutions undermine India's competitiveness globally. The need for a standardised and rigorous accreditation system is paramount to ensure and maintain quality standards in higher education institutions.
- **Research Discrepancy** While India produces a significant number of graduates, research output lags, impacting innovation and global recognition. A strategic approach involves allocating substantial funds to research initiatives, encouraging collaboration between academia and industry.
- **Outdated Curriculum** The rigidity of the current curriculum, often detached from industry needs, renders graduates less employable. Curriculum reform should be an ongoing process, adapting to evolving industry requirements.
- **Infrastructure Gaps** Insufficient resources and outdated infrastructure impede the effective delivery of education and research. A holistic approach involves both digital and physical infrastructure upgrades.

Strategic Approaches

Quality Enhancement

- **Accreditation Reforms** Implementing stringent accreditation processes ensures and maintains quality standards in higher education institutions. Transparency and accountability in the accreditation system are vital.
- **Faculty Development** Continuous training and development programs for educators enhance teaching methodologies and research capabilities, fostering a culture of academic excellence.

Research and Innovation

- **Increased Funding** Allocating substantial funds to research initiatives encourages high impact projects, collaborative research and the development of cutting-edge technologies.
- **International Collaboration** Fostering global partnerships facilitates knowledge exchange, collaborative research projects and exposure to global best practices, elevating India's research standards.

Curriculum Reformation

- **Industry Integration** Curricula should be revised in consultation with industries to align academic programs with industry requirements. Regular industry-academia interactions bridge the gap between theoretical knowledge and practical application.
- **Skill-Based Learning** Emphasising skill-based learning ensures that graduates possess practical skills, enhancing employability and fostering an entrepreneurial spirit.

Infrastructure Upgradation

- **Digital Transformation** Leveraging technology for online education, virtual labs and e-resources narrows the digital divide, making education accessible across diverse socio-economic backgrounds.

- **Physical Infrastructure** Investments in state-of-the-art laboratories, libraries and other amenities create a conducive learning environment, enhancing the overall educational experience.

Initiatives

Several initiatives exemplify positive strides in transforming higher education

- **National Education Policy** (NEP) **2020** Envisages a holistic approach, emphasising flexibility, multidisciplinary learning and increased focus on research and innovation. The effective implementation of NEP can reshape India's educational landscape.
- **Institutes of Eminence** (IoE) Recognising institutions for global competitiveness, IoE status encourages academic autonomy and facilitates global collaborations. IoE status can serve as a model for other institutions to emulate.
- **Research Consortia** Collaborative efforts like the SERB-DST Joint Project in Science and Technology empower researchers, fostering a culture of impactful research. Expanding such initiatives can contribute significantly to India's research output.

Way Forward

The vision for the future of higher education and research in India necessitates sustained commitment and concerted efforts

- **Global Collaboration** Actively engaging with global institutions fosters research partnerships, faculty exchange programmes and collaborative projects. This global perspective enriches the educational experience for students and researchers alike.
- **Inclusive Policies** Developing policies that ensure equitable access to education, catering to diverse socio-economic backgrounds, is crucial. Scholarships, grants and outreach programmes can promote inclusivity and diversity in higher education.
- **Industry-Academia Synergy** Strengthening ties with industries through initiatives like internships, joint research and skill development programmes bridges the gap between academic knowledge and industry requirements. Industry participation in curriculum design ensures relevance.
- **Technology Integration** Embracing emerging technologies like artificial intelligence, big data and virtual reality for advanced learning experiences prepares students for the demands of the modern workforce. Investments in technology infrastructure are imperative.

Conclusion

India's journey towards transforming higher education and research demands a comprehensive and collaborative approach. By addressing challenges, implementing strategic reforms and leveraging successful initiatives, India can emerge as a global leader in academia and research. The synergy between quality education, cutting-edge research, and innovative policies will propel India into a future where its intellectual prowess is recognised and celebrated worldwide.

As India navigates the evolving landscape of higher education, the emphasis should be on creating an ecosystem that nurtures creativity, critical thinking and excellence, ensuring a bright future for generations to come.

60. The destiny of a nation is shaped in its classrooms.

The adage "The destiny of a nation is shaped in its classrooms" encapsulates the profound influence education holds in sculpting the future of a country. As the cornerstone of intellectual development, classrooms serve as the crucible where the ideals, knowledge and values that define a nation are imparted.

The Power of Education

Education, the driving force behind societal progress, contributes significantly to a nation's economic, social and cultural fabric. A well-structured and inclusive educational system is paramount for fostering innovation, critical thinking and a collective sense of identity.

- **Building a Knowledge Economy** Educational institutions play a pivotal role in shaping the human capital that propels a nation towards a knowledge-based economy. According to UNESCO, countries with higher literacy rates tend to exhibit higher economic growth. Investing in quality education ensures a skilled workforce, fostering innovation and competitiveness on the global stage.
- **Fostering Civic Responsibility** Classrooms are not just spaces for academic learning; they are crucibles for cultivating civic responsibility and ethical values. Citizenship education is vital for nurturing responsible, informed and actively engaged citizens who contribute positively to the nation's social and political landscape.
- **Equitable Access to Education** Ensuring universal access to quality education is imperative for inclusive nation-building. Disparities in educational opportunities based on gender, socio-economic status or geography hinder a nation's holistic development. Robust policies must be in place to bridge these gaps and provide equal educational opportunities for all.
- **Cultural Preservation and Diversity** In diverse nations, classrooms serve as arenas for preserving and celebrating cultural heritage. Education becomes a medium through which the rich tapestry of traditions, languages and histories is passed down to successive generations, fostering a sense of unity in diversity.

Challenges in Educational Systems

- **Quality Disparities** Variations in the quality of education across regions and institutions undermine the potential of education to shape a nation positively. Standardising and enhancing the quality of curriculum delivery is essential.

- **Technological Divide** The digital divide poses a challenge to equitable access to education. Bridging this gap through technology integration in classrooms and digital literacy initiatives is crucial for ensuring that no section of society is left behind.
- **Teacher Training and Motivation** The role of educators is pivotal in shaping the destiny of a nation. Ongoing teacher training programmes, competitive remuneration, and recognition are essential to motivate and empower educators.
- **Curriculum Relevance** Aligning curricula with the evolving needs of society and the job market ensures that education remains relevant. Continuous updates to curricula and introducing vocational training enhance the employability of graduates.

Success Stories and Initiatives

- **Finland's Education System** Renowned for its student-centric approach, Finland's education system focuses on personalised learning, minimal standardised testing, and highly qualified teachers. This model underscores the importance of pedagogical methods in shaping successful educational outcomes.
- **Digital India Initiative** India's Digital India campaign aims to transform classrooms into tech-enabled spaces, bridging the technological divide. Integration of e-learning tools, online resources and digital infrastructure enhances the learning experience.
- **National Education Policy** (NEP) **2020** The NEP 2020 emphasises a holistic and multidisciplinary approach to education, promoting critical thinking, creativity and flexibility. The policy envisions classrooms as dynamic spaces nurturing well-rounded individuals.

The Role of Teachers

Teachers, the architects of a nation's intellectual foundation, wield unparalleled influence within classrooms. Their dedication, competence and passion are instrumental in instilling values, igniting curiosity, and inspiring the next generation of leaders.

Conclusion

In conclusion, the destiny of a nation is indeed shaped in its classrooms, where the seeds of knowledge, values and aspirations are sown.

By addressing challenges, leveraging successful initiatives and prioritising equitable access to quality education, nations can ensure that their classrooms become crucibles of progress, unity and enlightenment.

As we navigate the complexities of the 21st century, the focus must remain on nurturing classrooms that empower individuals to contribute meaningfully to the collective destiny of their nations.

In doing so, we lay the foundation for a future where education becomes the catalyst for holistic nation-building, steering societies towards prosperity, inclusivity, and global relevance.

61. A Good Life Is One Inspired By Love And Guided By Knowledge

In the intricate tapestry of human existence, the pursuit of a good life unfolds as a harmonious interplay between two powerful forces–love and knowledge. Love, the emotional compass that guides our connections, intertwines with knowledge, the intellectual lighthouse illuminating our path. These twin pillars, when cultivated in tandem, forge a life that is not just good but resonant with purpose, meaning and societal impact.

- **Love : The Heartbeat of a Fulfilling Life** At the core of a good life lies love – a force that transcends boundaries, cultivates empathy and binds communities together. Research indicates that individuals who experience strong social connections and emotional bonds tend to lead healthier and more fulfilling lives. Love, whether expressed in familial, platonic, or romantic relationships, fosters emotional well-being, resilience and a profound sense of belonging.
- **The Impact of Love on Mental Health** Studies highlight the crucial role of love in mental health. Positive relationships contribute to lower stress levels, decreased risk of mental health disorders, and enhanced overall psychological well-being. As the world grapples with rising mental health concerns, recognising the role of love becomes imperative for societal well-being.

Knowledge : The Guiding Light of Enlightenment

Knowledge, the pursuit of truth and understanding, acts as the intellectual foundation of a good life. A well-informed mind navigates challenges with resilience, embraces diversity, and contributes meaningfully to societal progress. As societies evolve, the acquisition and application of knowledge become essential for informed decision-making and innovative problem-solving.

- **The Socioeconomic Impact of Education** Education, a key conduit for knowledge acquisition, plays a pivotal role in shaping societies. According to UNESCO, education is a powerful tool for poverty reduction, economic growth, and social development. Nations with higher literacy rates and well-educated populations are better equipped to address complex challenges, fostering environments conducive to a good life for all citizens.

The Interplay between Love and Knowledge

The synergy between love and knowledge creates a dynamic framework for a good life. In personal relationships, understanding and empathising with others require both emotional intelligence (love) and cultural awareness (knowledge). Societies that value education often cultivate environments where inclusivity, empathy and love can flourish.

Challenges in Achieving a Good Life

- **Digital Disconnect** In an era dominated by technology, the digital-disconnect poses challenges to genuine human connections. Striking a balance between virtual interactions and authentic, emotionally rich relationships becomes essential.

- **Knowledge Inequality** Disparities in access to education and information create knowledge gaps, hindering the realisation of a good life for marginalised populations. Addressing these inequalities is crucial for societal progress.
- **Erosion of Values** In the pursuit of knowledge, there exists a risk of neglecting the moral compass guided by love. Ethical considerations and the cultivation of virtues are vital components for a genuinely good life.

Success Stories and Initiatives

- **Bhutan's Gross National Happiness (GNH) Index** Bhutan's unique development model emphasises holistic well-being over material wealth. The GNH Index incorporates factors like psychological well-being, community vitality and cultural diversity, recognising the importance of love, knowledge and interconnectedness in defining a good life.
- **Social-Emotional Learning (SEL) Programs** Educational initiatives globally are incorporating SEL programs to foster emotional intelligence, empathy and interpersonal skills alongside traditional academic learning. These programs recognise the integral role of love in the educational process.

Conclusion

Overall, a good life emerges not as a solitary pursuit but as a symphony orchestrated by the harmonious blend of love and knowledge. Love, with its emotional richness, anchors us in a shared humanity, fostering connections that transcend the boundaries of time and space. Knowledge, with its illuminating power, propels us towards enlightenment, equipping us to navigate the complexities of the world. The interplay between love and knowledge, guided by ethical considerations, forms the bedrock of a life that transcends personal fulfilment to contribute positively to the collective good.

As we navigate an era marked by unprecedented challenges, the quest for a good life beckons societies to prioritise the cultivation of emotional intelligence, the pursuit of knowledge, and the preservation of shared values. By weaving the threads of love and knowledge into the fabric of our individual and collective lives, we forge a narrative that celebrates not just personal success but the well-being of humanity. In embracing this symbiotic dance, we embark on a journey towards a future where the pursuit of a good life is synonymous with the flourishing of compassion, wisdom, and the common good.

62. Self-reliant India in Amrit Kaal

In the midst of the 21st century, India stands at a pivotal juncture, embarking on a transformative journey dubbed *Amrit Kaal*, the era leading to the centenary of India's independence. The vision of a self-reliant India or *Atmanirbhar Bharat*, is not just an economic policy but a clarion call towards comprehensive national development.

Foundation of Self-Reliance

The concept of self-reliance is deeply ingrained in India's socio-economic policies, signifying a shift from being a market-driven economy to one that prioritises strengthening its internal capacities. This paradigm shift is underpinned by the following pillars

- **Promotion of Local Manufacturing** Initiatives like 'Make in India' have been revitalised to focus on local manufacturing, reducing dependency on imports and making Indian products globally competitive.
- **Infrastructure Expansion** With the National Infrastructure Pipeline (NIP), India envisages a whopping investment worth trillions to overhaul its infrastructure, thereby fostering a conducive environment for growth across sectors.
- **Technological Advancements and Innovation** The emphasis on digital India and support for startups reflects the nation's commitment to embracing modern technology and innovation, making technology a pivotal element of self-reliance.
- **Fiscal Prudence and Governance** Implementing policies that ensure efficient governance and financial stability underscores the approach towards building a resilient economic framework.

Economic Resilience Through Diversification

Economic diversification is central to achieving self-reliance. India is making concerted efforts in various sectors as follows

- **Agriculture** The Indian Government is coming up with reforms aimed at improving farmers' income and ensuring food security. Initiatives that encourage organic farming, crop diversification and modern agricultural practices are being devised and implemented.
- **Energy Security** Investments in renewable energy sources, such as solar and wind, are being prioritised to reduce fossil fuel dependency, aiming for energy self-sufficiency.
- **Technology and Innovation** Support for R&D, particularly in emerging technologies like AI, blockchain, and space technology, positions India as a global innovation hub.

Boosting Human Capital

Human capital is acknowledged as India's most valuable asset. Enhancing health, education and skill development is vital for a self-reliant India

- **Education** The National Education Policy (NEP) 2020 emphasises skill development, critical thinking and adaptability, preparing a workforce for the future.
- **Healthcare** Schemes like Ayushman Bharat ensure affordable healthcare, aiming for a healthy workforce, which is crucial for economic productivity.
- **Skill Development** Programmes are in place to reskill and upskill the workforce, making them adaptable to the changing global job landscape.

Strengthening Social Infrastructure

The vision of self-reliance extends beyond economic measures to strengthening social infrastructure, ensuring that every citizen benefits

- **Social Equity** Policies aim at reducing income inequality and ensuring equitable growth across socio-economic strata.
- **Women Empowerment** Empowering women through education, entrepreneurship and participation in the workforce is crucial for holistic development.

Global Integration, Not Isolation

Self-reliance does not imply isolation. India envisions playing a significant role on the global stage

- **Export Promotion** A focus on enhancing export capabilities in various sectors, including technology, pharmaceuticals, and textiles, positions India as a key player in global supply chains.
- **International Cooperation** Strengthening diplomatic ties and engaging in multilateral organisations highlights India's commitment to global peace and development.

Conclusion

In conclusion, the journey towards a self-reliant India in Amrit Kaal is comprehensive, inclusive, and forward-looking. By focusing on local strengths, while embracing global best practices and fostering international cooperation, India seeks to not only accelerate its own development but also contribute significantly to global progress. This multifaceted approach, embedded in the principles of sustainable development and equity, ensures that the vision of Atmanirbhar Bharat transcends economic metrics, heralding a new era of prosperity and resilience for India and the world at large.

63. Indian Populations - Challenges and Solutions

India, with its burgeoning population, stands at a demographic crossroads, presenting both opportunities and challenges. At this juncture, it becomes imperative for us to understand the multifaceted aspects of India's demographic scenario, analysing the challenges posed by its large population and proposing strategic solutions to harness the demographic dividend effectively.

Demographic Landscape

India's current population exceeds 1.3 billion, making it the second-most populous country globally. While the demographic dividend – a youthful population – holds immense potential for economic growth, it also poses formidable challenges in areas such as healthcare, education, employment, and resource management.

Challenges

- **Education and Employment** The sheer magnitude of India's population places immense pressure on its education and employment sectors. Ensuring quality education for all and creating job opportunities commensurate with the demographic bulge are imperative to avoid a demographic disaster.
- **Healthcare Burden** A large population puts a strain on the healthcare infrastructure. The challenge lies not only in providing basic healthcare services but also in addressing the unique health needs of a diverse population spread across urban and rural landscapes.
- **Urbanisation Strain** The rapid pace of urbanisation, fuelled by population growth, leads to challenges such as inadequate housing, overburdened transportation systems and environmental degradation. Sustainable urban development becomes crucial to mitigate these challenges.
- **Resource Management** Meeting the needs of a vast population strains natural resources. From water scarcity to land-use conflicts, managing resources sustainably requires innovative strategies that balance development with environmental preservation.

Solutions

- **Investing in Education** Prioritising education is fundamental to addressing many challenges. Investments in schools, vocational training, and higher education can equip the burgeoning youth population with the skills needed for gainful employment.
- **Healthcare Reforms** Strengthening healthcare infrastructure and implementing comprehensive health programmes are essential. A focus on preventive healthcare, maternal and child health and disease management can ensure a healthier population.
- **Employment Generation** Promoting entrepreneurship, fostering a conducive business environment and investing in sectors with high employment potential are vital for absorbing the growing labour force into gainful employment.
- **Smart Urban Planning** As urbanisation is inevitable, adopting smart urban planning strategies that prioritise sustainability, efficient public transportation and green spaces can enhance the quality of life in cities.
- **Population Awareness** Encouraging family planning through awareness campaigns, ensuring accessibility to contraceptives and addressing socio-cultural factors influencing family size are crucial steps toward stabilising population growth.
- **Technology Integration** Leveraging technology for education, healthcare delivery and resource management can significantly enhance efficiency and effectiveness in addressing demographic challenges.

Conclusion

To conclude, India's demographic scenario encapsulates a paradox – the potential for a dynamic, youthful workforce coexists with the challenges of resource strain and socio-economic disparities. The path forward demands a comprehensive and multi-dimensional approach that integrates education, healthcare, employment and sustainable development. As India strives to harness its demographic dividend, strategic policymaking, innovative solutions and a collaborative effort from all stakeholders will be instrumental in steering the nation towards a future where its population becomes a driving force for inclusive growth rather than a constraint.

Balancing the demographic equation is not merely a national imperative; it is a global responsibility, as India's trajectory will significantly influence the world's socio-economic landscape. In navigating these demographic waters, India has the potential to transform its challenges into opportunities and emerge as a demographic powerhouse that propels itself and the world toward sustainable and equitable development.

64. Role of Media in Bringing Change

Media, in its diverse forms, has emerged as a potent force capable of shaping public opinion, influencing policy and sparking societal transformations.

Thus, media plays a multifaceted role as a harbinger of change, weaving together the threads of information dissemination, advocacy and public discourse. The various ways through which it brings change are

- **Awareness as the Precursor to Change** Media acts as a primary conduit for disseminating information to the masses. From print journalism to digital platforms, it plays a pivotal role in creating awareness about societal issues, thereby setting the stage for change. The widespread coverage of pressing problems, such as climate change, social inequality, or health crises, serves as a catalyst for public consciousness and engagement.
- **Exposing Injustices and Fostering Accountability** Investigative journalism, a cornerstone of media, unveils hidden truths and exposes societal injustices. Instances of corruption, human rights violations or political malfeasance are brought to light, fostering a sense of accountability.
  The #MeToo Movement, driven by media revelations, exemplifies how exposing systemic issues can spark a collective call for change.
- **Amplifying Marginalised Voices** Media provides a platform for marginalised voices, enabling them to reach a wider audience. Through documentaries, articles and interviews, it amplifies narratives that might otherwise be overshadowed. The coverage of movements like Black Lives Matter exemplifies how media can be a megaphone for those seeking justice and equality.
- **Promoting Social Causes and Philanthropy** The influence of media extends to philanthropy and social causes. Campaigns, telethons and awareness drives organised and promoted by media outlets contribute significantly to fundraising efforts.
  The extensive coverage of humanitarian crises, both at the local and global levels, galvanises public support and donations.
- **Shaping Public Opinion** Media plays a crucial role in shaping public opinion by providing diverse perspectives and analyses. Op-eds, debates and expert panels contribute to a vibrant public discourse, allowing citizens to form informed opinions. The role of media in influencing public sentiment during elections or policy debates is particularly pronounced.
- **Navigating the Digital Age** In the era of social media, the influence of media has become more nuanced. Platforms like Twitter, Facebook and YouTube serve as arenas for real-time discussions and debates. However, the digital landscape also poses challenges, including misinformation and echo chambers, emphasising the need for media literacy to navigate the complex web of information.

Media's Role in Social Movements

- **The Arab Spring and Beyond** The Arab Spring, fuelled in part by social media, demonstrated the transformative potential of media in mobilising masses for political change. The instantaneous spread of information and images catalysed movements across borders, illustrating the interconnectedness facilitated by digital media.
- **Environmental Activism and Climate Change Awareness** Media has played a pivotal role in environmental advocacy, raising awareness about climate change and its consequences. Through documentaries, news coverage, and campaigns, it has contributed to the global dialogue on sustainability and the urgent need for environmental action.

Challenges and the Way Forward

- **Combatting Disinformation** The rise of fake news and disinformation poses a significant challenge. Media organisations, alongside technological interventions, must prioritise fact-checking and accuracy to maintain credibility.
- **Ensuring Diversity and Inclusivity** Media must strive for diversity in representation, both in its workforce and the stories it tells. Inclusivity ensures that a wide array of perspectives is presented, fostering a more comprehensive understanding of societal issues.

Conclusion

As an unparalleled force shaping narratives and catalysing change, media stands at the forefront of societal evolution. Its influence extends from creating awareness to mobilising movements, from exposing injustices to shaping public opinion. However, this power comes with responsibilities—combatting disinformation, ensuring inclusivity and adapting to the challenges of the digital age. In navigating these complexities, media emerges not only as an observer but as an active participant in the unfolding story of societal transformation. The continuous evolution of media's role underscores its potential to be a driving force for positive change in the quest for a more informed, just and equitable world.

65. India's Decade of Transformation

Over the last decade, India has witnessed a profound transformation across various sectors, driven by ambitious government initiatives, strategic policies and a commitment to inclusive development. The key areas of transformation as reported by data and government sources are

- **Economic Growth and Reforms** The Indian economy has experienced significant growth and reforms in the last decade. According to the Ministry of Statistics and Programme Implementation, India's GDP grew at an average rate of around 7% per annum during this period. The introduction of transformative measures like the Goods and Services Tax (GST) and the Insolvency and Bankruptcy Code (IBC) has streamlined economic processes, fostering transparency and ease of doing business.
- **Financial Inclusion and Digital India** The Pradhan Mantri Jan Dhan Yojana (PMJDY) has played a pivotal role in promoting financial inclusion. As per official data, over 43 crore bank accounts have been opened under PMJDY, providing access to formal banking services for the previously unbanked. Simultaneously, the Digital India initiative has accelerated the adoption of digital technologies, with a substantial increase in internet penetration and online transactions. India's digital payments landscape has seen an unprecedented surge, with UPI emerging as a global leader. The Bharat Interface for Money (BHIM-UPI), IMPS and other digital payment methods have facilitated a shift towards a cashless economy. The seamless integration of digital payments is reflected in India's leadership, accounting for 46% of global real-time payments in 2022.
- **Swachh Bharat Mission** Launched in 2014, the Swachh Bharat Mission aimed to achieve open-defecation-free (ODF) status and ensure cleanliness and sanitation. Government data indicates that over 10 crore toilets have been constructed, leading to the declaration of rural India as ODF. This initiative has not only improved public health but also enhanced the quality of life for millions.
- **Healthcare Reforms** The Ayushman Bharat – Pradhan Mantri Jan Arogya Yojana (PMJAY) has been a transformative step in ensuring healthcare accessibility. With over 2.5 crore beneficiaries and the provision of financial protection against catastrophic health expenses, PMJAY has made significant strides in universal health coverage.
- **Renewable Energy and Climate Action** India's commitment to sustainable development is evident in the progress made in renewable energy. According to the Ministry of New and Renewable Energy, India's renewable energy capacity has more than doubled in the last decade, reaching a commendable 150 GW. Initiatives like the International Solar Alliance (ISA) further underline India's role in global climate action.
- **Skill Development and Employment** Skill India Mission has been instrumental in addressing the skills gap and enhancing employability. The Ministry of Skill Development and Entrepreneurship reports that over 5 crore people have been trained under various skill development programmes, aligning the workforce with evolving industry demands.
- **Infrastructure Development** Massive strides have been made in infrastructure development, encompassing areas such as roads, railways, and urban amenities. Government data reveals a substantial increase in the length of national highways, improved rail connectivity, and the implementation of flagship programs like the Smart Cities Mission.
- **Education Initiatives** The last decade has witnessed a focus on quality education through initiatives like the Samagra Shiksha Abhiyan. Government statistics indicate an increase in school infrastructure, teacher training and efforts towards ensuring equitable access to education.
- **Rural Development Initiatives** Recognising the importance of uplifting rural communities, the government has implemented schemes to address the unique challenges faced by those residing in remote areas. One such initiative is the Pradhan Mantri Gram Sadak Yojana (PMGSY), aimed at enhancing rural connectivity through the construction of all-weather roads. Additionally, the Mahatma Gandhi National Rural Employment Guarantee Act (MGNREGA) has played a crucial role in providing livelihood opportunities to rural households.

  This flagship program has not only ensured financial inclusion but also contributed to sustainable development by focusing on asset creation and environmental conservation. The integration of rural electrification schemes, such as the Deen Dayal Upadhyaya Gram Jyoti Yojana (DDUGJY), has brought about a transformative change in the lives of those residing in remote areas. Access to electricity has not only improved the standard of living but has also opened up new avenues for economic activities, education and healthcare.

Conclusion

In conclusion, India's transformation over the last decade is a testament to the government's commitment to holistic development. As India continues its journey towards becoming a global economic powerhouse, these transformative efforts serve as a foundation for sustained and inclusive growth.

66. India : A Digital Nomad's Oasis – Unveiling Hidden Horizons

The COVID-19 pandemic reshaped our approach to work, giving rise to a surge in digital nomadism- a lifestyle where one leverages remote work to travel and live in varying, often affordable locations around the world. While traditional nomadic havens like Bali, Mexico, Indonesia and Lisbon have long been established, India, an unconventional contender, is emerging as a potential hub. With hidden gems like Goa, Himachal, Kerala, Darjeeling, and Udaipur gaining traction, India presents a unique blend of rich culture, diverse landscapes and a burgeoning tech ecosystem, making it a compelling destination for digital nomads.

India's Unique Appeal for Digital Nomads

Despite its vast landscapes, a thriving urban working population and a relatively strong passport, India struggles with limited awareness among potential foreign and domestic digital nomads.

The nation, however, boasts of unparalleled offerings

- **Cultural Diversity** India's rich cultural tapestry, manifested in places like Goa, Himachal and Kerala, provides a unique experience for digital nomads seeking inspiration and cultural immersion.
- **Affordability** The cost of living in India is significantly lower than in many Western countries, offering a high standard of living without financial strain, making it an attractive proposition for digital nomads.
- **Thriving Tech Ecosystem** Cities like Bangalore and Hyderabad serve as global IT hubs, providing digital nomads access to cutting-edge technology and a robust digital infrastructure.
- **Co-living and Co-working Facilities** The rise of co-living and co-working spaces across metropolitan cities cater to the specific needs of digital nomads, fostering networking and collaboration among like-minded individuals.
- **Culinary Diversity** India's culinary diversity, from street food to gourmet cuisine, adds a unique dimension to the overall experience of digital nomads.

Challenges and Opportunities

While India holds immense potential, challenges such as bureaucratic hurdles and infrastructural gaps need addressing. Collaborative efforts between the government and private sectors can streamline processes and enhance the appeal of India as a digital nomad hub. Other challenges include biases regarding sanitation practices, language barriers, and food habits.

However, the nation is on the verge of a revolution. India's growing gig economy and the rise of startups indicate a shift towards remote work, creating opportunities for digital nomads. India offers a perfect blend of heritage exploration, improved connectivity, favourable currency exchange rates and climatic diversity, providing an enriching experience for digital nomads. The expanding infrastructure and the ongoing internet revolution in India contribute to creating an environment conducive to remote work.

As India continues to navigate these challenges and capitalise on opportunities, the unfolding narrative represents the nation's commitment to embracing digital nomadism. With the allure of heritage, affordability and technological advancement, India stands at the crossroads of redefining itself as a haven for the modern-day nomad.

67. India's Pioneering Role in COP28

India's robust engagement in COP28 showcased visionary initiatives and proactive measures, illustrating the nation's commitment to combatting climate change. India's Initiatives at COP28 include the Green Credit Initiative and Leadership Group for Industry Transition (LeadIT 2.0), promoting sustainable practices. The Global River Cities Alliance (GRCA) emphasised river-centric development and the Quad Climate Working Group (QCWG) focused on localised climate action.

The COP28 promised many positive outcomes which are as follows

- **Comprehensive Stocktake and Loss and Damage Fund** The global stocktake mandated countries to submit heightened emission reduction targets by mid-2025 for COP30, ensuring continual reassessment. The operationalisation of the Loss and Damage Fund ensures climate justice for vulnerable countries, addressing the urgent need for support.
- **Fossil Fuels and Phase-Down of Coal** COP28 formally acknowledged fossil fuels' role in global warming and called for a phase-down of coal. This signifies a global commitment to transition away from high-emission energy sources, paving the way for cleaner alternatives.
- **Focus on Renewable Energy and Adaptation** The Global Renewables and Energy Efficiency Pledge adopted at COP28 aims to reduce emissions by about 7 billion tonnes by 2030. COP28 emphasised common adaptation goals crucial for the world, reflecting a global perspective on adapting to climate change challenges.
- **Call for Enhanced Climate Finance and Diverse Participation** COP28 underscored the need for enhanced climate finance, emphasising the responsibility of developed nations. Diverse participation from various groups enhanced transparency in climate change negotiations.

COP28 introduced new goals and pledges, but substantial follow-up actions are crucial. The way to achieve the target involves

- **Introduction of New Indicators** Identifying new tangible indicators is crucial to measure progress on each global goal. Clear assessment indicators will gauge the effectiveness of implemented measures.
- **Establishment of Financial Mechanism** A robust financial mechanism must be promptly established to meet the estimated $500 billion requirement. Developed nations should adhere to financial obligations, ensuring equitable support to developing countries.
- **Binding Commitments and Clarity on Phase Down of Fossil Fuel** Intensified efforts should make renewable energy pledges binding on all member countries. Additionally, future COPs should prioritise establishing clarity on the timeline and targets for the phase-down of fossil fuels, which is pivotal for global adherence to sustainable energy practices.

- **Upholding Common but Differentiated Responsibility (CBDR)** The guiding principle of Common but Differentiated Responsibility (CBDR) must continue to be the cornerstone in upcoming climate negotiations. Acknowledging varied responsibilities ensures a fair and just approach to climate action.

Conclusion

India's comprehensive efforts at COP28 and the positive outcomes underscore the need for continued collaboration and decisive actions to address climate change. The path forward necessitates vigilance, commitment, and collective responsibility to shape a sustainable and resilient future for the global community. This holistic approach ensures that India, along with the global community, remains at the forefront of sustainable climate action.

68. India's Agricultural Transformation: Navigating Towards Evergreen Revolution

India's agricultural landscape stands at a critical juncture, demanding transformative measures to ensure sustainable productivity and the well-being of farmers. The concept of an 'Evergreen Revolution,' coined by Dr. MS Swaminathan, encapsulates a strategic approach to enhance output and productivity while ensuring long-term environmental sustainability.

Evergreen Revolution: Objectives and Components

The primary objectives of the Evergreen Revolution revolve around employing high-yield variety seeds, leveraging informational and communication technology (ICT) to enhance food productivity, doubling farmer incomes and maintaining environmental sustainability. Components such as improving soil health, utilising high-yielding seeds, implementing lab-to-land demonstrations and embracing rainwater harvesting play a pivotal role in achieving these objectives.

Challenges of the Past : Green Revolution and its Limitations

The Green Revolution, initiated in 1965, marked a significant chapter in India's agricultural history. Led by Dr. M.S. Swaminathan, it aimed to boost productivity through modern tools and techniques. However, the Green Revolution had its drawbacks, such as soil fertility loss, overuse of water leading to salinisation and a shift towards cereal-centric agriculture. The need for an Evergreen Revolution emerged as a response to the failures and shortcomings of its predecessor.

Evergreen Revolution and Food Security

As the global population grows, the urgency to increase food grain output becomes paramount. The Evergreen Revolution addresses this challenge by emphasising environmentally sustainable productivity growth. It aims to ensure a consistent increase in grain production, making food more accessible and affordable, thereby enhancing food security.

Evergreen Revolution and Nutrition Security

Beyond food security, the Evergreen Revolution recognises the multidimensional aspects of nutrition security. It emphasises a holistic approach, integrating agriculture, nutrition and health. Initiatives such as community hunger fighters and biofortified plant gardens are envisioned to combat malnutrition and ensure a balanced diet for all.

NITI Aayog's Roadmap for Evergreen Revolution

Recognising the urgency for agricultural reform, the NITI Aayog has outlined a three-year strategy to elevate farmer income and propel Indian agriculture to new heights. This roadmap emphasises increased food crop production, utilisation of wasteland, model contract farming, adoption of advanced technologies, promotion of deep-sea fishing, and cropping intensity enhancement through rice fallow areas.

Government Initiatives : Towards Sustainable Agriculture

Several government initiatives contribute to the vision of an Evergreen Revolution, like-

- **Pradhan Mantri Fasal Bima Yojana** (PMFBY) Provides risk coverage and financial support to farmers in case of crop failure, encouraging them to adopt modern agricultural practices.
- **Paramparagat Krishi Vikas Yojana** (PKVY) Promotes organic farming and sustainable practices, aligning with the principles of the Evergreen Revolution.
- **National Mission for Sustainable Agriculture** (NMSA) Focuses on sustainable practices, soil health management, and resource conservation to ensure long-term environmental sustainability.
- **National Agriculture Market** (e-NAM) A digital platform connecting agricultural produce markets, fostering transparency and efficient trading.
- **Agriculture Accelerator Fund** The Agriculture Accelerator Fund will be set up to encourage agri-startups by young entrepreneurs in rural areas, which will aim at bringing innovative and affordable solutions for challenges faced by farmers. It will also bring in modern technologies to transform agricultural practices, and increase productivity and profitability.
- **Atmanirbhar Horticulture Clean Plant Programme** The Government will launch an Atmanirbhar Clean Plant Programme to boost the availability of disease-free, quality planting material for high-value horticultural crops.

Conclusion

The integration of modern technologies, sustainable practices and farmer-centric policies is essential for realising this vision. As India charts its course towards a sustainable and prosperous agricultural future, the Evergreen Revolution becomes not just a strategy but a guiding philosophy for a resilient and harmonious coexistence with nature.

Previous Years' QUESTIONS

Directions (Q. Nos. 1-60) *Write essays on the following topics in about 300 words each.*

1. Digital Economy : Opportunities and Challenges

CAPF AC 2024

Our lives, works have been transformed by 21st century digital economy, driven by the rapid advancement of information and communication technologies. Digital Economy is a type of economic activity that results from billions of everyday online connections among people, business, devices, data and processes. It circumscribes a wide range of economic activities that utilise digital technologies as well as e-commerce, digital marketing, online banking, etc. This changeabout presents numerous opportunities and challenges.

Opportunities

Modernisation and Growth New business models and services are advanced and enabled by this great emergence of digital economy. Startups and small business have got an opportunity to compete globally with minimal investment, promoting new job creation and a comprehensive economic goal.

New Business Models Many innovative business models such as e-commerce, gig economy platforms, etc. have been raised by the advancement of digital economy and these models enable business and market places to compete a global audience with minimal overhead costs.

Upgraded Customers Experience Digital economy is the key source of higher customers satisfaction and loyalty. Through this businesses can leverage data to understand customer preferences and tailor their offerings accordingly.

Efficacy and Productivity Digital tools have simplified business operations by reducing costs and enhancing productivity.

Access to Global Markets Digital Economy is the greatest platforms mainly for the SMEs (Small and Medium Enterprises) as now those are able to compete on a global scale. Digital platforms breakdown geographical barriers, allowing to reach a global audience indeed. And this access to international markets significantly boosts sales and revenues and per capita income of a country's economy.

Challenges

IPR (Intellectual Property Rights) It is a complication of digital economy for the enforcement of Intellectual Property Rights. Sometimes, it becomes the reason of revenue losses for the creators as it becomes challenging to protect IPR as there is a lot of way for the ease of copying and distributing digital contents.

Management Challenges Often the policy makers and the government face challenges, in creating rules and regulations that balance innovation with consumers protection and fair competition.

Employment Displacement Inspite of creating an opportunity for new job creation, this also leads to job displacement of traditional sectors. Automation and digitalisation are the main reasons for job obsolete of skilled workforce.

Data Privacy and Security Since this new technological fit heavily relies on data, it is the matter of concern for data security and privacy. Cyber Security threat data breaches, personal information mis-management are the common risks in this economy to individuals as well as business.

Though digital economy presents a wealth of opportunities for innovation, efficiency and global connectivity, it is also challenge that needs to be advanced and addressed to ensure comprehensive and sustainable growth.

1. डिजिटल अर्थव्यवस्था: अवसर और चुनौतियाँ

CAPF AC 2024

21वीं सदी की डिजिटल अर्थव्यवस्था ने हमारे जीवन और कार्यप्रणाली में परिवर्तन कर दिया है, जो सूचना और संचार प्रौद्योगिकियों के तेजी से हुए विकास का परिणाम है। डिजिटल अर्थव्यवस्था एक प्रकार की आर्थिक गतिविधि है, जो लोगों, व्यवसाय, उपकरणों, डेटा और प्रक्रियाओं के बीच रोज़ाना अरबों ऑनलाइन कनेक्शनों से उत्पन्न होती है। यह आर्थिक गतिविधियों की एक विस्तृत, श्रृंखला को सीमित करती है, जो डिजिटल तकनीकों के साथ-साथ ई-कॉमर्स, डिजिटल मार्केटिंग, ऑनलाइन बैंकिंग आदि का उपयोग करती हैं। यह परिवर्तन कई अवसर और चुनौतियाँ प्रस्तुत करता है।

अवसर

आधुनिकीकरण और विकास डिजिटल अर्थव्यवस्था के इस उदभव से नए व्यवसाय मॉडल और सेवाएँ उन्नत और सक्षम हुई हैं। स्टार्टअप और छोटे व्यवसाय को न्यूनतम निवेश के साथ वैश्विक स्तर पर प्रतिस्पर्द्धा करने का अवसर मिला है, जिससे नए रोजगार सृजन और व्यापक आर्थिक लक्ष्य को बढ़ावा मिला है।

नए व्यवसाय मॉडल डिजिटल अर्थव्यवस्था की उन्नति से ई-कॉमर्स, गिग इकॉनमी प्लेटफॉर्म जैसे कई नए व्यवसाय मॉडल उभरे हैं। ये मॉडल व्यवसाय और बाज़ारों को न्यूनतम ऊपरी लागत के साथ वैश्विक दर्शकों के साथ प्रतिस्पर्द्धा करने में सक्षम बनाते हैं।

उन्नत ग्राहक अनुभव डिजिटल अर्थव्यवस्था उच्च ग्राहक सन्तुष्टि और निष्ठता का मुख्य स्रोत है, क्योंकि इसके माध्यम से व्यवसायी ग्राहक की वरीयताओं को समझने और उनके अनुसार अपनी पेशकशों को तैयार करने के लिए डेटा का लाभ उठा सकते हैं।

प्रभावकारिता और उत्पादकता डिजिटल उपकरणों ने लागत कम करके तथा उत्पादकता बढ़ाकर व्यवसाय संचालन को सरल बना दिया है।

वैश्विक बाजारों तक पहुँच डिजिटल अर्थव्यवस्था मुख्य रूप से एसएमई (लघु और मध्यम उद्यम) के लिए सबसे बड़ा मंच है, क्योंकि अब वे वैश्विक स्तर पर प्रतिस्पर्द्धा करने में सक्षम हैं। डिजिटल प्लेटफॉर्म भौगोलिक बाधाओं को तोड़ते हैं, जिससे वास्तव में वैश्विक दर्शकों तक पहुँचना सम्भव हो जाता है। और अन्तरष्ट्रीय बाजारों तक यह पहुँच किसी

देश की अर्थव्यवस्था की बिक्री और राजस्व तथा प्रति व्यक्ति आय को महत्त्वपूर्ण रूप से बढ़ाती है।

चुनौतियाँ

आईपीआर (बौद्धिक सम्पदा अधिकार) बौद्धिक सम्पदा अधिकारों का प्रवर्तन डिजिटल अर्थव्यवस्था की एक जटिलता है। कभी-कभी यह रचनाकारों के लिए राजस्व हानि का कारण बन जाता है, क्योंकि आईपीआर की रक्षा करना चुनौतीपूर्ण हो जाता है तथा डिजिटल सामग्री की प्रतिलिपि बनाने और वितरित करने में प्रायः आसानी के लिए कई प्रकार हैं।

प्रबन्धन चुनौतियाँ प्रायः नीति निर्माताओं और सरकार को ऐसे नियम और विनियम बनाने में चुनौतियों का सामना करना पड़ता है, जो नवाचार को उपभोक्ता संरक्षण और निष्पक्ष प्रतिस्पर्द्धा के साथ सन्तुलित करते हैं।

रोज़गार विस्थापन नए रोज़गार सृजन के अवसर पैदा करने के बावजूद भी इससे पारम्परिक क्षेत्रों में रोज़गार विस्थापन भी होता है। स्वचालन और डिजिटलीकरण कुशल कार्यबल की नौकरी के अप्रचलन का मुख्य कारण हैं।

डेटा गोपनीयता और सुरक्षा चूँकि यह नई तकनीकी डेटा पर बहुत अधिक निर्भर करती है, इसलिए यह डेटा सुरक्षा और गोपनीयता के लिए चिंता का विषय है।

साइबर सुरक्षा खतरा, डेटा उल्लंघन, व्यक्तिगत जानकारी का गलत प्रबन्धन इस अर्थव्यवस्था में व्यक्तियों के साथ-साथ व्यवसाय के लिए सामान्य जोखिम हैं।

हालाँकि डिजिटल अर्थव्यवस्था नवाचार, दक्षता और वैश्विक कनेक्टिविटी के लिए अवसरों का खजाना प्रस्तुत करती है, लेकिन यह एक चुनौती भी है, जिसे व्यापक और टिकाऊ विकास सुनिश्चित करने के लिए आगे बढ़ाने और सम्बोधित करने की आवश्यकता है।

2. Global Peace and National Defence Budget

CAPF AC 2024

Global peace and national security are inter-linked with defence budget that often plays a pivotal role in shaping the equilibrium. The reality of geopolitical tensions and security concerns necessitates important investment in national defence while, the hope for a peaceful world remains an universal goal. We may explore how defence budget or military expenditure impact international relations, national security in pursuit of global peace.

Enhancement of Military Expenditure

In 2023, global military expenditure reached a remarkable 2.44 trillion, making it nine consecutive growth years and this is the reason for heightened tensions, conflict and security concern worldwide.

In Indian context, we notice the Finance Minister announced an allocation of ₹ 6,21,541 crore for the Ministry of Defence and this marks a 4.3% increase from the previous year and constituting 13.04% of the Union Budget. This significant increasement in Defence Budget in India underscores its commitment to bolstering defence capabilities amidst growing security challenges.

Top Military Spenders : United States

US rank first in military expenditure with a budget of 916 billion, accounting for 37% of global military expenditure.

China that allocates 296 billion, accounting for 12% of global spending.

Russia 109 billion, accounting for 4.5% of global spending.

India India's defence budget is 3.4% global spending with 83.6 billion.

The Quest of Global Peace

Global peace is a state where the nations exists synchronically, resolving conflicts through diplomacy and cooperation rather than violence. To attain global peace, the processes are multifaceted with an involvement of organisation like UN (United Nations), treatise and several grassroots movements.

UN was established in 1945 and it plays a vital role in promoting peace through peace-keeping missions, conflict resolution through diplomacy and sustainable development goal.

Though historical animosities, territorial (disputes and ideological differences) often lead to conflicts. Additionally the proliferation of weapons, including nuclear arms, poses a significant threat to global stability.

The Role of National Defence Budget

This Budget actually funds the Military, Intelligent Agencies and other security related activities that are absolutely critical for ensuring countries's security and sovereignty. The primary objective for maintaining a substantial Defence Budget is to deter potential threats, protect national interests and ensuring the safety of the citizens. The challenges emerge while, balancing the pursuit of global peace with necessity of maintaining a robust national defence. Sometimes, Excessive Defence Budget divert resources from essential social services such as healthcare, education and infrastructure.

Though the target for achieving a peaceful world remains a noble goal, the real security threats necessitates substantial investment in national defence.

2. वैश्विक शान्ति और राष्ट्रीय रक्षा बजट

CAPF AC 2024

वैश्विक शान्ति और राष्ट्रीय सुरक्षा रक्षा बजट से जुड़ी हुई है, जो प्रायः सन्तुलन को आकार देने में महत्त्वपूर्ण भूमिका निभाती है। भू-राजनीतिक तनाव और सुरक्षा चिन्ताओं की वास्तविकता राष्ट्रीय रक्षा में महत्त्वपूर्ण निवेश की आवश्यकता है, जबकि शान्तिपूर्ण विश्व की आशा एक सार्वभौमिक लक्ष्य बनी हुई है। हम यह पता लगा सकते हैं कि रक्षा बजट या सैन्य व्यय वैश्विक शान्ति की खोज में अन्तर्राष्ट्रीय सम्बन्धों, राष्ट्रीय सुरक्षा को कैसे प्रभावित करते हैं।

सैन्य व्यय में वृद्धि

वर्ष 2023 में वैश्विक सैन्य व्यय 2.44 ट्रिलियन तक पहुँच गया, जिससे यह लगातार नौवाँ वृद्धि वर्ष बन गया तथा यह विश्व में तनाव, संघर्ष और सुरक्षा चिन्ता का कारण है।

भारतीय सन्दर्भ में हम देखते हैं कि वित्त मन्त्री ने रक्षा मन्त्रालय के लिए ₹ 6,21,541 करोड़ के आवण्टन की घोषणा की और यह पिछले वर्ष की तुलना में 4.3% की वृद्धि दर्शाता है और यह केन्द्रीय बजट का 13.04% है। भारत में रक्षा बजट में यह उल्लेखनीय वृद्धि बढ़ती सुरक्षा चुनौतियों के बीच रक्षा क्षमताओं को मजबूत करने की इसकी प्रतिबद्धता को रेखांकित करती है।

सर्वोच्च सैन्य व्ययकर्ताः संयुक्त राज्य अमेरिका

अमेरिका 916 बिलियन डॉलर के बजट के साथ सैन्य व्यय में पहले स्थान पर है, जो वैश्विक सैन्य व्यय का 37% है।

चीन 296 बिलियन डॉलर आवण्टित करता है, जो वैश्विक व्यय का 12 है।

रूस 109 बिलियन डॉलर आवण्टित करता है, जो वैश्विक व्यय का 4.5% है।

भारत का रक्षा बजट 83.6 बिलियन डॉलर के साथ वैश्विक व्यय का 3.4% है।

वैश्विक शान्ति की खोज

वैश्विक शान्ति एक ऐसी स्थिति है, जहाँ राष्ट्र एक साथ रहते हैं तथा हिंसा के बजाय कूटनीति और सहयोग के माध्यम से संघर्षों को हल करते हैं। वैश्विक शान्ति प्राप्त करने के लिए प्रक्रिया, संयुक्त राष्ट्र जैसे संगठन, सन्धि और कई जमीनी स्तर के आन्दोलनों की भागीदारी के साथ बहुआयामी है। संयुक्त राष्ट्र की स्थापना वर्ष 1945 में हुई थी और यह शान्ति-रक्षा मिशनों, कूटनीति के माध्यम से संघर्ष समाधान और सतत विकास लक्ष्य के माध्यम से शान्ति को बढ़ावा देने में महत्त्वपूर्ण भूमिका निभाता है। हालाँकि ऐतिहासिक शत्रुता, क्षेत्रीय विवाद और वैचारिक मतभेद अक्सर संघर्षों का कारण बनते हैं। इसके अतिरिक्त परमाणु हथियारों सहित हथियारों का प्रसार वैश्विक स्थिरता के लिए एक महत्त्वपूर्ण खतरा है।

राष्ट्रीय रक्षा बजट की भूमिका

यह बजट वास्तव में सैन्य, खुफिया एजेन्सियों और अन्य सुरक्षा सम्बन्धी गतिविधियों को निधि देता है, जो किसी देश की सुरक्षा और सम्प्रभुता सुनिश्चित करने के लिए महत्त्वपूर्ण हैं। पर्याप्त रक्षा बजट बनाए रखने का प्राथमिक उद्देश्य सम्भावित खतरों को रोकना, राष्ट्रीय हितों की रक्षा करना और नागरिकों की सुरक्षा सुनिश्चित करना है। वैश्विक शान्ति की खोज को एक मजबूत राष्ट्रीय रक्षा बनाए रखने की आवश्यकता के साथ सन्तुलित करते समय चुनौतियाँ सामने आती हैं। कभी-कभी अत्यधिक रक्षा बजट स्वास्थ्य सेवा, शिक्षा और बुनियादी ढाँचे जैसी आवश्यक सामाजिक सेवाओं से संसाधनों को हटा देता है।

हालाँकि एक शान्तिपूर्ण विश्व को प्राप्त करने का लक्ष्य एक महान लक्ष्य बना हुआ है, वास्तविक सुरक्षा खतरों के लिए राष्ट्रीय रक्षा में पर्याप्त निवेश की आवश्यकता है।

3. Tribal Resistance to Colonial Rule CAPF AC 2024

Tribal communities faced a significant challenge worldwide during the colonial era. Indigenous people met with significant challenges like grapling with new policies, land dispossession, economic exploitation and cultural merginalisation when foreign power started emerging.

Impact of Colonial Rule on Tribal Communities

Policies and diplomacies of colonialist have a profound impact on tribal communities. Their traditional land rights got disrupted by British administration and the officials imposed high land tax which affected their land revenue system badly in Indian context.

In India, the introduction of several foreign laws and exploitation by money lenders and traders is often seen as agents of the colonial government, further infuriated their plight.

Resistance

Tribals started resisting in several ways. Somewhere by armed uprising, somewhere by non-violent movements. They consistently protested for their rights.

Frontier Tribal Revolts

Khasi Rebellion and Naga Resistance The Khasi tribes in (1829-1833) protested against British administration by protesting them from building a road through their territory, which they saw as an encroachment of their territory and autonomy. They usually belonged to Meghalaya.

The Naga tribes of North-Eastern frontier revolted against British through Guerrilla warfare and maintained their independence for a significant period.

Santhal Rebellion (1855-1856) This Rebellion, led by Sidhu and Kanhu was one of the most significant uprisings during colonial era. It was a protest against the oppressive policies of the British and the exploitation by money lenders and landlords and the great Sepoy Mutiny of 1857 was greatly influenced by this Santhal Rebellion that time.

Characteristics of Tribal Resistance

Diplomacy and Legal Procedure Some communities tried to preserve their rights through diplomatic challenges and way of means they sorted legal channels to protect their rights and seek justice. But these communities were very minimal in number.

Preservation of Culture Tribal community's efforts to safeguard their cultural heritage, language and traditional practices was a form of resistance against colonial assimilation.

Leadership The colonial era witnessed some great heroes like Birsa Munda. Sidhu, Kanhu who emerged as messiah like figures who promised to end the suffering brought about by colonial rule.

It was a significant chapter in India's struggle for independence and was also a testament to the invincible spirit of the tribal communities who fought for their land, culture and way of life against all odds. Due to limited legacy and lack of superior military, they became unable to sustain the revolts. But their resistance challenged hegemony of British authority as well as it laid the groundwork for future movements advocating for tribal rights and developments.

3. औपनिवेशिक शासन के प्रति जनजातीय प्रतिरोध CAPF AC 2024

औपनिवेशिक काल में जनजातीय समुदायों को एक महत्त्वपूर्ण चुनौती का सामना करना पड़ा। जब विदेशी सत्ता उभरने लगी, तो स्वदेशी लोगों को नई नीतियों, भूमि अधिग्रहण, आर्थिक शोषण, सांस्कृतिक विलयन जैसी महत्त्वपूर्ण चुनौतियों का सामना करना पड़ा।

आदिवासी समुदायों पर औपनिवेशिक शासन का प्रभाव

उपनिवेशवादियों की नीतियों और कूटनीतियों का जनजातीय समुदायों पर गहरा प्रभाव पड़ा। ब्रिटिश प्रशासन द्वारा उनके पारम्परिक भूमि अधिकारों को बाधित किया गया और अधिकारियों ने उच्च भूमि कर लगाया, जिसने भारतीय सन्दर्भ में उनकी भूमि राजस्व प्रणाली को बुरी तरह प्रभावित किया। भारत में कई विदेशी कानूनों की शुरुआत और महाजनों व व्यापारियों द्वारा शोषण, जिन्हें प्रायः औपनिवेशिक सरकार के एजेण्ट के रूप में देखा गया, ने उनकी दुर्दशा को और बढ़ा दिया।

प्रतिरोध

आदिवासियों ने कई तरीकों से प्रतिरोध करना शुरू कर दिया। कहीं सशस्त्र विद्रोह से, कहीं अहिंसक आन्दोलनों से।

सीमान्त जनजातीय विद्रोह

खासी विद्रोह और नागा प्रतिरोध खासी जनजातियों ने 1829-1833 ई. में ब्रिटिश प्रशासन के खिलाफ विरोध प्रदर्शन किया, उन्हें अपने क्षेत्र से होकर सड़क बनाने से रोका, जिसे वे अपने क्षेत्र और स्वायत्तता पर अतिक्रमण के रूप में देखते थे। वे मुख्यतः मेघालय के थे।

उत्तर-पूर्वी सीमान्त की नागा जनजातियों ने गुरिल्ला युद्ध के माध्यम से अंग्रेजों के खिलाफ विद्रोह किया और एक महत्त्वपूर्ण अवधि के लिए अपनी स्वतन्त्रता बनाए रखी।

संथाल विद्रोह (1855-1856) सिद्धू और कान्हू के नेतृत्व में संथाल विद्रोह औपनिवेशिक युग के दौरान सबसे महत्त्वपूर्ण विद्रोहों में से एक था। यह विद्रोह अंग्रेजों की दमनकारी नीतियों और साहूकारों व जमींदारों द्वारा शोषण के खिलाफ था। 1857 का महान सिपाही विद्रोह संथाल विद्रोह से काफी प्रभावित था।

जनजातीय प्रतिरोध की विशेषताएँ

कूटनीति और कानूनी प्रक्रिया कुछ समुदायों ने कूटनीतिक चुनौतियों और साधनों के माध्यम से अपने अधिकारों को संरक्षित करने का प्रयास किया, उन्होंने अपने अधिकारों की रक्षा और न्याय पाने के लिए कानून की सहायता ली, परन्तु इन समुदायों की संख्या बहुत कम थी।

संस्कृति का संरक्षण आदिवासी समुदाय द्वारा अपनी सांस्कृतिक विरासत, भाषा और पारम्परिक प्रथाओं की रक्षा करने का प्रयास औपनिवेशिक आत्मसात के खिलाफ प्रतिरोध का एक रूप था।

नेतृत्व औपनिवेशिक युग में बिरसा मुण्डा, कान्हू जैसे कुछ महान नायक हुए, जिन्होंने औपनिवेशिक शासन द्वारा लाई गई पीड़ा को समाप्त करने में महत्त्वपूर्ण भूमिका निभाई।

यह भारत के स्वतन्त्रता संग्राम में एक महत्त्वपूर्ण अध्याय था और यह आदिवासी समुदायों की अजेय भावना का भी प्रमाण था, जिन्होंने सभी बाधाओं के खिलाफ अपनी भूमि, संस्कृति और जीवन शैली के लिए लड़ाई लड़ी।

सीमित विरासत और बेहतर सैन्य की कमी के कारण वे विद्रोह को बनाए रखने में असमर्थ हो गए, परन्तु उनके प्रतिरोध ने ब्रिटिश सत्ता के आधिपत्य को चुनौती दी और साथ ही आदिवासी अधिकारों और विकास की वकालत करने वाले भविष्य के आन्दोलनों की नींव रखी।

4. Importance of Tropical Rainforest — CAPF AC 2024

A massive variety of vegetation is found in several parts of the world as well as in India due to unequal distribution of rainfall and temperature as well as their seasonal variation, besides varied edaphic and biotic conditions. HG Champion, a renounced botanists and ecologists distinguished 116 types of vegetation in India. Later on, champion's classifications have been simplified by GS Puri (1960), SS Negi (1990). Along with four other types of vegetation, India and tropical rainforest with a total coverage of 169, 500 sq km and the world has its coverage of 3.6% of total Earth surface.

Tropical Rainforest is a type which grows in those areas having annual rainfall that exceeds 250 cm, annual temperature that is about 25°C-27°C and the average humidity exceeds 77% and the dry season which must be distinctly short. The trees often reach 45 metres in height and those are generally lofty, dense multi-layered forests with mesophytic evergreens. The total morphology of this rainforest looks like a green carpet when viewed from above. And it is almost impossible for the Sun to reach the ground, the undergrowth is formed mainly of tangled mass of canes, bamboos, ferms, climbers, etc. In India, true evergreen rainforests are found along the Western Ghats (Western side), in a strip running from North-East to South-East direction across Arunachal Pradesh, Upper Assam, Nagaland, Mizoram and Manipur.

This evergreen rainforest is often referred to The lung of 'The Earth' since it alone produces 20% of oxygen that helps to kept our 'Mother Earth' sound and healthy.

This rainforests are very crucial for the following aspects

Soil Protection Surprisingly, soil of rainforests is nutrient-poor so, those are basically stored in plants rather than soil itself. The tree roots bind the soil, that help in preventing erosion, while the canopy shield it form heavy rain. And the soil health is maintained when the trees die and their nutrients are recycled.

Climate Regulation/Balance As rainforests play an important role by absorbing CO_2 and producing oxygen (O_2) through photosynthesis and this cycle not only sustains our lives but also stabilises Earth's climate. And it also adds extra moisture to the atmosphere through transpiration that helps in forming clouds travelled worldwide.

Water Cycle Amazon, the greatest rainforest of the world alone, stores over half of planets rainwater, contributing to the global water cycle. So, without this water recycling, the world could have been faced droughts often leading to famine and disease.

Pharmacy for the Mankind 25% modern medicine are from forests; though we have explored only 1% of those remarkable species. And we must explore the left 99% of other species in near future that could be a live-saver for the mankind.

Commercial Purpose The timber of the forests is hard, durable and fine-grained which has a high commercial values. The important species of these forests are mesua, white cedar, toon, calophyllum, palaquium, hopea, etc.

So, we must say tropical rainforests are not just beautiful, they are extremely important for our well-being, biodiversity and health of the planet. We should always protect and cherish this invaluable ecosystem.

4. उष्णकटिबन्धीय वर्षा वन का महत्त्व CAPF AC 2024

वर्षा और तापमान के असमान वितरण के साथ-साथ उनके मौसमी बदलाव के अतिरिक्त विभिन्न मिट्टी और जैविक स्थितियों के कारण दुनिया के कई हिस्सों के साथ-साथ भारत में भी वनस्पति की विशाल विविधता पाई जाती है। एक प्रसिद्ध वनस्पतिशास्त्री और पारिस्थितिकीविद् एच.जी. चैम्पियन ने भारत में 116 प्रकार की वनस्पतियों की पहचान की। बाद में, चैम्पियन के वर्गीकरण को जी.एस. पुरी (1960) व एस.एस. नेगी (1990) द्वारा सरल बनाया गया। चार अन्य प्रकार की वनस्पतियों के साथ, भारत और उष्णकटिबन्धीय वर्षा वन कुल 169,500 वर्ग किलोमीटर और विश्व में पृथ्वी की कुल सतह का 3.6% कवरेज है।

उष्णकटिबन्धीय वर्षा वन एक प्रकार है, जो उन क्षेत्रों में उगता है, जहाँ वार्षिक वर्षा 250 सेमी से अधिक होती है तथा वार्षिक तापमान लगभग 25°-27°C होता है और औसत आर्द्रता 77% से अधिक होती है तथा शुष्क मौसम स्पष्ट रूप से छोटा होता है। पेड़ प्रायः 45 मीटर की ऊँचाई तक पहुँचते हैं और वे सामान्यतः ऊँचे, घने बहुस्तरीय जंगल होते हैं, जिनमें मेसोफाइटिक सदाबहार होते हैं। ऊपर से देखने पर इस वर्षा वन की कुल आकृति एक हरे कालीन की तरह दिखती है, जहाँ सूर्य के प्रकाश का जमीन तक पहुँचना लगभग असम्भव है। भारत में, सदाबहार वर्षा वन पश्चिमी घाट (पश्चिमी तरफ) के साथ अरुणाचल प्रदेश, ऊपरी असम, नागालैण्ड, मिजोरम, मणिपुर में उत्तर-पूर्व से दक्षिण-पूर्व दिशा में चलने वाली एक पट्टी में पाए जाते हैं। इस सदाबहार वर्षा वन को प्रायः 'पृथ्वी का फेफड़ा' कहा जाता है, क्योंकि यह अकेले 20% ऑक्सीजन का उत्पादन करता है और लगभग 50% से 75% जैविक प्रजातियाँ वर्षा वनों में मूल निवासी हैं। यह रोमांचक जैव विविधता जटिल पारिस्थितिक तन्त्र का समर्थन करती है, जिससे अनगिनत जीवों का अस्तित्व सुनिश्चित होता है।

मृदा संरक्षण आश्चर्यजनक रूप से वर्षा वनों की मिट्टी पोषक तत्त्वों से वंचित होती है, इसलिए, वे मूल रूप से मिट्टी के बजाय पौधों में संगृहीत होते हैं। पेड़ की जड़ें मिट्टी को बाँधती हैं, जो कटाव को रोकने में मदद करता है, जबकि पेड़ का आवरण इसे भारी बारिश से बचाता है और जब पेड़ सूख जाते हैं और उनके पोषक तत्त्वों का पुनर्चक्रण होता है, तब भी मिट्टी पोषक तत्त्वों से पूर्ण बनी रहती है।

जलवायु विनियमन/सन्तुलन वर्षा वन CO_2 को अवशोषित करके और प्रकाश संश्लेषण के माध्यम से ऑक्सीजन (O_2) का उत्पादन करके एक महत्त्वपूर्ण भूमिका निभाते हैं और यह चक्र न केवल हमारे जीवन को बनाए रखता है, बल्कि पृथ्वी की जलवायु को भी स्थिर करता है और यह वाष्पोत्सर्जन के माध्यम से वातावरण में अतिरिक्त नमी भी बनाए रखता है, जो बादलों को बनाने में मदद करता है।

जल चक्र अमेज़ॅन, दुनिया का सबसे बड़ा वर्षा वन, पृथ्वी के आधे से अधिक वर्षा जल को संगृहीत करता है, जो वैश्विक जल चक्र में योगदान देता है। इसलिए इस जल पुनर्चक्रण के बिना, विश्व को प्रायः अकाल और बीमारी का सामना करना पड़ सकता था।

मानव जाति के लिए फार्मेसी 25% आधुनिक दवाएँ वनों से प्राप्त होती हैं; हालांकि हमने उन उल्लेखनीय प्रजातियों में से केवल 1% का ही पता लगाया है और हमें निकट भविष्य में शेष 99% अन्य प्रजातियों का पता लगाने की आशा है, जो मानव जाति के लिए जीवन रक्षक हो सकती हैं।

वाणिज्यिक उद्देश्य जंगलों की लकड़ी कठोर और टिकाऊ होती है, जिसका वाणिज्यिक मूल्य बहुत अधिक होता है। इन जंगलों की महत्त्वपूर्ण प्रजातियाँ हैं– मेसुआ, सफ़ेद देवदार, टून, कैलोफ़िलम, पलाक्वियम, होपिया आदि।

इसलिए उष्णकटिबन्धीय वर्षा वन न केवल सुन्दर हैं, बल्कि वे हमारी, जैव-विविधता और पृथ्वी के स्वास्थ्य के लिए अत्यन्त महत्त्वपूर्ण हैं। हमें सदैव इस अमूल्य पारिस्थितिकी तन्त्र को सुरक्षित रखना चाहिए।

5. English in India : Deviance or Variance CAPF AC 2024

English was introduced to India during British colonial rule, primarily as a medium of communication for education and administration. And one of the most vital interests of British behind spreading English Education to India was to preach Christianity in East and South-Eastern Asia. Slowly and gradually English became entrenched in Indian Education System and was adopted by the elite as a language of power and prestige and supremacy. Britishers were also interested to make an elite class in India who will do flattery to Britishers. Wheather English in India represents a deviance from Standard English or a variance within the global English Speaking Community is complex and multifaceted and in post-independence English retained its importance, becoming one of the two official languages of India.

The tension between deviance or variance hinges on one's perspective of linguistic norms. Indian English might be seen as deviant from a standpoint which adheres strictly to the rules of British and American English, but it is a legitimate variance from descriptive and socio-linguistic perspective.

Socio-Economic Adhesion

English turned into a valuable skill in the Indian job market as it opened doors to better educational and employment opportunities. However it also externalises social inequalities, as access to quality English Education is often limited to urban and affluent populations.

Linguistic Features of Indian English

Indian English has developed its own distinct characteristics over time and is often regarded as IndE. Unlike stress-timed rhythm of British English, Indian English often exhibits syllable-timed rhythm and this includes unique phonological, syntactic and lexical features. Moreover, it communicates of words and phrases from Indian originated English, creating a rich, hybrid vocabulary.

We may say that English in India represents both deviance and variance as it initially introduced by British colonialism and then deviated from traditional English languages. Though over the time it has evolved into a variant that reflects the unique culture and linguistic blend of India. It incorporates, local vocabulary, grammar and pronunciation, creating a distinct form of language. This variance reflects the multifaceted and dynamic nature of English as it adapts to diverse cultural contexts. English basically serves as a bridge in India, showcasing its role as a global lingua franca while, embracing local nuances. It integrates into India's multi-lingual fabric shaped by interactions with other Indian languages.

English in India plays a pivotal role in social context by navigating historical legacies, social hierarchies and linguistic dynamism and it should be viewed as a variance rather than a deviance. It is so dynamic and evolving form of the language that reflects India's unique linguistic and cultural diversity and it plays a crucial role in shaping education, business, media, making it an essential part of India's multi-lingual fabric.

5. भारत में अंग्रेजीः विचलन या भिन्नता CAPF AC 2024

अंग्रेजी को भारत में ब्रिटिश औपनिवेशिक शासन के दौरान मुख्य रूप से शिक्षा और प्रशासन के लिए संचार के माध्यम के रूप में पेश किया गया था। भारत में अंग्रेजी शिक्षा के प्रसार के पीछे अंग्रेजों की सबसे महत्त्वपूर्ण रुचि पूर्वी और दक्षिण-पूर्वी एशिया में ईसाई धर्म का प्रचार करना था। धीरे-धीरे अंग्रेजी भाषा भारतीय शिक्षा प्रणाली में शामिल हो गई और अभिजात वर्ग द्वारा शक्ति, प्रतिष्ठा व वर्चस्व की भाषा के रूप में अपनाई गईं। अंग्रेज भी भारत में एक अभिजात वर्ग बनाने के इच्छुक थे, जो अंग्रेजों की चापलूसी करें। भारत में अंग्रेजी, मानक अंग्रेजी से विचलन का प्रतिनिधित्व करती है या वैश्विक अंग्रेजी बोलने वाले समुदाय के भीतर भिन्नता का प्रतिनिधित्व करती है। यह जटिल और बहुआयामी है।

स्वतन्त्रता के बाद अंग्रेजी ने अपना महत्त्व बनाए रखा, जो भारत की दो आधिकारिक भाषाओं में से एक बन गई। विचलन और भिन्नता के बीच तनाव भाषाई मानदण्डों के व्यक्ति के दृष्टिकोण पर निर्भर करता है। भारतीय अंग्रेजी को ब्रिटिश और अमेरिकी अंग्रेजी के नियमों का सख्ती से पालन करने वाले दृष्टिकोण से विचलन के रूप में देखा जा सकता है, परन्तु यह वर्णनात्मक और सामाजिक-भाषाई दृष्टिकोण से भिन्न है।

सामाजिक-आर्थिक जुड़ाव

अंग्रेजी भारतीय रोजगार बाजार में एक मूल्यवान कौशल बन गई, क्योंकि इसने बेहतर शैक्षिक और रोजगार के अवसरों के द्वार खोले है। हालाँकि यह सामाजिक असमानताओं को भी दूर करती है, क्योंकि गुणवत्तापूर्ण अंग्रेजी शिक्षा तक पहुँच प्रायः शहरी और समृद्ध आबादी तक ही सीमित होती है।

भारतीय अंग्रेजी की भाषाई विशेषताएँ

भारतीय अंग्रेजी ने समय के साथ अपनी अलग विशेषताएँ विकसित की हैं और इसे प्रायः इण्ड ई माना जाता है। ब्रिटिश अंग्रेजी की तनाव व समयबद्ध लय के विपरीत, भारतीय अंग्रेजी प्रायः शब्दांश-समयबद्ध लय प्रदर्शित करती है और इसमें अद्वितीय ध्वन्यात्मक, वाक्य-विन्यास और शाब्दिक विशेषताएँ शामिल हैं। इसके अतिरिक्त यह भारतीय मूल की अंग्रेजी से शब्दों और वाक्यांशों का संचार करती है, जिससे एक समृद्ध व संकर शब्दावली बनती है।

हम कह सकते हैं कि भारत में अंग्रेजी विचलन और भिन्नता दोनों का प्रतिनिधित्व करती है, क्योंकि इसे शुरू में ब्रिटिश उपनिवेशवाद द्वारा पेश किया गया था और फिर बाद में पारम्परिक अंग्रेजी भाषाओं से विचलित हो गई। हालाँकि समय के साथ यह एक ऐसे रूप में विकसित हो गई है, जो भारत की अनूठी संस्कृति और भाषाई मिश्रण को दर्शाती है। इसमें स्थानीय शब्दावली, व्याकरण और उच्चारण शामिल हैं, जिससे भाषा का एक अलग रूप बनता है। यह भिन्नता अंग्रेजी की बहुमुखी और गतिशील प्रकृति को दर्शाती है, क्योंकि यह विविध सांस्कृतिक सन्दर्भों के अनुकूल होती है। अंग्रेजी मूल रूप से भारत में एक सेतु का कार्य करती है, जो स्थानीय बारीकियों को अपनाते हुए एक वैश्विक भाषा के रूप में अपनी भूमिका दिखाती है। यह अन्य भारतीय भाषाओं के साथ बातचीत से आकार लेने वाले भारत के बहुभाषी ताने-बाने में एकीकृत होती है।

भारत में अंग्रेजी ऐतिहासिक विरासतों, सामाजिक पदानुक्रमों और भाषाई गतिशीलता का मार्ग प्रशस्त करके सामाजिक सन्दर्भ में एक महत्त्वपूर्ण भूमिका निभाती है और इसे विचलन के बजाय भिन्नता के रूप में देखा जाना चाहिए। यह भाषा का इतना गतिशील और विकसित रूप है, जो भारत की अनूठी भाषाई और सांस्कृतिक विविधता को दर्शाता है। यह शिक्षा, व्यवसाय तथा मीडिया को आकार देने में महत्त्वपूर्ण भूमिका निभाता है, जिससे यह भारत के बहुभाषी ताने-बाने का एक अनिवार्य हिस्सा बन जाता है।

6. Tribal Culture in the Age of Globalisation

CAPF AC 2024

Globalisation has profound impacts on various communities worldwide and it is mainly characterised by the inter-connectedness of economies, cultures and societies. The tribal communities are the indigenous who face inevitable challenges and opportunities in the rapidly changing landscape.

The Impact of Globalisation on Tribal Culture

Uprootedness and Identity Crisis Globalisation hurted tribal sentiments in many way, one of the significant impacts of globalisation is the erosion of traditional practices and identities. As global media and consumer penetrate ever the most remote areas, younger generations are increasingly exposed to lifestyles and values that differ totally from their ancestral traditions. This exposure often ends to cultural identity crisis, feeling of uprootedness where traditional practices are abondoned in favour of more modern, globalised ways of life.

Economic Pressures Exploitation of Resources Economic pressures has become one of the significant reason that threaten the livelihoods of tribal communities and has led to the exploitation of land traditionally inhibited by tribal people. It is not only dislocate the community but also disrupts their traditional ways of living, which are often closely tied to their natural environment. Like, the encroachment of logging and mining activities in Amazon has devastated and displaced many indigenous population.

Social Displacement Several advanced projects like dam construction, mining often result in the displacement of tribal populations. And this not only disrupts their way of life but also infuses social and psychological stress.

Education and Health One of the best sides of globalisation to tribal areas is the impact of modern health and education. Access to modern medical facilities and educational opportunities can enhance the quality of life for tribal people. Though these benefits are often unequally distributed and many tribes were deprived from the basic service.

Political Marginalisation Inspite of having a constitutional protection, tribal communities often face political marginalisation. So, there is a hope from globalisation that can exacerbate these issues by prioritising economic development over the rights and needs of indigenous populations.

Opportunities for Preservation and Empowerment

Cultural Revival Tribal knowledge and traditions can create a balance between progress and preservations. Lot of efforts through globalisation like documenting languages, promoting traditional crafts and celebrating tribal festivals have taken such initiatives to preserve and revive tribal cultures and there are several growing movements for tribal culture preservation.

Sustainable Development, Education and Advocacy

Education is the crucial factor here as it enables tribal leaders to better navigate. The complexities of globalisation and advocate for their communities rights. In such cases NGO's and government programmes play a pivotal role providing resources and support.

The age of globalisation has brought both opportunities and challenges for tribal culture. By leveraging the opportunities provided by globalisation. They may navigate the complexities while, preserving their identities and generations.

6. भूमण्डलीकरण के कालखण्ड में जनजातीय संस्कृति CAPF AC 2024

वैश्वीकरण के युग में जनजातीय संस्कृति वैश्वीकरण ने विश्व के विभिन्न समुदायों पर गहरा प्रभाव डाला है और इसकी मुख्य विशेषता अर्थव्यवस्थाओं, संस्कृतियों और समाजों का परस्पर सम्बन्ध है। जनजातीय समुदाय स्वदेशी हैं, जो तेजी से बदलते परिदृश्य में अपरिहार्य चुनौतियों और अवसरों का सामना करते हैं।

जनजातीय संस्कृति पर वैश्वीकरण का प्रभाव

जड़ता और पहचान का संकट वैश्वीकरण ने कई तरह से जनजातीय भावनाओं को चोट पहुँचाई है, वैश्वीकरण के महत्त्वपूर्ण प्रभावों में से एक पारम्परिक प्रथाओं और पहचानों का क्षरण है। जैसे-जैसे वैश्विक मीडिया और उपभोक्ता सबसे दूरदराज के क्षेत्रों में प्रवेश करते हैं, युवा पीढ़ी तेजी से ऐसी जीवन शैली और मूल्यों के सम्पर्क में आती है, जो उनकी पैतृक परम्पराओं से बिल्कुल अलग होती हैं। यह सम्पर्क प्रायः सांस्कृतिक पहचान के संकट, जड़ता की भावना को जन्म देता है, जहाँ पारम्परिक प्रथाओं को अधिक आधुनिक, वैश्वीकृत जीवन शैली के पक्ष में छोड़ दिया जाता है।

आर्थिक दबाव और संसाधनों का दोहन यह एक महत्त्वपूर्ण कारण बन गया है जो खतरे में डालता है। आदिवासी समुदायों की आजीविका और भूमि के दोहन को बढ़ावा मिला है, जो पारम्परिक रूप से आदिवासी लोगों द्वारा बाधित है। यह न केवल समुदाय को विस्थापित कर रहा है, बल्कि उनके पारम्परिक जीवन जीने के तरीकों को भी बाधित कर रहा है, जो अक्सर उनके प्राकृतिक वातावरण से निकटता से जुड़े होते हैं। जैसे- अमेज़न में लॉगिंग और खनन गतिविधियों के अतिक्रमण ने कई स्वदेशी आबादी को तबाह और विस्थापित कर दिया है।

सामाजिक विस्थापन बाँध निर्माण व खनन जैसी कई उन्नत परियोजनाओं के परिणामस्वरूप अक्सर आदिवासी आबादी का विस्थापन होता है। और यह न केवल उनके जीवन के तरीके को बाधित करता है, बल्कि सामाजिक और मनोवैज्ञानिक तनाव भी पैदा करता है।

शिक्षा और स्वास्थ्य आदिवासी क्षेत्रों में वैश्वीकरण का सबसे अच्छा पक्ष आधुनिक स्वास्थ्य और शिक्षा का प्रभाव है। आधुनिक चिकित्सा सुविधाओं और शैक्षिक अवसरों तक पहुँच आदिवासी लोगों के जीवन की गुणवत्ता को बढ़ा सकती है। हालाँकि ये लाभ अक्सर असमान रूप से वितरित किए जाते हैं और कई जनजातियाँ बुनियादी सेवा से वंचित रह जाती हैं।

राजनीतिक हाशिए पर संवैधानिक संरक्षण होने के बावजूद, आदिवासी समुदायों को प्रायः राजनीतिक हाशिए पर रखा जाता है, इसलिए वैश्वीकरण से आशा है कि यह स्वदेशी आबादी के अधिकारों और आवश्यकताओं पर आर्थिक विकास को प्राथमिकता देकर इन मुद्दों को और बढ़ा सकता है।

संरक्षण और सशक्तीकरण के अवसर

सांस्कृतिक पुनरुद्धार जनजातीय ज्ञान और परम्पराएँ प्रगति और संरक्षण के बीच सन्तुलन बना सकती हैं। वैश्वीकरण के माध्यम से बहुत-से प्रयास; जैसे–भाषाओं का दस्तावेजीकरण, पारम्परिक शिल्प को बढ़ावा देना और आदिवासी त्योहारों को मनाना, आदिवासी संस्कृतियों को संरक्षित और पुनर्जीवित करने आदि के लिए ऐसी पहल की गई है तथा आदिवासी संस्कृति संरक्षण के लिए कई बढ़ते आन्दोलन हैं।

सतत विकास, शिक्षा और वकालत शिक्षा महत्त्वपूर्ण कारक है, क्योंकि यह आदिवासी नेताओं को वैश्वीकरण की जटिलताओं को बेहतर ढंग से समझने और अपने समुदायों के अधिकारों की वकालत करने में सक्षम बनाती है। ऐसे मामलों में एनजीओ और सरकारी कार्यक्रम संसाधन और सहायता प्रदान करने में महत्त्वपूर्ण भूमिका निभाते हैं।

वैश्वीकरण का युग आदिवासी संस्कृति के लिए अवसर और चुनौतियाँ दोनों लेकर आया है। वैश्वीकरण द्वारा प्रदान किए गए अवसरों का लाभ उठाकर वे अपनी पहचान और पीढ़ियों को संरक्षित करते हुए जटिलताओं को दूर कर सकते हैं।

7. Cyber-attacks - a new kind of warfare CAPF AC 2023

Meaning of Cyber-Attacks

Cyber-attack refers to a spiteful and deliberate attempt by an individual or organisation to break through the information system of another individual or organisation. The attacker's intent is usually to seek some type of benefit from disrupting the victim's network. When used as a means to cause a war, it means the use of digital attacks — like computer viruses and hacking — by one country to disrupt the vital computer systems of another, with the aim of creating damage, death and destruction. The emergence of such dangerous wars and the increasing scope as well as expanse of cyber-attack is a result of rapidly increasing technological developments.

Cyber-Attack and Reliance on Technology

The modern societies are too reliant on computers systems. Today, computers are running almost everything from financial services to transport networks to defence systems. It is this reliance on technology due to which hackers can easily shut down these systems just like traditional military troops can disrupt a nation's peace with guns and missiles. Moreover, unlike traditional warfare, a cyber attack can be launched instantaneously from any distance and with little obvious evidence. Such an attack will be extremely hard to predict or trace back with certainty thus, rendering any kind of retaliation almost impossible.

Conclusion

A cyber war can be prevented and prepared against by the government by improving policies and creating a stronger defence.

Installing the best anti-virus and maintaining a staff well-versed in cyber attacks can further ensure that no such attacks take place. However, cyber-warfare is still a thing to be feared and thus, only by limiting our reliance on technology can we truly put an end to it and protect ourselves.

7. साइबर हमला-एक नया प्रकार का युद्ध। CAPF AC 2023

साइबर हमला क्या है?

'साइबर हमला' शब्द का प्रयोग आतंकवादी गतिविधियों में इण्टरनेट के माध्यम से किए जाने वाले हमलों के सन्दर्भ में किया जाता है। इनमें कम्प्यूटर वायरस जैसे साधनों के माध्यम से कम्प्यूटर नेटवर्क में जानबूझकर वृहत पैमाने पर इण्टरनेट से जुड़े निजी कम्प्यूटरों में व्यवधान उत्पन्न किया जाता है। वास्तविक दुनिया के बुनियादी ढाँचे, सम्पत्ति तथा किसी के जीवन को हानि पहुँचाए बिना किसी कम्प्यूटर नेटवर्क को लक्षित कर उसे क्षति पहुँचाना ही साइबर हमला है। इसे हैकिंग के नाम से भी जाना जाता है।

साइबर हमले की चुनौतियाँ

वर्तमान वैश्विक परिदृश्य में हथियारों द्वारा लड़े जाने वाले युद्ध की अपेक्षा साइबर हमला कहीं अधिक खतरनाक है, क्योंकि साइबर हमले से किसी व्यक्ति, संस्था या राष्ट्र के सन्दर्भ में उसकी व्यक्तिगत और खुफिया जानकारियों को चुरा कर उसका दुरुपयोग करने की सम्भावना बढ़ जाती है।

आज 21 वीं सदी में हर देश अपने दुश्मनों पर हैकिंग या अन्य प्रकार के साइबर हमले करवा रहा है, जैसा कि चीन, भारत में अपने मोबाइल फोन, एप्लीकेशन या अन्य प्रकार से साइबर हमलें करवाता रहता है। साइबर हमला अत्यन्त खतरनाक होता है, क्योंकि अन्य प्रकार के हमलों के लिए तो सेना और पुलिस मौजूद हैं, किन्तु साइबर हमलों से निपटने में अधिकांश देश स्वयं को अक्षम पाते हैं।

साइबर हमला एक ऐसी ऑनलाइन ठगी है जिसका शिकार एक व्यक्ति, कोई कम्पनी या सरकार भी हो सकती है। साइबर हमलों का उद्देश्य गोपनीय जानकारी चुराने से लेकर महत्त्वपूर्ण बुनियादी ढाँचे को बाधित करने और ऑनलाइन फिरौती माँगने जैसा कुछ भी हो सकता है।

साइबर हमले के प्रकार

साइबर हमले के कई प्रकार होते हैं जिनमें शामिल हैं

मालवेयर अटैक यह एक malicious सॉफ्टवेयर है जिसे कम्प्यूटर सिस्टम को नुकसान पहुँचाने to उसका फायदा उठाने के लिए डिजाइन किया गया है।

फिशिंग अटैक यह एक सोशल इंजीनियरिंग रणनीति है जिसका उद्देश्य व्यक्तियों को एक भरोसेमन्द इकाई के रूप में प्रस्तुत करके पासवर्ड और क्रेडिट कार्ड नम्बर जैसी संवेदनशील जानकारी को जुटाना होता है।

डिस्ट्रीब्यूटेड डेनियल ऑफ सर्विस (DDOS) अटैक DDOS हमले का उद्देश्य किसी नेटवर्क या वेबसाइट को ट्रैफिक से भर देना है, जिससे की वह यूजर्स के लिए अनुपलब्ध हो जाता है।

इसके अतिरिक्त SQL इंजेक्शन अटैक, मैन-इन-द-मिडल (Mitm) अटैक, क्रॉस-साइट स्क्रिप्टिंग (XSS) अटैक तथा पासवर्ड अटैक आदि विभिन्न प्रकार के साइबर अटैक होते हैं।

साइबर अटैक से कैसे बचें?

इण्टरनेट पर मौजूद किसी फोरम या फालतू वेबसाइट पर अपनी जानकारी को बेवजह किसी तीसरे को शेयर न करें

स्पैम, मैसेज और ईमेल को न खोले और न ही जवाब दें।

इण्टनेट का मौजूदा सोशल साइट; जैसे-फेसबुक, ट्विटर, इंस्टाग्राम, यूट्यूब इत्यादि पर अपनी निजी सूचना शेयर न करें।

इण्टरनेट के किसी भी प्लेटफार्म पर बनाए गए अकाउण्ट की यूजर आईडी, पासवर्ड इत्यादि को किसी दूसरे के साथ शेयर न करें।

SMS के माध्यम से आने वाले लिंक, जिसके बारे में आपको जानकारी नहीं है, पर क्लिक न करें।

साइबर सुरक्षा से जुड़े भारतीय कानून

साइबर सुरक्षा नीति राष्ट्रीय साइबर सुरक्षा नीति, 2023 को भारत के नागरिकों को और व्यवसायों के लिए सुरक्षित और लचीला साइबर स्पेश बनाने के लिए विकसित किया गया था।

आईटी अधिनियम 2000 वर्तमान में सूचना अधिनियम, 2000 देश में साइबर अपराध और डिजिटल वाणिज्य से निपटने के प्राथमिक कानून है।

भारतीय साइबर अपराध समन्वय केन्द्र (14) केन्द्र सरकार ने देश में साइबर अपराध से सम्बन्धित मुद्दों को व्यापक और समन्वित तरीके से सँभालने के लिए भारतीय साइबर अपराध समन्वय केन्द्र (14C) की स्थापना के लिए एक योजना शुरू की है।

साइबर सुरक्षा की सुदृढता हेतु भारत सरकार के प्रमुख कदम साइबर और सूचना सुरक्षा (CIS) की स्थापना, साइबर सुरक्षित भारत पहल की शुरुआत, साइबर काइम वालण्टियर्स की नियुक्ति, साइबर क्राइम रिपोटिंग पोर्टल की स्थापना, साइबर स्वच्छता केन्द्र की स्थापना आदि के माध्यम से भारत सरकार साइबर सुरक्षा को सुदृढ करने का प्रयास करती है।

साइबर सुरक्षा को बेहतर बनाने के प्रयास

समन्वय में वृद्धि अन्तर्राष्ट्रीय, राष्ट्रीय, राज्य और स्थानीय स्तर पर समन्वय एवं सुधार की जरूरत है। इस सम्बन्ध में एक महत्त्वपूर्ण कदम भारत सरकार द्वारा साइबर अपराधों पर हुए बुडापेस्ट कन्वेंशन पर हस्ताक्षर करना हो सकता है।

बुनियादी ढाँचे का विकास इसमें अधिक साइबर सेल, साइबर कोर्ट, फोरैन्सिक लैब बनना शामिल होगा, ताकि उल्लंघन करने वालों के लिए उचित दण्ड का प्रावधान किया जा सके।

कानून प्रवर्तन एजेन्सियों का मजबूत प्रशिक्षण सरकार को साइबर सुरक्षा और सुरक्षित इण्टरनेट हैण्डलिंग तकनीकों पर विशेष ध्यान देने वाली कानून प्रवर्तन एजेन्सियों और व्यक्तियों को निरन्तर, मजबूत और प्रभावी प्रशिक्षण प्रदान करने की आवश्यकता है।

सूचना प्रौद्योगिकी नियम में संशोधन

स्वतन्त्र एजेन्सियों द्वारा अनिवार्य साइबर सुरक्षा ऑडिट को शामिल करने के लिए आईटी अधिनियम में संशोधन किया जा सकता है, जैसा कि विगत वर्ष 2021 में हुआ था, लेकिन अभी इससे भी कठोर नियम की जरूरत है।

निष्कर्ष निष्कर्ष रूप से यह कहा जा सकता है कि साइबर हमलों की बढ़ती बारम्बारता ने सभी देशों के सामने एक प्रमुख चुनौती पेश की है, जिसके लिए सरकार को लोगों को इसके प्रति जागरूकता तथा अधिक कठोर कानून बनाकर इस पर लगाम लगाने की आवश्यकता है।

8. India as an emerging leader in the new world order CAPF AC 2023

India : An Aspiring Moral Power

India has never aspired to be a dominating power but a moral power. This was proven when the world was hit with a deadly pandemic and India did not shy away from shouldering its moral responsibility by exporting over 66 million doses of vaccines to nearly one hundred countries under Vaccine Maitri programme. By doing so, the nation lived up to its reputation as the 'pharmacy of the world' and reaffirmed its belief in the notion of '*Vasudhaiva Kutumbakam*', i.e., the world is one family.

Through this act, India led the fight against the pandemic and thus, emerged as a very strong leader in the world.

Leading at International Panorama

Furthermore, India hosted the prestigious G-20 presidency in 2023, which provided an opportunity for India to shape global economic and development agendas. India selected the theme of 'One Earth, One Family, One Future' which signaled the need for unity of purpose as well as the unity of action. India is also becoming one of the world's fastest growing economies in 2023. The nation led in digital payments in 2022, accounting for 46% of the global real-time transactions. The country's exports also reached a record $770.18 billion in 2022, coupled with a 50% increase in electronic goods exports. The nation has also played a huge role in countering terrorism, especially by repeatedly calling for a unified global response to terrorism.

The nation also holds considerable influence in World Bank, IMF and the WTO. It is the seventh-largest member in terms of voting power at the IMF and World Bank as of 2022 and uses its prominent voice for developing nations, advocating for fair trade rules for them. India is also leading in the field of defence as it has one of the largest and most advanced security forces in the world. It has a strong navy, army and air force which is not only protecting our countries but also engaged in UN's peace keeping process.

Conclusion

These achievements exemplify India's increasing global influence and its commitment towards addressing international challenges; thus, making the nation an emerging leader in the new world order.

8. नई विश्व व्यवस्था में भारत का उभरता नेतृत्व CAPF AC 2023

भारत ने कभी भी एक प्रभुत्वशाली शक्ति नहीं, बल्कि एक नैतिक शक्ति बनने की आकांक्षा की है। दुनिया हाल ही में कोविड महामारी से प्रभावित हुई थी और भारत में वैक्सीन मैत्री कार्यक्रम के तहत लगभग एक सौ से अधिक देशों को टीकों की 66 मिलियन से अधिक खुराक निर्यात करके अपनी नैतिक जिम्मेदारी निभाई। ऐसा करके भारत ने 'विश्व की फार्मेसी' के रूप में अपनी प्रतिष्ठा कायम रखी और वसुधैव कुटुम्बकम अर्थात् दुनिया एक परिवार है, की धारणा में अपने विश्वास की पुष्टि की। इस अधिनियम के माध्यम से, भारत ने महामारी के खिलाफ लड़ाई का नेतृत्व किया और इस तरह दुनिया में एक मजबूत नेता के रूप में उभरा। इसके अलावा भारत अब 2023 में G-20 की अध्यक्षता की मेजबानी कर रहा है, जो भारत को वैश्विक आर्थिक और विकास एजेंडा को आकार देने का अवसर प्रदान करेगा। भारत ने एक पृथ्वी, एक परिवार, एक भविष्य की थीम चुनी है जो उद्देश्य की एकता के साथ-साथ कार्यवाही की एकता की आवश्यकता का संकेत देती है।

भारत 2023 में दुनिया की सबसे तेजी से बढ़ती अर्थव्यवस्थाओं में से एक बना है। देश 2022 में डिजिटल भुगतान में अग्रणी रहा, जो वैश्विक रियल टाइम लेन-देन का 46% था। इलेक्ट्रॉनिक सामान के निर्यात में 50% वृद्धि के साथ, 2022 में देश का निर्यात भी रिकॉर्ड 770.18 बिलियन डॉलर तक पहुँच गया। राष्ट्र ने आतंकवाद का मुकाबला करने में भी बहुत बड़ी भूमिका निभाई है, विशेषकर आतंकवाद के प्रति एकीकृत वैश्विक प्रतिक्रिया का बार-बार आहवान करके। विश्व बैंक, आईएमएफ और डब्ल्यूटीओ में भी देश का काफी प्रभाव है। यह 2022 तक आईएमएफ और विश्व बैंक में मतदान शक्ति के मामले में सातवां सबसे बड़ा सदस्य है और विकासशील देशों के लिए अपनी प्रमुख आवाज का उपयोग करता है एवं उनके लिए निष्पक्ष व्यापार नियमों की वकालत करता है।

भारत रक्षा के क्षेत्र में भी बहुत अग्रणी है, क्योंकि इसके पास दुनिया की सबसे बड़ी और सबसे उन्नत सुरक्षा बलों में से एक है। इसके पास एक मजबूत थलसेना और वासुसेना है, जो न केवल हमारे देश की रक्षा करती है, अपितु संयुक्त राष्ट्र की शान्ति स्थापना प्रक्रिया में भी अपना महत्त्वपूर्ण योगदान देती है। ये उपलब्धियाँ भारत के बढ़ते वैश्विक प्रभाव और अन्तर्राष्ट्रीय चुनौतियों से निपटने के प्रति इसकी प्रतिबद्धता का उदाहरण देती है; इस प्रकार राष्ट्र नई विश्व व्यवस्था में एक उभरता हुआ नेतृत्वकर्त्ता बन जाएगा।

9. The Indian Diaspora and its contribution to post independent India. CAPF AC 2023

Indian Diaspora

The term 'Diaspora' is derived from Greek verb *diaspeiro* which means 'I scatter' or 'I spread about'. Diasporas essentially are a symbol of pride for a nation and they represent the country internationally. They help in building country's value through their huge success stories. The Indian Diaspora is an umbrella term for people who have migrated from parts of India and thus, comprises the Non-Resident Indians (NRIs), Persons of Indian Origin (PIOs) and Overseas Citizens of India (OCI).With over 25 million Indians living abroad and dispersed across the world's major continents, it is not surprising that India has the world's second-largest Diaspora.

Contribution of Indian Diaspora

The knowledge that the Indian Diaspora is so great, its ability to spread Indian soft power, lobby for India's national interests, and contribute economically to India's rise is now well-recognised. The Indian Diaspora spread the Indian culture and traditions, like Yoga and Ayurveda in other nations and thus, benefiting India in general. They also serve as a bridge for a nation through which it can access knowledge, expertise and resources of the world. According to the World Bank, the Indian Diaspora is the largest earner of remittances in the world currently. It is a source of large inflows of remittances which has been helping balance the current account. It further aids in socio-economic development and poverty reduction.

Conclusion

The Indian Diaspora's future contribution can further improve. PIOs frequently travel back to their homes to visit their family.

Promoting tourism should receive more attention among PIOs of the second generation. In this way, the Diaspora can significantly aid India's tourism industry in expanding. With the versatile role of Diaspora, India can fulfil its cherished dream of being a super power and it can make much head way in its international and foreign affairs. The Diaspora can also provide the requisite strategic impulse which makes it all the more important to unlock their potential.

9. आजाद भारत में प्रवासी भारतीयों का योगदान CAPF AC 2023

'डायस्पोरा' ग्रीक शब्द डायस्पेरो से लिया गया है, जिसका अर्थ है 'मैं बिखेरता हूँ' या 'मैं फैलता हूँ'। भारत में, यह अनिवासी भारतीयों (NRI), भारतीय मूल के व्यक्तियों (PIO) और भारत के विदेशी नागरिकों (OCI) को सन्दर्भित करता है जिनमें से भारतीय मूल के व्यक्तियों (PIO) और भारत के विदेशी नागरिकों (OCI) के कार्ड धारकों को 2015 में एक श्रेणी OCI के तहत विलय कर दिया गया था। भारतीय डायस्पोरा उन लोगों के लिए एक व्यापक शब्द है जो भारत के कुछ हिस्सों से प्रवास करके आए हैं।

भारत में विश्व का दूसरा सबसे बड़ा प्रवासी निवास है। 25 मिलियन से अधिक भारतीय विदेशों में रहते हैं और वे दुनिया के सभी प्रमुख महाद्वीपों में फैले हुए हैं, प्रवासी एक राष्ट्र के लिए गौरव का प्रतीक है और वे अन्तर्राष्ट्रीय स्तर पर अपने देश का प्रतिनिधित्व करते हैं। वे अपनी सफलता की कहानियों के माध्यम से अन्तर्राष्ट्रीय स्तर पर देश का मान बढ़ाने में मदद करते हैं।

भारतीय सॉफ्ट पावर का प्रसार करने, भारत के राष्ट्रीय हितों की पैरवी करने और भारत के उत्थान में आर्थिक योगदान देने की प्रवासी भारतीयों की क्षमता अब अच्छी तरह से मान्यता प्राप्त है। उन्होंने योग और आयुर्वेद की तरह भारतीय संस्कृति और परम्पराओं को अन्य देशों में भी फैलाया और इस प्रकार सामान्य रूप से भारत को लाभ हुआ। वे किसी राष्ट्र के लिए एक पुल के रूप में कार्य करते हैं जिसके माध्यम से वह दुनिया के ज्ञान, विशेषज्ञता और संसाधनों तक पहुँच बना सकता है। विश्व बैंक के अनुसार भारतीय प्रवासी वर्तमान में दुनिया में सबसे अधिक धन कमाने वाले व्यक्ति है। यह प्रेषण के एक बड़े प्रवाह का स्रोत है जो चालू खाते को सन्तुलित करने में मदद कर रहा है।

प्रवासन का कार्य केवल भौगोलिक सीमाओं तक सीमित नहीं है, बल्कि यह एक सांस्कृतिक विस्तार है। सिख समुदाय भरत के सबसे बड़े प्रवासियों में से एक है। ये यूके, कनाडा और कई अन्य देशों में निवास कर रहे हैं तथा भारतीय संस्कृति से पूरे विश्व को परिचित करा रहे हैं।

सक्रिय प्रवासी भारतीयों के साथ सम्बन्धों के पोषण और सामाजिक आर्थिक विकास में वृद्धि करने में तकनीकी क्षेत्र का प्रमुख योगदान रहा है। कई बड़ी बहुराष्ट्रीय कम्पनियों में भारतीय मूल के व्यक्ति निर्णायक पदों पर आसीन है जिनमें गूगल, माइक्रोसॉफ्ट पेप्सिको इत्यादि शामिल है। प्रवासी भारतीयों के समर्थन से संयुक्त राष्ट्र सुरक्षा परिषद् में भारत की स्थायी सदस्यता एक वास्तविकता बन सकती है। राजनीतिक स्तर, मन्त्रिस्तरीय और राजनतिक स्तर की पैरवी के अलावा भारत सुरक्षा परिषद की सदस्यता का समर्थन करने के लिए विभिन्न देशों में मौजूद अपने प्रवासी भारतीय समुदाय का लाभ उठा सकता है।

भारतीय प्रवासियों का भविष्य में योगदान और बेहतर हो सकता है। भारतीय मूल के व्यक्ति (PIO) अक्सर अपने परिवार से मिलने के लिए अपने घर वापस जाते रहते हैं। दुसरी पीढ़ी के PIOs के बीच पर्यटन को बढ़ावा देने पर अधिक ध्यान दिया जाना चाहिए। इस तरह प्रवासी भारतीय भारत के पर्यटन उद्योग के विस्तार में महत्त्वपूर्ण भूमिका अदा कर सकते है। प्रवासी भारतीयों की बहुमुखी भूमिका के साथ भारत एक महाशक्ति बनने में अपने पोषित सपने को पूरा कर सकता है और यह अपने अन्तर्राष्ट्रीय और विदेशी मामलों में काफी प्रगति कर सकता हैं। प्रवासी अपेक्षित रणनीतिक आवेग भी प्रदान कर सकते हैं जिससे उनकी क्षमता को उजागर करना और भी महत्त्वपूर्ण हो जाता है।

10. Education and awareness are the critical pillars for the success of a democracy. CAPF AC 2023

President Franklin D. Roosevelt of the USA observed that Democracy "cannot succeed unless those who express their choice are prepared to choose wisely. The real safeguard of democracy therefore, is education."

Education vs Democracy

India has declared herself as the Sovereign Democratic Republic and takes an enviable credit for being the largest democracy in the world. It is a way of life and not just a form of government. In fact, it is the rule of the people, by the people, for the people and with the people. But unless the people are observant, aware and conscious of their rights and responsibilities, it can have no meaning and liberty cannot be safe-guarded. The result of this will be that individual freedom and dignity would be endangered and corruption, oppression and dictatorship would be widespread in the country. Education is thus, integral in making people alert and capable of discharging their duties efficiently.

Role of Education

The role of education is not limited to the circulation of knowledge. Its purpose is also to shape the very fabric of a nation. It should make people aware of what is happening around them while making them skilled and knowledgeable enough to challenge and question practices that are unjust, discriminatory and unlawful.

Conclusion

Education instills the ideas of freedom, self-independence, equality and justice in people which are integral to a democratic government. Moreover, properly educated individuals prove to be better voters and decision makers and thus, will choose better representatives for themselves, further strengthening the very core of democracy.

10. शिक्षा व जागरूकता प्रजातन्त्र की सफलता के मुख्य स्तम्भ हैं CAPF AC 2023

संयुक्त राज्य अमेरिका के राष्ट्रपति फ्रैकलिन डी रूजवेल्ट ने कहा था कि लोकतन्त्र तब तक सफल नहीं हो सकता जब तक की जो लोग अपनी पसन्द व्यक्त करते हैं, वे बुद्धिमानी से चयन करने के लिए तैयार नहीं होते। इसलिए लोकतन्त्र की वास्तविक सुरक्षा शिक्षा है।

भारत ने स्वयं को सम्प्रभु लोकतान्त्रिक गणराज्य घोषित किया है और विश्व में सबसे बड़ा लोकतान्त्रिक राष्ट्र होने का गौरव लेता है। लोकतन्त्र जीवन का एक तरीका है न कि केवल सरकार का एक रूप। वास्तव में यह जनता का, जनता द्वारा, जनता के लिए और जनता के साथ शासन है। लेकिन जब तक लोग अपने अधिकारों और जिम्मेदारियों के प्रति चौकस एवं जागरूक नहीं होंगे, तब तक इसका कोई अर्थ नहीं हो सकता है और स्वतन्त्रता की रक्षा नहीं की जा सकती है। इसका परिणाम यह होगा कि व्यक्तिगत स्वतन्त्रता और गरिमा खतरे में पड़ जाएगी और देश में भ्रष्टचार, उत्पीड़न और तानाशाही व्यापक हो जाएगी। इस प्रकार शिक्षा लोगों को सतर्क और अपने कर्तव्यों का कुशलतापूर्वक निर्वहन करने में सक्षम बनाने में अभिन्न अंग है।

शिक्षा की भूमिका ज्ञान के प्रसार तक सीमित नहीं है। इसका उदेदश्य राष्ट्र के ताने-बाने को आकार देना भी है। इसे लोगों को जागरूक बनना चाहिए कि उनके आस-पास क्या हो रहा है, उन्हें कुशल और जानकार बनाना चाहिए कि वे अन्यायपूर्ण, भेदभावपूर्ण और गैर-कानूनी प्रथाओं को चुनौती दे सकें और उन पर सवाल उठा सकें।

शिक्षा लोगों में स्वतन्त्रता, आत्म-स्वतन्त्रता, समानता और न्याय के विचार पैदा करती है जो एक लोकतान्त्रिक सरकार के अभिन्न अंग है। उचित रूप से शिक्षित व्यक्ति बेहतर मतदाता और निर्णय लेने वाले साबित होते हैं और इस प्रकार, वे अपने लिए बेहतर प्रतिनिधि चुन सकेंगे, जिससे लोकतन्त्र की जड़ को मजबूती प्राप्त हो सकेगी। अतः कहा जा सकता है कि जनता में शिक्षा तथा जागरूकता लाकर एक लोकतन्त्र को मजबूत बनाया जा सकता है। बड़े स्तर पर जनता को जागरूक करने के लिए और शिक्षा के स्तर को बढ़ावा देने के लिए इससे सम्बन्धित अभियान चलाए जा सकते हैं।

11. E waste: the dark side of the digital revolution.

CAPF AC 2023

E-waste

E-waste or electronic waste refers to discarded electronic products ranging from computers, equipment of Information and Communication Technology (ICT), home appliances and peripherals of these devices. The rapid boom in the IT industry has led to a surge in the usage of electronic gadgets. These gadgets become redundant and go out-of-fashion rapidly and are thus, discarded frequently. This leads to large amounts of toxic e-wastes.

Contribution of Indian Diaspora

E-wastes comprise a mix of hazardous chemicals like cadmium, lead, mercury, poly-chlorinated biphenyls, besides plastics and glass. These contents leach into the soil from landfills and contaminate water bodies. E-wastes when burnt, also release poisonous gases in air. If it is not handled properly, it can cause serious health hazards. According to National Centre for Biotechnology Information, these risks include silicosis, cuts from Cathode Ray Tube (CRT) glass, inhalation of mercury, tin and lead compounds from circuit boards, acid contact with eyes and skin and circulatory failure.

Present Scenario

E-waste has woven a large informal sector in Indian cities that is involved in segregation and dismantling electronic items. Ten states in India generate 70% of the total e-waste. Among developing nations, India is one of the largest producers of e-waste.

Also, India is the destination for many developed nations to ship out their own e-wastes. However, it has been found that dismantling units in India are poorly equipped, as a result of which less than 5% of the e-waste gets recycled. Also, workers here work in dangerous conditions, without any protection or safety measures.

Conclusion

Thus, with the revelation of the dark side of technology, the Government of India passed the E-waste Management and Handling Rules Law in 2012. The law states that agencies must have licenses and comply with pollution standards, and labour laws. A fine of up to ₹ 1 lakh and jail of up to 7 years would be announced on the violators.

11. इलेक्ट्रॉनिक कचरा डिजिटल क्रान्ति का एक अन्धेरा पक्ष है।

CAPF AC 2023

ई-कचरा या इलेक्ट्रॉनिक कचरा कम्प्यूटर, सूचना और संचार प्रौद्योगिकी (ICT), घरेलू उपकरणों और इन उपकरणों के बाह्य उपकरणों से लेकर छोड़े गए इलेक्ट्रॉनिक उत्पादों को सन्दर्भित करता है। आईटी उद्योग में तेजी से उछाल के कारण इलेक्ट्रॉनिक गैजेटस के उपयोग में वृद्धि हुई है। ये गैजेट अनावश्यक हो जाते हैं और तेजी से फैशन से बाहर हो जाते हैं और इस प्रकार उन्हें अक्सर त्याग दिया जाता है। इससे बड़ी मात्रा में जहरीला ई-कचरा निकलता है। ई कचरा इलेक्ट्रॉनिक-अपशिष्ट का संक्षिप्त रूप है और इस शब्द का प्रयोग चलन से बाहर हो चुके पुराने इलेक्ट्रॉनिक उपकरणों का वर्णन करने के लिए किया जाता है। इसमें उनके घटक, उपभोग्य वस्तुएँ और पुर्जे शमिल होते हैं।

ई कचरे में प्लास्टिक और काँच के अलावा कैडमियम, सीसा, पारा, पॉली-क्लोरीनेटेड बाइफिनाइल जैसे खतरनाक रसायनों का मिश्रण होता है। ये सामग्रियों लैंडफिल से मिट्टी में मिल जाती है और जल निकायों को प्रदूषित करती हैं। ई-कचरे को जलाने पर ये हवा में जहरीली गैसों को छोड़ता है। अगर इसे ठीक से हैण्डिल नहीं किया गया, तो यह गम्भीर स्वास्थ्य खतरे पैदा कर सकता है। नेशनल सेण्टर फॉर बायोटेक्नोलॉजी इन्फॉर्मेशन के अनुसार इन जोखिमों में सिलिकोसिस, कैथोड रे ट्यूब (CRT) ग्लास से कटना, सर्किट बोर्ड से पारा, टिन और सीसा योगिकों का सांस लेना, आँखों और त्वचा के साथ एसिड का सम्पर्क और संचार विफलता शामिल है।

ई कचरे ने भारतीय शहरों में एक बड़ा-अनौपचारिक क्षेत्र चुन लिया है जो इलेक्ट्रॉनिक वस्तुओं को अलग करने और नष्ट करने में शामिल है। भारत के दस राज्य कुल ई-कचरा का 70% उत्पन्न करते हैं। विकासशील देशों में, भारत ई-कचरे के सबसे बड़े उत्पादकों में से एक है। इसके अलावा, भारत कई विकसित देशों के लिए अपना ई-कचरा बाहर भेजने का गन्तव्य है। यद्यपि यह पाया गया है कि भारत में निराकरण इकाईयाँ खराब तरीके से सुसज्जित हैं, जिसके परिणामस्वरूप 5% से भी कम ई-कचरे का पुनर्चक्रण हो पाया है। साथ ही यहाँ श्रमिक बिना किसी सुरक्षा या सुरक्षा उपायों के खतरनाक परिस्थितियों में कार्य करते हैं।

वर्ष 2012 में सरकार ने ई-कचरा प्रबन्धन और हैण्डलिंग नियम कानून पारित किया, जिसमें कहा गया है कि एजेन्सियों के पास लाइसेंस होना चाहिए और प्रदूषण मानकों और श्रम कानूनों का पालन करना चाहिए। इसका उल्लंघन करने वालो पर 1 लाख का जुर्माना और 7 वर्ष की सजा का प्रावधान किया गया है।

भारत में ई कचरे का लगभग 90% से अधिक हिस्सा अनौपचारिक क्षेत्र द्वारा सम्भाला जाता है, जो ई-कचरे से संसाधनों को निकालने के लिए गैर-वैज्ञानिक और खतरनाक तरीके अपनाता है और बाद में इसे गैर-जिम्मेदार तरीके से डम्प कर दिया जाता है।

ई-कचरे से पारिस्थितिकी असन्तुलन के साथ-साथ जल, वायु, भूमि व मृदा और रेडियो सक्रिय प्रदूषण में वृद्धि हो रही है।

ई-कचरे की बढ़ती समस्या को ध्यान में रखते हुए प्रत्येक वर्ष 14 अक्टूबर को अन्तर्राष्ट्रीय ई-कचरा दिवस मनाया जाता है। वैश्विक स्तर पर ई-कचरे के दोगुने होने की दर लगभग 16 वर्ष है।

यूरोप अपने द्वारा उत्पन्न कुल ई-कचरे का अधिकतम तथा अफ्रीका न्यूनतम पुनर्चक्रण करता है।

भारत में अक्टूबर 2016 में 'ई-कचरा प्रबधन नियम' को अधिसूचित किया है।

इस प्रकार स्पष्ट है ई-कचरे का नियम न केवल भारत के लिए वरन सम्पूर्ण विश्व के लिए एक चुनौती बना हुआ है, जो अनेक प्रकार की स्वास्थ्य सम्बन्धी समस्याएँ पैदा कर रहा है। अतः आवश्यकता इस बात की है कि इसे सुनियोजित तरीके से रीसाइकिल करके इसे पुनः उपयोगी बनाया जाए तथा पर्यावरण अवनयन की समस्या को नियन्त्रित किया जाए।

12. The geographical and linguistic diversity of India is its real wealth. CAPF AC 2023

India as a country is well-known for its diversity and it holds a unique position in the world for this quality. It is a land of diversity in many ways. In the North, there are Himalayas, in the South there are coastal areas looking over blue seas. There are green plains as well as plateaus. There are green lands of Kerala and deserts of Rajasthan. Similarly, there is a variety of climate at one time.

At one place, it is very hot and at another place at the same time it may be raining or it may be very cold. Languages and clothes too vary from place to place. People follow several faiths or religions. There are Hindus, Muslims, Sikhs, Buddhists, Parsis, Jews and others. This diversity is perhaps unique for India.

A thread of cultural unity runs through this diversity. Despite diverse religions, languages, way of dressing up, we are one.

Moreover, we have the freedom to live as we like, practise any religion, go to any place of worship and speak any language or dialect. Our civilisation is old but it has survived over centuries as it is resilient and tolerant and has the capacity to assimilate and adjust. Rightly, this land has been termed as 'the epitome of the world'.

But this diversity in culture, races, language, religion, etc., greatly stood in way of political unity. As a result, from the earliest time India has been divided into several independent states. The rulers of these states were always engaged in wars with each other for supremacy.

Conclusion

This friction and disunity was always exploited by foreign invaders and the British. It serves us as warning that we must maintain our unity despite our diversity. This will keep our uniqueness alive.

12. भौगोलिक एवं भाषाई विविधता भारत की वास्तविक सम्पत्ति है CAPF AC 2023

एक देश के रूप में भारत अपनी विविधता के लिए जाना जाता है और इस गुणवत्ता के लिय यह दुनिया में एक अद्वितीय स्थान रखता है। यह कई मायनों में विविधता की भूमि है। उत्तर में हिमालय, दक्षिण में नीले समुद्र की ओर देखने वाले तटीय क्षेत्र है। यहाँ एक ओर हरे-भरे मैदान है, तो दूसरी तरफ पठार भी है। एक ओर जहाँ केरल की हरी भूमि है, तो वहीं दूसरी तरफ राजस्थान की रेगिस्तानी भूमि भी है। इसी प्रकार एक समय में विभिन्न प्रकार की जलवायु होती है।

एक स्थान पर बहुत गर्मी हो रही है और दूसरे स्थान पर एक ही समय में वर्षा हो रही है। यह बहुत ठण्ड हो सकती है। अलग-अलग जगहों पर भाषाएँ एवं पहनावे भी अलग-अलग हैं। लोग कई आस्थाओं और धर्मों का पालन करते हैं। यहाँ हिन्दू, मुस्लिम, सिख, ईसाई, बौद्ध, जैन, पारसी, यहूदी और अन्य लोग निवास करते हैं। यह विविधिता शायद भारत के लिए अद्वितीय है।

इस विविधता में सांस्कृतिक एकता का सूत्र चलता है। विभिन्न धर्मों, भाषाओं, पहनावे के तरीके के बावजूद हम एक है। इसके अलावा हमें अपनी इच्छानुसार रहने, किसी भी धर्म का पालन करने, किसी भी पूजा-स्थल पर जाने, कोई भी भाषा या बोली बोलने की आजादी है, फिर भी हम सब भारतीय हैं। हमारी सभ्यता पुरानी है, लेकिन यह सदियों से जीवित हैं, क्योंकि यह लचीली और सहिष्णु है और इसमें आत्मसात करने और समायोजित करने की क्षमता है। ठीक ही इस भूमि को विश्व का प्रतीक कहा गया है।

भारतीय संस्कृति के बारे में पं. मदनमोहन मालवीय का कहना है कि भारतीय सभ्यता और संस्कृति की विशालता और उसकी महत्ता तो सम्पूर्ण मानव के साथ तादात्म्य सम्बन्ध स्थापित करने अर्थात वसुधैव कुटुम्बकम की पवित्र भावना में निहित है।

भारतीय संस्कृति अपनी विशाल भौगोलिक स्थिति के समान अलग-अलग है। यहाँ के लोग अलग-अलग भाषाएँ बोलते हैं, अलग-अलग तरह के कपड़े पहनते हैं विभिन्न धर्मों का पालन करते हैं, अलग-अलग भोजन करते हैं, फिर भी उनका स्वभाव एक जैसा होता है। चाहे कोई खुशी का अवसर हो या कोई दुःख का क्षण, लोग पूरे दिल से इसमें भाग लेते हैं, एक साथ खुशी या दर्द का अनुभव करते हैं।

एक त्योहार या एक आयोजन किसी घर या परिवार के लिए सीमित नहीं है। पूरा समुदाय या आस-पड़ोस एक अवसर पर खुशियाँ मनाने में शामिल होते हैं। इसी प्रकार एक भारतीय विवाह मेल-जोल का आयोजन है, जिसमें न केवल वर वधू बल्कि दो परिवारों का भी संगम होता है। चाहे उनकी संस्कृति या फिर धर्म का मामला क्यों न हो। इसी प्रकार दुःख में पड़ोसी और मित्र उस दर्द को कम करने में एक महत्त्वपूर्ण भूमिका निभाते हैं।

भारतीय संस्कृति विश्व की प्रावीनतम संस्कृतियों में से एक है। यह माना जाता है कि भारतीय संस्कृति यूनान, रोम, मिस्र, सुमेर और चीन की संस्कृतियों के समान ही प्राचीन है। भारत विश्व की सबसे पुरानी सभ्यताओं में से एक है, जिसमें बहुरोगी विविधिता और समृद्ध सांस्कृतिक विरासत है। इसके साथ ही अपने आप को बदलते समय के साथ ढालती भी आई हैं।

भारतीय संस्कृति विभिन्न माहाधाराओं का संगम है, जिसमें सनातन संस्कृति से लेकर आदिवासी तिब्बत, मंगोल, द्रविड़, हड़प्पाई और यूरोपीय धाराएँ समाहित हैं। ये धाराएँ भारतीय संस्कृति को इन्द्रधनुषीय संस्कृति या गंगा-जमुनी तहजीब मे परिवर्तित करती है।

लेकिन संस्कृति, नस्ल, धर्म आदि में यह विविधता राजनीतिक एकता के रास्ते में बहुत बड़ी बाधा बनी। परिणामस्वरूप प्राचीन काल से ही भारत कई स्वतन्त्र राज्यों में विभाजित हो गया। इन राज्यों के शासक वर्चस्व के लिए सदैव एक-दूसरे से युद्ध में लगे रहते थे।

इस मनमुटाव और फूट का विदेशी आक्रमणकारियों और अंग्रेजों ने सदैव फायदा उठाया। यह हमें चेतावनी देता है कि हमें अपनी विविधता के बावजूद अपनी एकता बनाए रखनी चाहिए। इससे हमारी विशिष्टता जीवित रहेगी।

13. The campaign to save the endangered species.

CAPF AC 2022

A campaign is a constructive, planned and active attempt to raise awareness about a problem and urge people to take action.

A campaign to save the endangered species aims to raise public knowledge of and support wildlife protection and conservation, to prevent smuggling and to demand reduction for wildlife products. The global Wild for Life campaign by the UN Environment, which supports international action against the illegal wildlife trade, is another example of a campaign.

The emergence of campaigns in not news as history has seen campaigns against inhuman acts. However, campaigns for the conservation of wildlife have become a burning issue in the present times. Today, wildlife is threatened by hunting, poaching, loss of habitat, climate change and several other man-made or natural disasters. As per current status, about one-fourth of all mammals are endangered. Hence, there are many conservation campaigns being carried out on national as well international levels to protect our ecology.

Some campaigns initiated by the Indian Government are listed below

- **Project Tiger** It was launched for the conservation of the Indian Tiger whose population had reduced from 40000 in 1900 to a mere 1800 in 1972. It aimed to protect the species and its habitat as a natural heritage for benefit of the people. It also aimed to harmonise the right of tribals in and around such areas.
- **Project Elephant** It was launched as a centrally sponsored scheme in 1992 for the protection of elephants and their habitat. Elephant corridors are areas that connect habitats of elephant colonies. The North-Eastern India has the highest numbers while South India has the least disturbed corridors. Orissa, Chhattisgarh and Jharkhand have the highest mineral wealth and elephant corridors, which means high man-animal conflict. In addition to mining ivory hunting is a serious problem.
- **Project Hangul** The Kashmir stag, also called Hangul is a subspecies of Central Asian Red Deer. In Kashmir, it is found in the Dachigam National Park. To counter its declining population, Project Hangul was launched by the government of Jammu and Kashmir in collaboration with the IUCN and the WWF.

Conclusion

To further the campaign for wildlife conservation, the Indian government also established the Indian Bio-diversity Awards in collaboration with the UNDP India. With these campaigns along with the many other efforts by the government, NGOs and people, we expect to preserve and conserve the endangered species of India and on a larger scale of the world.

13. लुप्तप्राय प्रजातियों को सुरक्षित रखने का अभियान।

CAPF AC 2022

लुप्त प्राय : प्रजातियाँ ऐसी प्रजातियाँ होती हैं, जिनकी संख्या लगातार या विगत् कुछ वर्षों में कम हुई हैं अथवा संकट में हैं। ऐसी प्रजातियों को आई. यू. सी. एन. की रेड डाटा बुक में सूचीबद्ध किया जाता है, जिन्हें संकटाग्रस्त, गम्भीर रूप से संकटाग्रस्त, समाप्त होने योग्य या कम जोखिम वाली प्रजाति में सूचीबद्ध किया जाता है।

ऐसी प्रजातियाँ मानवीय गतिविधियाँ तथा प्राकृतिक दोनों से प्रभावित होती हैं। लगातार वनों का विनाश, वन्य जीवों का शिकार, आवास की हानि, जलवायु, परिवर्तन, प्राकृतिक आपदाओं से खतरा, आदि से जीव संकट में हैं। वर्तमान स्थिति के अनुसार लगभग एक-चौथाई स्तनधारी खतरे में हैं। इन्हें सुरक्षित रखने व संरक्षण करने के लिए विभिन्न कार्यक्रमों तथा अभियानों को संचालित किया गया है, जो लोगों में जागरूकता बढ़ाने, लोगों को संरक्षण में सहयोग करने का आग्रह करता है।

यह एक रचनात्मक, योजनाबद्ध और सक्रिय प्रयास है।

यह प्रयास राष्ट्रीय एवं अन्तर्राष्ट्रीय स्तर पर जारी है, जिसका उद्देश्य वन्यजीवों का संरक्षण करना, इनके लिए आवास, प्रजनन केन्द्र की व्यवस्था करना, अनुकूल पर्यावरण को पुनः स्थापित करना, जीवों की तस्करी की रोकथाम करना, वन्यजीव के उत्पादों (सींग, दाँत) की माँग में कमी करना तथा लोगों में जागरूकता बढ़ाना आदि हैं। इसके लिए राष्ट्रीय पार्क, अभयारण्य, स्व स्थाने एवं पर स्थाने संरक्षण आदि की व्यवस्था की गई हैं। इसके अलावा कुछ जीवों के विशेष संरक्षण हेतु अभियान एवं परियोजनाएँ संचालित की गई हैं।

भारत में जीवों के संरक्षण सम्बन्धी परियोजनाएँ

- **हंगुल परियोजना (1970)** हंगुल गम्भीर रूप से संकटग्रस्त श्रेणी में रखा गया रेण्डियर प्रजाति का हिरण है। यह जम्मू-कश्मीर राज्य का राजकीय पशु है, जोकि कश्मीर के दाचीग्राम राष्ट्रीय उद्यान में पाया जाता है। वर्ष 1970 में हंगुल परियोजना प्रारम्भ की गई।
- **कस्तूरी मृग परियोजना (1972)** कस्तूरी मृग उत्तराखण्ड का राजकीय पशु है। यह परियोजना वर्ष 1972 में कस्तूरी मृग संरक्षण के लिए उत्तराखण्ड के केदारनाथ अभयारण्य में प्रारम्भ की गई।
- **गिर सिंह परियोजना (1972)** एशियाई सिंह (Lion) केवल प्राकृतिक रूप से भारत में पाया जाता है। इसका एकमात्र अधिवास गुजरात का **गिर-वन** (सौराष्ट्र) है। इसके संरक्षण के लिए वर्ष 1972 में गिर सिंह परियोजना प्रारम्भ की गई।
- **बाघ परियोजना (1973)** वर्ष 1973 में वर्ल्ड वाइल्ड लाइफफोरम की सहायता से 'प्रोजेक्ट टाइगर' शुरू किया गया। वर्ष 2005 में टाइगर टास्क फोर्स की अनुशंसा पर राष्ट्रीय बाघ संरक्षण प्रधिकरण (NTCA) का गठन किया गया, जो प्रोजेक्ट टाइगर के प्रबन्धन का कार्य करता है।
- **गैण्डा परियोजना (1987)** काजीरंगा (असोम) में एक सींग वाला गैण्डा पाया जाता है। यह भारत के अतिरिक्त नेपाल की तलहटी वाले क्षेत्रों में भी पाया जाता है, जिसके संरक्षण के लिए वर्ष 1987 में यह परियोजना प्रारम्भ की गई।
- **हाथी परियोजना (1992)** झारखण्ड के सिंहभूम जिले में इस परियोजना को प्रारम्भ किया गया। इसके अतिरिक्त हाथियों के अवैध शिकार का निरीक्षण करने के लिए (Monitoring the Illegal Killing of Elephant, MIKE) कार्यक्रम वर्ष 2004 से प्रारम्भ किया गया है।

- **लाल पाण्डा परियोजना (1996)** यह पूर्वी हिमालय में 1500 से 4000 मी की ऊँचाई पर पाया जाता है। अरुणाचल में इसे 'कैट बीयर' के नाम से जाना जाता है। WWF के सहयोग से वर्ष 1996 में इसे प्रारम्भ किया गया।
- **गिद्ध संरक्षण परियोजना (2006)** भारत में गिद्ध की 9 प्रजातियाँ पाई जाती हैं। गिद्धों की लगातार घटती संख्या के लिए 'डिक्लोफेनेक' नामक दवा को उत्तरदायी माना गया है, जिसको वर्ष 2006 में प्रतिबन्धित कर दिया गया। वर्ष 2006 में नई दिल्ली में 'गिद्ध संरक्षण परियोजना' को प्रारम्भ किया गया।
- **प्रोजेक्ट हिम तेन्दुआ (2009)** प्रोजेक्ट हिम तेन्दुआ की शुरुआत वर्ष 2009 में की गई। इसके अन्तर्गत हिमालयी पर्वतीय क्षेत्रों को किया गया है। यह हिमरेखा से ऊपर ऊँची हिमालय की पहाड़ियों पर जम्मू-कश्मीर से लेकर अरुणाचल प्रदेश तक पाया जाता है।

अन्तर्राष्ट्रीय प्रयास

- **अन्तर्राष्ट्रीय प्रकृति संरक्षण संघ** (International Union for Conservation of Nature, IUCN) इसकी स्थापना अक्टूबर, 1948 में हुई थी। इसका मुख्यालय ग्लैण्डु, (स्विट्जरलैण्ड) में है। प्रकृति की संकटापन्न प्रजातियों से सम्बन्धित रेड डाटा बुक का प्रकाशन आईयूसीएन ही करता है।
- **साइट्स** कन्वेंशन ऑफ इण्टरनेशनल ट्रेड इन एनडेंजरड स्पीशीज (Convention on International Trade in Endangered Speices, CITES) नाम का यह विश्व का सबसे बड़ा वन्यजीव संरक्षण समझौता है। यह विश्व में होने वाले जीवों तथा उनके अंगों आदि के व्यापार पर नजर रखता है। यह वर्ष 1976 से लागू हुआ। यह विभिन्न देशों को उत्प्रेरित व निर्देशित करता है कि वे अपने-अपने देश में जीव व्यापार को नियन्त्रित रखें। साइट्स द्वारा भारत को अवैध वन्यजीव व्यापार के विरुद्ध अपने प्रयास के लिए प्रशस्ति पत्र से सम्मानित किया जा चुका है।
- **ट्रैफिक** द वाइल्डलाइफ ट्रेड मॉनिटरिंग नेटवर्क नाम का यह एक ऐसा संगठन है, जो वनस्पतियों और जीवों के वाणिज्य में उनकी खरीद-फरोख्त के अभिलेख का विश्लेषण करता है। यह वन्यजीवों के व्यापार सम्बन्धी अन्तर्राष्ट्रीय बाजारों; जैसे—अमेरिका, ब्रिटेन, मध्य अफ्रीकी देश, चीन आदि पर कड़ी नजर रखता है। पादपों तथा पशुओं के महत्त्वपूर्ण हिस्सों—हड्डी, दाँत, खाल आदि के व्यापार पर प्रभावी ढंग से नियन्त्रण रखने के लिए इसका गठन किया गया है

14. What can be done to stop wars? CAPF AC 2022

War, a state of armed conflict between different nations or states, is a devastating event that brings about immense loss of life and property. It disrupts the social, economic and political balance of the involved regions and leaves a lasting impact on the global community. The prevention of war, thus, is an important and complex task that requires international cooperation, diplomatic efforts and a deep understanding of the root causes of conflicts.

The first step towards preventing war is understanding its root causes. Wars often stem from unresolved conflicts, territorial disputes, economic disparities and ideological differences. By identifying these triggers, we can devise strategies to address them proactively. The various ways in which we can try to stop wars are

Strengthening International Institutions International institutions such as the United Nations play a crucial role in preventing wars.

These institutions provide a platform for dialogue and peaceful resolution of conflicts. Strengthening these institutions therefore, is critical.

Building Trust and Promoting Dialogue Trust-building is an essential component of war prevention. This can be achieved through open dialogue, transparency in international relations and the promotion of cultural exchange programs that help foster understanding and respect among different nations. By promoting dialogue, nations can address misunderstandings and miscommunications that often lead to conflicts.

Education and Awareness Education is a powerful tool in preventing war. By educating people about the devastating effects of war and the importance of peace, we can foster a culture of non-violence.

Additionally, education can help promote critical thinking and empathy, which are essential for understanding and respecting different perspectives.

Investment in Peacekeeping and Diplomacy Investing in peacekeeping forces and diplomacy is another effective strategy. Peacekeeping forces can help maintain peace in conflict-prone regions, while diplomacy can help resolve conflicts peacefully.

Preventing war is a collective responsibility that requires international cooperation, diplomatic efforts and a deep understanding of the root causes of conflicts.

By addressing these causes proactively, strengthening international institutions, building trust, promoting dialogue, educating people and investing in peacekeeping and diplomacy, we can create a more peaceful world.

14. रण संग्रामों को समाप्त करने के लिए क्या किया जा सकता है? CAPF AC 2022

युद्ध शान्तिरहित अवस्था का एक प्रकार है, जिसमें शान्ति भंग हो जाती है। सामान्यतः इसका अर्थ किन्हीं दो तत्वों अथवा प्राणियों के मध्य पारस्परिक विरोध के फलस्वरूप घात-प्रतिघात से लगाया जाता है। यह दो समूहों, राष्ट्रों, व्यक्तियों के मध्य हो सकता है।

हॉवेल के अनुसार, "युद्ध एक सामाजिक समूह द्वारा दूसरे समूह पर किया गया संगठित आक्रमण होता है, जिसमें आक्रमण समूह आक्रान्ता समूह के हितों की कीमत पर अपने हितों की वृद्धि जानबूझकर अपनी जान-माल की बर्बादी करके करता है।" इसके कई कारण पाए जाते हैं; जैसे- राजनैतिक कारण, आर्थिक कारण, सांस्कृतिक कारण, अन्तर्राष्ट्रीय कारण तथा मनोवैज्ञानिक कारण आदि।

इस प्रकार युद्ध (रण संग्राम) लोगों के लालच और स्वार्थ का परिणाम होता है। यह युद्ध तब तक नहीं रुक सकता है, जब तक लोगों की सोच में बदलाव नहीं आता है, जीवन के प्रति अपना दृष्टिकोण नहीं बदलते हैं, युद्ध तब तक होते रहेंगे, जब तक लोग एक-दूसरे के साथ प्रतिस्पर्द्धा करने के बजाय साझा करना और एक-दूसरे की मदद करना नहीं सीखते हैं।

युद्धों को रोकने (समाप्त करने) के कुछ प्रमुख तरीके या उपाय इस प्रकार हैं

- **शान्ति को बढ़ावा देना** मानव जीवन की हर गतिविधियों में शान्ति को बढ़ावा दिया जाना चाहिए। इससे संवाद को बढ़ावा मिलता है, जिससे प्रतिस्पर्द्धा की भावना कम होती है और शान्ति का मार्ग प्रशस्त होता है। युद्ध जैसी भावना को उत्पन्न होने का अवसर नहीं मिल पाता है।
- **मूल कारणों को समझना** किसी भी घटना, विवाद, संघर्ष, टकराव आदि के मूल कारणों को समझने व स्वीकारने का प्रयास होना चाहिए, जिससे यह विवाद युद्ध में न बदले। इससे सशस्त्र संघर्षों का नेतृत्व करने से पहले समाधान का अवसर मिल सकेगा। ऐसे कारणों के समझ के अभाव में युद्ध को बढ़ावा मिलता है।
- **युद्ध सम्बन्धी मुद्दे से अवगत** (शिक्षित) **होना** युद्ध जैसी घटनाओं के कारणों व परिणामों के सम्बन्ध में शिक्षित होना आवश्यक होता है। इसे युद्ध क्षेत्रों की ऐतिहासिक पृष्ठभूमि, प्रभाव को समय से पहले समझने का अवसर प्राप्त होता है, इससे कुछ हद तक युद्ध को रोकने में मदद मिल पाएगी।
- **युद्ध विरोधी उम्मीदवार को वोट करना** लोगों को राजनीतिक रूप से सजग्र होना चाहिए तथा युद्ध विरोधी उम्मीदवार को वोट करना चाहिए। इससे दूसरों को ऐसा करने से प्रोत्साहन मिलता है। इससे अशान्ति, युद्ध जैसी भावना को बढ़ावा नहीं मिलता है।
- **समुदाय को शिक्षित करना** समुदायों के बीच युद्ध विरोधी सामुदायिक मंचों को बढ़ावा दिया जाना चाहिए। इससे समुदायों के बीच शान्ति का मार्ग प्रशस्त होता है, जिससे युद्ध जैसी भावना को पनपने का अवसर नहीं मिलता है।
- **पाद्यचर्या में शान्ति-शिक्षा को शामिल करना** ऐसा करने से शान्ति का मार्ग विद्यालय स्तर से प्रारम्भ होता है, जिसका प्रभाव समाज पर पड़ता है। इससे बच्चों, लोगों की मानसिकता में बदलाव आता है और स्थायी शान्ति का मार्ग प्रशस्त होता है।

वैश्विक स्तर पर भी राष्ट्रों के बीच प्रतिस्पर्धी भावना को रोककर, संयुक्त राष्ट्र के आदर्शों व नियमों का अनुपालन करके शान्ति को स्थापित किया जा सकता है।

15. The emerging presence of women in the Indian Armed Forces. CAPF AC 2022

The Indian Armed Forces, traditionally male-dominated institutions, are witnessing a notable transformation in recent years as they embrace inclusivity and gender equality. The increasing Presence of women in the Indian Armed Forces is a positive development that reflects changing dynamics and progressive values within the nation.The Indian Army, Navy and Air Force have all taken steps to increase the recruitment of women, with the aim of achieving gender equality and diversity within the armed forces.

In 2015, the Indian Air Force inducted its first batch of women fighter pilots and in 2020, the Indian Navy welcomed its first woman pilot. The Indian Army has also opened up several combat support roles to women, including positions in the Corps of Engineers, signals and intelligence. In 2016,the Indian Air Force's (IAF) first female fighter pilots began piloting MiG-21 Bisons. These numbers are increasing exponentially every year.

This changing dynamic is a result of the challenging and breaking of stereotypes that hinder individuals from pursuing military careers. This shift to remove all gender biasness promotes diversity and inclusivity, fostering a broader range of perspectives and skills within the armed forces. Further, with women no longer confined to non-combat positions, they are now actively contributing as pilots, engineers, doctors and officers demonstrating their expertise and capabilities in various operations.

As a result, we have an ever increasing number of role models who encourage others to pursue careers in defence and security, empowering a new generation of female leaders. In addition, women's participation enriches the talent pool within the armed forces, bringing diverse skills, perspectives, and problem-solving abilities. This increased diversity enhances operational effectiveness, strengthening the forces' capabilities in facing multifaceted challenges.

The increasing presence of women in the Indian Armed Forces is a positive step towards gender equality and diversity within the profession.

However, there is still much work to be done to address the challenges and obstacles that women face. With the implementation of policies and guidelines that promote inclusivity and diversity, as well as address biases and stereotypes, we can work towards a future where women in the armed forces are valued and respected for their contributions to our nation's security.

15. भारतीय सशस्त्र बल में महिलाओं की उभरती हुई उपस्थिति। CAPF AC 2022

भारतीय सेना व सशस्त्र बलों में महिलाओं का योगदान लम्बे समय से रहा है, जो अपनी क्षमता को विभिन्न क्षेत्रों में सिद्ध कर चुकी है। भारतीय सेना में महिलाओं की भूमिका तब शुरू हुई थी, जब ब्रिटिश शासन के दौरान सैन्य नर्सिंग विभाग का गठन किया गया था।

वर्तमान में सशस्त्र बलों में महिलाओं की संख्या लगभग दोगुनी हो गई है। ये केवल चिकित्सा पेशे में काम करने के बजाय सैनिकों, लड़ाकू पायलटों और सेना कमाण्ड पोस्ट के रूप में सेना में शामिल हो गई हैं। सेना, वायु सेना और नौ सेना में वर्ष 1992 में महिलाओं को शॉर्ट सर्विस कमीशन (एसएससी) अधिकारियों के रूप में शामिल करना शुरू किया गया। यह पहली बार था, जब महिलाओं को मेडिकल स्ट्रीम से बाहर सेना में शामिल होने की अनुमति दी गई। पुरुष अधिकारियों के विपरीत महिलाएँ केवल एसएससी के माध्यम से शामिल हो सकती हैं।

भारतीय सेना में 3500 से अधिक महिलाएँ हैं। वर्ष 2015 तक महिलाएँ फ्रण्ट-लाइन लड़ाकू सेना में महिलाओं की भागीदारी प्रतिबन्धित थी। वर्तमान में पैरा ईएमई, पैरा सिग्नल, पैरा एएससी आदि के पैराटूप्स विंग में शामिल हो सकती हैं। हालाँकि पैदल सेना में युद्धपोत, टैंक और युद्धक क्षेत्र में अभी भी महिलाओं के लिए शून्य जोन है। नौ सेना में पायलट के रूप में महिलाएँ कार्यरत हैं। पर्यवेक्षक के रूप में महिलाएँ भूमिकाएँ निभा रही हैं। वर्ष 2016 में भारतीय वायु सेना महिला लड़ाकू पायलटों ने मिग-21 बाइसन का संचालन शुरू किया। आइ ए एफ महिला फाइटर पायलटों के अनुसार चुनौतियाँ सभी लिंगों के लिए समान हैं। भारत के सर्वोच्च न्यायालय ने सेना की तीनों सेवाओं में महिला अधिकारियों को स्थायी कमीशन के लिए नियुक्त करने का आदेश दिया है।

राष्ट्रीय रक्षा अकादमी ने महिला कैडेटों के प्रवेश को आगे बढ़ाया है, जिसके माध्यम से तीन वर्ष का प्रशिक्षण एवं एक साल के पूर्व कमीशन प्रशिक्षण को बढ़ावा दिया जा रहा है, जिससे महिलाओं को प्रोत्साहन भी मिला है। इस प्रकार से महिलाओं ने सेना के विभिन्न कार्यों में अपनी भागीदारी को सुनिश्चित किया है।

सेनाओं में महिलाओं की भूमिका

- कल्याणी सेन पहली महिला थी, जिन्होंने द्वितीय विश्व युद्ध के दौरान यूके में जाकर रॉयल इण्डियन नेवी में महिला रॉयल इण्डियन नेवल सर्विस में सेवा दी।
- डॉ. सीमा राव भारत की पहली महिला कमाण्डो ट्रेनर हैं, जो 15000 से अधिक बलों को प्रशिक्षित कर चुकी हैं।
- अनुराधा शुक्ल, स्नेहा कठायत, शिरीन चन्द्रन तथा वसुन्धरा, चौकसी केवी कुबेर होवर क्रॉफ्ट जहाज पर युद्धक की भूमिका निभा चुकी हैं।
- देवश्मिता चट्टोपाध्याय आर. पी. एफ. में पहली महिला सुरक्षा आयुक्त के रूप में कार्य कर चुकी हैं।
- भावना कंठ, पायलट के रूप में अपनी प्रतिभा को सबके सामने प्रस्तुत कर चुकी हैं।
- वैशाली एस हिवासे जून, 2021 से भारत-चीन सड़कों के सीमा सड़क संगठन में महिला कमाण्डिंग ऑफिसर के रूप में कार्यरत हैं।

इस प्रकार महिलाएँ सेवा के विभिन्न पदों पर स्थापित होकर अपनी क्षमता व प्रतिभा को सबके समक्ष प्रस्तुत कर रही हैं।

16. Price rise : Causes and Effects CAPF AC 2022

Inflation is an economic phenomenon that leads to a general increase in the price level of goods and services over time. India has experienced high inflation in recent years with an inflation of 79% in April 2022, which is highest since May 2014. It has stayed above the RBI's tolerance threshold of 6% for fourth consecutive month, as per data released by the National Statistical Office (NSO).

The causes for such increase in the levels of price are many. While some of these are static and do not change with circumstance, others are dependent on time and extraordinary situation. Some these causes are given below

- **Increase in Demand** When the demand for goods and services in an economy increases, there can be a dearth in the supply without enough goods and services to meet the demand. As a result, prices go up.
- **Increase in Production Costs** When the cost of producing goods and services goes up, producers pass on the higher production costs to consumers in the form of higher prices. Hence, inflation can be a result of price rise in the materials and service that are required for production.
- **Increase in the Money Supply** When there is too much money in circulation in an economy, it can cause inflation because the excess money chases out few goods and services, leading to higher prices. For example, if the government prints too much money, it can cause inflation.

An increase in prices inevitably affects the lives of the general population. Inflation can have various impacts on the economy, individuals and businesses. Some of the impacts of inflation are

- **Decreased Purchasing Power** Inflation decreases the purchasing power of money. As the general price level increases, the same amount of money can buy fewer goods and services.
- **Reduced Savings** Inflation can reduce the value of savings because the value of money decreases over time.
- **Increased Costs for Businesses** Inflation can increase the costs for businesses as they have to pay more for raw materials, labour and other inputs. This can reduce their profit margins and make it difficult for them to remain competitive.
- **Redistribution of Income and Wealth** Inflation can redistribute income and wealth in an economy. Those who have fixed incomes, such as pensioners or low-income earners, may find it difficult to cope with the rising prices, whereas those who have assets that grow in value during inflation, such as property or stocks, may benefit.

Conclusion

The state of the world's affairs as well as domestic events has an impact on the increase of price. While some elements are beyond anyone's control, governments must take action over things they can to limit significant price increases.

16. मूल्य-वृद्धि : कारण एवं प्रभाव CAPF AC 2022

किसी वस्तु का मूल्य बढ़ जाना ही मूल्य वृद्धि कहलाता है। किसी भी अर्थव्यवस्था की विकास प्रक्रिया में कीमतों का बढ़ना स्वाभाविक होता है। निरन्तर बढ़ती हुई जनसंख्या, सुरक्षा, प्रशासकीय, आविकास दबाव के कारण माँग में वृद्धि होती है, किन्तु माँग के अनुरूप पूर्ति में परिवर्तन नहीं हो पाता है, तो माँग तथा पूर्ति के बीच का अन्तर ही कीमतों की वृद्धि को बढ़ावा देता है।

कीमतों की इस वृद्धि को मुद्रास्फीति कहते हैं। अत्यधिक मुद्रास्फीति अर्थव्यवस्था के लिए हानिकारक होती है। इस मूल्य वृद्धि के लिए कई कारक जिम्मेदार होते हैं। मुद्रास्फीति मुख्यतः दो कारणों से होती है माँगजनित कारक एवं लागत जनित कारक।

मूल्य वृद्धि के कारण

मूल्य वृद्धि कई कारणों से होती है। इनमें कुछ महत्त्वपूर्ण कारण निम्न हैं

- **माँग की अधिकता** जब जनसंख्या वृद्धि दर तीव्र हो या अन्य किसी कारण से वस्तुओं की माँग में अधिक वृद्धि होती है, तो वस्तु का मूल्य बढ़ जाता है।
- **काला बाजारी** वस्तुओं को मानव के द्वारा (व्यापारियों के द्वारा) जब कृत्रिम रूप से कम कर दिया जाता है, तब माँग के कारण मूल्य में वृद्धि हो जाती है।
- **जमाखोरी** इसमें वस्तुओं का एक जगह भण्डार कर दिया जाता है और माँग को बढ़ाया जाता है। इससे भी मूल्य वृद्धि अचानक उत्पन्न हो जाती है।
- **भ्रष्टाचार** अनुचित एवं अवैधानिक रूप से आर्थिक लाभ के लिए वस्तुओं को गलत तरीके से बेचने से भी मूल्य वृद्धि की समस्या उत्पन्न हो जाती है।
- **उत्पादन में कमी** वस्तुओं का उत्पादन कम होने से, वस्तुओं की माँग बढ़ जाती है, जिससे वस्तुओं का मूल्य बढ़ जाता है।

मूल्य वृद्धि का प्रभाव

- वस्तुओं के मूल्यों में वृद्धि से देश की बड़ी आबादी को कठिनाइयों का सामना करना पड़ता है।
- जब बुनियादी वस्तुओं की कीमतें बढ़ती हैं, तो निर्वाह स्तर से ठीक ऊपर रहने वाले लोग भी गरीबी रेखा से नीचे खिसक जाते हैं।
- यह मूल्य वृद्धि निश्चित आय वाले व्यक्ति को मुख्य रूप से प्रभावित करती है।
- अमीर कीमतों की वृद्धि से प्रभावित नहीं होते हैं। इसलिए ऐसी स्थिति में अमीर और गरीब के बीच खाई चौड़ी हो जाती है।
- इस महँगाई का कृषक वर्ग पर अनुकूल प्रभाव पड़ता है, क्योंकि किसानों के उत्पादों का मूल्य पहले से बढ़ जाता है।
- मुद्रास्फीति से ऋणदाता को हानि तथा ऋणी को लाभ होता है।
- इससे निवेश करने वाली कम्पनियों पर प्रभाव पड़ता है। जिसका प्रभाव अर्थव्यवस्था पर पड़ता है।

इस प्रकार मूल्य वृद्धि का प्रभाव व्यापक होता है। ऐसी स्थिति में सरकार ही मुख्य रूप से इन समस्याओं के समाधान में सहायक होती है।

17. A synthesis of Eastern Wisdom and Western Science: a needed goal for humanity. CAPF AC 2022

In the present world, the term 'Global Village' has been a part of bigger debates that discuss a synthesis or amalgamation of the Western Science and the Eastern Wisdom. Coined by Marshall McLuhan, a Canadian media theorist in his book 'The Gutenberg Galaxy: Making of a Typographic Man' (1962) and 'Understanding Media' (1964), the term essentially signifies the interconnectedness between the Eastern and Western worlds and sheds light on the phenomenon of Global Existence which become possible with the exchange of thoughts, ideas and philosophy and interaction between varied cultures. This gave birth to the idea of a hybrid philosophy of Eastern Wisdom and Western Science which is being discussed today as an essential requirement for the holistic welfare of humanity.

The idea of bridging the distinction between Western civilisation and Eastern civilisation is not a new one. However, it has taken a different turn. Western civilisation that has always been commended for their rapid growth in Science, never believed that an amalgamation between Western Science and Eastern Knowledge is ever possible. They reasoned that while they were based on observation and experiment, the Eastern philosophy is majorly based on belief and spirituality.

In contrast, today with the coming of Zen Buddhism and Hinduism, the synthesis of these two opposite philosophies becomes inevitable. The various moral issues of society that never found an answer in Science became answerable with the merging. Issues of abortion, euthanasia, bioethics, etc., were easily address. Further, the answers to the complexity of the world with all its mysteries and supernatural forces along with many medical procedures can be found in the classical books of Eastern civilisation.

Thus, a healthy dialogue between Eastern Knowledge and Western Science can pave to a path to knowledge that can foster a happy and healthy living.

17. प्राच्य विवेक/प्रज्ञता एवं पाश्चात्य विज्ञान का संश्लेषण : मानवता के लिए आवश्यक ध्येय/लक्ष्य। CAPF AC 2022

पूर्वी एवं पाश्चात्य दोनों ही दर्शन अपने अपने ढंग से ज्ञान का विवेचन प्रस्तुत करते हैं। पाश्चात्य दृष्टिकोण में विश्लेषण पर बल दिया गया है, वहीं भारतीय दृष्टिकोण को संश्लेषण प्रधान माना जाता है। पाश्चात्य दर्शन बौद्धिक अधिक है, जिसमें मानव जीवन को स्पर्श करने वाले तत्व उसमें कम हैं, जबकि पूर्वी (भारतीय) दर्शन जीवन व जगत को स्पर्श करता है। पूर्वी दर्शन ज्ञान के वे केन्द्र हैं, जहाँ से जीवन पथ अवलोकित होता है। विद्या को मोक्ष का माधव माना गया है। यथार्थ विद्या जन्म मरण के बन्धनों से छुटकारा दिलाती है।

पूर्वी दर्शनों का विकास स्वतन्त्र रूप से हुआ है, जबकि पाश्चात्य दर्शनों की सामग्री अन्य अनुशासनों; जैसे– मानवशास्त्र समाजशास्त्र व राजनीतिक शास्त्र के आधार पर विकसित की गई है। इस प्रकार पूर्वी दर्शन में वास्तविक ज्ञान के स्वरूप की व्याख्या करने का प्रयास किया गया है, जबकि पाश्चात्य दर्शन समस्त ज्ञान-विज्ञान की व्याख्या करने का प्रयास करता है।

- बौद्ध धर्म दर्शन में स्वयं के अस्तित्व के सम्बन्ध में कहा गया है कि यह एक भ्रम है। इनका मानना है कि न कोई ईश्वर, न कोई पदार्थ और न ही कोई अभूतपूर्व दुनिया हैं। परिनिर्वाण की अवस्था में आत्म निषेध से स्वयं (Self) की प्राप्ति नहीं होती है।
- हिन्दू धर्म, धर्म के एक सार को दर्शाता है। इसके अनुसार आत्मा वह होती है, जिसका वर्णन नहीं किया जा सकता, लेकिन अनुभव किया जा सकता है। यह जीवन को पीड़ा युक्त मानता है।
- इस प्रकार पूर्वी दर्शन मानता है कि स्वयं एक सार के रूप में मौजूद नहीं है, जो वास्तविक प्रकृति की हमारी अज्ञानता के कारण है, जबकि पाश्चात्य दर्शन इससे सहमत नहीं होता है। भारतीय दर्शन आध्यात्मिक है। जबकि पश्चिमी दर्शन भौतिकवादी है, अतः दोनों के अपने-अपने अनुभव एवं अनुभूतियाँ हैं, जिसे तर्कों के द्वारा पुष्ट करने का प्रयास किया गया है।
- पूर्वी (भारतीय) दर्शनों का विकास मनुष्य के तीनों प्रकार के दुःखों आध्यात्मिक, अधिभौतिक तथा अधिदैविक से छुटकारा दिलाने के उद्देश्य से हुआ है, वहीं पाश्चात्य दर्शनों का विकास आश्चर्यजनक वस्तुओं एवं क्रियाओं को देखने से उत्पन्न कौतूहल को शान्त करने के प्रयत्न से हुआ है। पाश्चात्य दर्शन ऊर्ध्वाधर विकास का अनुसरण करता है, जिसे प्लेटो, सुकरात व अरस्तू की शिक्षाओं आदि से समझा जा सकता है।
- पूर्वी दर्शन में बौद्ध, दर्शन, जैन दर्शन, सांख्य दर्शन, योग दर्शन अपने अपने विचारों के आधार पर विकसित हुए हैं। पश्चिमी लोग अकसर व्यक्तिवाद के पूर्वी दृष्टिकोण के प्रति आकर्षित होते हैं, जबकि पूर्वी दृष्टिकोण दूसरों की जरूरतों और सामूहिकता पर अधिक विचार करते हैं। पश्चिमी दर्शन एक मानव स्वयं के अस्तित्व को स्वीकार करता है, कुछ अपवादों के साथ, वहीं पूर्वी दर्शन दृढ़ता से मानव स्वयं के अस्तित्व को नकारता है। स्वयं की ज्ञान धारणाओं को सबसे अच्छी तरह से बौद्ध धर्म तथा हिन्दू धर्म के विचारों के द्वारा दर्शाया गया है।

18. The Indian Armed Forces are a combination of strategic thinking and timely action. CAPF AC 2022

Importance of Military Actions

Military actions have the ability to shape and alter the course of war and subsequently geography and politics of a country. This in turn decides the faith of the millions of people. The effectiveness of military doesn't lie solely in their strength but also in their strategic thinking and timely action. Indian Armed Forces have proved that they are the combination of both.

Success Examples at war Front

India was able to counter the invasion of the Pakistan Forces in Kashmir Valley in 1947 due to timely action of Indian Armed Forces. They again proved their effectiveness in 1965 war when Pakistani Force came in India through Pok, Indian Armed Forces opened second front and reached up to Lahore.

It is this strategic thinking and timely action which made Pakistan Army withdraw from India and save its own backyard. In 1971 war, Indian Armed Forces acted in synergy and their military tactics and timely action led to liberation of Bangladesh. Recently in the face-off with China, Special Frontier Force (SFF) was able to capture the heights of Mt. Kailash which forced China to come to table and discuss the disengagement process.

Intance of Lack of Timely Action

These successes, however, do not mean that India has always won a war. There have been instances wherein the lack of timely action has result in severe losses. During Indo-China war of 1962, India faced a humiliating defeat and later, in 1999, Pakistani Army was able to capture several high posts in India.

Conclusion

The Indian armed forces need to be battle ready even on short notice, especially in view of the changing nature of the threat within military domains. But India's status as the world's biggest arms importer is a hurdle in achieving military superiority. Indian government is attempting to build an advanced defence industry which aims to turn the country into a defence manufacturing powerhouse. The Government is also focusing on enhancing the synergy among Indian armed forces for carrying out timely and effective response.

18. भारतीय सशस्त्र बल सामरिक सोच एवं समयोचित कार्यवाही का संयोजन है। CAPF AC 2022

भारतीय सशस्त्र बल और अन्य वर्दीधारी सुरक्षा बल देश की सुरक्षा प्रणाली की नीव हैं। इन्हें और सशक्त करने, रक्षा उत्पादन में आत्मनिर्भरता प्राप्त करने और विकसित हो रही प्रौद्योगिकी की माँगों को पूरा करने की दृष्टि से भारत सरकार द्वारा समय-समय पर रक्षा सुधारों की घोषणा की जाती है।

- भारतीय थल सेना काफी सशक्त है। इसलिए आधुनिक भारत की सैन्य रणनीति में उत्तरी महाद्वीपीय परिधि के खतरों का प्रबन्धन करने में थल सेनाओं की भूमिका महत्त्वपूर्ण पाई जाती है। भारत स्वतन्त्रता के पश्चात् पाकिस्तान तथा चीन के दो युद्ध भी कर चुका है। जिसमें चीन से हार का सामना करना पड़ता, जबकि पाकिस्तान को बुरी तरह हराया, साथ ही इनसे तनाव की स्थिति ने भारत को बदलाव एवं रणनीति के लिए प्रेरित भी किया है।
- भारत ने सामरिक सोच एवं समय को देखते हुए रक्षा उपकरणों के सम्बन्ध तथा वैश्विक विनिर्माण के रूप में अपने को स्थापित करने की दिशा में बढ़ रहा है। रक्षा क्षेत्र में मेक इन इण्डिया को बढ़ावा दिया जा रहा है। स्वतः मार्ग के अन्तर्गत 74 की एफ. डी. आई. की अनुमति दी गई है। इसमें भी घरेलू स्रोतों को विशेषकर प्रोत्साहित किया जा रहा है। रक्षा अधिग्रहण में गति और पारदर्शिता का नया युग स्थापित किया जा रहा है। विगत 10 वर्षों में सबसे अधिक बढ़ावा वर्ष 2020 में दिया गया, जिससे नये युग का प्रारम्भ माना जाता है। एसएसएमई के लिए ₹ 100 करोड़ तक की खरीद को आरक्षित किया गया है। स्टार्टअप को बढ़ावा देने से विशिष्ट रक्षा गतिविधियों में उनकी भागीदारी तथा परीक्षण की लागत एवं समय में काफी कमी आई है।
- लागत एवं आयात निर्भरता को कम करने के लिए गॉर्डन रीच शिपबिल्डर्स एण्ड इंजीनियर्स लिमिटेड कोलकाता के साथ स्वदेशी रूप से डिजाइन किया गया पहला मॉडयूलर पुल का निर्माण किया गया है। 10,000 फीट से ऊपर की ऊँचाई पर विश्व की सबसे लम्बी सुरंग अटल सुरंग, रोहतांग सुरंग को अक्टूबर, 2020 में खोल दिया गया, जो उत्तरी सीमाओं को सभी मौसम में कनेक्टिविटी प्रदान करती है।

भारत सरकार रक्षा बजट पर भी ध्यान दे रही है, ताकि सशस्त्र बलों को समय के साथ आधुनिक बनाया जा सके। केन्द्रीय बजट 2021-22 में निजी लोगों को आगे आने, उपकरणों के डिजाइन एवं निर्माण दोनों की जिम्मेदारी लेने का आग्रह किया।

सशक्त्र बलों के उचित आधुनिकीकरण के लिए फ्रांस से 36 राफेल जेट सौदे, रूस से 5S400 राइफल प्रणाली, रक्षा खरीद प्रक्रिया के तहत इजराइल एवं यूएसए से टर्मिनल हाई एल्टीट्यूड एरिया डिफेंस प्रोद्योगिकी का सौदा किया गया है। इस प्रकार से भारत समय के अनुरूप शस्त्रबलों को सशक्त एवं आधुनिकीकृत कर रहा है।

इसके बावजूद राष्ट्रीय शक्ति के अन्य घटकों के अनुरूप में खतरों, सम्भावित सैन्य उद्देश्यों, सैन्य शक्ति के उद्देश्यपूर्ण उपयोग की पहचान की आनश्यकता है, ताकि विजुअलाइजेशन का प्रभावी ढग से मुकाबला कर सके, साथ ही साइबर सुरक्षा, आन्तरिक युद्ध, आर्टिफिशियल इण्टेलिजेंस के नकारात्मक उपयोग जैसे खतरों से उचित आधुनिकीकरण तकनीकों से निपटने की आवश्यकता है।

19. Chinese economic policy in countries bordering India. CAPF AC 2021

India has witnessed China's escalation of investments in Asia, particularly in India's neighbours such as Sri Lanka. The unforeseen rate of investments is part of Xi Jinping's Presidential and Administrative ambitions, the Belt and Road Initiative (RBI) to create a Sino-centric Global Trading Network. The expansion of economic trade facilitates Beijing is its pursuit of territorial and maritime claims betraying their whim of reshaping the world order as well as administrative arrangements within neighbouring countries.

India is in a precarious geo-political situation with China's aggressive economic policies expanding through the major Asian countries like Pakistan, Sri Lanka and Nepal.

The various reasons for it are

- **Chinese Investments in Maldives subvert Democracy** India is concerned with massive Chinese investments in infrastructure, housing, power and the hospitality sector. Maldives had been under the influence of India since 2013. After Abdulla Yameen won the disputed election, Maldives have been brought under the sphere of Beijing. The 2015 Constitutional Amendment of Maldives allowed foreigners to own lands on the archipelago providing China with the scope of leasing the Feydhoo Island for the long term. In 2017 the Maldives government rushed through a free trade agreement with China. The research states that the three largest Chinese projects are worth 1.5 billion Dollars which constitutes 40% more than Maldives' GDP.
- **Sino-Pakistan: A Precarious Mortgage** The China-Pakistan Economic Corridor is a strategic move by China veiled as an economic passway. It will create grave political problems for India as war would be an apprehension. The so-called economic corridor is economically lucrative in the short run. China has invested $62Billion Dollars in the China-Pakistan Economic corridor and $42.6 billion in power projects. The investment came at an opportune time with the USA resigning as the major bank for Pakistan. This economic agreement is favourable for both Pakistan and China from a military perspective.
- **Sri-Lanka-Debt-Trapped** In addition to China aiding Pakistan economically, India's qualms increase as Sri Lanka to has replaced India with China as its biggest economic partner. China accounted for 30% of all Foreign Direct Investments in Sri Lanka from 2012-16. Sri Lankans are indebted to China for more than $11 Billion over 0% major projects including port construction and infrastructure development. Chinese Developmental loans cost Sri Lanka 6.5% interest as contrasted to 2.5% -3% from the Asian Bank.

In such a situation, India cannot emulate China's influence in Asia in the contemporary times. It can only build on its strengths. India needs to build the capacities and capabilities in manufacturing and in supply chain networks in the home country. The COVID-19 experience has added a new urgency to ensure access to artificial intelligence, 5G and digital technologies beyond the current reliance on Chinese technology firms in India. As the global scenario gets more complex and India's ambitions increase, a cohesive strategic vision would give substance and drive to India's pursuit.

19. भारत के सीमावर्ती देशों में चीन की आर्थिक नीति CAPF AC 2021

भारत के सीमावर्ती देशों में पाकिस्तान, नेपाल, भूटान, बांग्लादेश, म्यांमार, अफगानिस्तान तथा चीन शामिल हैं। चूँकि अफगानिस्तान की सीमा POK से लगी हुई है लेकिन इस क्षेत्र पर भारत और पाकिस्तान दोनों ही अपनी सहमति जताते हैं अतएव अफगानिस्तान भी भारत के सीमावर्ती देशों की सूची में शामिल है।

चीनी अर्थव्यवस्था का उत्थान

आर्थिक शक्ति के रूप में चीन के उदय को पूरे विश्व में जिस तरह से देखा जा रहा है, वह 1978 के बाद से जारी चीन की आर्थिक सफलता को एक महाशक्ति के रूप में दर्शाता है।

आर्थिक सुधारों की शुरुआत करने के बाद से चीन सबसे ज्यादा तेजी से आर्थिक वृद्धि की ओर अग्रसर है और माना जा रहा है कि इस वृद्धि दर के कारण वह 2040 तक विश्व की सबसे बड़ी आर्थिक शक्ति अमेरिका से भी आगे निकल जाएगा।

सीमावर्ती देश और चीन की आर्थिक नीति

- भारत के सीमावर्ती देशों में चीन-पाकिस्तान आर्थिक गलियारा सबसे महत्त्वपूर्ण है। इस बहुप्रतीक्षित परियोजना से पश्चिमी एशिया से तेल की सीधी आपूर्ति पाइपलाइन के जरिए चीन को होगी, जिससे चीन के अपेक्षाकृत कम विकसित पश्चिमी क्षेत्रों का विकास सम्भव हो सकेगा। साथ ही आरम्भिक आकलन के अनुसार, पहले ही साल में पाकिस्तान की जीडीपी में 1.5 फीसदी की बढ़ोत्तरी होगी और इस परियोजना के फलस्वरूप बिजली संकट सहित रेल और सड़क निर्माण भी सम्भव हो सकेगा। इसके अतिरिक्त, चीन भूमध्य सागर के रास्ते होने वाले भारत के व्यापार पर भी नजर रख सकेगा और भारत से तनाव की स्थिति में अरब सागर पर रणनीति बढ़त बना सकेगा।
- चीन, बांग्लादेश का विगत कुछ वर्षों में सबसे बड़ा व्यापारिक सहयोगी देश रहा है। दोनों देशों के बीच आपसी व्यापार 10 बिलियन डॉलर का है, हालाँकि व्यापार सन्तुलन चीन के पक्ष में है।
- चीन और नेपाल के बीच पूर्व से ही सम्बन्ध रहे हैं लेकिन वर्तमान परिप्रेक्ष्य में नेपाल, चीन को आवश्यक वस्तुओं का एक महत्त्वपूर्ण आपूर्तिकर्त्ता तथा देश की अर्थव्यवस्था को पुनः पटरी पर लाने के लिए एक सहायक के रूप में देखता है। गरीबी और बेरोजगारी जैसी आन्तरिक समस्याओं से निपटने के लिए नेपाल को चीन जैसी बड़ी अर्थव्यवस्था की सहायता की आवश्यकता है। चीन-नेपाल आर्थिक गलियारे के माध्यम से नेपाल, चीन के साथ अपने व्यापारिक मार्गों पर प्रभुत्व स्थापित कर द्विपक्षीय व्यापार को बढ़ाना चाहता है।
- चीन एकमात्र ऐसा देश है जिसके साथ भूटान का अभी तक कोई औपचारिक सम्बन्ध नहीं है। साथ ही, चीन और भूटान के बीच का सीमा विवाद किसी भी प्रकार की आर्थिक नीति की सम्भावना को नकारता है। वर्तमान समय में भूटान का सबसे बड़ा व्यापारिक भागीदार भारत है।
- चीन और म्यांमार के बीच आर्थिक सम्बन्ध काफी सकारात्मक रहे हैं। विगत वर्षों में चीन-म्यांमार आर्थिक कॉरिडोर की सहमति हेतु दोनों देशों के बीच हस्ताक्षरित पत्र जारी हुए। वर्ष 2017 में 'सिल्क रोड आर्थिक बेल्ट की रूपरेखा और 21वीं सदी के समुद्री सिल्क रोड पहल' के अन्तर्गत दोनों देशों के बीच समझौता ज्ञापन हुआ। साथ ही सड़क, दूरसंचार आदि सेवाओं में भी चीन म्यांमार का सहयोगी रहा है।
- चीन, अफगानिस्तान में सबसे बड़ा विदेशी निवेशक है, जिसने ताँबे के निष्कर्षण, तेल और गैस क्षेत्र और सड़क तथा रेल बुनियादी ढाँचे में निवेश किया है।
- चीन और अफगानिस्तान ने अफगानिस्तान के वक्खन कॉरिडोर के माध्यम से एक फाइबर ऑप्टिकल लिंक भी शुरू किया है।

चीन की इन सभी देशों में निवेश की नीति उसकी प्रमुख आर्थिक नीति का एक भाग है, जिसके माध्यम से यह दक्षिण एशिया में शक्ति के रूप में उभरते हुए भारत की गतिविधियों पर रणनीतिक रूप से नजर रखना चाहता है और अपनी स्थिति को और अधिक सुदृढ़ करना चाहता है।

20. Work From Home: A boon or a bane? CAPF AC 2021

The COVID-19 health crisis came as an unprecedented shock that is transforming the lives and livelihoods of individuals around the Globe. The combination of fear of infection, public guidelines and great uncertainty produced a sharp contraction in economic activity and a deep and widespread shock to the labour market. In addition, state-imposed lockdowns have had very significant impacts, with millions of workers across many countries experiencing a reduction in or the complete loss of livelihoods. As industries were forced to cease operations, employers reorganised their operations to enable remote working arrangements. Due to this change, many workers were able to continue working through remote working arrangements or Work From Home.

WFH stands for work from home or remote work arrangement that allows employees to work from home by using a dedicated laptop/PC connected to the internet and business applications to collaborate and communicate with their team members. Employees can set-up their workspace in their homes and manage their entire work right from inside their houses, without the need to necessarily go to the office.

There are multiple benefits associated with WFH. They are

- **Zero Commutation** When working remotely, a person doesn't have to step out of their home. So, it will reduce the time and fuel spent to and from the office commute. This increases productivity as the employee feels fresh and motivated to work.
- **Flexible Schedule** The WFH model allows an individual greater autonomy and flexibility in the organisation of work. A person can choose to schedule tasks that would otherwise be left out like spending time on hobbies or learning something new.
- **Larger Skill Pool** Employers can extend their reach to hire a better skill pool across the globe, rather than just relying on persons available locally.
- **Cost Efficient** WFH culture reduces the cost expenditure of both the employees and the employers. The employees save commutation money and other expenses they may have while travelling to workplace. For employers, it reduces the cost of office space, electricity, wifi, etc.
- **Better work life balance** WFH allows an individual to pay equal attention to all aspect of life. As an individual has spare time in hand due to no travelling, he/she can participate in things that make the person happy. This in turn reduces stress and anxiety related to jobs.

While WFH offers many benefits, it also faced many challenges. Some of these are

- **Increased Isolation** WFH hinders social interactions and communication. A person can become quite isolated if he/she spends the majority of the time by him/herself working independently.
- **Loss of Focus** Homes are comfortable, but they present their own challenges. Even with a strict schedule, it is difficult to not get involved with family work or responsibilities. Hence, often, an individual cannot completely concentrate on work at home leading to a loss of productivity.
- **Technological challenges** WFH can often be hindered by technological challenges due to lack of physical servers, testing tools, gadgets, etc.

Conclusion

Working from home can be exciting, empowering and even profitable; provided one is realistic about the pros and cons. Work from home can keep a business operating during a pandemic, weather interruption or any other situation that closes down headquarters. It can also help employees handle other responsibilities and perhaps be even more productive.

As long as employees know what you expect from them and have the right resources, it can be a success for everyone involved.

20. वर्क फ्रॉम होम : एक वरदान या एक अभिशाप? CAPF AC 2021

वर्क फ्रॉम होम : एक परिचय

कोविड-19 काल में 'वर्क फ्रॉम होम' शब्द का इस्तेमाल सबसे ज्यादा किया गया। एक बिजनेस फर्म की रिपोर्ट के मुताबिक, यह भारत में गूगल पर सबसे ज्यादा सर्च किया जाने वाला कीवर्ड है।

कोरोना के कारण देशभर में लगे लॉकडाउन ने जहाँ एक ओर छात्रों को ऑनलाइन पढ़ाई की ओर अग्रसर किया तो वहीं कम्पनियों के द्वारा वर्क फ्रॉम होम का चलन भी तेजी से चल पड़ा। इस लॉकडाउन ने यह साबित कर दिया कि कई क्षेत्रों में वर्क फ्रॉम मुमकिन है। आने वाले समय में इसका चलन बढ़ सकता है और रिमोट वर्क एक हकीकत बन सकता है। रिमोट वर्क का अर्थ है कि आप अपना काम दफ्तर के बजाय किसी अन्य स्थान से भी सुचारु रूप से कर सकते हैं।

वरदान या अभिशाप

यद्यपि भारत में यह नया है लेकिन विदेशों में यह चलन में है। वर्क फ्रॉम होम के अपने फायदे और नुकसान हैं। इसके लिए कम्पनी और कर्मचारी दोनों को विशेष ध्यान रखना होता है।

इन्जीनियर्स को वर्क फ्रॉम होम का प्रशिक्षण देने वाली प्रमुख कम्पनी पेस्टो के अनुसार, प्रारम्भ में यह चुनौतीपूर्ण प्रतीत होता है क्योंकि कर्मचारी इस व्यवस्था को बिना समझे ही अपने दैनिक उपयोग में लाते हैं जिस कारण थकान, कामकाज में नीरसता, क्षमता की क्षीणता आदि समस्याएँ उत्पन्न होने लगती हैं।

इसके अतिरिक्त देश में संचार व्यवस्था में बाधा तथा संसाधनों की कमी इस व्यवस्था में बाधा उत्पन्न करती है। लोगों के मध्य तकनीकी ज्ञान का अभाव भी 'वर्क फ्राम होम' में एक बाधा है। फिर भी इसके अन्य बहुत से निम्न लाभ हैं–

कई रिसर्च यह बताती है कि दिल्ली-मुम्बई जैसे बड़े शहरों में लोग जितना समय पूरे वर्ष के दौरान दफ्तर आने-जाने में नष्ट करते हैं, वह उनके एक महीने के कामकाजी घण्टे के बराबर हैं और ऐसे में उनकी उत्पादन क्षमता कम हो जाती है।

समुचित रूप से वर्क फ्रॉम होम प्रणाली को प्रारम्भ करने पर यह पता चलता है कि गैर-जरूरी कार्यों में खर्च किए समय का सदुपयोग यदि बेहतर कार्य योजना पर हो तो कार्य क्षमता के साथ-साथ कार्यवृद्धि दर भी उचित गुणवत्तापूर्ण होगी।

कम्पनी के नजरिए से बात की जाए तो इस प्रणाली के तहत् कार्य सुनियोजित और सुव्यवस्थित तरीके से सम्पन्न किए जाते हैं, जिसके कारण कर्मचारियों की सन्तुष्टि का स्तर बेहतर होता है।

वर्क फ्रॉम होम के दौरान कर्मचारियों में क्षमता का पूर्ण विकास होता है, जिससे उनकी व्यक्तिगत और वित्तीय वृद्धि बेहतर होती है और साथ ही उसका अनुकूल असर पारिवारिक जीवन के स्तर तथा सामाजिक समरसता के स्तर पर भी दिखता है।

स्वास्थ्य की दृष्टि से भी वर्क फ्रॉम होम की व्यवस्था बेहतर साबित होती है। यदि कार्य संचालन यथास्थान से हो तो व्यक्ति घर पर ही सुरक्षित रह सकता है और साथ ही यातायात में होने वाले व्यवधान पर भी अंकुश लग सकता है।

निष्कर्ष वर्क फ्रॉम होम वर्तमान परिस्थितियों की माँग है, जिसे भविष्य के निवेश के रूप में देखा जा सकता है। यदि व्यक्तियों द्वारा सुनियोजित ढंग से इसका उपयोग किया जाए तो यह हमारी कार्य कुशलता हेतु लाभकारी सिद्ध होगा।

21. Party politics in India is a flourishing family business. CAPF AC 2021

India after its independence on 15th August, 1947, choose the Parliamentary democracy, an arrangement of democratic administration of the nation where the executive gains its legitimacy of authority from its capacity to get support from the Legislature to a Parliament to which it is accountable. Indian Parliamentary Democracy is based on representations in Political Parties. The first Political Party of India, the Indian National Congress tended to follow the trend of ancestral ascendancy in the leadership of the party. Since 1978, the Indian National Congress had choosen its leaders from its family members, namely Indira Gandhi and Rajiv Gandhi, as the Chief executives of the Indian Government.

Types of Leaderships in Government

The various types of leadership prevalent in political parties are charismatic, traditional and legal authority. Traditional authority stems from conventions with a family leader choosen as the representative as in the case of Shiv Sena. The legal authority of leadership is derived from the office of position as in the case of the Narendra Modi led Bharatiya Janata Party. The leadership gained through personal charisma depends upon the merits and capabilities of the individual leader.

Lineage Based Party Politics

Apparently, parties may emulate the lineage-based pattern like family-owned businesses, the former have a unique set of challenges the businesses are devoid of. Once a business is set-up by the founder, the business transforms itself into the profession of the family. The success or failure of the business is dependent upon the character and astuteness of the successor of the business. In contrast, to occupy positions of leadership in politics, the successor would require amassing public acknowledgement and support for legitimising the candidate's administrative authority.

Conclusion

The successors of a family business have choices for the position and the degree of their association with the family business; they can opt to play either active or passive participants in the business. They can choose to be the proprietor, passive investors or active executive officers in their businesses. The political counterparts are incapable of having such options of active or passive involvement for they have to be completely politically engaged or not have political participation.

21. भारत में दलगत राजनीति एक फलता-फूलता पारिवारिक व्यवसाय है। CAPF AC 2021

भारत में स्वतन्त्रता प्राप्ति और उसके कुछ वर्षों बाद तक राजनीति जनता की सेवा और राष्ट्र निर्माण हेतु प्रयुक्त एक माध्यम थी। तत्कालीन समय में अनेक महान नेता थे, जिनका जीवन त्याग, तपस्या तथा बलिदान की प्रतिमूर्ति था तथा राष्ट्र के प्रति समर्पित था। इनका जीवन न केवल राजनैतिक आदर्श को प्रतिबिम्बित करता था, बल्कि राजनैतिक विचारों में अनुकरणीय था। कालान्तर में राजनीति का चरित्र पूरी तरह से बदल चुका है। यह अपने राजनैतिक आदर्शों के विपरीत एक पारिवारिक व्यवसाय के रूप में फलता-फूलता जा रहा है। एक ऐसा व्यवसाय जिसमें आशातीत घोटाले किए जा सकते हैं और तदुनुरूप बड़ी कमाई की जा सकती है।

वर्तमान राजनैतिक दलों का बदलता स्वरूप

चूंकि वर्तमान राजनीति एक व्यवसाय बन चुकी है जिसमें नए घरानों का उदय हो रहा है। राजनीति के व्यवसाय में संलग्न घरानों में करुणानिधि की डीएमके (DMK), मुलायम सिंह यादव की समाजवादी पार्टी, लालू प्रसाद यादव की राष्ट्रीय जनता दल (राजद), बाल ठाकरे की शिव सेना, प्रकाश सिंह बादल की अकाली दल, चौधरी अजित सिंह की आरएलडी (RLD), शरद पवार की एनसीपी (NCP), फारूख अब्दुल्ला की नेशनल कॉन्फ्रेंस और इन सबसे ऊपर कॉंग्रेस पार्टी प्रमुख है। इन सभी दलों ने राष्ट्रीय या क्षेत्रीय चेहरे के रूप में परिवार के सदस्यों को ही बढ़ावा दिया है और इन्हीं के विचारों के अनुरूप समस्त क्रिया-कलाप संचालित किए जाते हैं।

दलगत राजनीति में निहित उद्देश्य

वर्तमान दलगत राजनीति विचारधारा पर आधारित न होकर जातियों और धर्मों पर केन्द्रित हो चुकी है। कुछ दल पिछड़े वर्ग की राजनीति करते हैं तो कुछ दलित वर्ग की।

अन्य दलों का गठन व्यक्ति विशेष के इर्द-गिर्द किया जाता है। हमारा लोकतन्त्र विकृत हो चुका है, क्योंकि चुनाव आर्थिक नीतियों और विचारधारा के बीच न होकर जातिगत और धार्मिक गठबन्धनों पर आधारित है। इन सबका प्रमुख कारण राजनैतिक दलों का एक पारिवारिक व्यवसाय के आकार में परिणत होना है और सभी दल लाभ के उद्देश्य को पूर्ण करने हेतु स्तरहीन राजनीति का उपयोग कर रहे हैं।

भारत में दलगत राजनीति का बदलता स्वरूप राजनैतिक आदर्शों के नैतिक पतन के लिए मुख्य रूप से जिम्मेदार है जिसने न केवल राजनीति के अर्थ को बदल दिया है, बल्कि राजनीति में निहित उसके सारतत्वों और मूल्यों पर भी गहरा आघात किया है। अतएव वर्तमान राजनैतिक परिदृश्यों को देखते हुए सहज यह अन्दाजा लगाना ज्यादा कठिन नहीं है कि दलगत राजनीति में पारिवारिक व्यवसाय का समावेशन भारतीय राजनीति में पूँजीवादी अर्थव्यवस्था के प्रभाव को बढ़ा दे।

22. Unemployment and the New Education Policy.

CAPF AC 2021

Unemployment in India

Unemployment had been one of the major agendas of all discussion and debates in the past decade. As per government statistics, the unemployment rate of educated persons in India was at 11.4%.

Considering that half of India's population is under 25 and about 66% are younger than 35, this small percentage is a very large number. The United Nations (UN) even suggests that by 2027, India will represent almost one-fifth of the global workforce, which will automatically and by far, be the largest in the world. This in addition with youth's unrest growing and brain drain, made it necessary for the government to take an action that not only tackles the issues of unemployment but also affects its root cause- lack of skills required for the job.

In the present day India, the traditional modes of education do not guarantee job. In fact, education was removed from the job market wherein a child did not gain the skills and knowledge required to do a job. Hence, youth of the nation was unemployed. To address this, the government of India introduced the New Education Policy in 2020 that would align education with the job market.

Role of NEP in Curbing Unemployment

The National Education Policy of 2020 was announced by the Ministry of Human Resource and Development which aimed to bring about a change in the Indian education system to meet the employment needs of the 21st century and to wipe off unemployment.

While the NEP 2020 seems to be directed at education, it brought a paradigm shift as honing the skills required to live an independent life and upskilling became important. With NEP, children will now have ample opportunity during their schooling to pursue their own areas of interest and develop their skills accordingly.

Moreover, the policy emphasises the world class education that suits needs of global job market. For the same, there are possibilities of aligning and developing skill courses, establishment of Community Colleges in General Colleges and Polytechnics development of Vocational Studies programmes at the undergraduate level and introducing skill credit transfer to facilitate vertical/horizontal mobility.

Conclusion

The unemployment problem in India can be solved with the best implementation of NEP 2020. The youth will be benefitted by the policy as it is more student friendly. The purpose of NEP 2020 is to give what the students need and not the institution offers.

This would lead to interest-based education and need based learning. It is hoped that the complete implementation of policy would lead to great outcomes. Indian youth would be empowered with best vocational skills in future.

22. बेरोजगारी और नई शिक्षा नीति

CAPF AC 2021

सामान्य रूप से बेरोजगारी का आशय उत्पादन कार्य में न लगा होना है, परन्तु केवल कार्यहीनता से या अप्रयुक्त श्रमशक्ति की मात्रा से ही बेरोजगारी को नहीं मापा जा सकता है क्योंकि यह गैर-रोजगार की अवस्था भी हो सकती है।

भारत में बेरोजगारी का आधार

बेरोजगारी भारत की एक प्रमुख आर्थिक तथा सामाजिक समस्या है जिसके कारण निर्धनता, अकाल, कुपोषण एवं अल्पपोषण की समस्याएँ उत्पन्न होती हैं। इस समस्या के अध्ययन, मापन एवं समाधान के सम्बन्ध में उपाय प्रस्तुत करने के लिए वर्ष 1973 में बी. भगवती की अध्यक्षता में एक समिति गठित की गई थी। समिति ने बेरोजगारी की माप के सम्बन्ध में तीन अवधारणाओं– सामान्य स्थिति, चालू साप्ताहिक स्तर तथा चालू दैनिक स्तर को प्रस्तुत किया, जिसे NSSO के 27वें चक्र से प्रयोग में लाया जा रहा है।

भारत में बेरोजगारी की वर्तमान स्थिति

भारत में बेरोजगारी तीन दशक के सर्वोच्च स्तर पर पहुँच गई है। अन्तर्राष्ट्रीय श्रम संगठन (आईएलओ) की रिपोर्ट के अनुसार, गत एक दशक में भारत की बेरोजगारी दर अपने पड़ोसी देशों में सबसे ज्यादा रही है। वर्ष 2009 तक श्रीलंका में बेरोजगारी दर सबसे अधिक थी। कोरोना के संक्रमण काल में देश में रोजगार व काम-धन्धों पर बुरा प्रभाव पड़ा है, जिसके कारण भारत में बेरोजगारी दर बढ़कर 7.11 फीसदी हो गई है।

बेरोजगारी के निदान हेतु प्रयास

भारत में बेरोजगारी के निदान हेतु सरकार द्वारा विभिन्न कार्यक्रम तथा योजनाएँ संचालित की जाती रही हैं, जिससे लोगों को रोजगार के अवसर प्रदान कर समाज की मुख्य धारा में जोड़ा जा सके।

महात्मा गाँधी राष्ट्रीय ग्रामीण रोजगार योजना इस क्षेत्र में किया गया एक प्रमुख प्रयास है, जिसके द्वारा रोजगार के दोहरे लक्ष्य को प्राप्त किया जाता है। इस योजना के द्वारा सरकार ग्रामीण परिवार के उन सदस्यों को 100 दिन का रोजगार उपलब्ध कराती है जो प्रतिदिन ₹ 220 की सांविधिक न्यूनतम मजदूरी पर सार्वजनिक कार्य सम्बन्धित अकुशल मजदूरी करने के लिए तैयार होते हैं। इसके अतिरिक्त, राष्ट्रीय ग्रामीण आजीविका मिशन, स्वर्ण जयन्ती ग्राम स्वरोजगार योजना, आजीविका ग्रामीण एक्सप्रेस योजना, स्वर्ण जयन्ती शहरी रोजगार योजना आदि के माध्यम से भी रोजगार सम्बन्धी कार्यों को सम्पन्न किया जा रहा है।

नवीनतम योजनाओं में वर्ष 2020 में प्रारम्भ की गई प्रधानमन्त्री स्वनिधि योजना तथा आत्मनिर्भर भारत अभियान के द्वारा भी कोविड-19 महामारी के दौरान उत्पन्न हुए रोजगार सम्बन्धी समस्याओं के निदान हेतु समुचित प्रयास किए जा रहे हैं।

नई शिक्षा नीति

नई शिक्षा नीति, 2020 को अन्तिम राष्ट्रीय शिक्षा नीति, 1986 (जिसमें वर्ष 1992 में संशोधन किया गया था) के स्थान पर लाया गया है। पूर्व इसरो प्रमुख कस्तूरीरंगन की अध्यक्षता में विशेषज्ञों की एक समिति ने इसका मसौदा तैयार किया था।

नई शिक्षा नीति : प्रमुख तथ्य

- नई शिक्षा नीति के लागू होने के साथ ही मानव संसाधन विकास मन्त्रालय का नाम बदलकर शिक्षा मन्त्रालय कर दिया गया है।
- नई शिक्षा नीति में पाँचवीं कक्षा एक मातृभाषा, स्थानीय या क्षेत्रीय भाषा में पढ़ाई का माध्यम रखने की बात कही गई है। इसे आठवीं कक्षा या उससे आगे भी बढ़ाया जा सकता है। विदेशी भाषाओं की पढ़ाई सेकेण्डरी लेवल से होगी।

- वर्ष 2030 तक स्कूली शिक्षा में 100% GER (Gross Enrolment Ratio) के साथ माध्यमिक स्तर तक एजुकेशन फॉर ऑल का लक्ष्य रखा गया है।
- स्कूल से दूर रह रहे दो करोड़ बच्चों को दोबारा मुख्य धारा में लाए जाने की योजना और इसके लिए स्कूल के बुनियादी ढाँचे का विकास एवं नवीन शिक्षा केन्द्रों की स्थापना की जाएगी।
- स्कूल पाठ्यक्रम के 10 + 2 ढाँचे की जगह 5 + 3 + 3 + 4 की नई पाठ्यक्रम संरचना लागू की जाएगी, जो क्रमशः 3-8, 8-11, 11-14 और 14-18 उम्र के बच्चों के लिए है। इसमें अब तक दूर रखे गए 3-6 साल के बच्चों को स्कूली पाठ्यक्रम के तहत् लाने का प्रावधान है, जिसे विश्व स्तर पर बच्चे के मानसिक विकास के लिए महत्त्वपूर्ण चरण के रूप में मान्यता दी गई है।
- एनसीईआरटी 8 वर्ष की आयु तक के बच्चों के लिए प्रारम्भिक बचपन देखभाल और शिक्षा (एनसीपीएफईसीसीई) के लिए एक राष्ट्रीय पाठ्यक्रम और शैक्षणिक ढाँचा विकसित करेगा।
- स्कूलों में शैक्षणिक धाराओं, पाठ्येतर गतिविधियों और व्यावसायिक शिक्षा के बीच विशेष अन्तर नहीं किया जाएगा।
- सामाजिक और आर्थिक नजरिए से वंचित समूहों (SEDG) की शिक्षा पर विशेष जोर दिया जाएगा।
- जीडीपी का छह फीसदी शिक्षा में लगाने का लक्ष्य है, जो अभी 4.43 फीसदी है।
- नई शिक्षा नीति का लक्ष्य 2030 तक 3-18 आयु वर्ग के प्रत्येक बच्चे को गुणवत्तापूर्ण शिक्षा प्रदान करना है।
- इस शिक्षा नीति का प्रमुख लक्ष्य रोजगारों-मुखी शिक्षा है। अर्थात् इस शिक्षा नीति में ऐसी व्यावसायिक शिक्षा की व्यवस्था है, जो लोगों को रोजगार प्रदान करने में सहायक सिद्ध हो सके।

23. Urbanisation is hazardous to human health.
CAPF AC 2021

Urbanisation refers to the phenomenon of human populations shifting into specific distinguished areas in Urban centres for the want of a better livelihood. The belief that cities are often preferred for better employment, education, health care and culture makes people migrate to cities.

However, the phenomenon generally associated with human development and progress is now being associated with poverty, environmental degradation and population demands that outstrip service capacity.

The mass unplanned transfer of people from Rural to Urban areas can lead to significant inequalities and health problems. Some of these major problems are

- **Overcrowding** Overcrowding happens where there are more people in comparison to space. The lack of space results in people dwelling in cramped spaces that threaten the safety of human beings from a health and sanitation point of view.
- **Slums and other ill-developed settlements** The lack of housing and proper living spaces lead to the development of slums and other ill-developed settlements. These slums are positioned near open sewers and restricted to geographically dangerous areas. Further, these spaces have high human densities and lack of ventilation which make people living in them prone to communicable diseases as well as waterborne and vector-borne diseases.
- **Degradation of environmental quality** The presence of a huge population in cities requires a host of facilities such as residential places, public transport and industries. Deforestation occurs on a large scale to ensure these utilities result in air and water pollution. Hence, the tree cover reduces and the environmental quality takes a hit.
- **Lifestyle Diseases** Most of the jobs in urban centres require odd hours of work that promote a stressful environment along with unhealthy food habits leading to diseases such as obesity, diabetes and hypertension. Further, the rise of nuclear families especially makes urbanites vulnerable to psychological trauma and to mental disorders leading to dementia, depression, substance abuse, alcoholism and family disintegration.

Conclusion

The problems just mentioned needs to be tackled on an urgent basis as the rate of urbanisation is on the rise. For the same, we must develop strategies and schemes that creates jobs and helps in combating poverty. The government can create polices addressing slums and add urban environmental issues.

To conclude, urbanisation is inherently not a problem for it is a sign of development. However, unsustainable and unplanned urbanisation is certain to create health and sanitary problems. Every Urban centre needs to go through scientific planning to counter the anticipated problems.

23. शहरीकरण मानव स्वास्थ्य के लिए हानिकारक है CAPF AC 2021

शहरों का भौतिक विस्तार (क्षेत्रफल, जनसंख्या जैसे कारक) शहरीकरण कहलाता है। शहरीकरण भारत सहित समस्त विश्व में होने वाला एक वैश्विक परिवर्तन है। 'नवीन भारत' पहल को आगे बढ़ाने के उद्देश्य से शहरी बुनियादी ढाँचों में सुधार के लिए शहरीकरण के प्रति समग्र दृष्टिकोण की प्रक्रिया अपनाई जा रही है।

वर्ष 2011 की जनगणना के अनुसार, भारत में 53 ऐसे शहर हैं जिनकी आबादी 10 लाख से अधिक है। इसके अतिरिक्त दिल्ली, मुम्बई, कोलकाता, चेन्नई, बंगलुरु और हैदराबाद की आबादी लगातार बढ़ रही है, क्योंकि लोगों का गाँवों से इन शहरों में पलायन बेहतर भविष्य की तलाश में लगातार होता रहा है।

शहरीकरण से उपजी नकारात्मक परिस्थितियाँ

शहरीकरण से सम्बन्धित समस्याओं में आवास की समस्या, सामाजिक सुरक्षा का अभाव, पारिवारिक विघटन, आर्थिक असमानता, पर्यावरणीय समस्या, जनांकिकीय असन्तुलन की समस्या, सामुदायिक एकीकरण की समस्या आदि महत्त्वपूर्ण हैं। इन सभी समस्याओं का केन्द्र बिन्दु मनुष्य है, जिसके शहरों में पलायन के फलस्वरूप तमाम परिस्थितियाँ उपजती हैं।

मानव स्वास्थ्य और शहरीकरण

शहरीकरण की चुनौतियों में सबसे प्रमुख मानव स्वास्थ्य पर पड़ने वाला नकारात्मक प्रभाव है। शहरीकरण के फलस्वरूप उपजी आवास की समस्या शहरों में निवास कर रहे लोगों में अस्थमा, तपेदिक सहित अन्य संक्रामक रोग जैसे, फ्लू और दस्त की वाहक है और साथ ही शहरों में फैली गन्दगी जनित बीमारियाँ आर्थिक रूप से सक्रिय युवा आबादी की क्षमता को प्रभावित करती हैं।

शहरों में अत्यधिक आबादी के दबाव ने पेयजल आपूर्ति पर प्रभाव डाला है जिसके फलस्वरूप एक बड़ा वर्ग असुरक्षित पेयजल के सेवन से टायफॉयड तथा हैजा जैसी बीमारियों से ग्रसित होता है। शहरों में खानपान की असुरक्षित शैली ने लोगों में मधुमेह जैसी बीमारियों को बढ़ाया है। इन सबका सबसे प्रमुख कारण शहरीकरण के फलस्वरूप बढ़ती औद्योगिक इकाइयाँ हैं, जिससे निकलने वाले अपशिष्ट पदार्थ जल और वायु प्रदूषण के बढ़ने में महत्त्वपूर्ण भूमिका निभाते हैं, जिसका दुष्प्रभाव शहरों में निवास कर रहे लोगों के स्वास्थ्य पर पड़ता है।

हालाँकि सरकार द्वारा कई कार्यक्रमों को संचालित कर इन समस्याओं से निदान का प्रयास जारी है और निकट भविष्य में अन्य कई प्रकार की योजनाओं का विकास किया जाना भी प्रस्तावित है लेकिन शहरी पलायन को रोकने हेतु सरकार को ग्रामीण पृष्ठभूमि पर ध्यान देने की आवश्यकता है। ग्रामीण क्षेत्रों में रोजगार के समुचित उपाय इन सब में सबसे प्रमुख हैं। यदि शहरीकरण की प्रक्रिया यूँ ही चलती रही तो एक सर्वेक्षण के अनुसार, वर्ष 2050 तक लगभग भारत की 50% आबादी शहरी निवासित हो जाएगी अतएव सरकार को स्वास्थ्य सम्बन्धी चुनौतियों से निपटना अत्यन्त दुष्कर हो सकता है।

24. Infiltrators are a threat to India's security.

CAPF AC 2021

The challenges to the internal security of India are numerous and their extent and scope are complex, varied and vast. As India's economic and military profile grows wider in the Indo-Pacific region, it faces a range of intra-state and inter-state security challenges, which it has to manage. One such major challenge that poses a great threat to India's security is Infiltration. India shares 15,106.7kms of International borders with Bangladesh, China, Pakistan, Nepal, Bhutan and Bangladesh making it more vulnerable to infiltrations. Infiltration can be simply understood as illegal entry of people and goods with malicious intent into another country. It can lead to various problems which are listed below

- **Illegal Migration** India faces problem of illegal migration from its neighbouring countries which creates a pressure on resources creating a source of conflict in India. Illegal migration has also created ethnic conflict in North-East as local population in many states have been reduced to minority leading to a sense of insecurity.
- **Terrorism** India has been a major victim of cross border terrorism sponsored by Pakistan which is mostly executed through cross-border infiltration. Recent attacks in Pathankot, Uri and Pulwama underline the security challenges posed by infiltration.
- **Insurgency and Left Wing Extremism** External forces aid insurgency in the North-East by aiding the local militia with arms and ammunition and creating anti-India propaganda. Infiltrators influenced the locals of the North-Eastern people to initiate violent crises within the country. In addition to the North-East problems, infiltrators also extend support to the left-wing extremists.
- **Import of Counterfeit Currency and Drugs Smuggling** India faces significant menace of fake currency and drugs smuggling which is routed through borders due to easy cross-border infiltration.

Infiltration is a major threat to India's security and it needs to be dealt in a holistic manner focusing on both security infrastructure as well as socio-economic infrastructure. For the same, India should adopt an integrated and holistic solution for tackling problem of Infiltration. In addition to the deployment of the armed forces, India must legislate stringent inter-nations and border policies. Stricter laws must be imposed on inter-border trade and commerce.

Conclusion

To surmise, India has historically been subjected to internal security threats from its neighbouring nations for infiltrations and illegal trespassing in the Indian territory. India has initiated the construction of building strategic roads, advanced landing air-strips, a new infantry battalion and special strike corps to increase observation over its borders.

24. घुसपैठिए भारत की सुरक्षा के लिए खतरा है। CAPF AC 2021

घुसपैठिए का अर्थ उन लोगों के समूह से है, जो अवैध रूप से किसी स्थान पर प्रयत्न द्वारा या जबरदस्ती घुसकर अपना प्रभाव स्थापित करते हैं। इस प्रकार का जन समूह न सिर्फ किसी राष्ट्र के स्थानीय संसाधनों पर बोझ है, बल्कि राष्ट्रीय सुरक्षा के लिए भी खतरा है। भारत में घुसपैठियों का प्रवेश मुख्यतः बंगाल, असम व पूर्वोत्तर सीमा तथा जम्मू-कश्मीर के रास्ते देश के आन्तरिक भागों तक होता है। वर्तमान समय में भारत में मुख्य रूप से रोहिंग्या मुसलमान या अन्य रूपों में इसके समकक्ष या सदृश घुसपैठिए की श्रेणी में शामिल हैं।

रोहिंग्या मुसलमान

रोहिंग्या मुसलमान को मूल रूप से बांग्लादेश का नागरिक माना गया है, लेकिन इन्हें कुछ समय पूर्व म्यांमार से बाहर किया गया है, जिसका प्रमुख कारण इनकी हिंसक प्रतिक्रिया है। इसी आधार पर भारत सरकार ने भी उच्चतम न्यायालय से इन्हें बाहर किए जाने की अपील की है।

गौरतलब है कि म्यांमार सरकार ने वर्ष 1982 में राष्ट्रीय कानून बनाया था जिसमें रोहिंग्या मुसलमानों का नागरिक दर्जा खत्म कर दिया गया था, जिसके बाद से ही म्यांमार सरकार इन्हें देश छोड़ने के लिए मजबूर करती आ रही है।

भारतीय दृष्टिकोण में रोहिंग्या मुसलमानों की स्थिति

केन्द्रीय गृह मन्त्रालय की रिपोर्ट के मुताबिक, भारत में 40 हजार रोहिंग्या गैर-कानूनी तौर पर जम्मू-कश्मीर, हैदराबाद, हरियाणा, उत्तर प्रदेश, दिल्ली-एनसीआर और राजस्थान में रहते हैं। गृह मन्त्रालय ने राज्य सभा में दिए गए एक लिखित जवाब में बताया कि वर्ष 2018 से 2020 के बीच भारत में अवैध रूप से प्रवेश करने का प्रयास करने वाले तीन हजार लोगों को गिरफ्तार किया गया है, जिनमें सर्वाधिक संख्या बांग्लादेशी, पाकिस्तानी और रोहिंग्या घुसपैठियों की है। ये सभी राष्ट्र के भीतर देश व समाजविरोधी गतिविधियों में संलिप्त पाए गए हैं।

भारत में घुसपैठियों की स्थिति

भारत में बांग्लादेशी घुसपैठियों की संख्या सबसे अधिक है। भारत में रोहिंग्या मुसलमानों की सर्वाधिक आबादी जम्मू में है। एक अनुमान के मुताबिक देश में पचास हजार से एक लाख बर्मी-चीनी घुसपैठिए रह रहे हैं। इनमें ज्यादातर मिजोरम में है और कुछ दिल्ली में निवासित हैं।

2005 में सुप्रीम कोर्ट की एक बेंच ने गैर-कानूनी प्रवासियों पर कहा था कि बांग्लादेश से अवैध घुसपैठ ने असम व त्रिपुरा के लोगों के जीवन को पूरी तरह असुरक्षित बना दिया है। भारत में घुसपैठिए बड़ी संख्या में नियमित रूप से पश्चिम बंगाल के रास्ते तस्कर के रूप में भारतीय सीमा में प्रवेश कर माल और पशुधन की तस्करी में भी लिप्त हैं। इन घुसपैठियों की फर्जी दस्तावेजों के सम्बन्ध में निरन्तर जानकारियाँ मिलती रहती हैं। यह आन्तरिक और बाह्य सुरक्षा की दृष्टि से खतरनाक है।

भारत में घुसपैठियों के बे-रोकटोक के कारण बहुत से सीमावर्ती जिले मुस्लिम बहुल हो गए हैं, जिसमें वहाँ की स्थानीय सरकार बहुत हद तक जिम्मेदार है। वोट बैंक की राजनीति ने इन घुसपैठियों के आवागमन को बढ़ावा दिया है। घुसपैठियों की बढ़ती आबादी ने देश में जनसंख्या असन्तुलन की स्थिति को बढ़ा दिया है।

25. Emerging threats to India's internal security

CAPF AC 2020

"Enemy within is the biggest enemy"-Kautilya

Kautilya wrote in Arthashastra that a state can be at risk from four kinds of threats.

In India, a country plagued with myriad problems, the biggest and gravest of them are the internal security threats which are constantly hindering its journey to attain economic supremacy. Over the years, the challenges to our internal security have grown manifold and assumed alarming proportions.

Threats of Security of India

Endowed with diverse culture, language, ethnicity, religion etc., that fill us with pride, India faces severe security problems like separatism, communalism, etc. These internal security problems become more complicated with development which bring merits to one section at the cost of exploitation of others. Inequality in terms of income and resources along with displacement and encroachment in tribal land gave birth to Naxal problems.

These internal factors give chances to hostile entities which fuel the separatist activity in India by helping troubling elements in form of money, shelter and support. Linguistic riots, inter-state disputes, caste and ethnic tensions and international terrorism have become commonplace due to various other indirect security problems such as arms smuggling, drugs trafficking, hawala transactions, money laundering, etc. Further, the phenomenal growth of the internet and mobile communication has demonstrated that social media could play a vital role in spreading disinformation and fanning violence thus, leading to a new threat of Cyber security.

Conclusion

Concluding, India is chasing the dream by becoming economically and democratically strong. However, to sustain this pace, we need immediate solution of our internal security problem with the understanding that all these internal security challenges are different in evolution and nature and need a little different approach for solution along with political will power.

25. भारत की आन्तरिक सुरक्षा के समक्ष उभरते खतरे।

CAPF AC 2020

आन्तरिक सुरक्षा का अर्थ सामान्यतः एक देश की अपनी सीमाओं के अन्दर की सुरक्षा से होता है। आन्तरिक सुरक्षा एक अत्यन्त प्राचीन शब्दावली है, किन्तु समय के साथ-साथ इसके मामलों में भी बदलाव होते रहे हैं। स्वतन्त्रता से पूर्व जहाँ आन्तरिक सुरक्षा के केन्द्र में धरना-प्रदर्शन, रेडियो, धार्मिक उन्माद तथा साम्प्रदायिक दंगे होते थे, वहीं स्वतन्त्रता के पश्चात् विज्ञान और प्रौद्योगिकी के क्षेत्र में अभूतपूर्व विकास ने आन्तरिक सुरक्षा को और अधिक संवेदनशील तथा जटिल बना दिया है। परम्परागत युद्ध के स्थान पर अब छद्म युद्ध के रूप में आन्तरिक सुरक्षा अब देश के लिए एक बड़ी चुनौती बन गई है।

आन्तरिक सुरक्षा के तत्त्व

- देश में आन्तरिक शान्ति और सुरक्षा को बनाए रखना।
- शान्तिपूर्ण सहअस्तित्व और साम्प्रदायिक सौहार्द बनाए रखना।
- राष्ट्र की सम्प्रभुता की सुरक्षा करना।
- कानून व्यवस्था को चुस्त-दुरुस्त बनाए रखना।

आन्तरिक सुरक्षा के समक्ष उभरते खतरे

भारत की भू-राजनैतिक स्थिति, इसके पड़ोसी देश, विस्तृत एवं जोखिम भरी स्थलीय, वायु एवं जलीय सीमा के साथ इस देश के ऐतिहासिक अनुभव इसे सुरक्षा की दृष्टि से बहुत संवेदनशील बनाते हैं।

इस सन्दर्भ में आन्तरिक सुरक्षा के समक्ष खतरे निम्नलिखित हैं

आतंकवाद आन्तरिक सुरक्षा के खतरों में आतंकवाद का एक प्रमुख स्थान है। आतंकवाद ऐसे कार्यों का समूह होता है, जिसमें हिंसा का प्रयोग किसी प्रकार का भय व क्षति उत्पन्न करने के लिए किया जाता है। किसी भी प्रकार का आतंकवाद, चाहे वह क्षेत्रीय या राष्ट्रीय या अन्तर्राष्ट्रीय हो, देश में असुरक्षा, भय और संकट का वातावरण उत्पन्न करता है। आतंकवाद का कोई सीमित दायरा नहीं होता है। वर्तमान में आज विश्व के अधिकांश राष्ट्र आतंकवाद की समस्या से ग्रसित हैं। भारत में हिजबुल मुजाहिद्दीन, आई.एस.आई.एस., इण्डियन मुजाहिद्दीन जैसे आतंकी संगठन देश की आन्तरिक सुरक्षा को चुनौती दे रहे हैं।

नक्सलवाद नक्सलवाद का उदय भारतीय कम्युनिस्ट आन्दोलन के फलस्वरूप हुआ था। नक्सलवाद की उत्पत्ति पश्चिम बंगाल के नक्सलवाड़ी ग्राम से हुई थी। वर्ष 1967 में चारु मजूमदार एवं कानू सान्याल ने इस आन्दोलन को आगे बढ़ाया। बहुत ही कम समय में नक्सलवाद ने देश के कई राज्यों को अपनी चपेट में ले लिया है। इसके परिणामस्वरूप नक्सलवाद ने लाखों लोगों को मौत के घाट उतार दिया। आज नक्सलवाद देश की आन्तरिक सुरक्षा के लिए सबसे बड़ी चुनौती बना हुआ है।

संगठित अपराध प्रत्यक्ष अथवा अप्रत्यक्ष रूप से आर्थिक या अन्य लाभों के उद्देश्य से एक से अधिक व्यक्तियों का संगठित दल, जो गम्भीर अपराध के इरादे से बनते हैं, संगठित अपराध की श्रेणी में आते हैं। परम्परागत संगठित अपराधों में लूट और ब्लैकमेलिंग, अपहरण, जबरन वसूली, अवैध ढंग से शराब का कारोबार, डकैती आदि प्रमुख हैं, जबकि आधुनिक संगठित अपराधों में साइबर अपराध, मादक द्रव्य तश्करी, मानव तश्करी, हवाला कारोबार आदि आते हैं।

मादक द्रव्य कारोबार भारत के पूर्वी पड़ोसी देशों म्यांमार, थाइलैण्ड और लाओस तथा पश्चिम में स्थित पड़ोसी देश पाकिस्तान, अफगानिस्तान तथा ईरान की उपस्थिति के फलस्वरूप मादक द्रव्य का बढ़ता व्यापार भारत की आन्तरिक सुरक्षा के समक्ष एक चुनौती बनकर उभरा है।

मनीलॉण्ड्रिंग काले धन को सफेद बनाना ही मनीलॉण्ड्रिंग है। यह एक ऐसी प्रक्रिया है, जिसके द्वारा अवैध स्रोत से अर्जित की गई आय को वैध बनाकर प्रदर्शित किया जाता है। इसमें शामिल धन का मादक द्रव्य व्यापार, आतंकी फण्डिंग और हवाला इत्यादि गतिविधियों में प्रयोग होता है, जो भारत की आन्तरिक सुरक्षा को खतरा उत्पन्न करता है।

भ्रष्टाचार भ्रष्टाचार भी आन्तरिक सुरक्षा के समक्ष एक चुनौती बनकर उभरा है, क्योंकि यह राज्य के नियन्त्रण, विनियमन और नीति-निर्णयन क्षमता को प्रतिकूल रूप से प्रभावित करता है।

पड़ोसी देश या छद्म मित्र देश

- पड़ोसी देश या छद्म मित्रता प्रदर्शित करने वाले देश भी देश की आन्तरिक चुनौती के समक्ष समय-समय पर संकट उत्पन्न करते रहते हैं। ये ऐसे देश होते हैं, जो सैन्य उपकरणों या गैर-सैन्य उपकरणों के माध्यम से सुरक्षा संकट उत्पन्न करना चाहते हैं।
- वर्ष 2008 में मुम्बई पर हुए आतंकी हमले में पाकिस्तान की स्पष्ट भूमिका थी। चूँकि पाकिस्तान भारत से प्रत्यक्ष युद्ध में जीत नहीं सकता, अतः वह इस तरह के छद्म युद्धों का सहारा लेता रहता है।
- भारत जैसे देशों में अवैध घुसपैठ एवं शरणार्थियों की समस्या में भी पड़ोसी देशों का प्रत्यक्ष योगदान है, जो देश की आन्तरिक सुरक्षा को चुनौती दे रहे हैं।
- इसके साथ ही अलगाववाद भी देश की एकता तथा अखण्डता को चुनौती दे रहा है।

विभिन्न संस्थानों तथा संगठनों की भूमिका

- इसमें गैर-सरकारी संगठन, आतंकवादी संगठन, धार्मिक व नृजातीय संगठन, पार राष्ट्रीय प्रवासी समुदाय तथा अन्तर्राष्ट्रीय मीडिया आदि आते हैं।
- इसमें से कुछ समर्थक की भूमिका में, तो कुछ व्यवस्था विरोधी होते हैं। ये संस्थान तथा संगठन ऐसे हैं, जिनका विस्तार या प्रभाव वैश्विक स्तर पर देखा जा सकता है। अतः आज के परिदृश्य में इन संस्थाओं तथा संगठनों को समानान्तर सरकार के रूप में भी देखा जा सकता है।

आन्तरिक सुरक्षा को मजबूत करने के उपाय

- स्थानीय से राष्ट्रीय स्तर तक खुफिया तन्त्र में सुधार करने की आवश्यकता है।
- पाकिस्तानी खुफिया एजेन्सी ISI से उत्पन्न सुरक्षा खतरों के खिलाफ एक प्रभावी जवाबी रणनीति बनाने की आवश्यकता है।
- केन्द्र सरकार को सभी राज्य सरकारों को उनके द्वारा सुरक्षा प्रबन्धन के विषय को प्राथमिकता देने की आवश्यकता के सन्दर्भ में जागरूक किया जाना चाहिए।
- नक्सलवाद और आतंकवाद के खिलाफ अभियान के साथ-ही-साथ प्रभावित राज्यों में सरकार को विकास योजनाओं को क्रियान्वित करके वहाँ के लोगों को विकास की मुख्य धारा से जोड़ा जाना चाहिए।
- पुलिस एवं सुरक्षा बलों को अत्याधुनिक उपकरणों से लैस किया जाना चाहिए।
- भारत सरकार को एक समग्र राष्ट्रीय सुरक्षा नीति बनाने की आवश्यकता है।

26. Crime against women is an expression of male domination

CAPF AC 2020

As India emerges on the global forefront as the next 'world power', it silently crumbles in the face of gender inequality – a social menace that has restrained this mighty elephant from realising its full potential. It is ironic that in the Vedic Period India embodied a system which gave chief prominence and prerogatives to women. And so, went the saying "*Yatra Naryastu Pujyante, Ramante Tatra Devta*"– which translates to "where women are worshipped, God resides". Yet, centuries later, daughters of India have been denied their rightful place by a patriarchal society, entrenched in the archaic belief that women are a liability to the community.

Forms of Crimes Against Women

From female foeticide and infanticide to illiteracy and child marriage, women had gone through all forms of crimes and violence. While it is important to take measure to remove the menace of crimes against women, it is crucial to analyse the base and source on which the entire premise stands. The answer to this analysis focuses on male domination. Violence against women is a manifestation of historically unequal power relations between men and women, which have led to the domination over and discrimination against women by men. Therefore, the key components of the dynamics of crimes against women are the concepts of gender and power.

Reasons for Crimes Against Women

As a social group, men have greater power and status than women and abuse and violence is an important way by which they seek to maintain their dominant position. As such, this has been true as in most parts of the world. Men dominate positions of political, economic and social power. Even though more and more women are taking on leadership roles in many walks of life, from government to private companies, the norm remains that leadership still has a male face.

Women who go into politics or who seek senior positions in business are often stigmatised for not acting like proper women. Because women in these roles might be seen as challenging men or taking space away from men, they often face harassment and abuse from men, who are attempting to reinforce their own power and control.

Crimes against women then maintains and is maintained by ideas about and practices of patriarchal masculinities. Violence is used, mostly by men to keep girls and women in their position of having less economic, political and social power.

When women try to assert their claims to such power, they are often attacked, verbally and physically. Further, because to be female is to be identified as being weaker and lesser than the masculine, they are seen to be 'naturally' vulnerable to male violence and thus, in need of male protection.

These ideas about feminine vulnerability and masculine strength expose women to more violence.

Conclusion

Thus, the matter of violence committed against women in India is massive and widespread. It requires more attention and adherence than what it already deserves. The first step to be taken is to change the masculine thinking of superiority and remove the idea of power from gender roles.

26. महिलाओं के विरुद्ध हिंसा पुरुष के वर्चस्व की अभिव्यक्ति है।

CAPF AC 2020

भारतीय समाज में महिलाओं पर अत्याचार होना कोई नई बात नहीं है। यहाँ पुरुष वर्चस्व को बनाए रखने के लिए हमेशा महिलाओं के स्वाभिमान और उनके जीवन की आहुति दी जाती रही है। वह सब कुछ सहती हुई कभी अपने साथ हो रहे दुर्व्यवहार और अत्याचार के विरोध में अपनी आवाज नहीं उठा पाइ, क्योंकि कहीं-न-कहीं वह जानती थी कि इस पुरुष प्रधान समाज में उसकी व्यथा सुनने वाला कोई नहीं है, इसीलिए अपने इसी जीवन को अपनी नियति मानती हुई वह सब कुछ सहन करना ही अपने और अपने परिवार के लिए बेहतर समझती थी।

प्रायः देखा जाता है कि महिलाएँ परिवार के अन्दर ही कभी पिता तो कभी पति किसी-न-किसी रूप में पुरुष के दमन और शोषण का शिकार हो जाती हैं जिसका सबसे बड़ा कारण है कि प्रकृति ने महिला को पुरुषों की अपेक्षा शारीरिक तौर पर कमजोर बनाया है जिसकी वजह से वे जल्दी ही पुरुषों के क्रोध और ईर्ष्या का शिकार हो जाती हैं।

दूसरी ओर हमारे देश में यह माना जाता रहा है कि पति को पत्नी पर हाथ उठाने का अधिकार शादी के बाद ही मिल जाता है, लेकिन अब परिस्थितियाँ इसके ठीक विपरीत हो चुकी हैं।

हमारी संवैधानिक व्यवस्था महिलाओं के ऊपर होने वाली हिंसा और उनके शोषण के प्रति सचेत हो गई है, जिनकी सहायता से कभी अबला और असहाय समझी जाने वाली महिलाएँ आज अपने अधिकारों के प्रति आवाज बुलन्द करने लगी हैं।

वर्ष 2006 में भारत सरकार द्वारा घरेलू हिंसा महिला संरक्षण अधिनियम, 2005 लागू किया गया है, जिसके अनुसार महिला, वृद्ध अथवा बच्चों के साथ होने वाली किसी भी प्रकार की हिंसा अब अपराध की श्रेणी में आती है और इसका दोषी पाए जाने पर कड़ी सजा का प्रावधान भी है अर्थात् कोई भी महिला यदि परिवार के पुरुष द्वारा की गई मारपीट अथवा अन्य प्रताड़ना से त्रस्त है, तो वह घरेलू हिंसा की शिकार मानी जाएगी। अतः महिला संरक्षण अधिनियम 2005, महिला को घरेलू हिंसा के विरुद्ध संरक्षण और सहायता का अधिकार प्रदान करता है।

महिलाओं के विरुद्ध हिंसा के मुख्य कारण

हमारे समाज में बेटी पैदा होने से ही उसके साथ भेदभाव होना शुरू हो जाता है। उसकी स्वतन्त्रता को कुचल देना भारतीय पुरुषों की आदत रही है। कहीं यदि वह अपनी आजादी व अस्तित्व के लिए आवाज उठाती है, तो उसके साथ गलत व्यवहार और मारपीट कर उसे चुप करा दिया जाता है। इस प्रकार महिलाओं के विरुद्ध हिंसा के निम्नलिखित कारण होते हैं

1. **समतावादी शिक्षा का अभाव**

हमारे पुरुष प्रधान समाज में लड़कियों की शिक्षा को न्यूनतम महत्त्व दिया जाता है। शहरी क्षेत्रों में तो स्थिति तब भी थोड़ा ठीक है, किन्तु ग्रामीण क्षेत्रों में लड़कियाँ आज भी शिक्षा और जागरूकता से वंचित हैं। इसके अतिरिक्त हमारे परिवारों में पितृ सत्ता अत्यधिक महत्त्व रखती है।

2. **महिला को स्वावलम्बी बनने से रोकना**

पुरुष वर्ग महिलाओं को अपने अधीन रखने में ही विश्वास रखता है। उसे आर्थिक तौर पर आत्मनिर्भर बनने से रोकना महिला के खिलाफ हिंसा को जन्म देता है।

3. **शराब की लत**

शराब की लत व्यक्ति को कुछ भी करने को विवश कर देती है। वह सही गलत का फर्क किए बिना छोटे से झगड़े में ही अपनी पत्नी पर अपना वर्चस्व जमाते हुए उसके साथ मारपीट पर उतारु हो जाता है।

4. **पुरुष के निर्देशों का पालन न करना**

पुरुषों के निर्देशों का पालन न करना भी महिलाओं के प्रति हिंसा का एक कारण है। यदि महिलाओं द्वारा पुरुषों की कोई बात काट दी जाती है तो यह पुरुष को नागवार लगती है और वह हिंसा का सहारा लेता है।

इस प्रकार स्पष्ट है कि वर्तमान पुरुष प्रधान समाज में महिलाएँ सदैव ही पुरुषों के अधीन रही हैं। जैसा कि श्लोकों में भी कहा गया है कि महिलाएँ सदैव ही पुरुष के अधीन होती हैं—

पिता रक्षति कौमारे, पति रक्षति यौवने
पुत्र रक्षति स्थविरे भावे, नारी स्वातन्त्रयम न अर्हति

अर्थात् बचपन में नारी पिता के अधीन, यौवनावस्था में पति के अधीन, वृद्धावस्था में पुत्र के अधीन होती है और इस प्रकार वह कभी स्वतन्त्र नहीं होती है।

किन्तु समाज में सामंजस्य बनाए रखने हेतु यह आवश्यक है कि महिला एवं पुरुष एक-दूसरे का सम्मान करें, क्योंकि यह सृष्टि दोनों के सुखद संयोग पर निर्भर है। पुरुष द्वारा नारी को अर्द्धांगिनी मानकर उसे आधा हक प्रदान करने की आवश्यकता है, तभी सृष्टि का सही ढंग से संचालन सम्भव है।

27. Crisis of credibility in Indian electronic media

CAPF AC 2020

With more than 400 news channels, India, without any doubt, is the world's most over-served media market. The media in India has grown into an economic giant and matches the economic size of many individual industries in India.

It is considered the world's most dynamic media industry and one of the fastest growing anywhere. Not just economically, the media of the country has played a disproportionate role in shaping public perceptions of politics, electoral outcomes and the way power is exercised. In sharp contrast to its immense financial and political power, stands its indifferent and generally declining quality, reliability and authenticity, loss of diversity and pluralism, shallowness in reporting and comment on serious issues, and systematic violation of elementary norms of responsible journalism.

Credibility Crisis in Media

There is no denying that Indian electronic media industry is facing a credibility crisis. In recent years, the media has lowered the quality of India's public discourse. Media expansion has led to a shrinking of the public sphere and spread of elitist and socially retrograde values. This is producing a growing and potentially grave crisis of credibility. The low and falling quality of Indian journalism is evident in a number of ways. In this huge market, there is an alarming rise in the phenomena of paid news, fake news, biased news and unreliable news.

Trying to set an agenda for the country, most news television channels in India can easily be identified as either pro-government or anti-government. Not only this, the daily schedule of most news channels consists of talk shows, comedy programmes and music events, as if they are trying to turn into General Entertainment Channels. The Indian media has also often drawn flak from various quarters for 'sensationalism' and 'trivialisation'. Intemperate language used by some politicians and social activists reflecting their gender and community bias has invariably underlined the need for the media to scrupulously avoid devoting precious time to issues that do not serve the public interest.

Inadequacy of Media

The media no longer adequately performs the primary functions it is meant to, which give it public legitimacy namely, informing the public, telling the truth, analysing complex social, economic and political processes, providing a platform for public debate and acting as the people's watchdog or conscience. The mainstream journalistic paradigm in the Indian electronic media is shockingly insensitive to the real concerns of people.

Conclusion

India is at the cusp of both economic and social change and is considered to be one of the emerging Global superpowers. The time has come when some introspection by the Indian media is required to correct certain defects and thus, overcome crisis of credibility, thereby assisting India's growth in this period of transformation.

27. भारतीय इलेक्ट्रॉनिक मीडिया में साख का संकट | CAPF AC 2020

इलेक्ट्रॉनिक मीडिया का अर्थ विद्युत माध्यम या विद्युत संचार माध्यम होता है। इलेक्ट्रॉनिक साधनों के माध्यम से जो जनसंचार होता है, वह इलेक्ट्रॉनिक मीडिया है। इस माध्यम से हम सुन और देख सकते हैं। विशेष रूप से इलेक्ट्रॉनिक मीडिया एक ऐसी विधा है, जिसके माध्यम से व्यक्ति को देश और विदेश की खबरों के अतिरिक्त अन्य जानकारी मिलती है। इलेक्ट्रॉनिक मीडिया जनसंचार का एक प्रमुख माध्यम भी होता है। इसके अन्तर्गत रेडियो, सिनेमा, इण्टरनेट, टेलीविजन और मल्टीमीडिया इलेक्ट्रॉनिक मल्टीमीडिया के घटक हैं।

साख पर संकट का कारण

इलेक्ट्रॉनिक मीडिया ने जहाँ एक ओर समाज को अनेक सूचनाओं, घटनाओं, विवरणों तथा राष्ट्रीय और अन्तर्राष्ट्रीय स्तर की अनेक घटनाओं से अपडेट करने का कार्य किया है, वहीं दूसरी ओर इलेक्ट्रॉनिक मीडिया ने लालच, भय, द्वेष स्पर्द्धा, दुर्भावना एवं राजनैतिक कुचक्र के जाल में फँसकर अपनी भूमिका को कलंकित भी किया है।

व्यक्तिगत या संस्थागत निहित स्वार्थों के लिए यलो जर्नलिज्म को अपनाना, ब्लैकमेल द्वारा दूसरे का शोषण करना, चटपटी खबरों को महत्त्व देना और खबरों को तोड़-मोड़कर पेश करना, दंगे भड़काने वाली खबरे प्रसारित करना, लालच में सत्तारुढ़ दल की चापलूसी करना, अनावश्यक रूप से किसी की प्रशंसा और महिमा मण्डन करना और किसी दूसरे की आलोचना करना जैसे अनेक अनुचित कार्य इलेक्ट्रॉनिक मीडिया की साख पर बट्टा लगा रहे हैं। दुर्घटना एवं संवेदनशील मुद्दों को बढ़ा-चढ़ाकर पेश करना, ईमानदारी, नैतिकता, कर्त्तव्यनिष्ठा और साहस से सम्बन्धित खबरों को अनदेखा करना आजकल इलेक्ट्रॉनिक मीडिया का एक सामान्य लक्षण हो गया है। मीडिया के इस व्यवहार से समाज में अव्यवस्था और असन्तुलन की स्थिति पैदा हो गई है।

इलेक्ट्रॉनिक मीडिया के माध्यम से पश्चिमी संस्कृति का आगमन और प्रसार हो रहा है, जिससे समाज में अनावश्यक फैशन, अश्लीलता, चोरी, गुण्डागर्दी जैसी घटनाओं में वृद्धि हुई है। इस पतन के कारण युवा पीढ़ी भी पतन की गर्त में धँसती जा रही है। इण्टरनेट के माध्यम से असामाजिक क्रियाकलाप युवाओं तक पहुँच रहे हैं, जिससे उनमें नैतिकता, संस्कृति और सभ्यता की लगातार कमी आती जा रही है। इन सबकों देखते हुए आज इलेक्ट्रॉनिक मीडिया की भूमिका पर चर्चा करना आवश्यक हो गया है।

इलेक्ट्रॉनिक मीडिया की भूमिका कैसी होनी चाहिए?

इलेक्ट्रॉनिक मीडिया की भूमिका यथार्थ सूचना प्रारूपक एजेन्सी के रूप में होनी चाहिए। मीडिया द्वारा समाज को सम्पूर्ण विश्व में होने वाली घटनाओं की जानकारी मिलती है, इसीलिए इलेक्ट्रॉनिक मीडिया का यह प्रयास होना चाहिए कि ये जानकारियाँ यथार्थपरक हों। सूचनाओं को तोड़-मरोड़कर या दूषित कर प्रस्तुत करने का प्रयास नहीं होना चाहिए। समाज के हित एवं जानकारी के लिए सूचनाओं को यथावत् एवं विशुद्ध रूप में जनता के समक्ष पेश किया जाना चाहिए। इलेक्ट्रॉनिक मीडिया का प्रस्तुतीकरण ऐसा होना चाहिए कि जो समाज का मार्गदर्शन कर सके। सही एवं सटीक सूचनाएँ, ज्ञानवर्धक सूचनाएँ और श्रेष्ठ मनोरंजन आदि सामग्रियों का समावेशन होना चाहिए, ताकि समाज को सही दिशा प्रदान की जा सके।

इलेक्ट्रॉनिक मीडिया अपनी खबरों द्वारा समाज के सन्तुलन एवं असन्तुलन में बड़ी भूमिका निभाता है। मीडिया अपनी भूमिका द्वारा समाज में शान्ति, सौहार्द, समरसता और सौजन्य की भावना विकसित कर सकता है। सामाजिक तनाव, संघर्ष, मतभेद, युद्ध एवं दंगों के समय इलेक्ट्रॉनिक मीडिया को बहुत संयमित तरीके से कार्य करना चाहिए। राष्ट्र के प्रति भक्ति एवं एकता की भावना को उभारने में भी इलेक्ट्रॉनिक मीडिया की अहम भूमिका होती है। भूकम्प, बाढ़ या अन्य प्राकृतिक या मानवकृत आपदाओं के समय जनसहयोग उपलब्ध कराकर मीडिया द्वारा मानवता की बहुत बड़ी सेवा की जा सकती है।

निष्कर्ष आज इलेक्ट्रॉनिक मीडिया की बहुआयामी भूमिका को देखते हुए यह कहा जा सकता है कि इलेक्ट्रॉनिक मीडिया आज विनाशक एवं हितैषी दोनों तरह की भूमिकाओं में है।

अब आवश्यकता इस बात की है कि मीडिया अपनी शक्ति का सदुपयोग जनहित में करे और समाज का मार्गदर्शक करे ताकि वह भविष्य में भस्मासुर बनने से बच सके।

28. Securing India's international borders is a challenging exercise for the Indian armed forces CAPF AC 2020

With a continent of sub-continental proportions, India occupies a major strategic position in Southern Asia and governs the Northern Indian Ocean with a coastline that is 7,683 km long and an Exclusive Economic Zone that is over two million square km in size. India's land borders exceed 15,000 km which it shares with seven countries including a small segment with Afghanistan. With such a long border, the case of Indian borders is quite complex and thus, a good management of borders is extremely important for national safety. However in India, International border faces many issues that need appropriate addressal.

Challenge of Border Security in India

- The Border Security Scenario in India is marked by many threats, with different sectors of the border posing different challenges and complexities. The threats to India are arguably increasing, with principal threats coming from Pakistan, Bangladesh and China and noteworthy threats from Myanmar, Nepal and Bhutan.
- The Pakistan border sees cross-border terrorism and movement of armed militants and smuggling of goods and narcotics, while along the Bangladesh border, illegal immigration and smuggling problem of drugs, cattle, humans, artifacts, fake currency note etc., have been the main concern.
- The China border sees fairly regular armed intrusions. All these activities emphasise the need for extreme vigilance on the borders all the while strengthening the border guarding militaries.
- Unfortunately, in this scenario our border forces appear to be severely undermanned and under-equipped which is taking a heavy toll on economic, social and political stability of our country.
- The major problem faced while securing the international border include maritime boundaries. Maritime boundaries are still undefined and much of land borders are not determined on the ground.
- The disputed and unsettled nature of boundaries has made them a source of tension with their policing much more problematic. Since most of Indian borders are man-made artificial boundaries and not based on natural features such as rivers and watersheds, they are very permeable and easy to cross.
- The terrain and the landscape conditions make it difficult to keep the fencing sturdy. In addition, the diversity of forces on the same borders has unavoidably led to the lack of accountability as well as problems of identification, command and control.
- Further, in the 1980s, the Border Security Forces (BSF) obtained hi-tech systems such as Hand Held Thermal Imagery (HHTI) systems, Long Range Reconnaissance Observation Systems (LORROS) and Battle Field Surveillance Radars (BFSR) that greatly enhanced the detection ability of BSF personnel.
- Despite this modernisation process, however, there are still problems in the current system. Some shortcomings include significant gaps in the system at rivers, high-tech equipment not providing all-round security and border systems not always working in unfavourable climatic conditions.
- Largely, the current system is not integrated and communication between different paramilitary forces is reportedly scarce, consequently failing to provide a common operating picture at all levels.

Conclusion

To achieve stable and secure borders in India, robust technologies for border control and surveillance are required in order to combat real and alleged dangers to the country. At the ground-level, we need to visibly reinforce our positions. The Indian Army has to strategise and should revisit its rules of engagement on the borders, while being mindful that troops in tactical situations cannot be shackled by past treaties. Real-time intelligence, surveillance equipment and satellite imageries must be available to field formations that need to act on it. All these solutions do not solve the problems but they do help in better securing of the boundary.

28. भारत की अन्तर्राष्ट्रीय सीमाओं की रक्षा करना, भारतीय सशस्त्र सेनाओं के लिए एक चुनौतीपूर्ण कार्य है CAPF AC 2020

भारत एक सम्प्रभु राष्ट्र है और इसकी अन्तर्राष्ट्रीय सीमा की रक्षा करना भारत सरकार व भारतीय सशस्त्र सेनाओं का सर्वप्रमुख दायित्व है। हाल के कुछ वर्षों में सीमा विवाद ने एक व्यापक मुद्दे का रूप ले लिया है, जिस कारण इसकी रक्षा करना भारतीय सशस्त्र सेना के लिए चुनौतीपूर्ण हो गया है, जिसे हमारी सेना निरन्तर उत्तरदायित्वपूर्ण ढंग से निर्वाह कर रही है।

भारत की स्थलीय सीमा 15,106.7 किमी लम्बी है और द्वीपीय क्षेत्रों सहित इसकी तटीय सीमा रेखा 7516.6 किमी लम्बी है। देश के प्रति शत्रुतापूर्ण हितों के विरुद्ध देश की सीमाओं की रक्षा करना निश्चित रूप से एक चुनौतीपूर्ण कार्य है।

अन्तर्राष्ट्रीय सीमाओं की रक्षा करने के सन्दर्भ में भारतीय सशस्त्र सेना की चुनौती को निम्नलिखित बिन्दुओं के अन्तर्गत समझा जा सकता है
विरोधी तत्त्वों के विशेषकर चीन के पास नवीनतम तकनीक धन की प्रचुरता, संगठनात्मक ताकत, अन्य समान विचारधाराओं के साथ रणनीतिक गठजोड़ है। फिर चीन द्वारा उत्पादित इलेक्ट्रॉनिक एवं अन्य उपभोक्ता वस्तुओं की तस्करी की जा रही है। चीन का लद्दाख, अरुणाचल प्रदेश आदि क्षेत्र में सीमा विवाद है जिसे छिटपुट हमलों के सन्दर्भ में समझा जा सकता है।
इसी प्रकार कई स्थानों पर समुद्री और स्थलीय सीमाओं का उचित सीमांकन न होने के कारण संघर्ष की स्थिति बनी रहती है।
रेगिस्तानी, दलदली कच्छभूमि आदि क्षेत्रों वाली कृत्रिम सीमाओं पर घुसपैठ करना आसान हो जाता है।

फिर सीमा पार से आतंकवाद विशेषकर पाकिस्तान के द्वारा भारत को अस्थिर करने का प्रयास किया जाता है।

इसी प्रकार पूर्वोत्तर क्षेत्र में विद्रोहियों के लिए पड़ोसी शत्रु राष्ट्र सुरक्षित आश्रय स्थल के रूप में कार्य करते हैं। इन उग्रवादियों/विद्रोहियों को हथियारों की आपूर्ति करते हैं।

कई बार ऐसा भी देखा जाता है कि जब भारतीय सेना द्वारा आतंकवाद, उग्रवाद के खिलाफ कार्रवाई की जाती है तो स्थानीय लोगों द्वारा इसका विरोध किया जाता है, साथ ही अन्तर्राष्ट्रीय जगत भी मानवाधिकार का हवाला देकर इसकी निन्दा करते हैं।

चीन जैसे बड़े राष्ट्रों से तुलना करने पर हम देखते हैं कि हमारी सैन्य बलों की संख्या कम है, आधारभूत संरचना की कमी आज भी बनी हुई है, साथ ही नवीनतम तकनीक व हथियारों की तुलनात्मक रूप से कमी है।

इन सब चुनौतियों के बावजूद हमारी सशस्त्र सेना ने निरन्तर अपनी उत्तरदायी भूमिका का परिचय दिया है जिसे हाल के वर्षों में भी प्रत्यक्ष उदाहरण से देखा जा सकता है; जैसे–डोकलाम विवाद, गलवान घाटी में चीन को मुँहतोड़ जवाब, पाकिस्तान पर सर्जिकल स्ट्राइक, ऑपरेशन बालाकोट आदि।

साथ ही भारत सरकार निरन्तर रक्षा क्षेत्र को मजबूत करने के लिए प्रतिबद्ध है, जिसके लिए वह निरन्तर प्रयास कर रहा है। आज सेना के आवागमन के लिए आधारभूत संरचना पर बल दिया जा रहा है, नई-नई तकनीकें अपनाई जा रही हैं, विदेशों से हथियार आयात में हमारा दूसरा स्थान है, साथ ही अपने यहाँ भी नवीन हथियारों के निर्माण पर बल दिया जा रहा है। तीनों सेनाओं के बीच समन्वय के लिए 'चीफ ऑफ डिफेन्स स्टाफ' के पद का सृजन किया गया है। भारत सरकार विभिन्न देशों की सेनाओं के साथ व अपनी तीनों सेनाओं के मध्य परस्पर सैन्य अभ्यास को बढ़ावा देकर भारतीय सेना के शौर्य का प्रदर्शन कर रही है।

इस प्रकार कहा जा सकता है कि सीमित संसाधन, अपर्याप्त नवीन तकनीक, उचित सीमांकन के न होने के बावजूद भी हमारी सेना निरन्तर भारत की सीमाओं की रक्षा कर अपनी चुनौतीपूर्ण भूमिका को अन्जाम दे रही है, जिस कारण हमारी सशस्त्र सेना हमारे आदर्श व गौरव का प्रतीक बनी हुई है।

29. Parenting in a competitive Indian society is a challenge

CAPF AC 2020

In today's world where the pace of living the life we crave for takes a toll in us, the ultimate winner is one who believes in the survival of the fittest.

Competitive Race among Parents

From an early age, each generation has an extra burden to carry the expectations of the previous generation and produce a better result to outrun everyone and come on top. Thus, as soon as a child a born, he/she enters a competition and a rat race and each parents enables participation in it for the world moves ahead with the spirit of competition.

Though this competitive spirit is a huge factor and an equally important lesson in life, it somehow manages to deprive the little ones growing of their right to childhood. The common psychology of most parents lie in making their children the best in whatever they do-be it education or even a simple fancy dress competition. However, with India being the largest populated country, this competition becomes more complex and fierce having many disastrous effects.

Plight of Children vs Parents

Nowadays, children are exposed to struggle quite early. Instead of freedom and innocence to play, do mischief and enjoy the simplicity of life, syllabus and tests are their constant companions. Even the fun time activities are graded to see who did the best work. The children are made to work hard, too hard for something they are not even sure they want. They are robbed of simple, uncomplicated joys like lazing around, meandering-plain leisure. In addition, parents often send children to tuition centres and other extracurricular activities that span the entire day such that a child does not have any time to play.

As a result, the picture of a balanced childhood, kids going to school, doing a little of homework and playing fort, flying kites and playing in the streets games has become a myth. Today, more and more children have been suffering from clinical depression, sleep deprivation, eating disorders, stress and unnecessary worry to fulfill their parents' expectations. Consequently, children do not grow organically. In fact, they suffer from burnout, lose interest in hobbies and withdraw from friends and family.

Conclusion

The problem here, then, lies not with parenting but the challenge of parenting. While parents want their child to be successful in the future which will require them to face competition, there is also a fear of mental health related issues. Thus, doing away with competition is not practical, but we can put a capping limit on it. Parents should go for moderate parenting. They should moderate their questions about winning, marks obtained, rank secured, etc., and change to a system in which the kid enjoys the process.

29. प्रतिस्पर्धात्मक भारतीय समाज में शिशुपालन एक चुनौती है।

CAPF AC 2020

वर्ष 1991 में भारत ने अपनी नई आर्थिक नीति के तहत् उदारीकरण, निजीकरण एवं वैश्वीकरण को अपनाया, जिसके बाद हमारे समाज में क्रान्तिकारी परिवर्तन हुए। निःसन्देह इसके बाद भारतीय अर्थव्यवस्था को गति मिली व भारत विकास के पथ पर आगे बढ़ा, लेकिन इसका एक दूसरा पहलू भी है। भारत का परम्परागत समाज अब आधुनिक व प्रतिस्पर्धात्मक समाज में तब्दील हो चुका है, जिसका एक मुख्य दुष्प्रभाव शिशुपालन के सन्दर्भ में समझा जा सकता है।

शिशुपालन आज प्रतिस्पर्धात्मक समाज में एक चुनौती बन चुकी है। वैश्वीकरण तथा निजीकरण के कारण एक तरफ अमीरी व गरीबी के बीच खाई जहाँ और अधिक बढ़ गई है, वहीं दूसरी ओर लोग भौतिकतावाद के प्रति कुछ ज्यादा ही आकर्षित हो रहे हैं, जिस कारण लोग परिवार के रिश्तों को सम्भालने से ज्यादा अपनी आर्थिक सुरक्षा पर ज्यादा ध्यान दे रहे हैं। स्थिति आज यहाँ तक पहुँच गई है कि माँ अपने बच्चों को जन्म देने के बाद समय नहीं दे पा रही है।

गरीब महिलाएँ मेहनत मजदूरी के लिए अपने बच्चों को या तो अकेले या पड़ोसियों के सहारे छोड़कर घर के बाहर जाती हैं जिससे वे अपने बच्चों को उपयुक्त समय नहीं दे पाती हैं।

आज की महिलाएँ सार्वजनिक और निजी दोनों क्षेत्रों में निरन्तर नए नए मुकाम हासिल कर रही हैं और देश के विकास में उनका योगदान निरन्तर बढ़ रहा है, परन्तु यह भी सत्य है कि वे चाहकर भी अपने शिशु की देखभाल स्वयं नहीं कर पाती हैं, बल्कि अपने शिशु की देखरेख के लिए किसी दाय को अपने यहाँ नौकरी देती है, लेकिन सभी महिलाओं के लिए यह सम्भव नहीं है। फिर एक दाय तथा एक माँ के द्वारा शिशु की देखरेख में पर्याप्त अन्तर होता है। शिशु को अपने माँ का दूध तक नहीं मिल पाता है, जिस कारण बच्चों में कुपोषण जैसी समस्या बढ़ रही है।

हमारा समाज वर्षों से पुरुषवादी रहा है। पुरुषों का यह मानना है कि बच्चों का पालन माँ की जिम्मेदारी है, जो हमारी संकीर्ण मानसिकता को अभिव्यक्त करता है। पुरुषों को यह जिम्मेदारी स्वीकार करनी चाहिए कि यदि माँ काम पर गई है तथा वे बेरोजगार होकर घर पर बैठे हैं तो शिशुपालन उनका कर्त्तव्य है।

आज हमारे भारतीय समाज में शिशुपालन इसलिए भी एक चुनौती है कि आज हमारा समाज एकल परिवार आधारित हो गया है। संयुक्त परिवार खत्म हो रहे हैं, जिस कारण बच्चों को देखने वाला कोई नहीं होता है।

शिशुपालन की जिम्मेदारी से बचने के लिए वे सन्तानोत्पत्ति में विलम्ब करते हैं या फिर भ्रूण हत्या बढ़ती है। यदि बच्चे का जन्म हो भी जाए तो

शिशुओं के अच्छे लालन-पालन के अभाव में शिशु कुपोषित मानसिक-शारीरिक रूप से दिव्यांग भी हो जाते हैं। साथ ही अकेले रहने के कारण बच्चों को धीरे-धीरे परिवार से अलगाव हो जाता है, जिस कारण आगे जाकर वे गलत संगत में पड़ जाते हैं, जिससे परिवार व समाज पर संकट बढ़ता है।

इस प्रकार आज के प्रतिस्पर्धात्मक समाज में यह एक बहुत बड़ी चुनौती है। यद्यपि सरकार ने कुछ उल्लेखनीय प्रयास किए हैं; जैसे–मातृत्व अवकाश को बढ़ाकर 26 सप्ताह किया गया है और आँगनबाड़ी को इससे जोड़ा जा रहा है आदि।

इन प्रयासों के बावजूद अभी भी इस क्षेत्र में काफी प्रयास व सुधार करने की आवश्यकता है, साथ ही माता-पिता दोनों को यह जिम्मेदारी स्वीकार करनी चाहिए, क्योंकि यह उनका नैतिक दायित्व है।

30. Ensuring social justice is a human right

CAPF AC 2020

Social justice is defined as "justice in terms of the distribution of wealth, opportunities and privileges within a society." Often this is achieved through institutions or services that work to make sure people can equally access the benefits of social cooperation and guard against socio-economic inequality.

Human rights, on the other hand, are moral principles or norms for certain standards of human behaviour which are regularly protected in municipal and international law. These definitions state that social justice and human rights are two different concepts but in practice they are closely linked.

Social justice and human rights have a shared goal-human dignity and equality for all. The issues that make social justice difficult to achieve, such as poverty, exclusion and discrimination are in direct contradiction with human rights, which apply to all individuals indiscriminately.

Through various laws and policies, a government controls the activities of individuals or companies so as to ensure social justice. These laws and policies are what ensure human rights. Thus, when we ensure social justice, we ensure a human right.

This can be proven by the fact that private companies, contractors, business persons, in order to make higher profits, often resort to unfair practices such as ignoring the conditions of work and the damage to the environment as well as the people of the neighbourhood, etc.

A major role of the government and those laws that maintain human right, therefore, is to control the activities of such entities by making, enforcing and upholding laws so as to prevent unfair practices and ensure social justice.

Social justice then is undertaken by the government for bringing in behavioural changes in society and addressing the means of exploitation by engaging more with the basic socio-cultural issues such as gender-based discrimination, insensitivity towards disabled, etc. It ensures that the dignity of individuals is not being trespassed by focussing on the marginalised sections like the poor, illiterates, marginal farmers, tribals, etc.

Conclusion

Human rights, then, help fight all indignity. In addition to promoting equality generally, human rights protect against direct and indirect discrimination based on certain characteristics. Human rights provide a legal framework that allows individuals to hold government to account and requires the state to create conditions necessary for the achievement of social justice. Thus, it can be said that ensuring social justice is a human right.

30. सामाजिक न्याय की सुनिश्चितता एक मानवाधिकार है।

CAPF AC 2020

सामाजिक न्याय व मानवाधिकार वस्तुतः एक-दूसरे के पूरक हैं। सामाजिक न्याय के अन्तर्गत मनुष्यों को सभी आधारों पर समान माना जाता है। वहीं मानवाधिकार एक नैसर्गिक अधिकार है, जिसके अन्तर्गत व्यक्ति को अपने सर्वांगीण विकास के लिए समान अधिकार प्राप्त होते हैं। वस्तुतः मानवाधिकार का हनन यदि होता है, तो उस समाज में सामाजिक न्याय स्थापित नहीं हो सकता है। मार्टिन लूथर के अनुसार जहाँ भी अन्याय होता है अर्थात् मानवाधिकारों का हनन होता है, वहाँ हमेशा न्याय को खतरा रहता है। अतः किसी मनुष्य के साथ धार्मिक, सांस्कृतिक, सामाजिक पूर्वाग्रहों या अन्य किसी प्रकार के आधार पर भेदभाव नहीं किया जाना चाहिए, क्योंकि इस भेदभाव से एक तरफ जहाँ मानवाधिकार का हनन होता है, वहीं दूसरी ओर राष्ट्र और समाज में विभिन्न समस्याओं की उत्पत्ति होती है।

पश्चिमी राष्ट्रों में सामाजिक न्याय की अवधारणा विधि के समक्ष समता और विधि के शासन तक सीमित है, जबकि भारत जैसे विकासशील देशों में इस अवधारणा के अन्तर्गत सामाजिक कुरीतियाँ, दुराचार, निर्धनता, बेरोजगारी, बीमारी, भुखमरी आदि जैसी समस्या का निवारण भी सम्मिलित है।

भारत में सामाजिक न्याय तथा मानवाधिकार को स्थापित करने हेतु भारतीय संविधान में अनेक प्रावधान किए गए हैं, साथ ही सरकार अपने विभिन्न लोक कल्याणकारी सामाजिक-आर्थिक कार्यक्रमों के माध्यम से भी सामाजिक न्याय सुनिश्चित करने का प्रयास करती है।

भारत के संविधान की प्रस्तावना में सामाजिक न्याय का उल्लेख है, साथ ही प्रतिष्ठा एवं अवसर की समानता का उल्लेख भी किया गया है। इसी प्रकार भारतीय संविधान के भाग-3 में मौलिक अधिकारों का उल्लेख है, अनुच्छेद 14 से 18 तक समानता के अधिकार का वर्णन है। अनुच्छेद 15 के तहत् किसी भी व्यक्ति के साथ धर्म, जाति, लिंग, मूलवंश अथवा जन्म स्थान के आधार पर भेदभाव प्रतिबन्धित है, साथ ही इसी अनुच्छेद के तहत् सामाजिक-आर्थिक रूप से पिछड़े वर्गों तथा अनुसूचित जातियों व जनजातियों के सामाजिक उत्थान के लिए विशेष प्रावधान करने की छूट दी गई है।

इसी प्रकार अनुच्छेद 17 में संविधान द्वारा अस्पृश्यता जैसी सामाजिक बुराई को प्रतिबन्धित किया गया है तथा अस्पृश्यता के अनुसरण करने को दण्डनीय अपराध माना गया है। अनुच्छेद 23 के अन्तर्गत बेगारी, बन्धुआ मजदूरी आदि को प्रतिबन्धित किया गया है, जबकि अनुच्छेद 24 के माध्यम से बाल मजदूरी पर प्रतिबन्ध लगाया गया है।

संवैधानिक प्रावधानों के अतिरिक्त सरकार विभिन्न कानूनों; जैसे–दहेज अधिनियम, हिन्दू विवाह अधिनियम, तीन तलाक, घरेलू हिंसा अधिनियम, अनुसूचित जाति व जनजाति निवारण अधिनियम आदि के माध्यम से सामाजिक न्याय को सुनिश्चित करने का प्रयास कर रही है, जिससे मानवाधिकार की रक्षा हो सके।

इसी प्रकार केन्द्र व राज्य सरकार अपने लोक कल्याणकारी कार्यक्रमों के माध्यम से समाज में सामाजिक न्याय स्थापित करने का प्रयास करती है। उल्लेखनीय प्रयास के बावजूद आज भी हमारे समाज में सामाजिक न्याय स्थापित नहीं हो रहा है व मानवाधिकार का हनन हो रहा है। उदाहरण के लिए दलितों पर अत्याचार, लैंगिक असमानता, महिलाओं पर हिंसा, यौन शोषण, बाल मजदूरी, गरीबी, बेरोजगारी आज भी प्रमुख समस्या के रूप में विद्यमान हैं।

इस प्रकार कहा जा सकता है कि एक समतामूलक समाज का निर्माण करने के लिए समाज के सभी वर्गों को सामाजिक न्याय दिलाने के लिए कार्य करना होगा, जो प्रत्येक मनुष्य का मानवाधिकार है। यद्यपि इस दिशा में संविधान के प्रावधान व सरकार के प्रयास सराहनीय हैं, लेकिन इसे और प्रभावशाली बनाने की आवश्यकता है, जिसमें सरकार के साथ-साथ हम लोगों की भी परस्पर भूमिका हो।

31. The Earth is not for humans only — CAPF AC 2019

Earth is the only habitable planet out of the eight planets in our solar system with Pluto being discarded as a Dwarf planet by the International Astronomical Union in August, 2006. It is the only habitat for the predicted 8.7 Million species, of which 2.2 Million species are aquatic in nature. Out of these species, human beings have been unanimously acknowledged as the smartest inhabitants of the planet possessed with ample cognitive abilities, processing power and motor skills. The realisation of its superiority has led humanity to turn a blind eye to other inhabitants of the planet for their self-convenience. As a result, nature became man's monopoly.

The increase in human activities such as industrialisation from the 1780s till contemporary times has exploited the natural habitat and resources such as forests, water bodies as well as the climate.

Humans have consumed almost every resource present on the planet without any regard for other creatures.

Resultantly, other species who have the right to live on Earth are facing extinction. The new UN Global Assessment Report warned that bio-diversity is declining globally at unprecedented rates and will result in the extinction of one million out of eight million species found on Earth. This sixth major mass extinction is caused by humans whose anti-environmental actions demonstrate that humans have an exclusive right to live on Earth and use its wealth.

In Indonesia, the replacement of rainforest with palm oil plantations has ravaged the habitat of critically endangered orangutans and Sumatran tigers. The number of the Great Indian Bustard has now dwindled to just 150 due to the depletion of grassland.

The passenger pigeons, dodo birds and stellar sea cows are already extinct from the Earth. Global warming and its resultant rise in temperature have led to the destruction of the 'Island of Bramble Cay in the Great Barrier Reef' that sheltered the now-extinct species of Bramble Cay Melomys. These are just small examples. One can find many such examples of loss of flora and fauna on the planet.

In the light of this damage, the National Green Tribunal validated the aforementioned statement that 'The Earth is not for humans only' and that it is a shelter for all wildlife. Keeping in mind the damage already done and the impacts visible in its severe form, it is time that to put a cap on these exploitative activities. A fundamental reorientation of human consciousness, accompanied by action that is bornout of inner commitment, is very much needed.

31. धरती केवल मनुष्यों के लिए नहीं है — CAPF AC 2019

हिन्दू धर्म की 'वसुधैव कुटुम्बकम' की अवधारणा के अनुसार, पृथ्वी एक परिवार है तथा इस परिवार में पृथ्वी के सभी प्राणियों एवं पौधों को शामिल किया गया।

हिन्दू शास्त्रों में भी 'सन्तोषम् परमम् सुखम्' का दर्शन प्रतिपादित किया गया है। 'भगवत्‌गीता' में भी इस सिद्धान्त को रेखांकित किया गया है कि मानव को प्रकृति की संरचना में छेड़छाड़ करने का प्रयास नहीं करना चाहिए न ही इसे नष्ट करने की कोशिश करनी चाहिए। वस्तुतः भगवत्‌गीता में प्राकृतिक संरक्षण एवं जैव विविधता को बनाए रखने की शिक्षा दी गई है।

पृथ्वी या प्रकृति में जैव विविधता की पर्याप्त उपस्थिति पर्यावरण को सन्तुलित बनाए रखती है। प्रकृति में पाए जाने वाले सभी प्रकार के जीव-जन्तु तथा पेड़-पौधों की अपनी विशेष भूमिका जैव चक्र में पाई जाती है। जैव चक्र की सन्तुलित अवस्था पृथ्वी के अस्तित्व के लिए अत्यन्त आवश्यक है।

वर्तमान में पूरा विश्व पर्यावरणीय समस्याओं का सामना कर रहा है। इस पर्यावरणीय समस्याओं के कई कारण हैं। इसमें कुछ प्रमुख कारण हैं–मानव द्वारा पर्यावरण में उत्पन्न की गई अव्यवस्था जिसके कारण जलवायु परिवर्तन, वैश्विक तापन, ओजोन क्षरण, अम्ल वर्षा इत्यादि समस्याएँ उभर कर सामने आई हैं। मानव व जन्तुओं में परस्पर संघर्ष की स्थिति देखनें में आ रही हैं। यह संघर्ष भी वस्तुतः जन्तुओं द्वारा अपने अस्तित्व को लेकर हैं। मानव द्वारा कृषि कार्यों से सम्बन्धित भूमि विस्तार, शहरों के निर्माण एवं विस्तार के कारण जीवों के प्राकृतिक आवासों को नष्ट किया जा रहा है। ऐसी स्थिति में जीव-जन्तु अपने अस्तित्व हेतु संघर्ष कर रहे हैं। वर्तमान में ऐसी कितनी प्रजातियाँ हैं, जो या तो नष्ट हो गई या नष्ट होने की कगार पर हैं। भारत में शेर, चीता, घड़ियाल, हाथी इत्यादि जानवरों को संरक्षण हेतु विशेष कार्यक्रमों का संचालन किया जा रहा है। मानव ने अपने विकास की प्रक्रिया में बड़ी मात्रा में वनों को नष्ट किया है, जबकि ये पेड़-पौधे पर्यावरणीय चक्र के लिए अत्यन्त आवश्यक हैं। इसके अभाव में मानव ऑक्सीजन प्राप्त नहीं कर सकेगा, जो उसके जीवन के अस्तित्व के लिए आवश्यक है। वनों के विनाश ने जहाँ हरित क्षेत्र को कम किया है, वहीं जीव-जन्तुओं के प्राकृतिक आवास को क्षति पहुँचाई है। प्राकृतिक आवासों के अभाव में जीव-जन्तुओं के अस्तित्व पर संकट के बादल घूमने लगे हैं। वर्तमान में ब्राजील के अमेजन के वर्षा वनों में लगी आग के कारण बड़ी मात्रा में पेड़-पौधों को क्षति पहुँची है, कई प्रजातियों के खत्म होने के आसार उत्पन्न हो गए हैं। साथ ही पर्यावरण को बहुत बड़े स्तर पर नुकसान हो रहा है।

मनुष्य द्वारा धरती के उन संसाधनों का उपयोग तेजी से अपने लाभ के लिए किया जा रहा है जो समाप्य तथा मूल्यवान संसाधन हैं।

संसाधनों के दोहन में हम धरती के अन्य प्रजातियों की चिन्ता नहीं करते, जिनका जीवन हमारे अस्तित्व के लिए आवश्यक है। इस प्रवृत्ति के लगातार बढ़ने से संकट गहरा गया है। हमारे सामने अब जल, भूमि तथा वायु का संकट है। प्रकृति के मनुष्य की कलुषताओं के विरुद्ध चेतावनी देना आरम्भ कर दिया है।

धरती केवल मनुष्य की नहीं है। यह उन कोटिशः प्रजातियों की है जिसमें मनुष्य भी शामिल है। मनुष्य को ईश्वर ने जिस धरती का संरक्षक बनाकर भेजा था वही इसका भक्षक बन रहा है। मनुष्य को 'मानवता' को बचाए रखने के लिए यह जानना आवश्यक है कि पृथ्वी केवल उसका निवास स्थान नहीं है, बल्कि यहाँ जन्म लेने वाली सभी सूक्ष्म तथा वृहद् जीव तथा वनस्पति प्रजातियों की जीवन का आधार है।

32. The impact of social media on social relationships

CAPF AC 2019

The Greek legendary philosopher and political scientist, Aristotle professed, 'Man is by nature a social animal.' The quote signifies that social relations and their consequent social interactions are the very essences of human existence. However, the advent of social media platforms such as Facebook, Instagram, Whatsapp and Twitter has revolutionised the nature of social relations from real-life interactions to predominantly digital in nature.

Age of Social Media

It is the Age of the Internet and Social Media has emerged as an indispensable tool of maintaining social relations. Social media is the means to communicate, exchange ideas and information and stay connected virtually. It has become part and parcel of everyone's life irrespective of the age group. From connecting with friends on the other side of the globe to quickly sending money, from being able to attend meetings, conferences and events from any part of the world to attending online classes, social media has empowered us like none other.

While it is true to say that social media has brought a revolution, it will not wrong to point out that it has negatively impacted social relationships. According to research, globally, people spend an average of 2 hours 24 minutes every day on social media, if someone signed up at 16 and lived to be 70, they would have spent 5.7 years of their lives on it. People stay so engrossed on social media sites virtually that they tend to forget the essence of 'real' connections with real people. Despite bringing the world closer, somehow social media has driven people away from each other.

Social Media Addiction

Social media is addictive. This means that one is way more concerned by what is online or how many friends one has online than in real life. As a result, some social media users tend to suffer from anxiety and depression. Further, as one can easily connect with a person though internet, the need for face-to-face communication has reduced in all spheres of life. Be it work, education, family or friend, one can easily video call another, As a result, an individual is isolated and secluded. Such a person is socially awkward as he/she does not learn to build social relations. This person, then, might ignore the emotions, expectations and experiences of those near them, and eventually become less involved in activities that used to be interesting before. Due to this, the level of bonding will decline after a short period and eventually affect the stability of the relationship.

Social Media Risks vs Opportunities

The above analysis has identified modern technologies as inventions that present both opportunities and risks to every user. Those who are engaged in various relationships should utilise them sparingly to minimise cases of addiction and depression. Over reliance on social media will destroy partnerships by affecting people's social skills, triggering anxiety and discouraging them from communicating directly with their partners. These insights have the potential to guide more individuals to use modern technology cautiously if they want to have fruitful relationships.

Conclusion

Thus, it is imperative that we find a balance in how we use our social media. A right balance will not only help you start but also foster a healthy relationship.

32. सामाजिक सम्बन्धों पर सामाजिक माध्यम का प्रभाव

CAPF AC 2019

सोशल मीडिया ने समाज का एकीकरण किया है। इसने लोगों के बीच दूरियों को सीमित कर उनके बीच डिजिटल ही सही नेटवर्क स्थापित किया है। सोशल मीडिया के माध्यम से हम उन व्यक्तियों से भी सम्पर्क एवं सम्बन्ध स्थापित कर सकते हैं, जिनको हम प्रत्यक्ष रूप से नहीं जानते, जबकि इससे पहले हमें लोगों से सम्पर्क साधने हेतु दूरभाष यन्त्रों का सहारा लेना पड़ता था। इस माध्यम के द्वारा हमारी शारीरिक उपस्थिति नहीं हो पाती थी। वर्तमान में हम सोशल मीडिया से इतने प्रभावित है कि हमारे पड़ोसी हमसे दूर हो रहे हैं पर दूर के लोग पड़ोसी बन रहे हैं। सोशल मीडिया ने व्यक्तियों से सम्बन्ध स्थापित करने हेतु उनके सदैव उपस्थित रहने की अनिवार्यता को समाप्त कर दिया। वर्तमान में हम वीडियो-कॉलिंग के माध्यम से सैकड़ों या हजारों किमी दूर बैठे व्यक्ति से सम्पर्क स्थापित कर सकते हैं। प्रत्यक्ष रूप से हम उन्हें देख सकते हैं तथा बातें कर सकते हैं।

वस्तुतः सम्बन्धों को विस्तार देने के क्रम में सोशल मीडिया के विभिन्न माध्यमों का विकास हुआ है, जिसमें फेसबुक, टिवट्र, इन्स्टाग्राम इत्यादि प्रमुख हैं। इसके माध्यम से विभिन्न प्रकार के समूहों एवं व्यक्तिगत स्तर सम्बन्ध स्थापित करने में सहायता मिली है। इस सोशल मीडिया का प्रयोग प्रत्येक आयु वर्ग के लोगों द्वारा किया जा रहा है। छात्रों द्वारा अपने समकक्ष छात्रों से शिक्षण कार्यों में सहायता हेतु इस मीडिया का प्रयोग किया है।

सोशल मीडिया की उपस्थिति ने मानव सम्बन्धों को नकारात्मक एवं सकारात्मक दोनों रूपों में प्रभावित किया है। सोशल मीडिया ने सम्बन्ध स्थापन में दूरी को जहाँ खत्म किया है, वहीं व्यक्ति से व्यक्ति के प्रत्यक्ष सम्बन्धों को बहुत ही नकारात्मक रूप से प्रभावित किया।

सोशल मीडिया पर अपनी गलत पहचान के द्वारा लोगों से सम्बन्ध स्थापित करके उनका आर्थिक, शारीरिक, मानसिक शोषण का प्रचलन दिन-प्रतिदिन बढ़ता जा रहा है। सोशल मीडिया पर किसी धर्म, जाति, व्यक्ति विशेष के विषय में भ्रामक एवं गलत सूचना डालकर विभिन्न धर्मों, जातियों एवं व्यक्तियों के प्रति परस्पर विद्वेष की भावना को बढ़ाया जाता है। इस प्रकार लोगों, विभिन्न समूहों, विभिन्न धर्मों के बीच परस्पर सौहार्द्र पूर्ण सम्बन्ध को विद्वैषपूर्ण सम्बन्ध में बदल दिया जाता है। भारत में कई साम्प्रदायिक दंगे इन्हीं सोशल मीडिया के कारण से प्रारम्भ हुए। इन्हीं कारणों से कई बार प्रशासन द्वारा इनको कुछ समय के लिए बन्द करने का निर्णय लिया गया। सोशल मीडिया की लत भी मानव के लिए अत्यन्त हानिकारक है

जिसके फलस्वरूप वह अपने सामाजिक दायित्वों से दूर रहता है एवं समाज में अपनी सकारात्मक उपस्थिति से बचता है।

वस्तुतः हमें सोशल मीडिया पर सम्बन्ध स्थापित करने के स्थान पर प्रत्यक्ष व्यक्तिगत सम्बन्धों की स्थापना पर बल देना चाहिए। सामाजिक एवं सांस्कृतिक समारोहों पर अपनी सक्रिय उपस्थिति दर्ज करानी चाहिए।

33. Sustainable farming is the need of the hour than rhetorical promises **CAPF AC 2019**

The Indian Economy is an agricultural economy with monopoly of trade in wheat, rice, pulses and textiles such as cotton. Thus, Indian agriculture has served the dual purpose of commercial gain as well as for the sustenance of the common citizens and the farmers. However, excessive commercial agriculture to maintain the economy led to detrimental impacts on the soil and conditions for agriculture.

The introduction of chemicals such as fertilisers, pesticides and insecticides in farming got many delirious at the sight of what they could accomplish. However, it did not take long before the negative impact of chemical was seen not only in soil and the environment but also on the health of all living organisms on the planet. The soil started losing its fertility, the chemical leeched into underground resources and polluted water bodies and new diseases started afflicting humans and all other life forms.

In a world battered by new diseases and degradation of the environment, the demand for healthy and safe food is already showing an upward trend. This led to a need for another type of farming that not only meets the needs of the population but also maintains the ecological balance. Hence, the concept of sustainable farming came into being. Sustainable Agriculture refers to a substitute method of cultivation for conventional commercial agricultural practices. The Food and Agriculture Organisation (FAO) of the United Nations defines sustainable agriculture and Rural development as processes that meet the following criteria

- They meet the basic nutritional requirements of present and future generations.
- They provide durable livelihoods for all those engaged in agricultural production.
- They maintain the productive capacity of the natural resource base without disturbing the environment.
- They reduce the vulnerability of the agriculture sector to adverse conditions and strengthen self-reliance.

Sustainable agriculture replaces the orthodox agrarian practices that make overuse of High Yielding Variety (HYV) Seeds which leads to a gradual degradation of layers of soil, depletion of groundwater and endangering of bio-diversity.

By using domestic seeds and organic manure such as cow dung, rainwater harvesting and farming of naturally available crops, the aim of this form of farming is simple- to feed the world without damaging the environment or threatening human health.

As an eco-friendly approach, it reduces the reliance on limited natural resources and focuses on farming methods such as crop rotation, intercropping and companion planting, to help protect soil health and water quality while eliminating the need for damaging practices. Such a practice can create stronger local economies and economic opportunities for small-scale farmers, allowing them to produce more food with fewer resources. Further, it encourages social equity and helps create a more equitable food system.

In the face of food and health crisis faced by the world today, focusing only on higher yields at the expense of other sustainability pillars is not the food production system needed.

The world needs an integrated system that gives equal importance to all sustainability dimensions across the value chain and thus, helps establish a healthy and well-fed society. So, instead of empty rhetoric, the government should chalk out a long-term plan to implement sustainable agriculture all over the country.

33. संधारणीय कृषि शब्दाडंबरपूर्ण वादाओं की अपेक्षा इस समय की आवश्यकता है **CAPF AC 2019**

संधारणीय अथवा संपोषित कृषि की अवधारणा, प्राकृतिक संसाधनों तथा पर्यावरण संरक्षण पर विशेष बल देती है।

यह पृथ्वी के अस्तित्व को बनाए रखने के लिए आवश्यक है कि आर्थिक समृद्धि का स्वरूप सतत हो अर्थात् प्रकृति के संसाधनों का दोहन भविष्य की पीढ़ियों की आवश्यकता को देखते हुए किया जाए। आर्थिक समृद्धि का यह तरीका कृषि क्षेत्र में लागू होता है। कृषि क्षेत्र में रासायनिक तत्त्वों एवं विभिन्न प्रकार के खादों के प्रयोग ने जहाँ कृषि उत्पादन में तो वृद्धि की है, दूसरी ओर भूमि की गुणवत्ता को प्रतिकूल रूप से प्रभावित किया। कृषि उत्पादन के इस तरीके को सभी विकसित एवं विकासशील देशों द्वारा अपनाया जाने लगा है। गैर-धारणीय कृषि ने भूमि के अधिकतम शोषण को बढ़ाया है। फलस्वरूप भूमि में जैविक तत्त्वों की कमी होती जा रही है। कृषकों के द्वारा कृषि कार्यों में भूमि की वास्तविक आवश्यकता की जानकारी लिए असन्तुलित रूप से रासायनिक तत्त्वों एवं खादों का प्रयोग किया जा रहा है। कृषि का यह तरीका कृषि भूमि के अस्तित्व के लिए खतरे की घंटी है। ऐसी स्थिति में कृषि उत्पादन में कमी एक बहुत बड़ी जनसंख्या को भुखमरी की स्थिति में ला देगा।

वर्तमान परिदृश्य में अब आवश्यक है कि कृषकों को अपने पारम्परिक तरीकों में बदलाव लाते हुए धारणीय कृषि को अपनाना चाहिए। धारणीय कृषि की आवश्यकता को सभी राष्ट्रों एवं उनके राजनेताओं के द्वारा प्रोत्साहित किया जाना चाहिए।

संयुक्त राष्ट्र संघ के खाद्य एवं कृषि संगठन ने भी धारणीय कृषि की आवश्यकता को स्पष्ट करते हुए इसके विभिन्न मानकों का निर्धारण किया है।

धारणीय कृषि का महत्त्व इस सन्दर्भ में है कि इसके माध्यम से पर्यावरण को कोई क्षति नहीं होती है, जबकि वह मानव स्वास्थ्य के अनुकूल होता है अर्थात् इससे स्वास्थ्य को कोई नुकसान नहीं होता। पारिस्थितिकीय तन्त्र सन्तुलित रहता है। धारणीय कृषि के माध्यम से कृषक अधिक उत्पादन को प्राप्त कर सकते हैं। बिना किसी अधिक व्यय और पर्यावरण को क्षति पहुँचाए। धारणीय कृषि को किसी भी प्रकार के खेतों में सरलतापूर्वक

अपनाया जा सकता है। फलस्वरूप छोटे किसान भी इस कृषि को अपनाकर अपनी-अपनी जीविका चला सकते हैं।

परम्परागत कृषि तरीकों को छोड़ने हेतु सरकारों के द्वारा भी प्रयास किया जाना चाहिए। इसी को ध्यान में रखकर सरकार के द्वारा कई प्रकार के कृषि कार्यक्रमों की शुरुआत की गई है। कृषकों के लिए मृदा स्वास्थ्य कार्ड जारी किए गए हैं, जिसके माध्यम से मृदा के प्रकार एवं उसके अनुसार खाद प्रयोग की जानकारी प्राप्त की जा सकती है। टिकाऊ कृषि के लिए किसानों को तभी प्रोत्साहित किया जा सकता है जब उनके सुनिश्चित आय की प्रक्रिया को प्रभावी रूप दिया जाए। भारत सरकार ने प्रधानमन्त्री किसान सम्मान योजना (पीएम-किसान) के माध्यम से ऐसा करने का प्रयास किया है। किसानों के जीवन में बदलाव उन्हें कृषि प्रक्रिया को भी परिवर्तित करने का उत्साह देगा।

धारणीय कृषि की आवश्यकता मात्र भूमि के कार्बनिक गुणों को बचाए रखने के लिए नहीं अपितु कृषि-चक्र के लिए भी आवश्यक है। इसलिए सरकार के द्वारा पूरे भारत में इसे लागू करने का प्रयास किया जाना चाहिए।

34. The role of Indian Army in nation building

CAPF AC 2019

The Indian soldier is the epitome of courage and unflinching devotion to duty. With an ethos of hard work, simple needs and frugal habits, more than any other group or community in the country, the soldier embodies and represents the idea of India. He/she stands sentinel over the nation's borders in the high Himalayas in hail, sleet and snow, in icy blizzards and pouring rain. Despite the omnipresent danger, hardships and privations of life on the nation's troubled frontiers, he/she stands tall and firm. Thus, they create a secure environment for the country to prosper. This secure environment provided by the Army, ensuring the path to prosperity and development for the country as a whole, is only a part of the larger and ubiquitous role played by the Indian Army in nation building.

These various roles can be categorised as

- **Ensuring a Secure Environment** First and foremost, it is the secure environment provided by the army as a guarantor of national and territorial integrity that ensures the path to prosperity and development for the country as a whole. Today, the dimensions of conflict are manifold and not restricted to the border areas alone. Once again, it is this organisation which is combating the scourge of violence and terrorism unleashed by secessionist elements. As a vital organ of the state, it is the army, the ultimate arbiter of national safety and security, which ensures a safe environment for internal progress and prosperity.
- **Humanitarian Assistance** Another area where the army periodically occupies centre stage is humanitarian assistance and disaster relief. The Navy has played a stellar role in providing critical help on foreign shores and also evacuation of Indian citizens in distant lands during times of natural as well as human crisis. Due to its ingrained capabilities, equipment and disciplined application and its network of field hospitals, its transportation assets, engineer plant equipment and reconnaissance and communication resources with its nationwide reach, the army has saved countless lives and provided succour to the people of India, during many natural calamities.
- **Foreign Missions** In the international arena, military diplomacy in its various forms is a key element in engaging with other nations. The army has adequately leveraged its capacity of putting boots on ground by being the largest contributor to worldwide UN missions. It also provides invaluable support in terms of capacity building and capability development to various friendly foreign armies. Its training institutions have a sizeable presence of officers from such nations.
- **Trained Manpower** Within the country, the army has provided key support to the central armed police forces in terms of training, equipment and cross attachment of personnel for absorbing best practices. Outside its own organisation, the army has been a great facilitator in human resource development. The army is also a great reservoir of trained, skilled and disciplined manpower readily available for lateral absorption in other government organisations as well as the private sector. In that sense-development of human resource has always been a hallmark of the Indian army.

Conclusion

Concluding, democracy in India is continuing strongly and the Constitution of India remains respected. This has been facilitated by the armed forces as they have maintained, most scrupulously, the ideals enshrined in the Constitution. They have made a great contribution towards nourishment of democracy in the nation by not interfering in politics. The strength of the armed forces lies in their high standards of discipline and morale supported by a secular outlook and a non-political behaviour.

They have always provided support to the people in times of crisis, whether external or internal. Thus, the capability of the nation to maintain its most significant pillar of security has contributed significantly to the task of nation building.

34. राष्ट्र निर्माण में भारतीय सेना की भूमिका

CAPF AC 2019

"अगर कोई आपसे ये कहता है कि वो मौत से नहीं डरता है, तो या तो वो झूठ बोल रहा है या फिर वो भारतीय सेना के गोरखा रेजिमेंट का जवान है।"

मानिक शॉ का यह कथन भारतीय सेना की निडरता को परिलक्षित करता है। भारतीय सेना ने अपनी निडरता से राष्ट्र निर्माण में अहम योगदान दिया है। भारतीय सेना 15 जनवरी, 1948 को स्वतन्त्र रूप से अस्तित्व में आई थी। ब्रिटिश सरकार ने जनरल के. एम. कारियप्पा को भारतीय सेना की कमान सौंपी थी। तब से लेकर आज तक भारतीय सेना ने देश की रक्षा करने के साथ-साथ राष्ट्र निर्माण में भी अहम योगदान दिया है।

आजादी के बाद स्वतन्त्र रूप से अस्तित्व में आई भारतीय सेना ने सन् 1948, 1962, 1965, 1971 की लड़ाइयों के साथ-साथ सन् 1999 में कारगिल युद्ध में अदम्य साहस का परिचय दिया। इसके अतिरिक्त यह आतंकवाद, उग्रवाद, कानून व्यवस्था, दंगा, आपदा आदि के समय देश के काम आती है। भारतीय सेना धर्मनिरपेक्षता की मिसाल प्रस्तुत करती है। भारतीय सेना

में सभी धर्मों के व्यक्ति हैं। यह जाति, धर्म, सम्प्रदाय आदि के आधार पर भेदभाव नहीं करता है। यही कारण है कि यह एक एकीकृत बल है।

भारतीय सेना का प्राथमिक उद्देश्य राष्ट्रीय सुरक्षा और राष्ट्रवाद की एकता को सुनिश्चित करना, राष्ट्र को बाहरी व आन्तरिक खतरों से बचाना, देश की सीमाओं पर शान्ति और सुरक्षा को बनाए रखना है।

आपदा के समय जब प्रत्येक कोशिश विफल हो जाती है, तब भारतीय सेना काम आती है। जब पुलिस और अन्य एन्जेन्सियाँ, किसी भी स्थिति को नियन्त्रित करने में असमर्थ होती हैं, तो भारतीय सेना को उस स्थिति को नियन्त्रण करने के लिए कहा जाता है। कुछ महत्त्वपूर्ण दंगे, जिन्हें केवल सेना द्वारा नियन्त्रित किया गया था वें है–सिख दंगा (1984), मुम्बई दंगा (1992-93), गुजरात दंगा (2002) आदि।

बाढ़ और भूकम्प जैसी प्राकृतिक आपदाओं, जैसे—उत्तराखण्ड त्रासदी, केरल बाढ़, जम्मू-कश्मीर बाढ़ आदि के समय हम सेना का दमखम देख चुके हैं। यहाँ तक कि खेलों; जैसे—राष्ट्रीय खेल, एशियाई खेल, कॉमनवेल्थ खेल, ओलम्पिक खेल आदि में भी पदक के लिए हमें सेना पर निर्भर रहना पड़ता है। मिल्खा सिंह, राज्यवर्द्धन सिंह राठौर, विजय कुमार, मेजर ध्यानचन्द, जीतू राय, राम सिंह आदि खिलाड़ी इसके उदाहरण हैं।

वर्तमान समय में भारतीय सेना ने मुम्बई आतंकवादी हमला, बालाकोट अटैक, उरी अटैक आदि के समय देश की रक्षा की है। राष्ट्र निर्माण में भारतीय सेना के योगदान को विस्मृत नहीं किया जा सकता। इसके लिए भारतीय सेना ने अनेक कुर्बानियाँ भी दी हैं।

भारतीय सेना ने राष्ट्र निर्माण में अपनी भूमिका निभाई है। भारत का प्रत्येक भौगोलिक क्षेत्र सेना के महत्त कार्यों तथा साहसिक कारनामों की कहानियों से आवृत है। देश निर्माण में भारतीय सेना की भूमिका निर्विवाद है। देश को सम्मान और आत्म विश्वास देने में भारतीय सेना की अद्वितीय भूमिका रही है।

35. Online gaming is dangerously attractive to youth

CAPF AC 2019

In 1972, the world of entertainment was introduced the first video game home console, the Odyssey. Since then, the online gaming industry has become one of the major sunrise sectors of India. Today, online gaming in India has the potential to be a multi-billion-dollar industry with data revealing that the industry is worth ₹ 21 thousand Crore in 2023. At present, the children of our country play online games for an average of 218 minutes in a day.

The reasons for such a rapid growth are many starting from increase in smartphone penetration along with better internet connectivity, rising disposable income of Indians, large youth population and easily available online payment methods.

While this may seem to be a growth factor for the nation, it is detrimental to the growth and development of youth. With games resembling the real world and offering rewards and benefits to winners, overindulgence in online games had reached the level of addiction, causing change in lifestyle, priorities and routine. Consequently, the World Health Organisation, on 25th May, 2019, officially voted to include 'gaming disorder' as a behavioural addiction under the International Classification of Diseases.

The effects of this addiction can be seen in the data revealed by a survey conducted in the year 2020. According to the survey, 65 percent of children under the age of 20 believed that they are ready to give up food and sleep to play online games. Many children are even ready to steal their parents' money for this. Thus, online gaming addiction has had a great negative impact on a child. Some of the ill effects of excessive online gaming are as follows

- **Health Problems** Spending several hours playing online video games results in poor physical health. Today, most children and youngsters face the issue of obesity as they spend less time in physical activity. They develop body aches, headaches, poor body posture, etc. They also develop many diseases such as diabetes, heart problems and cholesterol among youngsters in and worldwide. Moreover, such children also find difficult in sleeping.
- **Lack of Concentration** Constant focus on the screen adversely affects one's concentration. Children who suffer from online gaming addiction have low level of concentration and focus. Thus, they cannot pay attention to their studies and then, display poor academic performance or performance in general.
- **Lead to Social Isolation** Children who have been addicted to video games are often socially disconnected. They do not develop great bonds with family and friends and prefer social isolation. Hence, they do not develop proper social skills and relationships.
- **Anxiety and Depression** Online gaming, to some extent, is good for children to learn several life skills, concentrate, multitask and make the brain active. However, gaming addiction gives the exact opposite result that affects the brain. Many game addictive are the ones who highly suffering from anxiety and depression.
- **Increased Aggressive Behaviours** Another harsh negative effect of online video games is increased aggression. A significant part of the content in online games is violence. If the youth spend a lot of time viewing this type of content, they may begin to understand that violence is acceptable to behaviour. Hence, when things don't go according to their plan, it becomes difficult to control their mental state. As a result, such children display aggression and are very violent.

While negative impact of online gaming addiction are many, it is important to note here that, when played in a controlled way, online games undoubtedly benefit physical and mental health. To tackle the rising issue of gaming addiction, the Indian government can learn from China which is also a huge market for online gaming. The Chinese government made new rules to protect children from its addiction in 2022. According to these new laws, online gaming companies of China will have to ensure that children get to play online games for only 3 hours in a week. There are provisions for taking action against those companies which do not do so. There is a need to make strict rules on this in India too.

35. ऑनलाइन खेल युवाओं के लिए जोखिम भरा आकर्षण है

CAPF AC 2019

मोबाइल, लैपटॉप आदि के द्वारा वीडियो गेम खेलना ऑनलाइन गेम के अन्तर्गत आता है। आज की युवा पीढ़ी बहुत ही खतरनाक तरीके से ऑनलाइन गेम की ओर आकर्षित हो रही है। युवाओं में बढ़ रही इस प्रवृत्ति के खतरनाक परिणाम सामने आने लगे हैं।

किसी भी चीज की लत तब होती है, जब आवश्यकता से अधिक उपयोग होने लगे और उसके बिना जिन्दगी में कुछ अधूरा-सा लगने लगे। चाय-कॉफी के एडिक्शन की तरह ही अब युवाओं को ऑनलाइन गेम्स का एडिक्शन भी होने लगा है। सुबह उठने से लेकर रात में सोने तक वे फोन या लैपटॉप की कैद में रहने लगे हैं। ऐसे लोग कई बार अपने गेम्स की दुनिया में इतना खो जाते हैं कि कभी-कभी उनकी जान पर बन आती है।

वर्तमान समय में लोकप्रिय ऑनलाइन गेम्स में पब्जी (PUBG, ब्लैयर ऑनलाइन वैटल ग्राउन्ड), MOBA, MMO, RTS, ब्लू व्हेल का नाम प्रमुखता से शामिल हैं।

युवाओं के बीच इन ऑनलाइन गेम्स की लोकप्रियता का कारण यह है कि ये ऑनलाइन प्लेटफार्म पर खेले जाते हैं, इनमें बहुत से प्लेयर एक साथ गेम खेलते हैं। इसमें रोमांच एवं एडवेंचर भरपूर मात्रा में उपलब्ध रहता है। प्रारम्भ में मनोरंजन के लिए शुरू किया गया गेम बाद में लत बन जाता है।

अति किसी भी चीज की हो, एक सीमा के बाद वह बुरी हो जाती है। तकनीक के विस्तार ने हर काम को जितना आसान बनाया है, उतना ही लोगों को आरामपरस्त भी। उसी तरह ऑनलाइन गेमिंग की लत व्यक्ति को शारीरिक व मानसिक रूप से बीमार कर रही है।

ऑनलाइन गेम्स खेलने से होने वाले नुकसानों में से प्रमुख हैं–आँखों पर बुरा प्रभाव, समय की बर्बादी, नींद नहीं आना, डिप्रेशन, तनाव, पाचन तन्त्र में गड़बडी, मोटापा, हिंसक स्वभाव, आत्महत्या की प्रवृत्ति, पैसों की बर्बादी, समाज से कटना, चिड़चिड़ापन आदि।

युवाओं के बीच ऑनलाइन गेम्स की बढ़ती लोकप्रियता और उससे हो रही क्षति के कारण सरकार को कभी-कभी कड़े कदम उठाने पड़ते हैं। उदाहरण के तौर पर 'ब्लू व्हेल' गेम के कारण जब बच्चे आत्महत्या करने लगे तो सरकार ने इस खेल पर प्रतिबन्ध लगा दिया। वहीं दिल्ली पुलिस ने वर्ष 2018 में राजधानी के तकरीबन 700 शिक्षकों को साइबर सुरक्षा के प्रति जागरूक किया, जो बच्चों को ऑनलाइन व्यवहार के बारे में तो बताएँगें ही, वहीं बच्चों को ऑनलाइन गेम्स की लत से बाहर निकालने में सहायता करेंगे।

इस प्रकार युवाओं में खतरनाक तरीके से लोकप्रिय हो रहे ऑनलाइन गेम्स के कारण न केवल व्यक्तिगत हानि हो रही है, बल्कि मानव संसाधन के रूप में राष्ट्र को भी क्षति पहुँच रही है।

36. The complexity and unpredictability of Indian politics

CAPF AC 2019

The inception of the Indian Political Structure occurred during a tumultuous socio-cultural context ushered by the partition on the brink of India's Independence on 15th August, 1947. The two major political parties, The Indian National Congress and the Muslim league were contesting for political hegemony thus, giving rise to a complex and unpredictable political scenario that is yet to be resolved.

Multiparty System Complexity

As India is a vast and diverse country with many social and geographical features, the members of Constituent Assembly felt that these diverse social and geographical features of the country could not be represented through two or three parties. Hence, to accommodate the vast population and to ensure that power goes into the hands of those who are trusted by most, the multi-party system was enshrined in the Constitution of India.

Instability of Political System

The Indian political system has resulted in political instability in the nation. First, the political situation has become a game of blame. Instead of focusing on the development of the country, the numerous political parties are more interested in defaming the other parties. Further, the introduction and implementation of a policy or decision may take much time due to the discussions and deliberations between various political parties.

In addition, there is a fear of a downfall of a government over a disagreement. This is the case of coalition governments wherein the party with the highest number of seats may try to gain power by taking the support of like-minded political parties and forming a ruling coalition. After forming the government, however, if one of the constituents of the coalition is not satisfied with the share of power it gets, it may withdraw support thus, leading to the downfall of the government.

Conclusion

To Conclude with accusations of corruption, scams, money laundering among others, the Indian politics becomes more complex and unpredictable.

36. भारतीय राजनीति की जटिलता एवं अप्रत्याशितता CAPF AC 2019

जॉन एडम्स ने कहा था-

"मुझे राजनीति और युद्ध का अध्ययन करना चाहिए, ताकि मेरे बच्चों के पास गणित और दर्शन का अध्ययन करने की स्वतन्त्रता हो।"

उनका यह कथन राजनीति की गम्भीरता की ओर इशारा करता है। यह दर्शाता है कि राजनीति कितना गम्भीर पेशा है। इसमें अच्छे लोगों का जाना कितना आवश्यक है। परन्तु आज की राजनीति में भ्रष्टाचार इतनी चरम अवस्था पर है कि राजनीति को गलत पेशा माना जाने लगा है। भारतीय राजनीति की भी यही विडम्बना है।

भारत एक संघीय संसदीय लोकतान्त्रिक गणराज्य है। यह दुनिया का सबसे बड़ा लोकतान्त्रिक देश है। लोकतन्त्र में राजनीति की बड़ी अहम भूमिका होती है। राजनीति, राजनीतिक दलों में समस्या आने लगती है, तो लोकतन्त्र खतरे में पड़ने लगता है। भारतीय राजनीति में अनेक जटिलताओं एवं प्रत्याशितताओं का समावेशन है।

यदि हम भारतीय राजनीति की जटिलता की बात करें, तो हम पाते हैं कि बहुदलीय व्यवस्था, वंशवाद, राजनीति का अपराधीकरण, भ्रष्टाचार, साम्प्रदायिकता, क्षेत्रियता आदि भारतीय राजनीति की प्रमुख जटिलताएँ हैं।

भारत में बहुदलीय प्रणाली के कारण राजनीतिक अस्थिरता देखने को मिलती है। इसके चलते राजनीतिक दलों और इससे जुड़े लोगों में भ्रष्टाचार व्याप्त मिलता है। प्रान्तीय राजनीति और जातिवाद को इसके द्वारा बढ़ावा दिया जाता है। कई सारे प्रान्तीय दल अपने जनस्वार्थ के नाम पर भारत की धर्मनिरपेक्ष छवि को ठेस पहुँचाते हैं। दक्षिण भारत में राजनेताओं द्वारा हिन्दी भाषा के विरोध के नाम पर लोगों में द्वेष भरा जाता है।

जम्मू-कश्मीर के स्थानीय दल हमेशा भारत के विरुद्ध बात करते हैं तथा राजनीतिक अधिकारों के नाम पर उन्हें रोकना मुश्किल होता है।

इसी प्रकार यदि हम भारतीय राजनीति में अप्रत्याशितता की बात करें, तो हम पाते हैं कि प्रचण्ड बहुमत, गठबन्धन की सरकार, त्रिशंकु विधान सभा, सरकार का विघटन आदि इसकी प्रमुख अप्रत्याशितता है। कभी-कभी सरकारों को इतना प्रचण्ड बहुमत मिल जाता है, जिससे सरकारें लोकतान्त्रिक मूल्यों का हनन करते हुए तानाशाही की ओर बढ़ने लगती है। इसी तरह गठबन्धन की सरकारें कब गिर जाती हैं, इसका अन्दाजा लगाना मुश्किल हो जाता है। गठबन्धन की राजनीति के कारण कभी-कभी अप्रत्याशित रूप से त्रिशंकु विधान सभा की स्थिति उत्पन्न हो जाती है, जिससे सरकार का गठन नहीं हो पाता और यदि हो भी जाए, तो सरकारें बहुमत साबित करने में असफल हो जाती है।

भारत की राजनीतिक व्यवस्था तथा संविधान निर्माताओं की दूरदर्शिता ने भारतीय विविधता को एक सूत्र में बाँधने का महत्त्वपूर्ण प्रयास किया। भारतीय राजनीति में 'सबको प्रतिनिधित्व' प्रदान किया गया है। यह इसका सौन्दर्य है कि प्रत्येक विरोध का स्वागत यहाँ किया जाता है और इसे अवरोध की बजाय 'जन-मानस की आवाज' का रूप दिया जाता है। जटिलता के बीच यह अप्रत्याशितता भारतीय राजनीति का श्रेष्ठतम गुण है।

37. Civil wrong emerging from religious bigotry, constitutionally punishable CAPF AC 2018

The 42nd Constitutional Amendment Act of 1976 added the term 'secular' to the Indian Preamle emphasising that the state shall recognise and accept all religions and not favour or patronise any particular religion. Further, many articles in the Indian Constitution instate that the Indian Constitution provides equality to all, prohibits any discrimination on grounds of religion and allows the right to freely profess, practice and propagate a religion.

However, while the Indian Constitution declares the state being absolutely neutral to all religion, our society is steeped in religious bigotry, intolerance, fear and hatred towards the ones who are different from us. The recent Pew Research Centre analysis of 198 countries ranked India as 4th worst in the world for religious intolerance and bigotry.

One of the causes of the rise in such intolerance and bigotry is the mingling of religion and politics. The mobilisation of votes on grounds of primordial identities like religion, caste and ethnicity, have put Indian secularism in danger. Communal politics operates through communalisation of social space, by spreading myths and stereotypes against minorities, through attack on rational values and by practicing a divisive ideological propaganda and politics. Politicisation of any one religious group leads to the competitive politicisation of other groups, thereby resulting in inter-religious conflict.

One of the manifestations of communalism is communal riots. In recent past, communalism has proved to be a great threat to the secular fabric of Indian polity. Rise of Hindu Nationalism in recent years has resulted. The recent communal violence of Gujarat, the anti-Sikh campaigns during the mid-80s, the Mumbai Riots, the Ayodhya episode, the evacuation of Kashmiri Pandits, the attacks on the pilgrims on their way to pilgrimage are all blots on the secular fabric of the country.

Further, with love-jihad, crimes against women in the name of religion among other crimes have become the tell tale signs of how our society is deeply entrenched in religion paving the way for all sorts of bigotry and intolerance.

In a pluralistic society, the best approach to nurture secularism is to expand religious freedom rather than strictly practicing state neutrality. It is incumbent on us to ensure value-education that makes the younger generation understand and appreciate not only its own religious traditions but also those of the other religions in the country. There is also a need to identify a common framework or a shared set of values which allows the diverse groups to live together. The prerequisites to implement the social reform initiative like Uniform Civil Code are to create a conducive environment and forging socio-political consensus.

37. धार्मिक कट्टरताजन्य नागरिक अपराध, संविधान के अन्तर्गत दण्डनीय CAPF AC 2018

संविधान के अन्तर्गत दण्डनीय

भारत में संविधान तथा कानून द्वारा धार्मिक स्वतन्त्रता तथा धार्मिक एवं भाषायी अल्पसंख्यकों के संरक्षण की बात कही गई है। भारत एक पन्थनिरपेक्ष गणराज्य है, जहाँ सभी धर्मों को मानने वाले लोग एक विधि के तहत समान नागरिक अधिकारों का लाभ उठाते हैं। संवैधानिक तथा कानूनी संरक्षण के बावजूद भारत में धार्मिक कट्टरता तथा असहिष्णुता में वृद्धि हुई है। धार्मिक रूप से अल्पसंख्यकों को अपने से अलग मानने की प्रवृत्ति तथा उनके प्रति घृणा का माहौल हाल के वर्षों में अस्तित्व में आया है।

अप्रैल, 2017 में प्यू रिपोर्ट (यूएसए) के नवीनतम आँकड़ों में भारत की धार्मिक तथा सामाजिक भेदभाव तथा पाबन्दियों को स्पष्ट किया गया। विश्व के 198 देशों में भारत को चौथा सबसे खराब प्रदर्शन वाला राष्ट्र माना गया, जहाँ सरकारी तथा निजी स्तर पर धार्मिक भेदभाव को स्थान दिया गया तथा अल्पसंख्यकों में भय का माहौल पैदा किया गया। भारत लम्बे समय से धार्मिक कट्टरताजन्य अपराधों को झेलता आ रहा है।

भारत का विभाजन (1947-48), सिख विरोधी दंगे (1984), गुजरात तथा गोधरा दंगे (2002), मुजफ्फरनगर दंगे (2013) सामूहिक रूप से विरोधियों के प्रति कट्टरता के प्रदर्शन का उदाहरण हैं।

हाल के वर्षों में 'मॉब लिंचिंग' ने धार्मिक कट्टरता और असहिष्णुता को विमर्श का विषय बनाया है। 'गो-हत्या' के आरोप में लोगों को पीट-पीटकर मार डालने के अपराधों में तेजी से वृद्धि हुई है।

धार्मिक कट्टरताजन्य अपराधों में वृद्धि के निम्न कारण माने जा सकते हैं–

- कानून एवं व्यवस्था की स्थिति में गिरावट।
- धार्मिक सहिष्णुता तथा सांस्कृतिक विरासत की जानकारी का अभाव।
- कट्टरता को गलती से अलौकिक शक्तियों का संरक्षक माना जाना।
- धर्म की गलत व्याख्या तथा धार्मिक गुरुओं की असहज महत्त्वाकांक्षाएँ।
- राजनीतिज्ञों द्वारा चुनावों में धर्म आधारित वोट बैंक का निर्माण।
- धार्मिक रूप से असहिष्णु समूहों के कारण धार्मिक कट्टरताजन्य अपराधों में वृद्धि होती रहती है।

इस प्रकार के अपराधों के कारण समाज का बड़ा वर्ग प्रभावित होता है। यह सामाजिक सद्भाव को समाप्त कर देता है। बड़ी जनसंख्या ऐसी जगहों से पलायन कर जाती है, जहाँ धार्मिक अपराधों के कारण उनका जीवन संकटग्रस्त हो जाता है। यह लोकतन्त्र तथा मानव अधिकार के सिद्धान्तों की स्थापना का सबसे वृहद् बाधक तत्त्व है। इससे घृणा का माहौल निर्मित हो जाता है, जिससे अलगाववाद और पृथक्तावाद को पनपने का मौका मिलता है।

भारतीय संविधान की प्रस्तावना में 'पन्थनिरपेक्ष' शब्द तथा भाग III में वर्णित मूल अधिकारों के तहत अनुच्छेद-25 से 28 में धार्मिक स्वतन्त्रता की गारण्टी दी गई है। इन अधिकारों पर राज्य सरकारों को नियम बनाने के अधिकार दिए गए हैं। राज्य सरकारों ने समय-समय पर ऐसे अधिनियम पारित किए हैं, जो धार्मिक कट्टरता को नियन्त्रित करने में प्रभावी हैं।

भारतीय दण्ड संहिता (आईपीसी) में धार्मिक कट्टरताजन्य अपराधों का विवरण दिया गया है। आईपीसी की धारा खण्ड 295 (ए) के तहत धार्मिक भावनाओं को आहत करने वालों के लिए 'दण्ड' का प्रावधान है। सोशल मीडिया के माध्यम से कट्टरता को बढ़ाने के विरुद्ध भी आईपीसी में विधिक प्रावधान किए गए हैं। पृथक् धर्मों को मानने वालों पर हिंसात्मक अपराध के लिए कठोर सजा का प्रावधान किया गया है।

वस्तुतः दुनिया के सभी धर्मों में 'सहिष्णुता' की बात की गई है। सभी मतों के लोगों के साथ 'बन्धुत्व' को सबसे 'बड़ी आराधना' बताया गया है। भारत सदैव वैश्विक समता की संस्कृति वाला देश रहा है। हमारा सद्वाक्य 'वसुधैव कुटुम्बकम्' है, जो किसी प्रकार की कट्टरता का निषेध करता है।

38. Farm waiver is populistic and myopic strategy change needed CAPF AC 2018

India is an agrarian economy with the agriculture sector being one of the major contributors to the GDP. Agriculture is the primary source of livelihood as more than 58% of the population depend upon it directly or indirectly. Hence, After Independence, agricultural development was given the top most priority to attain self-sufficiency in food grains to feed the rapidly increasing population. Several public policies and investment decisions were taken particularly with regard to irrigation, fertilisers, land reforms and community development.

However, despite these reforms, the small and marginal farmers who are the backbone of our food security have become the victims of enormous debt. They hold more than 70 per cent of country's farmland but earn just enough to feed their families. This low income stands in contrast with rapidly growing costs and expenses of agriculture such as machinery, seeds and fertilisers. This situation is further worsened by the instability of monsoon and market. Hence, an Indian farmer lives a life of deprivation under the burden of huge debts which never reduce.

Hence, to relive the burden and pressure of faced by them, many farmers went to the government to seek farm waivers and the various State Governments conceded to farmers' demand by waiving off the loans. It is reported that India faces cumulative loan waiver of more than ₹ 3.1 lakh crore or 2.6% of the country's Gross Domestic Products (GDP).

The seeming relief given to the farmer, however is populist and myopic. Such a relief is no relief at all because in spite of the implementation of the massive loan waiver scheme, farm indebtedness has not receded and the real issues plaguing the industry were not addressed.

The real problem is the poor returns from the cultivation as the income from the farm is lower than the cultivating cost. In addition, lack of irrigation facilities, over-dependence on nature, infrastructural deficit, wrong and faulty practices, small and unviable holdings, dependence of too many people on farming, lack of efficient cold storage, exploitation by middlemen and inadequate insurance facilities are serious handicaps of the sector. Furthermore, this scheme doesn't cover those poor farmers who owe debt to moneylenders. To top it all, this scheme benefits the rich farmers who can afford to repay the loan but avail the loan with the aim of getting in waived off.

RBI only recently warned states against waivers which "impact credit discipline and vitiate credit cult" Borrowers will expect future loans also to be waived and lenders will be discouraged. The burden will actually be shifted from the borrowers to the tax payers which will affect the fiscal consolidation of states which have to deal with other challenges like the implementation of pay commission recommendations and the GST system. Further, according to RBI, farm waiver results in increase in interest rates that discourage private borrowers thereby reducing investments. This might lead to collapse of rural banking.

Thus, loan waiver is a temporary relief measure and long-term solution is needed to ensure economic welfare of our farmers. Lasting solutions like building irrigation capabilities and cold storage chains, increased crop insurance coverage, farm infrastructure building, tech-enabled productivity improvement and opening the sector to market forces and open trade can help the farmers in long run as a better option. Agrarian distress and farmers' income will be addressed much better if States undertake and sincerely implement long-pending reforms in the agriculture sector with urgency.

38. कृषि सम्बन्धी छूट लोकलुभावन एवं अदूरदर्शी : नीतिगत परिवर्तन आवश्यक CAPF AC 2018

लोकतान्त्रिक देश भारत में चुनावों से पूर्व किसानों से किए गए लोकलुभावन वादों और चुनाव के उपरान्त कृषि सम्बन्धी छूट वित्तीय व्यवस्था के लिए संकटपूर्ण परिस्थितियाँ उत्पन्न करता है। भारत में जनसंख्या कृषि पर आधारित है। किसानों तथा कृषि का भारतीय अर्थव्यवस्था पर महत्त्वपूर्ण प्रभाव होता है। सकल घरेलू उत्पाद (जीडीपी) के 17% हिस्से को कृषि से प्राप्त आय के रूप में देखा जाता है। देश के कुल निर्यात में कृषि तथा कृषिजन्य उत्पादों का हिस्सा 10.5% है।

छोटे तथा लघु किसानों के कारण भारत में 'खाद्य सुरक्षा' को महत्त्व प्राप्त हुआ है, खाद्यान्न उत्पादन के 70% हिस्से में इनकी भागेदारी है, किन्तु इस वर्ग की आय 'न्यूनतम' है। सीमान्त किसानों को खेती करने के लिए ऋण लेना होता है, जो बैंकों तथा साहूकारों से उन्हें प्राप्त होता है। सरकार द्वारा सार्वजनिक बैंकों के माध्यम से कृषि-ऋण देने की व्यवस्था की गई है। इसके अतिरिक्त 'फसल बीमा' योजनाओं को भी लागू किया गया है।

चुनाव के दौरान किए गए कर्जमाफी के वादों और किसानों की मूल समस्याओं को लेकर देश भर में किसानों के आन्दोलन हाल के वर्षों में

तीव्र हुए हैं। मार्च, 2018 में 35 हजार से अधिक किसानों ने महाराष्ट्र विधानभवन का घेराव किया था। राजस्थान, मध्य प्रदेश, उत्तर प्रदेश तथा दिल्ली भी ऐसे किसान प्रदर्शनों का गवाह बने हैं। यह प्रदर्शन तथा विरोध सरकार द्वारा कर्जमाफी के वादों तथा किसानों की बढ़ती पीड़ा से प्रेरित थे। भारत में किसानों की हालत बदतर हो रही है। फसलों के उत्पादन का उचित मूल्य उन्हें प्राप्त नहीं हो पा रहा है। सरकार द्वारा 'न्यूनतम समर्थन मूल्य' (एमएसपी) जो जारी किया जाता है, किन्तु फसल उत्पादों की खरीद के लिए प्रभावी व्यवस्था नहीं की जाती। सब्जियों एवं फलों के मूल्यों में तीव्र गिरावट से किसानों को अत्यधिक हानि होती है। सूखा तथा बाढ़ जैसी आपदाओं के कारण किसान अगली फसल की बुआई के लिए भी तैयार नहीं हो पाता।

कृषि कर्जों की माफी का असर 'विस्फोटक रास्ते' पर है। सार्वजनिक बैंकों में गैर-निष्पादित सम्पत्तियों (एनपीए) में तीव्र वृद्धि हुई। विभिन्न राज्य सरकारों ने वर्ष 2016-17 में किसानों की ऋण माफी की घोषणा की, जिसके तहत ₹ 3.1 लाख करोड़ के ऋण वसूली की प्रक्रिया को समाप्त कर दिया गया, जो भारत के कुल जीडीपी का 2.6% था। ऋण माफी से किसानों को तात्कालिक लाभ मिलता है, किन्तु दीर्घावधि में यह एक दुश्चक्र के रूप में किसानों के लिए संकट की स्थिति बन जाती है।

वर्तमान केन्द्र सरकार ने किसानों की आय वर्ष 2022 तक दोगुनी करने का लक्ष्य रखा है। यह नीतिगत सुधारों से ही सम्भव है। लोकलुभावन वादों के बदले सिंचाई संसाधनों का विस्तार, उत्पादों के उचित मूल्यों की प्राप्ति, उत्पादों के विनिमय की उचित व्यवस्था, भूमि सुधार जैसे दीर्घकालिक सुविधाओं पर ध्यान देना होगा। सबसे आगे एवं 'जीवन्त कृषि वित्तीय प्रणाली' को सामने लाना जरूरी है। किसानों की आशा और आकांक्षाओं को पूरा करने के उपरान्त ही भारत की धरती पुनः 'स्वर्णगर्भा' बनने की ओर अग्रसर होगी।

39. From economic growth to well-being a paradigm shift

CAPF AC 2018

Dynamic Changing World

The world is desperately seeking change. People sense that important social, economic and environmental shifts are afoot. There are now over seven billion people on the planet. Technology is helping us to communicate, organise and learn on a global scale. Emerging economies are rising in all continents and the 'global middle class' is larger than ever before.

Yet inequality between the world's rich and poor continues to grow, both between and within countries. Extreme weather events are more frequent and severe and adapting to changes in climate is now a reality. Demand for natural resources is increasing and contributing to the degradation of the environment. Food and oil prices set new records and acute debt crises cascade through the global economy. This new crises changed the focus of economy from economic growth and gross domestic product (GDP) to human well-being.

Economic Growth vs Nations Growth

The modus operandi of the past decades was economic growth. Here, economical success of the nation was treated as a true indication of development. Hence, the all credential was invested in excessive exploitation of natural resource.

Thus, economic prosperity was everything and a greater GDP was an indicator of a developed society. GDP was not simply used an economic metric but also as a performance assessment tool for society.

Countries were ranked in terms of GDP, international organisations and investors vet governments' policies through GDP, politicians and businesses are rated on their success at promoting GDP growth. This statistic had acquired a profound institutional power, providing the econometric backing for an economic model driven by industrial production, large corporations and mass consumption.

However, in the present world, the supremacy of GDP is being eroded, not only in the scientific community but also in policy circles and public debate. Many international agencies, including the UN, the Organisation for Economic Cooperation and Development, the World Bank and the European Commission, in their UN 2030 Agenda and the SDGs, provide a 'roadmap' for development which relies on the interconnectedness of social, environmental and economic dynamics and points towards the indivisibility of human and ecosystem wellbeing.

Sustainable Growth vs Economic Growth

The 17 Sustainable Development Goals laid out in the 2030, Global Sustainable Development Agenda within the desired 15 years is one without increasing 'GDP growth.' The Social Progress Index is now one of many 'development indices' that have been designed in response to a growing disenchantment with 'economic growth' as the one and only indicator and measure of 'development' of a society or country.

The economy, thus, is changing. A new system of accounting based on well-being rather than output has emerged to foster sustainable growth of the society. The list of beneficiaries of a shift to wellbeing includes families, communities, cooperatives, fair trade networks and many similar groups without any negative impact on anything.

Conclusion

This paradigm shift shows the future of a new and prosperous world. It has idealised the thought that "Development should be woven around the human and not the human around the Development". This human sensitisation of economics by various scholars has switched us to a new economic order where human development holds the steering.

39. आर्थिक विकास से खुशहाली की ओर : एक प्रतिमान परिवर्तन

CAPF AC 2018

भारत 2032 तक सकल घरेलू उत्पाद (जीडीपी) की दृष्टि से $10 ट्रिलियन की अर्थव्यवस्था वाला राष्ट्र हो जाएगा। विमर्श इस बात पर है कि देश के वित्तीय विस्तार के साथ क्या रोजगार के अवसरों में वृद्धि होगी? विश्व के अनेक देशों में जहाँ रोजगार के अवसर तेजी से बढ़ रहे हैं, वहीं भारत में जीडीपी की दरों में तीव्र वृद्धि के बावजूद रोजगार के अवसर उस गति से नहीं बढ़ रहे हैं।

भारतीय रिज़र्व बैंक (आरबीआई) के गवर्नर ने मौद्रिक नीति समीक्षा के दौरान अक्टूबर, 2018 में स्पष्ट शब्दों में कहा कि जीडीपी की उच्च वृद्धि दर वैज्ञानिक रूप से बेहतर अर्थव्यवस्था का मापदण्ड नहीं है। 'नैतिक अर्थव्यवस्था' (Moral Economy) वह है, जिसमें संवृद्धि का फल देश के सभी परिवारों एवं व्यक्तियों तक पहुँचे जिससे समाज में प्रसन्नता और खुशहाली का वातावरण तैयार हो। अपनी शास्त्रीय रचना **द स्ट्रक्चर ऑफ साइण्टिफिक रिवोल्यूशन्स** ('The Structure of Scientific Revolutions') में **थॉमस कोहन** ने 'आर्थिक विकास से खुशहाली' को एक प्रतिमान परिवर्तन के रूप में व्याख्यायित किया है।

आर्थिक नीतियों में प्रतिमान परिवर्तन (Paradigm sift) को वैश्विक स्तर पर महत्त्व दिया जा रहा है। पहले यह माना जाता था कि किसी देश की आर्थिक समृद्धि ही सब कुछ है, किन्तु अब इस अवधारणा को समर्थन नहीं मिल रहा है। विश्व बैंक भी अब आर्थिक समृद्धि की व्याख्या के लिए जिन संकेतकों को आधार बना रहा है, वह **प्रति व्यक्ति आय** तथा **औसत आय** है।

हाल के वर्षों में अर्थव्यवस्था को लोक कल्याण के रूप में देखने की प्रवृत्ति के साथ मानव अधिकार, मानव-कल्याण तथा हितवादी विचारों को महत्त्व मिलना आरम्भ हो गया है। लोक कल्याणकारी राज्य की अवधारणा को अधिक स्थायित्व प्रदान करने के लिए 'संयुक्त राष्ट्र विकास कार्यक्रम (UNDP) के तहत अमर्त्य सेन तथा महबूब-उल-हक ने मानव विकास सूचकांक (HDI) की प्रवृत्तियों का दिशा-निर्देश तैयार किया है। यह माना गया है कि जिस देश का मानव विकास सूचकांक अधिक होगा, उस देश का जीवन स्तर उच्च होगा, लोगों की **जीवन सम्भाव्यता** अधिक होगी, **शैक्षणिक स्तर** बेहतर होगा तथा **प्रति व्यक्ति जीडीपी** (प्रति व्यक्ति आय) उच्च होगी। विकास की इस संकल्पना को अत्यधिक समर्थन मिला है और इसे स्वीकार किया जाने लगा है कि यदि कोई देश 'मानव संसाधन विकास' तथा 'मानव पूँजी विकास' में निवेश करता है, तो दीर्घावधि में उसे श्रेष्ठ लाभ की आशा रहेगी। इससे लोगों के कौशल तथा कार्यदक्षता में वृद्धि होगी, ऐसी आशा की जा रही है।

यह प्रतिमान परिवर्तन यह दर्शाता है कि नए तथा समृद्ध विश्व का भविष्य बेहतर है। समावेशी तथा धारणीय विकास को महत्त्व मिलने से गति मिली है। यह स्पष्ट हो गया है कि विकास मनुष्य की योग्यता पर निर्भर करता है और मनुष्य विकास के परितः घुमने के लिए नहीं है। मानव केन्द्रित विकास ही निरन्तरता प्राप्त कर सकता है, यह स्पष्ट हो चुका है। इस विकासात्मक अवधारणा को महत्त्व मिल रहा है, जिससे आर्थिक विकास के माध्यम से मनुष्य की खुशहाली को गति प्रदान करना सम्भव हुआ है।

40. Reservation suppresses civil dynamism CAPF AC 2018

"The outcaste is a bye-product of the caste system. There will be outcastes as long as there are castes. Nothing can emancipate the outcaste except the destruction of the caste system." BR Ambedkar An essential component of the Indian Constitution framework is the introduction of Article 15,16,17,46 and 340 that vouch for establishment of a caste-less society. And it has worked.

The basic purpose of reservation is civil dynamism whereby every individual of deprived castes gets an opportunity to move upward through social hierarchy by ensuring equality of opportunities in education, Government jobs, etc., for all citizens irrespective of their caste, gender, race, religion, etc. When all individuals will have equal access to resources, the backward communities would also be able to uplift themselves in society. This in turn fulfills the very purpose of the Constitution as given under Articles 15 and 16 of the Constitution- building a casteless society.

However, it has been more than 70 years since the Constitution was framed and the social fabric of the society has changed. Today, the reservation policies set-up by the Constitution stand against the very ideals that it seek to counter. Reservation rather than reducing casteism, suppresses civil dynamism by creating deep resentment among those belonging to the General Category against the reserved ones.

The former assert that their exclusion from the reservation benefits is based on the false conviction of them all being economically sound and meritorious. Thus, the attempt to bring freedoms and opportunities to those deprived so, as to promote equality, has now resulted in a situation wherein the previously advantaged communities have becoming disadvantaged to a large extent due to the reservation conundrum.

Conclusion

Thus, the reservation policies made to drive the country towards an egalitarian society, has now entrenching the caste system into the social fabric of the society even more firmly. Thus, the need of the hour is to reconstitute the reservation policy and reconsider the objective it proposed to achieve.

40. आरक्षण नागरिक गतिशीलता का दमन करता है CAPF AC 2018

भारत में जाति व्यवस्था, वंशानुगत, कठोर तथा अगत्यात्मक है। जाति व्यवस्था के अन्तर्गत व्यक्ति का एक जाति से दूसरी जाति के बीच जाना असम्भव है। इस प्रतिबन्ध को समाप्त करने तथा नागरिक गतिशीलता को प्रभावी बनाने के लिए ही 'आरक्षण' की व्यवस्था की गई है। इस नागरिक गतिशीलता के तहत वंचित वर्ग के प्रत्येक व्यक्ति को सामाजिक संरचना में अवसर तथा सम्मान प्रदान करने की व्यवस्था की गई है। अनुसूचित जाति तथा अनुसूचित जनजाति के लिए राजनीतिक, शैक्षणिक, संस्थाओं तथा सरकारी सेवाओं के आरक्षण की व्यवस्था की गई है। अनुसूचित जाति तथा अनुसूचित जनजाति को लोकसभा तथा विधानसभाओं में सदस्यता के लिए सीटों का आरक्षण प्राप्त है। सरकारी शिक्षण संस्थाओं में प्रवेश तथा सरकारी सेवाओं में नियुक्ति के लिए आरक्षण की सुविधा इन वर्गों को प्राप्त है।

पिछड़े वर्गों को भी मण्डल आयोग की सिफारिशों के आधार पर सरकारी सेवाओं में आरक्षण दिया गया। 93वें संविधान संशोधन अधिनियम के पारित होने के बाद निजी शैक्षणिक संस्थानों में प्रवेश के लिए आरक्षण की व्यवस्था की गई है।

'आरक्षण' को जाति आधार पर रखने की जगह आर्थिक आधार पर देने की माँग लम्बे समय से की जाती रही है। केन्द्र सरकार ने जनवरी, 2019 में कमजोर आय वर्ग की सामान्य जातियों को आरक्षण की व्यवस्था पर जाति आधारित आरक्षण को लचीला बनाने का प्रयास किया है। पिछड़े वर्ग को आरक्षण देने में 'क्रीमी लेयर' के साथ आय को आरक्षण का आधार बनाया है। वर्तमान में क्रीमी लेयर का स्तर वार्षिक ₹ 8 लाख की आय है। आय का आधार केवल पिछड़े तथा सामान्य वर्गों के लिए रखा गया है। अनुसूचित जाति तथा अनुसूचित जनजाति को आरक्षण देने की प्रक्रिया में 'क्रीमी लेयर' की कोई संकल्पना नहीं है। इससे आरक्षण का लाभ विस्तारित रूप से पूरे समुदाय को मिलता है अथवा नहीं, यह विचारणीय विषय है।

कई महत्त्वपूर्ण विसंगतियाँ लगातार 'आरक्षण व्यवस्था' का पीछा कर रही हैं। कई जातियाँ स्वयं को अनुसूचित जाति अथवा पिछड़ी जाति में शामिल होने के लिए आन्दोलन कर रही है। हाल के वर्षों में भारत में ऐसे आन्दोलनों की गूँज सुनाई पड़ती है।

भारतीय संविधान में जिस पक्ष को देखते हुए आरक्षण की व्यवस्था की गई थी, आज उसे पूरा नहीं किया जा सकता है। जाति आधारित आरक्षण की व्यवस्था के बदले आर्थिक आधार पर कमजोर वर्गों को इसका लाभ देना ही अधिक प्रासंगिक है।

70 वर्षों में 'आरक्षण' का लाभ भारत को किस स्तर तक मिला है, उसे समाज में देखा जा सकता है। सरकारी सेवाओं में नियुक्तियों की संख्या नगण्य है। सरकारी संस्थाओं में प्रवेश के लिए सीटों की संख्या इतनी कम है कि बड़ी जनसंख्या में लोग इस व्यवस्था से लगातार बाहर ही हैं।

'आरक्षण' की व्यवस्था पूरे समुदाय का हितसाधक नहीं बन सकी है। यह सामाजिक विभाजन का आधार बन गई है और इस विभाजन ने नागरिक गतिशीलता को शिथिल किया है। समाज में दरार के कारण गतिशील प्रवृत्तियों को बनाए रखना असम्भव है।

आरक्षण ने नागरिक गतिशीलता का यदि दमन नहीं किया है तो इस गतिशीलता को मन्द करने में अवश्य ही अपनी भूमिका निभाई है।

41. Non-performing Parliament, unhealthy trend in Democracy CAPF AC 2018

When one steps inside the Parliament premises, right from the entrance point, where the statue of Dr. BR Ambedkar stands resolutely looking at the oval structure in front, to the corridors of the Parliament Library Building, the Annexe building and the main building – the Parliament House – one cannot help but celebrate the splendour of the highest legislative body of the country. However, for those who have been witnessing the working of the Parliament from close quarters over the last few years, the cruel irony of this splendor is not lost. For, if there is one institution whose functioning has been curtailed the most and which has been lowered the most in stature in recent years, it is our Parliament.

Decreasing Efficiency of Parliament

In the last 70 years, there has been a continuous decline in the efficiency of the functioning of the Parliament. The process of legislation has become slow and lagged. Laws are often passed in rush with little scrutiny and no follow- up rules. In some cases, it takes sessions together for a bill to become law. Number of days when the Parliament meets and discusses the relevant issues have also gone down. Even when the Parliament sits and meets, there is more noise than debate, more shouting than listening and more statements than engagement or debate.

Discourse and debate on issues of national importance were an attribute and highlight of Parliament during the first two decades of the republic, until around 1970. But this has eroded and diminished with the passage of time. There is discussion but it is often partisan—sometimes a dialogue of the deaf—between groups where party lines are sharply drawn.

Thus, differences lead to protests in the form of walk-outs or rushing to the well of the house. Further, the Parliament, which was meant to invoke accountability, has almost forgotten its role.

Role of Kinship, Money and Power in Polities

The factors underlying these developments and deterioration are not rocket science. The barriers to entry in politics are formidable. The only access comes from kinship, money or muscle power. Also, there are institutional constraints on the performance of MPs as well. The allocation of time for MPs to speak is proportional to the strength of their political party in the house and its leadership decides who gets to speak and for how long. Moreover, the Parliament does not meet or work long enough and there are institutional constraints on its performance while working.

Conclusion

Concluding, almost 70 years after we began life as a republic, there is a clear and present danger that we could be the world's most vibrant democracy with the world's least effective and perhaps most dormant, Parliament. It is time for MPs in India to reclaim their rights in Parliament as representatives of the people. Also, the time has come for citizens, whom it represents, to evaluate that performance. The need of the hour is to reaffirm the key Constitution value of deliberation, discussion and debate in the Parliament. Otherwise the people of India will soon loose trust in Indian Democracy.

41. अकर्मण्य संसद, प्रजातन्त्र में एक अस्वस्थ प्रवृत्ति CAPF AC 2018

स्वतन्त्रता संघर्ष के दौरान राष्ट्रीय नेताओं ने आजादी के बाद 'गणतन्त्र' स्थापना का सपना देखा था। संविधान सभा की बहसों के साथ यह स्पष्ट हो गया कि भारत एक 'लोकतान्त्रिक' देश बनने के रास्ते पर चल पड़ा है। संविधान में भारत को एक 'लोकतन्त्रात्मक गणराज्य' घोषित किया गया। यह घोषणा संविधान की 'प्रस्तावना' में वर्णित है।

संसदीय प्रणाली की सरकार का चयन करने का उद्देश्य हमारे नेताओं के लिए यह था कि यह जनता की सरकार का संचालन चाहते थे। जनता द्वारा अप्रत्यक्ष रूप से चुने गए प्रतिनिधियों के माध्यम से सरकार चलाने को श्रेष्ठ नीति माना गया। संसद में विभिन्न मुद्दों पर सहमति बनाने के लिए बहसों को महत्त्व दिया गया।

वर्ष 1951-52 में पहली लोकसभा की स्थापना के बाद विभिन्न कार्यक्रमों पर गम्भीर बहस को संसदीय कार्यनीति का प्रारूप बनाया गया, किन्तु विमर्श, बहस और सहमति की प्रक्रिया धीरे-धीरे धूमिल होती जा रही है। संसद में शोर-शराबे तथा कार्यों के संचालन को बाधित करना राजनीतिक दलों का फैशन बन चुका है। संसद तथा विधानसभाओं के भीतर राजनीतिज्ञों के व्यवहार में असहजता का समावेश हुआ है। सदनों की बैठक लगातार स्थगित की जाती रही है।

संसदीय प्रणाली की विशेषता यह है कि जिन समस्याओं को सरकार तक पहुँचाने के लिए सदनों को जन प्रतिनिधि अपना माध्यम बनाते हैं। वहीं इस प्रक्रिया में सदन की बैठकों के लगातार स्थगित होने के कारण उचित लाभ नहीं मिल पाता है। संसद के विभिन्न सदनों के लगातार स्थगित होने तथा संसद की अकर्मण्यता के कारण निम्न हैं–

- प्रधानमन्त्री कार्यालय तथा कैबिनेट के महत्त्व में वृद्धि के कारण संसद की गरिमा प्रभावित हुई है।
- विपक्षी दलों की नीतियों तथा कार्यक्रमों का केवल विरोध पर आधारित होना एक महत्त्वपूर्ण प्रक्रिया बनती जा रही है।

प्रजातन्त्र में संसदीय संस्थाओं का बेहतर तरीके से कार्य करना महत्त्वपूर्ण पहलू है। संसद का कार्य बाधित होना प्रजातन्त्र की अवधारणा के विरुद्ध है। जन-प्रतिनिधियों का निर्वाचन, चयन तथा नियुक्ति राज्यों तथा सम्बन्धित संसदीय क्षेत्रों की समस्याओं की उठाने तथा उसके उचित समाधान की प्रक्रियाओं को ढूँढने के लिए किया जाता है। इस वृहद उत्तरदायित्व का निर्वाह करना प्रतिनिधियों की प्राथमिकता है और इसे ध्यान में रखना जरूरी है, जिससे संसदीय मर्यादाओं का संरक्षण सम्भव हो सकता है। वस्तुतः संसद में काम-काज का ठप्प होना संसदीय संस्थाओं की प्रतिष्ठा को तो गिराता ही है, पर देश की जनता के कठिन परिश्रम से अर्जित पैसों का भी अपव्यय है। यह समय तथा धन दोनों की बर्बादी है। परम्परागत रूप से यह एक अस्वस्थ प्रजातान्त्रिक मूल्य को प्रोत्साहित करता है, जो 'लोकतान्त्रिक राजनीति' के लिए शुभ नहीं है।

42. Promoting innovative outlook in education

CAPF AC 2018

Independent India's first Minister of Education, Maulana Abul Kalam Azad stated that "Educationists should build the capacities of the spirit of inquiry, creativity, entrepreneurial and moral leadership among students and become their role model." According to him, the main objective of education is to inculcate a sense of inquiry through developing a scientific inquisitiveness of mind. However, the traditional classroom works in a very different manner.

Today's archaic 19th Century model of rote-based learning, or what we call traditional system of the 'chalk-and-talk' system, where the teacher talks endlessly and dictatorially and the student listens passively and submissively has discouraged questioning, discovery, experimentation and application in the school classroom.

The unfortunate results of this unimaginative factory-based model of education. are boredom, lack of involvement, low confidence and self-belief and an obsessive fear of failure. Not surprisingly, downbeat attitudes acquired at an early age have carried into adulthood resulting in a workforce that is, for the most part, bereft of the temper, desire and energy to create, invent and innovate.

In the era of 'Startup India', despite the exciting birth of a lot of new businesses, we have not witnessed an equivalent number of original or innovative ideas at scale from India. Reflecting perhaps years of uncreative education, an almost instinctive urge to copy ideas from outside, seen as a more predictable and dependable way of making money, has precluded hundreds of Indians from investing their time and energy in new and original ideas with a long-term, and uncertain return. Hence, the Indian Education system needed an urgent change to focus on creativity, innovation and the overall growth of a child who will become the future of the nation.

This change was delivered with the National Educational Policy of 2020 which focuses on recognising and nurturing the exceptional capabilities of each student by encouraging critical and innovative thinking. It shifts the focus from theory to practice whereby children learn by experimenting, questioning and observing.

Children will be encouraged to be curious and ask innumerable whys and why nots. By encouraging curiosity and creativity, children will become independent, thinking individuals who discover and solve problems on their own, thus, nurturing their confidence and self-belief. The result of such an education will be a child who holds the power of transforming many societies from low to high productivity, from poverty to prosperity from being consumers to being producers of ideas.

42. शिक्षा में नवोन्मेष उन्मुख दृष्टिकोण को प्रोत्साहन **CAPF AC 2018**

"शिक्षा सबसे शक्तिशाली हथियार है, जिससे आप दुनिया में बदलाव ला सकते हैं"**–नेलसन मण्डेला**

बदलाव दुनिया की एक निरन्तर प्रक्रिया है। बदलाव की प्रक्रिया वैज्ञानिक स्तर पर 'नवाचार' कहलाती है। शिक्षा के माध्यम से ही 'नवाचार' एक बेहतर समाज का सृजन करने में सक्षम होता है। बहुधा यह कहा जाता है कि शिक्षा परिवर्तन की प्रेरक है। नवाचार, सामाजिक-आर्थिक समस्याओं का हल है। यह नई पीढ़ी के लिए नवीन अवसरों को प्रेरित करने का मार्ग प्रशस्त करता है। उदाहरण के तौर पर कम्प्यूटर नवाचार के माध्यम से ही हम तक पहुँच सका है। यह शिक्षा की गुणवत्ता को बढ़ाने का कारक रहा है।

जीवन के प्रत्येक क्षेत्र में नवाचार (Innovation) महत्त्वपूर्ण है। यह गुणात्मक परिवर्तन का कारक है। शिक्षा के क्षेत्र में नवोन्मेष उन्मुख दृष्टिकोण दक्षता में वृद्धि के साथ सीखने के अवसरों को प्रभावी बनाता है। इसके माध्यम से जिन कौशलों को प्राप्त कर सकना सम्भव होता है। उसमें सृजनात्मकता, कल्पनाशीलता, समीक्षात्मक व्यवहार इत्यादि शामिल हैं। इन कौशलों में वृद्धि के लिए 'उद्यम आधारित शिक्षा' को बढ़ावा देना जरूरी है।

सरकार शिक्षा के क्षेत्र में 'नवोन्मेष' को प्रभावी बनाने के लिए नीतिगत फैसले ले सकती है जिससे इसे 'उद्देश्यपरक' बनाया जा सकता है।

हाल के वर्षों में सरकार ने विद्यालयी शिक्षा के क्षेत्र में कई ऐसे कदम उठाए हैं, जो नवाचार को प्रोत्साहित करने में सक्षम है। विद्यालयों में डिजिटल प्रौद्योगिकी तथा सूचना एवं संचार प्रौद्योगिकी की शिक्षा को लागू किया गया है। तकनीक आधारित नवोन्मेष उन्मुख दृष्टिकोण ने विद्यालयों के वातावरण को प्रभावित किया है। इसने विद्यार्थियों के सीखने की प्रवृत्ति को भी बदल दिया है।

भारत सरकार ने उच्च शिक्षा क्षेत्र में नवोन्वेष उन्मुख दृष्टिकोण को प्रोत्साहन देने के लिए 'इनोवेशन सेल' का गठन किया है तथा प्रत्येक वर्ष 'नवाचार उपलब्धियों' के लिए अटल रैंकिंग' जारी करने की शुरुआत की गई है। इस रैंकिंग के माध्यम से देश के उच्च शिक्षा संस्थानों में प्रतिस्पर्द्धात्मक माहौल पैदा किया गया है। इसके अतिरिक्त 'स्किल एक्विजिशन एफ नॉलेज एवेयरनेस फॉर लिवलीहुड प्रोमोशन' (संकल्प) तथा स्किल स्ट्रेंथनिंग फॉर इंडस्ट्रीयल वैल्यू इनहेंशमेण्ट (स्ट्राइव) के माध्यम से कौशल विकास पर ध्यान दिया गया है।

प्रसिद्ध शिक्षाशास्त्री **ह्यूएरटा मेलकर** का मानना है कि सामाजिक परिवर्तन का एकमात्र रास्ता सुधार है और यह सुधार शिक्षा में नवाचार के माध्यम से किया जा सकता है। राजनीति, अर्थव्यवस्था, समाज तथा प्रशासन के क्षेत्र में

बदलाव तथा नए विचारों के 'समस्या समाधान' के लिए 'शिक्षा' एकमात्र साधन है।

भारत विश्व में सर्वाधिक युवा जनसंख्या वाला देश है, जिसके माध्यम से शिक्षा के क्षेत्र में विस्तृत अवसरों को स्थान दिया जा सकता है। शिक्षा के क्षेत्र में गुणवत्ता की कमी को समाप्त करने में भी यह वर्ग सक्षम है।

यह अनिवार्य है कि शिक्षा के क्षेत्र में उत्पन्न विशिष्ट समस्याओं की पहचान करते हुए, उसके समाधान के लिए 'नवोन्मेष उन्मुख दृष्टिकोण' के माध्यम से नवीन विचारों को समाधान की प्रक्रिया में शामिल किया जाए।

भारत में उपस्थित 'मानव संसाधन' को ध्यान में रखते हुए शिक्षा के क्षेत्र में नवोन्मेष उन्मुख दृष्टिकोण को अपनाना देश के तीव्र तथा समावेशी विकास के लिए 'सम्भव प्रक्षेपण-पथ' है।

43. The need for Common Civil Code in India

CAPF AC 2017

The term Common Civil Code suggests the idea of equal set of civil rules for its citizens regardless of their religion, caste, etc. The term is important for India as the nation is a state following a democratic form of government has no religion of its own and propagates the belief that all the religions are equal for the state. The Preamble of the Indian Constitution declares India as a secular state and Part IV, Article 44 lays down an important directive principle of state policy, namely, that the State shall endeavour to secure for its citizens, a common/uniform civil code throughout the territory of India.

In a country as diverse as India, UCC is essential for various reasons listed below-

- **Celebrating Diversity, Strengthening Unity** UCC promote national integration and secularism by removing the distinctions and contradictions based on religious personal laws and creating a common identity for all citizens.

  This creates a sense of unity and harmony among diverse communities.
- **Empowering Women through Uniformity** UCC ensures gender justice and equality by abolishing the discriminatory and oppressive practices against women in various personal laws such as-polygamy, unequal inheritance, etc.
- **Streamlining Laws for Legal Efficiency** India's current legal system is burdened with complex and overlapping personal laws, leading to confusion and legal disputes. A UCC would simplify the legal framework by consolidating and harmonising various laws into a single code. This would enhance clarity, ease of implementation and reduce the burden on the judiciary, ensuring a more efficient legal system.
- **To accommodate the aspirations of the young population** A contemporary India is a totally new society where 55% of its population is below 25 years of age. Their social attitudes and aspirations are shaped by universal and global principles of equality, humanity and modernity. Their view of shedding identity on the basis of any religion has to be given a serious consideration so, as to utilise their full potential towards nation building.

While UCC is essential for the reason mentioned above, it is not without problems. It raises huge concerns regarding the judicial backlogs and minority rights. However, at the end of the day, a Universal Civil Code is needed for the nation with such a great diversity. In its need, it can emerge through an evolutionary process, which preserves India's rich legal heritage, of which all the personal laws are equal constituents.

44. Cashless transactions Scope and future prospects in India

CAPF AC 2017

Virtually every aspect of our life has been impacted by the rapid digitalisation of recent years. The shift in India toward a cashless economy is one of the most recent implications. India's economy is transitioning to a cashless society, beginning with the overnight note ban of circulation of notes with the denominations of ₹ 500 and 1000 that was implemented in November 2016.

To put it another way, less paper transactions will be made and more digital ones will occur, thanks to internet banking, digital wallets, point-of-sale devices, credit and debit cards, etc. This change would have several benefits and drawbacks and have a variety of effects on the economy.

The Advantages of a Cashless Economy

In a world full of nefarious people, carrying around a wallet stuffed with cash is stressful. However, if we utilise our mobile device as a one-stop shop for all kinds of operations, including paying bills, fees, transferring money, recharging, etc. We can ensure that our money is safe and scame for any transactions. It also guarantees a 'black-money free India' which solves a myriad of problems affecting our nation. Since most terrorist actions are sponsored with black money, crime rates have already begun to decline. Along with this, other crimes including bank robberies, extortion and burglaries are also on the decline.

The lengthening of the Income Tax Period is one of the largest benefits of cashlass transactions. Since there isn't much cash involved, large transactions must be made through banks, where rigorous KYC verifications are carried out before banking transactions. As a result, it will be simpler for the government to monitor and correct income tax avoidance by dishonest people. Further, because digital currency does not require printing, manual security, or a finite lifespan, it also has a high cost-benefit ratio.

The Disadvantages of Digital Banking

Due to a surge in digital transactions, the cashless economy will experience a rise in the hacking of personal information such as credit and debit card numbers, PINs, passwords and other sensitive information over the internet. In other words, if appropriate internet security measures are not done, cybercrimes will increase like anything else.

The majority of India's poor people, who are excluded from the traditional banking system, internet facilities and depend entirely on cash for their daily income, would also suffer greatly. Sectors with a lot of large cash transactions, such real estate, retail, restaurants, cement and other MSMEs, will be severely impacted as well.

Future of Cashless Transactions

The number of smartphones in the country is going to increase manyfold and as this percentage increases, the number of people using digital payments would also multiply. In this light, India needs to have a consistent broadband network and power connection in order to include the Rural consumers. The government has already launched Bharatnet in this direction and background infrastructure for Rural area is expanding slowly.

Further, the government should facilitate payment of tolls, purchase of railway tickets, subsidy payments to farmers through a digital medium while creating Cash-In Cash-Out (CICO) machines instead of ATMs which are now becoming very bulky and difficult to build and maintain. CICO machines can operate with a sim card whereas ATMs require a broadband connection.

The switch to digital economy should not be based on compulsions and should be left on the market forces. Incentivising is better than imposing financial burden on either companies or banks.

Also, the policy framing in this regard should be more inclined towards the consumer and less on the digital companies. India's demographic dividend offers hope to this transition. Private sector participation and Rural inclusion should remain the focus areas while moving forward towards 'Digital India'.

45. India Vs China in the context of emerging economy in South Asia CAPF AC 2017

India has enjoyed substantial regional influence across South Asia due to its size, comparative economic might and historical and cultural relevance to the region. China's history of involvement in South Asia is limited in comparison, though its long-standing ties to Pakistan are a notable exception. But over the past decade, China has become a significant economic partner to countries throughout the region, forging particularly strong ties with smaller states through trade, diplomacy, aid and investment.

China's increased involvement in South Asia poses a challenge to India as the regional economic and diplomatic heavy weight. Despite recent headlines proclaiming India's eclipse by China, several threads of economic interaction continue to link India with its neighbours quite deeply. China has not eclipsed India across South Asia but it is catching up in its trade and investment and in some cases, its economic diplomacy has been accompanied by expanded strategic cooperation with India's neighbours.

As China steps up its engagement with the region and promotes Asian connectivity, largely through its Silk Road 'belt and road' vision, it can marshal extensive resources on initiatives such as the Asian Infrastructure Investment Bank that will likely outpace other financial sources.

India Vs China Trade Relations

- Due to its size and location, India was a natural top trading partner for South Asian countries for decades. India and Nepal share an open border; India signed its first free trade agreement with Sri Lanka, India and Bhutan share 'mutually beneficial economic inter-linkages' and India has been a major economic partner to Bangladesh since its independence in 1971.
- With the exception of China's extensive economic relationship with Pakistan, China's growing influence in South Asia is a relatively recent phenomenon. The China-Pakistan axis stands as a special and separate case, one that reflects a unique strategic logic unparalleled with other South Asia countries.
- In the past decade, China has emerged as a top exporter of goods to the region, including to India, breaking into South Asian markets with its export-led growth strategy. Around 2005, China overtook India as Bangladesh's top trading partner. China displaced many Indian goods in Bangladesh, offering cheaper Chinese products (especially cotton and other fabrics central to the government industry) without the visa, transport, and customs challenges that had limited trade between India and Bangladesh.
- China's trade with Nepal and Sri Lanka still lags behind India's but the gaps are narrowing. Sri Lanka is among India's top trading partners in South Asia and India is Sri Lanka's largest trade partner. Since 2005, however, Chinese exports to Sri Lanka have quadrupled coming closer to Indian levels.
- Given Nepal's strategic location, it attracts significant attention from both of its neighbours. A 1996 trade agreement between India and Nepal increased bilateral trade volume, which now accounts for more than half of Nepal's total trade. In 2005, at the peak of Nepal's Maoist insurgency, a low point in its relations with India, Sino-Nepali relations shifted both economically and politically. Chinese goods flooded Nepali markets as Nepal diversified its imports and lessened its dependence on India.
- In Afghanistan, both China's and India's trade volumes with the landlocked country are under $1 billion but expected to grow. However, increased Chinese involvement in Afghanistan and the completion of its economic corridor connectivity through Pakistan could alter trade dynamics by opening up routes to Afghan markets through Pakistan.

Conclusion

With an unresolved border and a contentious history, India often views China's activities in the South Asia neighbourhood warily. Yet China's and India's efforts in South Asia can overlap, such as in the development of the Bangladesh-China-India-Myanmar economic corridor, opening up new opportunities for constructive cooperation. India's 'Act East' policy aims to facilitate commerce, culture and connectivity throughout South-East Asia, an area that also captures China's focus. The two countries' efforts will likely be complementary since the region's infrastructure needs are so pressing and require trillions of dollars in capital. Greater connectivity will enable both China and India to tap further into Asian markets through trade and investment, although India will be hard-pressed to provide products as inexpensive and plentiful as China can in the near term.

46. The things that count as being civilised

CAPF AC 2017

If one were to look in many dictionaries, the meaning of the word civil would be different in each one. This is because a single definition cannot describe what it means to be civilised. The meaning is different for every person because every person's individual values and morals are different. However, in the modern epoch, the definition of civilised is the characteristics of a state of civilisation, especially characterised by taste, refinement or restraint. Now, from this definition, the meaning of civilisation is a relatively high level of cultural and technological development stage at which writing and the keeping of written records is attained.

However, being civilised is not just about being educated. Civilised people respect human beings as individuals and are therefore always tolerant, gentle, courteous and amenable. They have compassion for every being present on this planet. They are sensitive, sympathetic and kind. They don't tell lies even in the most trivial matters and always speak the truth no matter what.

Civilised people don't simply obey their baser instincts. They don't run themselves down in order to provoke the sympathy of others. They don't play on other people's emotions and respect everything around them. There is respect for the country and the countrymen in a civilised society.

The duties are obeyed and rights are respected. Laws are strictly followed and there lies a sense of belonging towards the country. Empathising with the population and the feeling of oneness are some of the virtues that help in bringing about unity in society.

Thus, a civilised person is a blend of every good character tic that makes him/her a valuable asset for the nation.

47. Cleaning and connecting the rivers in India

CAPF AC 2017

Cleaning of Northern India's Perennial rivers and Interlinking of Peninsular rivers of India is considered one of the most ambitious projects in the modern times. A stable supply of quality water is an essential requirement for guaranteeing socio-economic-political stability. Rapidly increasing population, rising standards of living and exponential growth of industrialisation and urbanisation have exposed water resources, in general and rivers, in particular, to various forms of degradation.

Government efforts for Clean Rivers Projects

- The Central Government had set-up the 'National Ganga River Basin Authority' (NGRBA) in 2009 as an empowered planning, financing, monitoring and coordinating authority for the Ganga river, to ensure effective abatement of pollution and conservation of the river Ganga by adopting a holistic approach with the river basin as the unit of planning.
- The Namami Gange program launched by Union Government on 13th May, 2015 is a comprehensive approach to rejuvenate the river Ganga and all tributaries under one Umbrella Programme. It should be done by consolidating the existing ongoing efforts and planning for a concrete action plan for the future with an allocated budget of ₹ 20,000 crore for 5 years.

Interlinking of Rivers

First mooted by the Chief Engineer of the Madras Presidency in 1919, Sir Arthur Cotton, the idea behind interlinking of rivers is to reduce the problems of droughts and floods faced by various parts of the country. The concept was envisaged on the fact that the Indo-Gangetic rivers are perennial since they are fed by rains as well as the glaciers from the Himalayas.

The Peninsular rivers in India are, however, not seasonal because they are rain-fed mainly from the South-West Monsoons. Due to this, the Indo-Gangetic plains suffer from floods and the peninsular states suffer from droughts. If this excess water can be diverted from the Plains to the Peninsula, the problem of floods and droughts can be solved to a large extent. Hence, the interlinking of rivers will bring about an equitable distribution of river waters in India.

To promote the interlinking of rivers, the National River Linking Project (NRLP) was commissioned. This project envisages the transfer of water from the water-excess basin to the water-deficient basin by interlinking 37 rivers of India by a network of almost 3000 storage dams. This will form a gigantic South Asian water grid which can control both floods and droughts, help in hydropower generation and augment the defence and security of the country through the additional waterline defence.

Conclusion

Concluding, the projects of cleaning and connecting the rivers are massive and require efficient implementation. We as citizens of the country can help the government in its success by not polluting our water bodies and control actions that bring severe environmental changes.

48. The recent achievements of India's nuclear scientists CAPF AC 2017

India ranks second in terms of contribution to high-quality scientific research. It is among the world's top 10 nations in the number of scientific publications.

Some of the key achievements are

- **Heavy Water Production** After initial failures, nuclear scientists of Department of Atomic Energy (DAE) have mastered Heavy Water production technology. India even become an exporter and has exported many countries including USA and China. For controlled and sustained nuclear chain reaction, fast neutrons produced from nuclear reactors must be slowed down. Hydrogen (in water) is a very efficient moderator but it absorbs more neutrons which in turn require relatively enriched fuel.
- **Bhabhatron I and II** DAE's scientists have also been developing tools and techniques for treating the killer disease. Bhabhatron, the indigenous telecobalt machine is one of the successful products developed by Bhabha Atomic Research Centre (BARC), Mumbai for Cancer Treatment.

  There are only about 430 Teletherapy machines operating in the country. Many of them are old, needing immediate replacement. Most of the cancer treatment facilities are located in Urban areas, while the vast Rural areas remain untouched. Bhabhatron was developed to meet the growing demand for affordable high-performance telecobalt machine.
- **KALI(Kilo Ampere Linear Injector)** It has been developed by Bhabha Atomic Research Centre (BARC) and Defence Research and Development Organisation (DRDO) as a very high speed electron gun which can be targeted towards enemy systems such as missiles to destroy their on board electronic systems.
- **Nuclear Desalination Demonstration Plant (NDDP)** A large scale Nuclear Desalination Demonstration Plant (NDDP), near Chennai, developed by BARC nuclear scientists which uses Multi Stage Flash Evaporation and Reverse Osmosis Technologies has been running successfully. It is coupled with Madras Atomic Power Station (MAPS) and cleans nearly 6.3 million liters of water every day.
- **Control Systems of Ship Borne Terminal** ISRO Telemetry Tracking and Command Network provide TTC (Telemetry, Tracking and Control) support for Launch Vehicles and Spacecrafts for all ISRO missions. BARC and ECIL developed this indigenous ship borne antenna terminal (SBT) to support ISRO missions which include tracking of reentry vehicles for future Indian manned missions to space.
- **Integrated Environmental Radiation Monitor and Automatic Weather Station** BARC and ISRO (Indian Space Research Organisation) under a collaborative programme designed and integrated Environmental Radiation Monitor (ERM, developed under IERMON programme by BARC) with Automatic Weather Station (AWS, developed by ISRO), as a single stand-alone ERM-AWS system. The system operates with solar powered battery backup and the data transmission is via satellite.

Conclusion

The roles of nuclear scientists in the development in latest Atomic research immense which is not limited to the core areas but it has been expanded into various field of researches. But still, there is much more scope of progress and development.

49. The onus of maintaining healthy relations with Nepal is on India CAPF AC 2016

Nepal is an important neighbour of India and occupies special significance in its foreign policy because of the geographical, historical, cultural and economic linkages that span centuries. It is but obvious that both the countries enjoy a relation of friendship and cooperation characterised by open borders between them and deep rooted ties between people. Traders, businessman, doctors, engineers, IT professionals, labourers, etc., from India reside in Nepal. Nepalese citizens enjoy unparalleled advantages in India, availing opportunities equal to Indian citizens. Relations with India has allowed the Nepalese citizens to enjoy freedom of movement to and from India without any hesitancy. India and Nepal share similar in terms of Hinduism and Buddhism with Buddha's birthplace Lumbini located in present day Nepal and both countries having various places of pilgrimages.

Consequently, it is not surprising that the Nepal holds important place in Indian context. It holds a strategic importance for India's National Security and by virtue of their place as Indian neighbours, it helps in understanding India's role in International politics. Thus, India shares great relation with Nepal with initiatives to promote people to people contacts in areas of culture, academics, media, etc. This relationship was strengthened by the Indo-Nepal Treaty of Peace and Friendship of 1950 which obligated both sides "to inform each other of any serious friction or misunderstanding with any neighbouring state likely to cause any breach in the friendly relations subsisting between the two governments."

However, there has been a certain trust deficit between India and Nepal. India-Nepal relations have faced a deterioration and tensions because of various reasons which include.

- **Political Instability** Nepal has witnessed periods of political instability including a 10 years violent insurgency which severely damaged Nepal's economy and development. This has significantly brought tensions between India and Nepal as there have been changes in the government which sometimes favoured China. Any opportunity grabbed by China in the Nepal region is a lost opportunity for India. There was an economic blockade during Madhesi protest in Nepal in 2014 where Nepal even accused India of instigating the protests. Thus, there has been a significant strain between both the countries.

- **Internal Security** India shares an open border with Nepal. It creates security challenges for India as the open border is often used for illegal activities. There is infiltration of North-Eastern insurgents, supply of arms, supply of fake Indian currency into the Indian territory.
- **China-Factor** Nepal has usually acted as a buffer state between India and China. Nepal has seen different regimes which were either Pro-India or Pro-China. However, with Chinese initiatives of Belt and Silk road and Maritime Silk road dominating the South Asian regions and China's increasing generosity towards Nepal, the nation is increasingly becoming Pro-China. In other words, China's growing influence in Nepal has resulted in declining tradional leverage of India in Nepal. The relationship is further strained because, Nepalese regime has been feeling insecure because of the upper hand that India seeks to play in the relations between two countries.
- **Border Dispute** Though Indo Nepal border has remained peaceful, there has been a dispute over the Kalapani region. The dispute emerged when Nepal government published a new map which showed Kalapani region as Nepal's territory. The remergence of dispute has been attributed to Chinese pressure on Nepal. Though it has led to the emergence of new tensions in India-Nepal relations, the border dispute is easily solvable as long as there is political goodwill exercised on both sides.

Conclusion

Nepal is strategically and politically important for India. Hence, India should seek to strengthen its ties with Nepal. Issues can be sorted out between both countries on account of special relations that both the countries enjoy with each other.

The open border should be managed so that it does not harm the interests of both the countries. There must be enhanced focus upon cultural ties and strengthening people to people contacts. India should mitigate Nepal's concerns by taking them into confidence. India should confidently invest in Nepal's infrastructure so that Chinese dominance can be reduced. A stable, secure and prosperous Nepal is in India's best interests. Normal relations with the most friendly neighbour will be a foundation of prosperity in both the nations.

50. Farmers' suicides in India; A sign of impending disaster CAPF AC 2016

India is an agrarian economy with the agriculture sector being one of the major contributors to the GDP. Agriculture is the primary source of livelihood for more than 58% of the population depend upon it directly or indirectly. India has largely achieved self-sufficiency in production of food grains, delivering strong and fast economic growth for past several years.

The country has unique competitive advantages with the largest arable land area which is 60.44% of an estimated 179.8 million hectares and diverse agro-climatic conditions supporting the cultivation of various crops. After Independence, agricultural development was given the top most priority to attain self-sufficiency in food grains to feed the rapidly increasing population. Several public policies and investment decisions were taken particularly with regard to irrigation, fertilisers, land reforms and community development.

Yet Indian farmers are committing suicide on a mass scale. As per the Central Government, despite a multi-pronged approach to improving income and social security of farmers, over 12,000 suicides were reported in the agricultural sector every year since 2013. Scholars have given various reasons such as monsoon failure, climate change, high debt burdens, government policies, mental health, personal issues and family problems for farmers' suicides in India. Some of these reasons are discussed below

- **The surge in input costs** A major cause of the farmers' suicides in India has been the increasing burden on the farmers due to inflated prices of agricultural inputs. Be it the fertilisers, crop protection chemicals or even the seeds for cultivation, farming has become expensive for the already indebted farmers. Using agricultural equipment and machinery like tractors, submersible pumps, etc., adds to the already surging costs.
- **Distressed due to loans** NCRB data points out that in 2474 suicides out of the studied 3000 farmer suicides in 2015 the victims had unpaid loans from local banks. Hence, stress due to non-payment of the previous dues and the increasing debt forces a peasant to commit suicide.
- **Lack of direct integration with the market** Although initiatives like the National Agricultural Market and contract farming are helping integrate the farmers' produce directly with the market, cutting the role of intermediaries, the reality is still lagging behind.
- **Lack of awareness** The digital divide, as well as the literacy gap, has made the marginal and small farmers particularly vulnerable due to their inability to utilise the positives of government policies. This is reflected in the continued unsustainable cropping practices – like cultivating sugarcane in water-deficit regions.
- **Water crisis** The concentration of these suicides in the water-deficit regions of states is a manifestation of how the water crisis and thereby, the failure to meet production demands have intensified the menace. What has added to the already prevalent crisis is the unwillingness to cater to each other's water needs amongst the states. Climate change has acted as the last nail in the coffin by resulting in furthering of the

uncertainties associated with the already uncertain monsoon system and hence agricultural production. While incidents like flash floods have led to crop losses, deferred monsoons have seen production shortfall year-in and year-out.

Conclusion

In essence, the factors sum up to crop failure, unsustainable production and subsequent farmer indebtedness leading to failure of strengthening the economic state of the farmer which is the driving force behind these suicides.

"Give a man a fish, he will eat for a day but teach him how to fish, he will eat for the rest of his life". The case of our Indian farmers is similar to this, what they need is a means to sustain throughout their lives without having the face the desperation that adversity drives them to and all-inclusive approach that integrates biological, chemical, mechanical and physical methodology should be used to prevent crop damage.

51. India needs to redefine the relations between the Centre and the States CAPF AC 2016

The Indian Constitution declares India as a federal state meaning that it is a Union of States where power is divided between centre and states and further below to local levels as per the procedure mentioned in the Constitution. In this three tier system, the Central Government has the final say in all the matters so that the nation remains united.

However, recent trends show that the relations between the Centre and the States have been in conflict and now have to be redefined vis-a-vis the changing complexities of the India Social fabric.

These problems that lead to the conflict between the Centre and States are given below.

- **Multi-Party System** Due to the multi-party system in India, many times as a result of political ambiguity, the Center uses Article-356 of the Constitution and can dismiss state assemblies. In the successive meetings of the Inter-State Council, there has been a demand from various sections to restrict the use of Article 356 to cases where there is a serious threat to the national unity or secular fabric of the country.
- **Appointment of Governor** The provision of the Governor appointed by the Center for the states is not in line with the federal democratic polity. The Governor is the constitutional head of the state but he is appointed by the Central Government. If there is a government of different parties in the Centre and the State, then the role of the governor has been in doubt.
- **Centre, Concurrent and State lists** In the Constitution, the subjects of the Center list and concurrent list are continuously increasing and the subjects of the state list are decreasing. The Central Government has infiltrated the state list not only by putting a subject like education from the state list to the concurrent list but also by the rapid increase in so-called centrally sponsored schemes.

Conclusion

In a country like India where problems like communalism, language based problems, religious hysteria, etc., exist, a united stand is needed. Hence, a balanced approach where more financial autonomy is given to the states for the increasing liability of the states is needed. Both the Centre and the State need practical change so, that the goal of citizen-centric governance can be fulfilled.

52. Is development possible at the cost of environment? CAPF AC 2016

The twenty first century capitalism can yield profit from any crisis. It doesn't just exploit crisis for profiteering interest, but also produce crisis to come up with a business solution. It wages war and then sells arms in the name of defence support, it pollutes the environment first and then offers costly technology and medicine as environmental mitigation.

Man in his belief of being superior and greed for more and more luxuries has managed to ruin the environment. He has already wasted and destroyed vast amounts of natural resources and over exploited whatever they could get their hands on in the name of development. Rainforests have been destroyed and wiped off of earth, natural calamities like floods, droughts, wildfires, rapid melting of glaciers, rising temperatures among many other phenomenon have removed entire ecosystems off the face of the planet. Water bodies are polluted and aquatic life is at risk. Many species of flora and fauna have been swiped from existence. Fertile lands are becoming barren and many cities are under the risk of drowning.

However, time and again we have been shown that the exploitative activities of man will lead to its downfall. The after effects of the ecological imbalance as mentioned, is taking man towards a time wherein its existence is impossible. Hence, it was important for man to realise that development is not possible without concern for environment. Realising this concern, the UN came up with the Sustainable Development Goals which focus on development with environmental preservation.

53. Revamping our banking system is the need of the hour CAPF AC 2016

History of Indian Banking System

Indian banking system has been in operation successfully for more than 200 yrs. Since, then it has been evolving on a continuous basis, from being exclusivist to becoming a carrier of social reform and financial inclusion. However, in recent times, the banking industry has experienced many issues. For instance, a decline in asset quality, financial soundness and efficiency has marred the functioning of the Indian banking industry. Given the current challenges of a growing population, the Indian Banking Sector is constantly modifying and coming out with reforms to overcome the issues faced by it while promotes its growth.

Recent Trends in Banking Sector

Until recently, the lack of competitiveness vis-a-vis global standards, low technological level in operations, over staffing, high NPAs and low levels of motivation had shackled the performance of the banking industry. As the international standards became prevalent, banks had to unlearn their traditional operational methods of directed credit, directed investments and fixed interest rates, all of which led to deterioration in the quality of loan portfolios, inadequacy of capital and the erosion of profitability. The banking sector is stressed mainly due to its rising NPA. The NPAs might rise further due to loans made under the government's flagship schemes like Pradhan Mantri Mudra Yojana and the Kisan Credit Card. Further, challenges like cyber-theft, banking frauds and decentralised currency (such as Bitcoins) pose a threat to banking sector which needs to be addressed. The NBFCs have caused credit crisis in the financial sector.

Need of Banking Reforms banking sector reforms were needed to revamp the system and provide necessary platform for the Indian banks to operate on the basis of operational flexibility and functional autonomy, thereby enhancing efficiency, productivity and profitability. Further, the reforms help in enhancing the competitive element in the market through the entry of new banks. Reforms also lead to increase in transparency of the bank's balance sheets through introduction of prudential norms and increase in the role of market forces due to the deregulated interest rates.

Though, major reforms have been undertaken to improve the condition of banking sector, a lot needs to be done to abate current and future risks that surround banking sector. The World Bank has suggested that India must undertake financial reforms in three key areas

- Sound regulations for Non-Banking Financial Companies (NBFCs).
- Allow private sector banks to expand in the banking sector.
- Deepen capital market to aid growth.

Conclusion

Concluding, the financial sector is the mainstay of any economy and it contributes immensely in the mobilisation and distribution of resources. Financial sector reforms have long been viewed as significant part of the programme for policy reforms in a nation. The Banking Sector reforms have provided the economy with a lot of resilience and stability and have boomed nearly every sector of the economy. Now banks are playing significant role in resource mobilisation.

54. Urbanisation of India is nothing but blind Westernisation

CAPF AC 2016

Urbanisation refers to the phenomenon of human populations shifting into specific distinguished areas in Urban centres for the want of a better livelihood. The belief that cities are often preferred for better employment, education, health care and culture makes people migrate to cities.

However, the Western phenomenon generally associated with human development and progress, is now being associated with poverty, environmental degradation and population demands that outstrip service capacity especially in a agrarian nation like India which is not well-equipped to tackle such large scale migration.

The mass unplanned transfer of people from Rural to Urban areas ca

n lead to significant inequalities and problems. Some of these major problems are

- **Overcrowding** It happens where there are more people in comparison to space. The lack of space results in people dwelling in cramped spaces that threaten the safety of human beings from a health and sanitation point of view.
- **Slums and other ill-developed settlements** The lack of housing and proper living spaces lead to the development of slums and other it developed settlements. These slums are positioned near open sewers and restricted to geographically dangerous areas. Further, these spaces have high human densities and lack of ventilation which make people living in them prone to communicable diseases, waterborne and vector-borne diseases.
- **Degradation of environmental quality** The presence of a huge population in cities requires a host of facilities such as residential places, public transport and industries. Deforestation occurs on a large scale to ensure these utilities result in air and water pollution. Hence, the tree cover reduces and the environmental quality takes a hit.
- **Lifestyle Diseases** Most of the jobs in urban centres require odd hours of work that promote a stressful environment along with unhealthy food habits leading to diseases such as obesity, diabetes, and hypertension. Further, the rise of nuclear families especially makes urbanites vulnerable to psychological trauma and to mental disorders leading to dementia, depression, substance abuse, alcoholism and family disintegration.

The reason why these problems exist is simple- India is not ready for such a phenomenon. To cut a long story short, India's current mechanisms of urbanisation offer few opportunities for its disadvantaged citizens, especially for its religious minorities, new migrants and poor. Cities are not only mimicking rural social and cultural structures of inequality and exclusion but they are also creating fault lines for future conflicts.

It is well known in development literature that such unequal access to resources – which are in India, basic services – can curb human development potentials, lower the quality of life, create conditions for communal political rhetoric and exacerbate development cleavages along religious and ethnic lines. Yet, urbanisation is celebrated as it is a Western concept. Such an ignorance displays that urbanisation is juts blind westernisation.

55. Sardar Patel's role in India's freedom movement and afterwards CAPF AC 2015

Sardar Vallabhbhai Patel was one of the greatest patriots and a selfless human being. He was born on 31st October, 1875 in a small village in Nadiad. His father Jhaverbhai Patel was a simple farmer and mother Laad Bai was a simple lady. This man of steel learnt early to be tough, for he was born as a middle child in an impoverished family.
Around 1915, he came across Mahatma Gandhi. The Swadeshi Movement was at its peak. He started participating actively in the freedom movement. The British government declared to confiscate all the land of farmers. He brought together the farmers and forced the government to amend the rules. He got the title of 'Sardar' and became famous.
In Gandhiji's political journey, Sardar had been a keen adviser and an active participant. He was an important player of the Indian Independence Movement. Earlier, he had given up his busy legal practice to work for the freedom movement. He had been active in the movements of Champaran, Kheda, etc. He played an important part in Quit India Movement as well.
His greatest contribution came after the independence. With great wisdom and political foresight, he consolidated the small kingdoms. He took up and successfully completed the mission of uniting the princely states. With the non-conforming states, he used hard diplomacy and also force and succeeded. His greatness was that although he was a senior to Nehruji, he didn't compete for the post of PM deferring to Gandhiji's advice.
In successive phases of his life, Sardar Patel showed the defiance of the oppressed, a lawyer's brilliance, the daring to give up a flourishing career, the discipline of a soldier in the battles of freedom, the strategies of a General, the firmness of a patriot and the farsightedness of a statesman. His strength of character, the sharpness of his mind, his organising skills and all his energy were offered for achieving the freedom of India and after independence for India's consolidation.

56. Financial inclusion is a must for inclusive growth CAPF AC 2015

Even after 70 years of independence, a large section of Indian population still remain unbanked. This malaise has led generation of financial instability and pauperism among the lower income group who do not have access to financial products and services. However, in the recent years the government and Reserve Bank of India has been pushing the concept and idea of financial inclusion simply because financial inclusion is must for inclusive growth of the nation.

Inclusive growth refers to economic growth that creates employment opportunities and helps in reducing poverty. It means having access to essential services in health and education by the poor. It includes providing equality of opportunity, empowering people through education and skill development. It also encompasses a growth process that is environment friendly growth, aims for good governance and helps in creation of a sensitive society.

In the light of understanding and fostering inclusive growth, financial inclusion becomes a prerequisite. Financial inclusion means greater access to financial services and an increase in savings which would help in decreasing income inequality and poverty and would lead to increase in employment levels.

As financial inclusion encourages the habit to save, it enhances capital formation in the country, giving it an economic boost. Also, the availability of sufficient and transparent credit from formal banking institutions will promote the entrepreneurial spirit among the people, leading to an increase in productivity and prosperity in rural areas. Hence, all sectors of the Indian economy and social structure would see a growth as the society becomes financially inclusive.

The government, understanding the importance of financial inclusivity, has come up with many policies that encourage people to open bank accounts. However, merely opening an account does not make sure that the account is used. Instead, the following things can be done for the proper utilisation of accounts.
Financial literacy programmes should be undertaken and backed by products that address the real needs of consumers, with the support to use the product.

People have to be imparted an ability to understand and execute matters of personal finance such as basic numeracy and literacy, financial awareness, knowledge and skills, attitude and behaviours needed to make sound financial decisions, budgeting, investing and risk diversification.

57. Role of Governor in Indian polity CAPF AC 2015

Part VI of the Constitution of India deals with the state executive. The State Executive consists of the governor, the Chief Minister, the Council of Ministers and the Advocate-General of the State Governor is the nominal Head at the State Level but he/she plays a dual role in Indian Politics- as the Constitutional Head of the State and as the agent or representative of the centre.
Appointed directly by the President under his hand and seal, the Governor serves as a representative of the Union Government and thus has various powers. The State's Governor will have executive, legislative, financial and judicial powers. He does not, however, have the diplomatic, military or emergency powers like India's President possesses.

Executive Powers

- In the name of the Governor, the Council of Ministers exercises the executive functions. As a result, the Governor is simply a ceremonial head, while the Council of Ministers is the real executive.
- He/she is the State's constitutional head and picks the majority party's leader as the Chief minister.

- He/she can ask the Chief Minister for any information that he/she wants.
- The Governor appoints the State's Attorney General, Chairman and Members of the State Public Service Commission.
- He/she has the authority to recommend to the President that a constitutional emergency be declared in the State.
- As an agent of the President, the Governor has significant executive powers during the President's administration in the State.

Legislative Powers

- The Governor is part of the State Legislature and no bill cannot become a law until he/she signs it.
- He/she can withhold a bill and send it to the President for consideration.
- He/she can also dissolve the State Assembly before the expiry of its term on the advice of the Chief Minister or as directed by the President.
- He/she causes the annual Budget to be presented in the State Legislative Assembly.

Judicial Powers

- The Governor appoints the district judges and is consulted in the appointment of the judges of the High Court by the President.
- He/she can, pardon, remit and commute the sentence of a person convicted by a State court.

Financial Powers

- He/she causes the annual budget to be laid before the State Legislative Assembly.
- No money bill can be introduced in the State Legislative Assembly without the Governor's prior approval.

Discretionary Powers

- If no party receives an absolute majority, the Governor can choose the Chief Minister at his/her discretion.
- In an emergency, he/she can override the advice of the Council of Ministers and in such situations, he/she acts as the President's agent and becomes the true ruler of the State.
- He/she utilises the discretionary authority to submit a report to the President on the State's activities.
- He/she can also withhold assent to a bill and refer it to the President for approval.

Conclusion

Thus, the Governor plays a key role in Indian polity. He represents the Centre in the State and the State at the Centre.

58. Disaster Management System in India CAPF AC 2015

Today's world is afflicted with disasters. Be it earthquakes, forest fires, tsunamis, cloud bursts, pandemics, etc. Natural disasters are becoming more and more frequent, growing more severe and affecting more people than ever before. The reasons vary but climate change and environmental degradation has further compounded the frequency and intensity of disasters along with increasing the vulnerability of key assets including people. This has been true especially in the case of India which is among the world's most disaster-prone countries with 27 of its 29 States and 7 Union Territories exposed to recurrent natural hazards. Considering the frequency of recurrent floods, droughts, severe weather or conflict in different locations across India, our institutions and systems need to create an effective and efficient disaster management plan.

An effective disaster management plan provides the technology, tools and practices that enable disaster response organisations to systematically manage information from multiple sources and collaborate effectively to assist survivors, mitigate damage and help communities rebuild. In other words, it includes all aspects of planning, coordinating and implementing all measures which are necessary or desirable to prevent, minimise, overcome, or to stop the spread of a disaster. The broad objective of any disaster management policy, then, is to reduce the loss of lives, social and community assets and contribute to sustainable development and a better standard of living for all.

As far as India is concerned Disaster management is not a novel concept. People in the Indian antiquity have been using various indigenous techniques and strategies to manage disasters. The Government of India enacted the Disaster Management Act, 2005 which mandated creation of National Disaster Management Authority (NDMA) with Prime Minister as the Chairman and State Disaster Management Authorities (SDMA) headed by the respective Chief Ministers to spearhead and implement a holistic and integrated approach to Disaster Management in India. District Disaster Management Authority (DDMA) will be headed by the District Collector, Deputy Commissioner or District Magistrate as the case may be with the elected representative of the local authority as the co-chairperson The act also provided for creation of National Institution of Disaster Management (NIDM). It will organise training, research, documentation and development and will network with other institutions. Besides, a Calamity Relief Fund has been constituted.

However, India lacks a proper Disaster Management plan which like all disaster management plans needs to have three phases. These phases are discussed below

- The First phase is **Pre-disaster stage.** In this stage, disaster prone areas need long term planning. It includes preparing hazard zonation maps, land use zoning, modern forecasting and warning systems and creating awareness through education and communication systems. Mitigation measures include construction of disaster resistant houses and fortification of old houses in the sensitive zones, rehabilitating people to safer places.
- The Second phase includes **rescue and relief operations.**
- The third stage, post-disaster, refers to **rehabilitation**, which does not only cover rebuilding or repairing houses

and roads but giving crucial importance to the region if it is disaster prone. It includes political and administrative support, focus on community values and education and health care systems, reviving the economy and preserving the environment.

For appropriate disaster management, it is essential that all these aspects are given due importance while formulating policies and implementing them. But past experiences reveal that while managing disasters, only politico-administrative and economic aspects are given due importance. The other two are either neglected or misunderstood. Further, there had been problems of resource crunch wherein the Central and State Governments are unable to bear the burden of huge expenditure for rehabilitation.

As communities and economies move from responding to a natural disaster to following the longer road of recovery, those involved have an opportunity to ensure that investments are designed for long-term sustainability and innovation.

This requires a degree of planning and reconstruction that's designed not only to rebuild a community to what it was before, by revitalising the culture but also to infuse new concepts of innovation and resiliency to increase economic vitality.

The private sector, public sector and nongovernmental organisation community must work together to deploy solutions in the most effective manner and to ensure that solutions are appropriate, sustainable and designed to achieve the best possible results.

Global disaster management and humanitarian assistance requires a multifaceted approach that leverages the skills, resources and commitments of corporations, government agencies, intergovernmental organisations, non-governmental organisations and individuals.

59. NET Neutrality is a must for Digital India

CAPF AC 2015

Digital Technologies have become an inseparable part of modern lives, so much so, that many essential services are now being delivered digitally. The internet has become a necessity for most day-to-day affairs. This digital ecosystem has been enabled by various stakeholders and gateways like telecom service providers, personal computers and smartphones, operating systems, App developers, etc. However, when these gateways restrict access to internet/networks, they become gatekeepers and threaten net neutrality and openness of the internet giving rise to the problem of net neutrality.

Net neutrality is essentially the principle that all internet traffic should be treated equally, without discrimination or preference given to any particular website, service, or application.

Net neutrality ensures that everyone has equal access to information and services on the internet, regardless of their financial resources or the size and power of the websites they use. It is an important principle that helps to ensure a level playing field on the internet, and to protect the free flow of information and ideas. The concept came into existence when the TRAI banned Facebook's Free Basics and Airtel Zero. Both Free Basics and Airtel Zero let users access certain apps and websites for free.

In the digital age wherein internet is required by one and all, net neutrality is essential. Lack of net neutrality can lead to a plethora of issues as mentioned below

- **Monopolising Internet** Without net neutrality, ISPs would have the ability to shape internet traffic to derive extra benefits from it. This would give them the power to charge companies like YouTube and Netflix for services that consume more bandwidth compared to a normal website.
- **Discourage Innovation** Lack of net neutrality could spell doom for innovation on the web. Startups would be at a disadvantage compared to established players who have the resources to pay for faster access. This could lead to a web that is dominated by a few large players, rather than an open and diverse ecosystem.
- **Package Plans for Consumers** The lack of net neutrality would also mean that instead of free access, there could be 'package plans' for consumers. For example, users may have to pay more to access international websites compared to websites based in their own country. This would create a tiered internet system where users who pay more get better access to content.
- **Access to Objectionable Content** Offensive, dangerous, illicit and illegal content is accessible to everyone through net neutrality and is difficult to remove. In the absence of net neutrality Internet service providers can filter dangerous content.

Apart from these, one important factor stating the importance of net neutrality is the digital transformation of the country.

Conclusion

Today, the government is moving towards doing everything digitally. In this light, net neutrality becomes essential to stop ISPs across the world from getting the power to shape and control the traffic.

60. Sino-Pak alliance and India's security **CAPF AC 2015**

'Higher than the mountains, deeper than the oceans, sweeter than honey', this is how China and Pakistan describe their relationship. With China-Pakistan Economic Corridor coming in the light adds, 'stronger than steel.' China and Pakistan have shared their geo-political and strategic interest for almost seven decades. Pakistan-China is the only bilateral relationship, other than with Saudi

Arabia perhaps, in which Pakistan is happy to play the junior partner. Such a budding relationship can take a heavy toll on India because of the presence of the CPEC.

The China–Pakistan Economic Corridor (CPEC) is biggest connectivity project aims to connect Gwadar Port in South-Western Pakistan to China's North-Western autonomous region of Xinjiang, via a network of highways, railways and pipelines to transport oil and gas. The economic corridor is considered central to China–Pakistan relations and will run about 3,000 km from Gwadar to Kashgar.

The Corridor is an extension of China's proposed 21st century Silk Road initiative. While the corridor seems to bring many benefits to China and Pakistan and some benefits to India, the latter nation opposed CPEC route and development of Gwadar port, since its very conception. The reason was that this geographical reality of the CPEC could potentially impinge upon India's geopolitical calculations and pose a strategic challenge.

Some other reasons for such opposition were as listed follows

- The planned CPEC route passes through POK and Gilgit-Baltistan, which India claims to be its own integral and indispensable territory. Further, the CPEC also somewhat legitimises Pakistan's ownership over disputed PoK which may lead to the internationalisation of Kashmir Issue which India doesn't want. Apart from this India feels that the high economic stakes in the project will push China to ally with Pakistan on the Kashmir dispute.
- With the complete realisation of CPEC, China will get a free corridor to move its armour and mechanised weapons which are a threat to India in the plains of Punjab and Rajasthan. In the guise of securing CPEC, China can permanently position troops on Pakistan soil not too far from the Indian.
- Despite clarifications from China and Pakistan that the port at Gwadar will be used only for economic purposes, India fears that China may establish a naval base at Gwadar to ensure Chinese maritime hegemony in the Indian Ocean. India considers Gwadar Port as part of China's String of Pearls' bases, that extends from its Eastern coast to the Arabian Sea.

Conclusion

In order to counter Chinese dominance in Gwadar Port, India has invested in Iran's Chabahar port which is very near to Gwadar. Also, India, Iran and Afghanistan signed a trade corridor deal giving India the land access to Central Asia from Chabahar, bypassing Pakistan. India can work on improving the relationship with Pakistan as it can provide the shortest land route for us to access Central Asia.

Therefore a good relationship with Pakistan can give a boost to our trade relations with Central Asian countries. India should keep in mind that realisation of CPEC is important as a stable and economically strong Pakistan is necessary for the peace and prosperity in the region.

Unsolved Topics for Essay

1. Need of patience for success in the competitive world
2. Striking a Balance: Analysing the Socio-Economic Impact of Defence Spending on National Development in India
3. Science without Humanity is a Roaring Chaos
4. Without deviation from the norm, progress is not possible
5. Social Media is Inherently selfish
6. Equality and Education Goes Hand-in Hand
7. Empowering Women in the Evolving Job Landscape of Tier II and Tier III Cities
8. India and SDG goals- Vision and Progress.
9. Relevance of Mahatma Gandhi in present times
10. India's Suspension of Free Movement Region (FMR) with Myamar

02 Developing Counter Arguments

SPECIAL FOCUS

In 'Developing Counter Arguments' pay special attention to
- Track of word count (200 words) • Fact based writing • Avoid ambiguity
- Correct usage of grammar.

Developing counter-arguments is a debate question to be answered by presenting both 'for' and 'against' the topics asked in the UPSC Paper CAPF AC Paper II. This section carries **40 marks**; 2 questions (20 marks each) are to be attempted and no choice is provided Word limit for Arguments in **200 words**.

Essentials of a Good Counter Argument

- Crisp and clear argument without confusion or ambiguity
- Good structure (point-wise)
- Good presentation
- Sufficient facts/information/data
- Fulfilling the complete demand of the question

Topics for Counter Arguments

Subjects of argumentative compositions are usually current social issues, political issues and subjects where the overall opinion of the public could be in favour or against something.

Some of the areas are

- Social issues like education, poverty, corruption, reservation for OBC, etc.
- Topics related to politics
- Topics related to moral issues

Guidelines for Developing Counter Arguments

- You should have **sufficient information** about the topic. For this **read and browse** as much as you can to gather valuable information.
- Think carefully and write down all the points, you can use both **for** and **against** the topic.
- Strengthen your **view-points** with facts, figures and historical evidence.
- Remember the word limit of the arguments for both 'for' and 'against' is **200 words.**
- Do not exceed this limit.

Format of a Counter Argument

The CAPF paper requires the candidate to present a balanced approach on a topic. Hence, it expects the students to answer counter argument in the given format.

- **Introduction** Start the counter argument with an introduction to the topic. This introduction should describe, explain or define the topic in very general terms without taking any sides.
  You can include a reference to news to introduce the topic.
- **Connecting Line** After the introduction, set the stage for your arguments. You can use 'Let's discuss the various viewpoints regarding the debate'.
- **Body** This part contains the actual arguments both for and against the topic. In this section, you are required to write 4-5 arguments for each side of the debate. It is suggested that you write the body is pointers instead of a paragraph.

Rule for FOR and AGAINST

FOR	AGAINST
Justify the given statement	Justify the opposite to statement

- **Conclusion** Just like the introduction, you need to end your counter argument with a general conclusion. It will include verdict or decision if there is any. It can also include way forward or strategies implemented.

TIME IT !

The maximum time taken to attempt counter arguments should be 30 minutes.
Try to finish each argument in 15 minutes.

■ Sample Question

Write arguments for and against the following **20 Marks**

A family without pets is an incomplete family

SAMPLE FOR COUNTER ARGUMENTS

Introduction

The topic of the presence of a pet has come into scrutiny with many news reports regarding the pet dogs biting people came into light. The idea of keeping a pet has always enamoured mankind. We all have seen many movies which have moved us with a representation of great bonds of love between a family and its pets. In fact, many of us might have come across families who share great love with its pets. In this light, the issue of whether a pet should become a part of a family has become an issue of debate. While many claim that pets bring a lot of positivity into the family, many other believe that pets bring along a lot of problems. Let us look at following different perspectives.

For the Motion

Pets provide companionship and help to reduce our loneliness. Sometimes playing with a pet reduces our stress level and makes us emotionally well. Hence, the presence of a pet in the family ensures a great physical, emotional and mental well-being of its members.

- Having a pet delivers a great sense of responsibility to the child. Feeding and caring for pet encourages childhood responsibility.
- Children with pets display improved impulse control, social skill and self-esteem. Kids with a pet go outside more frequently to go for walks, run and play in the park.
- Research shows children who live in homes with a dog can possibly have fewer ear infections, respiratory tract infections and require fewer antibiotics. The exposure to animals at a young age stimulates the immune system. Children who grow up in homes with pets have less risk of developing common allergies and asthma. Thus, pet owners require fewer doctor visits.
- Pets also teach kindness and compassion. Pets are a perfect stepping stone for teaching children empathy and how to take care of another living being.
- A pet offers unconditional support when anyone in the family is sad, angry or upset. We can always trust our pets as they would never betray us. Pets like dog give safety to our family and lots of entertainment to family members.

Against the Motion

- Most parents are working professionals and the children are busy with their schools and other activities. Nobody has time to play with pets or look after them. As a result, pets have to spend long hours inside homes without any companion. It makes them anxious and irritated.
- One has to maintain their health which includes expensive food items, immunisation and visits to the veterinarians. To solve these problems, some families appoint servants to look after pets. But these paid individuals are not kind to the pets.
- Some pets carry infectious diseases which can be harmful for the child below 10 years of age. Thus, parents have to be cautious while selecting pets for their family.
- A pet can also not be good for your family if you do not get the right kind of pet. If someone buys a dog like German Shepherd or Saint Bernard while living in a small flat, it is harmful both for the person and the pet. These large dogs need atleast 2 hours of exercise and need large space to run and play. If you cannot provide this, it will ruin the health of the dog.

Conclusion

The issue of keeping pets seems to have a simple solution. Families that love animals and can afford to keep pets in a healthy and loving environment, can keep pets and make them a part of their family. In the end, it is the person's/ family's own volition that decides whether keeping a pet is safe or not.

Practice EXERCISE

Directions (Q. Nos. 1-15) *Write an Counter Arguments on each of the given topic in about 200 words.*

1. Pre-poll alliances are better than post-poll partnership

Introduction

Indian history is replete is examples of alliances that have formed governments. These alliance have been made both pre-poll and post-poll. Each type of such alliances has brought us many benefits and at the same time displayed some drawbacks. Keeping these in mind people take sides on which type of alliance is beneficial for the nation.

According to many, pre-poll alliance is better than post-poll alliances.

Let us look at the beliefs of different groups on this issue.

For the Motion

- With elections since 1996 throwing up coalitions of a jumble of parties, each time making the race too close to call, it makes for sound political reason to thrash out differences between potential partners long before voters queue up to cast their ballots.
- Buoyed by the combined organisational strengths of two partners, pre-election alliances offer the electorate clear and meaningful choice on individual as well as collective stands of parties willing to work together.
- With strong pre-poll alliances, voters are spared the uncertainty of post-poll alliances which are essentially opportunistic partnerships. Thus, voters get a clear view to make their voting decision.
- With parties in post-poll arrangements more likely to renege on promises, voters feel cheated, making the exercise of government formation full of instability. Frenzied post-election negotiations to reach the simple majority mark are often messy and unethical, especially when last-minute deals are struck between former avowed enemies. This was in full display after Delhi assembly elections when AAP, with a minority of seats, picked Congress as its partner to form a government which fell in 49 days.
- Well-crafted pre-poll alliances are more robust and durable than post-election partnerships because they offer incentives for moderation between two or more parties who are better positioned to balance opposing issues and policy preferences.
- Convergence of goals at the very outset allows allies to more efficiently solicit and prioritise policy choices besides becoming the basis for stable government, which is the result of political unity and common agenda forged before election day.

Against the Motion

- West Bengal Chief Minister, Mamata Banerjee, was spot-on when she said contemporary politics favoured post-poll alliances over ones forged before elections. Electoral trends over the last three decades provide a foundation for her conclusion. In 1984, the last time a single party won a Lok Sabha majority, there were all of 38 parties contesting.
- By 2009, there were 370 parties in the fray and the average of margin of victory dipped to a record low. In such a fragmented polity, a post-poll alliance is almost an inevitable outcome. The argument that post-poll alliances represent a cynical aspect of contemporary politics does not hold water.
- When a little more than half the electorate is in favour of a political party that cannot conceivably form a national government on its own and is often competing against both national parties, a post-poll alliance is the only way out to form a stable government.
- It is not just in Lok Sabha elections that post-poll alliances become imperative; the trend has also begun to show up at the state level. Delhi's extraordinary post-poll alliance between AAP and Congress showed that voters left politicians with no choice but to team up despite obvious dissimilarities.

Conclusion

Thus, both pre-poll and post-poll alliances have their own benefits and drawbacks. The only case that matters is the situation in which the alliance is made and how it benefits the nation.

2. A casteless society becomes distant through issues raised by reservation policies

Introduction

Despite attempts to create an egalitarian and modern society, the caste system remains a prominent feature of Indian society. Historically, castes, which are often associated with certain occupations, were arranged in a hierarchy, with some castes considered superior to others and thus accorded more power and privileges than others. This system of social stratification and power relations has been a major problem in India as it has led to discrimination and inequality for those belonging to lower castes.

The Indian Constitution, which was made to push India towards an egalitarian society, introduced various articles that vouched for the establishment of a caste-less society. However, in the present set-up, reservation policies have become a source of debate as many have questioned the relevance of the policies in the light of the aim of a castles society.

Let us look at the various view-points in this debate

For the Argument

- It has been more than 70 years since the Constitution was framed and the social fabric of the society has changed. Today, the reservation policies set-up by the Constitution stand against the very ideals that it seek to counter.
- Reservation rather than reducing casteism increases it. This is so because the persons get classified into different categories of SCs or STs which further creates a caste-based society. By classifying people on basis of their caste, the government has retained the caste system instead of removing it which further has the tendency to strengthen social evils.
- In the world today, the economically weaker and minority sections of the society are climbing up the social ladder and becoming more and more empowered, reducing the need of reservation policies.
- However, the presence acts as an advantage to these people. Hence, they further embed the idea of caste into the society. People now make their caste visible so as to get a benefit that would have otherwise gone to a deserving candidate.
- Thus, the attempt to bring freedoms and opportunities to those deprived so as to promote equality, has now resulted in a situation wherein the previously advantaged communities have becoming disadvantaged to a large extent due to the reservation conundrum. Many upper castes are still plagued by poverty and illiteracy.

Thus, the reservation policies made to drive the country towards a casteless society, has now entrenching the caste system into the social fabric of the society even more firmly.

Against the Argument

- The basic purpose of reservation is to ensure equality of opportunities in education, government jobs, etc., for all citizens irrespective of their caste, gender, race, religion, etc. When all individuals will have equal access to resources, the backward communities would also be able to uplift themselves in society.
- This in turn fulfills the very purpose of the Constitution as given under Articles 15 and 16 of the Constitution-building a casteless society.
- Reservation brings the SCs and STs to an equal level to the others in society. As a result, all of them run the race from the same starting point. This ensures that there is complete fairness and no discrimination towards any individual or community.
- As a result, caste becomes an obsolete phenomenon as all sections start taking an equal role in the mainstream society. Those discriminated now enjoy adequate representation in government posts and educational institutions thereby increasing their participation in the general functioning of society. They are now no longer treated as outcasts and have rather become an indispensable part of society.

Conclusion

While there is a need to encourage meritocracy to address the issues associated with reservation and promote a competitive spirit among citizens, there is also a need to support those who have been secluded from society and promote their growth. This is only possible through reservation. Thus, the dream and vision of a casteless society can be fulfilled only by the reservation system.

3. Women empowerment in India so far is an urban phenomenon

Introduction

Women have always been the most vulnerable and oft-exploited section of the society in any age, time, place and society. In ancient times, due to the lack of opportunities and health facilities, the inferior status of women became a menace that India needed to get out of for its development. Since ages, women have been victims of humiliation, torture, exploitation and violence.

But with the passage of time, society is awakening to its responsibility towards women. Women are being empowered in every field and are encouraged to give their best. Thus, a new term called 'Women Empowerment' has been added to the gender dictionary. Women empowerment, essentially can be defined as promoting self-worth, their ability to determine their own choices and their right to influence social changes for themselves and others.

The difference between today's situation and the situation of women existing 10 years prior is that Indian women have increasingly refused to be trapped in a bad situation and have stopped shedding silent tears.

However, people have time and again found that this change has largely been urban and not rural. This has led to a debate wherein many believe that women empowerment is purely urban and not rural while other find that the phenomenon can be seen everywhere.

Let us look into the different viewpoints on the issue.

For the Argument

- Participation of women from urban section in the economy is much more than that seen in rural women.
- Lack of proper rural infrastructure, illiteracy, lack of financial independence, lack of awareness and the obstinate traditional mindset of the rural people hinder women empowerment in the rural regions.
- Women are still restricted to get educated and are married off at a young age. They are denied financial independence and are often subjected to heinous crimes. What is sad is that most of these women are brainwashed and think that any counter action would worsen their situation.
- In fact, in spite of knowing that the crime committed is punishable by law, they refrain from reporting the crime for the fear of social stigma.

In this light, the need of the hour is to focus special attention to empowering the rural women folk so that our society can be completely gender equal.

Against the Argument

- Women, from both rural and urban setups, today are coming out of the four walls of their houses, raising their voice against all injustices and fighting for their rights.
- They are taking higher positions, participating in each and every field at par with men and taking all roles equal to men.
- Law has become tool for women empowerment and their better representation, which is bringing a social change. One can looks at leadership positions held by women such as Draupadi Murmu and Niramala Sitharaman, sports such as Geeta Phogat, Mithali Raj, Karnam Malleswari, Deepika Kumari, etc., or any other field, women are excelling.

Conclusion

Given all the viewpoints, saying that women empowerment is an urban phenomenon is negating all the efforts of the rural women who have broken the shackles of the traditional male dominance. However, much more can be done to accelerate the process and bring women to their full potential.

4. FDI in retail in India is a bane for a small trader

Introduction

Foreign Direct Investment or FDI refers to capital inflows from abroad which are invested to enhance the production capacity of the economy by buying a company in the target country or by expanding operations of an existing business in that country. In other words, it is an investment made by an organisation into a business or corporation situated in another country with the intention of establishing ownership or controlling interest.

With the government liberalising the retail sector in India for Foreign Direct Investment, the impact of FDI on business had sparked a crucial debate on whether it is actually useful or not. Many believe that FDI is a bane for a small trader. Such a belief has been question by many. Let us look at the various perspectives on the debate to understand it more clearly.

For the Argument

- Domestic retail players might not be able to withstand the competition from MNCs and may be wiped out from the market or be absorbed by the bigger players. For example, WALMART, a multi-retailed store established in the US, currently established retail stores in India compelled the *Kirana* stores to close their business leading to a massive loss of jobs and discomfort to a large chunk of society.
- Also, to match up with the current technology war, these new stores are expected to be much more advanced and automated which is a bad news for our less skilled labours.
- Further, once an MNC gets a stronghold in the market, they can cause price rise and even the farmer who were benefitting initially, may also be at the mercy of these big retailers. Thus, FDI may seem a great step in building international economic relations; it is a bane for the small industries that make much of India's GDP.

Against the Argument

- India is a retailer's dream with an estimated worth of worth USD 1.1 trillion (2020) due to its large upwardly mobile population and impressive growth rate.
- With the domestic retail sector projected to grow exponentially in the coming years, India has consistently been rated as one of the most desirable destinations for global retailers across an array of surveys and market reports. In terms of economy, retail is one of the pillars of the Indian economy with the sector contributing to about 10% of the Gross Domestic Product (GDP).
- With the FDI, foreign companies are directly involved with day-to-day operations in the other country. This means they aren't just bringing money with them, but also knowledge, skills and technology.
- With the entry of FDI, the highly unorganised retail sector will become organised. As this sector becomes more and more organised, there will be less wastage especially in the food industry with the presence of efficient supply chains and adequate storage facilities. Thus, FDI will become catalyst in avoiding distress sale and erosion as well as wastage in quality and quantity of the produce. Further, as MNC's pay higher taxes to the Indian government, development in terms of infrastructure, real estate and banking is expected is expected to take place at a much faster pace.
- In addition, FDI can create competitiveness among business leaders and helps to improve business environment of the country. It will help in technology and better management practice transfer which will help small and large enterprises of or country to produce goods effectively and efficiently. As a result of which India will flourish in terms of quality standards and consumer expectations.
- FDI will also promote the welfare of farmers by agricultural growth and thereby increasing their income level by reducing the dominance of intermediaries. Because of the presence of the intermediaries, prices lack transparency due to which the farmers do not get their fair share.
- Indian farmers at present realise only one-third of the final price paid by the consumer as against the two-third price realised by the farmers in the countries with a greater share of organised retail.
- FDI promotes contractual farming which would mean improved and efficient farming practices as well as higher output and better prices. It would also generate employment opportunities in the wake of improved supply chains that would be set-up to cater to these retail stores.

Conclusion

Thus, while it is true that FDI poses risks for the small scale firms, it is also true that it brings much more to the nation. However, it does not mean that we can ignore the risks. The need of the hour is to find a balanced approach that reduces the risks to the small scale firms.

5. Control of social media is an anti-democratic proposition

Introduction

It is the age of the internet and social media has emerged as an indispensable tool. Social media is the means to communicate, exchange ideas and information, and stay connected virtually. It has become part and parcel of everyone's life irrespective of the age group. This all pervasiveness of social media has sparked debate on the need to control it for its various disadvantages.
Let us look into the various perspectives in this debate

For the Argument

- Social media has deeply impacted all of us. From connecting with friends on the other side of the globe to quickly sending money, from being able to attend meetings, conferences and events from any part of the world to attending online classes, social media has empowered us like none other. The world has become smaller and everything is just a click away, thanks to social media.
- Social media is one of the most potent and effective mediums given its wide reach, effective delivery mechanism. It is changing the way we perceive the world. It has the ability to mobilise public opinion by giving people a voice as a principle to lead our community.
- Social media acts as an instrument that can question the seemingly invincible governments, make them accountable and bring sustained change driven by people beyond one vote in years.
- Further, the implications of social media for civic engagement are profound, as many people tend to discuss and debate news over these platforms. All of these benefits associated with social media is a resultant of the democratic freedom of speech and expression. If this freedom is taken away, the power held by democracy will be lost as it will become similar to tyranny.

Against the Argument

In the present world, social media is no longer just an innocent space to connect with friends and family. Instead, it has metamorphosed into becoming an influential space for political activity and creating a new political dialogue.

- In a democratic society like India, social media plays a major role by giving information to the citizens and by reflecting their opinions at a large scale impacting different communities. Rumours and wrong information travel with the speed of light and social media is proving to be a good medium for this. Content on social media is devoid of any crosschecks for validity and veracity and due to easy accessibility by all, it is prone to be misused, to misguide people and to contribute to anti-social activities.
- Hateful contents against communities and religions harm communal harmony and raise a wall of mistrust and disgust among people. Sharing of religious conflicts, proving one religion/ community/ gender/ race better than the other, spreading hate, etc., give rise to conflicts among masses. These conflicts sometimes become so intense that people tend to become violent and start verbal or physical abuse.
- Terrorism, using the social media, has become one of the most concerning issues across the world. Terrorist organisations are using social media platforms for recruiting, training and communicating with their followers, supporters, donors, as it is cheaper, easier, faster and more effective method of communication.
- Further, social media is known to be promoting sensationalism and commercialisation where it tends to exaggerate facts related to events, which definitely result in serious communal tensions and conflicts. Instead of bringing communal unrest to normalcy, social media often plays an ignorant role in inciting agitations as a consequence of which large scale rioting, arson and pillage takes place.

Conclusion

Thus, social media amplifies human intent both good and bad. At its best, it allows us to express ourselves and take action. At its worst, it allows people to spread misinformation and corrode democracy. In this light, controlling the freedom of social media is essential.

6. Freedom of expression is an absolute right

Introduction

Article 19(1)(a) of the Constitution gives all citizens the fundamental right to freedom of speech and expression. This means that every citizen has the right to express their own beliefs and opinions freely through writing, printing, pictures, word of mouth (orally) or any other mode. This right includes the freedom of the press, the right to communicate and circulate information through any medium including print media, audio, television broadcast or electronic media and the right to receive and access information which helps in forming an informed opinion. However, in the world dominated by social media, people have questioned whether freedom of expression is an absolute right or not.
Let us look at the various view-points in this regard.

For the Argument

- People who accept the freedom of expression as an absolute right know that democracy works well only if the people have the right to express their opinions about the government and criticise it if needed. In a democracy, the voice of the people must be heard and their grievances satisfied.

- The absence of the freedom of expression, democracy is threatened. The government will become all-too-powerful and start serving the interests of a few rather than the general public. Heavy clampdown on the right to free speech and free press will create a fear-factor under which people would endure tyranny silently. In such a scenario, people would feel stifled and would rather suffer than express their opinions.
- Further, the Preamble of the Indian Constitution itself ensures to all citizens the liberty of thought, expression, belief, faith and worship. Hence, freedom of expression cannot be restricted in any case.

Against the Argument

Although each one of us have freedom of expression, we also have a duty to behave responsibly and to respect other people's rights. But the situation today has shown that many people do not take this responsibility seriously. Hence, the public authorities have been given approval to restrict this right if they can show that their action is lawful, necessary and proportionate in order to protect

- national security,
- territorial integrity (the borders of the state) or public safety,
- prevent disorder or crime,
- protect health or morals,
- protect the rights and reputations of other people,
- prevent the disclosure of information received in confidence and maintain the authority and impartiality of judges.

An authority may be allowed to restrict your freedom of expression if, for example, you express views that encourage racial or religious hatred.

Conclusion

Freedom to express is a basic human right. However, we must be careful of our utterances and keep in mind that our expression should ne cause mayhem in the society.

7. Old is Gold

Introduction

In the modern world wherein new technologies, systems, and phenomena are occurring every day, we have often heard our elders reminiscing about the olden days, songs, people and life. Hence, the proverb "Old is gold" became popular as people realised the significance and importance of the day gone by.

The proverb essentially highlights the value, relevance and importance of the old over the new. It states that our old systems, mechanisations and knowledge are way more valuable. However, with must development, a sect of people believing that old is not necessarily gold has sprung up.

Let us look at the various perspectives of people who believe in the proverb and those who don't.

For the Argument

- In the Indian social set-up and many other cultures, the experience of the older generations is valued and celebrated. Because they believe that the wisdom of life comes only by experience.
  - Further, many articles of decoration, pieces of art, paintings, etc., grow in artistic and monetary value over time. Articles from centuries ago, like paintings, sculptures, jewellery, furniture, tools, etc., are considered very valuable as antiques.
- Not to forget, many scientific principles are carried over from ancient cultures such as Chinese Medicine, Ayurveda, Yoga are turning out to be valuable even in today's world. Used in combination with modern systems, the value of this old knowledge is growing in multiples.
- One can even look at the remixes or remakes of the old classic movies and how they are dissed and criticised in favour of the old dongs. Hence, it is true that even with updations and modifications, the old will never lose value.

Against the Argument

- Progress and innovation have reshaped our society and redefined what is truly valuable.
- The rapid advancements in technology have revolutionised our lives. The digital age has brought about convenience, connectivity and boundless opportunities.
- The younger generation, with their fresh perspectives, embraces change and pushes the boundaries of what is possible, proving that new can indeed be gold.
- Further, there are many practices that do not hold value in the present world.
- Practices based on gender biasness, religious intolerance, slavery, etc., today stand against the values of equality and have no place in the present world.

Conclusion

Hence, old can be gold but only to a certain limits. Not everything old is gold.

8. Crime-based serials on TV lead to a reduction in crime

Introduction

Television crime dramas and serials are becoming very popular all over the world. This popularity is not bound to a certain age group, rather all the TV viewers like these serials.

With this increasing popularity, people in the media industry all over the world are coming up new shows in innumerable fields.

Be it thriller based crime shows or shows related to social taboos, industry does have a great impact on our society.

Keeping this fact in mind, more and more crime based shows are taking over the media industry. However, the nature of the impact of such shows has come to question. Many people believe that crime-based serials lead to reduction in crime while others disagree with it. Let us look at the different perspectives regarding it.

For the Motion

- These crime serials play a positive role in society by creating awareness and spreading information regarding crimes.
- The potential benefit of these crime serials is that they make people aware of crimes taking place in the immediate surroundings and how they can stay safe in such an environment. Consequently, this knowledge can definitely saves many lives by enabling them to take certain precautions.
- The end result of all these shows related to crime will amount to more awareness and information that would reduce criminal tendencies. There will be some exceptions where individuals develop an unhealthy obsession that isolates them from normal society or claim them as excuses for their own crimes but this is just as likely to occur with any form of entertainment.
- Also, the crime shows reflect the positive role of law enforcement agencies while alerting the people regarding such incidences. It shows how every time, a crime takes place, the law enforcement of our country is ready to take charge and catch the criminal. Such representation of the law agencies create an image of fear and a warning to those who have the criminal tendencies.
- Instead of inducing crime, the shows give a message that crime never pays and will always take one down. Criminal tendencies are repressed at the very start and appositive image prevails.

Against the Motion

- The trending crime shows and even movies show that criminal live a lavish lifestyle and enjoy their life to the fullest without any fear. Such a representation moulds the behaviour of the child and effect child brain negatively. Coupled with the knowledge of the free criminals, such children are more and more attracted to the world of crime and think of themselves as fearless.
- These shows give new and different ideas to evil minds to commit crime. More importantly, many criminals by watching these crime serials find loopholes in the laws through which they can evade punishment. They start believing that they too can live such a life without any fear of being caught and punished by the law.
- In addition, it is not just about one particular show, but about the innumerable such shows that exist on TV and over the various OTT platforms. The large number of such shows viewed by children is also at fault. Without any filter or adult supervision, children get stuck in the negative mindset produced by the shows and hence are pushed into the world of crime.

Conclusion

Thus, the excess of everything is bad is correct with regard to the issue. While crime based shows do bring awareness, excess of crime based shows can prove to be detrimental to our society.

9. Everyone should become vegetarian

Introduction

The debate regarding what is better- a vegetarian diet or a non-vegetarian diet has been going on for a long time. It divided people into segments with many promoting vegetarianism as a healthy and sustainable way of living and others pointing out the necessity of non-vegetarianism. Let us look at the various perspectives in this regard.

For the Motion

- Most of the scientific research agrees that vegetarianism is the way to go. People should consume more vegetables and fruits and as little meat as possible because intake high amount of meat can cause serious health issues. The consumption of a vegetarian diet is a better way to live a healthy life.
- Producing vegetarian food is more ecologically sustainable, and it reduces damage to the environment.
- One should be vegetarian because it is very cheaper, healthier and better for us and also for our environment. By becoming vegetarian, you live longer, stronger and stay fit. There is strong medical evidence which proves that the consumption of meat is very unhealthy. This also causes heart problems and diabetes.
- A vegetarian diet reduces the risk for chronic degenerative diseases such as obesity, coronary artery disease, high blood pressure and diabetes. Maintaining a good vegetarian diet also helps to reduce your calories and make you more slim and fit. We should consume fruits and vegetables because they are very rich in proteins and vitamins.

Against the Motion

- While vegetarianism has been accepted as an ideal diet for a sustainable future, one cannot disagree that vegetarian diets are devoid of the proteins and fats that animal meat contains. Hence, people should have meat in every their meals in order to have a good health.
- Vegetarians are likely to face some difficulties if they do not eat meat like lack of energy.
- Vegetarians believe that meat is unhealthy because of the diseases it has been connected with. However, there are strong arguments for eating meat. The first reason is that as humans we are designed to eat meat and we have been eating meat for thousands of years. For example, cavemen made hunting implements so that they could kill animals and eat their meat. Second, meat is a rich source of protein which helps to build muscles and bones.

- Vegetarians often have to take supplements to get all the essential vitamins and minerals. According to medical science, a diet constituting of sea food like fish, and eggs sharpen our intellect and promote the smooth functioning of our brain.
- This ultimately accelerates our wisdom. Also, vegetarians have a limited choice of food compared to meat eaters. They also face difficulties while travelling abroad as vegetarian food is not available at all places.

Conclusion

To sum up, no one should be forced to turn to a vegetarian diet. Although the overconsumption of meat could possibly be unhealthy, a balanced diet of meat and vegetables should result in a healthy body.

10. Democracy cannot survive without education.

Introduction

Thomas Jefferson said, "An educated citizenry is a vital requisite for our survival as a free people." In a democracy which is believed to be the best way for realising human rights, one cannot survive without education.

Democracy is a form of government in which all the power lies in the hands of the citizens and the representatives chosen by them. But whether its true realisation can only come with proper education or not has become a topic of contention between many. Let us look at the various view-points in this regard.

For the Motion

- The total adult literacy rate around the world in 2023 is 87%. This means that there were nearly 785 million illiterate adults in the world. This kind of ignorance and lack of knowledge can be very harmful, especially considering the numbers. It is only possible to make a serious decision like this when every single voter is properly educated.
- Education should be provided right from childhood because without it, a person's ignorance and vices would cost the nation dearly, creating a need to correct them later on in life.
- On the contrary, if children are educated, they would imbibe virtues which would enable them to contribute as responsible citizens to their nation. They would be able to make correct choices for the country.
- Along with providing children with the right information, education will also teach them honesty and integrity and for a democracy to prosper, it needs people with truth and integrity in all the departments.
- Thus, the key to a rich, progressive country is not democracy in itself, but proper and informative education.
- An ignorant crowd, if given the right to choose from a number of options, can inflict more damage to the state than a well-educated monarch or dictator.

Against the Motion

- Democracy is a process which took time to reach its goal of equality and even now we have not achieved it, though we are closer to it. For this purpose, we have to be educated enough to understand the political structure of our government. But, this does not apply to the Indian democracy, where political literacy matters, but education might not.
- How can we judge a politician by their educational qualifications? There have been many great leaders who were uneducated but did fantastic work for the country and the Indian people has succeeded in recognising them. Take, for instance, the current Prime Minister of India. PM Narendra Modi, though not highly educated, has proven to be a great and capable leader. He is the person India chose for two consecutive elections to be the nation's Prime Minister. He has proven to be a far-sighted visionary who has worked to improve the Indian economic growth globally and he was chosen by the masses of India. Several people, both educated and uneducated, vote to choose him as the leader of the country. They did so because they realised his potential through his past works and his tenure as the Chief Minister of Gujarat.

Conclusion

So, though education helps in making wise decisions, democracy itself can survive without education. If a person is hard working, simple, honest, devoted to his service and has a far-sighted vision of future, then, democracy also will outshine without education.

11. Today's youth is more practical and less swayed by emotions.

Introduction

With the world balancing intelligence quotient with emotional quotient, the understanding of how people work has changed. This has led to significant changes in how we work and succeed.

To understand these changes, many surveys are being conducted in various groups to analyse what drives the youth. In this regard, many claim that today's youth is much more practical while some place emotions as the top-most driver of the youth.

Let us look at the various perspectives regarding the issue

For the Motion

- Much unlike the earlier generations of youth who were easily swayed by emotions, the current generation of youth more practical and less swayed by emotions. They are much more aware of what is going on in the world due to the advancement of communication technologies like the internet. Their education has improved and so has their general knowledge. All this adds up to a more practical approach to events in their lives.

- The youth today are highly optimistic about what they can achieve in their lives. Most of them are highly ambitious and will take all pains to fulfill their dreams. This implies that they adopt a more practical approach to solving problems which come in the way of fulfilling their ambitions.
- One of the reasons for such practicality in today's youth is competition. The desire to stay at the top and be successful acts as a strong motivation to make today's youngsters work more practically and systematically. They go to great lengths to ensure that they become a source of pride for everybody in their circle, whether it is the family, friends or acquaintances.
- Whether it is academics or sports or literary and cultural activities, the youth of today finds the field in which they can excel and then go all out for doing their best in that field.
- During this activity, there is no place for any emotions to be displayed.
- The euphoria they get due to achieving their goal makes them forget all emotions displayed by others. Thus, they do not get swayed by emotions while focusing on achieving the difficult goals they may have set for themselves.

Against the Motion

- The youth today are much affected by emotions, particularly those displayed by their parents, classmates, friends and others who are close to them. This is particularly so in case they fail to achieve what goals they have set for themselves. They simply don't know how to handle failure. They may be practical as long as their path is smooth. However, when they encounter a bump, they start losing control based on emotions displayed by others in reaction to their failure. They may go into depression, or may even run away from their homes to escape the emotional wrath of their parents.
- We are very well aware about two adolescent diseases, anorexia nervosa and bulimia. Sometimes adolescent girls are afflicted by such diseases only due to adverse body shaming comments. Thus, they are swayed by the emotions of others and resort to 'dieting' to gain approval. In some cases, youngsters are so badly afflicted by some emotions that they become vulnerable to depression and other psychological disorders, ultimately leading them to take their lives.
- The newspapers and news channels are full of stories that depict children taking severe fatal steps soon after the Board Exam results are declared. Such youngsters give into the negativity displayed to them and instead of being practical and taking tangible steps to dispel the emotions, take wrong measures.

Conclusion

Thus, today's youth is as emotional as the youth of any previous generation. The only difference one can find with the current crop of youngsters is in the way the emotions are displayed and dealt with. Youth today seem to be more emotional about their friends, companions and their belongings. They express their emotions by either blurting out in anger or commenting on the social media. Those who aren't so outspoken can be seen having emotional breakdown in ways which were considered cowardly earlier. Thus, it is obvious that the majority of today's youth is not very rational and do get swayed by emotions.

12. The end justifies the means

Introduction

'The end justifies the means'. This statement means that a good result should be achieved in whatever way it is possible, even if it appears wrong in the eyes of the people. In simpler terms, this means that anything is reasonable if it leads to an important and meaningful result. If one is working on an important thing, even if the means used to achieve the target may not appear good, it may be necessary to achieve it for the overall good.

However, the validity of this statement has come into question as people believe the statement to be ethically wrong in many cases. Let us look at the different view-points of people who stand for the motion and who stand against the motion.

For the Motion

- A good example of validity of the proverb is 'War'. It is seen as evil by all, but it is a necessary evil. It is impractical, for the sake of peace, to abolish the army and wish others to keep peace with us. Wars are important to safeguard a country's freedom, people, boundary and resources. In a war, soldiers have to kill others and sacrifice their own lives. Deaths might be seen as ugly, but without the sacrifices of few brave men, a nation cannot survive. The identity of the entire nation can be at risk.
- If the end is necessary, we are justified in seeking it and using any means to achieve it. For example, a person is driving to the hospital to see his dying mother. In his hurry to get there, he breaks some traffic rules. It is of course illegal, but if he does it to get to his mother before she dies, the means used can be pardoned. Thus, in some circumstances, 'The ends justify the means'.

Against the Motion

- If one is allowed, one will justify all sorts of actions. For example, the Americans justified their dropping of nuclear bombs on two Japanese cities in 1945 by saying that many more lives would have been lost and the war in the Pacific would have dragged on if they had not done so. However, the atomic explosion can never be called just as it caused much more misery and suffering, even more than seventy years later.
- All just people respect important principles of ethics and morality. There are certain fundamental principles that are 'right' and 'good'. Nobody can justify violating them only because they have some 'right' or 'good' goal in mind. One cannot have justice unless one follows the principles of justice. It is wrong to do unjust things

simply because one has a good and morally right goal in mind.

- The concept of what is right for one person may not be so for another. The people who believe that the end justifies the means are responsible for the vast majority of all great evils in the past.
- One can think of the Hitler's motive to provide justice for the German. This led to some of the worst crimes in the history of mankind. The Nazis may claim that their end was justice for the Germans, but they brought great misery to the entire world. One cannot have justice at such a great cost.

Conclusion

No end justifies the means taken to achieve it, if it ignores basic human principles. The Right to Life and Dignity of man are Fundamental Rights that all civilised nations recognise.

All men are equal in the eyes of law. No one can be convicted for crimes that are not proven with proper evidence.. This is because 'No end justifies the means'.

13. International sports promote friendship between nations

Introduction

Any discussion of the power of sport includes its importance as a vehicle to teach our youth –the lessons of leadership, good health, teamwork, fair play, self-reliance and continuous improvement. But, sports has also been viewed as a unifier. It is found that sports doesn't just empower on an individual basis; it also unites and inspires people collectively which builds communities.

However, the realisation of this unifying quality of sports has divided people into two segments with one highlighting how they are unifying and the other pointing how it divides our society.

Let us look at the different view-points in this regard

For the Motion

- On the global scene, since long, world leaders have used sports as a means to promote peace and unity. Perhaps, the most well-known example of this is the 1971 Chinese-American reconciliation through ping-pong that ended two decades of unfriendly relations. Similar international sports have been found to leverage sports as a means to reopen diplomatic dialogue and make conciliatory international gesture.
- The massive appeal of sports makes it a social phenomenon. Regardless of age, gender or ethnicity, sports is enjoyed by all; its reach is unrivaled. It transcends the boundaries of language and culture. Sports also promote equality and serve as a platform to promote the value of diversity. At the grassroot or community level, sports can be seen to provide a useful way of creating an environment in which people can come together to: work towards the same goal, show respect for others and share space and equipment. It creates friendships between people who would not normally communicate.
- One common example of how sports functions as a unifier is The World Cups. Nations bond to help each other and show off their support for the teams and the unification of people. Even the Olympic Truce calls for the strengthening of such bonds between nations.
- The importance of sports as a peacemaker had now been accepted by the UN which in its 2030 Agenda for Sustainable Development recognises the growing contribution of sports for development and peace. Thus, sport is a compelling tool to promote peace, tolerance and understanding, bringing people together across boundaries, cultures and religions.

Against the Motion

- While Olympic Games and all other sporting events stress the mission of 'building a peaceful and better world' and agree to uphold the principles of "peace, fair play and fair contest with the view to creating a peaceful society with less violence and competition", one cannot disagree with the fact that, most of the sports events held have failed to live up to the Olympic values.
- Sports events, especially the Olympics have often been used by national leaders for their political interests in ways far from promoting peace. Back in the Cold War era, US President Jimmy Carter boycotted the 1980 Moscow Summer Games to protest against the Soviet invasion of Afghanistan. The Soviets retaliated in the following Olympics hosted by the US by pulling out of the 1984 Summer Games blaming 'hostile anti-Soviet propaganda' designed in pursuit of American political aims.
- The world has also seen politically motivated terrorists taking advantage of the Olympic occasion to carry out attacks. Among the numerous incidents of terrorism, the most infamous have been a massacre during the 1972 Munich Summer Games and a pipe bomb explosion during the 1996 Atlanta Summer Games.
- From observing episodes of history, we now know that for any nation, promoting peace through the sports can't come before pursuing its political and economic interests at least not completely. Besides, ever since COVID-19 shook the world, it has become much harder to foresee cooperation among countries through the international sporting event.
- Likewise, it is only to be expected that the great noble cause of the Olympics, 'unity and peace,' as vague as it sounds, can be easily neglected and perhaps won't be enough to yield the world peace it professes.

Conclusion

Thus, while it can be accepted that sports brings people together, to remove its other negative implications would be incorrect.

14. 'Tour of Duty' the proposed short term military service should be made compulsory for all youth

Introduction

Tour of Duty or the Agnipath Scheme launched by the Union Government on 14th June, 2022 is a recruitment scheme for the Indian youth to serve in the armed forces. Under the Tour of Duty Army Scheme, soldiers get released after 4 years of service and only 25% of soldiers will be offered a full-time permanent job based on their performance and merit. In a country where more than 65% population is youth, the scheme seems to bring great benefits to the nation. However, the scheme has come under debate as people are suggesting that the scheme should be made compulsory for all. The debate question whether making the scheme compulsory for all would have the benefits that it seems to bring on a large scale.

Let us look at the various arguments in this regard.

For the Motion

- The programme builds a kind of orderliness that incorporates responsibility and love for the country within children leading them through their future lives. Young people gain important teamwork, problem-solving and leadership skills through military training and service that can be applied across different areas.
- Besides, by participating in Tour of Duty, young job seekers can improve their chances of getting employed in civilian and army sectors, through essential training that supplements their academic qualifications. With a structured lifestyle in place for them and a regimented environment, the youth are exposed to real life experiences which challenge them to be less vulnerable and more resilient than ever before; attributes that are highly sought after in the current labour market.
- In addition, mandatory military service enhances patriotism among young people from diverse backgrounds thereby fostering national cohesion and identity.
- Serving with peers also enables them to have a better understanding of their countries' values, hence contributing towards building strong social bonds and national integration.
- The Tour of Duty Programme addresses a number of socio-economic challenges such as unemployment and social instability by allowing young people to be involved in valuable engagement activities that can help them develop their skills.
- The programme helps minimise youth idleness, crime through engaging the participants in constructive exercises thereby instilling into them a sense of accountability to society.
- Equipping young citizens with necessary competencies enhancing patriotism and addressing socio economic problems could make Tour of Duty a significant player in shaping the brighter future for juveniles and nations.

Against the Motion

- Although military training could teach discipline and teamwork, it may not be appropriate for all people. It would be wrong to conscript young people into the armed forces because in doing so we would deny them freedom and independence and also an opportunity just to follow their dreams.
- Additionally, compulsory national service ignores how these same resources would produce diverse skills and contributions into other sectors such as schooling, entrepreneurship or social welfare programmes. By making it mandatory for all young individuals to join the army, we risk stifling ideas that can help spearhead progress in today's dynamic world.
- Enforcing mandatory military service may disproportionately affect disadvantaged communities who have few resources and opportunities available for advancement. Instead of promoting inclusivity and equality, such a policy could worsen existing disparities while furthering societal divisions.
- Additionally, a universal Tour of Duty Programme could have substantial financial and logistical implications that may render it infeasible for a country like India with limited resources and conflicting priorities. The military budget could be stretched by the costs of training, housing and supporting large numbers of new recruits, thereby taking away funds from other crucial sectors such as healthcare, education and infrastructure.
- Moreover, a democratic society that cherishes individual rights and freedom of choice may not accept mandatory military service. It is contrary to the principles of voluntary service and conscription in times of national emergency or defence.

Conclusion

Although military service can give individuals invaluable experiences as well as growth opportunities, imposing mandatory short-term militarism on all youth *via* the Tour of Duty Programme presents ethical dilemmas. Policy makers should abolish compulsory military service but focus on offering young people personal development choices as well as opportunities in their professional lives where they can explore their interests in order to make meaningfully varied impacts.

15. Development and creation of jobs must take priority over social development

Introduction

In the nation afflicted with many problems starting from social to economical, it is imperative to find solutions that promote the overall growth of the country while tackling the individual issues with careful consideration. However, such a mammoth task requires a priority list. People from all fields have opinions on which issue needs to be tackled first. While some people believe that development and creation of jobs is the key, other agree that social development is essential for the nation and should come first.

Body

Such a debate is inconsequential as development and creation of jobs would means social development. Lack of job or unemployment is explicitly related to the social fabric of society. Unemployment, causes disillusionment, frustration and dissatisfaction.

This gives rise to cynicism and dissipates the energy of the youth in destructive directions.

Thus, they resort to crime, violence, anti-social activities or even worse they try to take a short cut to achieve the much sought after social status. This explains the number of bank robberies, online money/financial frauds, etc. It further, has psychological impacts on an individual. An unemployed individual is likely to suffer from stress, anxiety and depression. Further, unemployment leads to poverty and loss of human resources.

Conclusion

Hence, for holistic socio economic development of nation it is important for government to take adequate and timely measure to provide employment opportunities. However, it should be kept in mind that it's not the quantity of jobs that should be created but also their quality.

Focus on skill based jobs, impetus to sunrise sector, startups, MSMEs, emphasis on making India a knowledge economy can be a key for leveraging demographic dividend productively.

(**Note** *This is a comprehensive topic which cannot have two sides. In this topic we will essentially write about how creation of jobs will foster social development*)

Previous Years' QUESTIONS

Directions (Q. Nos. 1-20) *Write counter arguments on the following topics in about 200 words each.*

1. Classical Literature should be a Component of the Curriculum **CAPF AC 2024**

Classical literature is the bed rock of Western literary tradition and it offers insights to cultural, historical and social contexts of ancient civilisations. Classical literature helps students to understand the roots of modern society and the constant influence of classical ideas on contemporary culture. Exposure to this text can improve vocabulary, comprehension and the ability to articulate ideas effectively. The sophistication of the language and rhetorical techniques in classical literature are able to enhance student's language skill also.

For the Motion

Universal Themes Classical literature often addresses universal themes of love, power, justice and human nature and tenacity through those texts belong to different era. And the spirit of the text resonates with readers across generations, fostering empathy and a deeper understanding of the human experience.

Having such attributes in its characteristics, classical literature may not always resonate with modern students. It can be inaccessible due to language barriers and back-dated societal norms.

A diverse range of literature instead including contemporary works and global voices, can better engage students and foster empathy and understanding of diverse perspectives. This approach prepares students for a multicultural world.

Against the Motion

Lack of Relevance Classical literature often reflects back-dated values, norms and issues of past societies, which may not resonate with modern students of this era. Modern literature on the other hand addresses relevant issues of contemporary life and society.

Engagement and Interest Students may not find any interest in this text as it is difficult to understand due to archaic language and outdated context.

Critical Thinking Classical literature can develop certain analytical skill but it is unable to address critical thinking sometimes and also unable to develop problem solving skills that is an inevitable skill needed in today's rapid world. Rather contemporary texts deal with current issues and can better prepare students for modern inevitable challenges.

Problem in Curriculum Flexibility Classical literature having so many complexities often creates an unyielding curriculum that students may find difficult to go with.

Cultural Sensitivity and Inclusivity Some classical texts is consisted of themes and languages that are now considered offensive or inappropriate. So, those texts can perpetuate harmful stereotypes and reinforce outdated social norms.

Conclusion

While, classical literature has its own indigenous attributes, it is essential to balance. The curriculum with modern, diverse and relevant texts that reflect the experiences and interests of today's students.

This approach basically foster inclusivity and prepare students comprehensively for the complexities of the contemporary world.

2. Housework is Unpaid Labour CAPF AC 2024

Housework, which is not directly compensated with a paycheck, holds significant value that contributes to the household economy.

Though it is often undervalued and taken for granted inspite of being essential for maintaining a healthy and comfortable living environment.

For the Motion

Housework is a natural part of family life and shouldn't be monetised as it has a belief that it is more a shared responsibility rather than a job.

- **Economic Feasibility** Sometimes, it appears economically challenging and impractical if someone is get paid for house work. And it seriously require significant changes to the current economic system.
- **Indistinct Lines** The definition and measurement of the household work has no clean lines so it is difficult to quantify the value that is variable in nature and effort.
- **Policy Implications** Housework being recognised as unpaid labour can lead to social welfare policy changes, such as providing financial support on social security benefits to those who perform it.

Against the Motion

- **Absence of Financial Compensation** Housework demands significant amount of time and effort, but it is not recognised and acknowledged and not provided financial compensation. This lack of monetary compensation/honorarium can lead to undervaluation of the work performed, despite its essential role in maintaining the household.
- **Gender inequalities** Housework is generally performed by women, which perpetuates gender inequalities. Acknowledging it as unpaid labour, highlights the need for more equitable distribution of domestic responsibilities and the importance of valuing all forms of work, regardless of gender.
- **Opportunity Costs** The time spend in household works could be invested for other activities which actually generate an employment and has monetary value. By refusing compensating housework, society actually fail to acknowledge the opportunity cost borne by those who perform the task.
- **Investment of Mental and Physical Effort** This unpaid labour requires both mental and physical effort, often leads to stress and fatigue and several vital health issues.
- **Lack of Social and Legal and Individual Recognition** Household works neither given social recognition nor it give the required respects to them who perform it and they become unrecognised figures of a family and role model to no-one.

Conclusion

By acknowledging its economic contribution, addressing gender disparities and valuing the time and effort invested in maintaining households are the actual way to make it little better and relaxing state to the performers. This perspective can lead to more equitable policies and a greater appreciation of the essential work that keeps homes and families safe and functioning smoothly.

3. Genetically modified crops are essential for food sufficiency CAPF AC 2023

Introduction

Genetically Modified (GM) crops are plants modified through genetic engineering which alters their DNA sequences to provide some beneficial characteristics. For instance, it can improve crop yield which increases the production of that crop.

Such crops can also resist drought, diseases and insect pests if engineered in such a way. If consumed, it will prove very beneficial and not at all harmful to people of any age. GM corn, for instance, has cut levels of naturally-occurring mycotoxin— a toxin that causes both health problems and economic losses — by a third.

The initial understanding of the GM crops seems to be completely beneficial. However, GM crops have become a source of tussle between people who find that GM crops has a detrimental impact on our health. It raises the questions of- What is our eventual goal - Sufficient food for everyone or nutritious, healthy and sufficient food for everyone?

Let us look at the various view-point in this debate

For the Motion

- Hunger is a major challenge for the world in this century. Global hunger continues to persist despite several measures and some improvements.
- Additionally, due to the changes in global climate and monumental environmental challenges we are facing, food security becomes a great challenge. Salinification and desertification, flooding and drought and natural disasters threaten agriculture across the globe.
- With changing temperatures, meanwhile, come new risks of pests and diseases. In such a situation, people look for any simple solution to prevent the deaths that are caused due to hunger and genetically modified crops are one of the those solutions.
- The need to grow more food crops, the extreme climate changes and the need to reduce the carbon emission and pollution is ever growing. These challenges cannot be dealt with same old crop breeding methods. Thus, genetic engineering offers us one tool for increasing yields and reducing agriculture's environmental footprint.
- As GM crops resist drought, diseases and insect pests it not only produces food in large quantities but the food produced is also not at all harmful to people of any age. Thus, genetically modified crops are essential for dealing with hunger and for food sufficiency.

Against the Motion

- Genetically Modified (GM) crops are associated with an increased use of chemicals, like glyphosate, that are toxic to the environment and humans. These chemicals not only contaminate our food and water supplies, but they also compromise soil quality and are actually associated with increased disease susceptibility in crops. This ultimately leads to an increase in the use of pesticides and further disrupts ecosystems.

- It is futile to argue that genetically modified crops have increased the yield of any major commercialised food source. In fact, soy — the most widely grown genetically modified crop — is actually experiencing reduced yields.
- Another important consideration in terms of food security is the reduction of waste. Many health commentators have argued that food waste is a key component in addressing the issue of food insecurity and thus, more integral to the cause than genetically modified crops. If we waste less food, everyone will be able to get their share and no human will go hungry.
- Once genetically modified plants have been introduced into the world, they often can no longer be retrieved: they can actively spread, multiply, passing on their genetically modified properties to other organisms. This has many unexplored consequences for the environment, animals and people.
- All new genetically modified crops have to be checked for harmlessness to humans, animals and the environment before they are approved, but many scientists describe the current regulations for risk assessment as insufficient. Thus, rather than solving the issue of food sufficiency, genetically modified crop can end up causing new, unforeseen problems as it is a relatively new field.

Conclusion

With the problems of hunger and malnutrition afflicting the world and the reduction of agricultural produce in the present, GM crops seem like a probable solutions. However, one cannot ignore the fact that GM crops may lead to more and new kinds of health and environmental problems which none might have solutions for. According to Scientists, food derived from GM crops poses no greater risk to human health than conventional food, but that each GM food needs to be tested on a case-by-case basis before introduction.

4. Capital punishment is a deterrent for heinous crimes CAPF AC 2023

Introduction

Capital punishment or death penalty as a means of giving justice has become one of the most controversial issues which pertain to the laws of our societies.

Death penalty is a legal process where a person is put to death by the state as a punishment for the crime he/she has committed. Ending a criminal's life has become the most talked about topic not only at the national level but also globally. Many find the punishment to be just, while other find it unethical.

Let us look at the various issues and understand the different perspective regarding capital punishment.

For the Motion

- Capital punishment is sure to act as a crime deterrent. Fear and dread of capital punishment can make the criminal think twice before committing a crime.
- Capital punishment serves as a means of fair justice. An old Mesopotamia law advocates 'a tooth for a tooth and an eye for an eye'. If a person takes away the life of a person, it is just logical that he must pay it with his life. Equal justice for both victim and perpetrator of the crime should be served without any favour.
- Capital punishment must stay for those hardcore offenders whose behaviour and mind set are not changeable.
- Another reason in favour of capital punishment is that the punishment for the culprit that fits the crime would soothe the victim's family. Executing a person certainly prevents recurrence of violence or quite possible the first occurrence of other murderous acts. If a criminal knows that the legal system will not hesitate to give him death penalty, the system may appear draconian to him. Hence, it can be possible that he may be less inclined to break the rules and kill.
- Thus, capital punishment can prove to be a deterrent for heinous crimes.

Against the Motion

- Saying that individuals are less likely to commit violent crimes if they know they will face punishment by execution is wrong. It assumes that criminals study and anticipate the consequences of getting caught, and decide that a long-term of imprisonment is acceptable, whereas execution is not. However, the truth is that most crimes are committed impulsively without leaving any consideration of punishment.
- Contrary to the popular belief that the death penalty reduces the crime rate, various surveys have shown that the threat of the death penalty does not in any way reduce the occurrence of violent crimes. In fact, it may even cause further violence. Execution is the ultimate sanction a state can inflict upon a person. Once criminals have knowingly committed a capital offence, they no longer have any interest in lessening their potential punishment by not committing further murders or other offences.
- In cases where people commit large-scale acts of violence (like terrorism), they do so knowing full well the consequences their acts will lead to. Therefore, they show no regard for their safety or loss of life. In such cases, capital punishment doesn't stop anything and deters no one. Execution, in such cases, might provide welcome publicity for the groups they belong to and create martyrs around which further support may be rallied for their cause.

Conclusion

With many arguments that questions the violent nature and the subsequent effect of capital punishment, many Countries across the globe maintains death penalty. However, India still continues with the laws. The Law Commission of India stressed on the reasoning that the conditions in India demands the contrary position to the proposition of 'abolition of death penalty' and concluded the death penalty should be retained. It said that the variety of upbringing, the diversity of the population, the disparity in the levels of education and morality and the paramount need for maintaining law and order were fundamental factors and issues that impede India from taking a favourable position to abolish the capital punishment.

5. Video games sharpen the mind CAPF AC 2022

Introduction

The world today has intertwined technology and entertainment as is evident in not only movies, shows and OTTs apps but also in video games that are available in abundance in every market. The popularity of this amalgamation is a result of the fact that they can easily help an individual distress. This is so especially for video games that provides instant gratification simple because it takes us away from the worries of real life.

However, the question arises – 'Is entertainment the only benefit of playing video games?' This question has divided people who have differing perspectives. Let us understand these different perspectives.

For the Motion

- In addition to relieving their stress, video games have a lot of benefits to offer to the young minds. They not only enhance computer fluency in the user but also develop hand-eye coordination.
- The games generally involve forming teams teach a person co-operation, communication, time management, decision-making under pressure, problem-solving skills, and creativity and teamwork.
- Now-a-days, video games serve as a fun and interactive platform to teach about several topics like cyber security and much more. These games are often employed by therapists to treat and manage children with attention disorders.
- Further, they also enhance focus and concentration. In addition, today, with the field expanding exponentially, playing video games have become a source of earning a good livelihood.
- Thus, even though playing video games might seem like wastage of time, it actually makes a person more observant and improves their mental strength.

Against the Motion

- With more and more games coming to the market, the activity done just for entertainment has now reached the levels of addiction causing change in lifestyle, priorities and routine.
- A survey revealed that 65% of children under the age of 20 believed that they are ready to give up food and sleep to play video games.
- Video games have had a great negative impact on a child. In the modern sedentary life, video games and its increasing popularity has led to a further reduction in physical activities leading to several health problems. Children today develop body aches, headaches, poor body posture, poor eyesight, etc. They also develop many diseases such as diabetes, heart problems and cholesterol among youngsters in and worldwide.
- Moreover, children who spend a considerable amount of time playing video games find difficult in sleeping. They have low levels of concentration and focus. Thus, they cannot pay attention to their studies and then display poor academic performance or performance in general.
- Constant need to play video games also isolates a person, separating them from the outside world and leading to social anxiety and disconnection. This can eventually lead to depression and poor emotional regulation.
- The addiction resulting from playing video games impacts a person's professional life, personal development and their interpersonal relations
- Another harsh negative effect of video games is increased aggression. When things don't go according to their plan, it becomes difficult to control their mental state. As a result, such children display aggression and are very violent. Thus, it is not good for a person's physical, emotional and mental health and the amount of time invested in playing video games should be kept in check.

Conclusion

There is no denying the fact that video games have many other benefits besides entertainment. However, too much of video games have displayed many negative impacts. In this light, it is important to have a balanced life where limits are set for video games so that they can become healthy tools of development.

6. United Nations Organisation has become redundant CAPF AC 2022

Introduction

The United Nations was established in 1945 with the purpose of maintaining international peace and security, protecting human rights, delivering humanitarian aid, preventing war, promoting sustainable development and upholding law. From an unprecedented pandemic ravaging households and hospitals worldwide to an increasingly pervasive climate crisis that threatens the livelihoods of millions, today, the United Nations faces a task far more arduous than anything else it has met in its history. While the UN has in the past played an irrefutably pivotal role in international arbitration, the present analysis of the organisation has left many divided on whether the international organisation aimed at maintaining global security and peace is becoming redundant or not.

Let us look at the various perspectives in it.

For the Motion

- UN's foremost stated aim is 'to maintain international peace and security', a task that lies with its most powerful body, the Security Council. Its success in this endeavour, however, is a contentious matter. In 2003, hints of weakness appeared when the Council deadlocked in the face of severe Iraqi aggression. More recently, failures to suppress the Syrian conflict and the retreat of nuclear non-proliferation mandate a re-examination of the SC's capabilities.
- Perhaps the most prevalent example of its incompetence is its inability in preventing a war was proven when it failed to end the conflict between Russia and Ukraine. Its action regarding the war was limited to diplomatically isolating and shaming Russia rather than actually engaging before or during the war.
- Another aim of the UN is 'to develop friendly relations between nations and encourage international cooperation'. However, representation in many bodies is dominated solely by an elite handful of nations with the United States at its helm. Several UN bodies are accused of being aggressively partisan 'majority coalitions', while regimes in South Africa and Chile have been unfairly targeted by UN resolutions in the past. Moreover, controversial members such as Israel have long suffered discrimination; Israeli participation in most councils today is heavily restricted. In the 21st century, with state politics and infighting dominating UN decisions, its ability to encourage global cooperation and friendliness is severely hindered.

Thus, United Nations has declined remarkably in its relevance in a wider global context. While some of its humanitarian missions have been met with adequate success, the UN's ability to live up to its other stated aims has been disappointingly insufficient.

Against the Motion

- Despite the challenges, failures and weaknesses, the long serving organisation, the United Nations assumes a significant job in the complexity of the world today. Founded on the principles of international peace, cooperation and development, UN plays a key role in keeping up harmony and security of the world nations.
- Several important specialised agencies of the UN work relentlessly towards global betterment. Today, the UN has been successful in pursuing its third aim, namely 'the improvement of human rights and liberties'.
- The United Nations Development Programme (UNDP) effectively works to achieve Sustainable Development Goals while eradicating poverty and improving the quality of life for all. The United Nations Environment Programme (UNEP) supports the governments in establishing and implementing necessary laws, policies, and programs for achieving sustainable development at the nation and international level.

Conclusion

The UN since its inception is actively working for maintaining peace, ensuring development, and cooperation among nations and has devised various initiatives to prevent conflict.

Without this integral peace-keeping organisation, military capacity will become the only way of protection against aggression. Thus, its relevance cannot be denied in the present world. However, times have changed and threats have emerged. Keeping the new trends in mind, it is important for the UN to become an organisation equipped with all the means the face the challenges of the present times.

7. Elections in states should be held simultaneously

CAPF AC 2021

Introduction

Election Day in India witnesses a strong display of democracy, people's opinion and of chaos. For long, many recommendations have been made suggesting a more effective method of organising elections but none have succeeded. One suggestion that has been debated on for a long time is that of simultaneous elections. It refers to the process of electing representatives in governing body all at the same time. However, opinions regarding simultaneous elections are divided on various points. Let is look at these different opinions.

For the Motion

- Simultaneous elections would undoubtedly minimise the time and the expenditure that is spent during the elections.
- The staff appointed for election duty, the paramilitary forces deployed to make sure that the process is conducted in a non-violent spirit, the election booths and the voting machines will be more easily and efficiently available if simultaneous elections are held throughout the states. It would also reduce the manpower that goes into organising an election, especially for a prolonged period.
- Conducting elections at the same time would ensure that the ruling parties focus more on the governance rather than being constantly occupied with campaigning for the elections.
- Although, the idea of simultaneous elections throughout the nation has not taken life yet, it concurs with PM Narendra Modi's "One Nation, One Election" concept. The elections in Assam, Kerala, Tamil Nadu, West Bengal and Puducherry, held in March-April 2021, that are thought to have contributed to the second wave of COVID-19 have only increased the need to solve this issue as early as possible.
- Thus, organising elections at the same time would be beneficial for the Election Commission, the officials involved and the entire population of India, at large.

Against the Motion

- According to a report drafted in 2018 by the Law Commission of India, if a few amendments are made to the Constitution, simultaneous elections can be conducted in the country in an organised and controlled manner. However, this step has not yet been approved and brought into action due to the various drawback it holds.
- It can't be denied that it will be a huge step that would require several measures including certain states and assemblies having to adjust the timing of elections in order to synchronise among themselves and with others. Now, this can only lead to a disruption among the governments of the states. It would be chaotic, to say the least.
- Separate elections as that is the custom since long has many benefits.
- The security forces deployed in more than a million polling booths all over the country do not have to face diversified and probably adverse climatic and geographical conditions, all at the same time. This ensures proper security of the nation.
- Several state political parties are also national and having to prepare and face the electorate more than once in five years assures their accountability and also keeps them in check. It requires them to come up with more opportunities for the people, like jobs that are created during elections.
- Further, state-wise election brings focus on the problems specific to the state. If simultaneous elections are held, they would shift the focus to national problems.

Conclusion

Hence, if the Election Commission makes a decision regarding this, it will have to consider all these aspects and come up with proper solutions to any obstacle that they or the citizens might face during elections, which is very probable considering the large population of India and the steps that are involved in this process.

It is sufficed to say the simultaneous election are desirable but not essential.

8. Farmer protests are politically motivated

CAPF AC 2021

Introduction

The battle that the farmers fought in November 2020 did not show any hopes of coming to an end till the government repealed the three acts that led to the protest, in November 2021 and again in the beginning of 2024. While the protest, at first glance may seem to have social impact, many have observed these protests as being prolonged by some political leaders and parties. This participation of leaders have raised the issue of the actual nature of farmer protests.

Let us look at the differing perspectives

For the Motion

- According to many, these protests are being prolonged by some political leaders and parties who only want to further their agenda through these farmers.
- The issues that the farmers seem to have with the bill were solvable. These issues included the fear of APMC *mandis* being completely overtaken by private *mandis* run by corporate giants who will only exploit the farmers further and the eventual abolishment of purchasing of crops at the Minimum Support Price. These issues were not being solved because of the continuous exploitation by the politicians.
- This fact was pointed out by the Chief Minister of Punjab who met with the Prime Minister and stated that these prolonged protests had the potential to affect the social fabric of the entire nation. The Punjab government also said in a statement that few Pakistan-backed anti-India forces were looking for ways to exploit the farmers' dissatisfaction with the government and pose threat to the nation.
- What began as a way to show disapproval of the bills had completely turned into a political strategy to criticise the government for one's own personal interest. Few politicians and parties were using the farmers' disgruntlement as a means to attack the government and establish themselves as sympathisers, who would have never done so if they were in power.

Against the Motion

- The farmers believed that the provisions in the farm laws would open the sale of agriculture products in private markets beyond the scope of APMC *mandis*, which would lead to their eventual exploitation at the hands of big corporate companies. They also feared that these private *mandis* would, in the future completely replace the public *mandis* and the security that the wholesale markets provide will be lost.
- The farmers also feared that if the APMC mandis are dismantled, it will encourage the companies to exploit them and abolish the purchase of their crops at the MSP. This is a big scare for the farmers who already don't have enough to sell owing to lack of storage infrastructure and high debts. If their fears come true in the future, it will lead to them losing their lands and homes due to the loans and debts.
- Along with their justified fears, there is also the fact that the farmer did not allow any political leader or party to share the same stage as them. Further, the farmers outline their demands clearly. Thus, saying that the protests were politically motivated is like saying that the farmers have no reason to fight, even when their livelihood is at stake.

Conclusion

The debate of whether the farmer protests were politically motivated or not are inconsequential in the light of the plight of the farmers. The central issue that requires urgent redressal is ensuring that the insecurities faced by farmers are dispelled.

9. Solitude during a pandemic is not unwelcome

CAPF AC 2020

Introduction

With the onset of the global pandemic, social distancing and the eventual lockdowns became a necessary precautionary step in containing its spread. Thus, various months were spent at home establishing feelings of loneliness and isolation in many. This state of isolation has divided people into two sects- one who believes that the solitude was necessary and the other who believes that solitude was detrimental to many. Let us look at theses perspectives in detail.

For the Motion

- While many people believe that this isolation had great negative impacts on an individual, studies conducted all across the globe reveal the contrary. Data revealed by these surveys suggest that the solitude brought by the isolation was a welcome event in this fast paced world on all levels. Be it individually, socially and environmentally, the solitude that came with social distancing brought them various benefits.
- People became open to many things. They were exercising, participating in their hobbies and doing things just for fun. It bought along a time of relaxation wherein people learnt different skills like painting, gardening, cooking, etc., and expanded their skills sets. Solitude as such led to a bonding with family- as bonding which was not a characteristic of the urban modern society. In other words, people starting valuing the time they had to themselves and felt peaceful when alone. Rather than feeling isolated, some actually felt even more connected to other people.
- Last but not the least, this solitude worked in the favour of mother Earth. As each and every one of us stay indoors closing out all those factories and industries that harm the environment, it is not hidden that Mother Earth healed itself. Clear skies, clean water, the chirruping of birds, etc., all around the globe made the solitude worthwhile.

Against the Motion

- The Pandemic induced lockdown, social distancing and isolation, changed the numbers of people suffering from this disorder and not in a good way. The number increased as multiple cases of anxiety, isolation and feelings of despair, complaints about not being able to endure the distance from friends and family, have had many people breaking down, made one realise that the solitude and isolation that came with the pandemic had severe negative impact on people.
- In the modern world where man has always known what to do next, with their lives generally following a regular trail, this sudden cataclysmic turn of events have brought them face to face with a dire reckoning –how to live with oneself doing nothing except work. Thus, an individual easily became prone to many mental disorders like depression, anxiety, adjustment disorder, chronic stress, insomnia or even late-life dementia.
- Further, apart from health concerns, this solitude brings a question mark on employment condition prevalent. With most small scale business being almost shut during the pandemic times, people are rendered to a point wherein not only are they susceptible to health concerns mentioned above but the economy of the country suffers. People are rendered jobless without any security benefits.

Conclusion

Thus, while solitude was essential to control the pandemic and in a long term for our and the nature's benefit, long term isolation is not desirable.

10. Political awareness among the social elite is inconsequential

CAPF AC 2020

Introduction

The introduction of the printing press in 15th century, Europe revolutionised the social landscape, helping information spread further and faster than never before. This had a deep link with the spread idea of democracy all over the world. In the present era, social media represents a similar paradigm shift.

Today, social media plays a crucial role in facilitating and distributing content related to all the matters that have a larger influence on public opinion and subsequently on democracy. Prominently, the role of social media leads us to the role of social elites. While it is easy to say that social elites have a large influence on people and their choice, their political awareness has time and again raised debates whether it is consequential or not.

Let us look at the differing perspectives on the issue.

For the Motion

- The influence of political influence of social elites has never been a central topic of discourse. In fact, it is considered inconsequential for all the apt reasons. First, elites have everything they need and even the things that they seldom need. Hence, they are self-absorbed in their lives and do not care for the grievances of the masses.
- They are not only uninformed but they support those who supports them. Further, their opinion is something that has mass appeal. Not to forget, they are side with the ruling regime for the various benefits that they receive. In this light, even if they make a comment, they cannot be blindly believed.
- Further, even though much of social elites are a part of political discourse, their knowledge and awareness does not seem to be affecting the overall growth and development the nation. As a matter of fact, their entire presence seems to be based on their social position and popularity.

Thus, political awareness among the social elite is inconsequential

Against the Motion

- Politics is one of the most important social constructs in history that holds a great influence in everyone's life. An individual's society and life are molded by decisions taken by the elected representatives. Thus, it is imperative that each of us stay up to date with what is happening in the political world and act upon it in a democratic way. And we do but in the process of make our choice; our decisions are greatly affected by the social elites of our societies.
- The social elites of our societies are those rich and privileged people who have the honour of meeting and interacting first-hand with the political leaders of any nation. This interaction may mean that they can better judge the leader and have a better awareness of whether the leader will promotes growth and development of the nation in comparison to the common masses.
- Further, their popularity and the effect their opinions have on the people, makes the government accountable for an action. A statement against the political leader can put the pressure on the government to address the grievance and check the activities of the leader. History is replete with figures belonging to social elite who have changed our society for the better.
- Social elites can encourage people to participate in political discourses and increase the political awareness of an individual. Hence, political awareness among the social elite is not inconsequential.

Conclusion

Social elites have garnered many roles in history. They have acted as heroes and villains whose views and opinions have had far-reaching consequence on the nation. Thus, to say that their views are inconsequential would be incorrect. However, we need to be wary of their views and make sure that the views are just before taking sides.

11. Digital technology may replace books with computers CAPF AC 2019

Introduction

The internet provides access to humungous amount of information and this can cater to possibly every set of audience. Youngsters have got hooked on to internet and computers for finding out information as it is not only portable but can also provide instant updates on any development. This pervasiveness of internet and digital technology has led to the metamorphosis in the techniques of reading and learning. This is led to conversation wherein people have question if digital technology can replace books. Let us look at different perspectives on this issue

For the Motion

- Digital technology has the capability of replacing books completely at the rate that developments are taking place in it. For many people, it has already started as they use a Kindle tablet to read e-books. Whenever they need specific information, they use the internet to get the information, otherwise, they read Wikipedia pages or watch YouTube videos on their computers. The latest news can be read on their smart phones.
- Hence, while books continue to be the most important source of learning in major part of the world, digital devices have permeated fast into our lives changing the we read and learn. Today the traditional pen, paper and blackboard classroom has converted to a Google classroom wherein printed books are no longer needed. Soft copies or e-books are easily available to teachers as well as students which provide a comfortable reading experience.
- There is also no need to wait for printing of a particular book as now these books are available on the internet as e-files which can be carried anywhere in you smart devices without the burden of carrying printed books.

Thus, while we cannot say for sure when it would happen but, it is sure that digital technology may replace books with computers.

Against the Motion

- The internet, a result of the development of digital technology, takes time away from other pursuits, provides entertainment and information, besides fulfilling many other useful purposes. But in no way, can it compare with the warm, personal experience of reading a good book.
- Books provide the in-depth knowledge of a subject that sitting in front of a computer cannot provide. We can download the text of a book from the internet but the downloaded text has no aesthetic qualities. The aesthetics of a well-designed book enhances the reading experience and brings another kind of pleasure.
- The book is still the most compact and inexpensive means of conveying a dense amount of knowledge in a convenient manner. The easy portability of the book is what makes it the most user-friendly format for knowledge ever invented. The idea that one can carry in one's pocket a play by Shakespeare, a novel by Charles Dickens or Plato's Dialogues in a small paperback edition is mind-boggling. We take such uncommon convenience for granted, not realising that the book itself has undergone quite an evolution.
- Another important reason why digital technology will never replace books is because, those who wish to become writers want to see their works permanently published in books.
- This is because books are something you can hold, see, feel, skim through and read at one's leisure. The writer may use a word processor instead of a typewriter or a pen and pad, but the finished product must eventually end up, as a book if it is to have value to the reading public. The writer may use the internet in the course of researching a subject just as he may use a library for that purpose, but the end product will still be a book.

12. Homework should be banned at primary level education CAPF AC 2019

Introduction

Boasting of one of the best education systems in the world, Finland focuses on more learning and less homework. Finland's education has no homework till primary level. This concept has sparked a debate among many about the relevance and utility of homework in primary level homework.

Let us look at the debate regarding the issue

For the Motion

- Studies have often showed that homework adds nothing to standardised test scores for primary level pupils. International comparisons of older students have found no positive relationship between the amount of homework set and average test scores. Hence, time and again people have realised that homework at the primary level of education has little educational worth and adds nothing to the time spent in school. As a result, some schools and some countries don't bother with homework at all.
- Homework is essentially almost always done every day as an overtime study when a child is already tired from a long day at school. Consequently, homework ends up being done in a hurry by students fighting fatigue which results in poor quality work. This makes the students, who have been up late trying to finish off their homework, come tired to school the next day leading to ineffective learning.
- Setting homework does little to develop good study skills. It is hard to check whether the homework that students produce is really their own. Some students have always copied from others or got their parents to help them do it.
- Further, overtime studies take away the free and playtime students which are crucial for their overall development. Thus, homework puts students off learning as they feel it to be a burden because of many factors which include homework.
- Learning should always be fun and enjoyable for primary students and never a burden. Thus, homework should not be given at the primary level of education.

Against the Motion

- Homework is a vital and valuable part of education. There are only a few hours in each school day at the primary level of education. This is not enough to cover properly all the subjects that children need to study. Giving homework extends study beyond school hours, allowing a wider and deeper education.
- It also makes the best use of teachers, who can spend lesson time teaching rather than just supervising individual work that could be done at home. Tasks such as reading, writing essays, researching, doing Math problems, etc., are best done at home, away from the distractions of other students.
- Having homework also allows students to really imbibe into their minds the work they have done in school. Doing tasks linked to recent lessons helps students to strengthen their understanding and become more confident in using new knowledge and skills. For children at the primary level, this could be practising reading or learning multiplication tables.
- Homework prepares students to work more independently as they will have to do so later on in life. Everyone needs to develop skills in personal organisation, working to deadlines, being able to research, etc. If students are always 'spoon-fed' knowledge at school, they will never develop study skills and self-discipline for the future.
- If homework puts students off learning, then it has been badly planned by the teacher. The best homework tasks engage and stretch students, encouraging them to think for themselves and follow through ideas which interest them. Over time, well planned homework can help students develop good habits, such as reading for pleasure or creative writing.

Conclusion

Education is a partnership between the child, the school and the home. Homework is one of the main methods in which the students' families can be involved with their learning.

Many parents value the chance to see what their children are studying and to support them in it. Additionally, schools need parents' support in encouraging students to read at home, to help with the practising of multiplication tables and to give them opportunities to research new topics. So, homework should not be banned at the primary level of education.

13. Privacy is an elitist idea CAPF AC 2018

Introduction

The right to privacy is about the freedom to make one's choices, freedom to dissent or move or think and protection from state surveillance. A nine-judge bench of the Supreme Court of India held unanimously that the right to privacy was a constitutionally protected right in India. It is granted to each and every individual. However, the situation in the ground reality points a discrepancy leading to contrasting views regarding privacy. These views are

For the Motion

- Indian privacy is essentially an elitist idea which is applicable to the only few who belong to the elite, rich class.
- India is a poor country where around 270 million people are below poverty level. They require state assistance for their basic needs such as food, shelter and clothes. They hardly know what privacy is all about and do not care about it as their main concern is to meet their basic needs. Apart from this, around 26% (more than one-fourth) of India's population is illiterate. They are

not even aware of their basic rights let alone privacy right.

- Further, almost every day we hear about violation of privacy right of the common man in India. There are incidents of harrassment, social intolerance, gender discrimination, etc., which clearly show that the common man has no privacy at all. Now, majority of these incidents go unreported or unnoticed because people know that it will be vain and not action would be taken. However, when the rich and the powerful are involved, such violations become national agenda. Constant debates and discussion regarding a high profile happens when a powerful person is involved.

Thus, the right of privacy is limited to the elite only in India

Against the Motion

- The Supreme Court verdict that privacy as an incident of fundamental freedom or liberty is guaranteed under Article 21 which provides that: "No person shall be deprived of his life or personal liberty except according to procedure established by law." However, many in India believe that privacy is an elitist concern which is untrue.
- The right to privacy is an inherent right and it does not move from individual to individual in matters of class, colour, creed or religion. It does not exclude the poor and the illiterate. In fact, the judgment demolished the argument that privacy is an elitist construct imported from Western countries.
- It categorically rejected the premise that the poor in the third world were more concerned with 'economic well-being' and 'privacy is a privilege for the few'. It also provides that every individual in society irrespective of social class or economic status is entitled to the intimacy and autonomy which privacy protects.

Conclusion

Those who say that privacy is an elitist idea do not understand what is meant by privacy. Privacy means the right to do anything you want, but the right to be respected in your choices, beliefs, in the company, in the clothes that you wear, in matters of love and choice of your partner, in your work, etc.

So, privacy is a concern that will apply to anyone and is not limited to the elite, rich or any other particular class in a democracy.

14. Note-ban, effective tool against black money

CAPF AC 2018

Introduction

Demonetisation or note-ban is the withdrawal of currencies or other valuables by the central bank to be used as the legal tender in the nation. Such currencies either turn into scrap or are deposited in the banks and replaced by the new currencies. Governments of many countries across the world have taken this drastic measure to curb black money and stop the counterfeiting of currency notes. Such a measure was taken by the Indian government too.

On the heels of The Undisclosed Foreign Income and Assets (Imposition of Tax) act of 2015 and the Income Disclosure Scheme of 2016, the Narendra Modi government announced demonetisation of ₹ 500 and ₹ 1000 currency, which has been referred to as a masterstroke by many experts. Many have appreciated the efforts while other have found the act to be problematic.

Let us see the difference between these two perspectives

For the Motion

- An attempt made by the government to flush out black money from the Indian capital circulation and expansion of the formal sector of the market, demonetisation led to a significant dump in fake currency notes; thus making it a successful attempt for various reasons.
- In accordance with the statements of the Reserve Bank of India, more than 99% of the invalid money was returned to banks which assisted government officials in tracking the source of unaccounted cash. Individuals with a huge chunk of money had to disclose their source of income and pay taxes on them.
- Demonetisation in India put a full stop to the funding of terrorist groups and all unlawful activities.
- It also curbed the money laundering acts and it was now easy for the income tax department to trace the money and made the path difficult for illegal money laundering. It also effectively turned India towards a cashless economy.

Against the Motion

- The sudden announcement of demonetisation in India caused panic and chaos in the country. It was done in a haphazard way which caused a lot of problems to the common man across India and even though, it claims to be successful in its attempt to curb blank money, the new notes that came into circulation do not in any way guarantee that the black money will be stooped completely.
- In fact, it paved the way for people to look for other ways to accumulating and using black money.
- Further, the note-ban decision affected the daily wagers, peasants, small and medium business, etc., adversely. These people who were paid for their work had to stand in queues leaving their livelihood behind to make sure that their income and their savings were safe. Many were out of work as their employers could not pay them in cash due to the cash crunch.
- The demonetisation also increased the inflation in the country because of the cash shortage. The unemployment rate stood at a four-year high from 2016 to 2017 when demonetisation was undergone. The cash crunch also affected businesses and caused a slowdown in the economy for some time.
- The central bank spent ₹ 21,000 crore in handing the mechanics of note-ban (demonetisation). This included the printing of new notes which reduced the profit of the Reserve Bank of India (RBI) resulting in lesser dividend being paid to the Central Government.

Post-Demonetisation, RBI's dividend declined by more than half.

- Another point worth mentioning is that most black money was held in the form of real estate (and not in cash) and hence demonetisation (note-ban) could not in any way help in this regard.

Conclusion

While note ban has many far reaching positive outcomes, its negative impacts point that it can only be effective if it is followed by stringent policies and strong institutions that help to alleviate the problems.

15. The youth in India are getting addicted to Android mobiles CAPF AC 2017

Introduction

We all are living in 21st century which is the age of science and technology. All the scientists of the world are inventing newer technologies every day to ease our life and give us comfort. One such technology is the Android mobiles. Mobile phones or smart phones were invented to allow us to connect with out near and dear ones at any time of the day. However, with new updations, the devices today can do everything; from clicking pictures to calculating. Today, with internet, the knowledge of the world is a fingertip away. This all pervasiveness of androids had led to debate of android and internet addiction. Let us see what the debate entails.

For the Motion

- While these devices became a necessary part of the present day world, it reached addictive heights for the youth. Young boys and girls seem to have become inordinately addicted to them always scrolling though social media sites and continuously texting. They are thoughtlessly and uselessly wasting their precious time on them neglecting their studies as well as social life.
- Children get hooked to the gaming apps and social media sites, becoming passive and killing their creativity. They spend less time in playing sports, exercise and outdoor activities.
- The overuse of mobile has posed serious health issues. Radiation caused by network towers as well as mobile phones, affect not only eye sight but also causes difficulty in concentration, fatigue, headaches and sleep disturbance that can further trigger health complications.
- Owing to late night use of mobile phones, the youngsters skimp on sleep which has made them aggressive and irritated.
- Another major disadvantage of the increasing use of mobile is the spread of undesirable information. Not only is such information confusing but they are also not age appropriate.
- Our youth is the future of our nation. We cannot allow this youth to waste their precious time on android mobiles.

Against the Motion

- Mobiles are so versatile that not just updated information, we can even get books, important educational documentaries and tours online.
- It is comprehensive device with a clock, stopwatch, timer, telephone directory, etc facilities at just a click of a button. It is a wonderful device that provides useful learning apps, a medium of connecting and bonding and entertainment in one's palm.
- In addition, we can get all facilities through the various applications, a mobile has to offer. Thus, we are always attached to our mobiles and are in despair when in it is lost or stolen.
- In this light, saying that the youth in India are getting addicted to Android mobiles is wrong.

Conclusion

Shakespeare has very wisely said: "There is nothing either good or bad, but thinking makes it so." Similarly, android mobile phones in themselves are neither good nor bad; however, how we use them makes them good or bad.

16. Power flows from the barrel of the gun CAPF AC 2017

Introduction

The phrase coined by Chinese communist leader Mao Zedong 'Political power grows out of the barrel of a gun' means that force, coercion and violence is the source of power. In other words, those with the weapons and the power to force their will on people are the rulers, the political leaders. The statement made during the Chinese Civil war, has become a source of contention among people who question its validity.

Let us look at the various viewpoints in it

For the Motion

- History is witness that if need arises, force has been used either for self-protection or for expanding the empire. When India got independence in spite of all efforts of peaceful integration, it was compelled to use the force against Pakistan supported fighters, Nizam of Hyderabad and for integration of Goa.
- Again in 1965 and during Bangladesh liberation war of 1971, India had to use the force to show their supremacy to the world.
- Further, a government with a powerful army and military will have greater control and can better govern the society. It can be a uniform mediator of issues which can unify the country.
- Use of force ensures disciplined and effective governance and leaves no room for anarchy. We all know that violence against the state must be fought back with violence; hence the need for guns and force is essential to fight back bad elements.
- Power also acts as a catalyst of change. Without power, revolution is impossible.

- Further, sometimes display of power is essential to bring about peace. War becomes essential for peace in the longer run.

Against the Motion

- Today, the use of force does not bring about true governance. Rather it leads to unrest and frustration within the masses. If force is applied to bend the masses to the will of the government, a rebellion will rise leading to civil war as in the case of South Sudan and Syria of modern times.
- Further, weapons only bring death and destruction to human resources. Their only use is to bring justice.
- The true power lies in thought and mind. A country like India has given great minds to the world. Lead positions across the world are held by Indians. This shows that true power of the nation. Thus, nations should have faith in themselves rather than force or guns.

Conclusion

Hence, we can say that power is somewhat essential to the maintenance of the civil society.

17. India needs to focus on imparting quality education instead of merely increasing its Gross Enrollment Ratio CAPF AC 2016

Introduction

India has the third largest education system in the world. This in itself is a remarkable achievement though the severity of challenges that the system faces are exceedingly high, daunting and times look insurmountable. The challenges confronting the Indian higher education system are challenging, complex and have different hues. In this regard, different opinions focusing on different aims have come into play leading to a debate.

Let us look at what the debate is about

For the Motion

- The education system has seen a scorching growth over the last decade with the system trebling in size. If we look at enrollment numbers the achievement looks stunning with enrollments doubling in the last decade. However, the state of affairs looks dismal if we dig deeper and try to understand the system better with the lack of quality education.
- If we look at the number of educated students getting jobs, we will find that a majority of graduates remain unemployed simply because their education did not teach them the skills required for the job. In fact, if one goes to the educational institutes, one will find that teachers are not equipped to bridge the gap between education and skills.
- Further, a major aspect of our education system is the focus on examinations that evaluation learning of theories and facts easily found in books instead of application of those theories. In addition, huge importance is given to marks scored.
- Hence, such a system, promotes cramming, rote learning and mugging.
- It is important to understand that without quality education, India cannot make progress in research and development.
- In addition, to organise the workforce, quality education is a necessity

Against the Motion

- Today, the focus has shifted to quality education with the hopes that the Gross Enrollment Ratio will keep in increasing as it has been in the past decade and will reach 50% by 2030.
- In a nation where the poor do not send their children to schools for the want of a better livelihood, the focus on encouraging people to get educated should remain a priority. If the focus is removed, the condition may revert back to what it was.
- India's literacy rate is still low and for women, it is lower. If the focus shifts entirely to quality education, the percentage will further reduce which will hamper the growth of the nation.

Conclusion

The knowledge that India has the greatest resource in the form of youth, it is imperative that the nation focus on increasing the quality of education while ensuring the Gross Enrollment Ratio increases. Thus, the NEP 2020 understanding the need for quality education as well as the increase GER is a good step ahead.

18. The trend of nuclear families will make old age homes in India increase in number CAPF AC 2016

Introduction

Gone are the days when the traditional norms and values of Indian society laid stress on showing respect and providing care for the elderly and the older members of the family were normally taken care of in the family itself. With the advent of modernisation, industrialisation, urbanisation, occupational differentiation, education and growth of individual philosophy, the society has changed and joint families have been replaced by nuclear families.

The rise in nuclear families and the increasing number of old age homes have been related in a manner that the former is believed by many to be the cause of the latter. This belief has divided people. Let us look at how people have various viewpoints on the topic

For the Motion

- A nuclear family is essentially a family comprising four to five member including the parents and children. There is no place for the grandparents in this family and hence, the elderly are moved to old age homes. With more and more people preferring nuclear families, it is expected that the number of old age homes will increase in India.
- Our elderly need great care and attention. They need someone to talk to pass their time. Such an attention is

not possible in a nuclear family as everyone is busy in their own lives.

- Further, as the elders are incapable of contributing to household work or monetarily, they are often considered as a liability. As a result, they are subject to abuse and neglect and eventually in some worse case scenarios abandoned without a penny to their name.
- In this situation, people prefer sending the elderly to old age homes as they provide all the necessary facilities, along with a warm and a friendly atmosphere for the elderly. They can be a secure place for the parents of those children who are working out of India or in some other distant city where they cannot visit or look after their parents regularly.
- Not just facilities, the old age homes also offer companionship which if often missing in nuclear families.

Against the Motion

There is no against the motion for this topic.

19. Large population of India is more of a bane than a boon. CAPF AC 2015

Introduction

India, the largest democracy in the world has added one more stud as the world's most populous country amongst the comity of nations. United Nations data shows India is world number one in population which grew by 1.56% to reach 142.86 crore, overtaking China which is at 142.57 crore. It has been predicted that India would reach this figure only in 2027, however, reached four years earlier (2023). The changes in the population growth have sparked many debates regarding the implication of this data.

For the Motion

- This rapid rise of population has led to various socio-economic problems in the country.
- Socially, population explosion leads to migration of people from rural to the urban areas leading to the growth of slum areas. People in slums live in the most unhygienic and insanitary conditions which gives birth to number of diseases. Migration also leads to several associated problems such as overcrowding, traffic congestions, frequent accidents and pollution.
- Further, increase in population increases the pressure on land and crop production which is compensated by using synthetic fertilisers, insecticides and pesticides which in turn pollute land, water and air.
- Population explosion also acts as a hurdle in addressing the problems of poverty, hunger and malnutrition effectively. This leads to an intensification of the existing problems of a nation.
- In addition, it puts a pressure on the several resources leading to the overall shortage in land, jobs, capital, housing transportation, employment and health services. To cater to the demands of an ever increasing population, building the subsequent infrastructure for providing basic necessities like health, education and water becomes a challenge for various government authorities.
- For feeding a large population, we need more production of food. Even though new techniques of agriculture have increased our productions, there is still malnutrituon reported in parts of our country. Population explosion ultimately leads to the decrease in the per capita income and standard of living of the people.

Against the Motion

- A country's power lies in the hands of citizens and India's growing population can mark India's rising power. After becoming the world's most populous nation, the role of population in India's future has become central.
- With majority of its population comprising the youth, India seems to have a great future ahead as it will have a larger number of working population. This larger working population provides a greater manpower. If this manpower is utilised efficiently in different sectors, it can lead the country towards prosperity and growth. This will decrease the dependency rate and add savings and investments in the country as more people are in employable age group. This will bring economic prosperity in the long run.
- Further, greater population means more consumers for industries. With more demand, the supply needs will require a growth of industries. This leads to greater competition and eventually leads to a fall in the prices of many goods.
- Moreover, a greater population paves the way for more people of multiple talents in the fields such as sports, music, art, etc. If a country invests well in human resources and provides enough opportunities to the people, it can come up with a vast pool of talented people.

Conclusion

Thus, population can be our strength only when we have resources and power to feed, provide the basic facilities, healthcare and jobs. This will mould them into an asset.

20. Democracy slows down the pace of development CAPF AC 2015

Introduction

In the new modern and globalised world, many theorists argue that the role of the government important in translating growth into development and how the state does so, depends on the type of political system. Hence, development and democracy have had a strong correlative and interactive relationship. Thus effects of this relationship has often been under debate with many claiming that democracy hinders development.

Let us look at the various view-points in this debate

For the Motion

- The fact that democracy hinders development is especially true for the modern society wherein money, muscle power and forces run the world. Today, democracy has been threatened, questioned and demanded by the same force which gives freedom to every individual. Thus, it has been said that the weakness of democracy is democracy itself.
- Indian Constitution provides for electoral system based on universal adult franchise which has become challenging with each day in the form of criminalisation of politics, breeding ground of corruption and source of violence in the name of caste, religion and language among other.
- Democracy talks about secularism; however, the freedom to practise religion has become the question of contention and communal disturbance and violence in the society. Indian Constitution provides for special care and privileges for weaker section of the society. However, the freedom has become the source of division and fragmentation in the society with more and more caste demanding privileges on superficial ground. It has also become the source of perpetual deprivation and thus perpetuation of caste based discrimination which is manifested in the form of violence against Dalits. Women are subjected to violence, rape and acid attack among others.
- The economic development has been the backbone of India ever since its independence. It is still required even more than before with huge socio economic obligation to fulfil the objectives of the preamble. However, it has been subjected to challenge from various quarters. Land acquisition has become the subject of political football. Displacement of the people has not been addressed properly and has become the breeding ground of Maoism, radicalism and propagation. RTI and PILs have been used extensively and delay of projects due to court's intervention has been the story of contemporary India.

  With exploitation, corruption and poor implementation, democracy is our Achilles heel dragging down our developmental agenda.

Against the Motion

- In a government of the people, by the people and for the people, the ability of the people to have a voice in the running of the state, in the economy, health, education, infrastructural development, etc., creates a balanced environment for governance to thrive; this can only be achieved in democratic governance.
- Democratic states have the right to vote for their government by deciding the policy of their nation and what their nation should be like. They have more freedom of speech and expression than in autocracies. In particular, they are free to criticise their own government.

  The government represents the views of the people who elect them and the same people can throw them out if the government does things that the people do not approve of. Unlike other forms of government democracy is about the common man, rather than the elite that are often disconnected from ground realities.
- Democracy is more about having checks and balances and having transparency of decision-making, than about elections and the populace throwing governments out of power.

Conclusion

In a democracy, the parliament, the media and sometimes the judiciary all keep an eye on what is being done with people's money. They are therefore able to keep a check on things that are detrimental to the country, are immoral or even illegal.

Even where such actions are not visible on the surface, there are separate institutions that have the power to investigate and watch any 'secret' deals or actions that are going on, away from public view. With these functions, a democracy supports the goals of development for the nation. Thus, development and democracy go hand-in-hand.

Unsolved Counter Arguments

1. Technology hinders human creativity.
2. India should focus more towards its own interests rather than international cooperation.
3. A college degree is needed to success in life.
4. Films should be made to escape from reality, not to remind us of how grim life is.
5. The Indian mindset regarding gender has really changed.
6. Humanities should be given a priority in the curriculum.
7. Self-interest should come first for India not International cooperation.
8. Digital everything can help us fight global warming.
9. English should not be allowed to be a formal medium of communication in India.
10. Economic growth and development are shaped by the societies in which they operate.
11. Skills would always be above knowledge in our society.
12. Evaluation should be both ways- by students and by teachers.
13. Minimalism should become a norm for sustainability.
14. Westernisation has a debilitating effect on the Indian society.
15. Wars are essential for peace.

03 Report Writing

SPECIAL FOCUS

In Report Writing pay special attention to
- Correct format
- Unbiased writing
- Track of word count (200-250 words)
- Avoid ornamental language

A report is factual, brief and an objective account of an incident that had already taken place.The purpose of writing a report is to give first-hand information of an event of general interest to people.

In the UPSC CAPF AC exams, 2 questions based on report writing are asked. These are to be attempted in **200 words** each. This section carries **20 marks** (10 × 2 marks) and no choice is provided.

Types of Report

In the CAPF exam, questions from two kinds of reports are generally asked.

They are

1. **Incident based** reports such as Facebook data leak, Operation Raahat, etc.
2. **Issue based** reports such as depletion of water table levels in major cities, increasing presence of women in Indian sports, etc.

Do Not Forget To Include!

Incident Based Report	Issue Based Report
• Event	• Causes / Reason
• Time	• Solutions
• Place	• Suggestions
• Effects, if any	• Conclusion
• Fatalities, if any	
• Conclusion	

TIME IT !

The maximum time taken to attempt report should be 20 minutes.
Try to finish each report in 10 minutes.

Making of a Good Report

We can easily make a good report if we know its characteristics. Remember, a good report ....

- is written a **straight forward** manner.
- presents **sufficient facts and figures** associated with the topic.
- is written in **clear** and **concise language**
- answers WHAT, WHEN, WHY and HOW of the event
- follows the **format and structure**
- makes use of data from **authentic sources**

Format of Report

Title/Heading

XYZ (Writer/Reporter Name)
Date : DD/MM/YY
Place : XXX

Para 1 Introductory paragraph mentioning the crucial information regarding the topic day, date, place, what, and timings. It includes the W's namely WHAT, WHEN, WHERE, WHO and WHY.

Para 2 Brief detail about place/cause/consequence/ effects/guests.

Para 3 Main steps/people involved/activities.

Para 4 Concluding para reactions/ promises by authorities.

Sources (From which data have been taken)

- Data for reports of authority figures such as name of ministers, government officers and departments.
- Statements given be field experts such as NGQs, scientists, academicians, etc.

Guidelines for Writing a Report

- Always provide a short and clear headline or title to the report.
- Be factual and provide only necessary information. Be unbiased
- Arrange the data given in the brief in a logical and a coherent order.
- Follow the correct format in your report
- Do not write your name in the report. Use XYZ or PQR as your name.

■ Sample Question

Write report on the following in about 200 words. **10 Marks**

Implementation of National Rural Health Mission (NRHM) in your district

SAMPLE REPORT

Implementation of National Rural Health Mission (NRHM) in your district

By ABC

21st August, 20XX, XYZ

The National Rural Health Mission (NRHM) was launched by the Prime Minister on 12th April, 2005, to provide accessible, affordable and quality health care to the rural population, especially the vulnerable groups. The essence of NRHM is a health delivery system that functions independently, is community-owned and decentralised.

The mission that aimed to deliver constant support to those who contribute to the social determinants of health found success in PQR district, XYZ.

The mission brought Accredited Social Health Activists ASHA volunteers who made the people aware of some common maladies and also suggested ways to prevent them. Some of them opened medical centers who could be contacted any time of the day for medical help. These institutions provided provisions of a range of free services related to maternal health, child health, adolescent health, family planning, universal immunisation programme and for major diseases such as Tuberculosis, vector borne diseases like Malaria, Dengue and Kala Azar, Leprosy, etc. The mission also brought Auxiliary Nurse Midwives (ANMs) to some deprived villages.

These ANMs carried Stethoscope, blood pressure measuring equipment, weighing mission to provide antenatal care and other related health care services to the mother and child.

One of the major undertaking of the mission was that it trained the Panchayat Raj Institutions (PRIs) to own, control and manage public health services and creates Village Health Committees to support public health management system.

With this, health became an important criterion of good living amongst the villagers which is a small step. But these small steps bring a positive change.

Sources

- The National Rural Health Mission (NRHM) Report
- Citizens of PQR district

Practice EXERCISE

Directions (Q. Nos. 1-15) *Write reports on the following in about 200 words each. Do not mention any name or address in the report, use XYZ/ABC if needed.*

1. 5G: Beginning of A New Era of Connectivity

By ABC

21st August, 20XX, XYZ

Every minute worldwide, an average of over 4 million videos are viewed on YouTube, 2 million Snapchats are sent and 50,000 photos are posted on Instagram. In a few years, connectivity has progressed at an astonishing pace and has taken hold of all aspects of human life. Wireless communication has now become an integral part of all parts of our lives, from connected refrigerators to locking our homes, road safety to remote open-heart operations.

The rapidly developing means of technology and communication promises instant and omnipresent data. To fulfill this promise, a new 5G network finally had reached a point of success. 5G, as one can easily gather, is the 5th generation mobile network after 1G, 2G, 3G and 4G networks. It is a new global wireless standard network that is designed to connect virtually everyone and everything together including machines, objects and devices.

5G network will provide very high bandwidth, increasing the maximum bandwidth of 4G from 1 Gbit/s to 10 Gbit/s. This will enable users to download an 8GB High Definition (HD) movie in about 6 seconds, whereas with 4G LTE, it can take almost 7 minutes and with 3G almost 70 minutes at peak speeds. Higher performance and improved efficiency means that the network will deliver higher multi-Gbps peak data speeds, ultra-low latency, more reliability, massive network capacity, increased availability, and a more uniform user experience to more users.

With 5G networks, one can certainly see a significant improvement in the field of cloud telephony and the internet phone system. 5G not only facilitates a smoother connection and prevents network delays but also improves the user experience and eliminates any factor that affects the bottom line. It will also aid you to make sure that the data transmitted over the 5G network is secure while also strengthening the network endpoints.

Concluding, the 5G network will create significant change and enable innovations. The potential for vast improvements in connectivity through 5G will have an impact on all aspects of our lives. However, these promises will only be fulfilled if the hardware, software and human architecture that support 5G delivers an extremely high level of data security and reliability for the services offered.

Sources

- News reports and blogs
- Expert opinions
- Ministry of Communication of India

2. Digital Banking in India

By ABC

21st August, 20XX, XYZ

Virtually every aspect of our life has been impacted by the rapid digitalisation of recent years. The shift in India toward a cashless economy is one of the most recent implications.

India's economy is transitioning to a cashless society, beginning with the overnight note ban of circulation of notes with the denominations of 500 and 1000 rupees that was implemented in November 2016.

To put it another way, less paper transactions will be made, and more digital ones will occur, thanks to internet banking, digital wallets, point-of-sale devices, credit and debit cards, etc. As digital banking has found its way in India, the nation's economy is moving towards becoming completely cashless.

At the moment, UPI is the most popular type of digital banking. By using a virtual payment address (VPA), UPI enables users to send money without providing their bank account information or IFSC code. There are no time constraints on the 24/7 transfer and receipt of funds. BHIM, PhonePe and Google Pay are UPI-based apps available in India.

Further, mobile wallets have made it unnecessary to carry loose currency, enter CVV codes or recall four-digit card pins.

They save bank account and card information so users may simply add money to their wallets and pay for goods and services from other businesses who offer compatible applications. Paytm, Freecharge, Mobiwik and others are well-known mobile wallets.

With our mobile devices, now we have a one-stop shop for all kinds of operations, including paying bills, fees, transferring money, recharging, etc. It will also guarantee a 'black-money free India'.

While digitisation has brought many benefits, it is not free from problems. With to a surge in digital transactions, the cashless economy will experience a rise in the hacking of personal information such as credit and debit card numbers, PINs, passwords and other sensitive information over the internet. In other words, if appropriate internet security measures are not done, cybercrimes will increase like anything else.

Thus, the path to digitisation has begun and is progressing at a fast pace in India.

Sources

- News Reports
- Expert opinions
- Department of Financial Services

3. Need to Ban Liquor Shops

By ABC

21st August, 20XX, XYZ

When people think about alcohol, they think about a strong colourless liquid that is the intoxicating constituent of many hard drinks.

Liquor is often considered as a luxurious commodity that has become one of the major contributors of not just economy but also death and disease. Hence, it is widely used and abused by many people all over the world.

Looking at the increasing number of negatives many states including Gujarat, Bihar, Nagaland and Manipur and the Union Territory of Lakshadweep have welcomed the move of banning liquor shops. Such a move is highly appreciated as it will help to promote the physical and mental well-being of society in general.

Drinking and continued alcohol consumption cause many health problems. People who abuse alcohol develop several problems affecting not only his family but also the society. It not only decreases the productivity of an individual and increases family problems but is also one of the major causes of broken relationships. People who drink heavily develop a physical and emotional dependency on alcohol.

Even though many people argue that alcohol consumption should be legal to the older population health care experts have raised concerns over the misuse of alcohol among teenagers during entertainment. Many teenagers die while driving under the influence of alcohol. Not just that alcohol also contributes to a larger percentage of crimes and road rage.

There is no doubt that alcohol is the leading cause of public disorder in the modern society. The government has imposed complete ban for a social cause to create an alcohol-free environment.

Through this ban they hopes to improve the standard of living. While promoting good health and productive economy. It also reduces the incidents of road rage. It is thus, commendable that the government is ready to forgo the revenue from liquour shops. Thus the government should be appreciated and applauded.

Sources

- State reports
- Expert opinions
- National Institute of Health

4. Application based Services

By ABC

21st August, 20XX, XYZ

A while back, the online and offline worlds were vastly different. With many technological changes, the barrier between online and offline is fast blurring as e-commerce, particularly mobile e-commerce, grows in popularity. However, this blurring became distinct as life came to a standstill during the COVID-19 pandemic.

There are applications and online services available for any type of need that a person might have. There are food delivery applications which have changed the dining experience for many. Ready-to-eat food delivery has emerged as a significant market thanks to the development of enticing, user-friendly apps and tech-enabled driver networks, as well as shifting consumer expectations. Further, most of these food delivery apps have also started delivering groceries and other essential items.

Nowadays, taxi apps have begun to surpass traditional taxi services and people have started to shift from personally-owned transportation modes toward mobility solutions as a service (MaaS). This has also made car-pooling easier which can relieve traffic congestion and better air quality. Not only that, app based ride-hailing services are more secure and safe given the GPS-enabled in-app location sharing.

These days, a variety of services, including AC servicing, cleaning and repair, refrigerator repair, washing machine repair, plumbing repair, electrician repair and home cleaning, are just a click away. Applications like these offer a one-stop shop where local businesses and consumers can handle all of their household service needs.

These are just some of the many application based services which is emerging today. These applications are becoming the new fad for the many benefits that they offer. They provide an ease of doing business as one can work from anyplace at any time. It not only creates employment opportunities but is also cost and time effective. For business, it brings a larger profit as the owners do not have to spend a fortune on marketing and advertising. Consumers get huge discounts on services along with a faster reddressal of demands and grievance. They also get a quick and easy support which makes these services much more preferable.

One may wonder if application based services have any negative impacts. There have been concerns of safety and exploitation but they are only rare. So, it important for us to know that while the growth of application based services is inevitable, it is importance for us to use it in a productive and a positive manner.

Sources

- Ministry of Communication and Information Technology
- News reports

5. Admission Tests for Undergraduate Courses

By ABC

21st August, 20XX, XYZ

A new trend has developed in the process of admission for professional courses in some colleges. This is the written entrance test, which is necessary to be cleared before any candidate is called for counselling. Some candidates and their parents feel that it is totally unnecessary because admission to other courses does not need any entrance test.

They think that it would result in being too strict for students opting for such a course.

The debate regarding the trend came after it was announced that The University of Delhi, along with 41 other central varsities, is conducting CUET with the help of the National Testing Agency (NTA). Students will be admitted to undergraduate programmes based on their performance in the online exam. Each university will release its separate merit list based on the marks obtained by students.

According to many educationalists, such tests are required for many reasons. It is said that the aptitude of students for a subject or profession is never tested in schools. Clearing the Board exams does not reveal the true potential of the child, as they can be passed by rote learning in most cases. Instead, entrance tests try to bring out the student's true capabilities. Only those students who are serious about the course will prepare and take the tests. So, these entrance tests for professional courses are necessary and should be introduced by all colleges offering professional courses.

Sources

- Ministry of Human Resource Development
- National Testing Agency

6. Crisis of Ethics in the Game of Cricket

By ABC

21st August, 20XX, XYZ

It is surprising to see that the sports which is considered another religion and is seen as a 'gentleman's game' was accused of unfair play and unethical practices. Cricket took a beating when the match-fixing scandal erupted in 2000 and the sport is still reeling from the aftermath. The revelations made in the scandal brought fair play and ethics at the center of cricket and lead to disillusionment among millions of fans and causing the game's integrity to be questioned.

Though there was already doubt that illegal Indian bookies were trying to influence players and games, Delhi Police stunned the global game when it filed a case on 7th April against some cricketers charging them with cheating and criminal conspiracy.

The officials found texts and conversations that brought out the dishonesty of many international cricketers. The data revealed match fixing, a term denoting influencing performance in games to go in a certain direction in return of money. The scandal brought a crisis as further probes found not some but many international iconic players to be unfair and unethical in their game.

As a result of the scandal, all sports and players are highly scrutinised for any such unethical practices. If a sportsperson is found guilty, he/she is immediately debarred from playing.

Sources

- Delhi Police
- Expert opinion

7. Skill Development : The need of the Hour

By ABC

21st August, 20XX, XYZ

India is one of the fastest growing economies but according a recent research by Tata Institute of Social Science, India is also one of the countries whose growth is hindered by unskilled workforce. The survey mentioned that more than 35% of the Indian youth in cities are unskilled. This makes by companies and as a result the job is filled in by others. The status of Indian villages is even worse. More than 75% of the Indian youth in villages are struggling because of lack of skills. Basically, it needs to be clearly understood that mere educational certificates will not suffice. Men have to accept the fact that it's not about how many thick and complicated books that one has read. The news era demands skill the ability to produced productive output. And productive output is possible only when skills are enhanced along with proceeding age.

It is now necessary for the government to make more and more awareness campaigns about initiatives like 'Skill India' and other such courses experience is the only thing that can help India overcome such a situation. Let's walk forward to make India skilled.

Sources

- Tata institute of Social Sciences
- Government of India

8. Solar Power : Solution to Energy Crises

By ABC

21st August, 20XX, XYZ

In the modern world where population and requirements are always increasing, the demand for energy has been on a constant rise. In this light, it is not unknown to us that our conventional sources of energy are depleting at an alarming rate. Consequently, the need of the hour to switch to renewable energy sources has time and again been taken up. Finally, we have a solution : solar power.

Solar power or Solar energy is the most abundant and readily available source of energy on Earth. As a renewable source of energy, solar power offers various benefits to its users. First, it helps to reduce energy bills significantly. Once the initial installation cost is covered, solar energy is virtually free. Second solar energy is completely clean and creates no pollution.

It is carbon free and emits no harmful gases. Hence, it is environmentally friendly and sustainable. Furthermore, solar energy requires low maintenance. It only needs to be cleaned periodically to remove dust and dirt. It is a one-time investment that has long-term benefits. Solar panels have a lifespan of 20-30 years they can be used to generate electricity for a long period.

To conclude, solar power is an apt global solution for the energy crisis. It is renewable. environmen-friendly and cost effective.

Governments and individuals must take necessary steps towards shifting to solar power to ensure a sustainable and greener future. It is high time we realised the importance of renewable energy sources and take action towards creating a brighter and cleaner future.

Sources

- Wikipedia
- Ministry of New and Renewable Energy

9. Waste Management Infrastructure

By ABC

21st August, 20XX, XYZ

Management of waste is an important facet of environment protection and conservation. A lack of proper waste disposal facilities and equipment can pose risk to environment, human and wildlife health, as well as property. Management and proper disposal of waste is a major environmental concern in India that has only been made worse by growing urbanisation. According to a Central Pollution Control Report, the total waste produced in a day in Mumbai was 6500 tonnes, in Delhi was 5800 tonnes and in Kolkata was 3670 tonnes.

Improper waste management is the cause of a plethora of problems we face today. Decomposition of waste produces methane which is not only a leading cause of global warming but is a highly combustible substance. It hence increases the likelihood of localised explosions and uncontrolled fires. Heaps of waste present in the open are breeding grounds for infectious microbes, flies and mosquitoes. Pathogens can also mix with potable water or contaminate the water table. These factors combined can lead to epidemics in pockets of a city. Often, people resort to burning of waste in such cases which increases the level of harmful pollutants in the air, further causing respiratory issues.

To maintain urban centers clean, local authorities throughout the nation offer solid waste management wherein they randomly dispose of solid trash to a dumpyard either inside or on the outskirts of a city. This system for managing and disposing of waste is essentially defective.

Local bodies and municipalities need to take responsibility for waste management, with the heads of such organisations taking command over waste management systems. There needs to be sustainable and suitable financing for waste management systems which will only happen if Indian society deems waste management as a necessary, indispensable and crucial service.

In addition to investments, there also needs to be strict enforcement of rules and regulations for the common public since littering is a serious issue in India. A waste tax, like the Swach Bharat Cess implemented in 2015, can lead to collection of significant funds that, if utilised properly, can improve and provide effective waste management infrastructure throughout India.

Waste management just needs a strategic system to be implemented. With it, not only will we have a cleaner surrounding but also a healthier environment to live in.

Sources

- Central Pollution Control Report
- Swach Bharat Cess Survey Report

10. Threats to the Environment

By ABC

21st August, 20XX, XYZ

Environmental degradation is one of the most pressing issues of our time. Threats to the environment are becoming more serious by the day which may not only cause irreversible environmental damage but also adversely affect the quality of life of all life forms.

Increased human activity, vehicular pollution, and industrial waste introduce harmful elements in the environment. These also lead to an increase in the levels of carbon dioxide and other greenhouse gasses which trap the radiation and heat of the Sun in the atmosphere. As a result, global temperatures are higher, unpredictable weather patterns are becoming common, habitats and ecosystems are destroyed and oceans too now are warmer. Overhunting and poaching are also increasing the threat of endangered species going extinct. Further, to meet the energy demands of a growing population, the levels of naturally occurring resources like gas, oil, coal, petrol are depleting fast.

Given the rate at which the environment is deteriorating, it is imperative that large scale changes are initiated to stop any more damage. However, small scale changes can always begin at home. One can inculcate mindfulness in using resources like water, electricity and petrol. Not being wasteful of these resources can reduce several adverse effects. Frequent use of public transport, odd-even vehicle use and carpooling are some ways in which vehicular emissions can be controlled and reduced. Using cloth bags and biodegradable carry bags as well as packaging can significantly lessen the threats posed by plastic.

Since, climate change is a global-level phenomenon, concerted efforts by countries all over the world has become the need of the hour. Afforestation, awareness and policy changes to reduce environmental threats can set the path to undoing the damage that has already been done. More countries need to come forward with a strong commitment to stop the ticking time bomb that is climate change. There needs to be a serious consideration of the fact that there is no planet B. A failure to control environmental threats and hazards may lead to extreme and inhabitable conditions for human beings. It may trigger tipping points and undo all progress that mankind has made so far.

Sources

- Environmentalist opinions
- Ministry of Environment

11. The Grand Pran Pratishtha in Ayodhya

By ABC

21st August, 20XX, XYZ

The grand Pran Pratishtha ceremony in Ayodhya was a historic moment for India's cultural and religious landscape, signifying the end of the long process that had been needed to rebuild Ram Mandir at Ram Janmabhoomi. Held on 22nd January, 2024, the awaited event was graced by the Prime Minister of India Narendra Modi, who inaugurated it along with millions of devotees from various parts of the country.

The importance of the Pran Pratishtha ceremony could not be exaggerated as this is what countless Hindus have been waiting for all over the world. For decades, the site where Ram Janmabhoomi is situated, has been subject to prolonged legal and socio-political wrangles. In a background that had seen emotional turmoil amongst thousands of India, the temple and its inauguration is seen as an expression of the resilience, faith and unity of the Hindus residing in India.

The ceremony itself was one big spectacle showing 'bhakti' (devotion) and reverence with priests and spiritual leaders performing elaborate ceremonies to purify the temple and invite Lord Rama's presence there.

Chanting Vedic hymns, pouring oblations into sacrificial fire, installing consecrated idols were some ways through which they ensured that the temple had divine power. The Pran Pratishtha ceremony was also attended by political leaders and celebrities who hailed it as a significant milestone in the cultural and civilisational journey of the nation.

This is a new era of religious concordance signified by Pran Pratishtha wherein Indian culture is rejuvenated; national unity is being sought after again hence reviving India as a country whose character could be traced through various traditions deeply rooted in spirituality over centuries.

Sources

- News reports

12. Rise of Electric Vehicle in India

By ABC

21st August, 20XX, XYZ

India is a country with one of the biggest automobile markets in the world and the growing number of electric vehicles (EVs) represents a significant shift towards sustainable transport. This past decade, India has seen escalating usage and recognition of EVs, pushed by government regulations, technological improvements and an increasing environmental awareness among customers.

The Economic Survey 2023 predicts that India's domestic electric vehicle market will see a 49% Compound Annual Growth Rate (CAGR) between 2022 and 2030, with 10 million annual sales by 2030.

This prediction heavily relies on the government's decision to encourage cleaner fuels and automobiles to meet the COP28 commitments. The government's initiatives and policies that are targeted at promoting electric mobility have been instrumental in driving this increase.

The Faster Adoption and Manufacturing of Hybrid and Electric Vehicles (FAME) Scheme launched in 2015 extended provides financial incentives, subsidies and tax breaks for both hybrid vehicle manufacturers and also buyers. With these incentives up to 30% can be taken off EV's initial costs which attract more people.

Furthermore, ambitious goals have been set by governments in relation to electric vehicle uptake with a target of attaining an electric vehicle penetration rate of 30% within the country's automotive market by 2030. Such targets led to investments as well as innovations being made in the EV sector leading to development of new technologies as well as infrastructure meant for support purposes on electric mobility.

The growing sophistication of batteries especially in the area of lithium-ion high-energy density has made electric vehicles more usable and affordable. This can include battery technology that allows for longer driving ranges as well as shorter charging periods, with which problems like range anxiety and lack of charging network can be addressed. In addition, firms from various countries teamed up to make the establishment of EV manufacturing plants possible.

India's future in electric vehicles appears bright as seen by a government committed to this directive and an industry undergoing rapid technological strides. Eventually, as infrastructure develops and the EV eco-system matures, these vehicles are expected to have a large presence in the Indian transportation system thus providing an environmentally sustainable alternative to conventional gas-powered cars.

India's adoption of electric vehicles points towards its commitment to reducing carbon emissions, improving air quality and sustaining growth. Further support from the government would see technology advancements take place and more uptake among consumers who would adopt them into their daily commute hence leading India towards cleaner greener future.

Sources

- Road and Transport Ministry
- Economic Survey 2023
- Scientists opinion

13. Legalising Same Sex Marriage

By ABC

21st August, 20XX, XYZ

On 17th October, 2023, India's Supreme Court declined to legalise same-sex unions, dashing the hopes of millions of LGBTQ+ people seeking marriage equality. The controversial decision of the Supreme Court is a major decision disappointing many who were hoping for an egalitarian society which respects every individual irrespective of their choices. The same-sex marriage legalisation in India is a major step towards equality and justice for the LGBTQ+ community in India. Inspite of its historical evidence which points to the presence of same sex relationships, Indian has been grappling with stigmatisation, prejudice, discrimination as well as legal issues which affect the LGBTQ+ community.

Currently, same-sex marriages are not recognised anywhere on Indian soil. Indian Penal Code Section 377, which prohibited consensual sexual acts between people of the same sex was overturned by the Supreme Court of India in 2018 through a landmark judgment. However, this ruling did not explicitly address the matter of gay marriage. The push to legalise same sex marriage in India faces many challenges such as deeply entrenched social cultural norms that do not favour homosexuality.

By legalising same-sex marriages, India would not only affirm the rights and dignity of the LGBTQ+ individuals, but it would also be seen as marking an important milestone in India's journey towards more inclusivity and acceptance. This would have far-reaching consequences for LGBT individuals and their families. This will result in formal recognition of their relationships including inheritance rights, property ownership rights and healthcare rights among others.

To make sure same-sex marriage will be allowed in India, there is a need for continuous advocacy, dialogue and legislative action. Thus, even if the progress is slow or gradual it is important to keep sensitising people, fighting against the unfair laws and promoting those changes that would be beneficial both for human beings rights and dignity regardless of who they are.

Legalising same sex marriages in India acts as a major move towards equality, dignity and justice among LGBTQ+ members. Inclusivity, acceptance principles affirming this milestone would go down as a landmark on India's path towards constructing a more just society where all its citizens can feel valued. So therefore, as the country transforms itself further and celebrates diversity more significantly than ever before; recognition of same sex marriages becomes an essential part of ensuring that every individual gets equal opportunities to succeed in life.

Sources

- Supreme Court Releases
- BBC releases
- Sociologists opinion

14. Cop28: Key Outcomes and Analysis

By ABC

21st August, 20XX, XYZ

The United Nations Framework Convention on Climate Change (UNFCCC) Conference of Parties 28 OR COP 28 UN Climate Change Conference ended on a momentous note with the first 'global stocktake' of the world's efforts to address climate change under the Paris Agreement. Held in Dubai, the United Arab Emirates with about 85,000 participants including more than 150 Heads of State and Government, the, Conference from 30th November to 13th December, 2023.

COP 28 closed with an agreement that signals the 'beginning of the end' of the fossil fuel era by laying the ground for a swift, just and equitable transition, underpinned by deep emissions cuts and scaled-up finance. As COP 28 President Dr Sultan Al Jaber pointed to the direction of travel in the energy transition, and that the scale and pace of change can't be stopped or reversed. The 'global stocktake' contains every element that was under negotiation and can now be used by countries to develop stronger climate action plans due by February 2025. The stocktake recognises the science that indicates global greenhouse gas emissions need to be cut 43% by 2030, compared to 2019 levels, to limit global warming to 1.5°C.

The two-week-long conference got underway with a historic agreement on the operationalisation of funding arrangements for addressing loss and damage, including a new dedicated fund under the UNFCCC – the first time a substantive decision was adopted on the first day of the conference.

The establishment of the fund, with commitments totalling USD 661 million to date, is an important symbol of global solidarity reflecting both the urgency of the climate emergency and a step forward in international climate justice.

Parties also agreed on targets for the Global Goal on Adaptation (GGA) and its framework. It reflects a global consensus on adaptation targets and covers the themes of water, food, health, ecosystems, infrastructure, poverty eradication and cultural heritage.

The Green Climate Fund (GCF) received a boost to its second replenishment with six countries pledging new funding at COP28 with total pledges now standing at a record USD 12.8 billion from 31 countries, with further contributions expected.

Further, discussions continued on setting a 'new collective quantified goal on climate finance' in 2024, taking into account the needs and priorities of developing countries. The new goal, which will start from a baseline of USD 100 billion per year, will help support the implementation of a new round of national climate plans that need to be designed and submitted by early 2025.

All the decided efforts are to be aligned with the goals of the Kunming-Montreal Global Biodiversity Framework, which was agreed at the 15th meeting of the Conference of the Parties (COP 15) to the UN Convention on Biological Diversity in Montreal, Canada in December 2022.

Among these, many other decisions were undertaken to solve the climate crisis. Regarding the unprecedented problems brought by global warming, COP conferences have a crucial place in driving forward to a more sustainable, fairer future that is stable enough for everyone.

Sources

- The United Nations Framework Convention on Climate Change (UNFCCC)
- COP 28 President Dr Sultan Al Jaber
- UN Climate Change Executive Secretary Simon Stiell

15. Impact of Social Media on National Security

By ABC
21st August, 20XX, XYZ

The internet is the largest experiment involving anarchy in history. 'It is a source for tremendous good and potentially dreadful evil, and we are only just beginning to witness its impact on the world stage.' - Eric Schmidt, Executive Chairman, Google and Jared Cohen, Director, Google Ideas

Social networking sites have changed the manner in which information is passed on, thus promoting instantaneous interaction and global connectedness. Nonetheless, as much as social media brings with it countless advantages, its influence on national security has become a major concern for governments, policymakers and security agencies around the globe. The impacts of social media are so wide-ranging as they head from influencing public opinion to enabling cyber-attacks.

One of the most important ways in which social media influences national security is through shaping public discourse and opinion. These platforms are tools that can be used to quickly disseminate news, opinions and narratives. However, this freedom of expression also makes it vulnerable to exploitation by malevolent parties intending to spread misinformation or propaganda. In the scope of national security, dissemination of false or misleading information can undermine trust among citizens, divide people and even manipulate public sentiment (including political sentiments), hence threatening democratic institutions and societal unity.

Risks of cyber security are another thing that social media presents in addition to influencing people's opinions as well as promoting radicalism. Today, through the use of social media, criminals organise attacks on critical government infrastructure and private companies. The extent of threats posed by social media range from hacking email accounts and scattering malware to coordinating cyber espionage operations. In fact, the inter-connectedness that defines these sites makes it easier for non-state actors and other individuals to interfere with national security operations and destabilise democratic processes.

The impact of social media on national security necessitates a multi-dimensional approach. Governments and their agencies have to create strong national strategies geared towards detecting and preventing threats that emerge from online platforms such as Facebook, Twitter among others. This will involve investment in emerging technologies as well as advanced analytical tools designed to arrest or disrupt cybercrime activities occurring online too often today.

Law enforcement agencies across the globe are using a superior form of "Open Source Intelligence" to engage, collate, analyse and predict, and share intelligence using data gleaned from social media networks, also known as Social Media Intelligence (SOCMINT). With all the measures, it is hoped that social media threats are bound to reduce making the internet a safe place for all.

Sources

- Eric Schmidt, Executive Chairman, Google
- Jared Cohen, Director, Google Ideas
- R. Gupta and H. Brooks, Using Social Media for Global Security

Previous Years' QUESTIONS

Directions (Q. Nos. 1-20) *Write reports on the following in about 200 words each. Do not mention any name or address in the report, use XYZ/ABC if needed.*

1. Voter Turnout in an Election **CAPF AC 2024**

By XYZ (Staff Reporters of West Bengal)
Place : ABC
8th August, 2024

Voters turnout is a crucial factor of domestic elections that indigates citizen engagement and the legitimacy of the electoral process. This report investigates the factors influencing voters turnout, its significance and strategies to improve participation. The factors that affects voter turnout indeed are

1. **Demographics** That displays the age, education, income and employment status and its impact.
2. **Political Engagement** That denotes interest, efficacy and satisfaction with government influence participation.
3. **Electoral Systems** That mainly signifies the proportional representation, voter registration and voting methods affect turnout. However social unrest, cultural factors also impact voter participation.

Sometimes high turnout validates election that results election results and government authority. Accountability of voter's turnover encourages elected officials to respond to constituent needs and in the context of democratic health. That indicates citizen, engagement and trust in the democratic process.

In the context of Lok Sabha Election 2024, 65.79% turnout in Lok Sabha polls, according to a report published by Election Commission.

Lakshadweep recorded the highest voter turnout at 84 followed by Assam (81%) and the lowest turnout was recorded in Bihar at 56.19%, UP (56.92%) and Mizoram (56.87%).

And the last Lok Sabha election saw a total voter's turnout of 65.79%. And the final voters turnout of 2019 Lok Sabha was 67.40%.

Mr. Kumar, alongwith two other ECs met President Draupadi Murmu and submitted the list of MPs elected to the 18th Lok Sabha.

Voter turnout is critical to democratic electrons, influenced by several factors. And we are looking forward to strengthen democratic legitimacy, representation and accountability by addressing these factors and implementing strategies to improve participation.

Sources

- Election Commission
- Wikipedia

2. Rehabilitation of War Victims — CAPF AC 2024

By XYZ (Staff Reporters of West Bengal)

Place : ABC

8th August, 2024

War leaves profound scars on individuals and communities, causing physical, psychological and social trauma. So, rehabilitation of war is a dynamic process aimed at restoring their health, dignity and functionality. This reports talks about various aspects of rehabilitation including medical, psychological and social interventions and highlights the importance of a holistic approach to recovery.

Physical Rehabilitation focuses on treating injuries and disabilities caused by war that includes Medical treatment, prosthetics and orthotics (providing artificial limbs and supportive devices to help victims) physiotherapy and psychological rehabilitation is the most profound and needed treatment that a post-war era actually demands. Psychological impact leaves the deepest scars in the mind of war victims that often leads to condition like PTS, depression and anxiety.

And the key components that become essential to overcome these phases are

- Counselling and therapy
- Support Groups or peer
- Mental Health Education and Counselling

Also integrating war victims into society is also crucial for their comprehensive recovery. That mainly focuses on

- **Vocational Training** That provides skills to the victims and help them to become self-sufficient.
- **Education** That ensures access to education for children and adults affected by war.

Rehabilitation efforts generally face numerous challenges, including limited resources, ongoing conflict and cultural barriers. Additionally commitment and sustainable funding are crucial for successful rehabilitation programmes.

In response of recent ongoing conflict between Ukraine and Russia, the world witnessed several losses. So, as a rehabilitation programme ERP (Emergency Response Plan) of the FAO tried to manage US 150 million to assist 8,21,050 people of war victims.

Rehabilitation is a complex process itself that generally requires a comprehensive approach. By addressing the medical, psychological and social needs of war survivors, we can help them rebuild their lives and contribute the recovery and stability of their families.

Sources

- United Nations
- World Bank

3. Depletion of Water Table Levels in Major Cities — CAPF AC 2023

By ABC

3rd September, 20XX, XYZ

There's nothing more essential to life on Earth than water. However, the UNESCO United Nations World Water Development Report of 2023 has encapsulated global concern over the sharp rise in freshwater withdrawal from streams, lakes, aquifers and human-made reservoirs, impending water stress and also water scarcity being experienced in different parts of the world.

One of the reasons for the same is the depletion in the water table.

A water table can be defined as an underground boundary where atmospheric pressure and water pressure are equal. It is the boundary between the soil surface and areas of sediments and rocks where groundwater gets saturated. Depletion of the water table means a significant reduction in the amount of groundwater as the rate of underwater withdrawal is much higher than the water seeps into the soil and recharges the aquifers.

Besides over withdrawal, deforestation, irregular climate conditions, increased agricultural needs and decreased recharging time of aquifers are some of the many reasons for the depletion of the water table.

Several steps have been taken by the Indian government to control and stop this depletion. For instance, the Government of India launched Jal Shakti Abhiyan (JSA) in 2019, a time bound campaign intended to improve water availability including ground water conditions in the water stressed blocks of 256 districts in India. In this regard, teams of officers from Central Government along-with technical officers from Ministry of Jal Shakti were deputed to visit water stressed districts and to work in close collaboration with district level officials to undertake suitable interventions. The citizens of the nation can also lend a hand in resolving this issue. More trees can be planted to get sufficient amount of rainfall and over pumping of the ground can be stopped.

Sources

- UNESCO United Nations World Water Development Report of 2023
- Ministry of Jal Shakti

4. Increasing Presence of Women in Indian Sports

CAPF AC 2023

by ABC

3rd September, 20XX, XYZ

"Woman is the builder and moulder of a nation's destiny. Though delicate and soft as a lily, she has a heart, far stronger and bolder than that of a man..."

— Dr Rabindranath Tagore

Women have proven to be equals and in some cases, even better than men. It is indeed remarkable considering the many restrictions that are placed on one half of mankind. Despite the discrimination, however, it has been witnessed that many women are participating in initially male-dominated fields like sports.

Female athletes have finally received recognition as a result of their perseverance, hard work and desire to prove themselves. Perhaps, women's incredible progress is a wonderful result of their commitment and aspirations. Sports have the ability to transform lives, the capacity to promote gender equality by instilling in women and girls the values of cooperation, independence, fortitude and self-assurance.

Women, who excel in athletics challenge gender conventions and prejudices, serve as positive role models and promote equality for both sexes. Sania Mirza, Mary Kom, Mithali Raj, PV Sindhu, Saina Nehwal and more female athletes have made the country proud with their illustrious triumphs in a variety of sports. They have moved beyond the realm of athletics that was formerly controlled by males.

Women have battled their way out of the dominant society throughout the years. They have achieved success in their lives despite being marginalised thanks to their consistent perseverance and will to succeed. Women have made a significant presence in the sports business and their persistence has paid off.

Sources

- Department of Women and Child Development, Government of India
- Sociologist, PQR

5. Evidences of Fellow Feeling During the COVID-19 pandemic.

CAPF AC 2022

By XYZ

17th August, 20XX, ABC

The Covid-19 pandemic saw the worst and the best come out of each individual, and every organisation and country. On one hand, we faced financial crisis, loss of lives, rise in mental health problems and an overall aggressive behaviour, on the other, we saw an emergence of sympathy and understanding for the suffering of others.

From a single case of the pandemic reported in China in 2019 to suffering the 3 consecutive waves, the world is still reeling from the shock. Even after following the various WHO guidelines as well as the guidelines given by the Ministry of Health and Family Welfare in India, the world was devastated. Yet cooperation on both global and local levels became a powerful tool to combat this devastation. Many people went an extra mile to help others. Take, for instance, medical professionals, who put their lives on the line to treat and care for the diseased. Many doctors even lost their lives in this process.

This is a ground level example of a much bigger feeling of fellowship that was demonstrated by several nations. India, for instance, provided vaccine assistance to more than 90 countries including Nepal, Bangladesh, Myanmar, Iran, Maldives, Brazil and Egypt, under its Vaccine Maitri initiative. The nation also gifted 200,000 doses of Covid-19 vaccine to the UN Peacekeepers to be distributed.

Correspondingly, several countries came forward to help India during the second wave of Covid-19, providing medicines and equipment including oxygen cylinders, ventilators (BiPAPs), which were not immediately available in the country. The US, for instance, sent several shipments of relief material, and the UK sent many oxygen concentrators to India. This goes to show the extent of empathy and fellowship a human being feels for another and proves that in a crisis situation, we stand together. It should be ensured that this camaraderie extends beyond the pandemic we faced.

Sources

- Ministry of Health and Family Welfare in India
- World Health Organisation

6. Green Energy Progress in India

CAPF AC 2022

By XYZ

22nd August, 20XX, ABC

In the world battered by ecological imbalance and dwindling resources, the need for better sustainable alternative sources of energy had become a necessity. The recently held 26th Climate Change Conference by the United Nations highlighted the climate change thrust and the need to shift to green energy. Consequently, all nations across the world have been taking up the task of finding green energy resources and India is among the top to do so. As of 2020, India ranks fourth in wind power, fifth in hydroelectric power, fifth in solar power and fourth in renewable power installed capacity. The country is targeting about 450 Gigawatt (GW) of installed renewable energy capacity by 2030 and about 280 GW (over 60%) is expected from solar. Additionally, India initiated the International Solar Alliance (ISA), an alliance of 121 countries. India is world's first country to set-up a ministry of non-conventional energy resources (Ministry of New and Renewable Energy (MNRE) in early 1980s.

India also announced that it aims to reach net zero emissions by 2070, which is a significant decision in the world's fight against climate change. India already has a numerous policy measures in place that – if fully implemented – could address some of these challenges by accelerating the shift to cleaner and more efficient technologies.

Subsidies for petrol and diesel were removed in the early 2010s, and subsidies for electric vehicles were introduced in 2019. India's robust energy efficiency programme has been successful in reducing energy use and emissions from buildings, transport and major industries. Government efforts to provide millions of households with fuel gas for cooking and heating are enabling a steady transition away from the use of traditional biomass, such as burning wood.

As such, a large developing economy with over 1.3 billion people, India's climate adaptation and mitigation ambitions are not just transformational for India but for the entire planet. Several organisations are in place to aid the nation's green energy progress.

Sources

- Ministry of New and Renewable Energy
- COP26, United Nations Conference on Climate Change

7. Oxygen Cylinders Crisis in Delhi — CAPF AC 2021

By XYZ
14th May, 20XX, ABC

The month of April and May 20XX saw many deaths all over the nation due to the lack of beds and oxygen cylinders in the hospital. The oxygen crisis in Delhi has been unprecedented as many COVID-19 patients died without oxygen support while several met their demise because of oxygen shortage. By the 1st of May, 20XX, Delhi had already reported more than 20,000 new infections and hundreds of death.

None of the hospitals had enough tankers and the government failed to meet their needs till the 29th of April. It was only when the crisis had reached its peak and received media attention that hospitals were provided with oxygen.

The reason for this crisis is still up for debate. According to the government, the fixed quota of oxygen was just 300MT. The Delhi Government said that it did not receive enough cylinders from the Centre and even after the Supreme Court's directions to provide Delhi with 700 MT oxygen, only 71% of it was received.

Yet, its failure in providing the hospitals with oxygen cylinders and lack of any planning to do so has equally resulted in the crisis, if not more. In the end, it doesn't matter who was at fault, the loss of lives was regrettable. It remains to be seen how the authorities will manage the situation should it rise again.

Sources

- Delhi Government
- Ministry of Health and Family Welfare in India

8. Poll Violence in West Bengal — CAPF AC 2021

By XYZ
05th August, 20XX, ABC

Violence ensued in West Bengal after the announcement of the assembly election results in May. What followed was a horrifying image of death and destruction. Multiple houses were ransacked, several villages were attacked and many people were beaten and killed for no fault of theirs. The aftermath of the violence revealed that around 40 families in Jadavpur had fled due to the fear for their lives. Further, internal sources revealed that 17 political workers belonging from the political parties of BJP and TMC lost their lives in the violence that shook West Bengal.

The Calcutta HC asked the NHRC to look into the matter and the result was a report submitted in July that slammed the newly formed government for letting matters get out of hands, informing that many victims were being threatened seven days later. It also recommended a CBI probe to look into the matter. As the result, the case is now filed with more than 40 FIRs.

In defense, the newly formed TMC government said that the NHRC's report was biased, greatly exaggerated and also politically motivated. Currently, the court has reserved verdict in the matter while the citizens await justice and live in threat, away from their homes.

Sources

- Calcutta HC
- TMC government
- NHRC Report

9. Provisions for Primary Education Sector in the New Education Policy — CAPF AC 2020

By XYZ
21st September, 20XX, ABC

The old debate regarding the need of overhauling the traditional system of education to meet the need of market demand came to a stop with the revelation of the New National Educational Policy 2020 by the Ministry of Education (earlier Ministry of Human Resource Development (MHRD)) on Wednesday, 29th July. The new policy is a landmark decision that seeks to introduce and implement a sea of changes across all levels of education in India, including the essential understanding of education in the country.

It also seeks to implement changes in the way the facilitators of education – schools, colleges and teachers – are trained and how they approach education. The policy, based on the pillars of 'access, equity, quality, affordability, accountability', aims to transform India into a 'vibrant knowledge hub' with a great focus on primary education.

In the new 5+3+3+4 structure of education, the policy makes primary schooling, the foundation of learning. Through various strategies, it hopes to create a strong base of Early Childhood Care and Education (ECCE) from age of 3 years onwards to promote better overall learning, development and well-being.

To do so, it calls for a flexible, multi-faceted, multi-level, play-based, activity-based and inquiry-based learning, comprising of alphabets, languages, numbers, counting, colours, shapes, indoor and outdoor play, puzzles and logical thinking, problem-solving, drawing, painting and other visual art, craft, drama and puppetry, music and movement.

This gives young children enables to participate and flourish in the educational system throughout their lives. The policy also directs the educators to focus on developing social capacities, sensitivity, good behaviour, courtesy, ethics, personal and public cleanliness, teamwork and cooperation.

The new ECCE shall be delivered through a significantly expanded and strengthened system of early-childhood education institutions consisting Anganwadis and pre-primary schools. Experts believe that the NEP 2020 combines all the aspects of schooling, and brought all levels of education under a single regulation. Such a change will be a turning point in our education system.

Sources

- NEP 2020
- Ministry of Education

10. Impact of the New Agricultural Laws on Farmers CAPF AC 2020

By XYZ

21st September, 20XX, ABC

In a landmark decision to liberalise and privatise the great agricultural sector of the economy, President Ram Nath Kovind gave his assent to three agriculture bills – The Farmers' Produce Trade and Commerce (Promotion and Facilitation) Bill, 2020, The Farmers (Empowerment and Protection) Agreement of Price Assurance and Farm Services Bill, 2020 and The Essential Commodities (Amendment) Bill, 2020 on, 27th September, 2020.

Together these three bills aim to eliminate the dangerous middlemen, facilitate better realisations for farmers, attract investment and enhance technology in the sector. The Farmers Produce Trade and Commerce (Promotion and Facilitation) Bill allowed farmers to sell outside of their designated districts APMC, thereby advancing their interaction with the market directly.

The Farmers (Empowerment and Protection) Agreement of Price Assurance and Farm Services Bill focused on creating avenues for farmers to engage in contract farming through verbal or written contracts. It essentially paved the way for farmers to access national and corporate markets. The Essential Commodities Act, 1955 deregulates the production, storage, movement and distribution of cereals, pulses, oilseeds, edible oils, onions and potatoes. Thus, with these bills, the Union government intended to double a farmer's current average monthly income while offering them the freedom of choice to sell their produce without restraint.

While the bills seem to benefit farmers, they have been opposed by several farmer organisations for various reasons. Some of the farmer organisations have called the acts corporate-friendly and anti-farmer and have expressed that the new acts may hurt the farmers' interests as there is a fear of losing government procurement at the Minimum Support Price.

With many such issues, the farm laws lead to a year-long battle between the government and the farmers who opposed to bills. Finally, in December 2022, the laws were formally repealed by the government.

Sources

- Government of India
- All India Kisan Sabha

11. The Rising Juvenile Abuse CAPF AC 2019

By XYZ

21st September, 20XX, ABC

Childhood is the most precious time of everyone's life. But the sad fact is that not every child is blessed with the butterflies of childhood. Some have to face the harsh realities of life from the very beginning. In most cases, it is the unstable financial conditions of the home that generally forces a person to fall prey to child abuse which is alarmingly on the rise in the present day world.

According to WHO and the National Crime Record Bureau, nearly 3 in 4 children - or 300 million children - aged 2-4 years regularly suffer physical punishment and/or psychological violence at the hands of parents and caregivers and 1 in 5 women and 1 in 13 men report having been sexually abused as a child. Every year, there are an estimated 40,150 homicide deaths in children under 18 years of age, some of which are likely due to child maltreatment. This number almost certainly underestimates the true extent of the problem, since a significant proportion of deaths due to child maltreatment are incorrectly attributed to falls, burns, drowning and other causes.

The first and the foremost reason for child abuse is neglect by parents. It is the duty of every parent to take proper care of their children. An international study indicated that there is a direct connection between the economic disparities and the risk of abuse and neglect on children. Financial stress and instability of the job pushes a parent to become harsh towards a child.

Child maltreatment has often severe short- and long-term physical, sexual and mental health consequences. These include injuries, including head injuries and severe disability, in particular in young children; post-traumatic stress, anxiety, depression, and sexually transmitted infections (STIs) including HIV. It can affect cognitive and academic performance and is strongly associated with alcohol and drug abuse and smoking – key risk factors for non-communicable diseases (NCDs) such as cardiovascular diseases and cancer.

Although Government of India has enacted the Protection of Children against Sexual Offences Act 2012 (POCSO Act), it has failed to protect child from abuse. The need of the hour is to prioritise prevention activities against abuse, creating safe online environments for children, besides calling on all with a role to protect children to work together to dramatically improve the response.

Sources

- WHO
- Government Of India
- National Crime Record Bureau

12. Water Scarcity and Access to Drinking Water CAPF AC 2019

By ABC

21st August, 20XX, XYZ

There's nothing more essential to life on Earth than water. However, the UNESCO United Nations World Water Development Report of 2022 has encapsulated global concern over the sharp rise in freshwater withdrawal from streams, lakes, aquifers and human-made reservoirs, impending water stress and also water scarcity being experienced in different parts of the world. A NITI Aayog Report, 'Composite Water Management Index, 2018 has sounded a note of caution about the worst water crisis in the country, with more than 600 million people facing acute water shortages.

Thus, from Central Australia to sub-Saharan Africa and Asia's teeming megacities, people are or will soon be seen struggling to access the clean water they need for drinking, cooking, bathing, hand-washing and growing their food.

The water crisis facing the world has rendered man helpless. As the population of the world grows and the environment becomes further affected by climate change, access to fresh drinking water dwindles. Globally, 785 million people lack access to clean drinking water.

Every day, over 800 children die from dirty water, due to diarrhoea caused by poor water, sanitation and hygiene and scarce or unreliable water and sanitation facilities in many communities around the world.

Hence, in the present day world, water scarcity and access to water has become a major topic of discussion. In what could serve as an encouragement to step up the pursuit of policies to better conserve water, we all need to recognise that all water has value, regardless of its source. It includes managing that source in an integrated, inclusive and sustainable manner by including the community, business leaders, industries, farmers, conservationists, policymakers, academics and others for ecological and economic benefits.

Sources

- UNESCO United Nations World Water Development Report of 2022
- NITI Aayog Report

13. Data Leak from Facebook CAPF AC 2018

By ABC

21st August, 20XX, XYZ

In an eye opening news on right to privacy, new revelations were made when news of data leakage from the social media site Facebook emerged in the United States in 2018. This led to the leakage of the personal data of as many as 87 million people in the US.

Referred to as Facebook Cambridge Analytica data scandal, the data leakage was a major political scandal, Cambridge Analytica was the company involved in the data breach which accessed and misused the private data of users for political purposes. In this scandal, the personal information of the users of the Facebook including Name, Age, Location, Public Profit, Date of Birth, etc., were accessed. This data was detailed enough for Cambridge Analytica to create psychographic profile of the users which helped them to send advertisements to the users in a particular location for some political event.

The leakage incident led to an outcry across the United States as it had infringed upon the privacy rights of the users of the Facebook App by using their data inappropriately without their consent. As the result, the CEO of Facebook, Mr. Mark Zuckerberg, testified before a joint session of the US Senate and Judicial Committee. On their remark, they signalled that the status quo was not satisfactory and called for changes voluntary or mandatory to promote transparency and prevent abuse.

The Press Trust of India has contacted Cambridge Analytica seeking response of whether it is involved in the misuse of data of Indian Profiles. Earlier, the IT Ministry had also issues a warning to the social media giant of stringent action of such data theft.

All in all, such a data leaks call into question the IT laws, rules and regulations which require a change to accommodate the changing scenario of data.

Sources

- Facebook reports
- IT Ministry
- Press Trust of India

14. Violence in University Campuses During Student Elections CAPF AC 2018

By ABC

21st August, 20XX, XYZ

One of the major period of our life include our college years where a child learns to become an adult. However, in the recent years, this phase has been marred by the concepts of violence and bullying in the name of event like elections and fests. Recently, cases of violence on university campuses during elections came forward. One of the major ones include the violence in the recently held Jawaharlal Nehru University Student's Union (JNUSU) elections in September, 2018.

In this, the activists of Akhil Bhartiya Vidyarthi Parishad (ABVP) stopped the election process for more than 16 hours on 15th September, 2018 in JNU. It was done by occupying the room where the counting of votes was being done. A former journalist was severely beaten outside the police station when she went to lodge a complaint against them. All this happened when ABVP was losing the elections and several students were beaten after the results were declared.

Such incidents of violence during the student elections have been reported from all over India. These violent incidents not only hamper the day-to-day working of the university but also defeat the very purpose of a university which is to educate and enlighten the students. As such incidents happen, classes are suspended and the work in the university comes to a standstill. Beside physical and academic loss, such incidents are often the cause of mental stress.

Strict Laws should be formulated to prevent such violent acts during the college elections. Any student taking part in such violence in the campus should be expelled from the university or debarred from taking admission in any college in India.

Apart from this, police action must be taken against any offender which will serve as deterrence for other students taking part in such activities. Elections in colleges/universities should be seen as a platform to elect suitable candidates who will help in aiding the college administration activities and not as a stage to force one's views or ideologies on others.

Sources

- Akhil Bhartiya Vidyarthi Parishad (ABVP)
- Expert Journalists

15. Corruption in Politics — CAPF AC 2017

By ABC
21st August, 20XX, XYZ

India was considered one of the most promising giants developing markets during the 2000s due to its expanding economy. However, in 2012 the country's fast-paced development slowed to a decade low, with many analysts blaming political corruption wherein government officials abused their legally granted authority for personal benefit. There is no one-size-fits-all explanation for political corruption, and the amount of corruption, and the forms it takes, vary consistently with the political environment. The degree and nature of corruption vary depending on the sort of regime under which it occurs.

According to Transparency International's (TI) Global Corruption Barometer-Asia (GCB), India has the highest share of bribery in Asia (39%), as well as the greatest proportion of citizens exploiting personal connections (46%). Thus, India has the highest level of political corruption which is undermining the political body and the supremacy of the law that governs society.

However, the major cause of political corruption in India can be associated with the elections. Elections in India are not financed by the government, and winning elections. These days seems to be unrealistic, without spending a hefty amount of money on campaigning. Additionally, there are no restrictions on the amount of money that may be spent on election campaigns. The lack of active use of the Right to Information Act, 2005 by the Indian public encourages politicians to engage in blatant corruption. Further, all anti-corruption units are directly controlled by the government, which may explain why ministers and lawmakers often obtain a free pass by pressuring the anti-corruption units.

The Indian government has made a few initiatives to tackle corruption at the federal level. Citizens can now seek access to any public information under the Right to Information Act, 2005 which has been regarded as a major milestone in the battle against corruption, as it allows for penalties in any event of disobedience and mandates officials to digitise data. A more proactive judiciary has also adopted a tougher stance against corruption, with the Supreme Court ordering all trial courts in the country to expedite corruption cases in early 2011. Thus, it is safe to conclude that new legislative developments, as well as recent government initiatives, are sufficient for the time being; the most important issue currently is their effective implementation, as well as addressing the challenges that may arise in their enforcement.

Sources

- Transparency International's (TI) Global Corruption Barometer-Asia (GCB)
- Right to Information Act, 2005
- Government of India

16. Environmental Pollution — CAPF AC 2017

By ABC
21st August, 20XX, XYZ

Environmental degradation is one of the most pressing issues of our time. Threats to the environment are becoming more serious by the day which may not only cause irreversible environmental damage but also adversely affect the quality of life of all life forms. One of the main causes of such great damage to the environment is that every increasing rate of environment pollution.

Environmental pollution essentially is the addition of contaminants into the natural environment that causes detrimental effects to nature, natural resources and mankind.

It includes the presence of unnatural and negative changes in the chemical, physical, and biological characteristics of any component of the ecosystem (i.e. air, water or soil) which can cause harm to nature and its cycle.

While the concept of pollution is not new, the present day world and its advancement has brought along many difference types of pollution starting from noise pollution to radioactive pollution. Hence, the world is now privy to air pollution, water pollution, soil pollution and radioactive pollution which cause ecological imbalance.

Exhaust and fumes from vehicles, natural gas, burning of fossil fuels, nuclear accidents, destructive off gasses from things such as paint, plastic production and so on release many toxic gases which is the major cause of climate change and global warming. Untreated chemical water and other everyday human activities like washing clothes, throwing pesticides, etc., affect water quality and poses great risks to all life.

Deforestation, soil erosion, leaching of waste from landfills, and burning of crops after harvesting contaminate the soil which enter the food chain and pose risks to food security, water resources, and livelihood. E-wastes, leaking of radioactive materials from nuclear centres, use of radio isotopes for medical purposes, mining, cosmic rays and radioactive decay of waste products lead to radioactive pollution which destroys everything in its wake.

All of these pollutions not only disrupt the natural cycle of our ecology and environment but also pose great health risks to human lives like respiratory disorders and cancer. The need to mitigate pollution starts with rooting out its cause and finding sustainable ways to carry on with the development tasks. For the same, common masses and the government need to join hands. In 2017, the UN assembly recognised this reality and the world's highest level gathering on the environment put the menace of pollution at the top of the global political agenda.

Sources

- UN reports
- Government of India reports

17. Receding Glaciers CAPF AC 2016

By ABC

21st August, 20XX, XYZ

In a world where the population is ever on the rise, resources are ever reducing and the Earth's temperature has been on a rise, it was not a surprise that world glacier count is decreasing at a rapid pace. In its report published in March 2023, The UN's World Meteorological Organisation (WMO) revealed the world's glaciers melted at an unprecedented rate in 2022, making their salvation effectively impossible. Further, the International Commission for Snow and Ice (ICSI) in its recent study on Asian glaciers stated, "glaciers in the Himalaya are receding faster than in any other part of the world and if the present rate continues, the likelihood of them disappearing by the year 2035 is very high".

Considered to be the sensors of climate change, glaciers are huge blocks of ice that are mostly found in Polar regions and mountain regions closer to the Equator such as the Himalayas. Glaciers hold about 2% of the Earth's water and hold about 70% of the world's freshwater. Thus, the rapid decrease in the glaciers rings an alarm as not only are the sources of fresh water reduced but the ecosystem surrounding the glacier is also affected. With rapid melting, the sea water rises making the land near water bodies prone to flooding. Scientists have also predicted that many coastal cities will drown in the coming ten years.

Further, the reduction in glaciers leads to an increase in temperatures.

Scientists presenting these studies, however, believe that we can mitigate the concern with some steps. With green resources, afforestation, reducing carbon emissions, we can move towards protecting our glaciers from further reduction. It is essential to prioritise collective action to tackle climate change and reduce greenhouse gas emissions to ensure a sustainable future for all.

Sources

- UN's World Meteorological Organisation (WMO)
- International Commission for Snow and Ice (ICSI)
- Expert Scientists
- Satellite imageries

18. Ban on Alcohol in Bihar CAPF AC 2016

By ABC

21st August, 20XX, XYZ

With the change in the lifestyles of rich and poor alike in the modern world, many modern habits have developed. Partying, betting, gambling, smoking and drinking, which were earlier elitist activities, are now activities of the common. Today almost everyone participates in one of these activities with the most popular on being drinking alcohol. Alcohol may seem like a colourless liquid but in reality is the cause of many not only health problems but also many social and economic problems.

Data provided by various surveys reveal that people who drink often become addicted to it.

To fulfill their addiction, they participate in illegal means to acquire money or take the money meant for their household. Such people not only leave their houses in poverty but also are found to be perpetrators of domestic violence. Further, the greater rise in alcoholism fosters the illegal production of alcohol.

Keeping these issues in mind, the Bihar government notified the Bihar Prohibition and Excise Act, 2016 to ensure that the ban on sale and consumption of alcohol including Indian Made Foreign Liquor (IMFL) as well spiced and domestic liquor continued in the state.

As per the new liquor law, those found indulging in unlawful import, export, transport, manufacture, possession, sale, intoxicant or liquor could attract a minimum 10 years of jail term which may extend to imprisonment for life besides a minimum fine of ₹ 1 lakh which may extend to ₹ 10 lakh.

Within a year of prohibition, the effects of the ban could be seen. The number of murders and gang robberies decreased by 20%, the number of riots fell by 13% and traffic accidents were reduced by 10%. For the economy, spending per household rose: increase in sales of milk by 10%, cheese by 200%, two-wheeled vehicles by 30%, and electrical appliances by 50%. In villages, brick houses are gradually taking the place of more rudimentary cottages since state prohibition came into effect. However, while the social condition of Bihar seems to have improved, the ban could not deter alcohol consumption in the state. Soon, alcohol addicts started travelling to neighbouring states and countries to acquire alcohol.

The failure of Bihar liquor ban has shown that prohibition has little chance of success. Those habituated to drinking were willing to take huge risks. Therefore, there is a need of a collective effort to mitigate the problems associated with alcoholism.

Sources

- Expert opinions
- Surveys
- Bihar Prohibition and Excise Act, 2016

19. Operation Raahat in Yemen — CAPF AC 2015

By ABC

21st August, 20XX, XYZ

In yet another difficult and challenging operation titled Operation Raahat, the Indian Armed Forces evacuated 464 personnel of different nationalities from the war torn city of Aden, Yemen on 10th April, 2015. The Operation evacuated more than 4,640 overseas Indian citizens and 960 foreign nationals from more than 41 countries during the 2015 military intervention by Saudi Arabia and its allies during the Yemeni Crisis.

The operation was carried out as Yemen was a no fly zone during the crisis which began on 27th March, 2015 when the Royal Saudi Air Force led a coalition of Arab states in attacking the Shiite Houthi rebels.

India chose Djibouti as a centre for initial evacuation by sea and Indians in Yemen were advised to reach Sana'a and Aden. The Indian Navy redeployed the patrol vessel INS Sumitra (P59) and dispatched the destroyer INS Mumbai (D62) (Captain Rajesh Dhankhar) and frigate INS Tarkash (F50) (Captain Pradeep Singh) from Mumbai to provide protection and support to Indian ships and aircraft in the conflict zone.

In addition, the Indian Air Force deployed two C-17 Globemaster cargo aircraft with a capacity of 600 passengers and two ferries belonging to the Lakshadweep administration, MV Kavaratti and MV Corals, with a capacity of 1,500 passengers. In addition, two Air India Airbus A320 aircraft were also deployed to Muscat in neighboring Oman.

On 1st April 2015, INS Sumitra reached Aden to evacuate 349 Indians and when Air India was permitted to fly to Yemen on 3rd April, 2015 it evacuated people from Sana'a. Two C-17 Globemasters flew nine sorties to Mumbai and two to Kochi from Djibouti. According to the data presented by the Ministry of Defence and Ministry of External Affairs, of a total of 5,600 people, 2,900 Indians were evacuated by 18 special flights from Sana'a and 1,670 Indians by Indian Navy ships from four ports. The air evacuation ended on 9th April, 2015 while the sea evacuation ended on 11th April, 2015.

Sources

- PIN Reports
- Ministry of Defence reports
- Ministry of External Affairs

20. Acid Attacks on Women — CAPF AC 2015

By ABC

21st August, 20XX, XYZ

Women are the architects of society. There is no doubt that we are witnessing a revolution in the history of the treatment received by women. The evidence is everywhere whether it is academic excellence, scientific inventions, space and technology, politics, journalism, entertainment or sports, their success is ubiquitous. However, despite the remarkable progress women have made, a crime is committed against women every hour. One of these crimes is the menace of acid attack. The Human Rights Law Network estimates that there were 1000 acid attack cases per year in India, however, only around 250 cases are reported.

Acid attacks have been defined as a form of violence, in which acid or another corrosive substance is thrown at a person – usually, a woman or a girl – with the intention of maiming, torturing, or killing them. Such attacks beside causing psychological trauma, result in severe pain, permanent disfigurement, subsequent infections, often blindness in one or both eyes. There are social ramifications too. As the attacks usually leave victims disabled, they become increasingly dependent on the members of the family for even the most basic daily activities. Further, public and government apathy results in a double victimisation of the survivors. They are forced to repeatedly appear in court, recount their trauma and visit doctors even as they grapple with their personal tragedy of physical disfigurement, loss of employment and social discrimination.

To root out such a heinous crime, it is important to look at why it happens. A study examining Indian news reports, which depict the motivation of attacks, suggests that 35% of these occurrences were a result of revenge on women for rejecting romantic, sexual or marriage proposals. Further, the orthodox beliefs that women need to be suppressed and the easy availability of acid also allow the crime to take place.

It is really unfortunate that until 2013, India didn't have any specific legislation for dealing with the horrific crime of acid attacks. In the Criminal Law (Amendment) Act., 2013, sections 326A and 326B were included specifically for dealing with acid attacks and sections. Later in 2017, India revised its Rights of Persons with Disabilities Act and recognized acid attack victims as disabled. This would mean that acid attack victims could have more access and help with finding jobs.

Despite having laws to punish the offenders and putting regulations on acid selling, India fails to tackle acid attacks on women. India needs to begin to dismantle and change ideas at a cultural level. Education is a crucial tool for changing ideas over time. The normalisation of women in high positions such as leadership can help shift ideas at a cultural level and provide a safer future for women. Changing toxic male masculinity and misogyny needs a shift of culture and mindset.

Sources

- Human Rights Law Network
- News reports
- Criminal Law (Amendment) Act, 2013

Unsolved Report Writing

Write reports on the following in about 200 words each. Do not mention any name or address in the reports, use XYZ/ABC if needed.

1. National Strategy for Artificial Intelligence
2. Global Energy Crisis
3. Heat Waves
4. Brain Drain
5. Communal Violence in Manipur
6. Rise of Biofuels
7. Deepfake: Impacts and Consequences
8. South Africa's Genocide- A Diplomatic Win
9. The Family Health Survey 2023
10. ChatGPT v/s Google Gemini
11. India-Arab-Mediterranean Corridor
12. Need for Plastic Ban in India
13. Groundwater Depletion
14. Future of Cleaner Technologies
15. Status of Malnutrition in India

04 Precis Writing

SPECIAL FOCUS

In Precis Writing pay special attention to
- Track of word count (1/3 of the passage)
- Correct usage of grammar
- Main idea of the passage
- Punctuations

Precis is an art of compression or giving the gist of a passage. It is basically a very concise summary of a passage comprising its meaning and the main theme.

In the UPSC CAPF AC Examination, one question based on precis is asked where students are asked to reduce a paragraph of 300-400 word length into its **one-third** which is around 100-130 words. It carries **15 marks**.

Precis Writing basically trains the aspirants to read passages very carefully with full concentration and helps them in developing their skill to distinguish essential and non-essential data from the passage.

Steps by Step Guide to Write a Good Precis

- Look at the **total number of words** of the passage. It is generally given at the right hand corner at the end of the passage. Read the given paragraph carefully.
- **Underline** all important points and ideas while reading.
- Now, **skim and scan** those ideas before using in your precis.
- **Reread** the given passage as well as the precis you have written to see, if you have not missed anything.
- Herein, also make sure that you have not made any grammatical mistake in it.
- Now, count the number of words of your précis. It should be one-third of the original passage.

TIME IT !

The entire process of writing the precis takes 15-20 minutes. Practice is the best key to complete the precis within this time frame.

Dos and Don'ts of a Good Precis

Dos

- Begin with the **basic idea** of the passage to make the precis convenient to read.
- Give a **clear idea** pertaining to what the reader is about to read.
- Follow the **main idea** of the passage with the facts/points of improvement/ methods, etc. as mentioned in the comprehension.
- Use **punctuation** marks such as (, : ; ' / ? . " – _ !) while writing your Precis.
- Include all the important **keywords** and terms which are used in the passage.
- Keep a track of the **tenses** you use.
- Use third person **pronouns** (she, her, hers, herself, he, him, his, himself, it, its, itself, they, them, theirs, themselves.) and indirect speech.
- Remember that a precis is a single paragraph.
- Keep the information as precise as possible.

Don'ts

- Do not make **assumptions** or add information in the precis as per your own imagination.
- Do not give your **own opinion** or criticism over the comprehension.
- Do not using **abbreviations**.
- Do not focus on any one point for very long.
- Do not write the **title** to the précis. It is specifically mentioned in the question.

■ Sample Question

Attempt to write précis of the given passages in one-third of its length. Do not suggest a title. Write, as far as possible, in your own words. The precis must be written only on the precis sheets. **15 Marks**

'Brain Drain' means, migration of highly trained man power from one country to another. The ex-President of India, Dr. KR Narayanan, described brain drain a few years ago, as 'The flight of Intellectual Capacity'. Shri PN Haksar once remarked, "A society, which cannot place the highest value on knowledge and its acquisition, inevitably alienates itself from creating, transmitting and applying knowledge." The alienation leads partly to the visible brain drain, that is migration and invisible brain drain, that means loss of morale and creativity among those who still stay in India. Both visible and invisible brain drain produce a great national loss, which can't be calculated in terms of money. India suffers from both visible and invisible brain drain. We can find many IITians doing MBA and working as Marketing Executives in private companies or preparing for IAS, etc. This type of invisible brain drain is as dangerous as visible brain drain. Our country invests a lot of money on every student doing IIT or IIM, when they migrate to other countries, it gives a great loss to the India's exchequer. Some may call these students, traitors, but we have to think from the angle of these students also.

Are we able to provide them, suitable jobs? What propels them towards other countries? Dr. CV Raman was compelled to join IAS for a few years because he couldn't get a good scientists job.

A plethora of causes ranging from attraction towards foreign countries to monetary benefits are cited for brain drain. Monetary gain is the foremost cause for the brain drain. When the highly educated find no place or respect in Indian panorama, they go out of country, get good money and good recognition not only in Foreign country, but also in our country after returning. Take the case of Kalpana Chawla who died in space. What she achieved in USA, was impossible to achieve in India, whatever calibre she might have possessed. Anyone who goes to West for studies and remains there even for five or six years, finds it almost impossible to settle in Indian conditions. Our system does not allow lateral entry, every post is tailor made, no triangle can fit as a square and no hexagon as a triangle. The rigidity in the system does not allow people to return to India from abroad. The salary structure is also rigid and have no place for extra increments to the talented. In addition to the lower salary package, the working conditions in India, are also not homogenous and healthy for progress. Bureaucratic pressures and red-tapism frustrate the technocrats of high calibre who wish to return to their country. **(438 words)**

SPECIAL SHEET FOR PRECIS

Write one word in each division and five words in each line. Punctuate your passage in the usual way and divide it into paragraphs, if pages in the answer book. The rough work should be scored through before you hand over your answer book.

					Do not write on the margin	Candidates must not write on this margin.
Emigration	of technically sound	man power	from one	country to		
another is	called	brain drain.	Brain drain is	defined by	10	
various	luminaries	differently.	Visible	brain drain		
means,	migration to	another	country,	while	20	
invisible	brain drain	means	loss of	enthusiasm and		
confidence	among the	intellectuals	who	couldn't	30	
go abroad,	both are	equally	harmful	for our		
country.	Our	country	invests	huge	40	
amount on	the education	and	technical	training of		
the youth,	who	later on	migrate to	Foreign	50	
countries.	Reasons	for	such	migrations		
are to be	ascertained.	Attraction	towards	Foreign	60	
countries,	better	salary,	better	future prospects		
and	recognition are	some	of the	fundamental	70	
reasons of	brain drain.	Rigidity of	system,	no reward		
to the	talented,	lower	salary,	poor	80	
working conditions,	bureaucratic	hurdles and	red-tapism	prevailing		
in our	system	discourage	the immigration	of the	90	
talent	back	to its	own	country.		
					100	

Practice EXERCISE

Directions (Q. Nos. 1-10) *Attempt to write précis of the given passages in one-third of its length. Do not suggest a title. Write, as far as possible, in your own words. The precis must be written only in the precies-format given below.*

1. The belief that fashion alone should dominate opinion has great advantages. It makes thought unnecessary and puts the highest intelligence within the reach of everyone. It is not difficult to learn the correct use of such words as 'complex', 'sadism', 'oedipus', 'bourgeois', 'deviation', 'left' and nothing more is needed to make a brilliant writer or talker. Some, of these words represented much thought on the part of their inventors; like paper money they were originally convertible into gold. But they have become for most people inconvertible and in depreciating have increased nominal wealth in ideas. And so we are enabled to despise the paltry intellectual fortunes of former times.

The modern-minded man, although he believes profoundly in the wisdom of his period, must be presumed to be very modest about his personal powers. His highest hope is to think first what is about to be thought, to say what is about to be said and to feel what is about to be felt; he has no wish to think better thoughts than his neighbours, to say things showing more insight or to have emotions which are not those of some fashionable group but only to be slightly ahead of others in point of time. Quite deliberately, he suppresses what is individual in himself for the sake of the admiration of the herd. A mentally solitary life, such as that of Copernicus or Spinoza or Milton after the Restoration, seems pointless according to modern standards. Copernicus should have delayed his advocacy of the Copernican system until it could be made fashionable; Spinoza should have been either a good Jew or a good Christian; Milton should have moved with the times, like Cromwell's widow, who asked Charles II for a pension on the ground that she did not agree with her husband's politics. Why should an individual set himself up as an independent judge? Is it not clear that wisdom resides in the blood of the Nordic race or alternatively, in the proletariat? And in any case what is the use of an eccentric opinion, which never can hope to conquer the great agencies of publicity?

The money rewards and widespread, though ephemeral fame, which those agencies have made possible, laces temptations in the way of able men which are difficult to resist. To be pointed out, admired, mentioned constantly in the press and offered easy ways of earning much money is highly agreeable; and when all this is open to a man, he finds it difficult to go on doing the work that he himself thinks best and is inclined to subordinate his judgement to the general opinion. **438 words**

Answer

The belief that fashion should dominate opinion makes thought unnecessary and puts the highest intelligence within the reach of everyone, especially for modern man. The modern man, although he believes profoundly in the wisdom of his period, must be presumed to be very modest. He thinks first what is about to be thought, to say what is about to be said and to feel what is about to be felt. He hides his own self and considers his own judgement to be subordinate to be appreciated, mentioned and admired. **89 words**

2. Indian literature has a long tradition and is a reflection of its culture through the ages. This fact is often overlooked, since literature in English is popular amongst the urban middle class. The British attempted to categorise the main regional languages. Despite the Orientalists' admiration of the Sanskrit tradition, the need to communicate with the locals or convert them to Christianity prompted the British to learn the local languages. As a result, a number of grammar books were written to understand these better. The nationalists also recognised the importance of regional languages. Members of the Congress Party realised that if they only spoke in English, they would be alienated from their own people, as it was considered to be synonymous with cultural domination. In 1910, the Hindi Sahitya Sammelan (Conference on Hindi Literature) was held by the conservatives of the Independence Movement.

In 1916 the Benares Hindu University was founded with a similar ideological aim to defend the great Hindu tradition. Gandhi, who endorsed it in the era between the two world wars, disassociated himself from it in the 1940s and reproached the conservatives for promoting a very Sanskritised Hindi. He advocated a synthesis, Hindustani, which could be used by all the speakers of Urdu and Hindi. After Independence, the government supported Hindi, which eventually became the official language of the nation and the mass media promoted a very Sanskritised form. Later, the increasing power of the Hindu nationalists also encouraged the use of Hindi. Paradoxically, the English-speaking intelligentsia also encouraged it as they did not want the communalists to monopolise the cultural traditions of the country. The growing domination of Hindi, which is evident due to a demographic balance of power, has however not eclipsed other regional literatures. In 1954, the Sahitya Akademi was established by the government. It considers Indian literature as 'a literature in several languages.' Two of its fellows, UR Ananthamurthy and K Satchidanandan, write in Dravidian languages—in fact, Ananthamurthy was awarded the Jnanpith Award in 1994 for his work in Kannada. If the Akademi makes allowances for Hindi literature, notably by giving prizes, it supports all other regional literatures equally. It acknowledges more languages than the constitution, including Maithili, Dogri, Rajasthani and English and tries hard to support them by following an active publications policy. The States Reoraganisation Act of 1956 rearranged the States according to a linguistic principle. This too helped foster regional literature as the State Governments supported it. The Sahitya Akademi seeks to focus on the common cultural traits that underlie literature written in Indian languages. The unity is associated with the structure of Indian society, its caste divisions, its religious communities and gender inequality. This social dimension of Indian literature is important. **451 words**

Answer

Indian literature has long been appreciated around the globe. What started as the need to learn the local language by the Britishers and the creation of grammar books is now evidence to the importance of Indian languages. And this importance was soon integrated into the independence movement. Hindi was defended and endorsed by various political leaders and educational institutes. This carried on after Independence wherein Hindi became the official language of the nation. The power enjoyed by Hindi did not mean that other languages were ignored. The government set up the Sahitya Akademi in 1954 which seeks to focus on the common cultural traits that underlie literature written in Indian languages. In doing so, it recognised Indian literature as 'a literature in several languages.' **124 words**

3. 'The financial expert's office was under a banyan tree his office furniture an old tin box'. From the first pages of Mr. Narayan's novel The Financial Expert we are back in the town of Malgudi with which for nearly twenty years we have been as familiar as with our own birth-place. We know, like the streets of childhood, Market Road, the snuff stalls, the vendors of toothpaste, Lawley Extension with its superior villas, the Regal Haircutting Saloon, the river, the railway. We expect at any moment to see the Bachelor of Arts waving a long farewell to a friend from the platform, small Swami wrapped in his adventurous dreams coming down Market Road, Mr. Sampath at the door of his dubious film studio. It is through their friendly offices that we have been able to meet these new and rather doubtful characters. Margayya, the financial expert himself, who graduates from the banyan tree to publishing and back to more elaborate and more crooked banking (but how innocent is all his crookedness) Dr. Pal, 'journalist, correspondent and author' and Margayya's son Balu whose progress from charming childhood to spoilt frustrated manhood is perhaps the saddest episode Mr. Narayan has written. All Mr. Narayan's comedies have had this undertone of sadness. Their gentle irony and absence of condemnation remind us how difficult comedy is in the West today farce, savage, boisterous, satirical, is easy, but comedy needs a strong framework of social convention with which the author sympathises but which he does not share. Miss Compton-Burnett is forced to place her stories in the Edwardian or Victorian past Mr Henry Green substitutes elaborate conventions of his own for our social vacancies, so that his characters move in the kind of dance we learnt at kindergarten 'one step forward, one step to the right, twirl on the right toe'. But the life of Malgudi never ruffled by politics-proceeds in exactly the same way as it has done for centuries and the juxtaposition of the age–old convention and the modern character provides much of the comedy. The astrologer is still called in to examine the horoscopes for a marriage but now if you pay him enough he will fix them the way you want the financial expert sits under his banyan tree opposite the new Central Cooperative Land Mortgage Bank. To push away a tumbler of milk is to insult a goddess; the caste of a great grandfather is still of great importance, Margayya, astute about mortgages, consumed by the modern desire for wealth and motorcars, yet consults the priest of the Goddess Lakshmi and finds himself seeking a red lotus to pound up in the milk drawn from a smoke coloured cow (the forty days of prayer have results he becomes the owner of a pornographic manuscript called first Bed Life or the Science of Marital Happiness but afterwards, through the caution of the printer, Domestic Harmony).

Margayya—the sad ambitious absurd financial expert is perhaps the most engaging of all Mr. Narayan's characters. In his ambitions for his boy, his huge dreams, his unintended villainies and his small vanities, his domestic tenderness, he has the hidden poetry and the unrecognised pathos we so often find in Chekov's characters who on the last page vanish into life. **545 words**

Answer

From the very start of Mr. Narayan's novel 'The Financial Expert', we are back in the streets of Malgudi which we have known for long. We know the nook and corner of the town and it is within these corners that we come across the characters of Narayan's saddest story about Margayya, Dr. Pal, and Margayya's son Balu. All of Narayan's comedies have a undertone of sadness. They have a gentle irony and absence of condemnation which is missing from the comedies of the West. A comedy needs a strong framework of social convention with which the author sympathises, but does not share. Such a framework is found in Malgudi where nothing changes over years and in this setting is Margayya- the sad ambitious absurd financial expert who in his ambitions for his boy, his huge dreams, his unintended villainies and his small vanities and his domestic tenderness becomes realistic. **152 words**

4. In the last decades of the twentieth century, the end of the Cold War, the collapse of the Soviet Union, the transitions to democracy in scores of countries, plus the significant expansion of international trade, investment, transportation and communication, usually labeled globalisation profoundly changed America's external environment and had atleast three major consequences for American identity.

First, the collapse of the Soviet Union and of communism left America not only with no enemy but also for the first time in its history without any clear 'other' against which to define itself. For over two centuries the liberal, democratic principles of the American Creed had been a core component of American identity, American and European observers had often referred to this creedal component as the essence of "American exceptionalism." Now, however, exceptionalism was becoming universalism, as democracy became more and more accepted around the world, atleast in theory, as the only legitimate form of Government. No other secular ideology existed to challenge democracy as fascism and communism had in the twentieth century.

Second, the extensive international involvements of American business, academic, professional, media, non-profit and political elites lowered the salience of national identity for those elites, who now increasingly defined themselves, their interests and their identities in terms of transnational and global institutions, networks and causes. As we have seen, some American elites tended to attribute greater salience to subnational identities than did the American public. Many of these same elites also assigned greater salience to transnational identities than did the public, which remained highly nationalistic.

Third, the decline in the relevance of ideology increased the importance of culture as a source of identity. The collective counterpart to the growing number of individuals with dual identities, dual loyalties and dual citizenships was the growing number and importance of diasporas. Diasporas are cultural communities cutting across the boundaries of two or more states, one of which is viewed as the homeland country of that community. Immigrant ethnic groups promoting their interests within American society have been a reality since the mid-nineteenth century.

Immigrants now, however, can much more easily maintain ties, interactions and communications with people in their origin country and thus see themselves as members of a diaspora. In addition, homeland Governments now view their diasporas as key sources of financial and other support and as sources of influence on host country Governments. Hence, they promote the expansion, mobilisation and institutionalisation of their diasporas.

The absence of an other until 2001, the spread of democracy, the denationalisation of elites and the rise of diasporas all blur the distinction between national and transnational identities.

432 words

Answer

The collapse of Soviet Union and the end of Cold War, the acceptance of democracy in many countries and globalisation profoundly changed America's external environment and had three major consequences for American identity. First, America was left with no enemy and has no clear 'other' against which to define itself. Second, the extensive international involvements of American elites lowered the salience of national identity for them. They increasingly defined themselves in terms of transnational and global institutions, networks and causes. Third, decline in the relevance of ideology increased the importance of culture as a source of identity. The diasporas grew in number and importance. Immigrant ethnic groups started promoting their interests within American society and became key sources of financial and other support. The absence of another until 2001, the spread of democracy, the denationalisation of elites and the rise of diasporas blurred the distinction between national and transnational identities.

150 words

5. Nations are built by the imagination and untiring enthusiastic efforts of generations. One generation transfers the fruits of its toil to another which then take forward the mission. As the coming generation also has its dreams and aspirations for the nation's future, it therefore adds something from its side to the national vision which the next generation strives hard to achieve. This process goes on and the nation climbs steps of glory and gains higher strength.

Any organisation, society or even a nation without a vision is like a ship cruising on the high seas without any aim or direction. It is the clarity of national vision which constantly drives the people towards the goal.

Our last generation, the glorious generation of freedom fighters led by Mahatma Gandhi and many others, set for the nation a vision of free India. This was the first vision, set by the people for the nation. It, therefore, went deep into the minds and hearts of the masses and soon-become the great inspiring and driving force for the people to collectively plunge into the struggle for freedom movement. The unified dedicated efforts of the people from every walk of life won freedom for the country. The next generation has put India strongly on the path of economic, agricultural and technological development. But India has stood too long in the line of developing nations. Let us, collectively, set the second national vision of Developed India. It means the major transformation of our national economy to make it one of the largest economies in the world; where the countrymen live well above the poverty line, their education and health is of a high standard, national security is reasonably assured and the core competence in certain major areas gets enhanced significantly so that the production of quality goods, including export, rises and brings all-round prosperity for the countrymen. **313 words**

Answer

Nations are built by well-directed and properly thought and imagined efforts of many generations. Every generation inherits the outcome of hardwork as well as aspirations of previous generations and takes the mission of development and prosperity forward. As a result of these efforts, the nation grows and gains strength. For proper development, people of a nation must have a vision. Our last generation set a target of free and unified India and the next generation put India strongly on the path of economic, agricultural and technological development. Now, it is time to set the vision of Developed India. **98 words**

6. We all know what we mean by a 'good' man. The ideally good man does not drink or smoke, avoids bad language, converses in the presence of men only exactly as he would if there were ladies present attends church regularly and holds the correct opinions on all subjects. He has a wholesome horror of wrong doing and realises that it is our painful duty to castigate Sin. He has a still greater horror of wrong thinking and considers it, the business of the authorities to safeguard the young against those who question the wisdom the views generally accepted by middle-aged successful citizens. Apart from his professional duties, he spends much time in good works : he may encourage patriotism and military training; he may promote industry, sobriety and virtue among wage earners and their children by seeing to it that failures in these respects receive due punishment. Above all, his 'morals', in the narrow sense, must be irreproachable.

It may be doubted whether a 'good' man in the above sense, does, on the average, any more good than a 'bad' man. I mean by a 'bad' man the contrary of what we have been describing. A 'bad' man is one who is known to smoke and to drink occasionally and even to say bad word when someone treads on his toe. His conversation is not always such as could be printed and he sometimes spends fine Sundays out of doors instead of at church. Some of his opinions are subversive; for instance, he may think that if you desire peace you should prepare for peace, not for war.

Towards wrong doing he takes a scientific attitude, such as he would take towards his motor-car if it misbehaved; he argues that sermons and prison will no more cure vice than men a broken tyre. In the matter of wrong thinking he is even more perverse. He maintains that what is called 'wrong thinking' is simply thinking, and what is called 'right thinking' is repeating words like a parrot. **338 words**

Answer

An ideal man has a lot of good qualities. He does not drink or smoke, avoids bad language, attends church regularly and holds the correct opinions on all subjects. He rejects Sin and any other wrong actions and believes in authority. He participates in good works, encourages patriotism and military training and promotes industry, sobriety and virtue among wage earners. On the contrary, a bad man occasionally smokes, drinks, abuses and talks nonsense. His opinions are subversive and thinking is person. For him 'wrong thinking' is simply thinking and what is called 'right thinking' is repeating words like a parrot. **100 words**

7. The ongoing conflict between Russia and Ukraine has far-reaching implications for geopolitics, regional stability and international relations. The war, which began in 2014, has significantly altered the political landscape and raised concerns about territorial integrity, sovereignty and the balance of power in the region.
One of the major impacts of the Russia-Ukraine war is the deterioration of relations between Russia and the West. The annexation of Crime by Russia and its support for separatist movements in Eastern Ukraine have resulted in economic sanctions, diplomatic tensions and a renewed focus on NATO's Eastern flank. The conflict has heightened geopolitical rivalries and deepened divisions between Russia and Western powers, leading to an era of strained relations and increased military posturing.
Furthermore, the war has sparked a reevaluation of security dynamics in Eastern Europe. It has prompted countries in the region to enhance their defense capabilities and seek closer ties with Western allies. NATO has bolstered its presence in Eastern Europe through increased troop deployments and military exercises, aimed at deterring potential aggression and ensuring the security of its member states. The conflict has redrawn security alliances and redefined the strategic calculus in the region.
The Russia-Ukraine war also has significant humanitarian implications. The protracted conflict has resulted in the displacement of thousands of people, loss of lives and widespread destruction of infrastructure. Humanitarian crises, such as the lack of access to basic services, food and healthcare, have emerged as major challenges. The war has strained international relief efforts and placed a burden on neighboring countries that have accommodated a large number of refugees.
Additionally, the conflict has rekindled discussions about energy security. Ukraine serves as a crucial transit route for Russian natural gas exports to Europe. The war has raised concerns about the reliability and vulnerability of energy supplies, prompting efforts to diversify energy sources and reduce dependence on Russian gas. This has led to the exploration of alternative pipelines and the promotion of renewable energy sources, shaping the energy dynamics of the region. **332 words**

Answer

The Russia-Ukraine war has significant geopolitical implications, impacting regional stability and international relations. It has strained Russia's relations with the West, prompted security reevaluations, caused humanitarian crises and raised concerns about energy security. The conflict has heightened geopolitical rivalries and reshaped alliances, leading to strained relations and increased military posturing. Humanitarian challenges and displacement have emerged and discussions on energy diversification have gained prominence. Efforts for diplomatic resolutions and international cooperation are essential to address the ongoing conflict's geopolitical impact. **80 words**

8. There is a fatal imbalance between what man is and what he wishes to be. This discord is responsible for our unrest. We talk like wise men but act like lunatics. We cannot prepare for war and at the same time for a world community. We are tormented by inner uneasiness and pangs of conscience. The warring sides of our nature require to be reconciled. If, we are to defeat fratricidal tendencies in us, we must break our self-will, the pride of egoism, which is widespread in all sides of our life. In man, there is always an urge to self-transcendence, but until it becomes absolute unselfishness, narrow loyalties and destructive rivalries will prevail. The unrest in the world is a reflection of our inner disharmony.

People are saved not by their military leaders or industrial magnates or by their priests and politicians, but by their saints of implacable integrity. Religion is the discipline by which we are helped to overcome the discord in our nature and integrate our personality. If, we reflect on the history of religious development, we will be surprised at the amount of intellectual ingenuity, passion and zeal spent on the task of defining the Supreme, to which silence or poetry would seem to be the most appropriate response. Self-righteousness breeds fanaticism. None but fools and fanatics are quite certain of their views of God with crusaders, there is no arguing. Before God, there is neither Greek nor barbarian, neither rich nor poor, neither master nor slave. They are all citizens of the one commonwealth, members of one family. A truly religious person cannot hold back but should lead. He cannot remain silent, when he should speak up. He should not compromise, when he should stand fast. Ethical values have relevance to social facts. We must face up to the ugly facts of sin, pride and greed. Human nature is essentially good and it is opposed to tyranny, injustice and authoritarianism. Religion appeals to the hearts of men to root out fear, guilt and faith in force. The tradition of tolerance, not merely in a negative, but in a positive sense, that is an appreciation of other faiths, has been with us for centuries. Tolerance is not apathy, but is conviction without condescension. Aggressiveness is not an essential part of human nature. Combativeness can be replaced by meekness and gentleness. The Cross indicates that the love, which suffers is more powerful than the force, which inflicts suffering. **411 words**

Answer

If a person is determined to achieve what he wishes, the difference of peace in his mind and heart must be resolved. He/She must find a balancing technique to take a practical decision. In the process of self-betterment, he/she needs to realise the importance of inner harmony. It is impossible to work towards peace and prepare for war at the same time. Saints are saviours who guide people to follow the religious and spiritual path. The efforts taken by them, to define the supreme power of divinity, are reflected in the history of religion. A truly religious person is filled with ethical values. It is human nature to oppose tyranny, injustice and domination. Tolerance on the other hand is also graded high by as it takes high spirit to respect other faiths. It is, thus said, that love that suffers and is polished after facing troubles is more powerful than the evil forces. (152 words)

9. Mining companies are dumping more than 180 million tonnes of hazardous mine waste each year into rivers, lakes and oceans worldwide, threatening vital bodies of water with toxic heavy metals and other chemicals poisonous to human beings and wildlife. The amount of mine waste dumped annually is 1·5 times as much as all the municipal waste dumped in US landfills in 2009.

Mine processing wastes, also known as tailings, can contain as many as three dozen dangerous chemicals including arsenic, lead, mercury and processing chemicals such as petroleum by-products, acids and cyanide. Waste rock, the extra rock that does not contain significant amounts of ore, can also generate acid and toxic contamination. The dumping of mine tailings and waste rock pollutes waters around the world, threatening the drinking water, food supply and health of communities as well as aquatic life and ecosystems. In a world, where climate change, ocean acidification, overfishing and recurring tragedies like the Gulf of Mexico oil spill are already disrupting water and food supplies, polluting the world's waters with mine tailings is unconscionable and the damage it causes is largely irreversible. No feasible technology exists to remove and treat mine tailings from oceans; even partial cleanup of tailings dumped into rivers or lakes is prohibitively expensive.

There is but one workable solution: Mining companies must stop dumping into natural bodies of water. In some cases, safer waste management options exist: putting dry waste in lined and covered landfills (a process called dry stacking) and putting tailings back into the pits and tunnels the ore came from (called backfilling). In other cases, even land-based tailings disposal is too risky. Some places, where companies want to dump tailings are simply inappropriate for mining and should be no dumping zones. The protection of such areas must be coupled with more efficient use of metals and support for sustainable development and livelihoods that do not endanger communities' health and safety.

A number of nations have adopted prohibitions or restrictions on dumping mine tailings in natural bodies of water. Nations with some restrictions on dumping including the United States, Canada and Australia - are home to major mining companies that use practices internationally that they wouldn't be allowed to use at home. Even these national regulations, however, are being eroded by amendments, exemptions and loopholes that have allowed destructive dumping in lakes and streams.

Non-governmental initiatives to promote responsible-mining by corporations can play an important role in helping close regulatory loopholes. Civil society organisations working to encourage more responsible mining are calling on mining companies to end water-based tailings dumping. In turn, the mining industry as a whole must, share our collective responsibility to protect water and aquatic ecosystems by pledging not to dump mine wastes in Earth's most precious resource: water. **462 words**

Answer

Mining companies have become major contributor of environment pollution through water based tailing dumping. Mining waste contains number of hazardous chemicals that pollute the natural water bodies, thereby, threatening drinking water, food supply and health of communities. With uncontrollable problems, mining companies should rise to alter their dumping patterns to cease the irreversible harm they are causing to the environment. The only helpful solution is to adopt safer waste management.

They should segregate their dumpings - dry waste in the landfills and tailings to be backfilled in the mines. There should be specific zones where such activities can take place and these places must be endowed with better use of metals. We should join hands with nations, who have prohibited water based tailing dumpings. Though the regulations and laws enforced has certain loopholes that allow partial water based dumpings, mining companies should realise their social and environmental responsibility to protect the aquatic ecosystem by pledging not to dump mine waste into natural water bodies. **164 words**

10. A secular state is constitutively tied to the value of religious liberty that has three dimensions. The first refers to the liberty of members of any one religious group (feature b). It is a fact that in most religious communities, one or two interpretations of its core beliefs and practices come to dominate. Given this dominance, it is important that every individual or sect within the group be given the right to criticise, revise or challenge these dominant interpretations. The second aspect of this important liberty in a secular state (feature c) is that it is granted non-preferentially to all members of all religious communities. It is entirely possible that non-preferential treatment by the state that accords religious liberty to its members is also found in states which respect multiple establishments. But religious liberty is not part of the core principles of multiple establishments.

However, it is a constitutive feature of the secular state. The third dimension of religious liberty (featured), unthinkable in states with multiple establishments, is that individuals are free not only to criticise the religion into which they are born, but at the very extreme, to reject it and further, given ideal conditions of deliberation, to freely embrace another religion or to remain without one. Religious liberty, when understood broadly, is one feature of a secular state.

To understand its other crucial ingredient, it is necessary to grasp the point that liberty and equality in the religious sphere are all of a piece with liberty and equality in other spheres. It is not a coincidence that the disestablishment clause in the first amendment to the American Constitution institutes not only religious freedom, but also the more general freedom of speech, of peaceful assembly and political dissent. It is entirely possible that a state which respects multiple establishments permits religious liberty and equality, but forbids other forms of freedom and equality.

For instance, a person may challenge the authority of the religious head of his own denomination, but not be free to challenge the authority of the state. This is impossible in a secular state which is committed to a more general freedom and equality. Thus, the second value to which a secular state is constitutively linked is the equality of free citizenship. **365 words**

Answer

Religious liberty is a fundamental aspect of a secular state, encompassing three dimensions. First, it grants individuals within religious groups the right to criticise or challenge dominant interpretations of their beliefs. Second, this liberty is non-preferentially extended to all members of all religious communities. Unlike multiple establishment states, a secular state's core principle includes the freedom to reject or embrace different religions, as well as the freedom to remain without one. Further, a secular state upholds the principles of freedom and equality in other spheres. A secular state, committed to broader freedom and equality, enables individuals to challenge both religious and state authority. Thus, the second value inherent to a secular state is the equality of free citizenship, where individuals enjoy equal rights and liberties across different domains. **128 words**

Previous Years' QUESTIONS

Directions (Q. Nos. 1-10) *Attempt to write précis of the given passages in one-third of its length. Do not suggest a title. Write, as far as possible, in your own words.*

1. Immigrants are people who arrive under an immigration policy which gives them the right to become citizens after a relatively short period of time-say, three to five years-subject only to minimal conditions (e.g., learning the official language and knowing something about the country's history and political institutions). This has been the traditional policy governing immigration in the three major countries of immigration-namely, United States, Canada and Australia.

Historically, immigrant groups have responded very differently to majority nation-building from national minorities. Unlike national minorities, the option of engaging in competing nation-building has been neither desirable nor feasible for immigrant groups in Western democracies. They are typically too small and territorially dispersed to hope to recreate their original societal culture from scratch in a new country.

Instead, they have traditionally accepted the expectation that they will integrate into the larger societal culture. Indeed, few immigrant groups have objected to the requirement that they must learn an official language as a condition of citizenship or that their children must learn the official language in school. They have accepted the assumption that their life-chances and even more the life-chances of their children, will be bound up with participation in mainstream institutions operating in the majority language.

Western democracies now have over 200 years of experience concerning how such groups integrate and there is little evidence that legal immigrants with the right to become citizens pose any sort of threat to the unity or stability of a liberal democracy. There are few (if any) examples of immigrant groups mobilising behind secessionist movements, nationalist political parties or supporting revolutionary movements to overthrow elected governments. Instead, they integrate into the existing political system, just as they integrate economically and socially.

So, immigrants have not resisted majority nation-building campaigns to integrate them into the mainstream society. However, what immigrants have tried to do is to renegotiate the terms of integration. Indeed, many recent debates over 'multiculturalism' in immigrant countries are precisely debates over renegotiating the terms of integration. Immigrants are demanding a more 'tolerant' or 'multicultural' approach to integration that would allow and support immigrants to maintain various aspects of their ethnic heritage even as they integrate into common institutions operating in the majority language. Immigrants insist that they should be free to maintain some of their old customs regarding food, dress, recreation, religion and to associate with each other to maintain these practices.

This should not be seen as unpatriotic or 'un-American'. Moreover, the institutions of the larger society should be adapted to provide greater recognition and accommodation of these ethnic identities e.g., schools and other public institutions should accommodate their religious holidays, dress, dietary restrictions and so on.

451 words

CAPF AC 2024

Answer

United States, Canada and Australia have a traditional policy of immigration.

'Historically immigrant groups' response is very different to majority nation-building from national minorities. In Western democracies 'immigrants' engagement in competing nation-building is not desirable as they are too small territorially to hope to recreate their indigenous social culture. They gradually accepted to integrate into a larger societal culture. Though few immigrants demanded opportunity for them to learn official languages, which is a basic requirement to get citizenship. And they have accepted that they as well as their next generation will face difficulties as they will be bound up with participation in mainstream institution operating in the majority language.

Western democracies have 200 years of experience visualising those groups of immigrants integrating with the traditional/Indigenous citizens and that often poses a sort of threat to the unity or stability of a liberal democracy. Immigrants are generally harmless. There are very few cases secessionist movements, revolutionary activities to overthrow the running government from theirs end, instead. They try to adopt themselves to the existing political system.

So, immigrants have always tried to integrate them into the mainstream society.

Their requirement and appeal is to provide them liberty in terms of food, dress, recreation, religion and to associate with each others to maintain the practises and not to consider it 'Un-American' approach. Moreover, the institutions of larger society must provide these ethnic groups schools, other public institutions, accommodating their religious holidays and so on.

150 words

2. The relationship between art and technology has been long a subject of debate, with some arguing that the two are incompatible, raising questions about the nature of creativity, aesthetics, and the role of the artist and others seeking to integrate technology into the artistic process. The question of whether the harmonisation of art and technology is possible is a complex and multifaceted one that requires careful consideration of the potential benefits and drawbacks of such an integration.

On the one hand, technology has the potential to expand the possibilities for artistic expression in new and exciting ways. Digital technologies, for example, have opened up new avenues for artists to experiment with interactive and immersive installations, augmented and virtual reality experiences and other forms of multimedia art. Technology, can also provide artists with new tools and techniques for creating and manipulating images, sounds, and other sensory inputs. At the same time, there are concerns that technology can undermine the traditional values and practices of art. Some critics raise the argument that technology can result in the commodification of art, turning it into a mass-produced product that can be easily replicated and distributed.

Others worry that technology can dehumanise the artistic process, reducing the role of the artist to that of a mere technician or programmer. The question of harmonisation of art and technology is further complicated by the fact that technology is constantly evolving, which means that its possibilities and limitations are always changing. As a result, the relationship between art and technology is a dynamic one that requires ongoing exploration and experimentation.

Philosophers have provided a range of interpretations of art created through artificial intelligence, offering insights into the ethical, epistemological, and ontological implications of this new art form. One of the key philosophical debates surrounding artificial intelligence ,art concerns the nature of creativity. Some philosophers believe that artificial intelligence cannot be truly creative, since it is ultimately the product of a machine rather than a human being.

While there is no consensus on the philosophical implications of artificial intelligence, the debates surrounding this new art form have opened up new avenues for philosophical inquiry arid reflection. By exploring these questions, we can better understand the implications of artificial intelligence for human creativity and artistic expression.

Using deep learning techniques, machines are able to learn from massive amounts of data and produce unique pieces of art that can range from abstract compositions to realistic portraits. Artificial intelligence-generated art is often a reflection of the data it has been trained on, leading to unexpected and unique results. In this way, artificial intelligence art provides a new lens through which we can view the world and inspire new perspectives on traditional art forms. **451 words**

CAPF AC 2023

Answer

People have always argued over the relationship between art and technology, with some saying that the two are incompatible and others hoping to include technology into the artistic process. It is so because technology can expand the possibilities for artistic expression in innovative ways. It can provide new ways to the artists to manipulate their artwork. Simultaneously, however, it can undermine traditional values and result in commercialisation of art. It can dehumanise the process. Thus, their relationship is dynamic and it urges the philosophers to further interpret art created through artificial intelligence. Their argument concerns the nature of creativity seeing as such artworks are a product of machine and not human being. This has opened the path for new philosophical inquiry. The art created through artificial intelligence is often a reflection of the data which can lead to unique results and thus can provide a new lens to view the world. **150 words**

3. Only that person can be healthy who feels happiness and happiness can only be felt by the person who has peace of mind. Fulfillment of basic needs, peace and happiness are the three things desired by man. These can be prioritised. To regulate the journey of life, fulfilling basic needs are a priority.

Happiness is a priority for the agreeable feelings it generates. And comforts cannot give happiness to a person unless he has peace. Rather than seek the gratification of desires, the Indian ethos espouses its antithesis—contentment—as the source of happiness. Contentment in this context refers to a state of mind in which the potential psychic energy, known as Libido in Western psychology, is transformed into a serene mental quality, rather than actualised as a desire that needs to be gratified or repressed.

A craving for fame and wealth often results in moral depravity and in many cases personal, destruction. The greatest of woes comes from not knowing contentment; the greatest of faults comes from craving for gains. The nature of humanity and, for that matter, of all creatures, was to live in a simple way, partaking no more than what was needed to maintain the healthy growth of the organism. Beyond that limit were selfish cravings and extravagances. A sage is free from excessive pursuit, enjoyment and expectation. A sage is not the product of moral cultivation but simply someone who lives according to his authentic nature. Alienation from this life of simplicity is the root cause of all human problems. What are the implications of contentedness for modern people?

First of all, one may raise the point that, unlike animals, human needs extend far beyond the physiological realm to cover psychological, emotional and spiritual needs. Even physiological needs change as civilisation progresses. For example, several decades ago, people were content with riding a bicycle, but today driving a car has become a necessity for many of them.

The biggest folly of our times is that the young have been presented with a plethora of objects. The youth are not taught that achieving peace is impossible without limiting the demands of the senses and the mind. Since childhood, we see and hear things which indirectly endorse an attachment to worldly possessions. The infatuation of the young with worldly pleasures grows so strong that it becomes virtually impossible for them to reject the demands of the senses and the mind. The attitude of indifference to worldly pleasures (Vairagya) has become an alien concept. **416 words**

CAPF AC 2022

Answer

Health, happiness and peace go hand-in-hand. Thus, if a person wishes to be healthy, their priority should be seeking peace. This further brings a realisation that its neither gratification of desires nor contentment with what one has that will bring about peace. A quest to fulfill all that one desires takes one towards moral depravity and sometimes personal destruction. In a similar manner, contentment with what one has is only ephemeral because every human being has an innate need to transcend their situation and aspire for more. Thus, the biggest problem lies in the youth's obsession with material possessions. They have failed to understand that it is not in objects that they can find peace; rather peace lies in an attitude of indifference towards worldly pleasures. **126 words**

4. For anyone living in Delhi, March is surely the season of the gods. The fresh wintry breeze, the trees in new leaf, the flower making a 'riot of colour' - all this evokes grateful surprise in a populace used to dust storms on the one hand and polluted winter evening on the other. It is also a time for birds, since many trees are not in leaf, the flitting and darting and pirouetting of small shapes seems to be all around us. As I sit here I can see Rose-ringed Parakeets flying into the neem trees, their long tail gleaming blue in the Sun. The peepul tree by the *varanda*, whose leaves are still tightly curled, harbours a family of Crimson-breasted Barbets. On the hibiscus bush outside my window a Tailor Bird is looking for nesting material, perhaps, along with an Ashy Wren Warbler. And on top of the hedge a Magpie Robin, glossily black and white and as self-assured as Clinton himself, is singing his heart out, because it is the courtship season too.

Further away, a tall pale tree is preparing to shed its leaves and cover itself with a washed lilac colour which could belong inside a Japanese painting. Because we have this blessing too - that when the freshness of March gives way to the sadder suns of summer, the flowering trees leap into colour and they are colours so amazing that we should seriously consider banning them. The red silk cottons are already aflame and alive with sunbirds, flower-peckers, bulbul and mynahs. Then it will be the stunning yellow of the laburnums, and after that the frothy, whites and pinks of bauhinias. Around our house some unnamed horticultural official, on whom be peace, has ensured that during the most despairing weeks of summer we are treated to a vision of purple jacaranda in full bloom.

And, of course, for the rest of the summer life is worth living only because of the *gulmohurs*. For the last two or three years, the advent of March has seemed to me peculiarly unexpected. The gentle message which it brings, i.e., that you never have a single season but a cycle, that every wheel comes full circle and today is not all, now appears both more reassuring and harder to believe.

And that, I suspect, is because we live in a world where, increasingly, today is in fact all. The print media and the television, those two dictators of our lives, scream about today in a way which drowns out both yesterday and tomorrow. Thus, in our personal lives, in our social life and in the national life, we grab for today with a vehemence which is out of all proportion to its importance. And, as recent events have shown, we sometimes somersault right back into yesterday. Whoever planted the jacaranda was thinking about tomorrow, and contemplating it now may teach us more than we imagine. **487 words**

CAPF AC 2021

Answer

Delhi in March, during the Spring season is delightful. It's in stark contrast to the rest of the year when one can only witness dust storms and fog. During Spring, one gets to enjoy the calming, fresh breeze and the budding flowers all in beautiful colours.

Trees are adorned with new leaves and nests, and a robin is perched on the top singing constantly. As March is the month that is going to dissolve into the summer heat, it is also the month of colours. As a pale tree is readying itself to adorn the lilac colour, other tress are coloured in red and yellow. And all of these trees come to life with the birds that surround them. The world, it seems has become a palette of colours. Every year, March comes as a reminder of the entire year and not just one, which is hard to believe as today's world has only taught us to think about the present. **161 words**

5. For Gandhi, respect and toleration were related and virtually indistinguishable. This might appear strange. To 'tolerate', in the classical 17th century meaning of the term, is to refrain from interference in the activities of others even though one finds them morally repugnant and despite having the power to do so. Here one puts up with, even suffers the morally reprehensible activities of others. At best, the powerless other escapes interference of the powerful because the latter shows mercy towards them. This is hate-based toleration–I hate but still tolerate.

Gandhi's 'toleration' is different. How? Parents often put up with the blemishes of their children which they would not suffer in others. We choose to overlook a fault in our spouse, lover, or close friend that we would not excuse in others. We might endure differences with fellow citizens because we value fraternity. In short, we tolerate some disagreeable beliefs and practices of persons or groups because we identify with many of their other beliefs and practices. In all such cases, we put up with dislikeable states of others even if we have some power to do something about them simply because we have love or love-like feelings for them. Others are tolerated not despite hate but rather because they are loved–I love, so I tolerate. This is Gandhi's love-based toleration, entirely consistent with respect.

Unlike the mainstream, hate-based conception of toleration that presupposes that oneness with significant others is achieved by abolishing the radical other, by eliminating plurality, for this second, Gandhian conception, oneness is attained by accepting all radical others as equally significant because they variously manifest one Supreme Being. Thus, to tolerate is to refrain from interfering in the life of others not despite our hatred for them, but because we love them as alternative manifestations of our own selves or because we deeply care for some basic norm common to all of us. We may not be able to be what they are, we may even dislike some of their beliefs and practices but we recognise that they are translations of our own selves or of God within each of us. This, Gandhi believed, binds us together in a relationship of lasting affection. **367 words**

CAPF AC 2020

Answer

Gandhi strangely believes that respect and toleration are related and virtually indistinguishable. To tolerate is generally related to the hate-based concept of toleration wherein a powerful individual tolerates and shows mercy to the activities that for him are morally reprehensible. In contrast, stands Gandhi's love-based concept of toleration according to which we tolerate because we love others. According to Gandhi, we tolerate because we love the alternative we love some other basic norm and belief that ultimately they all are alternatives of our own selves or God. This relation, thus, binds us together in a bond of affection. **98 words**

6. Religion, according to Gandhi is more or less a way of life, and as such is the personal concern of the individual who has to choose his way of life. But, if an individual has the freedom to take to the religious way of his own liking, he must also have a tolerance and a respect for the points of view that others might have chosen for themselves. Therefore, he recommends that the attitude towards different religions must be one of tolerance and respect. In his own case, it is much more than that. Although, sometimes an impression is created that he has a special liking for Hinduism, his attitude towards other religions is one of reverence. He was born in a Hindu family and so the way and the atmosphere in which he grew and developed implanted in his mind the elements and tenets of Hinduism. Naturally, the Gita and the Ramayana became his two invariable companions.

But he made a study of many great religious scriptures–of the Bible and the Quran-and he came under the influence of a number of saints and religious teachers. All these led him to believe that different religions are the different ways of apprehending the Truth. Gandhi believes that every religion contains good precepts and noble teachings, he also finds that some of the interpretations and commentaries have degraded religion and distorted it.

He also finds that almost every religion has given rise to some fanatic and unreasonable practices. Therefore, his conviction is that all religions are good as well as bad, basically good-good in conceiving its ideal, but bad in giving rise to hatred, crusades and fanaticism. The experience of communal riots in India strengthened his belief.

Therefore, he suggests that religions-historical religions-must not be allowed to cross the limits of reason of 'sober reason', as he calls it. He is convinced that this element of 'rationality' will be able to bring about, what can be called, 'a fellowship of all religions' or, 'the kingdom of God'–a Christian expression which he also approvingly uses on various occasions. **347 words**

CAPF AC 2019

Answer

According to Gandhi, religion is a person's way of life. So every person should tolerate and respect others religions, just as they want others to respect theirs. Gandhi followed Hinduism because he was born into a Hindu family. As Gandhi read the holy books of other religions and interacted with their holy people, he understood that all religions explain truth in different ways. Gandhi realised that all major religions were based on excellent principles, but these principles had been distorted by those who interpreted them. Hence, he suggested that people of all religions should moderate their teachings to rational levels so that a 'fellowship of all religions' can be created. **110 words**

7. Language as culture has three important aspects. Culture is a product of the history which it in turn reflects. Culture in other words is a product and a reflection of human beings communicating with one another in the very struggle to create wealth and to control it. But culture does not merely reflect that history or rather it does so by actually forming images or pictures of the world of nature and nurture. Thus, the second aspect of language as culture is as an image-forming agent in the mind of a child. Our whole conception of ourselves as a people, individually and collectively, is based on those pictures and images which may or may not correctly correspond to the actual reality of the struggles with nature and nurture which produced them in the first place. But our capacity to confront the world creatively depends on how those images correspond or not to that reality, how they distort or clarify the reality of our struggles. Language as culture is thus mediating between me and my own self; between my own self and other selves; between me and nature. Language is mediating in my very being. And this brings us to the third aspect of language as culture.

Culture transmits or imparts those images of the world and reality through the spoken and the written language, that is through a specific language. In other words, the, capacity to speak, the capacity to order sounds in a manner that makes for mutual comprehension between human beings is universal. This is the universality of language, a quality specific to human beings. It corresponds to the universality of the struggle against nature and that between human beings. But the particularity of the sounds the words, the word order into phrases and sentences, and the specific manner or laws, of their ordering is what distinguishes one language from another. Thus, a specific culture is not transmitted through language in its universality but in its particularity as the language of a specific community with a specific history. Written literature and orature are the main means by which a particular language transmits the images of the world contained in the culture it carries.

Language carries culture and culture carries, particularly through orature and literature, the entire body of values by which we come to perceive ourselves and our place in the world. **394 words**

CAPF AC 2018

Answer

Language as manifestation of culture has three important aspects. First, language is the means through which people communicate with each other in a specific community for their survival. Second, language helps a child to acquire a set of attributes—beliefs, knowledge, values, habits pertaining to a particular culture.

Third, language is the spoken or written medium through which a particular culture is manifested and understood by the rest of the world. Thus, while culture as a whole is transmitted very largely through language, different cultures transmit their predominant order through their language, Written Literature and public speeches are major mediums through which any specific culture, history, beliefs, etc. are transmitted to others. Hence, language and culture are interdependent on each other. **121 words**

8. During the launching of a satellite, the rocket must travel in exactly the right direction and at exactly the right speed. Radio signals are automatically sent back to Earth from the rocket. These signals tell men on the ground how the rocket is travelling and help them to make sure that it is going as it should. The signals go to special calculating machines called computers that work very fast. The computers work out whether the rocket is travelling correctly. If it is not, they calculate what correction is needed. Radio signals send the correction to the rocket and make it automatically change its direction or speed as necessary.

Artificial satellites are used for many things. By sending them through the upper parts of the atmosphere we can find out more about the atmosphere. The more air there is, the more slowly the satellite will travel, until it falls to Earth. By sending satellites round the Earth at different heights, we can find out how much air there is at each height.

We can find out more about the shape of the Earth by means of satellites, If the Earth is not perfectly round, its gravity will not be the same everywhere. Because the pull of the Earth's gravity keeps the satellite in its orbit, any change in the gravity will change the orbit. By watching the way a satellite travels, we can find out whether the Earth's gravity changes anywhere. If it does, we know that the shape of the Earth is different at that place. In this way artificial satellites have shown us that the poles of the Earth are flattened, and that the South Pole is flattened more than the North.

Satellites can give us information about the weather. By sending up satellites with television cameras on board, we can get pictures of the clouds below. Each picture shows an area the size of one or more whole countries. By looking at these pictures, we can see bad weather before it comes to us. By getting warning of hurricanes or typhoons in this way, people can get ready to shelter from them. Weather satellites can also show us when rain will come. Men are now trying to forecast weather all round the world with the help of satellites. **381 Words**

CAPF AC 2017

Answer

It is necessary for a rocket with a satellite to travel in exactly the right direction and at exactly the right speed. This is ensured with radio signals which not only inform us about the speed variations of the rocket but also calculate, control and correct the same if required to change speed or direction. Artificial satellites are sent to different heights to check availability of amount of air at different points in the atmosphere. Besides this, satellites also reveal the shape of the Earth and the variation in gravity. Further, satellites inform us about weather changes and predict hurricanes or typhoons along with rain. Entire world weather forecast by satellites is also being worked upon. **127 words**

9. There is no better illustration of human folly that aware of the story of this incorrigible fool who choose to ignore the sane advice of a passer-by of not cutting the same branch on which he himself was sitting. Obviously fools fail to learn from others' experiences and pay a heavy price in the process. They have use neither for their own intelligence nor for that of others. They live in their own world, while apparently they may be in the middle of a group of people.

Fools by nature are enemies of thinking, both reflective and prospective. They never doubt their intelligence and are cocksure of their sense of judgement. They think they are benefactors of society and are anguished that the world fails to recognise their talent. All fools possess a degree of impatience in their desire to make the world realise their worth, wishing to improve its lot by setting a personal example before it. They are sure that the folks around them lack an innate sense of discretion and require to learn from.

Fools have been immortalised by literature across the world. Like Sheikh Chilli's account in India, the legend of Don Quixote, the fictional Spanish knight, is equally famous in the West. He is known for thriving in a make-believe world where he is the lone saviour of humanity. The good thing is that these self-proclaimed Samaritans often inhabit the world of imagination, limiting their capacity to cause damage to the real world and producing in the process hilarious effects through their irrationality. But there are instances when such fools have come to occupy the centre stage of history. Their actions then had disastrous effects on our welfare, as well as on our existence. We all know how people like Hitler brought the world to the brink of destruction through their disastrous leadership. The condition of the world continues to be precarious and its future insecure due to foolish scientists who have handed over the destructive secrets of nuclear power to vicious politicians. There goes a saying that it is no use crying over spilt milk. Now what we need to become vigilant about is the danger posed by fools to our survival. Academic curricula across the world need to educate learners about the negative potential of fools to challenge the safety and security of planet Earth. **392 words**

CAPF AC 2016

Answer

Fools by nature are neither reflective nor prospective. Such people do not learn from experience and use their intelligence. Instead, they live in a world of their own wherein they are sure of their judgement. They think they are benefactors of society and are anguished that the world fails to recognise their talent. Many such fools can be found in literature. These fools are so engrossed in their imagination that they do not cause harm to the real world. They only produce humour. However, sometimes fools take a crucial role and bring destruction to human welfare. Hence, it is time that we become vigilant and learn about the negative potential of fools to challenge the safety and security of planet Earth. (121 words)

10. There is a fatal imbalance between what man is and what he wishes to be. This discord is responsible for our unrest. We talk likewise men but act like lunatics. We cannot prepare for war and at the same time for a world community. We are tormented by inner uneasiness and pangs of conscience. The warring sides of our nature require to be reconciled. If we are to defeat fratricidal tendencies in us, we must break our self-will, the pride of egoism which is widespread in all sides of our life. In man there is always an urge to self-transcendence, but until it becomes absolute unselfishness, narrow loyalties and destructive rivalries will prevail. The unrest in the world is a reflection of our inner disharmony.

A people are saved not by their military leaders or industrial magnates or by their priests and politicians, but by their saints of implacable integrity. Religion is the discipline by which we are helped to overcome the discord in our nature and integrate our personality. If we reflect on the history of religious development, we will be surprised at the amount of intellectual ingenuity, passion and zeal spent on the task of defining the Supreme to which silence or poetry would seem to be the most appropriate response. Self-righteousness breeds fanaticism. None but fools and fanatics are quite certain of their views of God. With crusaders there is no arguing.

Before God there is neither Greek nor barbarian, neither rich nor poor neither master nor slave. They are all citizens of the one commonwealth, members of one family. A truly religious person cannot hold back but should lead. He cannot remain silent when he should speak up. He should not compromise when he should stand fast. Ethical values have relevance to social facts. We must face up to the ugly facts of sin, pride and greed. Human nature is essentially good and it is opposed to tyranny, injustice and authoritarianism. Religion appeals to the hearts of men to root out fear, guilt and faith in force.

The tradition of tolerance, not merely in a negative, but in a positive sense, that is an appreciation of other faiths, has been with us for centuries. Tolerance is not apathy, but is conviction without condescension. Aggressiveness is not an essential part of human nature. Combativeness can be replaced by meekness and gentleness. The cross indicates that the love which suffers is more powerful than the force which inflicts suffering. **411 words**

CAPF AC 2015

Answer

It is our inner disagreement that causes unrest in the world. There is difference in what we are and what we want to be. Hence, there is inner anxiety and strong feelings of conscience. This inner unrest can be seen in the unrest that can be seen in the world. Religion helps us in overcoming the disagreement in our nature and uniforms our personality. It appeals to the hearts of men to root out fear, guilt and faith in force. Tolerance, then, is based on appreciation of other faiths. Basic human nature is not aggressive. Hence, we should be quiet, calm and kind. **103 words**

Unsolved Precis Writing

Directions (Q. Nos. 1-8) *Attempt to write précis of the given passages in one-third of its length. Do not suggest a title. Write, as far as possible, in your own words.*

1. All living things, from cabbages and cockroaches to kings, are adjusted or 'tuned', to a 24- hour day. Our bodies follow a certain rhythm: there are periods of great activity, when every cell seems to be working busily, followed by periods of rest.

These 'cycles' seem to follow the cycle of day and night. For example, the temperature of the body rises and falls at regular hours, as if controlled by an alarm clock. It is highest by about 10.00 a.m. but comes down to its lowest point a few hours after midnight – which is why you reach, in your sleep, for that extra sheet or blanket at 4.00 am similarly, our kidneys seem to be controlled by the clock. They are busy throughout the day, but 'go to sleep' at night, producing very little urine. Imagine how uncomfortable you would be if your kidney were not 'switched off' at night!

All our activities – our habits of sleep, work and hunger – follow the 'biological clock' which controls the rhythms of the body. If these rhythms are disturbed, there is trouble. High speed travel, which is one of the gifts of modern science, seems to be one of the greatest enemies of these natural rhythms.

In the old days, when people travelled from one place to another at gentle speeds, the body was able to adjust itself to changes in 'local' time; but jet planes which travel almost as fast as the sun give the body no time to re-set its biological clock.

Todays, as more and more people travel round the world at high speeds, the problem of jet lag is receiving a great deal of attention. The people who suffer from it most are jet pilots, who are constantly on the move, from one 'time zone' to another but even an ordinary traveller, who may have to fly not more than once in a fortnight, can suffer the effect of jet lag. **323 words**

2. The question of whether India needs more missiles or more industries is a complex and multifaceted one. It involves considerations of national security, economic development and strategic priorities.

India, as a rapidly developing nation, faces the challenge of balancing its defence requirements with its aspirations for economic growth and industrialisation.

On one hand, the need for a strong defence capability cannot be ignored. India shares borders with several neighboring countries and faces security challenges in the region. It is essential for the country to maintain a credible deterrence and protect its territorial integrity. Therefore, investing in missile technology and defence infrastructure is crucial to ensure national security and safeguard its interests. On the other hand, India also recognises the importance of economic development and industrialisation. To achieve sustainable growth and improve the living standards of its citizens, the country needs a robust and diversified industrial base. Industries generate employment, contribute to GDP and promote technological advancements. They also strengthen the overall resilience and self-sufficiency of the economy.

Finding the right balance between defence needs and economic development is a delicate task. It requires a comprehensive approach that prioritises both sectors without neglecting one at the expense of the other. India has been striving to achieve this balance by pursuing a policy of indigenous defence production and encouraging domestic industries. The aim is to build a strong defence manufacturing base that not only meets the country's defence requirements but also contributes to its economic growth.

Additionally, there is a growing recognition of the importance of dual-use technologies, where advancements in defence research and development can have spin-off benefits for civilian industries. This approach allows for the synergy between defence and industrial sectors, fostering innovation and promoting economic diversification.

In conclusion, the question of whether India needs more missiles or more industries is not an either/or proposition. The country needs to prioritise both national security and economic development. Striking the right balance between defence requirements and industrial growth is crucial for India's progress. By investing in indigenous defence production, promoting dual-use technologies and nurturing a strong industrial base, India can ensure both its security and economic prosperity in the long run. **359 words**

3. Today, mass media, specifically the visual media, plays pivotal role in creating an atmosphere of awareness among the society. Media refers to different communication channels or ways through which, knowledge and information is transmitted to the viewers or the readers. Visual media refers the media that conveys, knowledge and information to the viewers, through their eyes, it includes, television, cinema, posters, etc. Whatever is supplied through the visual media, has instant and longer lasting effect on the minds of the viewers.

With rapid development of information and technology, the visual media, in the shape of cable TV, with multitudes of domestic and foreign channels has reached almost every house, playing vital role in moulding the public opinion in various ways. It plays very crucial role in educating and entertaining the masses. The cable TV has changed the means and modes of entertainment, education.

Sitting before a TV, one can pass and enjoy his free time, listening to music, viewing movies, learning techniques of body building, hearing sermons of religious saints, learning about lives of wild animals, birds, water creatures, knowing about space and what not. During election period, one can know the electoral positions of political parties, their leaders, from all parts of the country and its impact on the election campaign and all facts of electioneering, just sitting before the TV.

Youngsters and teenage students are now a days seen viewing the channels, as per their likings; if some are viewing the music, some are seen quenching their thrust of knowledge, viewing channels like 'Discovery' or 'National Geography' or 'History', etc. The image on the small screen thus has a significant impression on all, more particularly on the gullible children and on the teens. The young mind takes the reel as real and thus is more often and more easily moulded and motivated by the visual media.

The present day fashion, hair dressing, sexual liberties, dating and awakening towards the right of youth, awareness among the women to their rights are because of the role visual media is playing in the society. In a hysterical effort to excel from others, some channels are showing such scenes and images, which are of no importance or have an adverse effect on the minds of viewers. Showing of sexual and rape cases, with minute details by the anchor and showing brutal scenes of murder the channels have crossed the limit of ethics and morality. The TV coverage of; massacre of Gandhi Nagar Akshardham, Godhra's burnt railway bogies, with burnt and churned bodies of victims lying in the bogies and outside coaches, creates feeling of hatred among the communities and motivates others to wreak vengeance. Obsessed by the mono aim of making fast bucks the channels are competing with one another to stop to any kind of absurdity, without considering even for a minute as to what effect such visuals have on the society.

480 words

4. Our constitution guarantees certain basic rights to every citizen of the country in the chapter on Fundamental Right. It is also a virtual fact that fundamental rights of people as a whole cannot be subservient to the fundamental rights of a group or section of the people. There cannot be any right to strike, which interferes in the lives of common people and also causes huge loss to the national economy.

In a democracy like ours, Government employees are part and parcel of the government machinery and so, owe duty and responsibility towards the society. Too many strikes and bandhs are very disastrous for the smooth running of Government and cause lot of hardships and create problems to the common people. In our country everyone is fond of talking of his rights in democracy but forgets the fundamental duties enshrined in the same constitution.

From worker's point of view, strikes are ultimate weapons, which are only resorted to by them when all other means of struggle and negotiation have been exhausted. In recent Indian experience, the working class as whole has been relatively responsible and only used strikes in extreme cases when negotiations have failed completely or when employers have appeared to be completely insensitive to genuine demands of labour.

Denial of this right would lead to a massive deterioration of the bargaining power of workers, which has already been weakened by various macroeconomic processes, such as-global integration and the withdrawal of the state from important areas of regulation and provision. In any society, the socio-economic rights of all citizens, including workers, have never really been freely gifted by the state or employers their recognition and implementation have always been the result of prolonged struggle on the part of workers and other groups.

Nobody says that the government employees should not have right to form, their associations to protect and further their interests. The trouble arises when this right is misused and they resort to Strikes, Hartals and Bandhs, thereby bringing the everyday life of common men to a halt.

342 words

5. Many people believe that there is something bigger than us. That there is a reason for everything. Some believe that everything is a coincidence. Some believe that coincidence is real and not fate. However, none of this can ever be truly proven. Coincidence is a seemingly planned sequence of accidentally occurring events. One might think the collision of events was fated to occur, but one is mistaken. It signified nothing. But searching like we all do for an explanation and a sense of importance, one creates his fate by spelling out meaning from a jumble of coincidences.

We've all had it happen to us. We think about someone who we haven't seen in a while and later on, the same day, we bump into them. We have an ominous feeling that something bad is going to happen and it does. We have a dream that predicts our future. We look back at events in our lives and we see them fitting together like a puzzle. It all seems connected somehow or is it just coincidence?

To many, fate only occurs on a personal level. Chain reactions exist, certainly, where one person's behaviour results in a massively far-reaching effect, but they are not ruled by fate. Incidents and chain reactions with a broader range of impact, such as the butterfly effect, have no intended purpose.

It is fate that can play the triggering role within the intimate confines of a single person's life. Sometimes, there are certain events in our lives that are just meant to happen. Those events that happen for some reason in some person's lifetime, are meant to influence only the person they happen to. None can say, what exactly is the difference between fate and coincidence.

No doubt coincidences happen, too. Not every occurrence in a person's life is fated. (303 words)

6. Honesty in business dealings or in other areas are not the only measures of morals and values. The strength of character of a person is also measured by uncompromising a version to cowardice, intrigue, envy, ambiguity, falsehood, disloyalty, treachery, in short, all undignified actions. There are, in reality, few human beings endowed with a truly spotless character. This is because an almost immaculate character does not exist until the last lives in human form. Educated individuals are not necessarily endowed with good morals and values. In fact, some of them use education and their intellect as a tool for deceit. However, the advantages and the need for education and culture cannot be denied.

They contribute largely for the development of intellectual ability and the power to reason, which are the means by which the spirit analyses, compares, infers and arrives at conclusions in the search for truth about the meaning of life. The most precious assets of the soul are its morals and values, but they are not easy to build. The character of each person requires longer periods of thoughtfulness, reasoning and the practice of those values, during many reincarnations, in the course of which, ideas sink in under life experiences.

It is only after enduring much disillusionment, grief, injustice and ingratitude for many successive corporeal lives, that a person will be able to measure, in the innermost recesses of his soul, the extent of human moral misery. Then, disgusted, he rebels against it and opens the door to a more ethical and honourable life. Thus, having known and experienced suffering, the spirit, in countless reincarnations, gradually frees itself from evil actions and through enlightenment and conviction follows the rigid tracks of a flawless conduct.

It is of great significance to talk about morals and values but it is also crucial to define the lines of character that everyone should consider in their lives. Some of the most important ones are good judgement, fairness, common sense, punctuality, loyalty, courage, magnanimity, dignity, gratitude, politeness, faithfulness, moderation, truthfulness, self-respect, respect for others etc. All these qualities, if properly cultivated, compose a prime set of dignifying virtues, which accounts for a refined character. e.g. we all make mistakes and to err is human. However, once an honest person is advised and becomes convinced of his mistake, he should admit it and try not to repeat it. Unfortunately, it is common practice to conceal one's mistakes, instead of avoiding them.

This is very detrimental to spiritual growth. Most people seldom use impartiality and justice in the innermost evaluation of their own actions. Even those, who are too harsh in the judgement of other people's actions, for whom they always have words of criticism and reproach, do not escape the usual tendency. When their own faults are concerned, they find a full, lenient, absolvent, justification. In this way, not only it denotes lack of character, but mistakes often end up incorporated to human habits. By acting this way, an individual loses his self-respect and his sense of character and dignity and becomes corrupted. What everyone should do, is to face up his mistakes and avoid new mistakes, by improving his sense of morals and values, with the help of his will-power. **536 words**

7. People write and publish autobiographies and autobiographical sketches for a number of reasons. One of these reasons is to put on record the events of a famous or influential career. But not all autobiographies, not even the autobiographies most frequently and widely read, are by famous or extraordinary men. Another reason is to hand on to others, wisdom won through experience and hard labour. Yet, many fine autobiographers seem to have little concern to teach or to persuade. A third reason is to distill from past experience events, persons and situations, which hold a firm place in memory and to put true values on them.

In this sense, autobiography is, as Somerset Maugham has said, a 'summing-up' and its first utility is to its author himself. Whatever its purpose or the fame of the man who writes it, autobiography is a thing created out of the recollections of life. It is not life itself. Whether it be valuable or useless depends upon whether it is well or ill-made. Good autobiographies can be mined from inconspicuous lives. For, autobiography is the inclusive and summary form of what we call 'themes of experience'.

It may contain reminiscences, descriptions of places, of animals, of people, the identification of characteristic preferences and prejudices and other matters as well. It has the traits of all these minor forms.

An autobiography is objectively true, but is not indiscriminately inclusive. It presents a selection of detailed episodes with sufficient fullness to preserve their essential qualities. It is usually written within the framework defined by a consistent point of view. It presents its subject in more than two dimensions, fusing the person and his actions with setting, manner and purpose. One further trait of autobiographical writing raises a few special problems: by its nature autobiography tempts its author to proceed chronologically. The events sort themselves, by the calendar and it is a natural impulse of every autobiographer to begin with the words "I was born on ....."

Strict chronological arrangement poses a discipline of some force. It is by no means easy to "begin at the beginning, go until you come to the end and then stop." Considerations, other than the calendar, have a way of forcing their way to notice. With due care, however, a chronological autobiography can be accomplished. It is important to remember that chronology is not the only principle, by which autobiography can be organised. Benjamin Franklin, whose procedure in his autobiography is basically chronological, does not hesitate to recognise the Philadelphia girl, who laughed at him as the very one, who subsequently became his wife. Joseph Conrad prefers the pattern of walking tour to that of the calendar and his richly imaginative account is stored with pertinent associations of the past with the present and future.

Often, to the autobiographer, it seems that life does not pass so much as it accumulates. Qualities emerge as identities independent of time. For this reason, we should not, as we write feel compelled to maintain a steady rate of advance through the time marks of our stories. Like Hazlitt on his journey, we linger over a choice adventure or a valued friend and then; if we choose, we skip a few years to catch up. **540 words**

8. Child is the father of man." This line, which has since taken the shape of a proverb, really occurs in the famous poem 'My heart leaps when I behold' of Wordsworth, the great poet. It implies that the qualities and characteristics shown by a child often indicate, what the child is going to be as a grown up man. The childhood is the reflection of future personality. The habits, traits, qualities of a man are usually the development of the habits, traits, qualities he had as a child. A careful study of the characteristic and qualities in a child can help us to foretell his future prospects.

The child is the father of man, is proved true in many cases. See the example of Shivaji, who during his childhood, loved so much to hear the stories of famous heroes of Ramayana and Mahabharata, became later a great warrior himself. Michael the famous sculptor and painter, during his childhood used to make drawings on the pots, easels, stools and other things belonging to an old painter. The old painter had said, "One day this boy will beat me. "A Young Italian lad, Titian, was very fond of painting pictures, but had no paints to colour with. He was so genius, he made his own paints. Nelson, the daring Naval Commander of British Navy, showed his traits of courage and fearlessness during his childhood.

Many more examples like that of Florence Nightingale, Macaulay, etc, can be quoted to prove the veracity of the proverb that 'The Child is the father of man', but we can find hundreds and thousands other examples, where childhood of a man did not reflect anything about the grown up personality of a man. Sonia Gandhi, never thought to entangle in the political arena. In her childhood, none could imagine that one day she would be in a position to become the Prime Minister of India, the world's largest democracy. Though, she did not accept the position of Prime Minister. Lal Bahadur Shashtri, never showed any such trait in his childhood. He was an average student from a poor and simple family. George Bernard Shaw was known as a hopeless dullard. Mahatma Gandhi was inclined to become a rich Barrister. Shelley, the great poet and writer never showed such traits during his childhood. Amitabh Bachchan the great Super Star of today, didn't show such traits and qualities in his childhood.

Inspite of apparent exceptions, it is generally observed that the characteristic and qualities nursed during childhood are developed in the grown up personality of a man. Circumstances can change the life of a person. Fate and coincidence play a great role in developing qualities of a person. The childhood ordinarily reflects the calibre of a person, but in changed circumstances, with several coincidences and the destiny, which is predetermined, can change everything. An average child can reach the highest position and a brilliant may have to survive in rectitude.

An old proverb, "As the twig is bent, so the tree will grow," endorses the saying, "Child is the father of man." **513 words**

05 Reading Comprehension

SPECIAL FOCUS

In Reading Comprehension pay special attention to

• Main idea of the passage • Correct usage of grammar • Punctuations • Vocabulary

Comprehension is defined as the understanding of a passage or a text. A comprehension passage is a text set for testing the reader's ability to comprehend or understand the meaning of the matter and to comprehend the style as well as the theme of the passage.

In the UPSC CAPF Exam 5 **Questions of 20 Marks** (each carrying 4 mark) are asked from this section. Candidates are asked to answer these 5 questions in their own words after reading and understanding the given paragraph.

Topics of Passages

One of the most important aspects of a reading comprehension is the knowledge of the topics on which the passage may be asked.

As such there is no specific criterion to adjudge the topic or type of the passage. However, it is noted that the comprehension is generally based on a piece of recent news on various topics.

Some spheres from which the topic for reading comprehensions may be picked are

- Current Events
- Social Sciences
- Philosophy and Psychology
- Fiction based
- Excerpts from Literature

TIME IT !

The entire process of solving the reading comprehension should take 15-20 minutes. Do not spend more time on reading comprehension. Practice as many passage as you can to be able to solve the passage in this time.

Step by Step Guide to Solve the Comprehension Passage

Keep the following steps in mind while attempting an unseen comprehension

Step 1 Skim Through Passage

- Skim (Quick read) through the passage to understand the main theme of the passage.

Step 2 Read the Questions First

- Read the questions carefully to understand what has been asked in the questions.

Step 3 Read the Passage Again

- Read the passage again. This reading should be thorough as you want to find the answers to the questions.
- Underline the words/phrases related to the questions.

Step 4 Write Answer

- Start answering the questions.
- While writing the answers, remain precise and to-the-point. Do not make general or vague statements.
- Aim to write 4-5 lines for each answer.
- Do not write your opinions or information that is not mentioned in the passage as it will lead to negative marking.
- Write the answers in your own language and expression. Never copy the exact language of the passage.
- Try to attempt vocabulary related questions first as they are much easy to solve.

Sample Question

Read the following passage and answer the questions that follow **20 Marks**

SAMPLE FOR COMPREHENSION

1. Very often, we do not take the first step towards a good cause because we say to ourselves, 'The task is so big. What can I do alone?' So nothing gets done. There is much talk about environmental protection, air pollution and saving our forests. Do we really care? If we do, here are a few things we can do to make our surroundings more pleasant.
2. It is good to adopt a two-uses-attitude. By putting an article to a second use, we are giving it a longer lease of life and using up less raw material from nature. One of the worst things we do is the abuse of paper. The clean sides of envelopes can be used to write small notes, lists and reminders around the house. The more paper we use, the more trees will have to be cut down. For the same reason, we should avoid the use of paper napkins or paper plates. Cloth napkins are just as good, for they can be washed and used over and over again.
3. Another area which needs the most urgent attention is effective garbage disposal. People who are conscious about it follow rules and laws strictly. As a result, their neighbourhood is clean and beautiful. Similarly, each one of us can contribute to a cleaner environment. All kitchen waste should be collected separately. Those of you who have green fingers can turn this into valuable manure. Dig a pit and put the kitchen waste into it. When the pit is a little over half full, cover it up with mud. Let nature do the rest. Within three or six months, we will have a good garden manure. It can also be done as a community project by digging a large pit in the colony). Do take help of all the members, for nothing succeeds like cooperation.
4. A lot of people don't care about the environment because they don't understand the adverse effect that society has on it. It is important to convince people to care about the environment. The first step would be to convince people to change by providing simple alternative solutions and ways' of doing things. The internet is a powerful tool and a group on social media of like-minded people can be formed. People can share environmental stories and issues, as well as pool in solutions and alternatives to educate one another. With the current state that our planet is in, it is imperative that people actively care about the environment and most importantly to act now.

1. Comment on the writer's statement that 'we do not take the first step towards a good cause'.

Answer The given statement by the writer indicates that the writer blames each one of us as individuals for the lack of change in anything. The writer believes that our lack to take initiatives, because we feel that the task is too big and we cannot do anything alone, had resulted in our condition as far as the environment is concerned.

2. What can we do to avoid the abuse of paper?

Answer To avoid the use of paper, we can use the blank sides of any used paper like the clean sides of an envelope to write small notes, lists and reminders around the house. Further, we must avoid using paper napkins and replace them with cloth napkins which are reusable.

3. What procedure can one adopt for kitchen waste? How long does it take to make good garden manure?

Answer All the kitchen waste should be collected separately and turned into manure. People can dig a pit and put kitchen waste into it. When the pit is half full, put some mud over it. After some time, we will have good manure to be used. It takes 3-6 months to make good garden manure.

4. List the ways in which the internet can be used towards the cause of the environment.

Answer The internet is a powerful tool that can be used towards the cause of the environment. A group of like-minded people on social media can be formed so that people can share environmental stories and issues as well as pool in solutions and alternatives to educate one another.

5. How can making of garden manure be done as community project?

Answer People of an area can convert making garden manure into a community project by digging a large pit in the colony and then, throwing kitchen waste into it.

Practice EXERCISE

Directions *Read the following passages and answer the questions that follow.*

PASSAGE 1

1. All of Earth's oceans share one thing in common: plastic pollution. Discarded plastic bags, cups and bottles make their way into sea. Today, it seems that no part of the ocean is safe from plastic trash. In recent years, oceanographers have searched in vain for a pristine marine environment. They have found plastic everywhere they have looked, "It is a common global problem, we cannot point to a single habitat or location with no plastic."
2. Plastic harms wildlife and introduces dangerous chemicals into marine ecosystems– communities of organisms interacting with their surroundings. Once plastic enters the environment, it lasts a long time. Scientists are working to prevent plastic pollution from entering sea.
3. When people litter or when trash is not properly disposed of, things like plastic bags, bottles, straws, foam, beverage cups get carried to the sea by winds and waterways. About 80% of ocean plastic originates on land. The rest comes from marine industries such as shipping and fishing.
4. In 2015, Engineer Jenna Jambeck at the University of Georgia and other researchers calculated that at least 8 million tonnes of plastic trash is swept into the ocean from coasts every year. That's the equivalent of a full garbage truck of plastic being dumped into the sea every minute. If current trends in plastic production and disposal continue, that figure will double by 2025. A report published by the World Economic Forum last year predicts that by 2050, ocean plastic will outweigh all the fish in the sea.
5. In today's world, plastic is everywhere. It is found in shoes, clothing household items, electronics and more. There are different types of plastics, but one thing they all have in common is that they are made of polymers–large molecules made up of repeating units. Their chemical structure gives them a lot of advantages : they are cheap and easy to manufacture, lightweight, water-resistant, durable, and can be moulded into nearly any shape.
6. Unfortunately, some of the properties that make plastics great for consumer goods also make them a problem pollutant. Plastic's durability comes in part from the fact that unlike paper or wood, it does not biodegrade or break down naturally. Instead it just fragments or breaks into tiny pieces over time. These tiny pieces, known as microplastic, can potentially stick around for hundreds or perhaps even thousands of years.
7. Another problem with plastics is the other chemicals they contain, like dyes and flame retardants. When plastic is not disposed of properly, these additives end up in the environment. Plastic also tends to absorb harmful chemicals from its surroundings. 'It is like a sponge for persistent organic pollutants.' These long-lasting, toxic substances include pesticides and industrial chemicals. If plastic absorbs the chemicals and marine organisms eat the plastic, they may be exposed to higher concentrations of these contaminants.
8. One of the biggest impacts of plastic pollution is its effect on sea life. Seals, sea turtles, and even whales can become entangled in plastic netting. They can starve to death if the plastic restricts their ability to move or eat. Or the plastic can cut into the animals' skin causing wounds that develop severe infections.
9. Sea turtles eat plastic bags and soda-can rings, which resemble jellyfish, their favourite food. Seabirds eat bottle caps or chunks of foam cups. Plastic pieces may make an animal feel full, so it does not eat enough real food to get the nutrients it needs. Plastic can also block an animal's digestive system, making it unable to eat.
10. Plastic and its associated pollutants can even make it into our own food supply. Scientists recently examined fish and shell-fish bought at markets in California and Indonesia. They found plastic in the guts of more than a quarter of samples purchased at both locations. In organisms that people eat whole, such as sardines and oysters, that means we are eating plastic too. In larger fish, chemicals from plastic may seep into their muscles and other tissues that people consume.
11. One way to keep the ocean cleaner and healthier is through cleanup efforts. A lot of plastic waste caught in ocean currents eventually washes up on beaches. Removing it can prevent it from blowing out to sea again. Beach clean-up is ocean clean-up.
12. Clean-up efforts cannot reach every corner of the ocean or track down every bit of microplastic. That means it is critical to cut down on the amount of plastic that reaches the sea in the first place. Scientists are working toward new materials that are safer for the environment. For example, Jambeck and her colleagues are currently testing a new polymer that breaks down more easily in seawater.
13. "Individual action make a big difference," says Jambeck, disposing of plastic properly for recycling or trash collection is a key step. "And simple things like reusable water bottles, mugs and bags really cut down on waste,"

she says. Skipping straws or using paper ones helps too. Ocean pollution can seem overwhelming, but it is something everyone can help address. This is a problem we can really do something about.

1. What is the biggest impact of plastic pollution on sea life?

The biggest impact of plastic pollution on sea life is that seals, sea turtles, and whales can become entangled in plastic netting. They can starve to death as the plastic can restrict their ability to move or eat. The plastic can also cut into the animals' skin, causing wounds that develop severe infections.

2. How does plastic waste enter the oceans?

When people litter or when trash is not properly disposed of, plastic waste such as plastic bags, bottles, straws, foam beverage cups, etc., get carried to the sea by winds and waterways. It also enters the oceans due to the marine industry which generally includes fishing and shipping.

3. How is it true to say that plastic is everywhere in today's world?

It is true to say that plastic is everywhere in today's world because it is found in shoes, clothing, household items, electronics and other items of daily use. There is no single habitat or location which is devoid of plastic.

4. Which property of plastic makes it a problem pollutant?

The property of plastic which makes it a problem pollutant is that it is not biodegradable or it does not break down naturally. Instead it just fragments or breaks into tiny pieces over time. These tiny pieces can potentially stick around for hundreds or perhaps even thousands of years. Further, it has the tendency to absorb, harmful chemicals from surroundings.

5. What has scientist Jambeck suggested for having cleaner and healthier oceans?

For having cleaner and healthier oceans, scientist Jambeck has suggested that disposing of plastic properly for recycling or trash collection is a key step. She also says that we should use reusable water bottles, mugs and bags to reduce waste. Straws should be avoided or only paper straws should be used. According to her, individual actions make a huge difference.

PASSAGE 2

I believe that the civilisation India has evolved is not to be beaten in the world. Nothing can equal the seeds sown by our ancestors. Rome went, Greece shared the same fate; the might of the Pharaohs was broken; Japan has become Westernised; of China nothing can be said; but India is still, somehow or other, sound at the foundation. The people of Europe learn their lessons from the writings of the men of Greece or Rome, which exist no longer in their former glory. In trying to learn from them, the Europeans imagine that they will avoid the mistakes of Greece and Rome. Such is their pitiable condition. In the midst of all this India remains immovable and that is her glory. It is a charge against India that her people are so uncivilised, ignorant and stolid that it is not possible to induce them to adopt any changes. It is a charge really against our merit. What we have tested and found true on the anvil of experience, we dare not change. Many thrust their advice upon India and she remains steady. This is her beauty: it is the sheet-anchor of our hope.

Civilisation is that mode of conduct which points out to man the path of duty. Performance of duty and observance of morality are convertible terms. To observe morality is to attain mastery over our mind and our passions. So doing, we know ourselves.

The Gujarati equivalent for civilisation means 'good conduct'. If this definition be correct, then India, as so many writers have shown, has nothing to learn from anybody else and this is as it should be. We notice that the mind is a restless bird, the more it gets the more it wants and still remains unsatisfied. The more we indulge our passions the more unbridled they become. Therefore, our ancestors, set a limit to our indulgences. They saw that happiness was largely a mental condition. A man is not necessarily happy because he is rich or unhappy because he is poor. The rich are often seen to be unhappy, the poor to be happy. Millions will always remain poor.

Observing all this, our ancestors dissuaded us from luxuries and pleasures. We have managed with the same kind of plough as existed thousands of years ago. We have retained the same kind of cottages that we had in former times and our indigenous education remains the same as before. We have had no system of life-corroding competition. Each followed his own occupation or trade and charged a regulation wage. It was not that we did not know how to invent machinery but our forefathers knew that, if we set our hearts after such things, we would become slaves and lose our moral fibre. They, therefore, after due deliberation decided that we should only do what we could with our hands and feet. They saw that our real happiness and health consisted in a proper use of our hands and feet.

They further reasoned that large cities were a snare and a useless encumbrance and the people would not be happy in them, that there would be gangs of thieves and robbers, prostitution and vice flourishing in them and that poor men would be robbed rich men. They were, therefore, satisfied with small villages. They saw that kings and their swords were inferior to the sword of ethics and they, therefore, held the sovereigns of the Earth to be inferior to the Rishis and the Fakirs.

1. Give the meaning of the following words in the passage: Life-corroding, sovereigns, anvil, indigenous.

Life-corroding–Gradually Weakening or destroying life
Sovereigns– A supreme ruler (king or queen)
Anvil–a difficult experience that changes someone or leads to something good

2. Why was India vis-a-vis other countries charged for not being developed?

In the relation to other countries, India remained immovable and believed in its glory. This led to the charge that the people of India are uncivilised, ignorant and rigid and it was impossible to induce or adopt any sort of changes for the sake of development.

3. What is the relationship between civilisation and morality?

According to the passage, civilisation is the mode of conduct that points out the right path of duty to man. Performance of duty is similar to morality which is to attain mastery over our mind and our passions. Thus, civilisation is almost equivalent to morality.

4. What is the foothold of Indian civilisation according to the author?

According to the author, the foothold of Indian civilisation is its belief in its glory. Due to this belief, India has remained rigid in its traditions and culture and has managed with the same kind of plough that existed thousands of years ago. It has retained the same kind of cottages that it had in former times and its indigenous education remains the same as before. It has learned that it does not need to change.

5. What justification does the author advance for practising ancestral occupation and why?

According to the author, each individual in India follow his/her own occupation or trade and charges a regulation wage as earlier. This lack of change is not because we did not know how to invent machinery but because our forefathers knew these things very well. They know that we could become slaves and lose our morality. Therefore, our ancestors, decided that we should only do what we could physically and manually. They found that our real happiness and health lies in a proper use of our hands and feet. So, the real containment is our mental satisfaction which comes by our hard work.

PASSAGE 3

1. We often make all things around us the way we want them. Even during our pilgrimages we have begun to look for whatever makes our heart happy, gives comfort to our body and peace to the mind. It is as if external solutions will fulfil our needs, and we do not want to make any special efforts even in our spiritual search. Our mind is resourceful—it works to find shortcuts in simple and easy ways.
2. Even pilgrimages have been converted into tourism opportunities. Instead, we must awaken our conscience and souls and understand the truth. Let us not tamper with either our own nature or that of the Supreme.
3. All our cleverness is rendered ineffective when nature does a dance of destruction. Its fury can and will wash away all imperfections. Indian culture, based on Vedic treatises, assists in human evolution, but we are now using our entire energy in distorting these traditions according to our convenience instead of making efforts to make ourselves worthy of them.
4. The irony is that humans are not even aware of the complacent attitude they have allowed themselves to sink to. Nature is everyone's Amma and her fierce blows will sooner or later corner us and force us to understand this truth. Earlier, pilgrimages to places of spiritual significance were rituals that were undertaken when people became free from their worldly duties. Even now some seekers take up this pious religious journey as a path to peace and knowledge. Anyone travelling with this attitude feels and travels with only a few essential items that his body can carry. Pilgrims traditionally travelled light, on foot, eating light, dried chickpeas and fruit or whatever was available. Pilgrims of olden days did not feel the need to stay in special AC bedrooms or travel by luxury cars or indulge themselves with delicious food and savouries.
5. Pilgrims traditionally moved ahead, creating a feeling of belonging towards all, conveying a message of brotherhood among all they came across whether in small caves, ashrams or local settlements. They received the blessings and congregations of yogis and mahatmas in return while conducting the dharma of their pilgrimage. A pilgrimage is like penance or *sadhana* to stay near nature and to experience a feeling of oneness with it, to keep the body healthy and fulfilled with the amount of food, while seeking freedom from attachments and yet remaining happy while staying away from relatives and associates.
6. This is how a pilgrimage should be rather than making it like a picnic by taking a large group along and living in comfort, packing in entertainment and tampering with environment. What is worse is giving a boost to the ego of having had a special *darshan*. Now alms are distributed, charity done while they brag about their spiritual experiences.
7. We must embark on our spiritual journey by first understanding the grace and significance of a pilgrimage and following it up with the prescribed rules and rituals—this is what translates into the ultimate and beautiful medium of spiritual evolution. There is no justification for tampering with nature.

8. A pilgrimage is symbolic of contemplation and meditation and acceptance, and is a metaphor for the constant growth or movement and love for nature that we should hold in our hearts.
9. This is the truth.

1. What change has taken place in our attitude towards pilgrimages?

Our attitude towards pilgrimages has changed tremendously. Today, pilgrimages are converted into opportunities for tourism. In them, we have started looking for what makes our hearts happy, bodies comfortable and minds peaceful.

2. What happens when pilgrimages are turned into picnics?

When pilgrimages are turned into picnic, the essence of the pilgrimage as sadhna is lost. Then, it serves the purpose of a social gathering wherein one lives in comfort and boosts ones ego. Thus, spiritual upliftment, is not achieved.

3. Why are we complacent in our spiritual efforts?

We are complacent in our spiritual efforts because we do not want to make any special efforts in our search for spirituality.

4. How does nature respond when we try to be clever with it?

When we try to be clever with nature, it responds by causing widespread destruction, washing away all imperfections and forcing human beings to understand that they have become complacent in their attitudes.

5. In olden days, with what attitude did people go on a pilgrimage?

In the olden days, people went on pilgrimages with the attitude that they were rituals undertaken after people became free from their worldly duties and that they were on a path to achieve peace and gather spiritual knowledge.

PASSAGE 4

Ever since the dawn of civilisation, class inequality has existed. Among savage tribes at the present day, it takes very simple forms.

There are Chiefs and the Chiefs are able to have several wives. Savages, unlike civilised men, have found a way of making wives a source of wealth, so that the more wives a man has the wealthier he becomes. But this primitive form of social inequality soon gave way to others more complex. In the main, social inequality has been bound up with inheritance and therefore, in all patriarchal societies, with descent in the male line. Originally, the greater wealth of certain persons was due to military prowess. The successful fighter acquired wealth and transmitted it to his sons.

Wealth acquired by the sword usually consisted of land and to this day land-owning is the mark of the aristocrat, the aristocrat being in theory the descendant of some feudal baron, who acquired his lands by killing the previous occupant and holding his acquisition against all comers. This is considered the most honourable source of wealth. There are others slightly less honourable, exemplified by those who, while completely idle themselves, have acquired their wealth by inheritance from an industrious ancestor and yet others, still less respectable, whose wealth is due to their own industry.

In the modern world, the plutocrat who, though rich, still works is gradually ousting the aristocrat, whose income was in theory derived solely from ownership of land and natural monopolies. There have been two main legal sources of property: one, the aristocratic source, namely, ownership of land; the other, the bourgeois source, namely, the right to the produce of one's own labour.

The right to the produce of one's own labour has always existed only on paper because things are made out of other things and the man who supplies the raw material exacts a right to the finished product in return for wages or where slavery exists in return for the bare necessaries of life. We have thus three orders of men–the land-owner, the capitalist and the proletarian.

The capitalist in origin is merely a man whose savings have enabled him to buy the raw materials and the tools required in manufacturing and who has thereby acquired the right to the finished product in return for wages. The three categories of land-owner, capitalist and proletarian are clear enough in theory; but in practice the distinctions are blurred.

A land-owner may employ business methods in developing a seaside resort which happens to be upon his property. A capitalist whose money is derived from manufacture may invest the whole or part of his fortune in land and take to living upon rent.

A proletarian in so far as he has money in the savings bank or a house which he is buying on the instalment plan, becomes to that extent a capitalist or a land-owner as the case may be. The eminent barrister who charges a thousand guineas for a brief should, in strict economics, be classified as a proletarian. But he would be indignant if this were done and has the mentality of a plutocrat.

1. How is social inequality bound with inheritance?

Social inequality is bound with inheritance in all patriarchal societies as man inherited a female's money. Therefore, wives became a source of wealth. In other words, the more wives a man has, the wealthier he becomes as he inherits his wife's money.

Thus, high ranking and respected people had more wives and consequently, more wealth. This inheritance is further passed on to the male heir. Thus, social inequality was permeated across generation through inheritance

2. What is the irony in the most honourable source of wealth?

The irony regarding the most honourable source of wealth is that it resulted from murder. This wealth is acquired by the descendant of a feudal baron who had acquired the lands by murdering or killing the previous occupant as well as holding his acquisition against all comers.

3. What are the two legal sources of property?

There have been two main legal sources of property these are as following

- The aristocratic source (ownership of land)
- The bourgeois source (the right to produce of one's own labour)

4. How does the writer distinguish the three orders of men?

According to the passage, the writer has described three orders of men which are as follows

- A landowner who may employ business methods in developing a seaside resort upon his property.
- A capitalist whose money is derived from manufacture may invest the whole or part of his fortune in land and take to living upon rent.
- A proletarian has money in the savings bank or will buy a house on the installment plan. He becomes to that extent a capitalist or a land-owner as the case may be.

5. Who is a plutocrat?

Plutocrat is a member of wealthy elite. In the modern world, the plutocrat, though rich, is gradually ousting the aristocrat. Their income was in theory derived solely from ownership of land and natural monopolies.

PASSAGE 5

1. In 1939, the French Director, Jean Renoir made one of his best known films 'Rules of the Game'. Film critics at that time failed to grasp that it was an amazing exception among films made for commercial release. One reason for this lack of proper evaluation could be that the film was screened only for a short while.
2. The first noticeable thing in Rules of the Game is that it has no single central character. It does not have a plot, but the story does move to conclusion. What Renoir had done in this film was to expose an unpleasant, but true aspect of the wealthy upper-middle class of French society. Vehement protests were made against the films and consequently, it was removed from the various cinema-halls.
3. There are many scenes which show two or three characters in a room. At the same time, through an open door, it is possible to see another set of characters in a room, involved in a different event. Since, the camera could not maintain the same distance from both sets of characters, Renoir was faced with a challenge. When shooting indoors, if objects close to and far from the camera must remain equally and clearly visible, it is necessary to use a large number of lights. No one used to do it, because it had been unanimously accepted that it was the foreground that was of primary interest and the background was secondary. Renoir was the first to use extra lights and maintain an equal focus on both. Today, such a technique is known as Deep Focus.
4. After 3 years Rules of the Game, a new film appeared in America. It was Citizen Kane, directed by Orson Welles. Like Jean Renoir, it showed a huge deviation from the established norms of film making. It has a central character, a typical American, a tycoon. Usually, Americans harbour a feeling of reverence towards such characters. Orson Welles tried to expose the real nature of such a character and forced the public to open its eyes to the truth.
5. Until that moment, every director in Hollywood had accepted as gospel truth that the audience should not be taxed too much. Welles struck a blow at these beliefs, without displaying the slightest of qualms. Visually, Citizen Kane was short with a harsh sharpness which permeated every scene. Traditionally, every make-up man and cameraman in Hollywood had to keep a careful eye on the appearance of the heroine, in case blemishes on her skin became obvious. Welles refused to follow this practice in the case of his own heroine. For the first time, dialogue was presented in a realistic form and mentally the audience was totally taken aback by a new style of flashback.
6. Citizen Kane has been universally acknowledged as an epoch-making creation in the history of cinema. Orson Welles made 'The Magnificent Ambersons' after that.
7. However, both films were in advance of their time. Consequently, they failed commercially and a disappointed Welles was forced to make thrillers to survive. His later films bear plenty of evidence of his originality in terms of technique, but the seriousness and social consciousness shown in the choice of subject in Citizen Kane, The Magnificent Ambersons, is not discernible in these later films.

1. Explain the reasons for the failure of 'Rules of the Game'.

The reasons for the failure of 'Rules of the Game' movie were many. The film had no plot, but the story moved to a conclusion.

There was no central character in the film. Further, as Renoir tried to expose true but unpleasant aspect of the wealthy upper middle class of the French society, there were many protests. As a result, the movie was removed from many places.

2. Why was Orson Welles forced to make thrillers? Which aspect of his earlier films was still evident in his later films?

Orson Welles was forced to make thrillers to survive in the film industry. The films lacked the social consciousness shown in his earlier films.

3. Which aspects did the later films of Orson Welles had which aspect did they lack?

Orson's later films like Citizen Kane, The Magnificent Ambersons show his originality in terms of technique, but the seriousness and social consciousness shown in the subject, is not discernible in later films.

4. What is 'deep focus'?

'Deep focus' is a technique which involves the use of extra lights and maintaining an equal focus on the foreground and the background. It was first used by Renoir.

5. Describe the new techniques used in the films of Jean Renoir and Orson Welles.

The new technique, in which background was equally important to the character in focus, was used in the films of Jean Renoir and Orson Welles. Due to this divided focus, the real nature of the character was exposed and public was forced to see the truth. The new technique was called 'Deep Focus' and it was used where extra lights were used to maintain equal focus on the foreground and the background.

PASSAGE 6

Gandhi's experience in South Africa was decisive: not only in his political, family and social life, but also for his culture and religion. Two of his most faithful collaborators there, Henry Polak and Hermann Kallenbach, were secular Jews. Gandhi had occasion to meet exponents of diverse religions and denominations, including Christian ones; he held long discussions with them and some tried to convert him. It was a Jainist poet and thinker from Bombay, Raychandbhai, who confirmed Gandhi in the faith of his fathers.

Gandhi met him on his return to India from England and continued to correspond with him from South Africa, until the poet's premature death. In his autobiography, Gandhi wrote that only once in his life had he come close to choosing a personal guru: yes, Raychandbhai. He considered him 'the best Indian of his time' and freely acknowledged his debt to the Jain. If his Christian friends in London had awakened in him "the thirst for a religious quest," Raychandbhai had taught him that religion was essentially the control of one's own spirit and liberation from any attachment or aversion to people or things.

It was principally during his South African years that Gandhi became acquainted with writers whom he would consider masters for the rest of his life: Ruskin, Thoreau, Carpenter, Tolstoy. In 1904, he read Ruskin's 'Unto This Last', A book identifying the individual good with the common good and speaking of the importance of work as the cornerstone of life; for Ruskin, all types of work have equal dignity and value, whether they be intellectual or manual, noble or humble. In 1907, Gandhi read Thoreau's 'On the Duty of Civil Disobedience' and was struck by its central theme: one's duty to refuse to obey a country's laws if one believes them to be unjust. Two years later, while in London, he read a volume written by the idealistic socialist, Edward Carpenter: Civilisation: Its Cause and Cure. He found it 'enlightening,' excellent in its analysis of civilisation. An advocate of the return to a simple life in harmony with nature, carpenter condemned modern civilisation as degrading and corrupting; like Ruskin, he exalted the joy of manual work, which industrialism had separated from the creative project.

However, the author that struck Gandhi more than any other was Tolstoy. All during the rest of his life, Gandhi would recognise his debt to the Russian writer. He probably read Tolstoy for the first time during the London years of his youth, when he greatly admired the author's ideas and work. But his first great encounter with Tolstoy dated back to 1894, in South Africa, when a friend gave him a copy of God's Reign is Within You. Gandhi's reading of it left an indelible impression on him. He felt for the book and its author the same admiration that he had held for the Sermon on the Mount. He found in it an admonition against responding to evil with violence, an exhortation to love one's neighbour and practise pacifism and a confirmation of the ancient Indian commandment (Jainist, in particular) of ahimsa. He also found a brief story of the forerunners of non-violence and a catalogue of its advocates and 'militants' at that time: from the Quakers to Tom Paine, from the American abolitionists to the Russian duchobors.

In other books, by Tolstoy which he read in the years that followed, Gandhi was led to agree more and more adamantly with the Russian's distillation of Christianity and of every religious faith to the commandment to love one's neighbour; the aspiration toward a profound moral rebirth of man; a highly critical attitude toward progress, science, luxury and wealth, as well as toward the city, a place of alienation and destruction of man's deepest values.

1. Why was Gandhi's experience in South Africa decisive?

Gandhi's experience in South Africa was quite decisive because he had several occasions to meet exponents of diverse religious and denominations. Apart from these, he held long discussions with the mass.

2. Who was Gandhi's personal guru and why did he consider him so?

Gandhi's personal guru was Raychandbhai. He considered him to be the best Indian of his time and acknowledges his debt to the Jain. Raychand bhai had taught him that religion was essentially the control of one's own spirit and liberation from any attachment or aversion to people or things.

3. Who were the writers whom he considered as masters? Mention the works of the writers that influenced Gandhi?

The writers whom Gandhi considered as masters were Ruskin, Thoreau, Carpenter and Tolstoy. The works that influenced Gandhi were

- **Ruskin** Unto This Last
- **Thoreau's** On the Duty of Civil Disobedience
- **Carpenter** Civilisation: Its Cause and Cure
- **Tolstoy** God's Reign is Within You and The Sermon on the Mount

4. How did these masters influence Gandhi?

Gandhi was drastically influenced by his masters- Ruskin, Thoreau, Carpenter and Tolstoy. Ruskin's 'Unto This Last,' taught him how to identify the individual good with the common good and that all types of work have equal dignity and value, whether they be intellectual or manual, noble or humble. Thoreau's 'On the Duty of Civil Disobedience' taught him that it is one's duty to refuse to obey a country's laws if one believes them to be unjust. Carpenter's Civilisation: Its Cause and Cure helped him in the analysis of civilisation. Tolstoy's God's Reign is Within You left a deep impact on him.

5. How much was Gandhi impressed by Tolstoy?

Gandhi was impressed by Tolstoy for his matchless creation. This was the author who struck Gandhi more than any other. Gandhi recognised his debt throughout his life. He greatly admired his ideas and work. After reading God's Reign is Within You, the book had left an indelible impression on him.

PASSAGE 7

1. The art of living is learnt easily by those who are positive and optimistic. From humble and simple people to great leaders in history, science or literature, we can learn a lot about the art of living by having a peep into their lives. The daily routines of these great men not only reveal their different, may be unique life styles but also help us learn certain habits and practices they followed.
2. A private workplace always helps. Jane Austen who asked that a certain squeaky hinge should never be oiled so that she always had a warning whenever someone was approaching the room where she wrote. William Faulkner, lacking a lock on his study door, detached the doorknob and brought it into the room with him. Mark Twain's family knew better than to breach his study door-they would blow a horn to draw him out. Graham Green went even further, renting a secret office; only his wife knew the address and the telephone number. After all, everyone of us needs a workplace where we can work on our creation uninterruptedly. Equally we need our private space too.
3. A daily walk has always been a source of inspiration. For many artists, a regular stroll was essentially a creative inspiration. Charles Dickens famously took three hour walks every afternoon, and what he observed on them fed directly into his writing. Tchaikovsky made do with a two-hour jaunt but wouldn't return a moment early; convinced that doing so would make him ill. Ludwig van Beethoven took lengthy strolls after lunch, carrying a pencil and paper with him in case inspiration struck. Nineteenth century composer Erik Satie did the same on his long hikes from Paris to the working-class suburb where he lived, stopping under street lamps to jot down ideas that came on his journey; it's rumoured that when those lamps were turned off during the war years, his music declined too.

   Many great people had limited social life too. One of Simone de Beauvior's close friends puts it this way. "There were no receptions, parties. It was an uncluttered kind of life, a simplicity deliberately constructed so that she could do her work." To Pablo the idea of Sunday was an "at home day".
4. The routines of these thinkers are difficult. Perhaps it is because they are so unattainable. The very idea that you can organise your time as you like is out of reach for most of us, so I'll close with a toast to all those who worked with difficulties. Like Francine Prose, who began writing when the school bus picked up her children and stopped when it brought them back; or TS Eliot, who found it much easier to write once he had a day job in a bank than he had as a starving poet and even F. Scott Fitzgerald, whose early books were written in his strict schedule as a young military officer. Those days were not as interesting as the nights in Paris that came later, but they were much more productive and no doubt easier on his liver.
5. Being forced to follow someone else's routine may irritate, but it makes it easier to stay on the path. Whenever we break that trail ourselves or take an easy path of least resistance, perhaps what's most important is that we keep walking.

1. What did Jane Austen like?

Jane Austen liked having a private working space when she was writing. Therefore, she preferred that the certain squeaky hinge is not oiled so that she would get a warning whenever someone was coming to her room.

2. Why do you think Graham Green hired a secret office? Did anyone know about it?

Graham Green hired a secret office for the need of privacy. He needed a private space wherein he could work on his creation without any interruption.

No one except Green's wife knew about this office and its telephone number.

3. What do you think inspired Erik Satie? What was the rumour about Erik Satie's productivity?

Erik Satie, the nineteenth century composer was inspired by the strolls he took. He went on long hikes from Paris to the working-class suburb where he lived. He stopped under street lamps to jot down ideas that came on his journey. The rumour regarding Erik Satie was that when the street lamps that he would come across on his hikes were turned off, his music too declined.

4. How did her limited social life affect Simone de Beauvior?

The limited social life led by Simone de Beauvior without any receptions and parties, added simplicity to her life wherein she could easily concentrate on her work.

5. In what way did TS Eliot's day job help him to write? What makes it easier for one to stay on the path?

TS Eliot's day job helped him concentrate on his writing as he did not have to starve because of the lack of a livelihood. Following a routine and living an organised life makes it easier for one to stay on one path.

PASSAGE 8

The power of the state is only limited internally by the fear of rebellion and externally by the fear of defeat in war. Subject to these restrictions, it is absolute. In practice, it can seize men's property through taxation, determine the law of marriage and inheritance, punish the expression of opinions' which it dislikes, put men to death for wishing the region they inhabit to belong to a different State and order all able-bodied males to risk their lives in battle whenever it considers war desirable. On many matters disagreement with the purposes and opinions of the state is criminal. Probably the freest states in the world, before the war, were America and England yet in America no immigrant may land until he has professed disbelief in anarchism and polygamy, while in England men were sent to prison in recent years for expressing disagreement with the Christian religion or agreement with the teaching of Christ. In time of war, all criticism of the external policy of the state is criminal. Certain objects having appeared desirable to the majority or to the effective holders of power, those who do not consider these objects desirable are exposed to pains and penalties not unlike those suffered by heretics in the past. The extent of the tyranny thus exercised is concealed by its very success few men consider it worthwhile to incur a persecution which is almost certain to be thorough and effective.

Universal military service is perhaps the extreme example of the power of the state and the supreme illustration of the difference between its attitude to its own citizens and its attitude to the citizens of other states. The state punishes, with impartial rigour, both those who kill their compatriots and those who refuse to kill foreigners. On the whole, the latter is considered the graver crime. The phenomenon of war is familiar and men fail to realise its strangeness to those who stand inside the cycle of instincts which lead to war it all seems natural and reasonable.

But to those who stand outside the strangeness of it grows with familiarity. It is amazing that the vast majority of men should tolerate a system which compels them to submit to all the horrors of the battlefield at any moment when their government commands them to do so. A French artist, indifferent to politics, attentive only to his painting, suddenly finds himself called upon to shoot Germans, who his friends assure him, are a disgrace to the human race.

A German musician, equally unknowing, is called upon to shoot the perfidious Frenchman. Why cannot the two men declare a mutual neutrality? Why not leave war to those who like it and bring it on? Yet if the two men declared a mutual neutrality they would be shot by their compatriots. To avoid this fate they try to shoot each other. If the world loses the artist, not the musician, Germany rejoices; if the world loses the musician, not the artist, France rejoices. No one remembers the loss to civilisation, which is equal whichever is killed.

1. What does the author mean when he says that the power of the state is absolute but subject to certain restrictions?

By saying that the power of the state is absolute but subject to certain restrictions, the author means to say that the state can exercise power to control the lives of its citizens through taxation, marriage and inheritance laws, send men to war to risk their lives, punish and kill people, etc. This power is absolute. However, it is limited internally by the fear of rebellion and externally, by the fear of defeat in war.

2. What examples of America and England does the author cite to indicate the power of the state?

The author cites some examples from America and England to indicate the power of the state. Accordingly, in America, no immigrant may land until he has professed disbelief in anarchism and polygamy. While in England, men were sent to prison for expressing disagreement with the Christian religion or with the teaching of Christ.

3. Explain the term 'graver crime' used in the second paragraph.

The term 'graver crime' means that in war, refusing to kill foreigners is a bigger crime than killing one's own compatriot. If a man declares neutrality with the opposition in war, he will be killed by his compatriots.

4. What are the citizens supposed to do when their government asks them to participate in war?

According to the passage, in times of war, if the government commands the citizens to participate in war, the citizens are supposed to accept it and submit to all the horrors of the battlefield at any moment.

5. Explain the term 'mutual neutrality' used in the second paragraph.

Mutual neutrality refers to the state of feeling wherein two men from opposite forces declare neutrality and kill no one. Such people decide to leave the war to those who like it and decide not to kill the opponent.

PASSAGE 9

1. Archaeology is the scientific study of the remains of past human culture. Archaeologists investigate the lives of early people by studying the objects those people have left behind. Such objects include buildings, artwork, tools, bones and pottery. Archaeologists may make exciting discoveries, such as a tomb filled with gold or the ruins of a magnificent temple in the midst of a jungle. However, the discovery of a few stone tools or grains of hardened corn may reveal even more about early people.
2. Archaeological research is the chief means to learn about societies that existed before the invention of writing about 5,000 years ago. It also provides an important supplement to our knowledge of ancient societies that left written records. In America, archaeology is considered a branch of anthropology, the scientific study of humanity and human culture. European archaeologists, however, think of their work as closely related to the field of history. Archaeology differs from history in that historians mainly study the lives of people as recorded in written documents. Archaeologists look for information about how, where and when cultures developed. Like other social scientists, they search for reasons why major changes have occurred in certain cultures. Some archaeologists try to understand why ancient people stopped hunting and started farming. Others develop theories about what caused people to build cities and to set up trade routes. In addition, some archaeologists look for reasons behind the fall of such early civilisations as the Mayas in Central America and the Romans in Europe.
3. Archaeologists examine any evidence that can help them explain how people lived in past times. Such evidence ranges from the ruins of a large city to a few stone flakes left by someone making a stone tool long ago.
4. The three basic kinds of archaeological evidence are artefacts, features and eco facts. Artefacts are objects that were made by people and can be moved without altering their appearance. Artefacts include objects like arrowheads, pots and beads. Artefacts from a society with a written history may also include clay tablets and other written records. Features consist mainly of houses, tombs, irrigation canals and other large structures built by ancient peoples. Unlike artefacts, features cannot be separated from their surroundings without changing their form. Ecofacts reveal how ancient people responded to their surroundings. Examples of ecofacts include seeds and animal bones. Any place where archaeological evidence is found is called an archaeological site. To understand the behaviour of the people who occupied a site, archaeologists must study the relationship among the artefacts, features and ecofacts found there. For example, the discovery of stone spearheads near bones of an extinct kind of buffalo at a site in New Mexico showed that early human beings had hunted buffalo in that area.
5. If objects are buried deep in the ground, their position in the Earth also concerns archaeologists. The scientists study the layers of soil and rock in which objects are found to understand the conditions that existed when the objects were placed there. In some places, archaeologists find many levels of deposits called strata. The archaeological study of strata, called stratigraphy, developed from the study of rock layers in geology. Archaeologists use special techniques and equipments to gather archaeological evidence precisely and accurately. They also keep detailed records of their findings because much archaeological research destroys the remains being studied. Locating sites is the first job of the archaeologist. Sites may be above ground, underground or underwater. Some large sites are located easily because they are clearly visible or can be traced from descriptions in ancient stories or other historical records. Such sites include the pyramids of Egypt and the ancient city of Athens in Greece.
6. Archaeologists use systematic methods of discovering sites. The traditional way to find all the sites in a region is through a foot survey. In this method, archaeologists space themselves at measured distances and walk in preset directions. Each person looks for archaeological evidence while walking forward. Scientific methods are used to help discover underground sites. For example, Aerial photography can reveal variations in vegetation that indicate the presence of archaeological evidence. Archaeologists describe, photograph and count the objects they find. They group the objects according to type and location. Three steps are followed to interpret the evidence found. They are classification, dating and evaluation.

1. What is archaeological research?

Archaeological research is the chief means of learning about societies that existed before the invention of writing. It also provides an important supplement to our knowledge of ancient societies that left written records.

2. How do archaeologists find out how people lived in the past ?

To find out how people lived in the past, archaeologists study the remains of past human cultures, the objects left behind by them and by locating sites. They also study the relationship between the behaviour of the people with the objects found in the sites.

3. How is archaeology different from history?

Archaeology is different from history as it looks for information about how, when and where cultures developed while history studies the level of the people as recorded in written documents.

Further, archaeology is a scientific and systematic study of the past of human culture while history studies the lives of people as recorded in written documents.

4. What are features and how are they different from artefacts?

While features and artefacts are archaeological evidence, they are very different in nature. Features are those objects which cannot be removed without changing their form like houses, tombs, etc. In contrast, artefacts can be moved without altering their appearance like arrowheads, pots, beads, etc.

5. How do archaeologists study the behaviour of people from a particular place?

To understand the behaviour of people from a particular place, archaeologists study the relationship among artefacts, features and ecofacts. For example, the discovery of stone spearheads near bones of an extinct kind of buffalo at a site in New Mexico showed that early human beings had hunted buffalo in that area.

PASSAGE 10

It is several years now since we reached the reductio ad absurdum of our examination system. The leakage of question papers and the consequent postponement of examinations, are the least disturbing of the reports in this regard that the newspapers publish. At Fatehgarh, some time ago, the superintendent and ten invigilators at an examination withdrew from their duties in protest against 'inadequate security arrangements'. Earlier, a mixed crowd of students and outsiders had invaded the examination centre on the very first day of the examination and adopted a threatening attitude when their attempts to pass on prepared answers to the candidates were thwarted. A day or two later a crowd climbed the roof of the examination hall and indulged in the most unspeakable acts of wretchedness. Many candidates were caught cheating. The news agency added that the administration appeared to be reluctant to handle the situation firmly as sons of some prominent citizens were said to be involved in these malpractices.

Our examinations, instead of bringing out the best in students, seem to bring out the worst. Everyone is agreed that the system should be reformed. But if one may indulge in a piece of levity on so grim a theme, the situation is rather like what Oscar Wilde said about the weather, namely, that everyone complains about it and no one does anything about it. The pace of reform is so unhurried as to be imperceptible. Meanwhile, examinations on the mass scale have at best become feats of organisation by the Registrar's office and their academic value as tests of proficiency has become negligible.

The only skills that they bring out are the ingenious ways which candidates employ for cheating. In the High School and Intermediate examinations of Uttar Pradesh, about 4,000 cases of the use of 'unfair means' are detected every year. A minister of education, while deploring this, pointed out, however, that considering the four hundred thousand that take the examinations the proportion of such cases cannot be considered large.

Reforms have no chance of success if they are based, as at present, on a wholly wrong view of the malady. The two most commonly recommended reforms, namely 'internal assessment' and 'objective tests', although they often carry the blessings of the same experts, proceed from two opposite views in regard to the validity of the old-fashioned type of examinations. Internal assessment is based on the recognition that if a teacher is good enough to teach, he is also good enough to examine his students. Objective tests, on the other hand, are intended to eliminate the chancy and subjective element in the older methods of academic evaluation. If the objective tests are really objective, it should make no difference whether their source is internal or external. In fact they eliminate the personal judgement of the teacher and their logical evolution is towards the machine-scored tests of the Educational Testing Service at Princeton.

Like other examinations these tests are useful if we are clear in our minds as to what we are testing. An academic examination should ordinarily be expected to test the student's judgement, his powers of expression and his memory–in that order. The trouble with our present examinations is that with the passage of time, this order has been reversed and the student's judgement is now left out of account altogether. We have now reached a stage where the annual external examination, on which so much depends, seems to the student a big gamble.

The evils of a final external examination at the end of a course have been exaggerated. Since, the American way of internal assessment and the piling up of credits is what finds favour with reformers today, it would perhaps be wise to have a look at what the British educator has to say about his own system.

It is wrong to suppose that we have to choose between internal assessment and external examinations. We should have both. The former will ensure that the student applies himself to his studies throughout the year and the latter will have the advantages that Harrison talks of. However, it would however be a mistake to add internal assessment scores to the external; this may tempt institutions to inflate the internal scores. The Education Commission suggests giving the two separately in the student's record. To the extent that institutions establish a name for reliability, their internal grades may protect a student from mishaps in the external examination.

The internal grades will also give the student greater confidence and eliminate the tensions that are partly responsible for those mishaps.

As for what happens in many examination centres, from rowdyism to murder, the cure is not examination reform but firm handling of wrongdoers. Now that the hooligans have discovered that they can get away with anything, an improvement in the reliability of examinations will not induce them to desist. Education had better conserve its energies for matters purely educational, leaving it to the law to deal with crime.

1. What is the significance of Oscar Wilde's complaint about the weather?

Oscar Wilde's complaint on weather, that everyone complaints about it and no one does anything about it, can be compared to the present situation of our examination system. The academic value of our examinations as tests of proficiency has become faulty. Our examinations, instead of bringing out the best in students, seem to bring out the worst. Not only are the candidates coming up with ingenious unfair means to pass the examination, but the nature of the present examination structure is also under question altogether.

2. What are the advantages recognised in the internal assessment and objective test respectively?

Internal assessment is based on the recognition that if a teacher is good enough to teach, he/she is also good enough to examine his/her students.

It ensures that the student applies himself / herself to his /her studies throughout the year. Objective tests, on the other hand, are intended to eliminate the subjective element in the older methods of academic evaluation. They eliminate the personal judgement of the teacher.

3. What is the order of priority ordinarily expected of an academic examination to test the students?

The exams are ordinarily expected to test the student's judgement, his powers of expression and his memory - in the given order.

4. What is the cure, recommended in the passage, other than the examination reforms?

According to the passage, the cure is not examination reform but firm handling of wrongdoers. The law of the land needs to deal with the crimes taking place in the examination centres. The hooligans should not feel that they can get away with anything.

5. Specify the words from the passage meaning: condemning, distorted.

Condemning – Reductio and absurdum, Distorted – Exaggerated

6. Use the following words/phrases in your own sentences: imperceptible, get away with.

Imperceptible The colour difference in the two shirts was so small that it was imperceptible.

Get away with The criminal should not be allowed to get away with the crime so easily.

PASSAGE 11

1. I know many friends of mine who drink coffee regularly but do not know that coffee exists in different forms other than instant coffee. There are many who swear by Nescafe Classic or Bru Gold, which they consider premium coffee. I may sound offensive but instant coffee is not the only way; in fact it's a very bad way of making coffee! Instant coffee cannot match up to brewed coffee's flavour nor does it have Arabica beans. It uses Robusta beans that are lower in flavour. Don't know the difference? Read on...
2. That plant might be a genius. It created a chemical that would keep pests away. Fortunately for us and unfortunately for the plant – that plan did not work the way it intended to. The chemical might have averted a few pest attacks, but attracted far greater threat – human beings. The plant I am talking about is coffee and chemical is caffeine.
3. To begin from the beginning – coffee is from a more mature part of the tree – the seed – unlike other stimulants. The ripe berry is picked and de-pulped leaving us with a seed called 'green bean' or 'green coffee'. Green bean is uncharacteristically bland with a taste nowhere close to that of coffee, but it is valued for its higher antioxidant levels.
4. It's an interesting phenomenon to see how this bland green bean turns to a flavourful coffee bean. Coffee bean is a seed and like any other seed is rich in proteins, fats and all necessary ingredients for giving birth to a new plant. When exposed to heat, the fats and carbohydrates in the bean turn into essential oils, which give the characteristic taste and aroma to the coffee bean. The degree of roasting depends on the need or purpose of use.
5. These beans are ground so that the surface area of the bean is increased, which makes extraction easier. The bean can be ground or crushed but making the particles uniform will ensure equal extraction, or else the smaller particle will get over extracted and the larger one under extracted. Hence, the burr grinder is used to ensure that the coffee bean gets ground in a uniform way in which all particles are of similar sizes.

6. Does under extraction give a lighter coffee and over extraction a stronger one? No. For a lighter or stronger coffee less or more coffee powder has to be used. Why? Under extraction will not get all the flavours of the coffee as the water runs too quickly. It will not get what you want – It will taste sour. Over-extraction will bring out all unnecessary flavours rendering the taste bitter.

1. Comment on the writers reference to the unique feature of coffee plant.

The writer's reference to the unique feature of the coffee plant, which is its ability to produce caffeine as a chemical to protect itself from pests, adds depth to the discussion of coffee and its role in human culture and biology. The reference to this unique feature highlights the complexity of the relationship between the coffee plant and humans, and how it has evolved over time to meet the needs of both.

2. List the reason why the author refers to humans as great threat to coffee plants.

The author refers to humans as a great threat to coffee plants because of the chemical that the plants had originally produced to ward off pests. This chemical- caffeine- is happily consumed by humans all over the world leading to the increased demand of coffee. The increased demand can lead to deforestation, habitat loss and other environmental impacts. Additionally, it can lead to unsustainable farming practices and the use of harmful chemicals to grow and process coffee, further endangering the coffee plant and its ecosystem.

3. Comment on the writer's reference to the interesting phenomenon of the green bean turning into a flavourful coffee bean.

The writer does an excellent job of describing the interesting phenomenon of the green bean turning into a flavourful coffee bean. The writer explains that the green coffee bean is uncharacteristically bland with a taste nowhere close to that of coffee, but is valued for its higher protein and fat content. When the bean is exposed to heat, the fats and carbohydrates turn into essential oils which give the characteristic taste and aroma to the coffee bean. This transformation is indeed an interesting phenomenon that showcases the transformative power of heat and the complexity of coffee production.

4. Over-extraction does not give a stronger coffee. List one method to get stronger coffee.

One method to get stronger coffee is to use more coffee powder. This will ensure that the water has enough time to extract all the flavours from the coffee beans, giving you a stronger cup of coffee.

5. Why is it fair to say that the right degree of extraction of coffee is important?

The right degree of extraction of coffee is important because it will determine the flavour, aroma and overall taste of the coffee. If the extraction is done incorrectly, the coffee will either taste sour or bitter and over-extracted. The right degree of extraction requires precise control over the amount of coffee and the time it is exposed to water. Only then can you create the perfectly balanced cup of coffee.

PASSAGE 12

The work which Gandhiji had taken in hand was not only the achievement of political freedom but establishment of a social order based on truth and non-violence, unity and peace, equality and universal brotherhood and maximum freedom for all. The unfinished part of his experiment was perhaps even more difficult to achieve than the achievement of freedom. In the political struggle, the fight was against a foreign power and all could or did either join in it or at least wish it success and give to it their moral support. In establishing the social order of his pattern, there was a lively possibility of a conflict arising between groups and classes of our own people.

Experience shows that man values his possessions because here he sees the means of perpetuation and survival through his descendants even after his body is reduced to ashes. That new order cannot be established without radically changing men's mind and attitude towards property and at some stage or other the haves have to yield place to the have-nots. We have seen in our time attempts to achieve a kind of egalitarian society.

But this was done by and large by the use of physical force. In the result, it is difficult to say that the instinct to possess has been rooted out or that it will not reappear in an even worse form under a different face. It may even be that like gas kept confined within metallic containers under great pressure, or water held behind a big dam, that breaks the barrier, reaction will one day sweep back with violence equal in extent and intensity to what was used to establish and maintain the outward egalitarian form. This enforced egalitarianism contains in its bosom the seed of its own destruction.

The root cause of class-conflict is possessiveness or the acquisitive instinct. So long as the ideal that is held up to be achieved is one of securing the maximum of material satisfaction, possessiveness is neither suppressed nor eliminated but grows by what it feeds upon. Nor does it cease to be such-it is possessiveness still whether it is confined to a few only or is bared by many. If egalitarianism is to endure, it has to be based not on the possession of the maximum of material goods whether by few or by all but on voluntary, enlightened enunciation—denying oneself what cannot be shared by others or can be enjoyed only at the expense of others.

This calls for substitution of spiritual value, for purely material ones. Mahatma Gandhi showed us how the acquisitive instinct inherent in man could be transmuted by the adoption of the ideal of trusteeship by those who have for the benefit of all those who have not so that instead of leading to exploitation and conflict, it would become a means and incentive to the amelioration and progress of society.

1. What, according to the author was the unfinished part of Gandhiji's experiment?

The unfinished part of Gandhiji's experiment relates to the establishment of a social order based or truth, non-violence, unity and equality, a sense of brotherhood and for maximum freedom for all.

2. Why is a change in men's attitude to property necessary for establishing a new social order?

The change in men's attitude to property is necessary for establishing a new social order because man values his possessions. He sees the means of perpetuation and survival through his descendants.

3. Why does the author say that enforced egalitarianism contains the seeds of its own destruction?

According to the author, an enforced egalitarian society was achieved by the use of physical force. This does not ensure that the instinct to possess has been rooted out or that it will not reappear in an even worse form under a different face.

4. How can the acquisitive instinct of man be made a tool for social progress?

The acquisitive instinct can be transmitted by the adoption of the ideal of trusteeship by those who have for the benefit of all those who have-not. This is to ensure that instead of leading to exploitation and conflict. It can become a means of amelioration and progress of society.

5. Why does man value his possessions more than his life?

According to the passage, man values his possession more than his life because for him his property is a means for perpetuation and survival of his descendants/ future generations even after his death.

PASSAGE 13

The happy man is the man who lives objectively, who has free affections and wide interests, who secures his happiness through these interests and affections and through the fact that they, in turn make him an object of interest and affection to many others.

To be a recipient of affection is a potent cause of happiness but the man who demands affection is not the man upon whom it is bestowed. The man who receives affection is, speaking broadly, the man who gives it. But it is useless to attempt to give it as a calculation, in the way in which one might lend money at interest, for a calculated affection is not felt to be so by the recipient.

What then can a man do who is unhappy because he is encased in self? So long as he continues to think about the causes of his unhappiness, he continues to be self-centered and therefore does not get outside the vicious circle. If he is to get outside it, it must be by genuine interests, not by simulated interests adopted merely as a medicine. Although this difficulty is real, there is nevertheless much that he can do if he has rightly diagnosed his trouble. If, e.g., his trouble is due to a sense of sin, conscious or unconscious, he can first persuade his conscious mind that he has no reason to feel sinful and then unconscious mind, concerning himself meanwhile with some more or less neutral activity. If he succeeds in dispelling the sense of sin, it is possible that genuine objective interests will arise spontaneously. If his trouble is self-pity, he can deal with it in the same manner after first persuading himself that there is nothing extraordinarily unfortunate in his circumstances.

If fear is his trouble, let him practise exercises designed to give courage. Courage has been recognised from time immemorial as an important virtue and a great part of the training of boys and young men has been devoted, to producing a type of character capable of fearlessness in battle. But moral courage and intellectual courage have been much less studied; they also, however, have their technique. Admit to yourself everyday at least one painful truth, you will find it quite useful.

Teach yourself to feel that life will still be worth living even if you were not, as of course you are, immeasurably superior to all your friends in virtue and intelligence. Exercises of this sort prolonged through several years, will at last enable you to admit facts without flinching and will, in so doing free you from the empire of fear over a very large field.

1. What kind of affection can be a potent cause of happiness?

To be recipient of affection is a potent cause of happiness. A man who lives objectively, who has free affections and wide interests, who secures his happiness through these interests and affections and through the fact that they, in turn make him an object of interest and affection to many others, is a happy man.

2. How can a 'self-encased' person get out of his sense of unhappiness?

A 'self-encased' person can get out of his sense of unhappiness by coming out of his self-centeredness. One can come of this self-centeredness by genuine interests, not by simulated interests adopted merely as a medicine.

3. How can a person overcome his feeling of self-pity and fear?

A person can overcome his feelings of self-pity by persuading himself that there is nothing extraordinarily unfortunate in his circumstances. He can get out of his fear by learning courage.

4. Explain the various kinds of courage mentioned by the author.

The author mentions three types of courage in the passage. First is the courage of fearlessness in battle which is the outcome of physical training and strength. The other two types are- moral courage and intellectual courage which can be learnt by teaching oneself to feel that life will still be worth living even if you were not immeasurably superior to all your friends in virtue and intelligence.

5. According to the passage, how can we build our courage?

The author of the given passage suggests various ways to build courage. They are

- Admit at least one painful truth every day.
- Feel that life will still be worth living.
- Feel that you are immeasurably superior to all your friends in virtue and intelligence.

PASSAGE 14

They were once everywhere. Chirping and flapping their wings at the window sills, on top of cupboards and on the branches of trees. Where have all the little sparrows gone? The association between humans and the house sparrow dates back to several centuries. It is a bird that evokes fond memories of childhood and adds freshness to households through its presence.

Many bird watchers and ornithologists recall with fondness how the house sparrows gave flight to their passion for observing birds. The nests of sparrow dotted almost every house in the neighbourhood as well as public places like bus stands and railway stations, where they live in colonies and survived on food grains and tiny worms. Unfortunately, the house sparrow has now become a disappearing species and their numbers are declining across their natural range. A study conducted by the Andhra University, Visakhapatnam highlighted that the population of sparrows fell by over 60% even in the Rural areas of coastal Andhra Pradesh. A survey conducted by the British Trust for Ornithology showed that the house sparrow population in Britain has declined by about 58% since 1970.

Certainly, there is no single reason for the decline of the house sparrow. Scientists and experts say that severe changes in the Urban ecosystem in recent times have had tremendous impact on the population of house sparrows. Mobile tower radiation and excessive use of chemical fertilisers are aggravating the problem and have been identified as potent sparrow killers.

It is said that sparrow chicks, which require insect food for their survival in their early days, have not been getting adequate supply from their parents. Urban landscape too, has been dramatically altered over the years. Old houses, with courtyards in front and backyards, have made way for concrete multistories with little greenery. No longer are sparrows able to find the tiny nooks, crannies and holes where they used to build their nests. Typically, sparrows were never an issue of concern for us with their diminutive presence in our household. Perhaps, it is this diminutive presence because of which even their gradual disappearance has gone unnoticed. Mohammed Dilavar is rightly called the 'Sparrow Man of India' as he has been successful in drawing the attention of the world towards the declining number of house sparrows.

1. "The association between humans and the house sparrow dates back to several centuries." Why does the author says so?

The author says so because since time immemorial a house sparrow has evoked fond memories of childhood and added freshness to households through its presence.

They have been a part of every neighbourhood and nook and cranny of the city where they existed in large numbers in their colonies without hampering daily life of humans.

2. What reasons does the author give for the declining house sparrow population?

The author gives several reasons for declining sparrow population. They are

- Severe changes in the urban ecosystem in recent times
- Mobile tower radiation and excessive use of chemical fertilisers
- Inadequate 'insect food' for the sparrow chicks

3. How has the urban landscape added to the dwindling population of the house sparrow?

Urban landscape has added to the dwindling population of the house sparrow because of the changing infrastructure of the urban city. Modern houses in a city lack greenery. There are no courtyards or backyards which prove to be a major hindrance for sparrows. Now, the sparrows are unable to find the tiny nooks and crannies where they could build their nests.

4. Why is Mohammed Dilavar called the Sparrow Man of India?

Mohammed Dilavar is called the Sparrow Man of India because he had been successful in drawing the attention of the world towards the declining number of house sparrows. Before him, the reduction in the numbers of house sparrows and their gradual disappearance had never been a central topic of discussion.

5. Why do you think that the declining numbers of house sparrows has gone unnoticed?

The declining number of the house sparrows has gone unnoticed because they had peacefully coexisted with humanity. They had never been a nuisance or disturbed the day to day activities of mankind. Their presence was never seen as a problem.

PASSAGE 15

Every year in the town of Silkeborg, in Denmark, thousands of visitors walk past a murder victim lying in a glass case. No one will ever know his name. It is enough to known that 2000 years ago he was as human as ourselves. That face has moved men and women to poetry and to tears. Last year, I visited this Danish town surrounded by lakes and looking at that face in a small museum, I felt a deep respect for it, for every wrinkle on that face tells a wonderful and terrible tale from Denmark's distant past. The rope which cut off the man's breath is still around his neck. Yet it is a surprisingly peaceful face, difficult to understand, and one that you cannot forget.

This strange and ancient murder mystery began 28 years ago, on 8th May, 1950, when two brothers, Emil and Viggo Hojgaard, were digging in Tollund Fen (or Bog), near Silkeborg, for peat to be used as fuel for cooking, and to keep their homes warm in the trees near the bog, where only bushes and thick grass grew.

Then, at a depth of 2.75 m, their spades suddenly struck something. They were gazing, with fear and wonder, at a human face under the soil. The body was naked except for a cap; it was resting on its side as if asleep, arms and legs bent. The face was gentle, with eyes and lips closed. There was a short growth of hair on the chin. The brothers, who did not known what to do, called the Silkeborg police.

Arriving on the scene, the police did not recognise the man as anyone reported to be missing. Cleverly guessing that the brothers might have discovered an unknown page from Europe's past, the police called in some archaeologists. Enter Professor Peter Glob, a famous archaeologist from nearby Aarhus University. Professor Glob carefully removed a lump of peat beside the dead man's head.

A rope made of leather hung round his neck. He had either been strangled to death or hanged. But when, and by whom? Professor Glob ordered a box to be built around the dead body and the peat in which it lay so that nothing would be disturbed. Next day, the box, weighing nearly a ton, was lifted out of the bog on to a horse drawn cart, on its way for examination at Copenhagen's National Museum. One of Professor Glob's helpers fell down and died with the huge effort. It seemed to be a sign of bad luck, as if some old god wanted the life of a modern man in place of a man from the past.

Bodies found in the bog were nothing new. So far, Denmark's bogs have produced no fewer than 400 of them, all in excellent condition because of the humid acid present in peat, which preserves the bodies.

But not until the nineteenth century did scientists and historians begin to understand that the bodies belonged to some dark, unknown corners of European pre-history. Once the bodies belonged to some dark, unknown corners of European pre-history.

Once the bodies were dug up, they crumbled quickly, after being exposed to the sunlight and air. Some of them were buried again. When peat-digging was started again during and after the Second World War, many more bodies were found in the bogs – first, in 1942 at Store Arden and then in 1946, 1947 and 1948 at Borre Fen.

The tools and other objects found beside them showed that they were people from Denmark's Early Iron Age (400 BC to 400 AD). Therefore, none of the bodies, was less than 1500 years old, and some were probably much older. The first of the bodies discovered in Borre Fen – a full – grown male – became specially important now. This man, too had died violently, with a rope around his neck, strangled or hanged. And his last meal had been of grain.

1. Why do thousands of visitors go to Silkeborg to see the murdered man?

Thousands of visitors go to Silkeborg to see the unknown murdered man kept in a glass case to get inspiration. These visitors know that the man lived like us (humans) about 2000 years ago. This makes the man a source of poetry for many men and women.

2. How did people known that the man was murdered?

The people/ tourists and the archeologist who found the body of the unknown man believed he was murdered because a rope made of leather, which cut off the man's breath, hung round the man's neck. This made people ascertain that the man had either been strangled to death or hanged.

3. Why did the people call in some archaeologist when the murdered man was found?

The people called in some archeologist when the murdered man was found because the police could not recognise the man to be a person reported to be missing. Further, they guessed that the Hojgaard brothers might have discovered an unknown page from Europe's past.

4. How did the people come to known that none of the bodies were less than 1500 years old?

People came to know that the bodies found while digging for peat were less than 1500 years old because the tools and other objects found beside them showed that they were people from Denmark's Early Iron Age (400 BC to 400 AD).

5. Make sentences with the following words used in the passage to bring out their meaning.

(i) Wrinkle (ii) Mystery
(iii) Strangled (iv) Exposed

(i) **Wrinkle** means a slight line or fold in something, especially fabric or the skin of the face.

Deven got botox treatment to get rid of the wrinkle on his face.

(ii) **Mystery** means something that is difficult or impossible to understand or explain.

I want to understand the mystery surrounding the Bermuda Triangle.

(iii) **Strangled** means having died as a result of having the neck squeezed or constricted.

The marks on her neck show that she was strangled to death.

(iv) **Exposed** means to make visible.

Rhea's lies were exposed through the video.

PASSAGE 16

It is often said that the Ghaznavid and Ghurid soldiers regarded death in a war against infidels as martyrdom in the cause of Islam. But it is more likely that the real draw was the attraction of plunder, the likes of which they had not seen in campaigns in more arid lands. For Indian Commanders, apart from plunder, battles incorporated the niceties of a sport with its own rules of play.

Immortalising the heroism of kings in battle, the poets and bards emphasised the rules of war and chivalry. To apply the chivalric code in minor campaigns may have relieved the tedium of war, but the campaigns against the Ghurids were of an entirely different nature and this may not have been realised initially. Notions of honour and devotion were often placed above expediency and gradually the astrologically determined auspicious moment for attack took precedence over strategy and tactics. Inflated claims to valour, such as the hero who could defeat a thousand warriors simultaneously, began to enter the rhetoric of courtly literature.

The organisation of Indian armies added to their weakness. Each army had as its permanent core the standing army, but many of the soldiers were local levies or soldiers supplied by Samantas where this was part of the latter's obligation to the suzerain.

In addition, mercenaries were a visible section of the armies of these times. Such a collection of soldiers had not always been trained to fight as a consolidated army. It was possibly also the dispersed character of the army that gave it a license to plunder indiscriminately. Villagers were harassed and looted by armies on the march, particularly if the campaign coincided with the harvesting of the crop, as it often did. For peasants and merchants, war was a nightmare that disrupted the routine of earning a livelihood. Laying waste vast tracts of inhabited and cultivated land, merely because it was a part of the enemy's territory, was a proud boast attributed to Prithviraj Chauhan on defeating the Chandella ruler.

Historians have sometimes commented, perhaps more from hindsight, on why Indian rulers did not make a conjoint effort through the centuries to defend the North Western passes. Time and again invaders came through these passes, yet little was done to prevent this, the defence of the region lying arbitrarily in the hands of the local rulers. It appears the construction of a series of fortifications along the passes was not thought feasible.

Perhaps the need for defence was not given priority, the area being viewed as a natural frontier. Alternatively, given the mountainous terrain the only routes for pastoralists and caravan were through the passes and it was therefore thought better to leave them open. The local kings and chiefs who controlled the passes derived an income from this trade. There would have been familiarity too with those coming across the passes and therefore a slow recognition that sometimes friendliness had turned into hostility. The effectiveness of mountains as a frontier was also thwarted by the many occasions when the Punjab was conquered from across the borders or was involved in the politics of Afghanistan and Central Asia. This closeness militated against a properly focused perspective on political developments across the borderlands and in Central Asia.

Invasions by outsiders are known in many parts of the world: the Huns attacking Rome, the Arabs invading Spain or the Spanish and Portuguese conquering Latin America. The potentialities of invasions were recognised only in Hindsight. These invasions were mounted by alien peoples who were little known, if at all, to the societies they invaded. But the Turks had been a contiguous people, familiar from trade in horses and other commodities and from the Turkish mercenaries employed in some Indian Armies. However, the historical scene in Central Asia and West Asia had now changed, with new political ambitions after the rise of Islam. For the rulers of Northern India, to recognise this would have required an understanding of a wider range of politics beyond the areas enclosed by the immediate frontiers. This does not appear to have been an Indian concern. Indians who travelled to different parts of Asia on a variety of assignments wrote little about what they observed, remaining silent on the politics of other lands. It was almost as if the exterior landscape was irrelevant Political interests therefore tended to be parochial.

This marks a striking contrast to the world of the Chinese and the Arabs, both made aware of distant places through the detailed accounts of travellers and traders. The Arabs had a fascination for the geography of other lands and the Chinese were wary of happenings in their neighbourhood in Central Asia.

1. What was the nature of campaign against Ghurids?

The campaigns against the Ghurids were of an entirely different nature in comparison to others. For others, practicality, morality and convenience were crucial. In contrast, in the campaign against Ghurids, notions of honour and devotion were often placed above expediency. Further, the astrologically determined auspicious moment for attack took priority over strategy and tactics.

2. According to the passage 'the Indian rulers did not find it necessary to the North-Western Pass'. Why?

The Indian rulers did not find it necessary to the North-Western Pass because these passes were the only routes of travel for pastoralists and caravans which led the kings and rulers to receive taxes. Further, as these passes were viewed as a natural frontier for all, so the Indian rulers did not feel the need to defend these passes and any law that defended them were not considered convenient.

3. Explain the statement "The potentialities of invasions were recognised only in hindsight".

The given statement indicates that even though the invasions by outsiders are known in many parts of the world, Indians did not pay much attention to it. This was so because these invasions were done by alien people who were little known to the societies they invaded. Further, they lacked the wider range of politics beyond the areas enclosed by the immediate frontiers because the Indian who travelled to different parts of Asia wrote very little about it.

4. Why were the Chinese and the Arabs aware of distant places?

The Chinese and the Arabs were aware of the distant places because their travellers and traders wrote detailed accounts of the places they visited.

This was because the Arabs were curious to understand the geography of other lands and the Chinese were sceptical of happenings in their neighbourhood in Central Asia.

5. Mercenaries were a visible section of the armies of these times. Justify.

The author of the given passage asserts that mercenaries were a visible section of the armies of these times because most of the Indian soldiers had not been trained to fight as a consolidated army but were given a license to plunder villagers.

Villagers were harassed and looted by armies on the march. Further, for peasants and merchants, war was a nightmare that disrupted the routine of earning a livelihood.

Previous Years' QUESTIONS

Directions *Read the following passages and answer the questions that follow each passage.*

PASSAGE 1

The diverse conceptual elements of religion, capital, nature, metaphysics, rationality, science, were tied together in a highly deliberate integration that is to say in deliberately accruing worldly alliances. Newton's and Boyle's metaphysical view of the new science won out over the 'freethinkers' and became official only because it was sold to the Anglican establishment and in an alliance with that establishment, to the powerful mercantile and incipient industrial interests of the period in thoroughly predatory terms. Terms which stressed that how we conceive nature may now be transformed into something, into the kind of thing, that is indefinitely available for our economic gain by processes of extraction, processes such as mining, deforestation, plantation agriculture intended essentially as what we today would call 'agribusiness'. None of these processes could have taken on the unthinking and yet systematic prevalence that they first began to get in this period unless one had ruthlessly revised existing ideas of a world animated by a divine presence. From an anima mundi, one could not simply proceed to take at whim and will. Not that one could not or did not, till then, take at all. But in the past in a wide range of social worlds, such taking as one did had to be accompanied by ritual offerings of reciprocation which were intended to show respect towards as well as to restore the balance in nature, offerings made both before and after cycles of planting and even hunting. The point is that, in general, the revision of such an age-old conception of nature was achieved in tandem with a range of seemingly miscellaneous elements that were brought together in terms that stressed a future of endlessly profitable consequences that would accrue if one embraced this particular metaphysics of the new science and build, in the name of a notion of rationality around it, the institutions of an increasingly centralised political oligarchy (an incipient state) and an established religious orthodoxy of Anglicanism that had penetrated the universities as well, to promote these very specific interests. These were the very terms that the freethinkers found alarming for politics and culture, alarming for the local and egalitarian ways of life, which some decades earlier the radical elements in the English Revolution such as the Levellers, Diggers, Quakers, Ranters and other groups had articulated and fought for. Gandhi, much later, spoke in political terms that were poignantly reminiscent of these radical sectaries and, in Hind Swaraj and other writings, he wrote about science and its relations to these political terms in ways that echoed the alarm of the somewhat later scientific dissenters. **CAPF AC 2024**

1. How did the metaphysical view of the new science become official?

The metaphysical view of the new science became official only because it was sold to Anglican establishment and in an alliance with that establishment to the powerful mercantile and incipient industrial interests of the period in thoroughly predatory terms.

2. What was nature reconceived as?

The nature was reconceived as the process of extraction, processes such deforestation, mining, plantation agriculture intended essentially as what we today would call 'agribusiness'.

3. How was the balance in nature restored in the past?

The balance in nature was restored by a wide range of social works, such taking as one did had to accompanied by ritual offerings of reciprocation that were intended to show respects and by offerings made by both before and after cycles of planting and even hunting in past.

4. What were the kinds of institutions that helped the reconceptualisation of nature?

The institutions of an centralised oligarchy (an incipient state) and an established religious orthodoxy of Anglicanism were the kinds of institutions that helped the reconceptualisation of nature.

5. Why did the freethinkers find the transformation of nature alarming?

The freethinkers found the transformation of nature alarming since it may be harmful to the locals and egalitarian ways of life that Gandhiji much spoke in political terms about science and its relations to these political terms are an echo of the alarm.

PASSAGE 2

Bombay was initially seven islands. As the population grew; the islands were joined to create more space and they gradually fused into one big city. Bombay was the commercial capital of colonial India.

As the premier port on the Western coast it was the centre of international trade. By the end of the nineteenth century, half the imports and exports of India passed through Bombay. One important item of this trade was opium that the East India Company exported to China.

Indian merchants and middlemen supplied and participated in this trade and they, helped integrate Bombay's economy directly to Malwa, Rajasthan and Sind where opium was grown. This led to the growth of an Indian capitalist class. Bombay's capitalists came from diverse communities such as Parsi, Marwari, Konkani Muslim, Gujarati Bania, Bohra, Jew and Armenian.

When the American Civil War started in 1861 cotton from the American South stopped coming into the international market. This led to an upsurge of demand for Indian cotton, grown primarily in the Deccan.

Once again Indian merchants and middlemen found an opportunity for earning huge profits. In 1869, the Suez Canal was opened and this further strengthened Bombay's links with the world economy. The Bombay government and Indian merchants used this opportunity to declare Bombay Urbs Prima in Indis, a Latin phrase meaning the most important city of India.

From the mid-nineteenth century there was a need to expand railways and shipping and develop the administrative structure. Many new buildings were constructed at this time. These buildings reflected the culture and confidence of the rulers.

The architectural style was usually European. This importation of European styles reflected the imperial vision in several ways. First, it expressed the British desire to create a familiar landscape in an alien country, and thus to feel at home in the colony. Second, the British felt that European styles would best symbolise their superiority, authority and power. Third, they thought that buildings that looked European would mark out the difference and distance between the colonial masters and their Indian subjects.

Initially, these buildings were at odds with the traditional Indian buildings. Gradually, Indians too got used to European architecture and made it their own. The British in turn adapted some Indian styles to suit their needs. One example is the bungalow which was used by government officers in Bombay and all over India. The name bungalow was derived from bangla a traditional thatched Bengali hut. The colonial bungalow was set on extensive grounds which ensured privacy and marked a distance from the Indian world around. The traditional pitched roof and surrounding veranda kept the bungalow cool in the summer months. The compound had separate quarters for a retinue of domestic servants. The bungalows in the Civil Lines thus became a racially exclusive enclave in which the ruling classes could live self-sufficient lives without daily social contact with Indians. **CAPF AC 2023**

1. How did Bombay develop into a commercial hub in the nineteenth century?

Bombay was a premier port on the Western coast. This made it the centre of international trade. Half of India's imports and exports passed through Bombay by the end of the nineteenth century. Thus, Bombay developed into a commercial hub in the nineteenth century.

2. How did the demand for Indian cotton escalate?

The export of cotton from the American South into the international market stopped at the start of the American Civil War in 1861. Due to this, the demand for Indian cotton escalated.

3. Why did European architecture dominate the skyline of Bombay in the mid-nineteenth century?

When the British settled in Bombay, they wished to create a familiar landscape and to feel at home. They further felt that European styles would best symbolise their superiority, authority and power and isolate them from their subjects. Thus, European architecture dominated the skyline of Bombay in the mid-nineteenth century.

4. How did the British adapt the Indian 'Bangla' to suit their needs?

Both Indians and Britishers adapted each others' architecture and styles as per their needs. The British adapted the 'bangla' which ensured privacy and marked a distance from the Indian world. It had a veranda which would keep the bungalow cool in summer and had separate quarters for domestic servants.

5. How did the bungalow symbolise colonial attitudes?

The bungalow symbolised colonial attitude by marking a distance from the Indian world around and by maintaining separate quarters for domestic servants.

PASSAGE 3

Properly regulated, the age-old system of apprenticeship could be developed as an alternative means of education rather than a system of exploitation. A blanket ban on children learning crafts would mean loss of a unique opportunity to create a skilled workforce of potential high earners. It would also imply the loss of an opportunity to generate self-employment in a country with rising unemployment and few employment avenues for rural youth, especially home-based women. However, every child under fifteen years should go to school and can learn the family craft while at home.

Sadly, in the craft sector in India, the choice is often between a craftsman's child learning ancestral skills (while on the job and contributing to the family income in the process) while remaining illiterate or getting a conventional education. Formal schooling might not actually equip him or her for any job in the future.

The crucial issue is not poverty, which is often cited as a justification for child labour but whether there are alternative educational opportunities available for the child that would give him/her the same employment opportunities. Can child labour be transformed — through legislation, innovative new planning and educational mechanisms — into a vibrant new form of training and empowerment?

Training in craft skills, whether at home or through the traditional guru-shishya relationship, should be recognised as industrial training and given the same support as other forms of technical and vocational education.

The family, master craftsperson, cooperative society, institution or NGO imparting the training should receive some stipend so that the child rather than the employer receives any money that he/she may earn during the period. Otherwise, there is the temptation, often succumbed to, of practising bonded labour of children under the guise of imparting a skill.

Craft skills should be on par with other forms of vocational training, especially in traditional crafts pockets and should be part of a properly structured curriculum, with trainers or parents paid to impart the skill, rather than using children as unpaid labour. Equally important is the issue of providing facilities for conventional education alongside those for teaching traditional skills, scheduling semesters and hours according to the work structures and seasonality of craft production. Most young craftspeople do not go to school because school hours and locations make it impossible to avail of both disciplines.

Much craft production is usually a seasonal affair, with peaks and lows according to market demands. School terms and curricula could be organised accordingly. In a country as diverse and multi-dimensional as India, there is no one single solution or methodology and we need to find ways for children of craft families to learn a craft and go to school.

CAPF AC 2022

1. What would 'blanket ban on children learning crafts' imply?

A 'blanket ban on children learning crafts' would imply a loss of the opportunity to generate self-employment in a country with rising unemployment and few employment avenues for rural youth, especially home-based women. It would mean that a unique opportunity of creating a skilled workforce would be lost.

2. What is the dilemma faced by a craftsman's child?

The dilemma faced by a craftsman's child is whether he/she should remain illiterate and learn the ancestral skills while working a job to contribute financially, or get formal education which might fail to ensure a future job for him/her.

3. Who should receive the stipend and why?

The family, master craftsperson, cooperative society, institution or NGO providing the training should receive the stipend. This should be done to make sure that the child receives the money he/she earns during the training period.

4. Why does child labour exist? What can make it a viable mode of employment?

There is no single cause of child labour. It is the result of several issues including poverty, lack of educational opportunities and viable alternatives.

Child labour can be made a viable mode of employment

1. by giving the organisations that provide training in craft skill a stipend so that the child earns money.
2. by making craft skills a part of a properly structured curriculum and providing facilities for conventional education.

5. What measures should be taken to encourage school education amongst children of craftsmen?

In order to accomplish the aim of encouraging school education among them, the following measures should be taken.

1. Making traditional craft skills a part of the curriculum.
2. Scheduling classes and semesters in accordance with the work structure and season of craft production.
3. Ensuring that the school is located nearby and is accessible to the children.

PASSAGE 4

One of the things that has long intrigued me about this country is its curious grudging relationship to money. I was reminded of this when, a few days ago, taking out a new 500-rupees note to pay a bill at a nursing home, I was made to notice a razor-thin tear in the paper, and given it back. "I just got this from an ATM," I said. The receptionist, noticing my look of exasperation, shared his own experience with me, "These days even banks aren't reliable…" and continued with words I could not hear properly.

I gave a flawless one this time and suppressed the question I would often ask: Why will a note with blemishes not do? People's responses are varied: some grin, others, pretend not to hear. I wondered whether I should go to a bank and exchange the note! Instead, I had a cappuccino at one of the coffee shops where the note changed hands without comment or scrutiny. Maybe the young man had not seen the tear or maybe he had noticed but both he and the coffee he served represented a new order to which the physical state of the bank note was irrelevant. The only other party that will accept a damaged note is the parking lot attendant. He will accept any kind of note, new or aged or separately. He represents the oddly accommodating nature of the old order.

The idea that the physical condition of a bank note is unimportant came to me during my years in England - as ragged five-or ten-pound notes, even rescued by a band of cellotape, changed hands without a word. In India, the symbolic worth of the note is heightened by its crisp look. And as the torn note threatens to fall apart, so does the value it represents.

This leads me to the other related mystery - the curiously perennial shortage of change. Give a 500-rupees note to a shopkeeper and he will look at you with an accusatory silence. And who can forget the auto driver who having been handed a large now, first rummage tiredly in one pocket, then in another and then takes out a carefully folded note.

A friend once gave me an insight into why the situation, as we know it, exists. Having arrived in the morning we had to pay the fare to the auto driver but not a single auto driver could give us change for a hundred rupees. "How cannot one of them have the money?" I asked. These people do not bring the last day's earnings when they return to work. They begin each day afresh. **CAPF AC 2021**

1. Which incident made the speaker think in terms of people's relationship to money?

Once, the speaker gave a slightly torn but a new 500-rupees note to pay the bill at a nursing home. It was returned because of the tear and consequently, he had to give a new, completely intact note which was accepted. This incident made the speaker question why the torn or blemished note was not acceptable as in his understanding the physical condition of the note was irrelevant.

2. What did the speaker do with the torn note of 500 rupees?

After having the note rejected at the nursing home, the speaker used the torn note to pay for a cappuccino at a coffee shop, where the note was accepted without any argument.

3. How are the young man at the coffee shop and the parking lot attendant different in their approaches towards a damaged note?

Even though both of these people are accepting of a damaged note, the young man represents a new order to whom the state of the note did not matter. In contrast, the parking lot attendant has an accepting nature of the old times when the physical appearance of things was not the ground of acceptance or rejection.

4. According to the speaker, what is the difference between the English and the Indian way of looking at a bank note?

While English people were unbothered with the physical state of the note, even if the notes were torn and made whole by a cellotape, Indians equate the worth of a note with its physical appearance. If a note is torn or blemished, its value is also reduced. This shows a difference in people's attitude towards a note in India and England.

5. Relate the experience of the speaker with the auto drivers vis-a-vis money.

While recalling his experience with notes, the author also mentions that the issue of scarcity of change is another mystery. The auto drivers never seem to have any change and though they try to find change in their pockets, they always come up empty handed. The speaker can't understand why they don't have change even in the mornings and concluded that it's because they earn daily and thus, don't bring the previous day's earning with them.

PASSAGE 5

After every party, it's time to clean up. Mount Everest is no different. The record number of climbers crowding the world's highest mountain this season has left a government clean-up crew grappling with how to clear away everything from abandoned tents to human waste that threatens drinking water.

Budget expedition companies charge just $30,000 per climber, cutting costs including waste removal. Everest has so much garbage–depleted oxygen cylinders, food packaging, rope–that climbers use it as a kind of signpost. But this year's haul from an estimated 700 climbers, guides and porters on the mountain has been a shock to the ethnic Sherpas who worked on the government's clean-up drive this spring.

The tents are littering the South Col or the Camp 4, which at 8000 m (26240 feet), is the highest campsite on Everest. The high winds have scattered the tents and trash everywhere. "The altitude, oxygen levels, dangerously icy and slippery slopes and bad weather of the South Col make it very difficult to bring such big things as tents down", said Dawa Steven Sherpa, who led an independent clean-up last month.

Exhausted climbers struggling to breathe and battling nausea often leave heavy tents behind. Dawa said the logos on the ice-embedded tents that identify the expedition companies were ripped out so that culprits could evade detection.

"It took us an hour to dig out just one tent out of the frozen ice and bring it down", he said. His expeditions have brought down some 20000 kg of garbage since 2008.

Dawa estimated 30 tents had been left on the South Col and as much as 5000 kg of trash. It is impossible to know exactly how much litter is spread across Everest because it becomes visible only when the snow melts. **CAPF AC 2020**

1. What does the garbage on Mount Everest consist of?

Garbage on Mount Everest consists of depleted oxygen cylinders, rope, tent material, food packaging material, food waste, human excreta and other used materials by climbers.

2. What is the task of the government clean-up crew?

The task of the government clean-up crew is to find the maximum possible wastes and garbage left by climbers and bring them back and make arrangements for their disposal so that Mount Everest can be kept clean and the water sources are clean.

3. Why is the clean-up task difficult?

The cleaning work is very difficult due to the bad terrain and bad weather. The high altitude, low oxygen levels, dangerous snow and slippery slopes make the clean-up task very difficult. In addition, many waste materials are sometimes buried in thick snow cover and become visible only when the snow melts.

4. Why do climbers leave their heavy tents behind on the mountain while returning?

While climbing, climbers have more energy and enthusiasm to reach the destination so they carry many heavy things up the mountain.

In contrast, when they are returning the climbers are exhausted, and due to difficulty in breathing and battling with nausea, they are often forced to abandon heavy objects like tents.

5. Why is it difficult to estimate the amount of garbage left behind by the climbers?

It is very difficult to estimate the amount of garbage left behind by climbers, as there is no proper record of what they have bought down and what they have left.

Further, things they have left are not visible and many tent parts are spread here and there with some parts buried deep down the ice sheets. These parts become visible only when the ice melts so it is very difficult to estimate the total amount of garbage.

PASSAGE 6

The literal meaning of the Sanskrit word Yoga/ Yuj is 'Yoke' which is joining of individual's soul energy with that of God (Supreme Soul).

Yoga allows us to look inward to nurture spirit and stay healthy in all spheres, as well as actively enjoy the life by balancing emotions.

Commonly perceived benefits include reduction of stress, weight management, resolving psychosomatic diseases, strengthen immune system, etc. Interestingly, Yoga is universal with no relation with caste, sex, religion, region, etc., Its daily practice is essential to understand the ongoing linkages in body and mind, as Yoga is evolutionary process to reach higher consciousness.

But the success is still limited. Only few educational institutes have promoted this as daily activity. People indulge in Yoga only when they suffer some ailments. Limited set of people are doing it from childhood in schools or as part of family tradition. Its actual benefits at the deeper levels in the form of attaining peace and everlasting happiness remain largely untouched.

Traditional Yoga techniques are being modified to suit modern lifestyles. Even medical practitioners advise their patients to opt for Yoga in their routine along with medicines. Now, due to rising risks of diabetes, heart diseases, cancer, etc, number of Yoga Ashramas and Studios are opening all around. Stress makes our body parts stiff and even teenagers find difficulty in bending and picking up things, touching toes, etc.

Health benefits of doing Yoga are immense for our physical body. For instance, this gradually loosens up our tight hamstrings, hips, etc., and makes them flexible enough. This improves our postures and prevents us from issues of alignment and pain in legs, back and other parts. Yoga is the most reliable and cheapest source to strengthen our muscles and bones which averts chances of continuous injuries, arthritis, neck pains, etc.

In fact, this supports our joints by maintaining cartilage. Face wrinkles also fade away with regular practice of yoga making us more young and attractive. Our body remains in shape. We know that spinal discs are our survival kit, but cannot stay in perfect shape without movement. Many backward, forward and twist Asanas such as Dhanurasana (Bow Pose), Adho Mukha Svanasana (Downward-Facing Dog Pose), Ardha Matsyendrasana (Half Lord of the Fishes Pose), respectively, are blessings to lengthen and strengthen spine. Yoga particularly improves body's blood circulation which further assists in normalising blood pressure and hypertension. In effect, levels of stress, hormone called cortisol are drastically reduced.

Good hormones namely dopamine, serotonin, etc, then flow in abundance which are essential to absorb food nutrients (vitamins, iron, calcium, etc.). **CAPF AC 2019**

1. What are the implications of the word 'Yoga'?

The implications of the word 'Yoga' are attaining peace and everlasting happiness, although the literal meaning of the Sanskrit word Yuj, from which Yoga is derived, means 'yoke' or 'the joining of an individual's soul energy with that of the Supreme Soul, i.e., 'God'.

2. How is 'Yoga' an evolutionary process?

Yoga is an evolutionary process to reach higher consciousness as its daily practice is essential to understand the ongoing linkages between body and mind.

3. What are the health benefits of 'Yoga'?

Health benefits of Yoga include stress reduction, weight management, resolving psychosomatic diseases, strengthening the immune system, etc. Besides, it generally loosens our tight hamstrings, hips etc. and makes them flexible. Further, it improves our postures, thus preventing alignment problems and pain in legs, back and other body parts. Additionally, it strengthens muscles and bones, thus preventing injuries.

4. What are some of the 'Asanas' and their benefits?

Asanas such as Dhanurasana (Bow Pose), AdhoMukhaShvanasana (Downward-Facing Dog Pose), Ardha Matsyendrasana (Half Lord of the Fishes Pose), respectively, aid us in spine related problems. They lengthen and strengthen our spine.

5. How is 'Yoga' a means to cure ailments?

Yoga is a means to cure ailments because it improves our body's blood circulation, helping in normalising our blood pressure and reducing hypertension. Yoga reduces stress levels which leads to reduction in the hormone called 'cortisol'.

As a result, good hormones such as dopamine, serotonin, etc, then flow abundantly and aid the absorption of nutrients from food.

Yoga also loosens up our tight hamstrings, hips, etc, and makes them flexible enough. This improves our postures and prevents us from issues of alignment and pain in legs, back, and other parts. It strengthens our muscles and bones which averts chances of continuous injuries, arthritis, neck pains, etc.

PASSAGE 7

The most essential and useful part to be played by our universities in free India is to educate public opinion, which is the foundation of Democracy. Everyone has a right to educate public opinion, and so every school of thought, in our own Republican Constitution, has been given ample freedom to win public opinion to its credit. It is here that true character is required and is tested.

Our country today needs such people who possess a strong character, who never stoop low to use questionable means under any circumstances. Those who cherish the idea of becoming good administrators must essentially possess a strong character. It should be the first and foremost function of our national universities to impress upon the minds of the future administrators of our country that in a true democracy there are no administrators but only servants of the people.

Another very essential and useful function of our universities should be to build the character of our future citizens. The greatest drawback in our educational institutions has been that sufficient attention was not paid to the moulding of character of the students.

True interest of a country and its people cannot be served simply by framing a Constitution. Constitution is just a set of rules and it can only be effective when persons responsible for its operation prove to be true reformers and real servants of the people and the nation.

Universities have to play a vital role. They should not teach politics to the students simply with the view to make them acquainted with the political structure of the country as well as of the world; but that it should be their function to impress upon them that they are to protect, guide, change and form the Constitution of their country and then of the world as true citizens and administrators of this democratic age, in body as well as spirit. **CAPF AC 2018**

1. What are the essential functions of universities?

The essential functions of universities, according to the passage are

- To educate students to have a public opinion
- To impress upon the minds of future administrators of our country that they should work as servants of people not as rulers or administrators
- To build the characters of students who are obviously future citizens of a country.
- To make the students acquainted with political structure of the country and the world. Students must learn to respect the Constitution of their country.

2. What is the major drawback in our educational institutions?

The major drawback of our educational institutions is that adequate attention has not been paid to the moulding of characters of the students. More attention is paid to the completion of syllabus and other activities like politics and elections.

3. Write the benefits of education imparted at universities.

The benefits of education imparted at universities can be manifold. Education can turn out students or future citizen as people of character who learn to serve people with honesty and integrity.

Through education, students can be taught to protect, guide, change and form the Constitution of their country in the best interest of all.

4. How best can the educated youth serve the people and the nation as administrators?

The youth of today can be taught to become good administrators by taking up the role as servants of people who want to reform the people and their nation in the interest of democratic ideals.

They learn not to be the egoistic rulers but humble administrators to protect the Democracy and the Constitution.

5. What is the contribution of the educated youth as enlightened citizens in a democracy?

The contribution of educated youth as enlightened citizens in a democracy is immense. The youth can lead by respecting its Constitution and Democratic ideals. The enlightened youth should be able to differentiate between the right and wrong. Such youths will do things to make their country better and stronger.

PASSAGE 8

If we look back at India's long history we find that our forefathers made wonderful progress whenever they looked out on the world with clear and fearless eyes and kept the windows of their minds open to give and to receive. And, in later periods, when they grew narrow in outlook and shrank from outside influences, India suffered a set-back, politically and culturally.

What a magnificent inheritance we have, though we have abused it often enough. India has been and is a vital nation, in spite of all the misery and suffering that she has experienced. That vitality in the realm of constructive and creative effort spread to many parts of the

Asian world and elsewhere and brought splendid conquests in its train. Those conquests were not so much of the sword, but of the mind and heart which bring healing and which endure when the men of the sword and their work are forgotten. But that very vitality, if not rightly and creatively directed, may turn inward and destroy and degrade.

Even during the brief span of our lives we have seen these two forces at play in India and the world at large - the forces of constructive and creative effort and the forces of destruction. Which will triumph in the end? And on which side do we stand?

That is a vital question for each one of us and, more especially, for those from whom the leaders of the nation will be drawn, and on whom the burden of tomorrow will fall. We dare not sit on the fence and refuse to face the issue.

We dare not allow our minds to be befuddled by passion and hatred when clear thought and effective action are necessary.

CAPF AC 2017

1. What hurdled the progress of India?

Narrow outlook, which makes us rigid and unreasonable and outside influences, which diverted our attention and energy from the clear targets, mainly hurdled the progress of India.

2. What is the uniqueness of the Indian vitality?

Indian vitality is unique in the sense that it has had the magnificent inheritance in the form of its culture and revered traditions which very few countries across the globe can boast of.

Further, this vitality belongs to the constructive and creative realms of mind and heart which bring healing to not only India but also many Asian and other countries around the world.

3. Why are the men of the sword and their work forgotten?

The men of sword and their work are forgotten in a short while because power, vengeance and hatred are not permanent and are bound to be irrelevant over a long period of time.

4. Why are the conquests of India always remembered?

Conquests of India are always remembered because they are not conquests of sword that caused war or destruction. Rather, they are the conquests of mind and heart which are constructive and creative efforts aimed at bringing healing.

5. What is the vital question referred to at the end of the passage and what is your answer to that question?

The vital question referred to at the end of the passage is regarding the force which will stand the test of time and survive. Who will survive? The forces of destruction or the forces of constructive and creative effort?

I, from the core of my heart, feel that the forces of constructive and creative effort will stand and live forever. Creative efforts live in memory and are always remembered to be passed on to posterity.

PASSAGE 9

It is an obvious trait of black incomes that they cannot be declared to the fiscal authority for fear of large penalties. As under- declarations multiply, the tax base shrinks and price controls begin to blunt the edge of fiscal policy. One instrument of control gets into the way of the other and makes it ineffective.

Tax evasion is large not necessarily because the rate of tax is high, as businessmen often proclaim, but because the income on which tax is to be paid and the activity follows that even if taxes were halved, so long as the income is black, taxes will be evaded.

However, to the extent taxation fails to catch undeclared incomes emanating from controls, it becomes a bad instrument for balancing aggregate demand and supply and for controlling inflation.

In an enthusiastic attempt to make taxation do the balancing trick, tax rates on honest tax-payers become penal. This leads to a second round of tax evasion, this time because tax rates are intolerably high.

More and more tax-payers at the margin avoid tax payment, become dishonest and in the course of time get used to dishonesty. While black money does so much damage to public policy, it also dries up the sources of real growth in the private sector of the economy.

The capital market, the main vehicle of growth, consequently dries up, and capital formation both in the public and private sectors suffers a serious decline. **CAPF AC 2016**

1. How is the circulation of black money detrimental for private entrepreneurs?

The circulation of black money is detrimental for the private entrepreneurs because black money causes financial leakage as unreported income that is not taxed which causes the government to lose revenue.

This creates problems for legitimate small firms to gain loans. Further, it dries up money in the capital market because of which capital formation, both in the public and private sectors, suffers a serious decline.

2. Why is not reduction of taxes useful for sprucing up taxes?

The reduction of the taxes is not useful because even if the taxes are halved, the taxes for the black income will not be paid and taxes will be evaded.

3. How do honest tax-payers suffer on account of tax evaders?

When the tax evaders do not pay the due taxes, then in order to balance the situation, the government penalizes or increases the tax rates which become a burden on the honest tax payers.

Now, the honest tax payers, especially those on the margins, have to either pay taxes or resort to the unfair tax practices. In majority cases, they will avoid taxes by dishonest means and hence, further foster tax evasion.

4. How does black income impact a nation's economy?

Black money negatively impacts the economy of a nation. First, it results in lesser collection of the taxes which ultimately reduces the overall revenue of the country. Second, it results in inflation that severely hits the poor. Further, the government has to change its public policy as a result of which honest tax payers have to suffer with the additional burden.

5. 'Large scale evasion of taxes takes place due to exorbitant taxes.' Argue for or against the statement on the basis of your reading of the passage.

Against the statement It is not true that large scale evasion of taxes takes place due to exorbitant taxes. Tax evasion takes place due to the presence of black money in the market. In this light, even if tax is reduced, the taxes for the black income will not be paid and taxes will be evaded.

PASSAGE 10

The most prominent obstacle to cultural unity is the variety of languages. When told that there are fourteen regional languages and many more dialects belonging to four different linguistic families in India, foreigners are inclined to think that Indians are not one people but, like the inhabitants of Europe, a motley group of peoples with different cultures showing some common elements.

There can be no doubt that on account of linguistic barriers, people from different parts of India generally meet as comparative strangers on all levels other than the religious one. Unless he happens to know English or Hindi, a man from the non-Hindi speaking regions finds it extremely difficult to make himself understood outside his own linguistic area.

No doubt if he spends sometime in a new place, he can pick up enough of the local language to get along but inspite of a common background of religious beliefs and thought in general, he cannot come in intimate contact with the people around him because there is no common medium for the exchange of deeper thoughts. So, until there is a link language and it is known throughout the country, an effective cultural unity is not possible.

But more variety of languages could not be a positive danger to the unity of India if it were not accompanied by linguistic communalism amounting in many cases to chauvinism. It is this poison in our social organism that makes the movement for linguistic states, which is perfectly justified on rational, historical and practical grounds, an object of great concern to all who have the good of the country at heart.

To avoid any misunderstanding we should make it clear what we understand by the term 'linguistic communalism'. The consciousness of a group of people speaking the same language that makes them form a distinct community is natural and legitimate.

But if it is associated with the feeling that those sons of the country living in the same area or an adjacent area who speak a different language are outsiders in the worst sense of the term and should be treated as such, then it assumes the ugly shape of linguistic communalism which is harmful to national unity and is highly objectionable. Far more harmful and objectionable, however is the tendency in a linguistic majority to withhold from the minority the safeguards guaranteed by the Constitution for preserving and promoting its language and culture, including the primary education of its children through the medium of the mother tongue or to discriminate against individual members of the minority in state services and other matters.

It is this chauvinism, unfortunately present in India, which has created a painful situation after the states were reorganised on a linguistic basis, the cultural and other rights of linguistic minorities in each state have been disregarded in many cases. So, when the question of redefining the boundaries of linguistic states comes up for consideration, one finds the worst tensions and conflicts in the border areas where each of two or more language groups agitates for the inclusion of the area of its domicile in the state where its own mother tongue would be the official language.

If groups living in each border area could be assured that to whichever state the area went they would all receive equal treatment and their constitutional rights would be safeguarded, a major difficulty besetting the problem of linguistic states would be removed. **CAPF AC 2015**

1. Why are the foreigners inclined to think that Indians are not 'one people'?

The foreigners are inclined to think that Indians are not 'one people' because of the variety of languages in India. There are numerous regional languages and many more dialects in India. Because of this linguistic variety, foreigners think that Indians are a mixed group of people with different cultures having some common elements.

2. "So, until there is a link language and it is known throughout the country, an effective cultural unity is not possible." Elucidate.

According to the passage, the chief hindrance to cultural unity in India is the variety of languages. While there may be a common background of religious beliefs and thought in general, a person cannot come in intimate contact with the people around him outside his linguistic community because there is no common medium for the exchange of deeper thoughts. This lack of communication prevents cultural unity. Hence, if there is a link language that is known throughout the county, India can be culturally united.

3. What according to the author is 'linguistic communalism'? When is it 'harmful to national unity'?

According to the author, 'linguistic communalism' is the awareness of a group of people speaking the same language that makes them form a distinct community and consider it natural and legitimate. The idea of linguistic communalism becomes harmful to national unity when people of a different linguistic community are considered an 'outsider' and discriminated.

As a result, the linguistic majority withholds from the minority the safeguards guaranteed by the Constitution for preserving and promoting its language and culture, including the primary education of its children through the medium of the mother tongue or to discriminate against individual members of the minority in state services and other matters.

4. What happens when the question of 'redefining the boundaries of linguistic states' crops up for consideration?

When the question of 'redefining the boundaries of linguistic states' crops up for consideration, the worst tensions and conflicts are found in the border areas. Each of the two or more language groups agitates for the inclusion of the area of its domicile in the state where its own mother tongue would be the official language.

5. How could the major difficulty besetting 'the problem of linguistic states' be solved?

The major difficulty besetting 'the problem of linguistic states' could be solved by assuring people that in whichever state they live in, they would all receive equal treatment and their constitutional rights would be safeguarded.

Unsolved Reading Comprehension

PASSAGE 1

Man, since antiquity, has been an inveterate traveller. Only the motivations for travel have changed. In ancient times, the main motivations for travel were trade, pilgrimage and conquest. It is not often realised how extensive were the contacts among the peoples several thousand years ago.

For instance, there was considerable interchange of ideas and knowledge between India and West Asia and the Graeco-Roman civilization. Travel became the means of acquiring culture in Europe. The tradition of the Grand Tour which started in the 17th century was more firmly established in the 18th and the 19th centuries by the emergence of an affluent mercantile class. After the Second World War, Europe lay in ruins.

The Marshall Plan which was introduced by the United States for the revival of the economies of European countries made tourism as one of its planks. It provided large amount of money for the reconstruction of hotels and tourism infrastructure of Western Europe. What was more significant was that for the first time tourism was viewed as an engine for economic development.

This made the governments start assuming responsibility for the promotion of tourism. Three technological inventions have fuelled the growth of travel on a large scale in successive periods. First, the steam engine which made travel by rail and steamship possible before 1914; then the internal combustion engine which popularise travel by automobile in the Inter-War years and lastly, the jet propulsion engine which has led to the international tourist explosion of the Post War era. The Government of India also took note of the new phenomenon of tourism and its economic implications. In 1947, the private sector consisted of a number of hotels and travel agencies in the main cities mainly owned and operated by foreign interests. As it happened in other industries after Independence, the control of many of these hotels passed into the hands of Indian entrepreneurs.

At the same time, a number of new indigenously owned and operated travel agencies and hotels started being set up. In the last 50 years, the Indian travel industry has shown remarkable enterprise. Some of the leading Indian hotel groups and travel agencies have branched out overseas and their performance is highly regarded in the international tourism remarks. The tourism revolution which started in full measure 50 years ago has not run its course. There are several reasons for taking a long-term optimistic view of tourism. First, the increase in leisure time in industrialised societies; paid holidays which were introduced as a social welfare measure have now become an accepted feature not only in industrialised countries but also in many developing countries. The length of paid holidays has increased.

The working week, both in public and private sectors, has come down to 40 hours spread over 5 days. Evidently governments will have to concern themselves with the quality of use of leisure. Tourism has become a preeminent form of recreation for the younger people. This is reflected in the increase in travel in the age group of 18 to 25 years. Second, the rise in literacy and educational standards. Third, better healthcare has made it possible for retired persons, above 60 years, to undertake travel for pleasure. Fourth, the increase in discretionary incomes in real terms in the last twenty years, partly due to income elasticity. Many research studies have established that increase in income level in real terms resulted in increase in propensity for travel.

And lastly, taking a vacation, generally twice a year, has become a way of life in modern societies.

1. What, according to the author, were the main motivations for travel in ancient times?
2. What was the state of tourism in Europe and the United States?
3. What part did technology play in the growth of tourism?
4. How does the author describe the state of tourism in the Post-Independence India?
5. Why does the author think that there is a bright future for tourism in modern societies?

PASSAGE 2

Proponents of the world system approach argue that in the eighteenth century the Indian economy or the Indian economies, became part of the new European-dominated world economy.

To account inter alia for the continued role played by Indian merchants in international trade, they come forward with the notion that India was part of the 'semiperiphery' of the world economy, that it played a role of relay and of intermediary between the centre of the world economy, Europe and its periphery, consisting of Africa, Asia and Latin America. There is in this thesis an underlying assumption about a decline in the role of Indian merchants in the world economy, which is open to question. It is not my intention here to deny that colonialism had many negative consequences for many Indian merchants. However, an objective assessment of its overall impact is no easy task.

There were wide differences in the way various merchant groups were affected: the time sequence is not without importance, as the merchant communities of West and North-West India had more time than their counterparts in the Eastern and Southern parts of the subcontinent to adapt themselves to the changes introduced by colonisation. This may be one of the reasons why merchants from these regions which were annexed in later times were on the whole more successful under the colonial regime than the merchants of the regions which were the first to be colonised. Between 1750 and the late nineteenth century the merchant world of India went through a complex and gradual process of redeployment, as merchants and bankers largely lost their functions, acquired in the eighteenth century, in the collection and transfer of state revenues. The change did not occur overnight.

The East India Company itself remained heavily dependent on the advances of Indian bankers for the first five or six decades of its rule; it is only around 1820 that it established a treasury system which allowed it to dispense with the *hundis* of the Indian *sahukars* and *sarrafs* in providing for the financial needs of its army and administration

1. When did Indian economy become a part of the Europe dominated world economy?
2. Why is objective assessment of colonisation not an easy task?
3. Why were the merchants from the West and North-West region more successful under colonial regime?
4. How did India go through redeployment?
5. How was the East India Company dependent on Indian bankers?

PASSAGE 3

Happiness is an electrifying and elusive state. Philosophers, theologians, psychologists, and even economists have long sought to define it. More than simply positive mood, happiness is a state of well-being that encompasses living a good life, one with a sense of meaning and deep contentment. Feeling joyful has its health perks as well. A growing body of research also suggests that happiness can improve your physical health; feelings of positivity and fulfillment seem to benefit cardiovascular health, the immune system, inflammation levels and blood pressure, among other things. Happiness has even been linked to a longer lifespan as well as a higher quality of life and well-being. Attaining happiness is a global pursuit. Researchers find that people from every corner of the world rate happiness more important than other desirable personal outcomes, such as obtaining wealth, acquiring material goods and getting into heaven. Happiness is not the result of bouncing from one joy to the next; researchers find that achieving happiness typically involves times of considerable discomfort. Genetic makeup, life circumstances, achievements, marital status, social relationships, even your neighbours—all influence how happy you are. Or can be. So do individual ways of thinking and expressing feelings. Research shows that much of happiness is under personal control.

Regularly indulging in small pleasures, getting absorbed in challenging activities, setting and meeting goals, maintaining close social ties, and finding purpose beyond oneself all increase life satisfaction. It isn't happiness per se that promotes well-being, it's the actual pursuit that's key. Happy people live with purpose. They find joy in lasting relationships, working toward their goals and living according to their values. The happy person is not enamoured with material goods or luxury vacations. This person is fine with the simple pleasures of life— petting a dog, sitting under a tree, enjoying a cup of tea.

Misperceptions abound when it comes to what we think will make us happy. People often believe that happiness will be achieved once they reach a certain milestone, such as finding the perfect partner or landing a particular salary. However, humans are excellent at adapting to new circumstances, which means that people will habituate to their new relationship or wealth, return to a baseline level of happiness and seek out the next milestone. Fortunately, the same principle applies to setbacks—we are resilient and will most likely find happiness again.

1. What can influence the happiness?
2. What are the characteristics of happy people?
3. What are the misperceptions about the happiness?
4. What does happiness encompass?
5. What are the benefits of happiness?

PASSAGE 4

History has a great variety of definitions and applications. In the broadest sense, it considers every action and every thought that man has had since his first appearance and records every significant advance or recession. It attempts to evaluate all the developments in science, in art, in literature, in philosophy, in architecture, in sociology, in politics, in war, in religion, and in law.

It sketches as complete a picture as possible of everything that has influenced man directly or indirectly. History, more than any other subject, has been enslaved and distorted for selfish purposes. Members of the clergy have used it to glorify and to promote the interests of the church, statesmen have utilised it to sway masses and writers have distorted facts to substantiate their conclusions. War spirit has been kindled through undue emphasis upon facts, if not falsification of them. The historian is likely to exaggerate the history of his own country – sometimes unintentionally – because of his environment and sometimes in order to facilitate the sale of his book. In all countries, there are zealots in responsible positions who cannot bear to have their fatherhood criticised.

Truth is frequently sacrificed at the altar of patriotism. Henry C. Lea, an outstanding American historian, declared that history should be "a serious attempt to ascertain the severest truth as to the past and set it forth without fear or favour." Michelet, a famous French historian, believed that "sacrilege and the mocking of false goods are the historian's first duty, his indispensable instrument for re-establishing the truth." The slight progress that we have made in the direction indicated by Lea and Michelet is rather discouraging, but there is a trend toward a broader and more inclusive point of view in the writing and teaching of history. World history, correctly interpreted, puts the individual state in the proper perspective and lessens the dangers of excessive nationalism. History has become more than war and politics. To make the story complete, the historian of the new school makes use of the work of the ethnologist, the anthropologist, the geographer and archaeologist, the geologist, the psychologist, the astronomer, the zoologist, the biologist, the chemist, the sociologist and the economist. He is concerned with man's cultural advances and his society, as well as with charters, constitutions and wars. There are dangers, as well as virtues, in the vast scope of the 'new history'. Over popularisation and under specialisation tend to cheapen history and to destroy some of its qualities as a basic and sober study.

There are decided advantages in the comprehension of the broad scope of history, but, in addition, the student should be able to appreciate the depth of the subject. Years of research have been spent and volumes have been written on a single topic. Without these specialised works, surveys would be of no particular value. However, some of the historians of the 'new history' have sacrificed important fundamental facts in order to make a chronicle of heroic persons and romantic occurrence.

They have overstepped the point where history and fiction should meet. The historian should make his description of the past lifelike hence, he should include grim realities as well as romantic incidents. One of the important aspects of the 'new history' is the emphasise upon man's cultural developments, popularly termed civilisation. Civilisation is difficult to define and evaluate. Just where it began and where man's actions and thoughts became human is impossible to determine. Man, like animals, has senses but some are less acutely developed; man has emotions, most of which are present but latent, in animals. Comfort seems to be the chief goal of the lower forms of animal life, but man pushes beyond that towards something that he has difficulty in defining.

This intangible something maybe called civilisation. Professor Lynn Thorndike believes that civilisation "is the product of our higher qualities as exercised first by original and superior individuals and then accepted or followed by a sufficient number of human beings to make it a social fact." Buckle held that moral and intellectual progress is the basis of civilisation. Emerson believed that civilisation is a progress and Bertrand Russell, a modern philosopher, thinks that it is the progress and predominance of science.

Perhaps we can agree that acknowledge of nature, progress in art, an ethical code, a government and a degree of material prosperity are essential in any form of civilised society. Civilisation became possible when chaos and insecurity were minimised.

Curiosity and constructiveness were encouraged when fear was overcome and man turned his attention toward the understanding and embellishment of life.

1. Why does the author consider history an all-inclusive area of study?
2. According to the author, how has history suffered distortions and why?
3. How does the author describe the new school of historians?
4. What are the dangers associated with 'new history'?
5. Why is it difficult to define and evaluate civilisation?

06 English Grammar

SPECIAL FOCUS

In Grammar section pay special attention to
Degree of Comparisons • Verbs/Tenses • Subject Verb Agreement • Prepositions • Conjunctions
Question Tags • Interchange of so... that to too ... to • Reported Speech • Voice • Phrasal Verbs

UPSC CAPF AC exam asks some questions based on simple English Grammar. Grammar related questions in the CAPF AC exam comprises three parts. (Sentence rewriting, making sentence using given phrase and correcting the sentence.) i.e., **Part (a)** carries 10 questions of 1 mark each. **Part (b)** carries 5 questions of 2 marks each and **Part (c)** carries 5 questions of 1 mark each. Thus, in CAPF AC exam, English Grammar carries 25 marks. The pattern of the questions is given below

Sample Question

(a) Rewrite the sentences as directed.

(i) Rabi said, 'I'll eat rice for lunch today'. (Rewrite the sentence using indirect speech)

(ii) The man was running the shop for long. (Rewrite the sentence using passive voice)

(iii) He was in Delhi. He did not meet his friend. (Rewrite by using though)

(iv) She is planning to go on a vacation to Maldives, ... (Add a suitable question tag)

(v) I went to the store .... the bakery and it was fabulous. (Supply a preposition)

(vi) I landed at the airport. It started raining. (Rewrite by using 'no sooner')

(vii) India can change only when education is reached to all. (Use 'unless')

(viii) People in a developing country .... (is/are) both rich and poor. (Choose the correct form of verb)

(ix) If you work hard you .... (will/would) achieve success.

(x) He is old. He cannot climb stairs. (Rewrite by using 'too')

(b) Write one sentence each using the following phrases to bring out their meaning clearly. Do not change the form of the given phrases.

(i) Make up
(ii) Turn down
(iii) Run over
(iv) Look down upon
(v) Carry on

(c) Correct the following sentences without-making any unnecessary changes.

(i) I wonder why people call the Taj Mahal the much beautiful mark of love.

(ii) Kranthi loves to swim at the local swimming pool in order that relieve his work stress.

(iii) The news that the examination were been cancelled upset all our plans.

(iv) In spite of being seriously handicapped, Stephen Hawking is one of most eminent modern scientists.

(v) The famous actor, along with his close family members, were attending the annual day function at his son's school.

Answers

(a) (i) Rabi said that she would eat rice for lunch that day.
(ii) The shop was being run by the man for long.
(iii) Though he was in Delhi, he did not meet his friend.
(iv) isn't she?
(v) beside
(vi) No sooner did I land at the airport than it started raining.
(vii) Unless education is reached to all, India cannot change.
(viii) are
(ix) will
(x) He is too old to climb stairs.

(b) (i) You should make an effort to make up with your friend.
(ii) I turned down the request of my friend to go to Shimla.
(iii) He was run over by a speeding car.
(iv) It is folly on your part to look down upon the poor students.
(v) Now it is difficult to carry on this business in the teeth of stiff competition.

(c) (i) I wonder why people call the Taj Mahal the most beautiful mark of love.
(ii) Kranthi loves to swim at the local swimming pool in order to relieve his work stress.
(iii) The news that the examination had been cancelled upset all our plans.
(iv) In spite of being seriously handicapped, Stephen Hawking is one of the most eminent modern scientists.
(v) The famous actor, along with his close family members, was attending the annual day function at his son's school.

To solve the questions asked in the exams, the knowledge of grammatical rules related to Verbs, Tenses, Subject Verb Agreement, Determiners, Conjunction, Preposition, Voice, Speech, Transformation of Sentences, etc is essential. Some of the important topics for the CAPF AC exam are discussed below.

NOUNS

Noun is the name of a person, place, animal, thing, idea and organisation.

Types of Noun

- **Proper Noun** When the name of a particular person, place, thing, animal or organisation is given, it is referred to as proper noun. e.g., Lakshay, Delhi, Alphabet.inc
- **Common Noun** When the general name of person, place, thing, animal or organisation is given, it is referred to as common noun. e.g., girl, city, company, etc.
- **Collective Noun** When a word is used to refer to a group of person, places, animals or things, it is referred to as collective noun. e.g., class, crowd, fleet, etc.
- **Abstract Noun** When a word is used to express an idea, quality or feeling, it is referred to as abstract noun. They can be felt but not seen or touched.

  e.g., love, hatred, innocence, etc.
- **Material Noun** When the name of a material or substance from which things are made is given, it is referred to as material noun. e.g., wood, iron, silver, etc.
- **Concrete Noun** When the name of anything that can be touched is given, it is referred to as concrete noun. e.g., book, table, phone, etc.
- **Compound Noun** When a name is given to a combination of two or more words used as one, it is referred to as compound noun. e.g., suitcase, bookworm, bus stop, etc.

Singular-Plural

The English language contains two types of numbers: the Singular and the Plural. The 'Singular' number refers to 'one' noun, while the 'Plural' number refers to 'more than one' noun. Formation of plural nouns from the singular noun.

1. **By adding 's' or 'es'.**

Chair	Chairs	House	Houses
Knife	Knives	Plant	Plants
Car	Cars	Table	Tables
Dish	Dishes	Pencil	Pencils
Desk	Desks	Window	Windows
Spoon	Spoons	Phone	Phones
Glass	Glasses	Pen	Pens
Fork	Forks	Cup	Cups

2. **By adding 's' to the nouns that end in 'o'.**

Piano	Pianos	Photo	Photos
Radio	Radios	Video	Videos
Studio	Studios	Solo	Solos
Cello	Cellos	Memo	Memos
Portfolio	Portfolios	Dynamo	Dynamos
Casino	Casinos	Kangaroo	Kangaroos
Logo	Logos	Tattoo	Tattoos
Cargo	Cargos	Ratio	Ratios

Exceptions

Hero	Heroes	Potato	Potatoes
Volcano	Volcanoes	Tomato	Tomatoes
Tornado	Tornadoes	Zero	Zeroes

3. **By substituting 'f' or 'fe' with 'ves' at the end.**

Knife	Knives	Life	Lives
Leaf	Leaves	Wife	Wives
Thief	Thieves	Shelf	Shelves
Calf	Calves	Half	Halves
Wolf	Wolves	Loaf	Loaves
Dwarf	Dwarves	Self	Selves
Hoof	Hooves	Scarf	Scarves
Sheaf	Sheaves	Staff	Staves
Belief	Beliefs	Chief	Chiefs
Leaf	Leave	Thief	Thieves

Exceptions

Belief	Beliefs	Chief	Chiefs
Cliff	Cliffs	Roof	Roofs
Proof	Proofs	Gulf	Gulfs
Reef	Reefs	Safe	Safes

4. **By changing the inside vowel**

Man	Men	Woman	Women
Foot	Feet	Tooth	Teeth
Goose	Geese	Mouse	Mice
Louse	Lice		

5. **By adding 'en' or 'ren'.**

Ox	Oxen	Child	Children

6. **Some nouns have the same singular and plural forms.**

Sheep	Deer	Moose	Fish
Series	Species	Aircraft	Trout
Salmon	Swine	Deer	Yoke

7. **Compound nouns generally form their plurals by adding 's' to the principal word.**

Bookshelf	Bookshelves	Cupcake	Cupcakes
Hairbrush	Hairbrushes	Sunflower	Sunflowers
Raincoat	Raincoats	Handbag	Handbags
Skateboard	Skateboards	Headphone	Headphones
Keyboard	Keyboards	Toothpaste	Toothpastes

8. **Foreign words**

Cactus	Cacti	Datum	Data
Medium	Media	Focus	Foci
Status	Statuses	Analysis	Analyses
Criterion	Criteria	Formula	Formulas or Formulae
Bacterium	Bacteria	Criterion	Criteria
Fungus	Fungi	Radius	Radii
Stimulus	Stimuli	Virus	Viruses
Medium	Media	Appendix	Appendices or Appendixes
Alumnus	Alumni (male plural)	Alumna	Alumnae (female plural)
Hypothesis	Hypotheses	Index	Indices or Indexes
Phenomenon	Phenomena		

PRONOUNS

Pronoun is a word that is used in place of a noun or noun phrase to avoid repetition.

Types of Pronoun

- **Personal Pronoun** When a pronoun is used in place of nouns referring to a person, place, animal or thing, it is referred to as personal pronoun. e.g., I, me, they, etc.
- **Possessive Pronoun** When a pronoun shows possession or ownership, it is referred to as possessive pronoun. e.g., his, mine, yours, etc.
- **Demonstrative Pronoun** When a pronoun is used to point to a particular person or thing, it is referred to as demonstrative pronoun. There are four demonstrative pronouns. e.g., this, that, these and those.
- **Interrogative Pronoun** When a pronoun is used to ask question, it is referred to as interrogative pronoun. Common interrogative pronouns include what, who, which and whose.
- **Relative Pronoun** When a pronoun is used to refer to the noun mentioned before it. e.g., who, that, which etc.
- **Distributive Pronoun** When a pronoun is used to refer to member of a group individually, it is referred to as distributive pronoun. Common distributive pronouns include each, either and neither.
- **Indefinite Pronoun** When a pronoun does not refer to a particular person or thing in a group, it is referred to as indefinite pronoun. e.g., anybody, all, every etc.
- **Reflexive Pronoun** When a pronoun is used to refer back to the subject in a sentence, it is referred to as reflexive pronoun. e.g., himself, herself, themselves, etc.
- **Emphatic Pronoun** When a pronoun is used to emphasise on the subject in a sentence, it is referred to as emphatic pronoun. e.g., myself, themselves, ourselves, etc.
- **Reciprocal Pronoun** When a pronoun is used to refer to two or more people involved in a mutual action, it is referred to as a reciprocal pronoun. There are two reciprocal pronouns-each other and one another.

Check Your Progress 1

Fill in the blanks with appropriate pronouns.

i. Who left .... umbrella by the door?

ii. Who do you think will win the game tonight, ... or ....?

iii. Did you hear .... talking about the new project during the meeting?

Give the plural form of the following words and make sentences using them.

iv. Cactus

v. Medium

ADJECTIVES

Adjective is a word that is used to modify a noun or pronoun by giving more information about it.

Types of Adjective

- **Adjective of Quality** When a word is used to describe the quality of a noun or a pronoun in a sentence, it is referred to as an adjective of quality. It answers the question of what kind? e.g., pretty, ugly, fresh, etc.
- **Adjective of Quantity** When a word is used to describe the quantity of a noun or a pronoun in a sentence, it is referred to as an adjective of quantity. It answers the question how much? e.g., some, more, enough, etc.
- **Adjective of Number** When a word is used to describe the exact quantity of noun or its position in specific numbers, it is referred to as an adjective of number. It answers the question how many and is used with countable nouns. e.g., nine, fifth, fourth, etc.
- **Demonstrative Adjective** When a word is used to express the relative position of a noun, it is referred to as demonstrative adjective. There are four demonstrative adjectives – this, that, these and those.
- **Possessive Adjective** When a word is used to indicate ownership or possession, it is referred to as possessive

adjective. There are seven possessive adjectives – his, her, my, your, its, their and our.

- **Interrogative Adjective** When a word is used to seek information and ask question about the noun in a sentence, it is referred to as interrogative adjective. There are three interrogative adjectives – which, whose and what.
- **Proper Adjective** When a proper noun is used as an adjective in a sentence, it is referred to as proper adjective. e.g., Belgium, Indian, Spanish, etc.

Degrees of Comparison

There are three degrees of adjectives. They are

- **Positive Degree of Adjective** When an adjective is used in its simple form, it is referred to as positive degree of adjective. e.g., good, happy, sad, etc.
- **Comparative Degree of Adjective** When an adjective is used to denote a higher degree than the positive while two things (or sets of things) are compared, it is referred to as comparative degree of adjective. e.g., better, happier, sadder, etc.
- **Superlative Degree of Adjective** When an adjective is used to denote the highest degree while more than two things (of sets of things) are compared, it is referred to as superlative degree of adjective, e.g., best, happiest, saddest, etc.

Order of Adjectives

When more than one adjective is used in a sentence, a particular order is adhered to. The order is

Opinion (Quality) > Size > Physical Quality > Shape > Age > Colour > Origin (Proper Adjectives) > Material > Purpose

e.g. The two huge old black cows walked across the street.

A long dark wooden table sat in the middle of the dining room.

Check Your Progress 2

Rewrite the sentences as directed.

i. Sonia is the most athletic girl in her class. (Use the comparative degree)

ii. Sam is taller than any other boy in the basketball team. (Use the superlative degree)

iii. This book is the most interesting book I've read this year. (Use the comparative degree)

iv. My cat is lazier than any other pet in the neighbourhood. (Use the superlative degree)

v. This car is the fastest car in its price range. (Use the comparative degree)

VERBS

Verb is a word that describes an action, possession or state of being in a sentence.

Types of Verb

On the basis of function it performs in a sentence, verb can be divided into three types.

- **Action Verb** When a verb tells what the subject does in a sentence, it is referred to as action verb. e.g., plays, eat, sing, etc. Two types of action verb are
  - **Transitive Verb** When an action verb requires an object to form complete meaning, it is referred to as a transitive verb. e.g., She bought me a dog.
  - **Intransitive Verb** When an action verb does not require an object to form complete meaning, it is referred to as an intransitive verb. e.g., Rhea screamed at him.
- **Linking Verb** When a verb serves as a link between the subject and the object, it is referred to as a linking verb. e.g., is, am, are, etc.
- **Helping Verb** When a verb supports the main verb in a sentence, it is referred to as a helping verb. It adds more detail to the main verb and is used to form tenses. e.g., is, are, were, etc. Two types of helping verb are
  - **Primary Auxiliary** Is, Are, Am, Were, Was, Do, Does, Did, Has, Have and Had
  - **Modal Auxiliary** Can, Could, May, Might, Must, Will, Would, Shall, Should, Ought To, Need To, Dare To and Used To.

Remember!

While linking verbs are complete in themselves, helping verbs require an additional (main) verb to give complete meaning.

On the basis of form, verb can be divided into two types

- **Finite Verb** When a verb changes its form according to the number or person of the subject and tense of a sentence, it is referred to as a finite verb.
  e.g., She loves to bake a cake.
  They love to bake a cake.
- **Non-Finite Verb** When a verb does not change its form according to the number or person of the subject and tense of a sentence, it is referred to as a non-finite verb.
  e.g., She loved to bake a cake.
  They love to bake a cake.

  Three types of non-finite verb are

  Infinitive When the to-form of a verb is used as a noun in a sentence, it is referred to as infinitive.
  e.g., I told him to write the letter.
  He was required to fill the form immediately.

- **Gerund** When the ing-form of a verb is used as a noun in a sentence, it is referred to as a gerund.
  e.g., Swimming is a great exercise.
  Lying is one of the seven sins.

- **Participle** When a verb is used as an adjective in a sentence, it is referred to as participle.
  e.g., The buzzing sound was incredibly irritating.
  The crooked neck of the doll made it scary.
  Having finished the project, they went to sleep.

ADVERB

Adverb is a word that is used to modify verbs, adjectives or other adverbs.

Types of Adverb

- **Adverb of Manner** When an adverb is used to indicate the manner in which an action takes place, it is referred to as an adverb of manner. It answers the question 'how'. e.g., bravely, fluently, quickly, etc.
- **Adverb of Time** When an adverb is used to indicate the time when an action takes place, it is referred to as an adverb of time. It answers the question 'when'.
  e.g., ago, after, since, etc.
- **Adverb of Place** When an adverb is used to indicate the place at which an action takes place, it is referred to as an adverb of place. It answers the question 'where'.
  e.g., inside, here, far, etc.
- **Adverb of Degree** When an adverb is used to indicate the intensity or degree of a verb, an adverb or an adjective, it is referred to as an adverb of degree.
  e.g., very, extremely, greatly, etc.
- **Adverb of Frequency** When an adverb is used to indicate how often an action is performed, it is referred to as an adverb of frequency. e.g., rarely, often, never, etc.
- **Interrogative Adverb** When an adverb is used to ask questions, it is referred to as an interrogative adverb. There are five interrogative adverbs – when, why, how, where and how often.
- **Relative Adverb** When an adverb introduces an adjective clause, while modifying the preceding verb, it is referred to as relative adverb. There are three relative adverbs – why, where and when.

Check Your Progress 3

Rewrite the sentences as directed.

i. Neither the students nor the professors .... present for the lecture. (Fill in the blank space with the appropriate form of the verb 'be')

ii. The marathon runners .... through the city streets. (Rewrite the sentence using the appropriate form of the verb 'run')

iii. Sarah and Tom .... lunch together yesterday. (Rewrite the sentence using the appropriate form of the verb 'eat')

iv. The choir members .... beautifully during the concert. (Rewrite the sentence using the appropriate form of the verb 'sing')

v. My cat and dog .... peacefully in their beds last night. (Rewrite the sentence using the appropriate form of the verb 'sleep')

TENSE

The tense of a verb tells 'when' an action takes place or is performed.

Types of Tense

Simple Present Tense

Type of Sentence	Structure	Example
Affirmative	Singular Subject + V1 + s/es + Object I/Plural Subject + V1 + Object	She lives in Delhi. They live in Delhi.
Negative	Singular Subject + does not + V1 + Object I/Plural Subject + do not + V1 + Object	She does not live in Delhi. They do not live in Delhi.
Interrogative	Does + Singular Subject + V1 + Object? Do + I/Plural Subject + V1 + Object?	Does she live in Delhi? Do they live in Delhi?

Present Continuous Tense

Type of Sentence	Structure	Example
Affirmative	Singular Subject + is/am + V1 + -ing + Object Plural Subject + are + V1 + -ing + Object	She is living in Delhi. They are living in Delhi.
Negative	Singular Subject + is/am + not + V1 + -ing + Object Plural Subject + are + not + V1 + -ing + Object	She is not living in Delhi. They are not living in Delhi.
Interrogative	Is/Am + Singular Subject + V1 + -ing + Object? Are + Plural Subject + V1 + -ing + Object?	Is she living in Delhi? Are they living in Delhi?

Present Perfect Tense

Type of Sentence	Structure	Example
Affirmative	Singular Subject + has + V3 + Object I/ Plural Subject+ have + V3 + Object	She has lived in Delhi. They have lived in Delhi.
Negative	Singular Subject + has + not + V3 + Object I/ Plural Subject+ have + not + V3 + Object	She has not lived in Delhi. They have not lived in Delhi.
Interrogative	Has + Singular Subject + V3 + Object? Have + I/ Plural Subject + V3 + Object?	Has she lived in Delhi? Have they lived in Delhi?

Present Perfect Continuous Tense

Type of Sentence	Structure	Example
Affirmative	Singular Subject + has been + V1 + -ing + Object I/ Plural Subject+ have been + V1 + -ing + Object	She has been living in Delhi. They have been living in Delhi.
Negative	Singular Subject + has + not + been + V1 + -ing + Object I/ Plural Subject+ have + not + been + V1 + -ing + Object	She has not been living in Delhi. They have not been living in Delhi.
Interrogative	Has + Singular Subject + been + V1 + -ing + Object? Have + I/ Plural Subject + been + V1 + -ing + Object?	Has she been living in Delhi? Have they been living in Delhi?

Simple Past Tense

Type of Sentence	Structure	Example
Affirmative	Singular/ Plural Subject + V2 + Object	She lived in Delhi.
Negative	Singular/ Plural Subject + did not + V1 + Object	They did not live in Delhi.
Interrogative	Did + Singular/ Plural Subject + V1 + Object?	Did they live in Delhi?

Past Continuous Tense

Type of Sentence	Structure	Example
Affirmative	Singular Subject + was + V1 + -ing + Object Plural Subject+ were + V1 + -ing + Object	She was living in Delhi. They were living in Delhi.
Negative	Singular Subject + was + not + V1 + -ing + Object Plural Subject+ were + not + V1 + -ing + Object	She was not living in Delhi. They were not living in Delhi.
Interrogative	Was + Singular Subject + V1 + -ing + Object? Were + Plural Subject+ V1 + -ing + Object?	Was she living in Delhi? Were they living in Delhi?

Past Perfect Tense

Type of Sentence	Structure	Example
Affirmative	Singular/ Plural Subject + had + V3 + Object	They had lived in Delhi.
Negative	Singular/ Plural Subject + had + not + V3 + Object	She had not lived in Delhi.
Interrogative	Had + Singular/ Plural Subject + V3 + Object?	Had they lived in Delhi?

Past Perfect Continuous Tense

Type of Sentence	Structure	Example
Affirmative	Singular/ Plural Subject + had been + V1 + -ing + Object	She had been living in Delhi.
Negative	Singular/ Plural Subject + had + not + been + V1 + -ing + Object	They had not been living in Delhi.
Interrogative	Had + Singular/ Plural Subject + been + V1 + -ing + Object?	Had they been living in Delhi?

Simple Future Tense

Type of Sentence	Structure	Example
Affirmative	Singular/ Plural Subject + will/ shall + V1 + Object	She will live in Delhi.
Negative	Singular/ Plural Subject + will/ shall + not + V1 + Object	They will not live in Delhi.
Interrogative	Will/ Shall + Singular/ Plural Subject + V1 + Object?	Will they live in Delhi?

Future Continuous Tense

Type of Sentence	Structure	Example
Affirmative	Singular/ Plural Subject+will/ shall be + V1 + -ing + Object	They will be living in Delhi.
Negative	Singular/Plural Subject+will/ shall not be + V1 + -ing + Obj.	She will not be living in Delhi.
Interrogative	Will/ Shall + Singular/Plural Subject+be+V1+ -ing + Obj	Will they be living in Delhi?

Future Perfect Tense

Type of Sentence	Structure	Example
Affirmative	Singular/ Plural Subject + will/ shall have + V3 + Object	She will have lived in Delhi.
Negative	Singular/ Plural Subject + will/ shall + not + have + V3 + Object	They will not have lived in Delhi.
Interrogative	Will/ Shall + Singular/ Plural Subject + have + V3 + Object?	Will she have lived in Delhi?

Future Perfect Continuous Tense

Type of Sentence	Structure	Example
Affirmative	Singular/ Plural Subject + will/ shall have been + V1+ -ing+Obj	They will have been living in Delhi.
Negative	Singular/ Plural Subject + will/ shall + not + have been + V1 + -ing + Object	She will not have been living in Delhi.
Interrogative	Will/ Shall + Singular/ Plural Subject + have been + V1 + -ing + Object?	Will they have been living in Delhi?

SUBJECT VERB AGREEMENT

In order to make a sentence be grammatically correct, the verb must agree with the subject in Number and Person. There are certain rules to ensure this and these rules are collectively known as the Subject Verb Agreement.

Rules of Subject Verb Agreement

- If the subject is singular, it takes a singular verb and if the subject is plural, it takes a plural verb.

  e.g., Rohan is my classmate.

  My friends are going to a party.
- When two or more nouns are joined by the conjunction 'and', a plural verb is used. e.g., Ruchika and Sneha are fighting again.

  When two subjects refer to one idea, a singular verb is used. e.g.,

  Pancakes and eggs is my comfort food.
- When there is one subject in the sentence and more than one verb, all the verbs must agree with the subject.

  e.g., Shruti doesn't like her and always fights with her.
- When two or more singular nouns are joined by 'or' or 'nor', a singular verb is used.

  e.g., Mother or father is going to attend the meeting.
- Two singular subjects connected by or, either/or, or neither/nor require a singular verb.

  e.g., Neither he nor I stole the money.
- When a singular and plural subject are connected by either/or or neither/nor, the plural subject should be placed last and a plural verb should be used.

  e.g., Neither the teacher nor her students have prepared for the assembly.
- When the subject has two nouns or pronouns joined by connectors like as well as, with, along with, in addition to and together with, the verb agrees with the first one.

  e.g., The minister along with her guards was unfazed by the threat.
- Uncountable nouns take a singular verb.

  e.g., Sugar is not good for health.
- Collective nouns take a singular verb.

  e.g., The jury is unanimous in its decision.
- **Exception** When the individual units of a collective are being referred to, a plural verb is used.

  e.g.,The jury are divided in their decision.
- We use plural verbs with quantifiers such as both, few and many. Much takes a singular verb.

  e.g.,Many students are not participating in competition.
- The words here, there and where are not subjects. They introduce a sentence in inverted order. The verb must agree with the subject of a sentence.

  e.g., Here is the book you were looking for.
- A singular verb must be used with the singular indefinite pronouns, such as each, neither, either, anyone, everyone, no one, someone, etc.

  e.g.,Someone is coming to help you.
- When two subjects are joined by not only. but also, the verb agrees with the subject that is closest to it.

  e.g.,Not only me but also my friends are going to perform.
- Titles of books, magazines and films take singular verbs, even if they contain plural nouns.

  e.g.,'The Silence of the Lambs' is a great book.
- Some subjects, although plural in appearance, are singular in meaning and take a singular verb.

  e.g.,Diabetes is a dangerous disease.
- A singular verb is generally used after words denoting an amount.

  e.g.,10 kilometres is not a very long distance.

Check Your Progress 4

Rewrite the sentences as directed.

i. They go to the gym everyday. (Change into Past Tense)

ii. He had finished his homework before dinner. (Change into Present Perfect Tense)

iii. Neither the cat nor the dog .... allowed on the couch. (Fill in the blank with the appropriate filler)

iv. She cooks dinner every evening. (Change into Future Perfect Tense)

v. Either the blue pen or the red pen .... missing. (Fill in the blank with the appropriate filler)

ARTICLE

Article is a word that is placed before a noun to indicate whether it is specific or general.

Types of Article

- **Indefinite Article** The indefinite articles 'a' and 'an' are used to refer to any non-specific singular noun.
- **Definite Article** The definite article 'the' is used to refer to a specific noun or a noun that has already been referred to.

Uses of 'A' and 'AN'

The article 'A' is used with words that start with a consonant sound. e.g.,

(i) I found a kitten in the garden.

(ii) He wants to become a doctor.

However, in some cases, the article 'A' is used before words that start with a vowel letter. This is so because the words begin with a consonant sound.

e.g., She is a European. (European starts with the sound of 'y')

- Please give me a ten-rupee note. (One- rupee note starts with the sound of 'w')
- I want to go to a university. (University starts with the sound of 'y')
- The article 'An' is used with words that start with a vowel sound.

  e.g.,

  (i) My mother gave me an orange to eat.

  (ii) I should carry an umbrella as it is going to rain.

However, in some cases, the article 'An' is used before words that start with a consonant letter. This is so because the consonant letter is silent and the word starts with a vowel sound.

e.g.,

(i) Vishal will be late by an hour.

(ii) My father is an honest man.

In these sentences, the sound of 'h' is silent. The words start with the sound of 'o'.

Uses of 'The'

- The is used before both countable and uncountable nouns.
  e.g., I failed to get him the watch.
- before a noun that has already been referred to before.
  e.g., Aarti has a pet cat. The cat is vicious.
- when a singular noun represents a whole class.
  e.g., The dog is a loyal animal.
- before some proper nouns, such as

Proper Nouns	Examples
Name of oceans, rivers and seas	the Indian Ocean, the Ganga, the Mediterranean Sea
Name of deserts	the Thar Desert, the Sahara Desert
Name of group of Islands	the West Indies,
Name of mountain ranges	the Himalayas, the Appalachians
Name of some countries	the Netherlands, the United Kingdoms
Name of some famous monuments	The Taj Mahal, the Eiffel Tower
Name of holy and classical books	the Bible, the Gita
Name of newspapers	the Hindu, the Indian Express
Name of organisations	the United Nations, the Red Cross Society
Name of unique things	the Sun , the Moon, the Earth

- before the superlative degree of adjectives.
  e.g., This is the greatest day of my life.
- before the people mentioned by their professions.
  e.g., The journalist asked that atrocious question.
- with ordinal numbers (first, second, third and so on).
  e.g., The first time I met him, I was only four years old.
- before the name of some musical instruments.
  e.g., My favourite instrument is the guitar.
- before names of decades, centuries and historic periods.
  e.g., The Elizabethan era was a golden age in the British history.
- with adjectives like poor, rich, elderly, unemployed, etc., to talk about groups of people.
  e.g., The elderly constitute a large and important part of our population.

Omission Of Articles

Articles are omitted

- before plural countable nouns used in a general sense.
  e.g., People often ignore their problems.
- before names of meals, diseases, months, festivals, etc.
  e.g., Breakfast is the most important meal of a day.
  Holi is just around the corner.
- before languages. e.g.,
  Chinese is a very complicated language.
- before names of relations. e.g.,
  Father asked me to make tea.
- before proper nouns (like name of a person, name of a company etc.) except those mentioned in the list above.
  e.g.,
  It is always cold in Canada.
  Richa works in Google.
- before material nouns. e.g.,

Rings made of gold never go out of style.

PREPOSITION

Preposition is a word that is used in a sentence to join the nouns, pronouns or phrases to other words.

Common Prepositions And Their Uses

Common Prepositions	Their Uses	Examples
On	To specify days and dates To refer to a surface To refer to devices	I will come back from my trip on Tuesday. My notebook is lying on the dining table. I will watch a movie on my laptop tonight.
At	To refer to a particular time To indicate a place	My brother called and said that he'll be home at eight o'clock. I am waiting for my family at home.
In	To specify day, month, season, year To indicate a location To be used while doing something	The winter vacations will start in December. My little sister hid my phone in her bag. We went to the museum in a cab.

Common Prepositions	Their Uses	Examples
To	To refer to a period To indicate direction	I will be home from Friday to Sunday. We are going to the New Delhi Railway Station.
For	To indicate the duration or time To indicate the receiver of something or to get the benefit of it	He has been ill for quite some time now. I've brought a cup of tea for you.
Of	To indicate relating to, belonging to To indicate being part of something To indicate measurement	A friend of mine is coming today. The lid of the box is not closed. 2 kilograms of potatoes cost rupees 30.
With	To indicate agent To indicate being together	I wrote the letter with a pen. I ordered a sandwich with a drink.
By	To indicate before the given time To indicate proximity To show means	The meeting should have finished by 4:30 pm. I live by the old building on the Main Street. Little children go to school by bus.
Into	To show a position in or inside something To show the direction of something	The thieves broke into the house. He jumped into the river to save the little boy.
From	To show the time period of action To show how far apart two places are	The doctor said, "I will see you from 12 to 1 pm tomorrow." His house is around a kilometre from my house.
Before	To refer to timed events To refer to a place	I will go for my coaching classes before the match. Please drop me at the bus stop before the railway station.
After	To refer to a 'later' time To show 'next to' a place	He will meet me day after tomorrow. What do those letters after your name mean?
During	To denote the length of time in which something happens.	During summer vacations, we went to the beach.
Above	To show that something is on the top of another thing	The plane is flying above the clouds.
Below	To show that something is on the lower level than another thing	She lives on the floor below mine.
Over	To show that something is in direct contact with or is covering another	They made her comfortable and put a blanket over her.

Common Prepositions	Their Uses	Examples
Under	To show that something is on the lower level	The cat is hiding under the table.
Between	To show the position of a thing in the middle of two things	The hotel is between the temple and the school.
Across	To show something on the other side	You can go on a ride across the country.
Along	To show that something is moving in a constant direction on a horizontal surface	The path is along the river.
Around	To show a movement taking place in a circular fashion	The girls danced around the bonfire.
Beside	To tell the location of something in relation. It means 'next to'.	The person sitting beside me is wearing a yellow hat.
Besides	In addition to	Besides these clothes, I don't own anything.

Check Your Progress 5

Fill in the blanks with appropriate prepositions.

i. 'Please hand in your assignment .... the end of the class.'

ii. "I'm interested .... joining the team."

iii. 'Can you please remind me .... the meeting on Friday?'

iv. We went to .... museum to see the new art exhibit.

v. She bought .... umbrella because it was raining outside.

CONJUNCTION

Conjunction is one or more words used to join phrases, clauses or sentences to form new sentences.

Types Of Conjunction

- **Coordinating Conjunction** When a conjunction is used to link two or more clauses or sentences of equal importance, it is referred to as coordinating conjunction. There are seven coordinating conjunctions – for, and, nor, but, or, yet and so.
- **Subordinating Conjunction** When a conjunction is used to introduce and join subordinate clauses to main clauses, it is referred to as subordinating conjunction. It comes at the beginning of a subordinate clause. e.g., if, as, because, since, whenever, although, etc.
- **Correlative Conjunction** When a pair of words is used to join two or more clauses or sentences of equal importance, it is referred to as correlative conjunction. e.g., both…and, not only…but also, either…or, neither…nor, no sooner…than, etc.

Question Tags

Questions tags are short questions that are added at the end of assertive sentences or statements.

e.g., The Sun rises in the East, doesn't it?

I was not feeling well, was I?

5G connection is available in Delhi, isn't it?

Rules For Making Question Tags

Rule 1 If the statement is positive, then the question tag is negative.

e.g., I will attend the function, won't I?

Rule 2 If the statement is negative, then the question tag is positive.

e.g., Virat couldn't play cricket today, could he?

Rule 3 Questions tags only contain pronouns. The nouns used in the statement are converted into their respective pronouns in question tags.

Transformation of Sentences

Transformation of sentences is a category of rules in a language that includes changing the structure/ syntax of the sentence without changing its meaning.

There are various ways in which we transform a sentence. These include

- Change of Voice
- Change of Narration (Direct-indirect speech)
- Change in the type of sentence (Simple, Complex, Compound)
- Interchange of sentences

Check Your Progress 6

Add a suitable question tag to the following sentences.

i. You will be going to the renaissance fair, ... ?

ii. They've already finished their homework, ...?

Connect the following sentences using an appropriate conjunction.

iii. She likes to swim. She doesn't like cold water.

iv. He studied all night. He still failed the exam.

v. The weather was bad. We decided to cancel the picnic.

VOICE

Voice refers to the form of verb that indicates when a subject is the doer or the receiver of the action.

Kinds of Voice

There are two kinds of voice

1. **Active** Where subject is the doer of the action. e.g., He plays cricket.
2. **Passive** Where action is done upon the subject. e.g., Cricket is played by him.

General Rules For Changing Active Voice Into Passive Voice

1. The subject of the verb in the active voice becomes the object in the passive voice sentences.

   e.g., Kanika is cleaning the house. (Active)

   The house is being cleaned by Kanika. (Passive)
2. The third form of the verb, (the past participle form of the verb) is used in the passive voice.

   e.g., Kanishk buys a pen every week. (Active)

   A pen is bought by Kanishk every week. (Passive)
3. Auxiliary verb 'be' (am, is, are, was, were) is added before the past participle according to the tense of the verb.

   e.g., The postman delivered the letters on time. (Active)

   The letters were delivered by the postman on time. (Passive)
4. Generally 'by' is used before the object of the passive voice sentences.

   e.g., The teachers are attending a meeting. (Active)

   A meeting is being attended by the teachers. (Passive)
5. Certain verbs take fixed prepositions after them instead of 'by'. Some of these verbs are- known to, surprised by/at, contained in, annoyed with/at, etc.

   e.g., The child's irrelevant pleadings annoyed his parents. (Active)

   His parents were annoyed at him for his irrelevant pleadings. (Passive)
6. The pronouns are changed into objective case while changing into passive voice.

   e.g., I water my plants everyday. (Active)

   My plants are watered by me everyday. (Passive)
7. If the subject of the sentence is not known, we can drop the subject into the passive voice.

   e.g., Someone has sent me a bouquet of flowers. (Active)

   A bouquet of flowers has been sent to me. (Passive)
8. Study carefully the use of interrogative pronoun while, changing active sentences into passive.

   'Which', 'What', etc., are placed as they are. However, When, 'What/Which' is used as a subject, it is changed into 'By what'. But 'Who' is changed into 'By whom' and 'Whom' is changed into 'Who'.

   e.g., What are you writing? (Active)

   What is being written by you? (Passive)
9. Sentences beginning with negative indefinite pronouns are converted into negative.

   e.g., Nobody can change destiny. (Active)

   Destiny cannot be changed. (Passive)
10. When principle clause is followed by noun clause as object the passive voice is made as follows

e.g., People consider that he is honest. (Active)
It is considered that he is honest. (Passive)

11. Verbs with two objects-sometimes verbs are used with two objects in active voice sentences. Passive voice can be made with either of the objects.

e.g., He gave me a book. (Active)
I was given a book by him, or A book was given to me by him. (Passive)

12. Infinitives

e.g., She is to write a letter. (Active)
A letter is to be written by her. (Passive)

13. Participles/Gerund

e.g., I remember my mother taking me to a doctor. (Active)
I remember being taken to a doctor by my mother. (Passive)

14. If a preposition or an adverb is used with a verb to convey specific meaning, it should not be removed while, making a passive voice.

e.g., (i) Mothers look after their children. (Active)
Children are looked after by their mothers. (Passive)

15. Imperative Sentences

(A) **Command and Order**

When object is given, use Let + object + be + Past participle.

e.g., Bring a book. (Active)
Let a book be brought. (Passive)

When no object is given, begin the sentence with you are ordered/commanded to.........

e.g., Go out at once. (Active)
You are ordered to go out at once. (Passive)

(B) **Permission, Request and Advice**

When object is given, make passive with object. Follow Object + Should + Past Participle

e.g., Obey parents. (Active)
Parents should be obeyed. (Passive)

When no object is given, begin the sentence with you are allowed, requested or advised ....

e.g., Please come soon. (Active)
You are requested to come soon. (Passive)

16. Sentences beginning with let

(A) **Permission**

When object is given make passive voice as follows

e.g., Let me play here. (Active)
I may be allowed to play here. (Passive)

(B) **Suggestion**

When object is given make passive voice as follows

e.g., Let us help him. (Active)
He should be helped. (Passive)

When no object is given, begin, the sentence, with .... It is suggested ....

e.g., Let us stay here. (Active)
It is suggested that we should stay here. (Passive)

Rules For Changes in Tenses

When a sentence is changed from active to passive voice, the tense remains the same. See the table given below

Tenses	Active Voice	Passive voice
Simple Present	Structure- S + V1 + O They watch a play.	Structure – O + am/is/are + V3 + by + S A play is watched by them.
Present Continuous	Structure- S + am/is/are/ + V1 + ing + O They are playing a game.	Structure- O + am/is/are + being + V3 + by + S A game is being played by them.
Present Perfect	Structure- S + have/has + V3 + O He has bought a pen.	Structure- O + have/has + been + V3 + by + S A pen has been bought by him.
Simple Past	Structure- S + V2 + O They won the game.	Structure- O + was/were + V3 + by + S The game was won by them.
Past Continuous	Structure- S + was/were + V1 + ing + O Kamna was reading stories.	Structure- O + was/were + being + V3 + by + S Stories were being read by Kamna.
Past Perfect	Structure- S + had + V3 + O He had done this work.	Structure- O + had been + V3 + by + S This work had been done by him.
Simple Future	Structure- S + shall/will + V1 + O You will pass the exam.	Structure- O + shall/will + be + V3 + by + S The exam will be passed by you.
Future Perfect	Structure- S + shall/will + have + V3 + O We shall have bought a house.	Structure- O + shall/will + have + been + V3 + by + S A house will have been bought by us.

Note Perfect Continuous tenses do not have passive voice.

REPORTED SPEECH

The act of reporting the words of a speaker is called narration. There are basically two ways in which the words of the speaker can be conveyed in writing.

(a) **Direct Speech** (Direct Narration) The reporting of the words of the speaker without making any changes to it is known as Direct Speech. Direct speech is written inside double quotation marks.

(b) **Indirect Speech** (Indirect Narration) The act of reporting the words of the speaker by making necessary changes to it is called Indirect Speech. While, narrating something, changes are made in the original words of the person. For instance, tense and pronouns are changed according to the reporting verb.

e.g.,

(i) My mother told me, " You have to work harder at school." (Direct speech)

(ii) My mother told me that I had to work harder at school (Indirect speech)

In sentence (i), we can notice that this is the speaker's direct narration as it is shown inside double quotation marks, but in sentence (ii), tense and pronouns are changed and quotation marks are removed.

Basic Rules of Speech and Conversion

(a) **In Direct Speech**

(i) Put the words spoken by the speaker within " " (double quotes or double inverted commas).

(ii) Separate the reporting verb from the direct speech by a comma.

(iii) Begin the first word inside inverted commas with a capital letter.

(b) **In Indirect Speech**

(i) Change the reporting verb according to the sense conveyed by the speech.

(ii) Do not change the tense of the reporting verb.

(iii) Remove the comma separating the reporting verb from the direct speech.

(iv) Remove inverted commas.

(v) Introduce the indirect speech by some connector like *that, if, whether, what, where, how, why* etc depending on whether you want to transform a statement, question or request, as the case may be.

(vi) Convert all kinds of sentences into assertive statements.

(vii) Make other necessary changes in person, verb forms, time, place and expressions.

Some Changes to Consider

(a) **1st person** (I, we etc) → change according to the subject of the reporting verb.

(b) **2nd person** (You, your etc) → change according to the object of the reporting verb.

(c) **3rd person** (He, she, it, they, his, her etc) → make no change.

(d) Change **1st person** into **3rd person** if the reporting verb has no object mentioned.

Rules for Changing Simple Direct Speech into Indirect Speech

Rules	Direct Speech	Indirect Speech
Remove separating comma, inverted commas and use the connector 'that' when there is no object in the sentence.	He said, "I work in a shipyard." Sheena said, "My teacher is highly educated."	He said that he worked in a shipyard. Sheena said that her teacher was highly educated.
The reporting verb 'said' becomes 'told' along with the subject and the connector 'that' when it is followed by an object.	Kamya said to me, "You have been a great help." He said to me, "I shall go to the party."	Kamya told me that I had been a great help. He told me that he would go to the party.

Changes into Reported Speech with Respect to the Tense

Rules of Conversion	Direct Speech	Indirect Speech
Simple Present changes into Simple Past	He said, "I do not like computers." They said, "We love our country."	He said that he did not like computers. They said that they loved their country.
Present continuous changes into past continuous	I said, "It is raining." She said, "I am not laughing."	I said that it was raining. She said that she was not laughing.
Present perfect changes into past perfect	She said, "He has finished his work." They said, "We have not gone to New York."	She said that he had finished his work. They said that they had not gone to New York.
Present perfect continuous changes into past perfect continuous	He said, "I have been studying since 3 o' clock." Radha said, "It has been raining for three days."	He said that he had been studying since 3 o' clock. Radha said that it had been raining for three days.

Past Tense

Simple past changes into past perfect	My teacher said to me, "You answered correctly." He said, "I didn't buy a car."	My teacher told me that I had answered correctly. He said that he had not bought a car.
Past continuous changes into past perfect continuous	They said, "We were enjoying the weather." He said, "Mohit was listening to the music."	They said that they had been enjoying the weather. He said that Mohit had been listening to the music.
Past perfect remains past perfect (tense does not change)	He said, "I had started a business." I said, "She had eaten the meal."	He said that he had started a business. I said that she had eaten the meal.

Future Tense

Rules of Conversion	Direct Speech	Indirect Speech
Simple future: *will* changes into *would*	He said, "I will study the book." They said to me, "We will send you gifts."	He said that he would study the book. They told me that they would send me gifts.
Future continuous: *will be* changes into *would be*	Shreya told him, "I will be waiting for you." He said, "He will not be flying kites."	Shreya told him that she would be waiting for him. He said that he would not be flying kites.
Future perfect: *will have* changes into *would have*	He said, "I will have finished the work." Narayan said, "I will have gone."	He said that he would have finished the work. Narayan said that he would have gone.

Rules for Changing Interrogative Sentences into Indirect Speech
(The reporting verb 'said' becomes 'asked' and 'to' is removed)

Rules	Direct Speech	Indirect Speech
Use 'if' or 'whether' in place of 'that' as a connector.	She said to me, "Do you like tea or coffee?"	She asked me whether I liked tea or coffee.
Remove the question mark while forming an assertive sentence.	She said to Shyam, "Do you have an extra copy?"	She asked Shyam if he had an extra copy.
The questions starting with question words like **when, why, where**, do not use 'if' or 'whether'. The question words are retained to introduce the reported question.	He said, "What is your problem?" She said, "Why are you not coming?"	He asked me what my problem was. She asked me why I was not coming.

Rules for Changing Imperative Sentences into Indirect Speech (Commands, Requests and Suggestions)

Rules	Direct Speech	Indirect Speech
Use conjunction 'to' instead of 'that'.	I said to Hari, "Do not pluck the flowers." The Principal said to the students, "Get out of the office."	I ordered Hari not to pluck the flowers. The Principal ordered the students to get out of the office.
In sentences beginning with 'Let', the reporting verb is changed to 'proposed' or 'suggested'.	He said, "Let us keep quiet in this matter."	He suggested that we should keep quiet in this matter.

Rules for Changing Exclamatory Sentences into Indirect Speech

Rules	Direct Speech	Indirect Speech
Words such as Alas, Bravo, Oh, Wow, Wah should be left out in indirect speech.	Ram said, "Alas! I have been ruined."	Ram exclaimed with sorrow that he had been ruined.
Forms of the verb 'wish' is used if the sentence conveys a wish.	She said, "If I were a bird."	She wished to be a bird./She wished that she were a bird.

Some Other Changes

Other Changes		
Time, Place, Expression and Other Changes		
now	—	then
ago	—	before
today	—	that day
last night	—	the previous night or the night before
next week	—	the following week
here	—	there
hither	—	thither
this	—	that
thus	—	so

Change the Type of Sentences

Interchanging Simple and Complex Sentences

A simple sentence can be changed to a complex sentence by expanding phrase or a group of words into a subordinate clause as explained below

(A) **Noun phrase/Noun to Noun clause**

e.g.,

(i) He hopes to succeed.(Simple)

(ii) Truth cannot perish. (Subject to verb)

(iii) Pay attention to his words. (Object to preposition)

(iv) My faith, about his success, is firm. (Case in apposition to noun)

(v) It is unfortunate to be cheated by friends. (Case in apposition to a pronoun 'it')

(vi) My wish is to do something useful. (Complement of a verb 'is')

Change of Noun Phrase/Noun to a Noun Clause

(i) He hopes that he will succeed.

(ii) What is true cannot perish.

(iii) Pay attention to what he says.

(iv) My faith, that he will succeed, is firm.

(v) It is unfortunate that one is cheated by friends.

(vi) My wish is that I should do something useful.

(B) **Adjective Phrase to Adjective Clause**

(i) He is a student of great promise.

(ii) I met my friend living in Mumbai.

Change of Adjective Phrase/ Adjective to an Adjective Clause

(i) He is a student, who holds great promise.

(ii) I met my friend, who is living in Mumbai.

(C) **Adverb phrase to Adverb or Adverb Clause**

(i) I shall do it in your presence.

(ii) Do not go till I return.

Change the Adverbial Phrase/Adverb into Adverb Clause

(i) I shall do it, when you are present.

(ii) Do not go until I return.

Interchanging Simple and Compound Sentences

Rule 1 Convert a word or phrase into a clause by using a coordinating conjunction.

e.g., Going home, she had dinner. (Simple)

She went home and had dinner. (Compound)

He was ill, but he went to work. (Compound)

In spite of his illness, he went to work. (Simple)

Rule 2 Use infinitives in simple sentence.

e.g., He brought some flowers and gave them to his wife. (Compound)

He brought some flowers to give to his wife. (Simple)

Interchanging Compound and Complex Sentences

Rule 1 Convert either of the independent clauses in a compound sentence into a dependent clause and replace the coordinating conjunction with the subordinating conjunction.

e.g., You should hurry or you will miss the chance. (Compound)

If you don't hurry, you will miss the chance. (Complex)

The teacher entered the classroom and the students opened their books. (Compound)

When the teacher entered the classroom, the students opened their books. (Complex)

Interchanging Affirmative and Negative Sentences

Generally, when a Affirmative Sentence is changed into negative like 'no' or 'not' we use words negative in the sentence.

e.g., She was writing poems. (Affirmative)

She was not writing poems. (Negative)

However, this is not the case with all sentences. We follow certain rules to convert different positive sentences to negative sentences.

Rule 1 Use antonyms in the sentence along with negative words like 'not', 'no', 'never', etc.

e.g., He is a bad man. (Affirmative)

He is not a good man. (Negative)

Rule 2 When the positive sentences contains words like only, everyone, everything, etc., it is replaced with words like none but (for person), nothing but (for thing), etc.

e.g., Only you can solve this question. (Affirmative)

None but you can solve this question. (Negative)

Rule 3 If a sentence contains an amount or magnitude or number of something then negative is made by adding 'no'.

e.g., She has a car. (Affirmative)

She has no car. (Negative)

Note it when there are changes in pronouns, verbs, adjectives or adverbs, it is to be checked that the meanings of the sentences are not changed.

Interchanging Assertive and Interrogative Sentences

Rule 1 If the question is seeking an answer in 'yes' or 'no', change affirmative question into a negative sentence and *vice-versa*.

e.g., There wasn't a notebook on the table. (Negative)

Was there a notebook on the table? (Positive Interrogative)

Rule 2 If the question is seeking an answer, that is, it is a real question, use phrases like 'I wonder', 'I want to know' or 'I would like to know' in the assertive sentence.

e.g., I wonder what he will think of the gift I gave. (Assertive)

What will he think of the gift I gave? (Interrogative)

Interchanging Assertive and Exclamatory Sentences

Rule 1 When changing an exclamatory sentence into an assertive sentence, words like 'very', 'great', 'extremely', etc, are added.

e.g., How beautiful this monument is! (Exclamatory)

This is a very beautiful monument. (Assertive)

Rule 2 Words expressing strong emotions like 'Hurrah!', 'Alas!', etc., in an exclamatory sentence are replaced by similar emotions in an assertive sentence.

e.g., Hurrah! We won the match.

It is a matter of joy that we won the watch. (Assertive)

Interchange of Degrees without Changing the Meaning

Rule 1 If we find 'as – as' in a positive degree, we will use 'not less-than' to convert it into a comparative.

e.g., Bikash is as brave as Milan. (Positive)

Bikash is not less brave than Milan. (Comparative)

Rule 2 If we get 'as soon as' in a positive degree, we will use "no sooner than" to change it into a comparative degree.

e.g., As soon as the man saw a tiger, he ran away. (Positive)

No sooner had the man seen a tiger than he ran away. (Comparative)

Rule 3 If we get 'No other' in a positive degree, we will use 'Any other' to transform it into a comparative degree and 'Of all' into a superlative degree.

e.g., No other metal is so bright as gold. (Positive)

Gold is brighter than any other metal. (Comparative)

Gold is the brightest of all metals. (Superlative)

Rule 4 If we get 'One of the' in the superlative degree, we will use 'many/most other' to convert it into a comparative degree and 'Only a few/ Very few' in the positive degree.

e.g.,

Sachin is one of the greatest Indian cricketers. (Superlative)

Sachin is greater than most other Indian cricketers. (Comparative)

Very few Indian cricketers are as great as Sachin. (Positive)

Rule 5 If the sentence is positive and we do not get 'One of the/Of all' in the superlative degree, we use 'no other' to transfer it into a positive degree and 'Any other' into the comparative degree.

e.g.,

Arjun is the best character in Mahabharata. (Superlative)

Arjun is better than any other character in Mahabharata. (Comparative)

No other character in Mahabharata is so good as Arjun. (Positive)

If the sentence is negative, we use 'Some other' to convert it into both positive and comparative degrees.

e.g. Ram is not the best boy in the class. (Superlative)

Ram is not better than some other boys in the class. (Comparative)

Or

Some other boys in the class are better than Ram. (Comparative)

Ram is not so good as some other boys in the class. (Positive)

Interchange of so That.... too ...to or Removal of too

The conjunctions 'so.. that' and 'too.. to' serve the same purpose. However, both the conjunction are used differently. Too...to...usually expresses a negative idea. When we connect two clauses with too...to... we get a simple sentence consisting of an independent clause and an infinitive phrase.

e.g., The tea is too hot for me to drink.

So… that… presents a positive connotation to make a complex sentence with one dependent clause and an independent clause.

e.g., The tea is so hot that I cannot drink it.

Hence, while transforming the sentence, we replace 'so' with 'too' and *vice-versa.*

use 'that' is used after the Adjective

replace 'to' with 'cannot' or 'could not'

e.g.,

(a) He is too old to work hard.

He is so old that he cannot work hard.

(b) The mother was too weak to control her sons.

The mother was so weak that she could not control her sons.

Check Your Progress 7

Rewrite the following sentences as directed.

i. Your talent in cooking greatly astonishes me. (Change the voice)

ii. The students were asked to submit their assignments by Friday. (Change to active voice)

iii. 'I will finish the report tomorrow,' said Mark. (Rewrite using Indirect speech)

iv. The cake was baked by Sarah for her sister's birthday. (Change to active voice)

v. 'We have completed the project,' announced the team leader. (Rewrite using Indirect speech)

CONFUSING WORDS

There are certain words within the extensive English vocabulary that are so similar in pronunciation or spelling that students are often confused by them. Such words are referred to as 'Confusing words'. Following is a list of most commonly used confusing words

1. **Affect/Effect** 'Affect' is usually a verb meaning to influence, while 'Effect' is usually a noun meaning the result of an action.
2. **Compliment/Complement** 'Compliment' is an expression of praise or admiration, while 'Complement' refers to something that completes or enhances something else.
3. **Principal/Principle** 'Principal' can mean a person who holds a high position or the main sum of money, while 'Principle' refers to a fundamental truth or belief.
4. **Accept/Except** 'Accept' means to receive or agree to something, while 'Except' means to exclude or leave out.
5. **Assure/Ensure/Insure** 'Assure' means to make someone confident or certain, 'Ensure' means to make sure something happens and 'Insure' refers to protecting against financial loss.
6. **Loose/Lose** 'Loose' means not tight or free from restraint, while 'Lose' means to misplace or no longer possess something.
7. **Stationary/Stationery** 'Stationary' means not moving or fixed in one place, while 'Stationery' refers to writing materials.
8. **Peak/Peek/Pique** 'Peak' can refer to the top of a mountain or the highest point, 'Peek' as a verb means to look secretively and 'Pique' means to stimulate or provoke.
9. **Their/There/They're** 'Their' is possessive, indicating ownership, 'There' indicates a place and 'They're' is a contraction of 'they are'.
10. **Passed/Past** 'Passed' is the past tense of the verb 'to pass', while 'Past' refers to a time before the present or beyond a certain point.
11. **Than/Then** 'Than' is used for making comparisons, while 'Then' is used to indicate time or consequence.
12. **Farther/Further** 'Farther' refers to physical distance, while 'Further' usually refers to figurative distance or to a greater extent.
13. **Cite/Site/Sight** 'Cite' means to quote or refer to, 'Site' refers to a location and 'Sight' refers to vision or something seen.
14. **Weather/Whether** 'Weather' refers to atmospheric conditions, while 'Whether' is used to introduce a choice between alternatives.
15. **Born/Borne** 'Born' is the past participle of 'bear', meaning to give birth to, while 'Borne' is the past participle of 'bear' in the sense of carrying or supporting.
16. **Allude/Elude** 'Allude' means to suggest or indirectly refer to something, while 'Elude' means to evade or escape from someone or something.
17. **Conscious/Conscience** 'Conscious' relates to being aware or awake, while 'Conscience' refers to one's inner sense of right and wrong.
18. **Counsel/Council** 'Counsel' can refer to advice or guidance or a lawyer, while 'Council' is a group of people convened for consultation or decision-making.
19. **Immigrant/Emigrant** 'Immigrant' refers to a person who comes to live permanently in a foreign country, while 'Emigrant' refers to a person who leaves their own country to settle permanently in another.
20. **Desert/Dessert** 'Desert' can mean a dry, barren area of land or to abandon, while 'Dessert' refers to the sweet course typically eaten at the end of a meal.

PROVERBS

A proverb is a simple, traditional saying that expresses a perceived truth based on common sense or experience. Proverbs are often metaphorical and use formulaic language. Following is a list of most commonly used proverbs

1. **Actions speak louder than words** What a person does is more significant than what they say. It emphasises the importance of deeds over mere promises or talk.
2. **All's fair in love and war** In situations involving intense emotions or conflicts, people are justified in using any means necessary to achieve their goals, even if those means might be considered unethical or unfair.
3. **Don't count your chickens before they hatch** Don't make plans or be overly confident about something that hasn't happened yet. It advises against premature celebration or assumption of success.
4. **Don't cry over spilled milk** Don't waste time worrying or being upset about something that has already happened and cannot be changed. Instead, focus on finding a solution or moving forward.

5. **Every cloud has a silver lining** Even in difficult or challenging situations, there is often a positive aspect or outcome. It encourages optimism and looking for the bright side.
6. **Fortune favours the bold** Taking risks and being courageous can lead to success and good fortune. It suggests that those who are willing to take bold actions are more likely to be rewarded.
7. **Haste makes waste** Rushing or acting too quickly can lead to mistakes or wasted efforts. It advises patience and careful consideration in actions and decision-making.
8. **If it ain't broke, don't fix it** Don't try to improve or change something that is already functioning well. It advocates for leaving things as they are when they are satisfactory.
9. **Kill two birds with one stone** Accomplish two tasks with a single action or effort. It highlights efficiency and productivity in completing multiple objectives simultaneously.
10. **Let sleeping dogs lie** Avoid stirring up trouble or reopening old conflicts. It advises against bringing up past issues that may cause unnecessary trouble or tension.
11. **Rome wasn't built in a day** Achieving significant goals or creating something substantial takes time and patience. It emphasises the importance of persistence and gradual progress.
12. **The early bird catches the worm** Being proactive and taking action early can lead to success or advantage. It underscores the benefits of being prepared and acting promptly.
13. **There's no smoke without fire** Rumors or suspicions often have some basis in truth. It suggests that where there is gossip or speculation, there is likely some underlying reality.
14. **Two heads are better than one** Collaboration or seeking input from others can lead to better solutions or decisions. It highlights the value of teamwork and collective intelligence.
15. **When in Rome, do as the Romans do** Adapt your behaviour or actions to fit in with the customs or norms of a particular place or group. It emphasises the importance of respecting local traditions or etiquette.
16. **You reap what you sow** The consequences of one's actions, whether good or bad, will eventually catch up to them. It underscores the principle of cause and effect or karma.
17. **A penny saved is a penny earned** Money saved through frugality or thriftiness is equivalent to money earned through work. It encourages wise financial management and saving.
18. **Don't put all your eggs in one basket** Avoid relying on a single source of income or investment. It advises diversification and spreading risk across multiple avenues.
19. **Better late than never** It's preferable to do something late than not at all. It suggests that it's better to take action, even if delayed, than to never take action.
20. **The early bird gets the worm** Those who act promptly or arrive early have an advantage over those who delay or arrive late. It emphasises the benefits of being proactive and punctual.

PHRASAL VERBS

A phrase or a phrasal verb is a small group of words comprising a verb and a preposition which together acts as an idiomatic expression (has a meaning other than its literal meaning).

(i) Fall out means quarrel.
(ii) Put up with means tolerate.

LIST OF IMPORTANT PHRASAL VERBS

1. Account for (explain the reason, answer for) I can't account for his unusual behaviour in this matter.
2. Ask after (ask about the welfare, inquire after) I met your brother at the party, he asked after you.
3. Ask for (request for) She asked for a glass of water.
4. Back out (withdraw from promise) He agreed to help but backed out at the last moment.
5. Bear on/upon (relevant) Your remarks have no bearing on the main problem.
6. Bear with (to show patience, cooperate) In view of the heavy losses suffered by the company, the shareholders were requested to bear with.
7. Blow out (extinguish) The candle blew out as the gust of wind came in.
8. Blow up (explode, start suddenly) The plan of the enemy to blow up the flyover was foiled by the police.
9. Break down (emotional collapse, stop functioning) While giving evidence in the court, she brokedown.
10. Break into (enter by force) The robbers broke into his house last night.
11. Break off (come to an end) The talks between India and China broke off.
12. Break out [spread (war, epidemic, fire, riots)] The fear that AIDS has broken out in India is not unfounded.
13. Break through (major achievement) There is no hope of a break through in the murder case of the famous actor, Sushant.
14. Break up [terminate (meeting, school, session)] The college will break up next week for summer vacation.
15. Bring about (cause to happen) The administration helped to bring about a peaceful settlement.

16. Bring out (explain the meaning) When asked to explain, she could not bring out the meaning of the poem.
17. Bring up (rear, educate) Fathers are beginning to play a bigger role in bringing up their children.
18. Call at (visit a place to meet) I called at the residence of my boss yesterday.
19. Call for (necessary, require) For the unity of the country, discipline among the people is called for.
20. Call in (send for help) The police were called in without delay by the residents.
21. Call off (suspend or abandon) We decided to call off the strike.
22. Call on (go and visit a person) It is a tradition for the Prime Minister to call on the President.
23. Call out (ask to come for help) The National Guards has been called out to render help in the flood affected areas.
24. Call upon (appeal, exhort) He was called upon to prove the correctness of the press reports.
25. Carry on (continue) Now it is difficult to carry on this business in the teeth of stiff competition.
26. Carry out (implement, obey, execute) It is not likely that your father will carry out the threat of disinheriting you.
27. Catch up with (make up for deficiency, overtake) He remained ill for many days but caught up with the pending work very soon.
28. Come across (meet or discover by chance) I came across my old friend in the market yesterday.
29. Come by (get) How have you come by such a precious diamond?
30. Come of (belong to) Reeta comes of a family of freedom fighters.
31. Come over (to suddenly experience a strong feeling) I don't know what came over me when I hit my best friend.
32. Come round/around (around, agree, recover from illness) My father at first refused to let me continue my studies but he came round in the end.
33. Come upon (get by chance) My friend came upon the evidence when he was searching his old papers.
34. Cut off (discontinue, die, remove) Gas supplies have now been cut off.
35. Die down [gradually disappear (riots, excitement, storm, etc.)] The wind has died down.
36. Die out (become out of use or existence) He thought that the custom of dowry had died out a long time ago.
37. Dispose to (willing, inclined favourably) My friend is disposed to discussing the problems thoroughly.
38. Do away with (eradicate) We should do away with social evils.
39. Do without (to manage without) We cannot do without a fan in summer.
40. Drop out (retire in the midst of doing something) She could not qualify for the selection as she dropped out while the race was in progress.
41. Fall back on (depend on) You must save money to fall back on it in old age.
42. Fall out (quarrel) The two friends appear to have fallen out over a minor issue.
43. Fall through (to remain incomplete, fail) For want of sufficient funds, your new project is likely to fall through.
44. Follow up (pursue after the first attempt) The idea has been followed up by a group of researchers.
45. Get ahead (go forward) You can get ahead of your rivals only by hard work.
46. Get along (be friendly) They just can't get along together because of their temperamental differences.
47. Get away (escape) The thieves got away on a scooter.
48. Get on (progress) How is your son getting on with his studies?
49. Get over (recover from an illness or shock, come over) He is still trying to get over the financial crisis.
50. Get through (pass through, succeed) It is not possible to get through any examination without working hard.
51. Give away (distribute) She has given away jewellery worth thousands of rupees to help the poor.
52. Give in (surrender, agree) At first she was adamant but at last she gave in to the request of her friend.
53. Give up (stop, abstain from) He gave up smoking to regain his health.
54. Go back on (withdraw, back out) One should not go back on one's promise.
55. Go on (continue) There is no need to go on arguing about it.
56. Go through (read hurriedly, endure) He didn't lend me the newspaper because he was going through it.
57. Hand out (distribute) Hand out the books to the students.
58. Hand over (give charge or authority) He has not handed over charge to the new manager.
59. Hold on (carry on, bear difficulties, persist) Inspite of financial difficulties, he held on and succeeded in the long run.
60. Jump at (accept happily) He jumped at the offer of his boss to accept the job abroad.
61. Jump to (arrive suddenly [conclusion]) You should never jump to conclusions.
62. Keep off (keep at a distance) There was a notice at the site, "Keep off the bushes."
63. Keep on (continue) She kept on crying in spite of my assurance of help.

64. Keep up (maintain) Always try to keep up the standard of life even in the face of crises.

65. Lay out (plan building, garden, etc.) A number of gardens were laid out by the Moghuls.

66. Let down (humiliate, to lower down) We should never let down our friends.

67. Let (somebody) in on (share a secret) I will not let her in on my plans.

68. Live on (depend for food) The lion is carnivorous and lives on flesh.

69. Live by (means/manner) You must learn to live by honest means.

70. Look about (in search of, on the watch) The thirsty crow was looking about water here and there.

71. Look after (take care of) In her old age, she has no one to look after her.

72. Look for (search for a person or lost thing) She was looking for her lost books.

73. Look down upon (hate, despise) It is folly on your part to look down upon the poor students.

74. Look into (investigate a matter) A committee was set up to look into the issue of child labour in Delhi.

75. Look over (examine carefully, go over) The examiner has yet to look over the practice note books.

76. Look out (watch out) Look out! there is a snake under the bush.

77. Look out for (in search of, on the watch) He is looking out for a decent job.

78. Look up (consult some book for a word, rise) Please look up this word in the dictionary.

79. Look up to (to admire or respect someone) His younger brother looks up to him and obeys his every order.

80. Look upon (consider, regard) We must look upon social evils as a nuisance.

81. Make off with/away with (run away, destroy) They made off with the cash and fled.

82. Make up (to end (a quarrel), compose) You should make an effort to make up with your friend.

83. Make up for (compensate for) After her long illness, she is trying her best to make up for her deficiency in studies.

84. Pass away (die, expire) On the passing away of his father, I sent him a message of condolence.

85. Pass oneself off (show off) The hypocrites always pass themselves off as honest persons.

86. Pass out (leave after completing education) The cadets will pass out next month after completing their training.

87. Pull off (succeed) India pulled off victory in the last stage of the match.

88. Pull through (recover from illness) I think she'll pull through her serious illness very soon.

89. Put on (wear, pretend) It is difficult to put on the appearance of innocence for a long time.

90. Put out (extinguish) The fire was put out suddenly.

91. Put up (stays) He is putting up at a hostel these days.

92. Round up (arrest) The police rounded up anti-social elements last night.

93. Run after (pursue, hanker after) We should not run after money.

94. Run out (come to an end) When the rations ran out, the head office was informed.

95. Run over (crush under) He was run over by a speeding car.

96. See off (to escort a guest for his/her departure) His friends were present at the station to see him off.

97. See through (discover something hidden, motive) Man has grown so clever that it is difficult to see through his tricks.

98. Send for (summon) She sent for a doctor when her husband fell ill.

99. Set in (begin) As soon as the summer sets in, the reptiles come out of hibernation.

100. Set off (to start a series of events, process, improve) Privatisation has set off the process of liberalisation in foreign trade.

101. Set up (establish) The factory was set up by his uncle.

102. Set forth (start on a journey, explain) The party will set forth its views on globalisation at a public rally.

103. Set out (start on a journey, set forth) No sooner was the hunter informed of a lion's presence in the forest than he set out.

104. Stand by (support, help) Although he promised to stand by me in difficulties, he did not live up to it.

105. Stand for (represent) TEC stands for Technical Education Certificate.

106. Stand out (to be different) She stood out from the crowd because of her amiable manners.

107. Stand up for (defend) It is your duty to always stand up for the poor.

108. Strike off (remove from the list) His name has been struck off the admission list.

109. Take after (resemble) She always reminds me of her mother since she takes after her.

110. Take down (write) She was busy in taking down the dictation which the teacher was giving.

111. (Be) Taken to (form a habit) He took to wearing black leather jackets.

112. Take up (start a hobby or study, occupy) He has taken up modelling as a career.

113. Take for (suppose to be, identify) I took the scoundrel for a noble person.

114. (Be) Taken aback (be surprised) I was taken aback to hear of the news of his failure.

115. Talk over (discuss a matter) I agreed to go home and talk over the matter.

116. Turn down (reject, strike down) I turned down the request of my friend to go to Shimla.

117. Turn out (prove, reveal, expel) Nothing ever turned out right for me in life.

118. Watch out (look out, be careful) If you do not watch out, the snake might harm you.

119. Wipe away (cleanse, remove) The marks of blood were wiped away by the accused.

120. Work out (solve the problem) He is very intelligent and can work out any difficult problem.

Check Your Progress 8

Rewrite the sentences as directed.

i. Don't .... before they are hatched. (Fill in the blank to complete the proverb)

Write one sentence each using the following phrasal verbs without changing their forms.

ii. Drop out

iii. Carry on

Use the following words in sentences of your own so as to bring out their correct meanings.

iv. Conscious / Conscience

v. Peak / Peek

Practice EXERCISE

Set 1

(a) Rewrite the sentences as directed.

(i) It is your duty to help the poor people in your parish. (Change the voice)

(ii) He said, "Let us go to the movie." (Rewrite the sentence using indirect speech)

(iii) You are allowed into the club only if you are a member. (rewrite the sentence using 'Unless')

(iv) You cannot lose what you never had, ...? (Add a suitable question tag)

(v) Do not look .... on women. (Supply the appropriate preposition)

(vi) This is one of his more readable books. (use the superlative degree)

(vii) It is sad to think that youth should pass away. (change into exclamatory sentence)

(viii) The stranger .... (creeps/ crept)in through the window last night. (Choose the correct option)

(ix) He has refused to help me. (begin the sentence with 'He said')

(x) We .... (must/ would)not hurry, we have got plenty of time. (Choose the correct form of the verb)

Answers

(i) The poor people in your parish are to be helped by you.

(ii) He proposed that they should go to the movie.

(iii) Unless you are a member, you are not allowed in the club.

(iv) Can you

(v) down

(vi) This is the most readable book of his.

(vii) How sad it is to think that youth should pass away!

(viii) crept

(ix) He said that he will not help me.

(x) must

(b) Write one sentence each using the following phrases to bring out their meaning clearly. Do not change the form of the given phrases.

(i) Deal in (ii) Call on

(iii) Get off (iv) Hold back

(v) Put up with

Answers

(i) His father deals in precious stones and also the jewellery business.

(ii) I was supposed to call on by my friend at his home but I forgot.

(iii) It is expected of India to get off to a flying start in the last match.

(iv) I held myself back during the tense situation and stopped it from escalating.

(v) I could not put up with her rude behaviour and dismissed her instantly.

(c) Correct the following sentences without-making any unnecessary changes.

(i) I had walked for most of the day to Kanpur and then get on the train by Mumbai.

(ii) The singer took the jury's harsh criticism in heart.

(iii) While driving, Satheesh always switches off his mobile phone and kept it in the dashboard.

(iv) No sooner he was brought to the hospital than he began panting heavily.

(v) If I was the President of India, I would work to ensure communal harmony.

Answers

(i) I had walked for most of the day to Kanpur and then got on the train by Mumbai.
(ii) The singer took the jury's harsh criticism to heart.
(iii) While driving, Satheesh always switches off his mobile phone and keeps it on the dashboard.
(iv) No sooner was he brought to the hospital than he began panting heavily.
(v) If I were the President of India, I would work to ensure communal harmony.

SET 2

(a) **Rewrite the sentences as directed.**

(i) The old man said to his son, "May God bless you!" (Rewrite the sentence using indirect speech)
(ii) Lemon tastes sour. (Change the voice)
(iii) Hari is so short that he cannot touch the ceiling. (replace 'so' by 'too')
(iv) The board of directors will decide the penalty, ...? (Add a suitable question tag)
(v) I am planning a get together .... Monday. (Supply the appropriate preposition)
(vi) No metal is as costly as gold. (use comparative degree of 'costly')
(vii) I doubt, if you have done it. (change into negative without changing the meaning)
(viii) If nature ....(continue/continues) to degrade, the world's economic output will suffer sooner or later. (Choose the correct option)
(ix) To make mistakes is easy. (begin the sentence with 'it')
(x) He is the patient .... (who/whom)called you in the morning. (Choose the correct option)

Answers

(i) The old man wished/blessed his son that God might bless him.
(ii) Lemon is sour when it is tasted.
(iii) Hari is too short to touch the ceiling.
(iv) Won't they
(v) on
(vi) Gold is costlier than any other metal.
(vii) I am not sure if you have done it.
(viii) continues
(ix) It is easy to make mistakes
(x) who

(b) **Write one sentence each using the following phrases to bring out their meaning clearly. Do not change the form of the given phrases.**

(i) Turn down
(ii) Do without
(iii) Fall back upon
(iv) Look over
(v) Mix up

Answers

(i) I turned down the request of my friend to go to Goa.
(ii) We cannot do without Air Conditioner in the summer months.
(iii) She has saved much money to fall back upon in old age.
(iv) I think, I may have made some typos in this report. Could you look it over?
(v) I didn't complete the assignment because I didn't know how. The directions mixed me up.

(c) **Correct the following sentences without-making any unnecessary changes.**

(i) Radha told her friends that she will discuss the project with her mentor when she would meet him tomorrow.
(ii) Not only did he sell his house but as well squandered his father's money.
(iii) The knight was received compliments from the king for his bravery.
(iv) Your sister will look after your son in your absence, isn't it?
(v) I read a novel by Sydney Sheldon within my illness.

Answers

(i) Radha told her friends that she will discuss the project with her mentor when she meets him tomorrow.
(ii) Not only did he sell his house but also squandered his father's money.
(iii) The knight received compliments from the king for his bravery.
(iv) Your sister will look after your son in your absence, won't she?
(v) I read a novel by Sydney Sheldon during my illness.

SET 3

(a) **Rewrite the sentences as directed.**

(i) She thought, "She will not go out with him." (Rewrite the sentence using indirect speech)
(ii) Do you trust me? (Change the voice)
(iii) Notwithstanding his hard work, he did not succeed. (rewrite the sentence using 'yet')
(iv) Today, students should be reconciled with the way things are changing., ...? (Add a suitable question tag)
(v) Mr. Obi put his whole life .... the work. (Supply the appropriate preposition)
(vi) Do this to escape sufferings. (make the sentence using 'lest')
(vii) Durga is a brave girl. (change to exclamatory sentence)
(viii) I In a classroom students are to be trained to love .... (each other/one another) .(Choose the correct option)

(ix) As soon as the bell rang, the train started. (rewrite the sentence using 'No sooner')

(x) Just as in a family it is the willing cooperation of its members that …… (brings/brought) happiness and contentment, so is it in the larger family of the nation. (Choose the correct form of the verb)

Answers

(i) She thought to herself that she would not go out with him.

(ii) Am I trusted by you?

(iii He worked hard yet did not succeed'.

(iv) Shouldn't they

(v) in

(vi) Do this lest you should suffer.

(vii) What a brave girl Durga is!

(viii) one another

(ix) No sooner had the bell rung, than the train started.

(x) brings

(b) **Write one sentence each using the following phrases to bring out their meaning clearly. Do not change the form of the given phrases.**

(i) Hang up

(ii) Iron out

(iii) Jack up

(iv) Knock out

(v) Look forward to

Answers

(i) I'd like to talk longer, but I'd better hang up. My sister needs to make a call.

(ii) Yes, I know, we disagree on lots of things, but we can iron them out.

(iii) We'll have to jack up the back of the car before we can change the tire.

(iv) The boxing match ended abruptly as no one expected him to knock his rival out.

(v) I really look forward for May to begin for it is vacation time.

(c) **Correct the following sentences without-making any unnecessary changes.**

(i) Every Saturday, your mother prepares a pudding, isn't she?

(ii) His idea of going to the picnic was universally accepted by all.

(iii) When she went for a walk Maya couldn't take off her scarf because it was too much windy.

(iv) You should tell these children to complete their projects himself.

(v) Jawaharlal Nehru was a scholar as well a statesman.

Answers

(i) Every Saturday, your mother prepares a pudding, doesn't she?

(ii) His idea of going to the picnic was accepted by all.

(iii) When she went for a walk Maya couldn't take off her scarf because it was too windy.

(iv) You should tell these children to complete their projects themselves.

(v) Jawaharlal Nehru was a scholar as well as a statesman.

SET 4

(a) **Rewrite the sentences as directed.**

(i) She said that she cooked vegetables and he fried rice. (Rewrite the sentence using direct speech)

(ii) It is necessary to help the poor. (Change the voice)

(iii) I did not spend as much money as you. (change into comparative degree)

(iv) I walked out …………… I wanted to breathe some fresh air. (Add a suitable conjunction)

(v) I organised my dressing table ………….. putting all the rubber bands in the drawer. (Supply the appropriate preposition)

(vi) He ran fast to reach the bus stop. (change into an interrogative sentence)

(vii) He drove too fast for the police to catch. (Remove 'too')

(viii) If you had consulted me, I would have …….. (adviced/ advised) you. (Choose the correct option)

(ix) He confessed that he was guilty. (change into a simple sentence)

(x) I'm sure I …….. them at the party last night. (Choose the correct form of the verb 'see')

Answers

(i) She said, "I cooked vegetables and he fried rice."

(ii) The poor are required to be helped.

(iii) You spent more money than I did.

(iv) because

(v) by

(vi) Did he run fast to reach the bus stop?

(vii) He drove so fast that the police could not catch him.

(viii) advised

(ix) He confessed his guilt.

(x) saw

(b) **Write one sentence each using the following phrases to bring out their meaning clearly. Do not change the form of the given phrases.**

(i) Account for

(ii) Cast away

(iii) Get through

(iv) Keep up

(v) Live by

Answers

(i) I can't account for his unusual behaviour in this matter.

(ii) We usually give our servants the old clothes, which we cast away.

(iii) It is not possible to get through the examination security without a full checkup.
(iv) The reason for their increasing debt is that they tried to keep up their standard of luxurious life.
(v) You must learn to live by honest means.

(c) **Correct the following sentences without-making any unnecessary changes.**
(i) Why you copying your homework from someone else?
(ii) Open your books at page tenth.
(iii) "Under no circumstances we can help you in this illegal work," said the Manager.
(iv) He said that he had forgot to lock the door before leaving.
(v) We don't really want a large house, we are looking for same comfort and same convenience on a moderate price.

Answers

(i) Why are you copying your homework from someone else?
(ii) Open your books at page ten.
(iii) "Under no circumstances can we help you in this illegal work," said the Manager.
(iv) He said that he had forgotten to lock the door before leaving.
(v) We don't really want a large house, we are looking for the same comfort and same convenience at a moderate price.

SET 5

(a) **Rewrite the sentences as directed.**
(i) She said to her mother, "Father had left before/when she reached home." (Rewrite the sentence using indirect speech)
(ii) This watch need not be winded up. (Change the voice)
(iii) To the best of my knowledge, he is a vegetarian. (begin the sentence: As far as ....)
(iv) I have ……… Lakshmi for the past twelve years. (Choose the correct word)
(v) The strike has been called ……… . (Supply the appropriate preposition)
(vi) She is more intelligent than her brother is. (use positive degree)
(vii) Only he is responsible for my failure in life. (change into negative without changing the meaning)
(viii) .... (whoever/whatever) wins this civil war there will be little rejoicing at the victory. (Choose the correct option)
(ix) Eat few rich dinners and you will need few medicines. (rewrite the sentence with 'if')
(x) There will be a rush for seats when the train .... (arrived/arrives) (Choose the correct form of the verb)

Answers

(i) She told her mother that father had left before/when she reached home.
(ii) You don't need to wind this watch.
(iii) As far as my knowledge does, he is a vegetarian.
(iv) Known
(v) off
(vi) Her brother is not so intelligent as she is.
(vii) None, but he, is responsible for my failure in life.
(viii) Whoever
(ix) If you eat few rich dinner, you will need few medicines.
(x) arrives

(b) **Write one sentence each using the following phrases to bring out their meaning clearly. Do not change the form of the given phrases.**
(i) Wipe out
(ii) Talk over
(iii) Set out
(iv) Round up
(v) Put on

Answers

(i) We must try to wipe out poverty from the country.
(ii) I agreed to go home and talk over the matter.
(iii) No sooner was the hunter informed of a lion's presence in the forest, than he set out.
(iv) The police rounded up anti-social elements last night.
(v) It is difficult to put on the appearance of innocence for a long time.

(c) **Correct the following sentences without-making any unnecessary changes.**
(i) Most of the carbon-trapping mechanisms that we have identified are based at limit studies.
(ii) It is a common misconception that every policeman badly behaves with the citizens.
(iii) I will make the payment either in cash else through cheque.
(iv) The earthy fragrance of soil after the first rain is always refreshing.
(v) Scientists have made dramatic progress in understanding the universe and the mechanisms of biology.

Answers

(i) Most of the carbon-trapping mechanisms that we have identified are based on limited studies.
(ii) It is a common misconception that every policeman behaves badly with the citizens.
(iii) I will make the payment either in cash or through cheque.
(iv) The earthy fragrance of soil after the first rain is always refreshing.
(v) Scientists have made dramatic progress in understanding the universe and the mechanisms of biology.

SET 6

(a) **Rewrite the sentences as directed.**

(i) She said, "If I am selected, I needn't study further." (Rewrite the sentence using indirect speech)

(ii) Autobiographies are written by people for various reasons. (Change the voice)

(iii) Shall we ever forget these happy days. (rewrite using 'never')

(iv) Wheat is not native to India and barley .... (Complete appropriately)

(v) Nadheeka was musing .... memories of the past. (Supply the appropriate preposition)

(vi) He is too arrogant to listen to ad vice. (change into a complex sentence)

(vii) It would be wonderful if we would go to Shimla. (change into an exclamatory sentence using 'how')

(viii) Just as in a family it is the willing cooperation of its members that...... (brings/brought)happiness and contentment, so is it in the larger family of the nation. (Choose the correct option)

(ix) This is the greatest discovery that the world has ever known. (begin the sentence with 'never')

(x) Ramappa .... (is elected/ will be elected) as the mayor of the town and he will assume charge this Friday. (Choose the correct form of the verb)

Answers

(i) She said that if she was selected, she would not have to study further.

(ii) People write autobiographies for various reasons.

(iii) I shall never forget those happy days.

(iv) isn't either

(v) on

(vi) He is very arrogant so he does not listen to advice.

(vii) How wonderful would it be if we go to Shimla.

(viii) brings

(ix) Never has the world known such a great discovery.

(x) is elected

(b) **Write one sentence each using the following phrases to bring out their meaning clearly. Do not change the form of the given phrases.**

(i) Make up for

(ii) Make out

(iii) Look up

(iv) Look after

(v) Jump to

Answers

(i) After her long illness, she is trying her best to make up for her lost opportunities.

(ii) The police could not make out the face of the criminal from the video.

(iii) Please look up this word in the dictionary.

(iv) In her old age, she has no one to look after her.

(v) You should never jump to conclusions.

(c) **Correct the following sentences without-making any unnecessary changes.**

(i) Most of the families in my research rely at phone calls for almost all of their communication.

(ii) I like reading fictional stories besides write poems.

(iii) He sat down in a darkly corner and covered his face, and would not say a single word to anyone.

(iv) She will be write her examination by this time tomorrow.

(v) There is many ways to make a stranger feel welcome in the community.

Answers

(i) Most of the families in my research rely on phone calls for almost all of their communication.

(ii) I like reading fictional stories besides writing poems.

(iii) He sat down in a dark corner and covered his face, and would not say a single word to anyone.

(iv) She will be writing her examination by this time tomorrow.

(v) There is many ways to make a stranger feel welcomed in the community.

SET 7

(a) **Rewrite the sentences as directed.**

(i) She said to me, "When I was a student, I could not go out alone." (Rewrite the sentence using indirect speech)

(ii) How can a fire be lit if you have no matches? (Change the voice)

(iii) The shirt is too loose for my body. (replace 'too')

(iv) It'll rain soon, ...? (Add a suitable question tag)

(v) Many things have happened .... I met you last. (Supply the appropriate preposition)

(vi) No other bowler in India is so famous as Kapil Dev. (Change to comparative degree)

(vii) Who can live more than 100 years? (change into assertive without changing the meaning)

(viii) Thomas worked very hard, ... (still/ but) he did not stand first. (Choose the correct option)

(ix) He is too weak to play game. (Use 'so..that')

(x) My father .... a newspaper every day. (Choose the correct form of the verb 'buy')

Answers

(i) She told me that when she was a student, she was not allowed to go alone.

(ii) How can you light a fire if you have no matches?

(iii) The shirt is so loose that it does not fit my body.

(iv) Won't it

(v) since

(vi) Kapil Dev is more famous than any other bowler in India.

(vii) No one can live more than 100 years.

(viii) still
(ix) He is so weak that he cannot play game.
(x) buys

(b) **Write one sentence each using the following phrases to bring out their meaning clearly. Do not change the form of the given phrases.**
(i) Watch out for
(ii) Throw away
(iii) Show up
(iv) Pitch in
(v) Nodded off

Answers

(i) There's a school at the end of this block. Watch out for children crossing the street.
(ii) You shouldn't throw those newspapers away; they're recyclable.
(iii) The boss was very upset when you didn't show up for the meeting.
(iv) We'll be finished soon, if everyone pitches in.
(v) The speech was so boring that several people in the audience nodded off before it was finished.

(c) **Correct the following sentences without-making any unnecessary changes.**
(i) My friends whom were preparing to climb Mount Everest have reached the base camp.
(ii) It's been many years have I left Mumbai and settled in Delhi.
(iii) The policeman asked many people but no one was knowing how the accident happened.
(iv) Alex picked up the boxes quite easily even they were heavy.
(v) Had you been to Mumbai, I would also go with you.

Answers

(i) My friends who were preparing to climb Mount Everest have reached the base camp.
(ii) It's been many years since have I left Mumbai and settled in Delhi.
(iii) The policeman asked many people but no one knew how the accident happened.
(iv) Alex picked up the boxes quite easily even though they were heavy.
(v) Had you been to Mumbai, I would have also gone with you.

SET 8

(a) **Rewrite the sentences as directed.**
(i) Lekha said, "Mansi, You must be silent." (Rewrite the sentence using indirect speech)
(ii) Were students being taught by Vinu? (Change the voice)
(iii) For more information contact the Secretary. (begin the sentence with 'should')
(iv) The rock band .... play very well last year, ...? (Add a suitable question tag)
(v) Shivaji fought .... every kind of aggression. (Supply the appropriate preposition)
(vi) Kolkata is larger than any other city in Asia. (use superlative degree)
(vii) He is not a wise fellow. (change into negative without changing the meaning)
(viii) I waited for him .... (as/ until) the clock struck seven. (Choose the correct option)
(ix) His success is sure. (use adverb)
(x) It is time we .... (acted/ act) with determination. (Choose the correct form of the verb)

Answers

(i) Lekha ordered Mansi to be silent.
(ii) Was Vinu teaching students?
(iii) Should you need more information, please contact the secretary.
(iv) don't they
(v) against
(vi) Kolkata is the largest city in Asia.
(vii) He is a foolish fellow.
(viii) until
(ix) He will surely succeed.
(x) act

(b) **Write one sentence each using the following phrases to bring out their meaning clearly. Do not change the form of the given phrases.**
(i) Drop by
(ii) Cut back (on)
(iii) Brush up on
(iv) Add up
(v) Turn-out

Answers

(i) If you're in town next month, we'd love to see you. Please try to drop by the house.
(ii) "You should cut back on the amount of coffee that you drink".
(iii) If you're going to travel to the UK, you'd better brush up on your English.
(iv) His theory seems, at first, to be plausible, but the facts in his research don't add up.
(v) There was a heavy turn-out for the opening ceremony.

(c) **Correct the following sentences without-making any unnecessary changes.**
(i) Although he was late but he stopped on the way to have coffee with his friends.
(ii) The manager took him at task for his negligence.
(iii) The recently hike in the price of petroleum products will hit household budgets severely.
(iv) Mr. Das, my friend and Principal of this college, have retired.

(v) The city turned out to be very different to what he had expected.

Answers

(i) Although he was late, he stopped on the way to have coffee with his friends.
(ii) The manager took him to task for his negligence.
(iii) The recent hike in the price of petroleum products will hit household budgets severely.
(iv) Mr. Das, my friend and Principal of this college, has retired.
(v) The city turned out to be very different from what he had expected.

SET 9

(a) **Rewrite the sentences as directed.**

(i) Rohan told her that he would leave Jaipur soon. (Rewrite the sentence using direct speech)
(ii) Ritika had finished her work. (Change the voice)
(iii) Unless you run fast you will miss the train. (rewrite using if)
(iv) I asked him for some paper, but he .... (Add a word/phrase)
(v) "Are you alone, my son ?"asked a soft voice close .... me. (Supply the appropriate adverb)
(vi) I am not well so I shall not come to the office. (change into complex sentence)
(vii) Alas! she died so young. (change into assertive without changing the meaning)
(viii) Today everyone wishes .... (to earn/ earning)money quickly. (Choose the correct option)
(ix) Rani is not more intelligent than Shalu. (use 'as....'as)
(x) I told him that I .... (shall/ ought to)leave next day. (Choose the correct form of the verb)

Answers

(i) Rohan said to her, "I shall leave Jaipur soon."
(ii) Her work had been finished by Ritika.
(iii) If you run fast, you will not miss the train.
(iv) had none
(v) behind
(vi) I shall not come to the office as I am not well.
(vii) It is sad that she died so young.
(viii) to earn
(ix) Shalu is as intelligent as Rani.
(x) ought to

(b) **Write one sentence each using the following phrases to bring out their meaning clearly. Do not change the form of the given phrases.**

(i) Take-over
(ii) Outset
(iii) Upkeep
(iv) Breakdown
(v) Hang of something

Answers

(i) The take-over of Sahara Airlines has been finalised.
(ii) The trainees were warned of the danger at the outset.
(iii) The upkeep of my office costs me a lot these days.
(iv) The breakdown of the car delayed our departure.
(v) As I entered the conference hall, I got the hang of conspiracy.

(c) **Correct the following sentences without-making any unnecessary changes.**

(i) What is the name of the Swami whom autobiography impressed you so much?
(ii) His father prevented him to go abroad for higher studies.
(iii) Scarcely has the train stopped at the platform than the passengers started pushing each other to enter the train.
(iv) A lot of food we serve are wasted.
(v) The bus broke down because we had to walk some distance.

Answers

(i) What is the name of the Swami whose autobiography impressed you so much?
(ii) His father prevented him from going abroad for higher studies.
(iii) Scarcely had the train stopped at the platform than the passengers started pushing each other to enter the train.
(iv) A lot of food we serve is wasted.
(v) The bus broke down so we had to walk some distance.

SET 10

(a) **Rewrite the sentences as directed.**

(i) He said to her, "I want to see you now." (Rewrite the sentence using indirect speech)
(ii) You have to do this immediately. (Change the voice)
(iii) Nobody will deny that she is honest. (use 'admit' in the sentence)
(iv) I need sugar for my tea, give me .... (Add a determiner)
(v) It became clear that the strangers were heading ....a serious disaster (Supply the appropriate preposition)
(vi) Reena has more money than brain. (use positive degree)
(vii) They found a little sugar in the kitchen. (change into negative without changing the meaning)
(viii) They said that movie was fantastic ....(and/ so) I watched it. (Choose the correct option)
(ix) I met him last, when his father died. (use 'since' for 'when')
(x) ....of robbers surrounded us. (Add the correct word)

Answers

(i) He told her that he wanted to see her then.
(ii) This has to be done by you immediately.
(iii) Everyone will admit that she is honest.
(iv) some
(v) towards
(vi) Reena has not as much brain as she has money.
(vii) They found not much sugar in the kitchen.
(viii) so
(ix) I haven't met him since his father's death.
(x) Gang

(b) **Write one sentence each using the following phrases to bring out their meaning clearly. Do not change the form of the given phrases.**
(i) Wind up
(ii) Turn up
(iii) See through
(iv) Go over
(v) Dispose of

Answers

(i) We were forced to wind up the business on account of the heavy loss.
(ii) Who can say what will turn up next?
(iii) Man has grown so clever that it is difficult to see through his tricks.
(iv) As I go over the balance sheet of the company, I am finding serious mistakes.
(v) She has decided to dispose of her old house.

(c) **Correct the following sentences without-making any unnecessary changes.**
(i) Cyclone Amphan roared into West Bengal on Wednesday leave behind a trail of devastation across a large area of the state.
(ii) Only five minutes are allowed for each speaker during the function.
(iii) The sports day events will be conducted from 3 : 30 pm and 5 : 30 pm on Saturday.
(iv) Airlines have increased fares because according to the new rules only limiting passengers are allowed.
(v) My mother generally reads the local newspaper to keep abreast of the local news.

Answers

(i) Cyclone Amphan roared into West Bengal on Wednesday leaving behind a trail of devastation across a large area of the state.
(ii) Only five minutes are allowed to each speaker during the function.
(iii) The sports day events will be conduction between 3:30 pm and 5:30 pm on Saturday.
(iv) Airlines have increased fares because according to the new rules only limited passengers are allowed.
(v) My mother generally reads the local newspaper to keep abreast of the local news.

SET 11

(a) **Rewrite the sentences as directed.**
(i) Both of them did not partake in the function. (Correct the sentence)
(ii) As soon as the bell rang, the train started.(Rewrite the sentence using 'No sooner')
(iii) She would not ...... how old she was. (say, tell)
(iv) If it does not stop raining we cannot play.(Begin with Unless')
(v) The cattle damaged both the fence and the crop.(Rewrite using 'not only .... but also')
(vi) He shouted, "Let me go."(Change to Indirect Speech)
(vii) Give the order. (Change the voice)
(viii) Notwithstanding his hard work he did not succeed. (Rewrite the sentence using 'yet')
(ix) Durga is a brave girl. (Change to Exclamatory Sentence)
(x) He is as strong as his brother.(Change the degree of comparison without changing the meaning)

Answers

(i) Both did not partake in the function.
(ii) No sooner had the bell rung than the train started.
(iii) tell
(iv) Unless it stops raining, we cannot play.
(v) The cattle not only damaged the fence, but also the crop.
(vi) He shouted to let him go.
(vii) Let the order be given.
(viii) He worked hard, yet he did not succeed.
(ix) What a brave girl Durga is!
(x) His brother is not stronger than him.

(B) **Use the following phrasal verbs in sentences of your own.**
(i) To do away with
(ii) To put up with
(iii) Turn down
(iv) Do without
(v) Fall back upon

Answers

(i) This chemical will do away with the stain in your sink.
(ii) You don't need to put up with her toxic behaviour.
(iii) Turn down the radio, please.
(iv) Jamie told me that she could do without that filthy looking rug.
(v) One should always have a plan B to fall back upon.

(c) **Correct the following sentences without-making any unnecessary changes.**
(i) The retention of a major portion of our earnings have helped build our new house.
(ii) Geeta suspects Seeta for stealing the pen.
(iii) She's used to get up early.

(iv) Jane thought she can win the prize.
(v) The gardener picked up flowers in the garden.

Answers

(i) The retention of a major portion of our earnings has helped build our new house.
(ii) Geeta suspects Seeta of stealing the pen.
(iii) She's used to getting up early.
(iv) Jane thought she could win the prize.
(v) The gardener plucked flowers from the garden.

SET 12

(a) **Do as directed**

(i) He was very tired. He did not go out for a walk. (Combine using 'too .... to')
(ii) As soon as the Chief guest arrived, the programme started. (Rewrite the sentence starting with 'No sooner')
(iii) Had I known you were not coming......... . (Complete the sentence)
(iv) It is very humid. It is better to wear cottons. (Combine these sentences starting with 'Considering')
(v) The mason is building the wall (Change the voice)
(vi) Why couldn't you complete the work in time? (Change the voice)
(vii) I admire her. I cannot agree with everything she does. (Combine the sentences using 'Much')
(viii) The reason why she is absent today is because her husband is ill. (Correct the sentence)
(ix) "Climb the mountain, cross the river and attack the enemy," said the Commanding Officer of the soldiers. (Change the narration)
(x) The teacher said to Rakesh, "What time will the train arrive?" (Change the narration)

Answers

(i) He was too tired to go out for a walk.
(ii) No sooner had the chief guest arrived than the programme started.
(iii) Had I known you were not coming, I wouldn't have come either.
(iv) We should wear cotton, considering that its very humid.
(v) The wall is being built by the mason.
(vi) Why wasn't the work completed in time by you?
(vii) Much as I admire her, I cannot agree with everything she does.
(viii) The reason she is absent today is because her husband is ill.
(ix) The Commanding Officer commanded the soldiers to climb the mountain, cross the river and attack the enemy.
(x) The teacher asked Rakesh what time the train would arrive.

(b) **Use the following words in sentences of your own so as to bring out their meanings.**

(i) coast/beach
(ii) contagious/infectious
(iii) famous/famed
(iv) incident/accident
(v) price/cost

Answers

(i) Coast- We walked along the coast for two miles.
Beach- Some tourists are sunbathing on the beach.
(ii) Contagious - If a person is contagious they have a disease that can be spread to other people by touching.
Infections- If a person is infectious, they have a disease that can be spread to others.
(iii) Famous - He is a famous artist.
Famed- He is a famed musician.
(iv) Incident - His bad behaviour was just an isolated incident.
Accident - He was killed in an accident.
(v) Price - He managed to get a good price for the car.
Cost - The plan had to be abandoned on grounds of cost.

(c) **Correct the following sentences without-making any unnecessary changes.**

(i) I wish I was as tall as my leader.
(ii) Sharmas will start after the breakfast.
(iii) I look forward to see him soon.
(iv) Each boy and each girl was in their best dress.
(v) Why is Ruby appearing so sad?

Answers

(i) I wish I were as tall as my leader.
(ii) Sharmas will start after breakfast.
(iii) I look forward to seeing him soon.
(iv) Each boy and each girl was in his and her best dress.
(v) hy does Ruby appear so sad?

Previous Years' QUESTIONS

2024

(a) Rewrite the sentences as directed.

(i) Let the door be shut. (Change the voice)

Ans. Shut the door

(ii) He told me that he had not gone there. (Change into direct speech)

Ans. He said to me, I did not go there.

(iii) He had not read the book, he had not seen it either. (Rewrite using 'neither', 'nor')

Ans. Neither had he read the book nor had he seen it either.

(iv) He (do) it for the last two days. (Use the correct form of the verb)

Ans. He **has been doing** it for the last two days.

(v) His brother is more intelligent. (Change into the negative without changing the meaning)

Ans. His brother is not less intelligent.

(vi) He is sitting the shade of a tree. (Insert the correct preposition)

Ans. He is sitting **under** the shade of a tree.

(vii) He is very strong. He can defeat his enemies. (Combine the two sentences using 'enough')

Ans. He is strong enough to defeat his enemies.

(viii) The cat jumped .... the fence. (Fill in the blank using the correct preposition)

Ans. The cat jumped **over** the fence.

(ix) He gave a modest answer to the question. (Rewrite the sentence changing the adjective into an adverb)

Ans. He answered the question modestly.

(x) It is difficult to get used to (eat) with chopsticks. (Use the correct form of the verb in the brackets)

Ans. It is difficult to get used to eating with chopsticks.

(b) Write one sentence each using the following phrases to bring out their meaning clearly. Do not change the form of the given phrases.

(i) Bring out

Ans. The new recipe made by my brother really brings out the flavours of the fresh herbs.

(ii) Give way

Ans. The crowd of the town had to give way as the parade marched through the entire streets.

(iii) Look into

Ans. I have promised my father to lookinto the matter and get back to him with a solution.

(iv) Get along

Ans. Despite of different point of views. The two colleagues managed to get along and work effectively as a team.

(v) Bring about

Ans. The new government budget is expected to bring about significant improvements in the healthcare system.

(c) Correct the following, sentences without making any unnecessary changes.

(i) He walked one and a half hours.

Ans. He walked for one and half hour.

(ii) He is always ready to pick up quarrels.

Ans. He is always ready to start quarrels.

(iii) I have ordered for dinners.

Ans. I have ordered dinners. 'For' is unnecessary here.

(iv) Let us discuss about the problems.

Ans. Let us discuss the problems. 'About' is unnecessary here.

(v) One cannot be too careful about what he says.

Ans. One cannot be too careful about what they say.

2023

(a) Rewrite the sentences as directed.

(i) Your behaviour greatly astonishes me. (Change the voice)

Ans. I am greatly astonished by your behaviour.

(ii) He said, "Where will I be this time next year !" (Rewrite the sentence using indirect speech)

Ans. He wondered where he would be that time the following year.

(iii) As soon as she reached her home, the messenger arrived. (Use "No sooner ... than")

Ans. No sooner had she reached her home than the messenger arrived.

(iv) He walks in an awkward fashion,........... ? (Add a suitable question tag)

Ans. doesn't he

(v) My son always confides......... me. (Supply the appropriate preposition)

Ans. in

(vi) He visits me rarely. (Change into a negative sentence without changing the meaning)

Ans. He doesn't visit me frequently.

(vii) He is so clever that he cannot be trusted. (Use "too......... to")

Ans. He is too clever to be trusted.

(viii) Neither of the plans......... (suit/suits) him. (Choose the correct option)

Ans. suits

(ix) Tanya is the most intelligent girl in her class. (Use the comparative degree)

Ans. Tanya is more intelligent than any other girl in her class.

(x) Deep snow........ (laid/lay) on the railway track. (Choose the correct form of the verb)

Ans. lay

(b) Write one sentence each using the following phrases to bring out their meaning clearly. Do not change the form of the given phrases.

(i) held up

Ans. She held her hands up in surrender.

(ii) carry out

Ans. He must have realised that it was impossible to carry out his plan.

(iii) take after

Ans. I pray that the newborn doesn't take after its uncle.

(iv) look down upon

Ans. You should never look down upon a man simple because he is uneducated.

(v) give in.

Ans. Her nagging bothered me so much that I decided to give in.

(c) Correct the following sentences without-making any unnecessary changes.

(i) Everyone, except the five boys, have reached the destination.

Ans. Everyone, except the five boys, has reached the destination.

(ii) Unless he does not return the library books, he will not be relieved from service.

Ans. Unless he does not return the library books, he will not be relieved of service.

(iii) They have arrived from Chennai yesterday.

Ans. They had arrived from Chennai yesterday.

(iv) Your answer is replete from errors.

Ans. Your answer is replete with errors.

(v) The book is missing from my room from yesterday.

Ans. The book is missing from my room since yesterday.

2022

(a) Rewrite the sentence as directed.

(i) Let the government punish the wrong doers. (Change the voice)

Ans. Let the wrong doers be punished by the government.

(ii) The policeman said to the man, "You are a trespasser and will be punished." (Rewrite the sentence using indirect speech)

Ans. The policeman told the man that he was a trespasser and would be punished.

(iii) The meeting started the moment the minister arrived. (Use 'as soon as')

Ans. The meeting started as soon as the minister arrived.

(iv) He does his work........without depending on others. (Fill in the blank space with an appropriate reflexive pronoun)

Ans. Himself

(v) A law-abiding citizen is one who abides........the laws of the land. (Supply the appropriate preposition)

Ans. By

(vi) I met a woman. Her purse was snatched by someone. (Combine these simple sentences into a complex sentence)

Ans. I met a woman whose purse was snatched by someone.

(vii) You aren't going out,........? (Add a suitable question tag)

Ans. Are you

(viii) He always remembers his well-wishers. (Change into a negative sentence without changing the meaning)

Ans. He never forgets his well wishers.

(ix) He drove too fast for the police to catch him. (Remove 'too')

Ans. He drove so fast that the police could not catch him.

(x) The book may be in the bag. It may be in the cupboard. (Join the two sentences using 'either ... or')

Ans. The book may either be in the bag or in the cupboard.

(b) Write one sentence each using the following words and phrases to bring out their meaning clearly. Do not change the tense form of the given words.

(i) Look up to

Ans. Many people in the world look up to the Indian Prime Minister Narendra Modi.

(ii) Let down

Ans. The families of the victims feel that the justice system has let them down.

(iii) Take up

Ans. Because of the medical emergency, she was unable to take up the London posting.

(iv) Turn down

Ans. It's hard to believe a person would turn down a trip to Barcelona.

(v) Break into

Ans. Do you think that Sahil plans to break into his parent's house tomorrow?

(c) Rewrite the following sentences correctly after detecting errors of any kind including mispositioning of words. Do not make unnecessary changes.

(i) One of the prisoner escaped from the prison van.

Ans. One of the prisoners escaped from the prison van.

(ii) How you could forget the name of your school?

Ans. How could you forget the name of your school?

(iii) Prices are increasing in leaps and bounds.

Ans. Prices are increasing by leaps and bounds.

(iv) No sooner I had reached the station than the train started.

Ans. No sooner had I reached the station than the train started.

(v) I avoid to go there.

Ans. I avoid going there.

2021

(a) Rewrite the sentences as directed.

(i) The flowers Rana gave to Meena have withered. (Change to passive voice)

Ans. The flowers given to Meena by Rana have withered.

(ii) The cushions do not match the couch. The curtains also do not match the couch. (Combine the sentences using 'neither…nor')

Ans. Neither the cushions nor the curtains match the couch.

(iii) Anil plays football in the evenings. He goes for swimming in the mornings. (Combine the sentence using 'not only … but also')

Ans. Not only does Anil play football in the evenings, but he also goes for swimming in the mornings.

(iv) Can your mother not go in the other car? (Change to affirmative)

Ans. Your mother can go in the other car.

(v) You never think of ………. . (Fill in the blank using a reflexive pronoun)

Ans. yourself

(vi) ……… she was talking on the phone, her purse fell from her hand. (Fill in the blank using the appropriate word - Because/While)

Ans. While

(vii) The godown is infested ……… mice. (Fill in the blank using a preposition)

Ans. with

(viii) A great poet and essayist ……… in this house. (Fill in the blank using the correct form of 'live')

Ans. lived

(ix) You are requested not to pluck the flowers. (Change to active voice)

Ans. Please don't pluck the flowers.

(x) Laavanya said to Pallavi, "Did Priyanka have lunch with Shilpy?" (Change to indirect speech)

Ans. Laavanya asked Pallavi whether Priyanka had lunch with Shilpy.

(b) Write one sentence each using the following words/phrases to bring out their meaning clearly. Do not change the form of the given words/phrases:

(i) back off

Ans. She was so tired after her day at the office that when the time came for her interview with the magazine, she told them to back off and leave her alone.

(ii) carried away

Ans. My father got carried away when he saw the little orphan girl taking care of a stray dog and brought both of them home.

(iii) log out

Ans. My friend's brother once forgot to log out of his Google account and someone hacked all his information from there.

(iv) drop in

Ans. When I was leaving, my aunt told me to drop in the next time I'm near her house.

(v) hold on

Ans. Long after Parker's death, Hachi would still hold on to his memories and run to the railway station to wait for him.

(c) Correct the following sentences without making any unnecessary changes:

(i) Help me to open the bottle.

Ans. Please help me open the bottle.

(ii) Ten kilometres are a long distance.

Ans. Ten kilometers is a long distance.

(iii) I, you and my brother will go to the movie tomorrow.

Ans. You, my brother and I will go to the movie tomorrow.

(iv) Hardly did he open the door when the lights went off.

Ans. Hardly had he opened the door when the lights went off.

(v) The sister and the brother congratulated one another on their success.

Ans. The sister and brother congratulated each other on their success.

2020

(a) Rewrite the sentences as directed.

(i) The inaugural ceremony of the Commonwealth Games was held ……… the Jawaharlal Nehru Stadium. (Fill in the blank space with a preposition)

Ans. at

(ii) I decided to buy ……… few paintings that were left unsold in the exhibition. (Fill in the blank space with an article)

Ans. a

(iii) My neighbour takes care of my dog in my absence. (Transform the sentence into passive form)

Ans. My dog is taken care of by my neighbour in my absence.

(iv) The foundation stone of this auditorium was laid by the Chief Minister. (Transform the sentence into active form)

Ans. The Chief Minister laid the foundation stone of this auditorium.

(v) Neither the driver nor the passengers of the bus .... injured in the accident. (Fill in the blank space with the appropriate form of the verb 'be')

Ans. were

(vi) The police spokesperson requested the media persons to allow him to complete his statement. (Rewrite the sentence using the direct speech form)

Ans. The Police spokesperson said to the media persons, "Please allow me to complete my statement."

(vii) If the police had reached the crime scene on time, the victim .... (Fill in the blank space with the appropriate form of the verb 'save')

Ans. would have been saved.

(viii) We need to take care of .... (Fill in the blank space with an appropriate reflexive pronoun)

Ans. ourselves

(ix) Give your statement to the police. It will enable them to arrest the culprit. (Write one simple sentence by combining the two sentences)

Ans. Give your statement to the police to enable them to arrest the culprit.

(x) He sings only in the bathroom. (Change this simple sentence into a complex sentence)

Ans. He sings that also only in the bathroom.

(b) Write one sentence each using the following words and phrases to bring out their meaning clearly. Do not change the tense form of the given words:

(i) takes after

Ans. Mahinder's son takes after him as far as looks are concerned.

(ii) put off

Ans. The Manager warned us not to put off out work for later during the match.

(iii) called off

Ans. The Principal of the School called off the meeting as she received the news of her mother's death.

(iv) called on

Ans. The teacher called on me, and I didn't know the answer.

(v) denied

Ans. After hearing the case and seeing the evidence, the judge denied bail to the criminal.

(c) Rewrite the following sentences correctly after detecting errors of any kind including mis-positioning of words. Do not make unnecessary changes in the sentences:

(i) He met all the concerned officers but failed to get the permission to hold the function.

Ans. He met all the concerned officer but failed to get permission to hold the function.

(ii) One of my colleagues is leading the officious delegation.

Ans. One of my colleagues is leading the official delegation.

(iii) The students organised a three days cultural festival in their college.

Ans. The students organised a three-day cultural festival in their college.

(iv) The landlord asked his tenant to evict his rented house if he could not pay the rent.

Ans. The landlord asked his tenant to vacate his rented house if he could not pay the rent.

(v) We need an affordable vaccine for everybody because we will only be safe if everyone else is safe.

Ans. We need an affordable vaccine for everybody because we will be safe only if everyone else is safe.

2019

(a) Rewrite the sentences as directed.

(i) They will be arriving soon, ... ? (Add a suitable question tag)

Ans. They will be arriving soon, won't they?

(ii) He is greater than I. (Change to a negative sentence using 'great')

Ans. I am not as great as him.

(iii) The police were taking him to prison. (Change the voice)

Ans. He was being taken to prison by the police.

(iv) I have nothing that I can offer. (Change to simple sentence)

Ans. I can offer nothing.

(v) Abdul is as strong as his brother. (Change to comparative degree without changing the meaning)

Ans. Abdul is not stronger than his brother.

(vi) He hanged himself .... a piece of cloth. (Write suitable preposition)

Ans. with

(vii) Sitting on the tree, a bee stung him. (Begin the sentence with : While he ...)

Ans. While he sat on the tree, a bee stung him.

(viii) Please excuse ...... being late. (Write the correct pronoun)

Ans. my

(ix) Gold and silver .... precious metals. (Use the correct verb form)

Ans. are

(x) He said, "We all are sinners." (Change to indirect speech)

Ans. He stated that all of them were sinners.

(b) Use the following words and phrases in sentences of your own so as to bring out their meaning clearly. Do not change the form of the word.

(i) iron out

Ans. Rishabh must iron out the flaws in his batting technique so as to stay longer at the crease.

(ii) nonchalant

Ans. The clown in the circus did a number of somersaults with nonchalant ease.

(iii) recalcitrant

Ans. Manish was recalcitrant and refused to budge from his stand.

(iv) all and sundry

Ans. All and sundry applauded Kohli's double century when he reached it.

(v) watch out

Ans. Watch out for that deep pothole on the road.

(c) Correct the following sentences without making any unnecessary changes.

(i) Gulliver's Travels were written by Jonathan Swift.

Ans. Gulliver's Travels was written by Jonathan Swift.

(ii) If anybody knows the truth let them tell it.

Ans. If anyone knows the truth, let that person tell it.

(iii) Please meet my Mrs.

Ans. Please meet my wife.

(iv) I shall pay you when I return back.

Ans. I shall pay you when I return.

(v) My heartfelt congratulations to the team.

Ans. Please convey my heartiest congratulations to the team.

2018

(a) Rewrite the sentences as directed.

(i) The teacher said to me, "Are you not ashamed of telling a lie?" (Change into indirect speech)

Ans. The teacher asked me if I was not ashamed of telling a lie.

(ii) You must complete the work by the end of this week. (Change the voice)

Ans. The work must be completed by the end of this week.

(iii) Few students knew the answers, ... ? (Put a question tag)

Ans. didn't they

(iv) The minister was annoyed that he had not carried out his orders. (Change into a simple sentence)

Ans. The minister was annoyed for not carrying out his orders.

(v) Shakuntalam is understood to be the best drama in Sanskrit. (Change to comparative degree without changing the meaning)

Ans. Shakuntalam is understood to be better than any other drama in Sanskrit.

(vi) As soon as he came, he made objections. (Rewrite using "No sooner ...")

Ans. No sooner had he come than he made objections.

(vii) The writer is evidently enamoured .... the subject. (Fill in the blank with the correct preposition)

Ans. by

(viii) The paper was very easy. He could score high marks. (Combine the sentences using 'enough')

Ans. The paper was easy enough for him to score high marks.

(ix) We seldom see .... as others see us. (Fill in the blank using a reflexive pronoun)

Ans. ourselves

(x) If I .... the Principal of the college, I would allow no indiscipline. (Fill in the blank using the correct form of the verb 'be')

Ans. were

(b) Use the following words and phrases in sentences of your own so as to bring out their meaning clearly.

(i) on the wane

Ans. His influence over his employees was on the wane.

(ii) gourmand

Ans. The party was really fantastic with incredible food selection that would make any gourmand happy.

(iii) debutant

Ans. He dazzled London society as the greatest debutant of his generation.

(iv) plutocracy

Ans. Financial plutocracy must give way to financial democracy.

(v) esoteric

Ans. The medical research was so esoteric that only a few physicians could actually understand the results.

(c) Correct the following sentences without making any unnecessary changes.

(i) I bid him to hold his tongue.

Ans. I asked him to hold his tongue.

(ii) She wasn't her usual ebullient at the party.

Ans. She was not her usual ebullient self at the party.

(iii) They did not provide us any chairs to sit.

Ans. They did not provide us any chairs to sit in.

(iv) Under no circumstances passengers are permitted to open the doors themselves.

Ans. Under no circumstances are passengers permitted to open the doors themselves.

(v) I am seeing her enter the room.

Ans. I saw her enter the room.

2017

(a) Rewrite the sentences as directed.

(i) .... university stands for humanism, tolerance, progress, etc. (Fill in the blank with the correct article)

Ans. A

(ii) He often gets .... trouble because of his carelessness. (Fill in the blank with the correct preposition)

Ans. into

(iii) I .... living in this town since 2007. (Fill in the blank with the correct auxiliary verb)

Ans. have been

(iv) They have complete the work. (Change into passive voice)

Ans. The work has been completed by them.

(v) The method of living happily must be known to you. (Change into active voice)

Ans. You must know the method of living happily.

(vi) My teacher said to me, "You should learn to live your life meaningfully and beautifully." (Change into indirect speech)

Ans. My teacher told/advised me that I should learn to live my life meaningfully and beautifully.

(vii) My mother advised me that I should give respect to elders. (Change into direct speech)

Ans. My mother said to me, "You should give respect to elders."

(viii) Educated and empowered women contribute richly for the development of our nation, ...? (Put the correct question tag)

Ans. don't they

(ix) People respect him because he is an exemplary leader. (Change into simple sentence)

Ans. People respect him for being an exemplary leader.

(x) The problem was so complicated that I would not solve it. (Rewrite the sentence using "too")

Ans. The problem was too complicated to be solved.

(b) Give the plural form of the following words and make sentences using the plural form.

(i) Alga

Ans. Algae
The old pond near the cottage is covered in green algae.

(ii) Child

Ans. Children
My father took all the children to the amusement park.

(iii) Formula

Ans. Formulae/ Formulas
The answers to the given questions can only be found after applying the correct formulas.

(iv) Syllabus

Ans. Syllabi
The professor distributed the syllabi for all of his courses on the first day of class.

(v) Thesis

Ans. Theses
This is the collection of theses written by all my students.

(c) Correct the following sentences without making any unnecessary changes.

(i) He finds fault in every one.

Ans. He finds faults with everyone.

(ii) He is one of the noble men who have sacrificed his life for the nation.

Ans. He is one of the noble men who had sacrificed his life for the nation.

(iii) One should always take care of his health.

Ans. One should always take care of one's health.

(iv) None of the five persons were found suitable for the job.

Ans. None of the five persons was found suitable for the job.

(v) My friend is younger than me.

Ans. My friend is younger to me.

2016

(a) Rewrite the sentences as directed.

(i) No.........., no gains. (Fill in the blank to complete the proverb)

Ans. pains

(ii) None of these books ..... in circulation today. (Fill in the blank with appropriate form of 'be')

Ans. is

(iii) Such rumours are commonly heard these days. (Change to active form)

Ans. We hear such rumours commonly these days.

(iv) He says, "I'm not coming to the function." (Convert into indirect statement)

Ans. He tells that he is not coming to the function.

(v) None other but Raj has done this mischief. (Correct the sentence)

Ans. None but Raj has done this mischief.

(vi) Neither she nor her husband was present for the ceremony. (Change into interrogative sentence)

Ans. Was she or her husband present for the ceremony?

(vii) They come to the park regularly. (Change to past tense)

Ans. They used to come to the park.
or They would come to the park.

(viii) They know you, ...? (Supply the question tag)

Ans. don't they

(ix) We fashioned these artefacts out of waste material. (Change into passive form)

Ans. These artefacts were fashioned by us out of waste material.

(x) 'Arch-enemy' means one's old enemy/worst enemy. (Strike out the wrong option)

Ans. worst enemy

(b) Give the plural form of the following words and make sentences using the plural form.

(i) Alumnus

Ans. Alumni
Many colleges and universities turn to their alumni for financial support.

(ii) Antenna

Ans. Antennas
Pack all those antennas properly so that they are intact.

(iii) Synopsis

Ans. Synopses
The synopses written by the children were collected for review.

(iv) Stratum

Ans. Strata

They claim to have a wide appeal to all strata of society and every class.

(v) Fungus

Ans. Fungi

Many trees are found to have their smaller roots invaded by fungi.

(c) Correct the following sentences, without making any unnecessary changes.

(i) Several defence aircrafts have crashed recently.

Ans. Several defence aircrafts have crashed recently.

(ii) She had come here but did not meet me for reasons best known to her.

Ans. She had come here but did not meet me for reasons best known to her.

(iii) He is one of the most promising pupil of my class.

Ans. He is one of the most promising pupils of my class

(iv) Cadets must get all items of clothes ironed before packing them for the excursion.

Ans. Cadets must get all items of clothing ironed before packing them for the excursion.

(v) Uneasy lies the head who wears the crown.

Ans. Uneasy lies the head who wears the crown.

2015

(a) Rewrite the sentences as directed making necessary changes without changing their meanings.

(i) The children said, "We went to the zoo this morning." (Change into indirect speech)

Ans. The children said that they had gone to the zoo that morning.

(ii) She said that they would have a party that night. (Change into direct speech)

Ans. She said, "We shall have a party tonight."

(iii) People say the bridge is unsafe. (Change the voice)

Ans. The bridge is said to be unsafe.

(iv) Although there is inflation, the standard of living has gone up. (Change into simple sentence)

Ans. Inspite of inflation, the standard of living has gone up.

OR

Despite inflation, the standard of living has gone up.

(v) The tutor has come. He will teach my son. (Combine the two sentences using 'to')

Ans. The tutor has come to teach my son.

(vi) You may either have an apple or an orange. (Correct the sentence)

Ans. You may have either an apple or an orange.

(vii) No sooner did the sunrise than the rain stopped. (Rewrite using 'as soon as')

Ans. As soon as the sun rose, the rain stopped.

(viii) Notwithstanding his hard work, he did not succeed. (Change into compound sentence)

Ans. Although he worked hard yet he did not succeed.

(ix) He was more sly than a fox. (Change from affirmative to negative)

Ans. A fox is not as sly as he.

(x) The man would not agree to my suggestion. He would not leave me in peace. (Make into a single sentence using 'neither ... nor')

Ans. The man would neither agree to my suggestion nor leave me in peace.

(b) Use the following words in sentences of your own, so as to bring out their meanings.

(i) Impetus/Impetuous

Ans. Impetus– His efforts have given a fresh impetus to this project.

Impetuous– He is an impetuous young man. He needs to be careful while taking decisions.

(ii) Allusion / Illusion

Ans. Allusion– His remarks were seen as an allusion to his friend's divorce.

Illusion– You are under the illusion that you will be selected for the post.

(iii) Collision / Collusion

Ans. Collision-Raman died in a mid-air collision.

Collusion– The officer was corrupt and was operating in collusion with the criminals.

(iv) Official / Officious

Ans. Official– This was his first official visit to Chennai.

Officious– She is a nasty officious lady.

(v) Imminent/Eminent

Ans. Imminent- Their business is in imminent danger of collapse.

Eminent- Sonu Nigam is an eminent singer of the Indian Music Industry.

(c) Fill in the blanks with appropriate prepositions.

(i) The post office will compensate us ... the loss.

Ans. for

(ii) The scene ...... of us is magnificent, isn't it?

Ans. in front

(iii) It is against my nature to pick a quarrel ... anyone.

Ans. with

(iv) I can't climb ...... that high roof.

Ans. up

(v) I haven't seen a movie ... the end of February.

Ans. since

Answers for Check Your Progress

1. i. Who left their umbrella by the door?
ii. Who do you think will win the game tonight, them or us?
iii. Did you hear them talking about the new project during the meeting?
iv. Cacti. In the desert, the resilient cacti thrive with their sharp spines and vibrant blooms.
v. Media. The media plays a crucial role in shaping public opinion and disseminating information.

2. i. Sonia is more athletic than any other girl in the class.
ii. Sam is the tallest boy on the basketball team.
iii. This book is more interesting than any other book I've read this year.
iv. My cat is the laziest pet in the neighbourhood.
v. This car is faster than any other car in its price range.

3. i. were, ii. ran, iii. ate,
iv. sang, v. slept

4. i. They used to go to the gym everyday.
ii. He has finished his homework before dinner.
iii. is
iv. she will have cooked dinner every evening.
v. is

5. i. by, ii. in, iii. of,
iv. the, v. an

6. i. won't you?
ii. haven't they?
iii. She likes to swim, but she doesn't like cold water.
iv. He studied all night, yet he still failed the exam.
v. The weather was bad, so we decided to cancel the picnic.

7. i. I am greatly astonished by your talent in cooking.
ii. The teacher asked the students to submit their assignments by Friday.
iii. Mark said that he would finish the report the next day.
iv. Sarah baked the cake for her sister's birthday.
v. The team leader announced that they had completed the project.

8. i. Don't count your chickens before they are hatched.
ii. Many students dropout of school due to various reasons such as financial constraints.
iii. Carry on my wayward son. There'll be peace when you are done.
iv. Conscious – She made a conscious decision to donate her entire salary to charity.
Conscience – Despite his actions, his conscience weighed heavily on him.
v. Peak – The climbers reached the peak of the mountain just as the sun began to rise.
Peek – She couldn't resist taking a peek at the surprise gift hidden in the closet.

Mock Tests (1-3)

CAPF (AC) Exam
Mock Test 01
GENERAL STUDIES, ESSAY AND COMPREHENSION

Time : 3 Hrs. MM : 200

Paper 2

General Instructions

- All the six questions are to be attempted.
- Question No. 1 is printed both in Hindi and in English
- Other questions are printed in English only and should be attempted in English only.
- The number of marks carried by a question/part is indicated against it.

1. Write essays on any *four* of the following in about 300 words each
निम्नलिखित में से किन्हीं चार पर लगभग 300 शब्दों (प्रत्येक) में निबन्ध लिखिए। **(20 × 4 = 80)**

(a) Elimination of Corporal Punishment in School (GECP)
स्कूलो में शारीरिक दण्ड का उन्मूलन (जीईसीपी)

(b) Geopolitical conflict is changing the world order
भू-राजनीतिक संघर्ष विश्व व्यवस्था को बदल रहा है।

(c) Gender Bias: has the Indian Mindset changed?
लैंगिक भेदभाव: क्या भारतीय मानसिकता बदल गई है?

(d) Skills and knowledge are a twin pillars of countries economic growth and social development.
कौशल और ज्ञान देश की आर्थिक वृद्धि और सामाजिक विकास के दो स्तम्भ हैं।

(e) Need of Patience for success in the competitive world
प्रतिस्पर्धी दुनिया में सफलता के लिए धैर्य की आवश्यकता

(f) Ethnocracy and concentration of power can derail even an affluent nation.
जातीयता और शक्ति का संकेन्द्रण एक समृद्ध राष्ट्र को भी पटरी से उतार सकता है।

2. Write an arguments *for* and *against* each of the following statements. **(20 × 2 = 40)**

(a) Government should regulate the media

(b) Quality of life is better than just longevity.

3. Write reports on the following in about 200 words each. Do not mention any name or address in the report, use XYZ/ABC if needed. **(10 × 2 = 20)**

(a) E-Waste management in India

(b) Water Future in a Climate risked world

4. Attempt a precis of the given passage in one-third of its length. Do not suggest a title. Write, as far as possible, in your own words. The precis should be attempted only on the precis sheets. **(15 × 1 = 15)**

Power and authority are mutually exclusive notions, but ones that are often difficult in practice to disentangle. Authority can best be understood as a means of gaining compliance which avoids both persuasion and rational argument, on the one hand, and any form of pressure or coercion on the other. Persuasion is an effective and widely used means of influencing the behaviour of another, but, strictly speaking, it does not involve the exercise of authority. Much of electoral politics amounts to an exercise in persuasion: political parties campaign, advertise, organize meetings and rallies, all in the hope of influencing voters on Election Day. Persuasion invariably involves one of two forms of influence: it either takes the form of rational argument and attempts to show that a particular set of policies 'make sense', or it appeals to self-interest and tries to demonstrate that voters will be 'better off' under one party rather than another. In both cases, the elector's decision about how to vote is contingent upon the issues that competing parties address, the arguments they put forward and the way they are able to put them across.

Quite simply, parties at election time are not exercising authority since voters need to be persuaded. Because it is based upon the acknowledgement of a 'duty to obey', the exercise of authority should be reflected in automatic and unquestioning obedience. In this case, political parties can only be said to exercise authority over their most loyal and obedient supporters – those who need no persuasion. Similarly, in its Weberian sense, authority can be distinguished from the various manifestations of power. If authority involves the right to influence others, while power refers to the ability to do so, the exercise of power always draws upon some kind of resources. In other words, power involves the ability to either reward or punish another. This applies whether power takes the form of pressure, intimidation, coercion or violence. Unlike rational argument or persuasion, pressure is reflected in the use of rewards and punishments, but ones that stop short of open coercion.

5. Read the following passage and answer the questions that follow. **(4 × 5 = 20)**

Happiness is an electrifying and elusive state. Philosophers, theologians, psychologists, and even economists have long sought to define it. More than simply positive mood, happiness is a state of well-being that encompasses living a good life, one with a sense of meaning and deep contentment. Feeling joyful has its health perks as well. A growing body of research also suggests that happiness can improve your physical health; feelings of positivity and fulfillment seem to benefit cardiovascular health, the immune system, inflammation levels, and blood pressure, among other things.

Happiness has even been linked to a longer lifespan as well as a higher quality of life and well-being. Attaining happiness is a global pursuit. Researchers find that people from every corner of the world rate happiness more important than other desirable personal outcomes, such as obtaining wealth, acquiring material goods, and getting into heaven. Happiness is not the result of bouncing from one joy to the next; researchers find that achieving happiness typically involves times of considerable discomfort. Genetic makeup, life circumstances, achievements, marital status, social relationships, even your neighbors—all influence how happy you are. Or can be. So do individual ways of thinking and expressing feelings. Research shows that much of happiness is under personal control. Regularly indulging in small pleasures, getting absorbed in challenging activities, setting and meeting goals, maintaining close social ties, and finding purpose beyond oneself all increase life satisfaction. It isn't happiness per se that promotes well-being, it's the actual pursuit that's key. Happy people live with purpose.

They find joy in lasting relationships, working toward their goals, and living according to their values. The happy person is not enamoured with material goods or luxury vacations. This person is fine with the simple pleasures of life— petting a dog, sitting under a tree, enjoying a cup of tea.

Misperceptions abound when it comes to what we think will make us happy. People often believe that happiness will be achieved once they reach a certain milestone, such as finding the perfect partner or landing a particular salary. Humans, however, are excellent at adapting to new circumstances, which means that people will habituate to their new relationship or wealth, return to a baseline level of happiness, and seek out the next milestone. Fortunately, the same principle applies to setbacks—we are resilient and will most likely find happiness again.

(a) What can influence the happiness?

(b) What are the characteristics of happy people?

(c) What are the misperceptions about the happiness?

(d) What does happiness encompass?

(e) What are the benefits of happiness?

6. (a) Rewrite the sentences as directed. **(1 × 10 = 10)**

(i) "You must write neatly," the teacher told her students. (Change into indirect speech)

(ii) After driving Professor Jones to the museum she dropped him at his hotel. (Change the voice)

(iii) I shouldn't have lost my temper, ... ? (Put a question tag)

(iv) He confessed that he had committed a crime. (Change to simple sentence)

(v) No other place in Maharashtra is as expensive to live in as Mumbai. (Change to superlative degree without changing the meaning)

(vi) As soon as Jayesh entered the courtroom, his cell phone rang. (Rewrite using "No sooner...than)

(vii) He travelled all .... the world when he was seventy years old. (Fill in the blank with correct preposition)

(viii) He earns very little. He cannot keep his family in comfort. (Combine the sentences using "too...to")

(ix) Be careful! You might electrocute ....! (Fill in the blank using a reflexive pronoun)

(x) Your friends' .... for you for over an hour. (Fill in the blank using the correct form of the verb 'wait')

(b) Write one sentence each using the following phrases to bring out their meaning clearly. Do not change the form of the given phrases. **(2 × 5 = 10)**

I. Add on.
II. Call in.
III. Fall off.
IV. Give up.
V. Knock out.

(c) Correct the following sentences without-making any unnecessary changes. **(1 × 5 = 5)**

(i) He is senior than me.

(ii) Each of the books were costly.

(iii) He gave me a ten rupees note.

(iv) We enjoyed at the party.

(v) Always tell the truth.

CAPF (AC) Exam

Mock Test 02

GENERAL STUDIES, ESSAY AND COMPREHENSION

Time : 3 Hrs. **MM : 200**

Paper 2

General Instructions

- All the six questions are to be attempted.
- Question No. 1 is printed both in Hindi and in English
- Other questions are printed in English only and should be attempted in English only.
- The number of marks carried by a question/part is indicated against it.

1. Write essays on any four of the following in about 300 words each
निम्नलिखित में से किन्हीं **चार** पर लगभग 300 शब्दों (प्रत्येक) में निबन्ध लिखिए। **(20 × 4 = 80)**

(a) The feminization of Agriculture
कृषि का नारीकरण।

(b) Our World is living in shadow of nuclear catastrophe
हमारा विश्व परमाणु आपदा की छाया में जी रहा है।

(c) Who looks inside awakes, who looks outside dreams
जो अन्दर देखता है वह जागता है, जो बाहर देखता है वह सपने देखता है।

(d) Violence in North-Eastern India: Problems and solutions
पूर्वोत्तर भारत में हिंसा: समस्याएँ और समाधान।

(e) India's rise as assertive power from just a soft power.
भारत का एक नरम शक्ति से मुखर शक्ति के रूप में उदय।

(f) Climate Change: Why countries are failing in mitigating its impact?
जलवायु परिवर्तन : देश इसके प्रभाव को कम करने में क्यो विफल हो रहे हैं?

2. Write an arguments for and against each of the following statements. **(20 × 2 = 40)**

(a) Books should be Replace by Electronic gazettes in Schools.

(b) Restrictions on freedom are necessary in the interest of social harmony

3. Write reports on the following in about 200 words each. Do not mention any name or address in the report, use XYZ/ABC if needed. **(10 × 2 = 20)**

(a) Infiltration of AI Chatbots

(b) Status of Single sue plastic ban

4. Attempt a precis of the given passage in one-third of its length. Do not suggest a title. Write, as far as possible, in your own words. The precis should be attempted only on the precis sheets.

The Renaissance in India was not like the Renaissance in Europe. It was not a return to India of the past. It was essentially a matter of spirit which produced striking changes in the realm of religion, society and culture along with a demand for natural regeneration. There arose a new self-consciousness among the people of India. The soul of India began to unfold itself and break the shackles of the past. It is maintained that the Renaissance in India stirred the Indian soul to its very depths and Modern India owes everything to the Renaissance which was followed by $ reformation movements all over India. It also paved the way to national a regeneration. The spirit of Renaissance and the subsequent reform movements affected almost all the aspects of national life. There were new developments in religious, social and political lives. There were new trends in the fields of education, literature, fine arts and science.

The view of Sir Jadunath Sarkar is that the Indian Renaissance was at first an intellectual awakening which profoundly affected our literature, education thought Sand art. In the next succeeding generation, it became a moral force and reformed the Indian society and religion. In the third generation it brought about the economic modernisation of India and ultimately political emancipation.

In his book entitled, "The Renaissance in India". Sri Aurobindo has attempted anve analysis of the Renaissance in India. He points out that the eighteenth and early go nineteenth centuries in India were periods of political decline, defeat and anarchy which practically killed the creative spirit in religion and art. India began to imitate Europe and forgot her own achievements in the past. However, the life breath of the mination moved as a subordinate under cup 6, and Punjab, in the political aspirations of Maharashtra and the literary activity of Bengal.

Sri Aurobindo points out that the Renaissance in India in the nineteenth century had three aspects. In the first place, it aimed at a recovery of the old spiritual gospel contained in the sacred groups of the country The researches of European Indologists helped the people in the West and India to understand and appreciate the achievements of the Indians in the past . Philosophers and thinkers like Schopenhauer Emerson Thoreau Royce highly praised India's wisdom in the past Indian saints and mystic leaders in India also helped the same process. Secondly, this re-invigorated spirituality inspired fresh activity in the fields of philosophy, literature, art etc.Thirdly, an attempt was made to deal in an original subway with modern problems in the light of the new inspiration.

Sri Aurobindo did not compare the Indian Renaissance with the European 36 Renaissance of the fifteenth Century. He compared it with the Celtic Renaissance 37 when Ireland wanted to go back to the older culture after a long period of British domination. In his analysis of the Indian Renaissance, Sri Aurobindo put great emphasis on the recovery of the spiritual tradition and heritage of the past. 40 According to him, the establishment of new religious sects in India was a central A event in the Indian Renaissance. The Brahmo Samaj, the Arya Samaj, Ramkrishna 42 Paramhans and Vivekananda, the neo-Vaishnavism of Bengal and the Renaissance in Islam tried to go back to the past and recover the light of old wisdom. Sri Aurobindo referred to the cosmopolitanism, eclecticism, religious rationalism and logic of the 4€ Brahmo Samaj. Of all the leaders of the Renaissance in India, Dayananda appealed most to Sri Aurobindo. He considered him as a unique personality which created a 69 Vigorous Aryan manhood in India. Aurobindo found a national instinct inthe reliance of Dayananda on Vedic wisdom. To quote Aurobindo, Dayananda "brings back an old Aryan element into the national character". Aurobindo gave credit to the Theosophical Society for getting some recognition in the West for some of the psychic, occult and esoteric achievements of the old Hindus. According to Aurobindo, Ramkrishna Paramhans was "the man who had the greatest influence and has done the most to regenerate Bengal". Vivekananda proclaimed to the world thatIndia was awake not only to exist but also to conquer. In India itself, Vivekanandawas a leader who wanted "preservation by reconstruction". Aurobindo alsoreferred me to the achievements of J. C. Bose and Rabindranath Tagore in the field of Indian Renaissance. Aurobindo believed that the spiritual and intellectual advance of India he was bound to come. To quote him, "The Renaissance in India is as inevitable as the rising of tomorrow's Sun and the Renaissance of a great nation of three hundred million with so peculiar a temperament, such unique traditions and ideas of life, so powerful an intelligence and so great a mass of potential energies cannot but be oneof the most formidable phenomena of the modern world."

5. Read the following passage and answer the questions that follow.

Man, since antiquity, has been an inveterate traveller. Only the motivations for travel have changed. In ancient times, the main motivations for travel were trade, pilgrimage and conquest. It is not often realised how extensive were the contacts among the peoples several thousand years ago.

For instance, there was considerable interchange of ideas and knowledge between India and West Asia and the Graeco-Roman civilization. Travel became the means of acquiring culture in Europe. The tradition of the Grand Tour which started in the 17th century was more firmly established in the 18th and the 19th centuries by the emergence of an affluent mercantile class. After the Second World War, Europe lay in ruins. The Marshall Plan which was introduced by the United States for the revival of the economies of European countries made tourism as one of its planks. It provided large amount of money for the reconstruction of hotels and tourism infrastructure of Western Europe. What was more significant was that for the first time tourism was viewed as an engine for economic development. This made the Governments start assuming responsibility for the promotion of tourism. Three technological inventions have fuelled the growth of travel on a large scale in successive periods. First, the steam engine which made travel by rail and steamship possible before 1914; then the internal combustion engine which popularise travel by automobile in the inter-War years and lastly, the jet propulsion engine which has led to the international tourist explosion of the post-War era. The Government of India also took note of the new phenomenon of tourism and its economic implications. In 1947, the private sector consisted of a number of hotels and travel agencies in the main cities mainly owned and operated by foreign interests. As it happened in other industries after Independence, the control of many of these hotels passed into the hands of Indian entrepreneurs.

At the same time, a number of new indigenously owned and operated travel agencies and hotels started being set up. In the last 50 years, the Indian travel industry has shown remarkable enterprise. Some of the leading Indian hotel groups and travel agencies have branched out overseas and their performance is highly regarded in the international tourism remarks. The tourism revolution which started in full measure 50 years ago has not run its course. There are several reasons for taking a long-term optimistic view of tourism. First, the increase in leisure time in industrialised societies; paid holidays which were introduced as a social welfare measure have now become an accepted feature not only in industrialised countries but also in many developing countries. The length of paid holidays has increased.

The working week, both in public and private sectors, has come down to 40 hours spread over 5 days. Evidently Governments will have to concern themselves with the quality of use of leisure. Tourism has become a preeminent form of recreation for the younger people.

This is reflected in the increase in travel in the age group of 18 to 25 years. Second, the rise in literacy and educational standards. Third, better healthcare has made it possible for retired persons, above 60 years, to undertake travel for pleasure. Fourth, the increase in discretionary incomes in real terms in the last twenty years, partly due to income elasticity. Many research studies have established that increase in income level in real terms resulted in increase in propensity for travel. And lastly, taking a vacation, generally twice a year, has become a way of life in modern societies.

(a) What, according to the author, were the main motivations for travel in ancient times?

(b What was the state of tourism in Europe and the United States?

(c) What part did technology play in the growth of tourism?

(d) How does the author describe the state of tourism in the post-Independence India?

(e) Why does the author think that there is a bright future for tourism in modern societies?

6. (a) Rewrite the sentences as directed.

(i) Rabi said, "I'll eat rice for lunch today". (Change into an indirect speech)

(ii) The man was running the shop for long. (Change into passive voice)

(iii) He was in Delhi. He did not meet his friend. (Rewrite by using though)

(iv) I landed at the airport. It started raining. (Rewrite by using 'no sooner')

(v) Though we were under the British rule we had a rich cultural heritage. (Change into a simple sentence)

(vi) India can change only when education is reached to all. (Use 'unless')

(vii) People in a developing country are both rich and poor. (Rewrite by using 'either' and 'or')

(viii) If you work hard you will achieve success. (Rewrite by using 'in order to')

(ix) Most of the corrupt politicians do not find themselves in Jail. (Change into acomplex sentence)

(x) He is old. He cannot climb stairs. (Rewrite by using 'too')

(b) Write one sentence each using the following phrases to bring out their meaning clearly. Do not change the form of the given phrases.

I. Abide by II. rule out

III. put out IV. kick off

V. jump in

(c) Correct the following sentences without-making any unnecessary changes.

(i) He enjoyed during the holidays.

(ii) Whoever works hard he will win.

(iii) The man who knocked at the door was stranger.

(iv) I asked my colleague when was he going to his home town.

(v) Besides clothes, the shopkeeper deals with cosmetics too.

CAPF (AC) Exam
Mock Test 03
GENERAL STUDIES, ESSAY AND COMPREHENSION

Time : 3 Hrs. MM : 200

Paper 2

General Instructions

- All the six questions are to be attempted.
- Question No. 1 is printed both in Hindi and in English
- Other questions are printed in English only and should be attempted in English only.
- The number of marks carried by a question/part is indicated against it.

1. Write essays on any four of the following in about 300 words each
निम्नलिखित में से किन्हीं चार पर लगभग 300 शब्दों (प्रत्येक) में निबन्ध लिखिए। **(20 × 4 = 80)**

(a) India must become a nation of job creators instead of being a nation of job seekers
भारत को नौकरी चाहने वालों के बजाय नौकरी देने वालों का देश बनना चाहिए।

(b) Dual Board Exams for 10 and 12 from 2025- Boon or Bane
2025 से 10वीं और 12वीं के लिए दोहरी बोर्ड परीक्षा-वरदान या अभिशाप।

(c) A society that has more justice is a society that needs less charity.
जिस समाज में न्याय अधिक होता है, उसे दान की कम आवश्यकता होती है।

(d) Scientific and technological progress cannot be equated with the progress of humanity
वैज्ञानिक और तकनीकी प्रगति की तुलना मानवता की प्रगति से नहीं की जा सकती।

(e) A parliamentary system of government rests on a functioning opposition as 'no democracy can do without it
सरकार की संसदीय प्रणाली एक कार्यशील विपक्ष पर टिकी होती है क्योंकि कोई भी लोकतन्त्र इसके बिना नहीं चल सकता।

(f) Our common humanity demands that we make the impossible possible
हमारी सामान्य मानवता की मांग है कि हम असम्भव को सम्भव बनाएं।

2. Write an arguments for and against each of the following statements.

(a) Security of Lives are more important than Economy Recovery.

(b) Ensuring quality education will give better pay offs than other social welfare schemes.

3. Write reports on the following in about 200 words each. Do not mention any name or address in the report, use XYZ/ABC if needed.

(a) Search for Rare Earth Minerals

(b) India Maldives Relationship Shift

4. Attempt a precis of the given passage in one-third of its length. Do not suggest a title. Write, as far as possible, in your own words. The precis should be attempted only on the precis sheets.

The work of a lawyer or a politician must contain in a more delectable form a great deal of the same pleasure that is to be derived from playing bridge. Here, of course, there is not only the exercise of skill but the outwitting of a skilled opponent. Even where this competitive element is absent, however, the performance of difficult feats is agreeable. A man who can do stunts in an aeroplane finds the pleasure so great for the sake of it he is willing to risk his life. I imagine that an able surgeon, in spite of the painful circumstances in which his work is done, derives satisfaction from the exquisite precision of his operations.

All skilled work can be pleasurable, provided the skill required is either variable or capable of indefinite improvement. If these conditions are absent, it will cease to be interesting when a man has acquired his maximum skill. A man who runs three-mile races will cease to find pleasure in this occupation when he passes the age at which he can beat his own previous record. Fortunately there is a very considerable amount of work in which new circumstances call for new skill and a man can go on improving, at any rate until he has reached middle age. In some kinds of skilled work, such as politics, for example, it seems that men are at their best between sixty and seventy, the reason being that in such occupations a wide experience of other men is essential. For this reason, successful politicians are apt to be happier at the age of seventy than any other men of equal age. Their only competitors in this respect are the men who are the heads of big businesses.

There is, however, another element possessed by the best work, which is even more important as a source of happiness than is the exercise of skill. This is the element of constructiveness. In some work, though by no means in most, something is built up which remains as a monument when the work is completed. We may distinguish construction from destruction by the following criterion. In construction, the initial stage of affairs is comparatively haphazard, while the final state of affairs embodies a purpose; in destruction, the reverse is the case: the initial state of affairs embodies a purpose, while the final state of affairs is haphazard, that is to say, all that is intended by the destroyers is to produce a state of affairs which does not embody a certain purpose.

Destruction, is of course necessary very often as a preliminary to subsequent construction; in that case it is part of a whole which is constructive. But not infrequently a man will engage in activities of which the purpose is destructive without regard to any construction that may come after. Frequently he will conceal this from himself by the relief that he is only sweeping away in order to build afresh, but it is generally possible to unmask this pretence, when it is a pretence, by asking him what the subsequent construction is to be.

5. Read the following passage and answer the questions that follow.

History has a great variety of definitions and applications. In the broadest sense, it considers every action and every thought that man has had since his first appearance and records every significant advance or recession. It attempts to evaluate all the developments in science, in art, in literature, in philosophy, in architecture, in sociology, in politics, in war, in religion, and in law. It sketches as complete a picture as possible of everything that has influenced man directly or indirectly.

History, more than any other subject, has been enslaved and distorted for selfish purposes. Members of the clergy have used it to glorify and to promote the interests of the church, statesmen have utilized it to sway masses, and writers have distorted facts to substantiate their conclusions. War spirit has been kindled through undue emphasis upon facts, if not falsification of them. The historian is likely to exaggerate the history of his own country – sometimes unintentionally – because of his environment and sometimes in order to facilitate the sale of his book. In all countries, there are zealots in responsible positions who cannot bear to have their fatherhood criticized. Truth is frequently sacrificed at the altar of patriotism. Henry C. Lea, an outstanding American historian, declared that history should be "a serious attempt to ascertain the severest truth as to the past and set it forth without fear or favour." Michelet, a famous French historian, believed that "sacrilege and the mocking of false goods are the historian's first duty, his indispensable instrument for re-establishing the truth." The slight progress that we have made in the direction indicated by Lea and Michelet is rather discouraging, but there is a trend toward a broader and more inclusive point of view in the writing and teaching of history.

World history, correctly interpreted, puts the individual state in the proper perspective and lessens the dangers of excessive nationalism. History has become more than war and politics. To make the story complete, the historian of the new school makes use of the work of the ethnologist, the anthropologist, the geographer, and archaeologist, the geologist, the psychologist, the astronomer, the zoologist, the biologist, the chemist, the sociologist and the economist. He is concerned with man's cultural advances and his society, as well as with charters, constitutions, and wars. There are dangers, as well as virtues, in the vast scope of the "new history". Over popularization and under specialization tend to cheapen history and to destroy some of its qualities as a basic and sober study.

There are decided advantages in the comprehension of the broad scope of history, but, in addition, the student should be able to appreciate the depth of the subject. Years of research have been spent and volumes have been written on a single topic. Without these specialized works, surveys would be of no particular value. However, some of the historians of the "new history" have sacrificed important fundamental facts in order to make achronicle of heroic persons and romantic occurrence. They have overstepped the point where history and fiction should meet. The historian should make his description of the past lifelike hence, he should include grim realities as well as romantic incidents. One of the important aspects of the "new history" is to emphasize upon man's cultural developments, popularly termed civilization. Civilization is difficult to define and evaluate. Just where it began and where man's actions and thoughts became human is impossible to determine. Man, like animals, has senses but some are less acutely developed; man has emotions, most of which are present, but latent, in animals. Comfort seems to be the chief goal of the lower forms of animal life, but man pushes beyond that towards something that he has difficulty in defining.

This intangible something maybe called civilization. Professor Lynn Thorndike believes that civilization "is the product of our higher qualities as exercised first by original and superior individuals and then accepted or followed by a sufficient number of human beings to make it a social fact." Buckle held that moral and intellectual progress is the basis of civilization. Emerson believed that civilization is a progress and Bertrand Russell, a modern philosopher, thinks that it is the progress and predominance of science. Perhaps we can agree that acknowledge of nature, progress in art, an ethical code, a government, and a degree of material prosperity are essential in any form of civilized society. Civilization became possible when chaos and insecurity were minimized. Curiosity and constructiveness were encouraged.

6. (a) Rewrite the sentences as directed.

(i) He was given a merciless thrashing at school. (Change the voice)

(ii) The nurse said to us;" Please wait outside the room." (Change into indirect narration)

(iii) Hold your tongue and you can hold anything else. (Make a simple sentence)

(iv) Lets go now. (Put a question tag)

(v) ....iron is ......chemical element.(Use appropriate article)

(vi) What an honest boy he is! (Make assertive)

(vii) It is not as expensive as you think. (change into comparative degree)

(viii) My mother didn't go to university. My father also didn't go to university. (Use neither .....nor)

(ix) If I had known you were coming, ...(complete the sentence with making a suitable clause of your own)

(x) neither of the choices ......attractive. (use correct form of verb be)

(b) Write one sentence each using the following phrases to bring out their meaning clearly. Do not change the form of the given phrases.

I. iron out   II. give in

III. Fall through   IV. end up

V. do without

(c) Correct the following sentences without-making any unnecessary changes.

(i) the essays of Bertrand Russel are not so popular.

(ii) Kamala asked Akshay if he is not ashamed of himself.

(iii) Excessive chocolate eating lead to decay of teeth.

(iv) When they reached the airport, the plane already took off.

(v) You must stop to chew tobacco.